RAW THOUGHT
RAW NERVE
INSIDE THE MIND OF AARON SWARTZ

NOT-FOR-PROFIT — THIRD EDITION

DISCOVERY PUBLISHER

Book Content: Copyright © Aaron Swartz, under
BY-NC-SA 4.0 license as stated by Dr Sean B. Palmer.

First Edition: 2014, Discovery Publisher
Second Edition: July 2016, Discovery Publisher
Third Edition: October 2016, Discovery Publisher

Author : Aaron Swartz
Editor in Chief: Adriano Lucchese

DISCOVERY PUBLISHER

616 Corporate Way, Suite 2-4933
Valley Cottage, New York, 10989
www.discoverypublisher.com
books@discoverypublisher.com
facebook.com/DiscoveryPublisher
twitter.com/DiscoveryPB

New York • Tokyo • Paris • Hong Kong

ABOUT THIS EDITION

In October 2014, Discovery Publisher released *Raw Thought, Raw Nerve: Inside the Mind of Aaron Swartz*. It was then the first publication introducing Aaron Swartz's lifetime work —see Page 3 for details.

In August 2015, the publishing company The New Press, claiming to have legally obtained exclusive copyright from Aaron's legal IP owner —Dr. Sean B. Palmer— took unlawful steps to shutdown our publication; shortly thereafter, The New Press published a scaled-down version of *Raw Thought, Raw Nerve*. A similar action was performed shorlty after the release of our second edition.

In an article titled "If I get hit by a truck...", Aaron stated "If I get hit by a truck [...] the contents of all my hard drives [should] be made publicly available". It should be noted that in all articles published by Aaron on his blog, he never claimed to be against commercial publishing. Aaron was, however, against abusive or restrictive copyright. As such, when the first edition of this book was released, we did not claim exclusive copyright. Our statement was the same as it is today: "The content of this book is copyrighted to Aaron Swartz".

Much has been said and written about the unlawful steps that The New Press took against Discovery Publisher; those actions have also been publicly qualified as unethical towards what Aaron stood for. To this day, The New Press has never made any public statement.

Very recently, however, Dr. Sean B. Palmer with the help of Aaron's family and close friends took legal steps to let Discovery Publisher (re-)publish *Raw Thought, Raw Nerve: Inside the Mind of Aaron Swartz* as well as corresponding translations into the French, Italian, Spanish, German, and Portuguese languages —which are presently being produced— under BY-NC-SA 4.0 license.

After a year of legal battle, we are very excited to introduce this not-for-profit third edition of *Raw Thought, Raw Nerve: Inside the Mind of Aaron Swartz*.

This book is in memory of Aaron and what he stood for.
Rest in peace, Aaron, your battles were not in vain.

The Discovery Team
October 2016

TABLE OF CONTENTS

SCIENCE & STUFF 194

WORK & TECH 234

RAW NERVE   498

FAREWELL   524

WHAT IS GOING ON HERE?

A WORD FROM THE PUBLISHER

I didn't know who Aaron Swartz was. Then, in June 2014, I watched *The Internet's Own Boy: The Story of Aaron Swartz*[1].

Aaron taught himself to read when he was three. At twelve, he created Info Network, a user-generated encyclopedia, which he later likened to an early version of Wikipedia. Not long after, Aaron turned his computer genius to political organizing, information sharing and online freedom.

In 2006, Aaron downloaded the Library of Congress's complete bibliographic dataset. The library charged fees to access them. However, as a government document, it was not copyright-protected within the USA. By posting the data on OpenLibrary.org, Aaron made it freely available. Eventually, the Copyright Office sided in favor of Aaron.

In 2008, Aaron downloaded and released 2.7 million federal court documents stored in the Public Access to Court Electronic Records (PACER) database managed by the Administrative Office of the United States Courts. *The Huffington Post* characterized his actions as: "Swartz downloaded public court documents from the PACER system in an effort to make them available outside of the expensive service. The move drew the attention of the FBI, which ultimately decided not to press charges as the documents, were, in fact, public."[2]

In late 2010, Aaron downloaded a large number of academic journal articles through MIT's computer network. At the time, Aaron was a research fellow at Harvard University, which provided him with an authorized account. Aaron's motivation for downloading the articles was never fully determined. However, friends and colleagues reported that his intention was either to publicly share them on the Internet or uncover corruption in the funding of climate change research. This time, faced with prosecutors being overzealous and a dysfunctional criminal justice system[3], Aaron was charged with a maximum penalty of $1 million in fines and 35 years in prison, leading to a two-year legal battle with the US federal government that ended when Aaron took his own life on January 11, 2013.

Soon after Aaron's death, director Brian Knappenberger, who was "inspired, infuriated and frustrated"[3] by his suicide, began filming *The Internet's Own Boy: The Story of Aaron Swartz*.

After watching the end of the documentary, I was saddened by this tragic story and left with many questions: Why did the US criminal justice system take such a strong and unprecedented stand on punishing Aaron? Why did Aaron find no other way out than ending his life? What legacy did Aaron leave behind him?

I discovered that between 2007 and 2011 Aaron read 614 books; one book every three days. Early on, Aaron made a point to write about his findings and reflection[4]. From the "Hello World"[5] post published on January 13, 2002 to the last known article written on November 1, 2012 "What Happens in *The Dark Knight*"[6], Aaron published 1,478 articles on his personal blog[7]; one article every three days.

Aaron dealt with a wide range of subjects going from politics, economics, science, sociology, through technology, education, nutrition, philosophy, among many others. But beyond that, I was struck by the clarity of Aaron's mind on the difficulty of the subjects he was dealing with at such a young age. When the typical 16 year-old college student worries about *fitting in* and mating, Aaron was tackling with a book publication[8] and wondered about what he should do with his life[9]. At 18 he read Noam Chomsky, and at 23 wrote the very impressive 12,000-word piece "A Summary/Explanation of John Maynard Keynes' General Theory"[10]. This article was dealing with such complexity that two days after its publication, it was followed by a *much* shorter and accessible version, titled "Keynes, Explained Briefly"[11].

After two months into Aaron's writing, I was convinced that what Lawrence Lessig said at the MIT Media Lab talk "A remembrance of Aaron Swartz: A statement from Tim Berners-Lee read by Lawrence Lessig"[12], was indeed the best way to describe Aaron : he was not after the money; he was on to making a better world for us all; a freer world.

Back in May 15, 2006, in the article "The Book That Changed My Life"[13] Aaron wrote:

> *[...] It's taken me two years to write about this experience, not without reason. One terrifying side effect of learning the world isn't the way you think is that it leaves you all alone. And when you try to describe your new worldview to people, it either comes out sounding unsurprising ("yeah, sure, everyone knows the media's got problems") or like pure lunacy and people slowly back away.*
> *Ever since then, I've realized that I need to spend my life working to fix the shocking brokenness I'd discovered. And the best way to do that, I concluded, was to try to share what I'd discovered with others. I couldn't just tell them it straight out, I knew, so I had to provide the hard evidence. So I started working on a book to do just that.*

Much has been written on the Internet about Aaron's decision to end his life. The article "Losing Aaron"[14,15] written by *Boston Magazine* after interviewing Aaron's father, Robert Swartz, gives a particularly precise and touching account of Aaron's struggles during that time.

On July 26, 2006, in the post "I Love the University"[16] Aaron wrote:

> *[..] I was once one of those kids, working there, and I think about why I left [the university] and why I miss it. I marvel at the pointlessness, the impracticality, the waste.*
>
> *The sky is overcast now, the crowds of students have thinned out, and those that remain scurry from place to place with their heads down. I'm tired now, I feel sadder, and I wonder how I lost so much so quickly.*
>
> *I want to feel nostalgic, I want to feel like there's this place, just a couple subway stops away, where everything will be alright. A better place, a place I should be in, a place I can go back to. But even just visiting it, the facts are plain. It doesn't exist, it never has. I'm nostalgic for a place that never existed.*

There have been numerous criticisms about Aaron's decision to end his life. Some agree with it, some don't. Whether he made the right decision is *certainly not* for me to comment on.

Instead, I've chosen to focus on the positive impact Aaron made on us all. This is why I decided to publish some of Aaron's best writings in the form of this present book.

Five months before his death, Aaron completed *Raw Nerve*[17], a series of articles reflecting on life, depicting an honest, painful and yet beautiful picture of the tragedy of life. Perhaps then, Aaron knew his time was drawing to an end...

RIP, Aaron Swartz.

Adriano Lucchese
Discovery Publisher
November, 2014

1. https://www.youtube.com/watch?v=vXr-2hwTk58
2. http://www.huffingtonpost.com/2013/02/07/darrell-issa-internet-freedom_n_2633197.html
3. http://www.biography.com/news/aaron-swartz-internets-own-boy-interview
4. *Raw Thought, Raw Nerve*, P.7
5. http://www.aaronsw.com/weblog/000081
6. *Raw Thought, Raw Nerve*, P.283
7. http://www.aaronsw.com/
8. http://www.aaronsw.com/2002/bookAuthorTips
9. *Raw Thought, Raw Nerve*, P.586
10. http://www.aaronsw.com/weblog/generaltheory
11. *Raw Thought, Raw Nerve*, P.209
12. http://www.media.mit.edu/video/view/aaronsw-2013-03-12-1
13. *Raw Thought, Raw Nerve*, P.590
14. http://www.bostonmagazine.com/news/article/2014/01/02/bob-swartz-losing-aaron/
15. *Raw Thought, Raw Nerve*, P.792
16. *Raw Thought, Raw Nerve*, P.547
17. *Raw Thought, Raw Nerve*, P.756

Disclaimer: The unedited content of *Raw Thought, Raw Nerve: Inside the Mind of Aaron Swartz* is available on Aaron's blog[7]. The pricing for this compilation and special edition has been purposely set at the lowest point on Kindle and paper, and free on iBooks. As we believe Aaron would have wanted it[9], this book is also available free of charge through the website archive.org.

WHAT IS GOING ON HERE?

In his 1959 classic, *The Sociological Imagination*, the great sociologist Charles Wright Mills told students of the discipline:

> *As a social scientist, you have to ... capture what you experience and sort it out; only in this way can you hope to use it to guide and test your reflection, and in the process shape yourself as an intellectual craftsman. But how can you do this? One answer is: you must set up a blog...*
>
> *In such a blog ... there is joined personal experience and professional activities, studies under way and studies planned. In this blog, you ... will try to get together what you are doing intellectually and what you are experiencing as a person. here you will not be afraid to use your experience and relate it directly to various work in progress. By serving as a check on repetitious work, your blog also enables you to conserve your energy. It also encourages you to capture 'fringe-thoughts': various ideas which may be byproducts of everyday life, snatches of conversation overheard in the street, or, for that matter, dreams. Once noted, these may lead to more systematic thinking, as well as lend intellectual relevance to more directed experience.*
>
> *... The blog also helps you build up the habit of writing. ... In developing the blog, you can experiment as a writer and this, as they say, develop your powers of expression.*

Actually, he called it a "file" instead of a blog, but the point remains the same: becoming a scientific thinker requires practice and writing is a powerful aid to reflection.

So that's what this blog is. I write here about thoughts I have, things I'm working on, stuff I've read, experiences I've had, and so on. Whenever a thought crystalizes in my head, I type it up and post it here. I don't read over it, I don't show it to anyone, and I don't edit it — I just post it.

I don't consider this writing, I consider this thinking. I like sharing my thoughts and I like hearing yours and I like practicing expressing ideas, but fundamentally this blog is not for you, it's for me. I hope that you enjoy it anyway.

Aaron Swartz
July 29, 2006

HELLO, WORLD.

Hello, world.

Aaron Swartz
January 13, 2002 05:21 AM

ECONOMICS, POLITICS & PARODY

A SAD DAY FOR AMERICA

CNN: Senate approves Iraq war resolution[1]. 'The president praised the congressional action, declaring "America speaks with one voice."'

I'm not sure how the president can call it one voice when half of America does not want to go to war[2].

Miguel[3] sent an email expressing his support to stop the war. He also told me about an article talking about how we have failed to learn from history[4]. He wrote: "most dumb laws are passed before an election and when there is a rush and no time to inform the American public, whoever takes the most hard-line position wins. The same thing happening now in congress." *Thanks, Miguel!*

I wish I had known that such horrible things were going to happen while I was D.C.; I might have been able to join some protests or something. I feel powerless, perhaps I should move to another country. However, I am heartened that my senator voted nay[5], I wonder if my fax last night may have done some good.

October 11, 2002

1. http://www.cnn.com/2002/ALLPOLITICS/10/11/iraq.us/
2. http://www.cnn.com/2002/ALLPOLITICS/10/07/iraq.poll/
3. http://primates.ximian.com/~miguel/activity-log.php
4. http://www.zmag.org/content/print_article.cfm?itemID=2462&sectionID=40
5. http://www.senate.gov/legislative/vote1072/vote_00237.html

UNSPEAKABLE THINGS

Paul Graham has written a fascinating article on *What You Can't Say*[1] — those ideas which are so heretical that people will shout you down and call you names for even daring to state them.

Soon after (but not intentionally because of) I said people have no right to make me pay to use their software[2] and was quickly shouted down as immoral, childish, and (especially funny) anti-capitalist/communist[3, 4, 5]. I don't want to discuss these things, but I do want to try to come up with a list of unspeakable things. What things qualify? It's hard to say precisely, but I think they should have a reasonable chance of being true yet you would be embarrassed to admit you believed them to your friends.

Here's the list so far:
- Democracy isn't a very good idea; lots of people shouldn't be allowed to vote.
- Sex with and in front of children/animals/multiple people is OK.
- Eugenics and suicide should be encouraged.

- Blacks and women are naturally not as smart as white men.

Can you think of things to add? Comment or email. I promise to do what I can to keep your suggestions anonymous; good ones will be added to this list and deleted from the comments.

January 05, 2004

1. http://www.paulgraham.com/say.html
2. http://www.aaronsw.com/2002/onPiracy
3. http://offlineblog.com/mtarchives/2004_01_04__181.php
4. http://www.docuverse.com/blog/donpark/EntryViewPage.aspx?guid=7a592614-ff21-4817-b7c0-3ea9a7007122
5. http://www.25hoursaday.com/weblog/CommentView.aspx?guid=9f3fa053-237f-4579-8cab-e418b9aecf70

MONEY AND POLITICS

Think money doesn't decide who wins elections?

Candidate name	% of vote	% of money	Difference
Bush	51	53	2
Kerry	48	46	2
Nader	0.3	0.5	0.2
Badnarik	0.1	0.3	0.2
Peroutka	0.1	0.1	0.0
Cobb	0.1	0.01	0.08

Think again.

November 03, 2004

- Washington Post: http://www.washingtonpost.com/wp-srv/elections/2004/page/295001/
- Center for Responsive Politics: http://www.opensecrets.org/presidential/index.asp

THE FACTS ABOUT MONEY AND POLITICS

The previous article, "Money and Politics", was meant as a somewhat humorous and thought-provoking piece of commentary about campaign spending.

However, for those who are truly curious about how money runs politics, I know of no better source than Thomas Ferguson's book *Golden Rule: The Investment Theory of Party Competition and the Logic of Money-Driven Political Systems.* The principle alluded to by the title is "to discover who rules, follow the gold" and Ferguson does just that. Using historical evidence including letters, contribution records, public statements, and other documents, Ferguson shows precisely how, from the very founding of the country, politics has been a game for and by large wealthy interests.

The underlying theory is really very simple: running a political campaign is expensive. Individuals are poorly organized to contribute with significant effects. That leaves large corporations who fund practically all viable candidates.

Of course, corporations are usually not monolithic, and political battles arise because of their conflicting interests. Some industries may prefer protectionism to secure the domestic market for themselves. Others may prefer free trade so they can sell and buy from foreign markets. These different corporate blocs coalesce around different candidates who then spend their money to do whatever it takes to get the populace to vote for them.

The key point about the theory is that issues which no corporations support, even if massively popular among the people, will never be raised in a political campaign. Were a candidate to make the mistake of supporting them, his money supply would quickly dry up and his campaign would wither. The result? All political policies enacted, from the New Deal to the invasion of Vietnam, are those supported by the wealthy corporations, not the people.

November 04, 2004

THE POLITICS OF LYING

It is a truism that politicians and political groups lie. Lies uncovered on one political side are frequently written off by saying "all politicians lie" or "the other side lies too". Indeed, uncovered lies on one side are sometimes used an argument to be skeptical of the other (as in, "since you've show the Whigs lie a lot why aren't you equally skeptical of the Tories?").

Does this really make sense? It helps to ask the all-important question: "Cui bono?" or "Who benefits?"

Take the issue of gun control. There are heated partisans on both sides of the issue who claim to have facts to back up their positions about how much harm is caused by guns. Let's say the gun-control advocates (the left) investigated and found that they were wrong and guns weren't really a problem after all. For them, this is good news — they no longer have to spend time and energy protecting people from guns, since they aren't a problem in the first place. Thus the left has little reason to lie.

The story is different for the right. If gun rights advocates discovered that guns really did kill lots of people, their position would not change. They would still be in support of giving people guns. The only problem is that much of the public might not be. Thus, there is a strong incentive for them to lie.

The facts bear this theory out. Conservative "scholar" John Lott has made up studies, falsified data, and done other things to prove that guns are actually a good thing. Despite all this, he continues to receive large grants from conservative patrons, prominent play in The *New York Times*, large sales for his erroneous book, and draws large crowds and acclaim from conservatives.

By contrast, Michael Besailles was found to have made some errors in citation in his pro-gun-conrol historical work. Besailles was promptly investigated, fired, exposed in the Boston Globe, had his book pulled from publication, and was torn to shreds in various public forums.

Not surprisingly, considering the rewards and punishments involved, new liars on the right pop up frequently while liars on the left are relatively rare.

Even more evidence supporting this theory can be found by looking at when the left does lie. Take, for example, the case of Ralph Nader. The left has raked Nader over the coals for his 2004 presidential campaign, suggesting he's getting funds and signatures from Republicans, attacked Michael Moore for being fat, and done other horrible things.

Yet, as the Nader campaign explains, they have worked hard to refuse signatures from Republicans, fighting lengthy court battles to get them ruled unnecessary. Only 51 Republicans, many of whom Ralph says he knows personally, have donated to the campaign and collectively they've donated even more to the Democrats. And Ralph merely expressed some concern about Moore's health towards the end of a letter.

The simplistic analysis would be to tout this as proof that the left does lie, but again it is interesting to look at the circumstances. When does the left lie? When it is attacking people even further to the left and is thus, in a very real sense, acting as the right.

The next time you hear a claim from a politician, don't just be skeptical. Ask who benefits — the left or the right?

October 25, 2004

SHIFTING THE TERMS OF DEBATE
HOW BIG BUSINESS COVERED UP GLOBAL WARMING

In 2004, Michelle Malkin, a conservative editorialist, published the book *In Defense of Internment.* It argued that declassified security intercepts showed that Japanese internment during World War II — the government policy that relocated thousands of Japanese to concentration camps — was actually justified in the name of national security. We needed to learn the truth, Malkin insisted, so that we could see how racial profiling was similarly justified to fight the "war on terror."

Bainbridge Island was the center of the evacuations; to this day, residents still feel ashamed and teach students a special unit about the incident, entitled "Leaving Our Island". But one parent in the district, Mary Dombrowski, was persuaded by Malkin's book that the evacuation was actually justified and insisted the school was teaching a one-sided version of the internment story, "propaganda" that forced impressionable children into thinking that the concentration camps were a mistake.

The school's principal defended the practice. As the Seattle Times reported:

"We do teach it as a mistake," she said, noting that the U.S. government has admitted it was wrong. "As an educator, there are some things that we can say aren't debatable anymore." Slavery, for example. Or the internment — as opposed to a subject such as global warming, she said.[1]

True, Japanese internment isn't a controversial issue like global warming, but ten years ago, global warming wasn't a controversial issue either. In 1995, the UN's panel on international climate change released its consensus report, finding that global warming was a real and serious issue that had to be quickly confronted. The media covered the scientists' research and the population agreed, leading President Clinton to say he would sign an international treaty to stop global warming.

Then came the backlash. The Global Climate Coalition (funded by over 40 major corporate groups like Amoco, the U.S. Chamber of Commerce, and General Motors) began spending millions of dollars each year to derail the Kyoto Protocol, the international treaty to help reduce global warming. They held conferences entitled "The Costs of Kyoto," issued press releases and faxes dismissing the scientific evidence for global warming, and spent more than $3 million on newspaper and television ads claiming Kyoto would mean a "50-cent-per-gallon gasoline tax."[2]

The media, in response to flurries of "blast faxes" (a technique in which a press release is simultaneously faxed to thousands of journalists) and accusations of left-wing bias, began backing off from the scientific evidence.[3] A recent study found only 35% of newspaper stories on global warming accurately described the scientific consensus, with the majority implying that scientists who believed in global warming were just as common as global warming deniers (of which there were only a tiny handful, almost all of whom had received funding from energy companies or associated groups).[4]

It all had an incredible effect on the public. In 1993, 88% of Americans thought global warming was a serious problem. By 1997, that number had fallen to 42%, with only 28% saying immediate action was necessary.[5] And so Clinton changed course and insisted that cutting emissions should be put off for 20 years.

US businesses seriously weakened the Kyoto Protocol, leading it to require only a

7% reduction in emissions (compared to the 20% requested by European nations) and then President Bush refused to sign on to even that.[6] In four short years, big business had managed to turn nearly half the country around and halt the efforts to protect the planet.

And now, the principal on Bainbridge Island, like most people, thinks global warming is a hotly contested issue — the paradigmatic example of a hotly contested issue — even when the science is clear. ("There's no better scientific consensus on this on any issue I know," said the head of the National Oceanic and Atmospheric Administration, "except maybe Newton's second law of dynamics.")[7] But all this debate about problems has kept us away from talk about solutions. As journalist Ross Gelbspan puts it, "By keeping the discussion focused on whether there is a problem in the first place, they have effectively silenced the debate over what to do about it."[8] So is it any wonder that conservatives want to do the same thing again? And again? And again?

June 6, 2006

1. http://seattletimes.nwsource.com/html/localnews/2002027639_bainbridge06m.html
2. http://prwatch.org/prwissues/1997Q4/warming.html
3. http://prwatch.org/prwissues/1997Q4/warming.html
4. http://fair.org/index.php?page=1978
5. Cambridge Reports, Research International poll. "Do you feel that global warming is a very serious problem…?", Cambridge Reports National Omnibus Survey, September 1993, in Roper Center for Public Opinion Research (0290350, 039). USCAMREP.93SEP, R40.
6. http://prwatch.org/prwissues/1997Q4/warming.html
7. Warrick, Joby. "Consensus Emerges Earth Is Warming — Now What?", Washington Post, 12 Nov. 1997: A01.
8. http://dieoff.org/page82.htm

MAKING NOISE
HOW RIGHT-WING THINK TANKS GET THE WORD OUT

Malkin's book on internment was no more accurate than the corporate misinformation about global warming. Historians quickly showed the book badly distorted the government records and secret cables it purported to describe. As just one example, Malkin writes that a Japanese message stated they "had [Japanese] spies in the U.S. Army" when it actually said they hoped to recruit spies in the army.[1] But it should be no big surprise that Malkin, who is, after all, an editorialist and not a historian, didn't manage to fully understand the complex documentary record in the year she spent writing the book part-time.[2]

Malkin's motives, as a right-wing activist and proponent of racial profiling, are fairly obvious. But how did Mary Dombrowski, the Bainbridge Island parent, get caught up in this latest attempt to rewrite history? Opinions on global warming were changed because big business could afford to spent millions to change people's minds. But racial profiling seems like less of a moneymaker. Who invested in spreading that message?

The first step is getting the information out there. Dombrowski probably heard about Malkin's book from the Fox News Channel, where it was ceaselessly promoted for days, and where Malkin is a contributor. Or maybe she heard about it on MSNBC's Scarborough Country, a show hosted by a former Republican congressman, which had Malkin as a guest. Or maybe she heard it while driving and listening to FOX host Sean Hannity's radio show, or maybe Rush Limbaugh's. Or maybe she read a review in the New York Post (which, like Fox News, is owned by Rupert Murdoch). Or maybe she read about it on a right-wing website or weblog, like Townhall.com, which publishes 10 new conservative op-ed columns every day.

All of these organizations are partisan conservative outlets. Townhall.com, for example, is published by the Heritage Foundation, a right-wing Washington, D.C. think tank. Most people imagine a think tank as a place where smart people think big thoughts, coming up with new ideas for the government to use. But that's not how Heritage works. Nearly half of Heritage's $30 million budget is spent on publicity, not research.[3] Every day, they take work like Malkin's that agrees with their ideological prejudices and push it out through the right-wing media described above (Fox News, Rush Limbaugh, New York Post) and into the mainstream media (ABC, NPR, *New York Times*, Seattle Times).

They use a variety of tactics. Heritage, for example, publishes an annual telephone directory featuring thousands of conservative experts and associated policy organizations. (The Right Nation, 161) And if looking up somebody is too much work, Heritage maintains a 24-hour hotline for the media, providing quotes promoting conservative ideology on any subject. Heritage's "information marketing" department makes packages of colored index cards with pre-printed talking points for any conservative who plans to do an interview. (The Right Nation, 167) And Heritage computers are stocked with the names of over 3,500 journalists, organized by specialty, who Heritage staffers personally call to make sure they have all the latest conservative misinformation. Every Heritage study is turned into a two-page summary which is then turned into an op-ed piece which is then distributed to newspapers through the Heritage Features Syndicate. (What Liberal Media?, 83)

It all adds up: a 2003 study by Fairness and Accuracy in Reporting, the media watch group, found conservative think tanks were cited nearly 14,000 times in major newspapers, television, and radio shows. (By comparison, liberal think tanks were cited only 4,000 times that year.)[4] That means 10,000 additional quotes of right-wing ideology, misleading statistics, distorted facts, and so on. There's no way that doesn't unfairly skew the public debate.

1. http://hnn.us/articles/7092.html
2. http://www.isthatlegal.org/Muller_and_Robinson_on_Malkin.html
3. http://www.fair.org/extra/9607/heritage.html
4. http://www.fair.org/extra/0405/think-tank.html

ENDORSING RACISM
THE STORY OF THE BELL CURVE

If you have any doubt about the power of the think tanks, look no further than the story of *The Bell Curve*. Written by Charles Murray, who received over 1.2 million from right-wing foundations for his work, the book claimed that IQ tests revealed black people to be genetically less intelligent than whites, thus explaining their low place in society. Murray published the 845-page book without showing it to any other scientists, leading the Wall Street Journal to say he pursued "a strategy that provided book galleys to likely supporters while withholding them from likely critics" in an attempt "to fix the fight ... contrary to usual publishing protocol." Murray's think tank, the American Enterprise Institute, flew key members of the media to Washington for a weekend of briefings on the book's content. (What Liberal Media?, 94)

And the media lapped it up. In what Eric Alterman has termed "a kind of Rorschach test for pundits," (What Liberal Media?, 96) every major media outlet reviewed the book without questioning the accuracy of its contents. Instead, they merely quibbled about its proposed recommendations that the dumb blacks, with their dangerously high reproductive rates, might have to be kept in "a high-tech and more lavish version of an Indian reservation" without such luxuries as "individualism, equal rights before the law," and so on. Reviewers proposed more moderate solutions, like just taking away their welfare checks. (What Liberal Media?, 94)

But such quibbles aside, the amount of coverage alone was incredible. The book received cover stories in Newsweek ("the science behind [it] is overwhelmingly mainstream"), The New Republic (which dedicated an entire issue to discussion of the book), and The *New York Times* Book Review (which suggested critics disliked its "appeal to sweet reason" and are "inclined to hang the defendants without a trial"). Detailed articles appeared in TIME, The *New York Times* ("makes a strong case"), The *New York Times* Magazine, *Forbes* (praising the book's "Jeffersonian vision"), the *Wall Street Journal*, and the *National Review*. It received a respectful airing on such shows as *ABC*'s *Nightline*, *PBS*'s MacNeil/Lehrer NewsHour, the *McLaughlin Group*, *Think Tank* (which dedicated a special two-part series to the book), *ABC*'s *PrimeTime Live*, and *NPR*'s All Things Considered. With fifteen weeks on the bestseller list, it ended up selling over 300,000 copies in hardcover.1

This wasn't just a media debate about the existence of global warming or the merits of internment, this was a full-on media endorsement of racism, which the American Heritage Dictionary defines as "The belief that race accounts for differences in human character or ability and that a particular race is superior to others." Nor did the media mention the work's political intentions. On the contrary, they presented it as the sober work of social scientists: Nightline's Ted Koppel lamented to Murray about how his "great deal of work and research" had become "a political football".[2]

Of course, this was almost certainly Murray's intention all along. In the book proposal for his previous book (Losing Ground, an attack on government welfare programs) he had explained: "Why can a publisher sell this book? Because a huge number of well-meaning whites fear that they are closet racists, and this book tells them they are not. It's going to make them feel better about things they already think but do not know how to say."[3] That's certainly what The Bell Curve did, replacing a debate over how to improve black achievement with one about whether such improvement was even possible.

There was just one problem: none of this stuff was accurate. As Professor Michael Nunley wrote in a special issue of the American Behavioral Scientist on The Bell Curve, after a series of scientific articles debunked all the book's major claims: "I believe this book is a fraud, that its authors must have known it was a fraud when they were writing it, and that Charles Murray must still know it's a fraud as he goes around defending it. ... After careful reading, I cannot believe its authors were not acutely aware of ... how they were distorting the material they did include." (What Liberal Media?, 100)

June 8, 2006

1,2,3   http://www.fair.org/index.php?page=1271

SPREADING LIES
HOW THINK TANKS IGNORE THE FACTS

But do the right-wing think tanks even care about the facts? In his autobiography, Blinded by the Right, David Brock describes his experience being recruited for one right out of college: "Though I had no advanced degrees, I assumed the grandiose title of John M. Olin Fellow in Congressional Studies, which, if nothing else, certainly impressed my parents. ... My assignment was to write a monograph, which I hoped to publish as a book, challenging the conservative orthodoxy on the proper relationship between the executive and legislative branches of government." This topic was chosen, Brock explains, because with "a squish like Bush in the White House ... the political reality

[was] that the conservative agenda could be best advanced by renegade conservatives on Capitol Hill." (79f)

Needless to say, paying fresh-faced former college students lots of money to write articles that serve political needs is not the best way to get accurate information. But is accurate information the goal? Look at John Lott, a "resident scholar" at the American Enterprise Institute — the same right-wing think tank that promoted The Bell Curve. Lott's book *More Guns, Less Crime* claimed that his scientific studies had found that passing laws to allow people to carry concealed weapons actually lowered crime rates. As usual, the evidence melted away upon investigation, but Lott's errors were more serious than most.

Not content to simply distort the data, Lott fabricated an entire study which he claimed showed that in 97% of cases, simply brandishing a gun would cause an attacker to flee. When Internet critics begun to point out his inconsistencies on this claim, Lott posted responses under the name "Mary Rosh" to defend himself. "I have to say that he was the best professor I ever had," Lott gushed about himself one Internet posting. "There were a group of us students who would try to take any class that he taught. Lott finally had to tell us that it was best for us to try and take classes from other professors."

Confronted about his alternate identity, Lott told the Washington Post "I probably shouldn't have done it — I know I shouldn't have done it". And yet, the very next day he again attacked his critics, this time under the new pseudonym "Washingtonian". (It later got so bad that one of Lott's pseudonyms would start talking about posts from another Lott pseudonym.)[1]

Lott, of course, is not the only scholar to make things up to bolster his case. For comparison, look at Michael Bellesiles, author of the anti-gun book *Arming America*, which argued guns were uncommon in early America. Other scholars investigated and found that Bellesiles had probably fabricated evidence. Emory University, where Bellesiles was a professor of history, begun an investigation into the accuracy of his work, eventually forcing him to resign. His publisher, Knopf, pulled the book out of print. Libraries pulled the book off their shelves. Columbia University revoked the Bancroft Prize the book had been awarded. The scandal was widely covered in academic circles. Bellesiles was firmly disgraced and has not shown his face in public since.

And what happened to Lott? Nothing. Lott remains a "resident scholar" at the American Enterprise Institute, his book continues to sell well, his op-ed pieces are still published in major papers, and he gives talks around the country.[2] For the right-wing scholar, even outright fraud is no serious obstacle.

June 9, 2006

1,2   http://timlambert.org/guns/Lott/

SAVING BUSINESS
THE ORIGINS OF RIGHT-WING THINK TANKS

Since the goal of these think tanks clearly isn't to advance knowledge, what are they for? To understand their real goals, we have to look at why they were created. After the tumultuous 1960s led a generation of students to start questioning authority, business decided something had to be done. "The American economic system," explained Lewis Powell in a 1971 memo for the U.S. Chamber of Commerce, "is under broad attack" from "perfectly respectable elements of society: from the college campus, the pulpit, the media, the intellectual and literary journals, the arts and sciences, and from politicians."

And business has no one to blame but itself for not getting these things under control: the colleges are funded by "contributions from capital funds controlled or generated by American business. The boards of trustees … overwhelmingly are composed of men and women who are leaders in the system." And the media "are owned and theoretically controlled by corporations which depend upon profits, and the enterprise system to survive." So business must "conduct guerilla warfare" by "establishing a staff of highly qualified scholars" who can be paid to publish a "steady flow of scholarly articles" in magazines and journals as well as books and pamphlets to be published "at airports, drugstores, and elsewhere."[1]

William Simon, president of the right-wing Olin Foundation (the same one that later funded Brock) was more blunt: "The only thing that can save the Republican Party … is a counter-intelligentsia. … [Conservative scholars] must be given grants, grants, and more grants in exchange for books, books, and more books." (Blinded By the Right, 78)

The Powell memo was incredibly influential. Soon after it was written, business began following its advice, building up its network of think tanks, news outlets, and media pressure groups. These organizations begun to dot the landscape, hiding behind respectable names like the Manhattan Institute or the Heartland Foundation. While these institutions were all funded by partisan conservatives, news accounts rarely noted this fact. (Another FAIR study finds The Heritage Foundation's political orientation — let alone its funding — was only identified in 24% of news citations.)[2]

As the conservative message machine grew stronger, political debate and electoral results begun to shift further and further to the right, eventually allowing extreme conservatives to be elected, first with Ronald Reagan and now with George W. Bush. More recently, conservatives have managed to finally win not only the White House but both houses of Congress. While their policy proposals, when understood, are just as unpopular as ever, conservatives are able to use their media power to twist the debate.

June 10, 2006

1. http://reclaimdemocracy.org/corporate_accountability/powell_memo_lewis.html
2. http://www.fair.org/extra/9805/think-tanks.html

HURTING SENIORS
THE ATTACK ON SOCIAL SECURITY

Recent events provide a compelling case study of how this process works. Conservatives have wanted to get rid of Social Security for years. The most successful anti-poverty program in history, it clearly shows how the government can be used to help people — anathema to conservative ideology. Now, with a secure lock on government, is their time to strike. As a White House deputy wrote in a memo that was later leaked, "For the first time in six decades, the Social Security battle is one we can win — and in doing so, we can help transform the political and philosophical landscape of the country."[1]

There's extremely strong public support for Social Security — conservatives could certainly never just come out and say they wanted to end it — so their plan is to deceive the public: First, persuade people that Social Security is facing some sort of crisis and won't be around for the next generation. Second, convince them to begin replacing Social Security with a privatized version. Privatization, the logic goes, will naturally keep increasing until all of Social Security is eliminated. The only problem is that Social Security isn't facing a crisis and any form of privatization, which would require both paying out to existing retirees and saving away money for the private accounts of the current generation, would worsen whatever financial problems Social Security does have.[2]

But think tanks have been preparing for this moment for years, floating privatization plans and doing their best to persuade the media that Social Security was in imminent danger. So when the Bush administration started up their anti-Social Security campaign, the media knew exactly what to say.

CBS, for example, presented a segment featuring man-on-the-street Tad DeHaven. "I don't expect to get anything from Social Security, OK?" said young DeHaven. "It's not going to be there — that's my assumption." DeHaven had good reason to say these things: for years, he's been one of the leading Republican activists in the fight to get rid of Social Security. CBS never mentioned the connection.[3]

A later CBS report boosted fears that Social Security was going bankrupt by displaying a graphic on the screen that read "2042: Insolvent = 0 benefits??" [sic] ("In 2042, Social Security will become insolvent, and today's young workers risk losing their benefits," a voiceover explained.) But this just isn't true: even the pessimistic Social Security Administration concedes that by 2042 Social Security will be able to pay nearly 80% of scheduled benefits, which is still far more than what it pays out today.[4]

Other networks were no better. NBC's report feature quotes from Bush saying the system would go "flat bust" and an interview with a Heritage Foundation scholar — identified only as a "social security expert" — but allowed no critics to contradict their claims.[5] Meanwhile, an ABC report claimed "One thing everyone agrees on, the Social Security system as it exists now won't be able to afford those payments for long after the Wilsons retire." In fact, it's quite the opposite: even the most pessimistic predictions say that Social Security will be fine until the Wilsons are statistically dead. Again, no critics...[6]

June 11, 2006

1. http://www.j-bradford-delong.net/movable_type/2005-3_archives/000119.html
2. http://www.fair.org/activism/cbs-cnn-social-security.html
3. http://www.fair.org/activism/cbs-cnn-social-security.html
4. http://www.fair.org/activism/cbs-social-security-update.html
5. http://www.fair.org/activism/nbc-socialsecurity.html
6. http://www.fair.org/activism/abc-socialsecurity.html

FIGHTING BACK
RESPONSES TO THE MAINSTREAM MEDIA

Unlike the conservative media, it does not appear the national media is intentionally partisan. But it exists in a very specific structural context. A recent study found that two-thirds of journalists thought bottom-line pressure was "seriously hurting the quality of news coverage" while around half reported their newsrooms had been cut. 75% of print and 85% of broadcast journalists agreed that "too little attention is paid to complex issues."[1] When you're short on staff and stories are shallow, reporters become even more dependent on outside sources — and the right-wing think tanks are more than willing to help out, while further pulling coverage to the right.

But one obvious solution — creating a matching set of left-wing think tanks — while perhaps helpful in balancing the debate, will not solve the problem. Media norms of balance mean that even qualified experts will always be presented as "just one side of the story," balanced directly against inaccurate conservatives — recall how the handful of corporate-funded global warming deniers are still balanced against the overwhelming scientific consensus.

Ideally, viewers would be able to hear both perspectives and decide which they thought was accurate. But since, as the journalists conceded, so little time is spent explaining complex issues, in practice very little information is presented that can help the viewer decide who's correct. So they're left to decide based on their existing ideological preferences, further splitting the country into two alternate realities.

Figuring out what is true — especially when it's so obvious, as in the examples above — is precisely what the mainstream media should be doing. Partisan pundits would be replaced with thoughtful scholars. Non-peer-reviewed books would be ignored, not endlessly promoted. Scientific facts would be given precedence over political arguments. Political commentary would be replaced by factual education.

Don't hold your breath. Six major companies own nearly 90% of all media outlets.[2] And they — and their advertisers — don't mind how things are going. Sumner Redstone, CEO of Viacom (Paramount, CBS, Blockbuster, MTV, Comedy Central, etc.), told a group of CEOs that "I look at the election from what's good for Viacom. I vote for what's good for Viacom." And, "from a Viacom standpoint, the election of a Republican administration is a better deal. Because the Republican administration has stood for many things we believe in, deregulation and so on."[3] Better news reporting wouldn't just be more expensive, it would threaten these business interests.

To get the straight story, it's necessary to turn to independent and community sources which don't have such conflicts of interest. One possibility is the daily news show Democracy Now!, hosted by Amy Goodman, which is funded only by viewers and foundations. Broadcast on 150 radio stations, 150 television stations, and the Internet, the show presents stories from activists, journalists, authors, and public interest organizations from around the world.

When outlets from ABC to the *New York Times* began claiming Iraq had weapons of mass destruction, Democracy Now! was one of the few sources to take a contrary view. It presented the testimony of Iraq's top weapons official, who defected to the US and explained that all the weapons had been destroyed. (Other stations, ironically, parroted the Bush administration in promoting the information he presented about the weapons Iraq had, without mentioning they had been destroyed.)4

And when US soldiers kidnapped Jean-Bertrand Aristide, the democratically-elected president of Haiti, and flew him to the Central African Republic where they locked him in a hotel room, he managed to quietly phone out while armed guards stood outside his door. Democracy Now! was alone in airing his incredible story. When Aristide was finally freed, he insisted on returning to his country and again Amy Goodman was the only US television journalist who dared to accompany him back.[5]

Still, Democracy Now!'s audience is rather small compared to that of the mainstream media. But stories from overseas hint at what could happen if enough people begun paying attention to such sources. In South Korea, the country with the highest rate of broadband adoption, politics has been turned upside down by OhmyNews, a five-year-old website. Founded by Oh Yeon Ho, OhmyNews has a feature unlike any other paper: more than 85% of its stories are contributed by readers.[6]

Almost anyone can write for OhmyNews: the site posts 70% of all stories that are submitted, over 15,000 citizen-reporters have published stories. OhmyNews copyedits their work but tries to leave their differing styles intact. The citizen-reporters write about things they know about and that interest them, together they end up covering most of the traditional spectrum. Yet their new voices end up providing coverage on things which typically get ignored by the mainstream media.[7]

This is most evident in their political coverage. Before OhmyNews, conservatives controlled 80% of Korea's newspaper circulation. Then OhmyNews gave a voice to progressives, inspiring massive nationwide protests against the government. The protests, in turn, led to the election of reformist Roh Moo Hyun, now known as "the first Internet president."[8] The furious conservative National Assembly responded by voting to impeach Roh on technical grounds. OhmyNews readers again organized and overthrew the Assembly in the next election, reinstating Roh. There's no reason why what happened in South Korea can't happen here. Overcoming the tide of misinformation is hard work, but working together committed citizens can make amazing progress, even when up against the most powerful interests. Out society has an extraordinary level of freedom and openness. Whether we use that freedom to seek out the truth or remain content with conventional platitudes is up to us.

June 11, 2006

1. http://people-press.org/reports/pdf/214topline.pdf
2. http://www.thevoicenews.com/news/2003/0411/Front_Page/C06_LaVoie-media.html
3. http://www.opinionjournal.com/extra/?id=110005669
4. http://www.democracynow.org/article.pl?sid=03/04/07/0320205
5. http://www.democracynow.org/article.pl?sid=04/03/01/1521216&mode=thread&tid=25
6. http://www.siliconvalley.com/mld/siliconvalley/business/columnists/5889390.htm
7. http://english.ohmynews.com/articleview/article_view.asp?article_class=8&no=201599&rel_no=1
8. http://english.ohmynews.com/articleview/article_view.asp?article_class=8&no=201599&rel_no=1

AN INCONVENIENT TRUTH

Al Gore's presentation on global warming is filled with graphs — Gore is fanatical about collecting evidence, even at one point going to the North Pole to persuade the scientists there to release their records of the ice shelves — but only one of them really matters. It comes early in the film, as Gore talks about the large ice core samples that scientists take to trace the history of the Earth's temperature and CO_2 ratings.

Gore shows the results of these samples and then says we can go back further. The screen expands in both directions to show a massive graph of CO_2 concentration going back 600,000 years. Its had its fluctuations over that time — large hills and then valleys. Underneath it, he then graphs temperature over the same period.

Temperature tracks CO_2 almost exactly, with a several-decade lag. Those large fluctuations? Those were the six ice ages we've had over the past 600,000 years. CO_2 in the atmosphere goes up and so does the temperature, the CO_2 trapping the sun's radiation inside our planet, where it heats the Earth.

These huge fluctuations are the difference between ice ages and where we are today. Then Gore shows the most recent trajectory of CO_2: straight up, more than doubled. "If that much CO_2 in one direction causes an ice age," Gore says, "imagine what it will do in the other direction." And then he shows the projections for the next 50 years. Again straight up, another doubling. "This is literally off he charts," he explains. He has to climb up to reach that peak.

"Not a single number in this graph," he says, "is in dispute." This is the inconvenient truth: unless we change, we will destroy the environment that sustains our species.

June 6, 2006

THE ATTRACTION OF THE CENTER

"Centrism" is the tendency to see two different beliefs and attempt to split the difference between them. The reason why it's a bad idea should be obvious: truth is independent of our beliefs, no less than any other partisans, centrists ignore evidence in favor of their predetermined ideology.

So what's the attraction? First, it requires little thought: arguing for a specific position requires collecting evidence and arguing for it. Centrism, simply requires repeating some of what A is saying and some of what B is saying and mixing them together. Centrists often don't even seem to care if the bits they take contradict each other.

Second, it's somewhat inoffensive. Taking a strong stand on A or B will unavoidably alienate some. But being a centrist, one can still maintain friends on both sides, since they will find at least some things that you espouse to be agreeable with their own philosophies.

Third, it makes it easier to suck up to those in charge, because the concept of the "center" can easily move along with shifts in power. A staunch conservative will have to undergo a major change of political philosophy to get a place in liberal administration. A centrist can simply espouse a few more positions from the conservatives and a few less from the liberals and fit in just fine. This criteria explains why centrists are so prevalent in the pundit class (neither administration is tempted to really force them out) and why so many "centrist" pundits espouse mostly conservative ideas these days (the conservatives are in power).

Fourth, despite actually being a servant of those in power, centrism gives one the illusion of actually being a serious, independent thinker. "People on the right and on the left already know what they're going to say on every issue," they might claim, "but we centrists make decisions based on the situation." (This excuse was recently used in a fund-raising letter by The New Republic.) Of course, the "situation" that's used to make these decisions is simply who's currently in power, as discussed above, but that part is carefully omitted.

Fifth, it appeals to the public. There's tremendous dissatisfaction among the public with the government and our system of politics. Despite being precisely in the middle of this corrupt system, centrists can claim that they're actually "independents" and "disagree with both the left and the right". They can denounce "extremism" (which isn't very popular) and play the "moderate", even when their positions are extremely far from what the public believes or what the facts say.

Together, these reasons combine to make centrism an especially attractive place to be in American politics. But the disease is far from limited to politics. Journalists frequently suggest the truth lies between the two opposing sources they've quoted. Academics try to distance themselves from policy positions proposed by either party. And, perhaps worst of all, scientists try to split the difference between two competing theories.

Unfortunately for them, neither the truth nor the public necessarily lies somewhere in the middle. Fortunately for them, more valuable rewards do.

Exercise for the reader: What's the attraction of "contrarianism", the ideology subscribed to by online magazines like Slate?

July 12, 2006

TALKING RIGHT

Government, John Dewey famously said, is the shadow cast by big business over society. And political language, Geoffrey Nunberg argues in *Talking Right*, is the shadow cast by government. Democrats, he points out, seem to think language has a talismanic power, that if only they can find the right catch phrase or slogan, they can pull people over to their side. "Liberal" must become "progressive", "family values" must become "valuing families". There's an intellectual cleverness to such stunts, and as a Berkeley linguist, Nunberg must want to believe in them. But he doesn't. The words, he explains, are just a side-effect of the larger political situation. Dewey explained that attempts to change the shadow will have no effect without a change in the substance, and Nunberg heartily agrees.

It's hard to see how it could be otherwise, but Democrats have suffered from a stubborn literalism in political discourse: thinking they can beat the charge of big government by launching programs cutting down on bureaucratic waste, thinking they can reclaim the issue of values by pointing to their love of tolerance and fairness, thinking they can dodge the charge of latte-sipping by donning a hunting cap and rifle. In reality, the issues go much deeper: big government is an attack on the notion that government can do good, values refers to a feeling of national morals run amok, and the latte-sipping charge is an attempt to distract voters from bigger issues of class. Nunberg even chastises his colleague George Lakoff for assuming that the current packages of political positions have any deeper meanings, rather than just being accidents of history.

Nunberg is an essayist — his commentaries for NPR's *Fresh Air* are a national treasure — and his style, while eminently readable, doesn't translate well to a long book, where his points get lost in a field of anecdotes. But beneath all the stories about how conservatives eat more brie and liberal used to be a mantle claimed by everyone, Nunberg's point is a familiar one: if the Democrats want to win, they must begin telling full-throated populist stories about how the economic elite are capturing the wealth of our country and how we need government to take it back. The point is no less true for being popular, and it's heartening to find that investigation from yet another perspective yields the same conclusions.

October 17, 2006

THE INVENTION OF OBJECTIVITY

Big media pundits are always wringing their hands about how upstart partisan bloggers are destroying the neutral objectivity our country was founded on. (If there's one thing pundits love to do, it's hand-wringing.) Without major papers giving everyone an objective view of the facts, they insist, the very foundation of the republic is in peril.

You can criticize this view for just being silly or wrong, and many have, but there's another problem with it: it's completely ahistorical. As Robert McChesney describes in *The Problem of the Media*, objectivity is a fairly recent invention — the republic was actually founded on partisan squabblers.

When our country was founded, newspapers were not neutral, non-partisan outlets, but the products of particular political parties. The Whigs had their paper, the Tories theirs, and both of which attacked their political opponents with slurs that would make even the most foul-mouthed bloggers blush. This behavior wasn't just permitted — it was encouraged.

You often hear the media quote Jefferson's comment that "were it left to me to decide whether we should have a government without newspapers, or newspapers without government, I should not hesitate a moment to prefer the latter." However, they hesitate to print the following sentence: "But I should mean that every man should receive those papers, and be capable of reading them." In particular, Jefferson was referring to the post office subsidy the government provided to the partisan press.

In 1794, newspapers made up 70% of post office traffic and the big debate in Congress was not over whether the government should pay for their delivery, but how much of it to pay for. James Madison attacked the idea that newspaper publishers should have to pay even a token fee to get the government to deliver their publications, calling it "an insidious forerunner of something worse." By 1832, newspaper traffic had risen to make up 90% of all mail.

Indeed, objectivity wasn't even invented until the 1900s. Before that, McChesney comments, "such notions for the press would have been nonsensical, even unthinkable." Everyone assumed that the best system of news was one where everyone could say their piece at very little cost. (The analogy to blogging isn't much of a stretch, now is it? See, James Madison loved blogs!)

But as wealth began to concentrate in the Gilded Age and the commercial presses began to lobby government for more favorable policies, the size and power of the smaller presses began to dwindle. The commercial presses were eager to be the only game in town, but they realized that if they were, their blatant partisanship would have to go. (Nobody would stand for a one-newspaper town if the one paper was blatantly biased.) So they decided to insist that journalism was a profession like any other, that reporting was an apolitical job, based solely on objective standards.

They set up schools of journalism to train reporters in the new notion. In 1900, there were no J-schools; by 1920, the major ones were going strong. The "church and state" separation of advertising and reporting became official doctrine and the American Society of Newspaper Editors (ASNE) was set up to enforce it.

The entire foundation of press criticism was rebuilt. Now, instead of criticizing papers for the bias of their owners, press critics had to focus on the professional obligations of their writers. Bias wasn't about the slant of a paper's focus, but about any slanting put in by a reporter.

So that was the line of attack the house press critics took when the world of weblogs brought back the vibrant political debates of our country's founding. "These guys are biased! Irresponsible! They get their facts wrong! They're unprofessional!" they squeal. Look, guys. Tell that to James Madison.

October 19, 2006

THE WORLD IS WATCHING

The World is Watching is an incredible and, to my knowledge, unique film about the making of news. Two film crews, one at ABC News headquarters in New York, the other with ABC's Central American Unit in Nicaragua, spend a day watching exactly how the clips that appear on the national nightly news are made. The result is revealing.

The crew begins the day by checking in with Washington to get the appropriate framing for the story. At the same time, they keep an ear out for tips and scoops. They hear about a village leveled by the contras (the US-funded group fighting Nicaragua's socialist government) and set out to get some film.

They interview a peasant. "You have to be angry," the reporter coaches his subject, who stubbornly remains calm and peaceful despite having been brutally attacked. This peasant, like every other one in the film, can clearly and eloquently explain exactly what's going on: Reagan is fighting a war by proxy against their government because it has dared to institute policies which favor the poor (that is, people like them) over the wealthy elites. They live in horrid conditions, they are brutally attacked by contra forces, they appear to be just poor and stupid peasants — yet they know exactly what's going on and tell the cameras as much.

The cameras, of course, know better. For the journalists and the folks at home, the events are seen through a different frame. Five Central American countries have signed a peace agreement promising to institute Democratic reforms in exchange for peace. Most of these countries are US client-states where the governments we instituted brutally terrorize civilians and suppress democratic freedoms. The media doesn't see that, though. Instead, Reagan literally directs their eyes elsewhere by delivering a heartfelt message to the media: they have an import responsibility — perhaps "one of journalism's great triumphs," he says — to ensure democracy flourishes... in Nicaragua.

The journalists unquestionably accept this frame, sending camera crews to Nicaragua, not the other countries. Once there they ensure everything that comes back is fit into this frame. We watch as Peter Jennings marvels at how the Sandanista government has managed to survive the democratic reforms. We watch as the Washington team carefully scrutinizes the voiceovers, blanching at the suggestion that the protesters in the street are somehow "anti-war". "It sounds like they're peaceniks or something," one reporter says. Pro-Sandanista protesters would be much better.

Once the piece hits air the peasant's words, so eloquent before, are chopped and translated for the larger audience. Now she is seen stupidly insisting that she does not see communism. This is just a backlash against being attacked by the contras, the voiceover helpfully explains, and anyway, she's just a peasant — what does she know? Meanwhile, the Sandanista government still refuses to negotiate with the contras and is thus presumably the cause of all this violence. The whole piece takes up just two minutes on the news.

At the same time the piece airs on ABC, the facts on the ground show a different story. Daniel Ortega, leader of the Sandanistas, is giving a speech to a large assembled crowd. He will negotiate with the Sandanistas, he says. It's too late — the piece has been filed and the ABC crew has already flown to the next day's location. The folks at home never hear the news.

October 24, 2004

MYSTERIES OF THE EARTH-BOUND HUMAN

In my short stay upon this planet I have noticed many things interesting and strange which I have written about in this and other periodicals. However, there are some things which are more than just unusual: they are simply incomprehensible. And yet they are widespread and almost universally beloved.

There are many silly and irrational things on this planet (I'm thinking of a major one in particular), but the irrationality of such things is generally acknowledged in the more intellectual circles and plausible explanations have been devised. No such thing is true of the following — it is the rare soul who would admit to agreeing with the following.

Sports. Humans find no end of amusement in sitting on their butts on uncomfortable metal benches in an ugly, dirty facility that stinks of alcoholic beverages and saliva-modified products and watching a bunch of other humans far below play any of a variety of bizarre games with sticks and balls. They sit (or, more accurately, stomp and scream) and watch this entirely boring display for hours on end, repeatedly. When they cannot make it in person they watch facsimilies which are beamed into their homes.

It is not simply that the humans have boring lives and appreciate any excuse from them. While that is undoubtedly true, it does not explain such a bizarre choice. There is no similar crowd who collects to observe the behavior of ants or even other humans (in constrained situations like malls, perhaps) even though both these things are far more interesting.

Nor is it that the humans enjoy thinking about games, since broadcasts of more intellectual games receive nowhere near the same audience. Instead, such obsession is reserved for what they call "sports" — games with organized teams under rigid rules that involve a great deal of athletic activity. No explanation for this obsession is ever provided. Indeed, even questioning the obsession is taboo.

Now let me be clear. I certainly find it enjoyable to play a good game, especially one that involves plenty of exercise. Yet even here, humans manage to inexplicably screw it up. When playing a game their goal is never to have fun, even though that is precisely what the game is good at. Instead, they become obsessed with the minutiae of following "the rules" and deciding who is "winning" — pastimes which generally practiced are antithetical to the aforementioned aim.

Rock concerts. A sizable segment of the human population spends their time involved in the production of things that amuse other humans, a field known as "entertainment". Some in this field create a certain type of interesting sounds, known as "music". I have nothing against this endeavor — many of the results are quite enjoyable, with interesting results on mood and emotion. (Although most of it, especially that noted as "popular", is quite bad.)

And I can certainly sympathize with the desire to become more involved with a group of "musicians" who make sounds that one things especially good. However, the humans once again take this reasonable pursuit and turn it towards the bizarre. It turns out that the tribute takes form in what they call a "rock concert".

A concert consists of going to listen to the humans make their good sounds. (Reasonable so far.) However, for most modern bands, it is apparently required to do this in a dark and poorly-cleaned basement, pressed up against the bodies of numerous other people who are talking and stuff, with the sounds played through speakers at a volume so loud that they sound absolutely dreadful. The alcoholic beverages and so on also again make an appearance.

Food. Like the humans, I require certain the consumption of certain objects in order to power the chemical reactions that allow me to functions (a process the humans call "eating"). While there are differences in our tastes (mine our smaller) and quantities (mine are larger), no one can object to doing these things which are necessary to live.

What is bizarre is how much enjoyment they seem to get out of it. In a recent informal survey, the humans told me that "eating" made up a large part of the enjoyment they derived from their lives. I was not able to discern the causes of such enjoyment.

In one incident, a subject explained how he looked forward fondly for the opportunity to consume a certain liquid. Interested in pursing such enjoyment, I decided to have some of the liquid with him. The liquid promptly proceeded to burn my innards, causing a distinctly unpleasant situation that lasted for some time. And yet this human is far from the only one who enjoys this liquid — facilities for distributing it seem to be on every block. But as far as I can tell humans do not enjoy burning their innards in any other situation. The fact that it's "food" seems to have a magical power over them.

Sex.

[*This section has been censored from the Earth edition of this publication because it was found too inflammatory in focus groups.*]

This is the greatest of all human oddities. Humans are simply obsessed with sex and sexual relations and other related things. They think about it, according to some accounts, nearly all the time and much of their entertainment is dedicated to the subject. Yet, by all accounts, it is a distinctly unpleasant affair involving activities so disgusting I dare not describe them to you here. While humans no doubt derive pleasure from such activities, surely it is not worth the enormous costs — pleasure can be found in other ways in their society.

Conclusion. I do not hold out much hope for solving these strange mysteries during my stay here. They are of some interest to me, but more as a sidenote than as anything I would devote my efforts to. Even if I were to investigate, I cannot even think of a plausibly effective way to proceed on these questions. So I write them up here and leave them as one of this planet's unsolved mysteries.

2005-10-28

TRIALS OF TESTING

Since many readers complained about the previous piece "Mysteries of the Earth-Bound Human" we have pulled it and provided this replacement. The things we do for you people!

It takes little courage to denounce men who believe they can harness the power of their minds to fly and use a space of universal consciousness to create world peace. And, in the long run, it is of little consequence. No one can recall the obscure psuedo-scientific claims of yesteryear.

But take the idea that underneath the skull lie a series of organs for human traits like acquisitiveness and amorousness which bulge and change the shape of the head with dominance. The idea seems equally preposterous but it held real sway in its era — the Massachusetts Medical Association and the president of Harvard threw their weight behind it (Paul, 7) and phrenology continues to be remembered today.

Such absurd ideas are not remnants of a bygone past — just replace "organs" with "genes" and you'll have the new "science" of evolutionary psychology (formerly sociobiology), an absurdity which Harvard University's own president has thrown the institution's weight behind. And yet one rarely sees "pro-science skeptics" challenging its claims. Indeed, scientific magazines write them up with only minor questioning, saving their ire for those who dare criticize the ideas.

But at least such fields have critics (and I count myself among them). There are related claims, however, that exercise much more power over our lives and (perhaps as a result) are far less challenged. One of their creators explained that they would "promote personal development", "manage conflict", and "increase human understanding worldwide." (Paul, 121) But instead of Vedic science, she was talking about here creation: the Myers-Briggs personality test.

I have written before about the failures of experiments to provide evidence in favor of our concepts of personality or intelligence and how despite this many continue to believe in them. One can discuss how even studies by proponents find that IQ lacks validity and that 47% of people have a different Myers-Briggs personality type on a second administration of a test. But this somehow seems not to convince. So let us try another tack: let us look at how these tests are made.

The history of the IQ test — along with a number of other supposed ways of measuring "intelligence" — is detailed in Stephen Jay Gould's classic *The Mismeasure of Man*. It was originally created by Alfred Binet to find children in French schools who might need special tutoring. Binet thought that by locating and helping these students, one could make sure that everyone learned all the material. Binet composed the test by throwing together whatever questions came to mind: things about shapes and numbers and words. He just wanted to see if some kids were having trouble, he made no attempt to make sure the result was a balanced measure of "intelligence".

Lewis Terman, a professor at Stanford University, imported the Binet test to America, added some more random things and mixed it all up a little, and called the result the Stanford-Binet intelligence test (a name which is still used today)[1]. One of the test's first applications was American Psychological Association president Robert Yerkes's attempt to classify the people recruited for the Army. Among the questions:

- Crisco is a: patent medicine, disinfectant, toothpaste, food product
- The number of a Kaffir's legs is: 2, 4, 6, 8
- Christy Mathewson is famous as a: writer, artist, baseball player, comedian

Recent immigrants, whose command of English might be understandably weak, were allowed to take a pictorial version: drawing "a rivet in a pocket knife, a filament in a light bulb, a horn on a phonograph, a net on a tennis court, and a ball in a bowler's hand (marked wrong, Yerkes explained, if an examinee drew the ball in the alley, for you can tell from the bowler's posture that he has not yet released the ball)." (Gould, 230)

Terman, meanwhile, conducted a longitudinal study of the people his IQ test marked as "gifted". Joel Shurkin, based on exclusive access to the records, documented the full story in his book *Terman's Kids*. Among the study's participants was a man named Jess Oppenheimer. "Gave the impression of being very pushy and forward although he did not show these characteristics during the interview," wrote one of Terman's assistants. "I could detect no signs of a sense of a humor." (Shurkin, 54) Oppenheimer went on to create and write the shows *I Love Lucy and Get Smart*.

The story of personality tests is little better. In her book *The Cult of Personality* (recently republished as *The Cult of Personality Testing*), Annie Murphy Paul (a former senior editor for mass bi-monthly *Psychology Today*) describes the history of all the major personality tests. Take the Minnesota Multiphasic Personality Inventory (MMPI), which was created in a similar way to the IQ test.

The test was created by psychologist Starke Hathaway and neuropsychiatrist J. Charnley McKinley by simply coming up with a bunch of true-or-false statements that they thought might indicate whether the respondent had a mental illness. Among them:

- I have never had any black, tarry-looking bowel movements.
- I have had no difficulty starting or holding my urine.

- I have never indulged in any unusual sexual practices.
- There is something wrong with my sex organs.
- I believe there is a Devil and a Hell in the afterlife.
- Everything is turning out as the Bible said it would.
- I think I would like to belong to a motorcycle club.
- Often I feel as if there were a tight band around my head.
- I loved my father.
- I like to flirt.
- I believe my sins are unpardonable.
- I have a good appetite.
- I think Lincoln was greater than Washington.
- Women should not be allowed to drink in cocktail bars.
- A large number of people are guilty of bad sexual conduct.
- If the money were right, I would like to work for a circus or carnival.
- (Paul, 53)

The resulting test was administered to the patients at the University of Minnesota mental hospital as well as the (presumably sane) staff there (all white, Protestant, Minnesotans who came to be known as the "Minnesota Normals"). Statistical analysis was then done to determine which questions more accurately predicted whether the user had a mental illness and more specifically, what kind.[2]

This was quickly generalized: people who scored above-average on the scales for Hysteria or Depression (but not high enough to actually have a mental illness) could be said to have hysterical or depressive personalities, even though there was absolutely no evidence to support this leap (not that it was on particularly sturdy ground to begin with).

The resulting test was used to analyze people in business, the army, court, high school, and at the doctor's. It was "used to screen job applicants, offer vocational advice, settle custody disputes, and determine legal status." (Paul, 58f) And while the test engendered some backlash, it continues to be used frequently today, often as the a requirement for getting or keeping a job. Paul notes "the MMPI (in an updated version) is employed by 86% of clinical psychologists and administered, by one estimate, to 15 million Americans each year." (63) For example, it is used by 60% of police departments to evaluate prospective officers. Meanwhile, studies show that such tests can reject as high as 60% of healthy applicants.

This is but one example — and one chapter in Paul's book — but all the others all have similar stories. An absurd test, concocted through absurd means, completely untested, ends up becoming a powerful societal force. All the more reason for us to speak out about them.

October 28, 2005

1. Incidentally, although Terman did not put his name on the test, his family continues to have a presence at Stanford. His son Frederick Emmons Terman was a professor of engineering (and later provost); the Terman Engineering Center, which was across the street from my dorm, is named in his honor. And down the hall from me in my dorm lived his daughter, who, in full disclosure, I ate meals with a couple times.
2. Not that this methodology is necessarily flawed, although it leads to some interesting conclusions. Paul writes that in one experiment, the question "that yielded some of the most useful information" about whether someone had a fascist personality was: "Obedience and respect for authority are the most important virtues children should learn." (Paul, 147)

THE TRUTH ABOUT DRUG COMPANIES

Whenever someone wants to talk about how great our society is, one example that always seems to come up is our many innovative and powerful new drugs invented by the pharmaceutical companies. Perhaps it's just the $54 billion a year the companies spend on marketing, much of it going to ads talking about how innovative and helpful drug companies are, bur it does seem like these life-saving wonder pills have really captured the public's imagination.

But in her new book, *The Truth About the Drug Companies*, Marcia Angell, former editor-in-chief of the respected New England Journal of Medicine, shows that much of what we thought about the drug companies is wrong. For one thing, they're not innovative. Believe it or not, drug companies simply do not do research into major new drugs. All the real research is done at universities and funded by the government.

Thanks to the Bayh-Dole Act, universities can then patent these medical discoveries made by their employees using public funding, which they then turn around and sell to the drug companies for a relative song. Often the universities have done all the work — including clinical trials — and drug companies just start up the manufacturing plants.

Because the drug companies have bought exclusive patent rights, they can now charge whatever they like for these drugs without fear of competition. And what little research the drug companies do mostly involves coming up with "me too" drugs — modifying an existing drug a little bit (even things as minor as changing the color or coating it) and then filing new patents on the result so that the exclusive profits keep rolling in. Thanks to armies of lawyers and various FDA patent loopholes, drug companies can use various patent tricks to keep generic competitors away for years.

Even when competitors do finally arrive, the drug company marketing campaigns start up, encouraging everyone to switch to their new, slightly-different-but-patented drug. For example, take AstroZeneca's heartburn drug Prilosec ($6 billion in annual sales): when its patent ran out, AstroZeneca took the inactive half off of Prilosec, repatented it, and marketed as Nexium. It then ran clinical trials which compared 20mg of Prilosec with 20mg of Nexium, but since half of Prilosec was inactive, this was like comparing 10mg of the old drug and 20mg of the new drug. Somewhat surprisingly, Nexium's double dose appeared to be only slightly more effective, but AstroZeneca touted these results in a massive marketing campaign involving tons of ads and gobs of free samples, enough to get doctors to switch most prescriptions before the Prilosec patent ran out.

These marketing campaigns are huge: $11 billion a year in free samples, over $6 billion on sales reps (one for every five doctors), $3 billion on vague ads to consumers. But on top of this are massive campaigns of deception: bribing doctors, bribing researchers, bribing universities, bribing HMOs, providing kickbacks, running "medical education courses" which state law requires doctors to attend, running in-hospital television networks which are one long drug ad, and funding deceptive studies (like the Nexium one) that wrongly make it appear that the company's new drug has amazing beneficial properties.

These studies are so pervasive that when the rare honest study is done, the results are incredible. The US government funded a massive study called ALLHAT (8 years, 42,000 people, 600 clinics) to compare different treatments for high blood pressure. It compared a series of different popular modern drugs (Norvasc, Cardura/doxazosin, Zestril/Prinivil/lisinopril) which worked in different ways and an "old time diuretic" or "water pill". The results were stunning: the diuretic was more effective and had less side effects than the expensive fancy new drugs — less heart failure and fewer strokes, so much so that the Cardura part of the trial had to be stopped early since so many people were getting heart failure. These expensive new drugs weren't just wasting people's money (as much as $678 a year per person), they were seriously hurting them.

But nobody prescribed diuretics, perhaps in part because nobody marketed them to doctors. Drug companies aren't required by the FDA to compare their new drugs to older treatments, so doctors had no way to know which was more effective. And drug companies aren't even required to publish the studies the FDA does require. For example, the study that led the FDA to approve antidepressants (like Prozac, Paxil, Zoloft, Celexa, Serzone, and Effexor) found that placebos were 80% as effective. But these studies weren't released until fifteen years later, when someone filed a Freedom of Information Act request against the FDA. There are even worse cases: for decades, women were prescribed estrogen and progesterone hormone replacement therapy because industry-sponsored studies said it would prevent heart disease. But a large NIH clinical trial found the therapy actually increases heart disease!

Our utopia of miracle pills is now beginning to look a bit like a nightmare. Drug companies use our tax money to pay for their research, turn around and sell the results to us at high prices, spend the resulting profits on massive campaigns to mislead us about their effects, which then encourage doctors to prescribe an expensive pill which may not help much and might even make things worse. Year after year, drug companies are by far the most successful industry. They use their stunning profits to buy off politicians and propagandize the public into maintaining this state of affairs.

Only by learning the true state of affairs can we begin to fight back.

March 25, 2005

THE CASE AGAINST LAWRENCE SUMMERS

> *Just between you and me, shouldn't the World Bank be encouraging MORE migration of the dirty industries to the LDCs [Less Developed Countries]? ... I think the economic logic behind dumping a load of toxic waste in the lowest wage country is impeccable and we should face up to that. ... countries in Africa are vastly UNDER-polluted*
>
> — Lawrence H. Summers[1]

On January 14, 2005, Harvard President Lawrence H. Summers offered "some attempts at provocation" at a conference on "Diversifying the Science & Engineering Workforce", specifically discussing "women's representation in tenured positions in science and engineering at top universities and research institutions".[2]

He begins by suggesting that under-representation isn't always due to discrimination:

Catholics are substantially under-represented in investment banking, which is an enormously high-paying profession in our society; that white men are very substantially under-represented in the National Basketball Association; and that Jews are very substantially under-represented in farming and in agriculture.

So, he says, we have to ask why women are under-represented and he offers three possibilities. The first is what he calls "the high-powered job hypothesis", namely that "young women in their mid-twenties make a decision that they don't want to have a job that they think about eighty hours a week". ("Is our society right [in these expectations and imbalances]?" He tables the question.) The second is "differential availability of aptitude at the high end" — that there is a difference in the variability of "mathematical ability, scientific ability" that is "not plausibly culturally determined" which, by his rough calculations, means there are five times as many male math/science geniuses as there are women math/science geniuses.

"I would far prefer to believe something else," Summers says, but "the combination of the high-powered job hypothesis and the differing variances probably explains a fair amount of this problem."

Could the differing variances be due to socialization? Summers doesn't think so. He says that "a hundred different kibbutzes" each independently decided to reverse course from a sexual egalitarianism and let "the men ... fix the tractors and the women ... work in the nurseries". And furthermore:

... my experience with my two and a half year old twin daughters who were not given dolls and who were given trucks, and found themselves saying to each other, look, daddy truck is carrying the baby truck, tells me something.

(Summers does not say whether two-person sample was also raised without TV and books and all the other images of socialization that say girls should play with baby dolls.)

Is it discrimination?

If it was really the case that everybody was discriminating, there would be very substantial opportunities for a limited number of people who were not prepared to discriminate to assemble remarkable departments of high quality people at relatively limited cost simply by the act of their not discriminating ... I think one sees relatively little evidence of that.

So, he says, the general problems of universities are those of the "high-powered job", the specific problems of the sciences are due to natural varying ability. "I would like nothing better than to be proved wrong," but "empirical psychology" and "the data" say otherwise. And our personal prejudices have to bow before the objectivity of science.

This is a tune that is by no means new. As Stephen Jay Gould points out in his fine book, The Mismeasure of Man, throughout history those who have tried to justify existing inequalities by blaming biological determinism have said the same thing.

Paul Broca, for example, who carefully weighed numerous brains to see which groups were intelligent and which were not, was truly sad to discover that the brains of blacks were smaller than those of whites. But, he argued, there was nothing he could do: "There is no faith, however respectable, no interest, however legitimate, which must not accommodate itself to the progress of human knowledge and bend before truth."

Despite such lofty principles, Gould shows that, quite aside from the false assumption that brain size is related to intelligence, Broca repeatedly and consistently manipulated his data to reach these conclusions. Gould believes such manipulation was unconscious, even though at times it was quite extreme. (As one example, Broca threw out entire systems of measurement when the inferior races scored too well on them.)

The tone is a theme through Gould's book, so it is no surprise to see it reappear today. But is it any more true?

Broca's major error was assuming that the size of someone's brain could tell you how intelligent they are. This is of course incorrect — people's brain size is mostly determined by the size and build of the rest of their body — and trouble the assumption seems absurd. Yet we believe in a notion that is just as silly — that IQ tests and math exams measure some sort of innate intelligence.

In the present context, a study by Claude Steele brings some of the problems into sharp relief. (I am working here from Steele's chapter in Young, Gifted, and Black.) Steele, with Steven Spencer and Diane Quinn, took some of the best and most dedicated math students they could find and gave them an extremely difficult math test. The men performed more than three and a half times as well as the women — an enormous gap. Then they gave students the same test, but told them this was a special test in which women always did as well as men. The gap closed almost entirely, with women's scores increasing dramatically. (Steele's research shows similar effects with other victims of stereotypes, like blacks.)

Steele suggests that women's scores are depressed by "stereotype threat" — a woman comes across a hard problem that they have trouble solving, and they begin to worry that people might think they're having trouble at math because they're female, and they begin to worry that this might be true. (Needless to say, comments like Summers's can't do much to alleviate these fears.) When they're told the stereotypes can't apply, the fears go away and they perform fine.

But the mechanisms involved are unimportant for our purposes. The key point is that the supposedly objective examination measure of intelligence is seriously flawed, even on a subject as supposedly objective as a math test. These tests are not just measuring intelligence; at the very least they're also measuring something like self-confidence.

As Gould argues, we are tempted to measure things and then we are tempted to assume the numbers that result refer to something real — that tests in math measure something called "mathematical ability". But this is a logical leap — the case must be carefully proven. There's no evidence that such a thing as "math ability" even exists, let alone that it can be measured.

Biological determinists like to respond to such arguments by saying that the speaker is denying the influence of biology, when all reasonable people know that both biology and environment have an impact — say 40% biology, 60% environment. But it is the determinists who are missing the point. Skills cannot be divided up in so absurd a manner.

Let us put aside brains for a second and imagine the arm muscle. Some people are born with a naturally skinny body type that doesn't build much arm muscle. Others naturally build muscle like crazy. Clearly biology plays a role. But it's absurd to say that it's 40% biology, or any other number — a muscular person whose arm is paralyzed will not be very muscular at all, while a weak person who works out incessantly will have huge biceps.

It's not hard to see how the brain could work the same way: people are born with natural tendencies, but work or environment can quickly change this "default" destiny.

In a real twist of irony, it turns out that it is exactly this confusion that causes the gender gap. Further research by Carol Dweck has investigated whether students believe that "mathematical ability" is a learned skill or an innate gift. A simple study shows the shocking effects of this belief. Students were given an obscure non-verbal IQ-style test that was designed to be easy for their age group. Afterwards, half were told "You got a great score. You must have worked really hard" and half were told "You got a great score. You must be really good at this." Then they asked kids if they wanted to try harder questions that might help them learn more. The ones who were praised for effort were happy to — one effort-based kid (in another study) rubbed his hands together, licked his lips, and exclaimed "I always love a challenge!" — but intelligence-based kids tried to avoid it, perhaps fearing they'd look stupid.

They were then given the harder problems, much too hard for them to solve. Then they were given more easy problems again. The gift kids did much worse on the third set of problems. When asked if they wanted to take more problems home, they said they already had them at home (an absurd lie). By contrast, the skill kids not only asked for some to take home, one even asked for the name of the tests "so my mom can buy more when I run out". The kids were also asked to write a note about the tests to other kids who might take them. The notes were anonymous, but there was a little place to put your score. Nearly 40% of the gift kids lied and exaggerated their scores. All this from just one little sentence — the kids were otherwise identical.

In other words, Dweck says, telling kids they're smart makes the stupid and liars.

Dweck's observations of classrooms find that boys are more often chided on the basis of effort ("Johnny, I know you'd do better if you just spent more time on this"), perhaps leading girls to infer that their ability is innate. Her studies find that girls are more likely to believe their ability is innate than boys and that it is these girls who are the cause of the gender gap in ability. Teaching these girls that mathematical ability comes from hard work can eliminate the gap.

[Personal note: Both Dweck and Steele have been recently hired away from Stanford and presented their results to my class.]

Looking at the long history of how even supposedly scientific evidence of the differences intelligence between groups has been false and distorted, one ought to be very careful before reviving such claims. Summers was not only not careful in his evidence, he didn't even bother to present evidence.

There are few worse things an intellectual can do than present false claims without evidence. If you present true claims, of course, there is no problem. And if you present false claims with evidence, one can evaluate the quality of the evidence. But if you simply state something as true, it has a way of seeping unquestioned into people's heads. And how much worse, then, to spread these falsehoods on such a subject, where they can do great harm.

I'll close with a bit from the question period after Summers's talk:

Q: I noticed [this is] being recorded so I hope that we'll be able to have a copy of it. That would be nice.

LHS: We'll see. (LAUGHTER)

1.   http://www.whirledbank.org/ourwords/summers.html
2.   http://www.president.harvard.edu/speeches/2005/nber.html

PHILIP ZIMBARDO
ON THE PSYCHOLOGY OF EVIL

Philip Zimbardo, the creator of the famed Stanford Prison Experiment (don't worry, I'll describe it later), is giving a lecture on terrorism and Abu Ghraib.

Zimbardo notes that he was a high-school classmate of Stanley Milgram, perhaps the best-known social psychologist. Milgram was the one who conducted the classic experiments on obedience to authority. He would invite a subject in and explain to them that they were helping him research the effects of memory. A confederate would be hooked up to an electrical chair in another room. The subject would then be asked by the lab-coat-wearing experimenter to give increasingly large electric shocks to the confederate as punishment for getting the memory questions wrong. In response, the confederate would scream in agony, ask to be let out, shout that he had a heart condition, and finally just stop responding.

At the time, conventional wisdom was that only a few people — the sadists — would go all the way, following the orders to increase the voltage even after the confederate stopped responding. Milgram quickly proved conventional wisdom wrong: 65% followed their orders and went all the way. As Zimbardo notes, the popular theory of the time was largely dispositional: people do things because that's their nature. Milgram provided clear evidence of situationism.

Milgram went on to do other pioneering research, including the small world experiment, where he would give people in Kansas a note for a friend in Cambridge, MA and ask them to get it there simply by passing it through friends. Milgram found that, again despite conventional wisdom of the time, it usually only six intermediaries to make it, which of course gave rise to the phrase "six degrees of separation".

Sadly, Milgram died of a heart attack at only 51.

Milgram likely moved on from the obedience experiments because they were highly controvertial — many considered them seriously unethical, even though Milgram went to great lengths to inform the subjects the true purpose of the experiment afterwards and make sure they were alright. Zimbardo, however, follows that same path.

Milgram did a number of variants on the Obedience experiments — moving subjects closer to their victims, trying the experiments in an office building away from the prestige of Yale, using women instead of men — but most had little or no success in lowering compliance rates. Two things, however, did change compliance rates. First, if the subject saw other subjects resisting, they became willing to resist as well. Second, if the subject did not throw the switches directly, but simply supervised someone who did, they became far more willing to continue.

The two discoveries clearly have larger societal messages (just a few people resisting can help mobilize others, but increasing bureaucratization can increase compliance in the name of evil), which of course have been confirmed by larger societal studies.

For this, Zimbardo draws the concept of the "good guard" — the man who doesn't hurt anyone but simply does his job and doesn't interfere with the hurting. The good guards, Zimbardo notes, are key to the whole thing because if they showed signs of resistance the bad guards would likely begin to resist too. (Again, it's not hard to extrapolate this to society.)

Zimbardo continues surveying the research and lays out the ten lessons he's drawn from it on how to get people to commit evil:

1. Create an ideology where the ends justify the means
2. Get a contract from the subjects where they agree to comply
3. Give participants meaningful roles with clear social value
4. Have the rules be vague and changing
5. Relabel actors and actions ("order control", not guards; "monsters", not people)
6. Diffuse responsibility so subjects don't feel liable
7. Start small but slowly increase the requirements, step by step
8. Make the leader seem compassionate at first
9. Permit verbal dissent ("I don't want to do this; I feel bad") as long as subjects continue complying
10. Make it difficult to exit

Further experiments find that people's inhibitions will be lowered if they or the subjects are "de-individualized" (e.g., they wear uniforms and masks; the subjects wear bags over their heads). In numerous experiments, this doubled the harm participants would voluntarily commit. (Anthropological studies confirm this, finding that cultures with costumes and masks are more violent.)

Similarly, changing how people think of their actions is key. In one experiment, where the experimenter called the victims "nice guys" the amount of punishment subjects inflicted went down. But when he called them "monsters" it went up.

Zimbardo put together all that he had learned into one experiment, the Stanford Prison Experiment, to see how far things could go. Volunteer subjects were recruited and half assigned to be prisoners and half assigned to be guards so that there would be no differences between the two groups. The prisoners were arrested at their home and taken to recently-redecorated basement of the Stanford Psychology department, where they were imprisoned.

There were no windows, so prisoners could not gauge time. Prisoners were strip-searched and forced to wear dress-like clothes. They were given leg shackles, a constant reminder of their status. Guards were given uniforms and mirror sunglasses (so no one could read their emotions) as well as minimal requirements or training.

On only the second day of the experiment, the prisoners tried to resist. Guards responded by calling in reinforcements, attacking the prisoners with fire extinguishers, placing the leaders in solitary confinement, and harassing the rest. They also created a privileged cell for the prisoners who most resisted the rebellion, with special benefits.

The next day, they reversed things, putting some of the leaders in the privileged cell (to imply the leader had sold out).

Soon enough, prisoners began going crazy. Guards became so evil and violent that the study had to be prematurely ended.

The relevance to Abu Ghraib should be obvious. And, sure enough, Zimbardo got a chance to testify before the court trying one of the Abu Ghraib guards, arguing that his sentence should be lowered because, as his research had shown, few could have resisted the powerful situational influences, which were surely even more powerful at a real prison with (presumably at least some) real criminals.

He went on to talk a bit about how the administration had weaponized fear with things like the terror alert system. The reason Al-Qaeda hadn't attacked again, he suggested, was because Bush was doing their job for them, scaring the population with vague threats without clear solutions.

October 31, 2004

WHY IS BIG MEDIA LOSING VIEWERS?

Watching the coverage of this week's Democratic National Convention, I've seen endless amounts of media handwringing about the coverage of this week's Democratic National Convention. Why are people turning to comedy news like The Daily Show? Why are people turning to partisan outlets like Fox News and talk radio? Why are people reading untalented webloggers?

After some consideration, Big Media has concluded it's the people's fault. They've become to partisan, shallow, and stupid to handle healthy, traditional news, so they've abandoned it for lesser outlets. While this storyline is no doubt convenient for the people espousing it (see, we're not doing anything wrong — it's their fault!) it doesn't seem quite right to me. The actual answer, which lies unspoken between the lines of all discussion on the subject, is much simpler: people are abandoning Big Media because it sucks.

Notice how the media simply refuses to acknowledge this possibility. Although evidence of the elite media's conservative bias is overwhelming (name one overtly liberal TV talk show host or regular pundit; read What Liberal Media? if you're still not convinced), the only kind of bias the media will acknowledge is a potential liberal one. Every article about webloggers ends with the platitude that bloggers won't be replacing journalists anytime soon. And when John Stewart was about to suggest that the regular media simply refused to do their job and call BS when they saw it, Ted Koppel quickly ended the interview.

No, in denial, Big Media will never admit it has a problem.

But it does. America is the only country with a media that refuses to analyze the news and draw conclusions. Instead, in the service of some notional "objectivity", American media will only repeat "facts" — that is, quotes provided by both sides. There is no memory, no analysis, no context, no conclusions, no opinions, no humanity at all. Is it any surprise that Americans look elsewhere for their news?

Big Media has a prepared response. Why, they say, the very pillars of civilization would crumble if opinion were allowed in the news! This is absurd. First, as I have noted, practically every other country allows analysis in their news, and they seem to be doing fine. Second, we already have opinion, it just comes in the form of vapid and partisan pundits. Letting actual journalists give us their opinions would certainly be an improvement over those guys. Third, Americans are already leaving Big Media for partisan sources or no news sources at all. Surely giving your viewers opinionated news is better than having no viewers at all.

This is not to say we should throw accuracy out the window and listen to whatever lies make us feel good. No, journalism's goal should be to be fair and accurate (the opposite of false and misleading), not "objective" and "balanced". A journalist should tell the whole truth and not try to mislead the reader. But as long they do so, they should be free to give whatever context and draw whatever conclusions they feel are appropriate. Once you've given side A and side B a fair shake, there's no harm — indeed, there's a great service — in telling which side you've chosen and why.

It seems clear to me that media with context and humanity is more popular than that with soulless objectivity. If Big Media wants to stop losing viewers to these supposedly less careful sources of information, they can start by adopting these goals as their own.

July 30, 2004

JEFFERSON
NATURE WANTS INFORMATION TO BE FREE

Since many have said that my view of copyright and patent law is childish and held merely because I grew up with Napster and do not write for a living, I thought I'd investigate some more respectable views on the subject. And who better than those of our thoughtful third President, Thomas Jefferson?

Judging from his letter to Isaac McPherson[1], Jefferson's thoughts are thus:

No one seriously disputes that property is a good idea, but it's bizarre to suggest that ideas should be property. Nature clearly wants ideas to be free! While you can keep an idea to yourself, as soon as you share it anyone can have it. And once they do, it's difficult for them to get rid of it, even if they wanted to. Like air, ideas are incapable of being locked up and hoarded.

And no matter how many people share it, the idea is not diminished. When I hear your idea, I gain knowledge without diminishing anything of yours. In the same way, if you use your candle to light mine, I get light without darkening you. Like fire, ideas can encompass the globe without lessening their density.

Thus, inventions cannot be property. Sure, we can give inventors an exclusive right to profit, perhaps to encourage them to invent new useful things, but this is our choice. If we decide not to, nobody can object.

Accordingly, England was the only country with such a law until the United States copied her. In other countries, monopolies may be granted occasionally by special act, but there is no general system. And this doesn't seem to have hurt them any — those countries seem just as inventative as ours.

(I am not directly quoting Jefferson here, I am translating what he said to modern English and omitting a bit, but I have not put any words in his mouth — Jeferson said all these things.)

The first thing to note is that Jefferson may have been the first to say, in essence, "information wants to be free!" (Jefferson attributed this will to nature, not information, but the sentiment was the same.) Thus, all those people who dismiss this claim as absurd have some explaining to do.

The second is that while Jefferson repeatedly says "idea", his logic applies equally to, say, a catchy tune or phrase and thus pretty much everything we commonly call "intellectual property law" (mostly copyright, trademarks, and patents).

The third is that, surprisingly (especially to me!), Jefferson is just as crazy as I am:

- By their very nature, ideas cannot be property.
- The government has no duty to make laws about them.
- The laws we do make aren't all that successful.

If Jefferson wasn't happy with the comparatively modest laws of 1813, can anyone seriously suggest that he wouldn't be furious with the expansionist laws of today? Forget the Free Software Foundation and the Creative Commons, Jefferson would be out there advocating armed resistance and impeaching the Justices that voted against Eldred![2] (OK, maybe not, but he'd certainly do more than write copyright licenses.)

It's true that in Jefferson's day there were no movies or networks, but there were certainly books and inventions. People made their livelihoods as writers or inventors. It's difficult to argue that Jefferson would change his mind now on economic grounds — if anything, I suspect that upon seeing the ease of sharing ideas over the Internet, he would argue for less restrictive laws — not more.

Jefferson thought these laws were contrary to human nature when they only affected people with large workshops or commercial printing presses — imagine how angry he would be when he saw that these laws restricted practically everyone, even doing perfectly unobjectionable things (like teaching your AIBO to dance or making a documentary[3]).

Now perhaps folks will find Jefferson as easy an argument for ad hominem attack as they found me. And just because Jefferson said it doesn't make it true — obviously his views were even the subject of some discussion at the time. But when the suggestions of our third president are called the "a ball of self-justification", "bullshit", "the far left", "selfishness", "shallow", that of a "moron", "disgusting", a "misunderstanding" of the law (!), and "immoral"[4], you sort of have to stop and wonder: what in the world is going on?

January 12, 2004

1. http://press-pubs.uchicago.edu/founders/documents/a1_8_8s12.html
2. http://www.pbs.org/wgbh/amex/duel/peopleevents/pande02.html
3. http://www.oreillynet.com/pub/a/policy/2002/08/15/lessig.html?page=3
4. http://www.docuverse.com/blog/donpark/EntryViewPage.aspx?guid=7a592614-ff21-4817-b7c0-3ea9a7007122

COUNTERPOINT
DOWNLOADING ISN'T STEALING

The *New York Times Upfront* asked me to contribute a short piece to a point/counterpoint they were having on downloading. (I would defend downloading, of course.) I thought I managed to write a pretty good piece, especially for its size and audience, in a couple days. But then I found out my piece was cut because the Times had decided not to tell kids to break the law. So, from the graveyard, here it is.

Stealing is wrong. But downloading isn't stealing. If I shoplift an album from my local record store, no one else can buy it. But when I download a song, no one loses it and another person gets it. There's no ethical problem.

Music companies blame a fifteen percent drop in sales since 2000 on downloading. But over the same period, there was a recession, a price hike, a 25% cut in new releases, and a lack of popular new artists. Factoring all that in, maybe downloading increases sales. And 90% of the catalog of the major labels isn't for sale anymore. The Internet is the only way to hear this music.

Even if downloading did hurt sales, that doesn't make it unethical. Libraries and video stores (neither of which pay per rental) hurt sales too. Is it unethical to use them?

Downloading may be illegal. But 60 million people used Napster and only 50 million voted for Bush or Gore. We live in a democracy. If the people want to share files then the law should be changed to let them.

And there's a fair way to change it. A Harvard professor found that a $60/yr. charge for broadband users would make up for all lost revenues. The government would give it to the affected artists and, in return, make downloading legal, sparking easier-to-use systems and more shared music. The artists get more money and you get more music. What's unethical about that?

Footnotes:

- "a fifteen percent drop in sales since 2000": This is from the RIAA's own chart[1]. In 1999, they sold 938.9M CDs, in 2002 they sold 803.3M. (938.9-803.3)/938.9 ~= .14 (so it's really closer to 14%, but we'll give them the benefit of the doubt and say 15%).
"a 25% cut in new releases": It depends on how you count. The RIAA says they released 38,900 new releases in 1999. According to SoundScan[2] the RIAA released 31,734 new releases in 2001, leading to an 18% drop. This isn't really fair, since we're using RIAA numbers for 1999 and SoundScan numbers for 2001, and SoundScan probably doesn't count as many albums as the RIAA does. However, the RIAA said in early 2003 that they released 27,000 new albums the previously year. Apparently embarassed by this information, they've since removed it from their website. But if you use their numbers, you get a 31% drop. I've split the difference and called it a 25% cut. But I could change this to 30% or 20% if you wanted; I don't think it would change the argument.
- "90% of the major label's catalog isn't available for sale": speech by Ken Hertz[3]
- "60 million people used Napster": according to the *New York Times*[4]
- "50 million voted for Bush or Gore": according to CNN[5]
- "A Harvard professor found that a $60 per year tax on broadband connections would make up for all lost music and movie sales": see Terry Fisher, Promises to Keep[6]. "Assuming that the ISPs pass through to consumers the entire amount of the tax, that average fee would rise by $4.88 per month" (p. 31) 4.88*12 ~= 59, so I say $60/yr.

January 08, 2004

1. http://www.riaa.com/news/marketingdata/pdf/year_end_2002.pdf
2. http://www.businessweek.com/technology/content/feb2003/tc20030213_9095_tc078.htm
3. http://www.xeni.net/images/boingboing/speech.htm
4. http://emoglen.law.columbia.edu/LIS/archive/mp3/18SONG.html
5. http://www.cnn.com/ELECTION/2000/
6. http://tfisher.org/PTK.htm

OUR BRAVE CENSORS

I'd like to take some time to recognize some especially brave Americans. These men and women work long hours, face harsh criticism, and receive little praise, yet they continue to do their work because they know it is right. I refer to, of course, the censors.

The folks at organizations at the Parents Television Council have the unrewarding job of watching endless quantities of television, carefully watching for sexual behavior (shown or implied). Often, they have to rewind and rewatch especially salacious scenes several times to understand it fully, before summarizing it and marking its location down in their notes for future reference. The task is arduous, and often requires hours of intense concentration, but yet these fearless warriors carry on.

Brave members of the ChildCare Action Project go see every new movie, marking down each every swear word spoken, every violent act, each appearance of drugs, and, again, all sexual content. And what rigor and detail! You'd think that an organization like this would see the name, or at most the trailer, for Austin Powers: Goldmember and write it off. But not these guys! They continue to sit through the entire movie, taking notes on everything. A lesson to us all.

Meanwhile the American Decency Association carefully goes through the Abercrombie and Fitch catalog, searching their pages for every last bare butt and breast, marking down the page numbers on which they appear, and putting the results on the Internet. But just doing this once isn't enough for them. Instead, they make sure to get a copy of every issue, and do the same for all of them. What persistance!

Why do these people take on this unrewarding job? We may never know. All I can do is think of them, sitting there in front of their television, movie screen, or nude photographs, carefully examining offensive and sexual content, and thank them for doing what most of us could not stomach. Continue on, brave censors.

November 28, 2003

BECAUSE WE CAN

When I first started studying the First Amendment — nearly a decade ago — I read about the different theories trying to make sense of it. Some scholars argued the First Amendment's goal was to create a robust marketplace of ideas: if everyone could share their opinion, the truth could come out through robust debate. Others concluded the First Amendment was a sort of logical safeguard: by protecting speech and assembly and petitions for redress of grievances, it guaranteed people the right to work against laws they disapprove of, kind of the way the Second Amendment is said to be a bulwark against totalitarianism.

These aren't just theoretical debates; the theories have practical consequences for how one interprets that key amendment. If you believe it's for a marketplace of ideas, then you will support regulation aimed at correcting market failures by suppressing certain kinds of problematic speech. If you believe it's a political safeguard, then you will not be too worried about speech regulation aimed at clearly nonpolitical speech.

Now, I'm not quite sure why such a theory is needed. The First Amendment always struck me as perfectly clear: "Congress shall make no law." No law meant no law (at least with regard to content; I'm more lenient when it comes to regulating other aspects). But if one has to have a theory, it struck me the right one was something completely different: Because We Can.

The Framers were very skeptical of government. The system they designed was full of checks and fetters, of which the First Amendment is probably the most extreme (unless you believe in a libertarian conception of the Tenth). They saw government as a necessary evil; they were willing to accept it, but they wanted to constrain it where they could.

And speech is a very obvious way to constrain it. A government needs to be able to stop violence and make war and so on or its people will get very badly hurt. But there's no reason it has to stop speech. As the old saying goes, sticks and stones may break my bones but words will never hurt me. Words do hurt, of course, but theirs is a tolerable pain. People, and society, march on even in the face of grievous insults. And so the Framers decided to exclude this class of regulation from the government's ambit. Not because speech is particularly good, but because it's not particularly bad. Because it's one thing they could safely exclude. Because we can.

The implications of this theory for interpretation are obvious: they lead to the most expansive conception of the First Amendment compatible with the other goals of government: a stable democratic body to promote the general welfare, and so on. That's certainly further than any court heretofore has gone and probably a bit further than I'd personally prefer, but isn't that what fetters are for?

October 20, 2009

I HATE THE NEWS

Some people start their day by reading The *New York Times*. Others end it by watching the nightly news. Some get it from The Daily Show. Others download it from a variety weblogs. Some keep up-to-the-minute by following CNN. Others have instant news updates automatically text messaged to their phone. But everybody seems to agree: it's a citizen's responsibility to keep up with the news. Everybody except me.

I think following the news is a waste of time.

Some people agree with me on a small scale. Some point out that the cable channels are obsessed with bizarre crimes that have little larger impact, that they worry too much about horse-race coverage of politics, that too much of the news is filled with

PR-inserted nonsense. But they do this because they think these are aberrations; that underneath all this, the news is worth saving. I simply go one step further: I think none of it is worthwhile.

Let us look at the front page of today's *New York Times*, the gold standard in news. In the top spot there is a story about Republicans feuding among themselves. There is a photo of soldiers in Iraq. A stock exchange chief must return $100M. There is a concern about some doctors over-selling a nerve testing system. There is a threat from China against North Korea. There is a report that violence in Iraq is rising. And there is concern about virtual science classes replacing real ones.

None of these stories have relevance to my life. Reading them may be enjoyable, but it's an enjoyable waste of time. They will have no impact on my actions one way or another.

Most people will usually generally concede this point, but suggest that there's something virtuous about knowing it anyway, that it makes me a better citizen. They point out that newspapers are a key part of our democracy, that by exposing wrong-doing to the people, they force the wrong-doers to stop.

This seems to be true, but the curious thing is that I'm never involved. The government commits a crime, the *New York Times* prints it on the front page, the people on the cable chat shows foam at the mouth about it, the government apologizes and commits the crime more subtly. It's a valuable system — I certainly support the government being more subtle about committing crimes (well, for the sake of argument, at least) — but you notice how it never involves me? It seems like the whole thing would work just as well even if nobody ever read the Times or watched the cable chat shows. It's a closed system.

There is voting, of course, but to become an informed voter all one needs to do is read a short guide about the candidates and issues before the election. There's no need to have to suffer through the daily back-and-forth of allegations and counter-allegations, of scurrilous lies and their refutations. Indeed, reading a voter's guide is much better: there's no recency bias (where you only remember the crimes reported in the past couple months), you get to hear both sides of the story after the investigation has died down, you can actually think about the issues instead of worrying about the politics.

Others say that sure, most of the stuff in the news isn't of use, but occasionally you'll come across some story that will lead you to actually change what you've been working on. But really, how plausible is this? Most people's major life changes don't come from reading an article in the newspaper; they come from reading longer-form essays or thoughtful books, which are much more convincing and detailed.

Which brings me to my second example of people agreeing with me on the small scale. You'll often hear TV critics say that CNN's up-to-the-minute reporting is absurd. Instead of saying, "We have unconfirmed reports that — This just in! We now have confirmed reports that those unconfirmed reports have been denied. No, wait! There's a new report denying the confirmation of the denial of the unconfirmed report." and giving viewers whiplash, they suggest that the reporters simply wait until a story is confirmed before reporting it and do commentary in the meantime.

But if that's true on a scale of minutes, why longer? Instead of watching hourly updates, why not read a daily paper? Instead of reading the back and forth of a daily, why not read a weekly review? Instead of a weekly review, why not read a monthly magazine? Instead of a monthly magazine, why not read an annual book?

With the time people waste reading a newspaper every day, they could have read an entire book about most subjects covered and thereby learned about it with far more detail and far more impact than the daily doses they get dribbled out by the paper. But people, of course, wouldn't read a book about most subjects covered in the paper, because most of them are simply irrelevant.

But finally, I'd like to argue that following the news isn't just a waste of time, it's actively unhealthy. Edward Tufte notes that when he used to read the *New York Times* in the morning, it scrambled his brain with so many different topics that he couldn't get any real intellectual work done the rest of the day.

The news's obsession with having a little bit of information on a wide variety of subjects means that it actually gets most of those subjects wrong. (One need only read the blatant errors reported in the corrections page to get some sense of the more thorough-going errors that must lie beneath them. And, indeed, anyone who has ever been in the news will tell you that the news always gets the story wrong.) Its obsession with the criminal and the deviant makes us less trusting people. Its obsession with the hurry of the day-to-day makes us less reflective thinkers. Its obsession with surfaces makes us shallow.

This is not simply an essay meant to provoke; I genuinely believe what I write. I have not followed the news at least since I was 13 (with occasional lapses on particular topics). My life does not seem to be impoverished for it; indeed, I think it has been greatly enhanced. But I haven't found many other people who are willing to take the plunge.

October 20, 2006

GOOGLE AND THE GRADIENT

For a long time it seemed like everything I heard about Google was even cooler than the last. Wow, it's a great search engine! Wow, they're not sleazy like other companies! Wow, they treat their hackers well! Wow, they *are* hackers!

The feeling peaked sometime last year when I was almost rolling on the floor hoping to work at Google. And I do mean peaked. Everything I've heard since then has been downhill, each time I hear about it Google seems less cool. I'm not saying the company is imminently doomed or that you should sell your shares, but I definitely don't think it's going to get any cooler.

Google is run like a socialist state. Its citizens are treated extremely well. There's free food, free doctors, free massages, free games, a limited workweek, etc. There are ministries to give projects free promotion and support. The government tries to avoid getting too much in people's lives. And Google is always coming up with more perks to give away. (There's also a strong class hierarchy, with abused temps and powerful acquirees.)

The problem with a system like this is that it's necessarily a bubble. Everybody inside gets treated grandly, but the outside world gets nothing. Indeed, because of Google's notorious secrecy, they barely even get to talk to the people inside. A friend who's a prominent free software developer says that every community member who's joined Google has stopped contributing to public projects. It's so bad, he says, that they're thinking of banning Google from buying a booth at their next conference. They can't afford to lose any more developers.

Which means that Google has to be careful about who they hire, but since they're growing so fast they need to hire people as quickly as possible. It's an impossible bind — you can hire lots of people or you can hire really good people, but even a company as prominent as Google is going to have a hard time doing both.

The solution, of course, is to pop the bubble. There's no reason being part of Google has to be a binary decision. Google has a wide variety of resources and while there are some they can't really give away to everyone (e.g. massages), there are others that should be easy (e.g. servers). Unfortunately for them, Google's mindset is so obviously set that this will never happen. Even a company as woeful as Amazon is already kicking their but in this space, giving away storage space and computer power, with more in the works.

But let's imagine you had the resources to do this right, what would you do? (I feel like I'm giving away a valuable secret here, but since nobody listens to me anyway, I doubt it will make any difference.) The right thing is to build not a bubble, with it's binary in-or-out choice, but to build a gradient, with shades of resources you make available as people achieve success.

So you have this organization dedicated to building cool web apps. The first thing you do is you start giving away free food in the middle of San Francisco. You have a nice cozy area with tables and bathrooms and Wi-Fi and anyone interested in starting a web site is encouraged to drop by and hang out. There they can eat, chat, hack, get feedback, get suggestions, get help.

Then you give them free hosting. Servers and bandwidth are cheap, good projects are invaluable. But not only will you host their app for free, throwing in servers to scale it as necessary, but you'll pay them for the privilege of hosting. Indeed, you'll pay them proportionately to the amount of traffic they get, in exchange for the right to run ads on it someday.

So now you've got all the bright, smart young things who want to start companies starting them on your servers, with clear and unambiguous incentives: get traffic, get paid. They don't need to worry about impressing anyone with their idea; anyone can use the hosting. And they don't need to sell out to investors anymore; as their traffic grows, you'll already be giving them the cash to grow the business.

Most of these sites, of course, will probably be failures. But who cares? Sites that don't get much traffic don't use up much in the way of resources. Meanwhile, a couple of the sites will actually take off. So what do you do with those? *Give them more resources.*

Put your promotional team behind them to spread the word about the ideas. Have your web designers, database jockeys, and JavaScript hotshots help them fix up the site. Encourage promising young programmers interested in helping out with something to write a feature or two.

And — this is where the gradient comes in — as they become more successful, you give them more resources. Let them move into the apartment building above to food/hangout space, so they can get more facetime with fellow successful hackers. Give them free offices to work in. Provide free massages and exercise equipment. Have your PR team set up interviews with the major media. Integrate their site with your other sites. Plus, of course, they're getting paid more for more traffic the whole time.

Some of the sites will be huge hits, another YouTube or Facebook. The founders will be raking in millions from the traffic. And at some point, they'll get tired of running the site and they'll let it go. You'll be there to take it over, slap some ads on it to recoup the investment, and give it to some new, junior developers to maintain and improve. And the cycle continues.

(Bonus for the truly adventurous: run the whole thing as a non-profit and have all the applications involved be open source.)

A bubble like Google can hire only so many people and there's no way of picking only the ones which will be successes. But everyone can be part of a gradient and the successes simply rise to the top. I know which one I'd work for.

Thanks to Emmett Shear for discussion and suggestions.

October 26, 2006

FOUNDER'S SYNDROME

The simplest way to do something, of course, is to do it yourself. But there's lots of stuff to be done and not enough you to do it. You can get around this a little bit by finding friends who are interested in doing some of it themselves, but at some point you're going to have to start "delegating", or getting somebody else to do it.

Now you're moving up in the world. If you're a decent manager, instead of running one project, you can run five or ten. Instead of simply directing your own labor, you can direct whole groups of people. Of course, it'll still be people doing what you wanted, but — funny thing — people are smart enough that they'll begin to get the gist of things on their own and, if you do it right, your delegation will become an organization. You can disappear for a week and things will keep on marching.

But make no mistake, even those organizations are still following the will of their erstwhile founder. Even as they get big, they betray facets of the founder's personality. The most obvious is in who is respected. My friend Emmett Shear has a theory that in each company only one class of people can be in charge and it's going to be the class of people the founders are in. At Apple, for example, the UI designers are in charge, because Jobs obsesses over UI design. At Google, it's the programmers, because Larry and Sergey used to code. Even though the founders aren't directly involved in every project, their surrogates still win the day.

Now the problem comes when the organization wants to grow beyond its founder. This is most common on non-profits, where they even have a name for it: founder's syndrome. See, once you have all these people carrying out your bidding, it's pretty difficult to want to give that up. Maybe you can have them do more projects, maybe you can give them more flexibility in what they choose, but I can't think of a single story where the guy in charge voluntarily gave up his power. And that has a severe cost (which I've come to calling the "power premium") because giving up your power is often the right thing to do.

In non-profits, for example, your organization is probably made up of a bunch of independent-minded young people with a strong belief in democracy. These people aren't too happy being told what to do all the time, especially when the instructions are pretty obviously not the best thing for the non-profit's mission. So they rebel against the founder, and the founder tries to hold on to power, and things get very messy. (I don't know how things usually turn out in this situation. Maybe you fight until the founder dies?)

Less well noticed is that the same mistake is made by for-profit corporations as well, it's just less obvious because the founder is the fellow holding all the cash, so you fight about it at your peril. But companies regularly do stupid things, even when if you asked all the people in the company about it they would have told you they were stupid. But in a capitalist economy, the founder has to maintain control.

But the power premium has a even more serious cost. While many people seem to be able to make the leap from doing something themselves to building an organization to do it, nobody seems to have been very good at taking the next step: going from an organization to a meta-organization, an organization that hires other organizations to do its work, rather than hiring people directly.

Why? Partly because few people get to be in charge of something the size of Google, where they need to take that next step to grow, and perhaps the trait of thinking that big is rare. But I think part of it is simply because the people at the top can't give up their power. Engaging organizations means you're no longer in charge of what people do or how they do it; the organizations have to be in charge of that. And that means you're no longer a delegator, but more of a moderator. It's founder's syndrome at the largest scale.

October 27, 2006

UP WITH FACTS
FINDING THE TRUTH IN WIKICOURT

I'm an optimist. I believe that statements like "Bush went AWOL" or "Gore claims to have invented the Internet" can be evaluated and decided pretty much true or false. (The conclusion can be a little more nuanced, but the important thing is that there's a definitive conclusion.)

And even crazier, I believe that if there was a fair and accurate system for determining which of these things were lies, people would stop repeating the lies. I would certainly try to. No matter how much I wanted to believe "Dean's state record sealing was normal" or "global warming does exist", if a fair system had decided against it, I would stop.

And perhaps most crazy of all, I want to stop repeating falsehoods. I believe the truth is more important than particular political goals, so I want to build a system I can trust. I want to know that when I make claims, I'm not speaking out of political distortion but out of honest truth. And I want to be able to evaluate the claims of other too.

So how would such a system work? First, large claims ("Gore is a serial liar", "Ronald Reagan was a great President") would be broken down into smaller component parts ("Gore claimed to have invented the Internet", "Ronald Reagan's economic plan created jobs"). On each small claim, we'd run The Process. Let's take "Gore falsely claimed to have invented the Internet".

First, some ground rules. Everything is open. Anyone can submit anything, and all the records are put on a public website.

We'd begin with collecting evidence. Anyone could submit helpful factual evidence. We'd get video tape from CNN of what exactly Gore said. We'd get Congressional records about Gore's funding of the Arpanet. We'd get testimony from people involved. And so on. If someone challenged a piece of evidence's validity (e.g. "that photo is doctored", "that testimony is forged"), a Mini-Process could be started to resolve the issue.

Then there'd be the argument phase. A wiki page would be created where each side would try to take facts from the evidence and use them to build an argument for their case. But then the other side could modify the page to provide their own evidence, expand selective quotatins, and otherwise modify the page to make it more accurate and less partisan. Each side would continue bashing the other side's work until the page gave the best arguments from each side, presented in such a way that nobody could object. (You may think that this is impossible, but Wikipedia has ably proven that it can work.)

Finally, there'd be the adjucation phase. This is the hard part. A group of twelve fairminded intelligent people (experts in the field, if necessary) would agree to put aside their partisanship and come to a conclusion based on the argument. Hopefully, most of the time this conclusion would be (after a little wiki-rewriting from both sides) unanimous. For example, "While Gore's phrasing was a little misleading, it is clear Gore was claiming to have led the fight for providing funding for research that was later developed into the Internet — a claim that is mostly true. Gore was one of the research's major backers, although others were involved."

The panel would be assembled by selecting people widely seen as fairminded and intelligent, but coming from different sides of the political spectrum. It is likely many would accept — all they'd need to do was read a page and spend a little time agreeing to summarize it. And in doing so, they'd provide a great contribution to political debate (as well as getting their side represented).

All of these phases would be going on essentially simultaneously — the argument could be updated as new evidence came to light, new evidence could be added to fill holes in the argument, and the adjudicating jury could keep tabs on the page as updated.

And once a decision on an issue was made, it could be cited as evidence in the argument for a related issue ("Gore is a serial liar").

Everything would be very fluid and wiki-like. We'd make up the rules as we went along, seeing what was necessary. And when we learned from our mistakes, we could go back and fix them.

This seems like an awful lot of effort for just coming to a decision on a couple of silly issues, but I think it's far more than that. The result would be a vast collection of trustable arguments for many of the hot-topics of the day, a collection that could be relied on through time to give you the fair truth — because everybody had essentially signed off on it (it is publicly-modifiable, after all) And if you look at the effort expended on these claims and political fights, spending a little time getting the facts right seems like a small price to pay.

What do you think?

February 19, 2004

WHAT JOURNALISTS DON'T
LESSONS FROM THE TIMES

Speech to the Bay Area Law School Technology Conference blogs panel, as prepared.

So I was asked to speak about bloggers and journalists — it seems like people are always finding an excuse to talk about this. In fact, the National Press Club had a panel on it just yesterday. Most of the discussion focuses on what bloggers do — is it trustworthy? is it right? — but I'd like to take a different tack. I'd like to discuss what journalists *don't*.

Last summer, during the election campaign, I decided to take on a little project. Every day for a month I would read all the political articles in the *New York Times* and take notes on them on a blog. A number of things stood out and I thought I would discuss them. Keep in mind that this is the *New York Times*, widely recognized to be the most serious of newspapers. So everything that applies to them applies to an even greater extent to all the lesser newspapers, the evening news, the talking head shows, and so on.

The first was the extreme conservative bias. One day, they ran a front page story that claimed Kerry was, quote, like a caged hamster. Another, claiming, quote, life is like high school, decided to interview various Kerry classmates. So they got two quotes. On the right was the guy who thought Kerry "seem[ed] ruthless" and on the left was the one who insisted "hatred is too strong a word" for what his classmates felt. These are just fun examples — I found hundreds of these things in just a month. And many were on more serious issues as well.

The constant theme was that Times reporters would repeat Republican talking points and images and so on. Kerry was elitist, Kerry was a flip-flopper, the Kerry campaign was failing. One reporter even had his own cottage industry in stories of that last type. Adam Nagourney ran 22 consecutive stories claiming Democrats were worried about themselves.

But we shouldn't forget the more important things as well. The Times was, of course, one of the major outlets for false claims that Iraq had WMDs. My understanding is that it's a sort of cardinal rule in journalism that if you're going to make a claim, especially a big, important front-page claim, you get two sources. Well, the Times didn't do that on WMDs — they just printed whatever the administration said. And when the administration used their bogus reporting to go to war, the Times did its best to ignore the fact that the war was a blatant violation of international law.

In all these areas, the blogs bested the Times. Some tracked the spreading meme that Kerry was elitist, others pointed out that Bush wasn't much of a down-home cowboy himself, still others carefully debunked each new right-wing myth. Blogs pointed to people like weapons inspector Scott Ritter, who correctly pointed out there were no WMDs, or the Iraqi defector who explained they had all been destroyed. Blogs 1, Times 0.

The second thing I noticed during my study was that reporters rarely pointed out Bush was lying, corrected his lies, or even conceded that an objective reality containing a truth existed. You don't have to trust me on this one; I spoke to Washington Post campaign reporter Jim VandeHei about it when he visited Stanford. Some things are undoubtedly true, he said — he got very animated — but editors won't let reporters print the facts. He wanted to do a piece where he compared Bush and Kerry's stump speeches to see how many lies they contained, but editors just wouldn't let him.

So instead you get the results so perfectly parodied by Paul Krugman, who commented that if the administration announced the Earth was flat, the lead story in the Times the next day would be "Shape of Earth: Views Differ". In fact, we don't really need to leave that sort of thing to the imagination anymore. The other month ABC ran a show which balanced people who claimed they had been abducted by aliens against respected doctors who explained that their experiences resulted from a condition called sleep paralysis. Who was right? ABC refused to say.

Even when facts are reported, they don't seem to stick. Just last month, a Harris poll found that 47% of adults think Saddam helped plan 9/11 and 36% think Iraq had WMDs. But if the media sends the message that it's unnecessary to check your beliefs against the facts, should we really be so surprised that so many Americans don't?

Blogs suffer from no such compulsions. They're happy to take tell you the facts and show you the evidence. They're happy to tell you that some things are just wrong and often furious against those who dare to lie. The incredible blog Media Matters, for example, diligently tracks right-wing lies spread through the media, citing all the sources that prove them false.

But the most important thing, and the thing that nobody really seems to talk about, was how completely empty the Times's coverage was. It was entirely focused on who the candidates were giving stump speeches to or what ads they were buying this week.

The only time an actual policy proposal was mentioned was deep inside a discussion of how a candidate played with a certain group. You know, 'Kerry has had problems with the Teamsters, even though they support his health care plan' or something. That was basically it. And this is supposed to be the high point of journalism! If the Times won't talk about policy then no one will.

And if nobody talks about policy then nobody votes on the basis of it. A September 2004 Gallup poll found that only 10% of registered voters said that they voted based on the candidates, quote, agenda/ideas/platforms/goals — 6% for Bush, 13% for Kerry.

And it's at this point that you really have to ask yourself: "is this really a democracy?" It's the most contested election of out time, coverage is lavished on the topic, the nation is closely divided, and yet the media completely ignores the issues. There's no policy debate. And if the media doesn't report the policy proposals and the media doesn't report the facts, then we're right back to my first point: vague emotional claims about Kerry being a rich elitist flip-flopper, or, from the other side, Kerry was a brave soldier who blew stuff up in the Vietnam war.

This wasn't your grand democratic election: The people didn't get together and look at the facts and have a debate about issues. They didn't look at facts and they didn't discuss issues at all! They sat in their houses, watched a bunch of fuzzy TV commercials, and took in news coverage that recited the same vague themes. And then they voted based on which fuzzy image they liked the best. There's a word for stuff like that. It's not pretty, but I think it's appropriate. It's called propaganda. This was an election on the basis of propaganda.

And so I believe blogs are important insofar as they help us move away from this sorry spectacle and towards a real democracy. Blogs, of course, can help spread propaganda — and no doubt, most do — but they can also help stem it. Political blogs can help pull people into politics, tell them things they wouldn't otherwise hear, and lead them to organize their own projects — like building support for Howard Dean or trying to save social security.

One of the most important things I think blogs do, though, is teach people. The media, as I've noted, is supremely unintelligent. But I don't think the people of this country are. And one of the most striking things about blogs to me is how they almost never talk down to their readership. Indeed most seem to think higher of their readership than they do themselves.

Atrios doesn't hesitate before explaining some piece of economics that the Washington Post finds too complex. Tim Lambert will teach you the statistical theory you need to understand why some right-wing claim is wrong. And Brad DeLong has taught me more about what it's like to be an economics guy in the government than I got from Paul O'Neill's book.

The media isn't going to come save from this nightmare. But maybe blogs can. Or at least they can help. The more people learn, the smarter they become. The smarter they become, the more they understand the way the world really works. The more they understand, the more they can do to fix things. And that is the truly important goal. Thank you.

* * *

So, what I did was I took the above speech, bolded the key words and numbers, and printed it out. Then I gave it mostly from memory, occasionally looking down to get the next bolded word or a particularly well-worded phrase. It worked really well, I think.

The speech touched quite a nerve, as I hoped. My two conservative co-panelists (Zack Rosen failed to show) immediately demanded a chance to respond and then cut off my rebuttals. One of them (Mike) started insisting there was no such thing as objective truth at which point I cut in and said 'Well, I can see why Republicans would want to deny that truth exists since it often cuts against them!' which was hailed as the best line of the night.

After the talk I got a lot of compliments and a guest blogger for Daily Kos said he'd talk to Markos about getting me an occasional spot on Daily Kos, which is something like the liberal blogger equivalent of a regular gig on the *Tonight Show*. So I think it went well. :-)

April 10, 2005

SOCIAL CLASS IN AMERICA

One night the other weekend I was walking back with my dad to the hotel. I think we were talking about college admissions and things when he said 'We don't have class in America.' 'What?' I said, stunned. 'We don't have a class system here. That's only in places like Britain.'

My dad has always found occasion to repeat the absurd propaganda he picks up from his daily doses of NPR and the *New York Times* — evolution is a fraud, global warming is perfectly normal, etc. — but this claim just floored me. How could anyone believe we didn't have social class in America? The evidence is all around us, all the time — it must take real training not to see it.

A large part of it is that the media pretends class doesn't exist. It never talks about it, except to say that we're all middle class or imply that class is a purely cultural construction, not an economic one. (It is this last thing that allows multimillionaire George W. Bush to become lower class by speaking in a Texas twang and wearing cowboy boots.) And the realities of other classes are never portrayed, except in a stereotyped, mocking tone. In the media, everyone is middle class.

The PBS documentary *People Like Us: Social Class in America* is the rare exception. While it too mostly ignores economic issues, through a series of local stories highlighting the mixtures and contradictions of class, it at least begins to build a portrait of what class cultures really looks like in America.

April 22, 2005

OUR NEXT SUPERJUMBO

The question seems rather less important now, but for a while I was working on a book about politics, especially how the Democrats could win elections. For those out there interested in the question, Rick Perlstein (author of *Before the Storm*, the highly-praised history of the rise of the Republican right) has written what is pretty much the definitive piece on the subject, now in paperback as *The Stock Ticker and the Superjumbo*.

In short: Perlstein recounts the strong evidence that there is very broad support for the economic platform of the Democrats. Nonvoters, independents, and even Republicans, he notes, support core Democratic principles. They just don't consider themselves Democrats, a party they think of as not standing for anything in particular. This is, of course, because Democrats have been busy chasing after the mirage of swing voters, running further and further to the right, following the ball Republicans are glefully pulling in front of them.

He argues that instead, the Democrats must build a strong and long-term political identity, building a new political landscape instead of trying to win on the old one, just as the right-wing Republicans did. Doing so requires a openness to the possibility of losing, at least initially, but in the end it is the only way to win.

This artless summary doesn't convey the depth of Perlstein's piece, so if you're interested you can:

A final note: Why is all this uninteresting? Because the Democrats aren't paid to win elections. They're paid to win policy for their corporate donors. Policy that hurts those companies, however popular with the public, simply will not be funded.

July 20, 2005

THE GOD WHO WASN'T THERE
(AND THE ONE WHO WAS)

"I was doing some research into the idea that Jesus never existed. When I first looked into it, I thought it was just a crackpot theory and I was curious why anyone would believe this," explains Brian Flemming. "To my surprise I found the evidence kept stacking up. The more I looked into it, the more that the facts aligned with those who said Jesus was just a legendary character. The shaky evidence and the poor reasoning were actually on the side of those who said that Jesus did exist."

And so Flemming (*Bat Boy: The Musical*, *Nothing So Strange*, *Fair & Balanced*, and all-around digital rights supporter) decided to make a movie. The result, which is currently being screened across the country in theaters and at atheist organizations and will be released on DVD soon, is a shockingly good film.

Flemming begins at the beginning: the popular story of Jesus. In a hilarious montage of old footage taken from the Prelinger archives underneath deadpan narration, he tells the story in six minutes. And then it's on to debunking it. Through interviews with various experts, illustrated with entertaining graphics, he tries to reconstruct the historical evidence for the story…only to find there isn't much and a lot doesn't add up.

Convinced the story is wrong, Flemming takes aim at the right-wing Christian fundamentalists who act based on it, the wishy-washy Christian moderates who enable them, and the rest of the system. He concludes by heading back home to the fundamentalist Christian school he attended as a child to confront the principal about what he's teaching children.

Flemming's previous film, *Nothing So Strange* (which I also reviewed) was interesting but, in fairness, rather amateurish. No such criticism can be made of this film, which has some of the best graphics I've seen in a documentary and a brilliant score composed from the Creative Commons-licensed Wired CD by the hertofore-unknown DJ Madson (a nom-de-plume of Flemming, I'm beginning to suspect) by remixing popular artists. The whole thing, from the interviews down to the promotional posters, hangs together so well that it's hard to believe Flemming is doing this all himself, but apparently he is, with no liberal atheist conspiracy to back him.

(Although, in full disclosure, Larry Lessig and former Creative Commons executive director Glenn Otis Brown receive special thanks in the credits. And in a remote Q&A via iChat after the screening here at Stanford, Flemming was wearing a Creative Commons shirt. So if you want to investigate a conspiracy, that's where I'd look.)

On the other hand, Flemming has always had what Bill O'Reilly might call a "parasitic" sense of self-promotion. His film *Nothing So Strange* received press largely because it included scenes of Bill Gates being assassinated. And during the California Recall, Flemming jumped into the fray on the platform "If elected, I will resign." (Thus making Lt. Governor Bustamante governor, since at the time he was refusing to run, thinking he'd draw support away from the actual governor.) When FOX sued Al Franken for using the phrase "Fair and Balanced", Flemming wrote a play with the name. When Arnold Schwarzenegger sued the makers of a bobblehead version of him, Flemming posted a photo of Arnold's penis.

Both times, he insisted the works were a form of political protest, but he still charged money for the products. He did the same when he released portions of *Nothing So Strange* under a Creative Commons license. It's one thing to support free speech; it's another to try to make money off of other people's support for it. What's unsettling about this film is not how Flemming is using various atheist groups to screen and promote it — that's perfectly reasonable, especially since he's giving the DVDs to the groups at outrageously low prices.

No, what's unsettling is a hidden feature on Flemming's site called the Grassroots Promotion Team or GPT. In general these things are nothing new — just personally, I remember volunteering for Apple when the iMac came out and joining a "Street Team" website to promote a Buffy DVD. The idea behind such sites is that your particular group of obsessive lonely fans will spend their free time promoting your products on various forums and websites in exchange for a chance to win some lame prizes.

It's sad when big corporations do this, but when independent political folks like Flemming do it, it becomes a little creepy. It's also problematic. Take the movie's soundtrack, which is sold on Amazon. Normally such obscure CDs have hardly any reviews. But this one not only had 11, but they were all amazingly glowing. "Wow, this CD must be really good," I thought. But when I saw Flemming was awarding 100 "points" for each Amazon review, it suddenly made sense. If everyone plays this game, Amazon reviews will quickly become meaningless, which is why I don't think it's a very good idea to start.

The film is valuable and grassroots promotion of it is certainly a good thing. I just wish it felt a little less like using well-meaning people to make money for Flemming and a little more like a cooperative community with the aim of spreading the Real News.

Brian Flemming responds:

Thanks for the kind words about the movie. I agree with some of your criticism of the street team, but I think your aim is off the mark with much of it.

1.   AMAZON REVIEWS. There's an old phrase in publicity, "I don't care if the review is positive or negative, just put the title in the headline." As an indie filmmaker always struggling to get the word out against competing messages backed by tens of millions of dollars, I definitely subscribe to this philosophy. It was never the design of the movie's street team to load up Amazon with praise (frankly, a mix of angry one-star reviews and passionate five-star reviews would be better). It's no secret that authors and their publishers and friends stack the Amazon book reviews (as has been documented), but I don't wish to add to that clutter. I've never asked anyone to post nice things on Amazon about the soundtrack CD for The God Who Wasn't There, or to withhold negative statements (and I have not posted a review myself). Street team members are given a free (digital) copy of the soundtrack and encouraged to go to Amazon and post a review of the music — that's it. About 5% of them do. There's no incentive to make the review positive or negative. However, while I think the street team members' reviews of the soundtrack CD on Amazon are sincere, and no harm has been done, this particular sample does naturally skew positive — if you're on the street team, you probably like the film/soundtrack you've decided to back with your time. But then again, reviews are inherently biased — and fans tend to be more motivated than others in posting. Most reviews on Amazon for most media products are positive for that reason. I'll freely admit to sending people to Amazon — but my goal is battling obscurity, not battling negative opinion. And I certainly can't stop anyone from posting a negative review.

2. THE STREET TEAM ITSELF. A "street team" is a group of volunteer supporters who distribute flyers and stickers and otherwise spread the word about a band or film online and offline. You say, "It's sad when big corporations do this, but when independent political folks like Flemming do it, it becomes a little creepy." Here's where I think your aim is considerably off the mark. To be opposed to a street team is nearly tantamount to being opposed to the very idea of promoting indie artists. I believe promotion should be honest and ethical, but promotion itself is not an evil. And organizing promotion is not an evil. To eliminate street teams would be largely to give up and turn over the marketplace to those who have the money to promote via advertising and other expensive means. It would strengthen messages backed by money and weaken messages backed by passion. I think the street team for The God Who Wasn't There is a great example of passion being organized into action, and I'm proud of it. I give theatrical rights away for free — and then a group like SF Atheists holds a screening and earns upwards of $1000 to help their extremely important efforts. Volunteers go to a website where grassroots action is made easier — and conversations all over the web get started over whether Jesus really did exist, a very legitimate question that is nonetheless the third rail of mainstream-media conversations about Christianity. Street teams aren't "creepy," and this one in particular is doing some very real, verifiable good.

3. MONEY. You write that when I attacked Arnold Schwarzenegger and Bill O'Reilly via Fair Use Press, I "insisted the works were a form of political protest, but [Flemming] still charged money for the products. He did the same when he released portions of Nothing So Strange under a Creative Commons license. It's one thing to support free speech; it's another to try to make money off of other people's support for it." Really, I'm just shaking my head in wonder at this accusation. I have never made any profit whatsoever from any of my Fair Use Press e-books. The Schwarzenegger attack was given away, with a high-res "premium" edition sold at first for $1 (both editions are free now and have been for about a year). I added a $1 price to that specifically to demonstrate fair use — that I wasn't taking a "noncommercial" copout, so Schwarzenegger and his attorney couldn't claim that's why they didn't sue. That's what my activism through Fair Use Press is about — demonstrating the limits of fair use. I want people to look at what I do, see that I got away with it, and then do more of the same. The commercial marketplace — where messages like Bill O'Reilly's already live — is an important battlefield in this fight. Just because I fight in that space doesn't mean I'm making a profit from Fair Use Press. I don't, and it certainly isn't part of the plan (I spend far more on promotion and advertising than I take in). And my best-case scenario for The God Who Wasn't There is to break

even on marketing expenses (production costs are already written off, gladly, as a loss). All of my indie-film work and free-culture activism operates in the red, subsidized by the Hollywood work-for-hire assignments I take that also pay my rent. I'm not, as you say, "using well-meaning people to make money." I'm putting in my own money and time to the same purpose as the people I'm working side-by-side with. The fact that we earn revenue to try to keep the project somewhat self-sustaining cannot reasonably be termed exploitation.

Criticism is a good thing, Aaron, and we free-culture activists of course do need to criticize each other where criticism is justified. And I certainly should be held publicly accountable for anything I publicly do. But in this case I really think you've gone overboard and made accusations that have little merit.

Aaron replies:

Thanks for responding. I can't say I'm glad to hear you don't expect to turn a profit on any of this, but it certainly allays any fears of exploitation.

But I feel like you missed my main point about the street team — the one I ended the article with: "I just wish it felt ... a little more like a cooperative community with the aim of spreading the Real News." There's nothing wrong with telling people about music or movies you like, or even putting up posters to promote them. Where it gets creepy is when this natural enthusiasm is co-opted and channeled into a structured, top-down sort of system. Now I'm not just expressing my opinions, I'm following orders so I can get goodies. That fundamentally changes things.

Maybe an analogy will help. My mom likes telling people about interesting things I've done. There's nothing wrong with this — the people she talks to like knowing this stuff. But you have to admit it would be creepy if I started providing my mom with a list of my achievements and awarding her points every time she found a way to mention them. Mom begins to feel used, her friends begin to feel duped, and I look like a narcissist.

There's no need to get rid of the promotion system, just scale it back a little. Provide a list of suggested actions, a forum where people can talk about what they're doing, and then offer to mail a t-shirt or something to people who work hard.

You see, contrary to popular opinion — even in the free culture community, oddly enough — rewards are incredibly destructive. Study after study shows they actually demotivate people, encourage people to cheat and lie, and cause them to make stupid decisions about trade-offs. For an excellent book on the subject, see *Alfie Kohn's Punished By Rewards*.

June 1, 2005

WHAT'S FREEDOM?

George Lakoff is a prominent cognitive scientist whose central insight (which is not to say that the idea originates with him) is that we can learn about the structure of our thoughts by looking carefully at the words we use to express them. For example, we think of time as a line, as you can see through phrases like "time line", "looking forward", "further in the past", etc. Similarly, we thinking is thought of as a kind of seeing: "do you see what I mean?", "pulled the wool over your eyes", "as you can see from the book", "his talk was unclear", "that sentence is opaque", etc.

Lakoff used these techniques to write a series of books describing the structures of various ideas (*Metaphors We Live By, Philosophy in the Flesh, Where Mathematics Comes From*, etc.) but after the Republican Revolution of 1994, he turned the technique on politics, resulting in his 1996 classic Moral Politics, which tries to explicate the cognitive models of Democrats and Republicans.

After the election of Bush, Lakoff began talking about how Republicans were better at "framing", or using language to get people to agree with them, than Democrats. Lakoff that the process goes both ways: language causes your mind to think of certain concepts which create certain pathways in your brain. Thus Republicans, he said, through massive repetition of certain phrases, were literally changing the brains of the electorate to be more favorable to them. ("If this sounds a bit scary," he writes, "it should. This is a scary time.")

Around the 2004 election, Lakoff skyrocketed to fame among Democrats, who were convinced by his argument that fighting Republicans required not just giving into Republican frames, but reframing the debate themselves. He rushed out the slender book Don't Think of an Elephant, a cobbled-together guide on his basic ideas and how progressives could use them. The book stayed on the *New York Times* bestseller list for weeks.

Now Lakoff is back with a more studied work, *Whose Freedom?*, which tries to focus in more detail on the differing views of one particular concept: freedom. Lakoff starts the book by noting that in his 2004 speech at the Republican convention, Bush used "freedom", "free", or "liberty" once every forty-three words. Most progressives think of this simply as a stunt — using feel-good symbols like flag and words like freedom to distract from the real issues. But Lakoff argues something much deeper is going on: Bush is trying to change the meaning of freedom itself.

So what is he trying to change it to? Right away, the book begins to fall apart. Lakoff's definition of freedom is so broad (it encompasses democracy, opportunity, equality, fairness, education, health, the press, the market, religion, the military, academia, and privacy) as to be fundamentally meaningless: "Every progressive issue is ultimately about freedom," he concludes. And yet freedom is kept on as the book's organizing principle: instead of chapters about economics, religion, and foreign policy, we have the chapters "Economic Freedom", "Religion and Freedom", and "Foreign Policy and Freedom".

This would be harmless if it was simply a rhetorical affectation, but Lakoff still seems to think is fundamentally about freedom. As a result, the chapters are not only weighed down with meaningless and silly attempts to connect the topic to freedom ("Life is a progressive issue, since progressive Christians are committed to promoting freedom, freedom from oppression and pain and freedom to realize one's dreams." — actual quote) but their actual substance is stripped bare, because it's not discussed in its own right, but merely as an aid to the book's discussion of freedom.

Thus instead of deriving his key theory of how family metaphors create political views, by showing how he discovered this and how it explains a lot about the world, he quickly asserts it and then tries to apply the idea to the empty void of "freedom". The result is a book that is fundamentally vacuous — its main idea has no substance and its supporting ideas have no explanation.

And for a linguist, Lakoff has a surprisingly tin ear for language. His suggestions (like using the term "freedom judges" to respond to "activist judges") are so bad that I assume they must not be meant to be taken literally ("judges that will fight for freedom" is more akin to what Lakoff means).

It's unclear how the book got into this sorry state, but the good news is there's hope. Lakoff's Rockridge Institute has been putting out thoughtful and valuable guides on how to think and talk about various issues and they plan to publish their major work, the Progressive Manual, this summer. Let us hope that book does what this could not.

Disclosure: I received a free review copy of Lakoff's book fedexed to me before the July 4 publication date.

June 23, 2006

FREAKONOMICS

I happen to be taking a class on sociological methods. The other day we had a section where the TA showed us how to use SPSS, a GUI statistical analysis program. Usually such computer demos are pretty boring — pull down this menu here, click this button here, and so on — but this demo was magical: it used real data.

The TA downloaded a listing of venture capitalists from the State of California. Then he downloaded the records of political campaign contributions from the Federal Election Commission. He merged the two files and calculated an index of party loyalty — how likely each person was to donate to the Democrats or Republicans. Then he graphed it. He found an anomaly in the data and went back and investigated it.

The whole performance was oddly enthralling and I went up to ask him questions afterwards. 'So you're interested in statistics?' he asked me and I said yes and began to think about why. I've decided it's because I like truth. If you like finding out the truth — which is often surprising — the best technique to use is science. And if you want to do serious science, sooner or later you'll probably need statistics.

In the field of surprising statistics, one name comes up frequently: Steven D. Levitt. And — surprise, surprise — Levitt has a new book out, Freakonomics. (As an aside, Levitt must have a great publicist because the book has been receiving tons of hype. It's a good book, but not as good as the hype would make it seem.[1] Nonetheless, I will put this aside in reviewing it.) The book consists of a popularization of the papers of Levitt and other interesting economists.

As a result, the book doesn't have much of a theme but covers a bunch of bizarre topics: how school teachers and sumo wrestlers cheat, how bagel eater don't, how real estate agents and surgeons don't have your best interests at heart, how to defeat the Ku Klux Klan, how The Weakest Link contestants demonstrates racism, how online daters lie, how drug dealing works like McDonalds, how abortion overthrows governments and fights crime, how to be a good parent, and what you can learn from children's names.

Despite his unusual interests and open mind, Levitt remains an economist and has the economist's typical right-wing assumptions: most notably, a strong commitment to incentives and an unquestioning faith in societal order. For the former, it makes fun of criminologists by insisting the evidence that punishment deters criminals is "very strong", but fails to provide a single citation (almost everything else in the book, even well-known facts, is scrupulously cited). For the latter, they simply assume that IQ is an accurate and inherited measure of intelligence, despite a rather glaring lack of evidence for this.

Furthermore, in a section that uses parental interviews to pick out which parenting techniques are most effective, the authors almost entirely ignore the possibility that parents are lying — an omission they don't make elsewhere. For example, they find no correlation between saying that you read to your children and your children doing well in school. From this they conclude that reading doesn't matter; a far more likely explanation seems to be that nearly all parents claim they read to their children. (Thanks to Brad Delong for this criticism[2].)

But it's still a fun and interesting book. However, I believe its most important point is one that's not stated explicitly: that through the proper investigation of the numbers we can better understand our world.

Sociologists write many amazingly well-written and fascinating books, even without the help of a professional co-author, yet none of them have seen anything like the publicity this book has. I don't think it's a coincidence that it took an economist to write a sociology book before it could be given publicity. Sociology raises too many problematic questions about society but an economist can do somewhat interesting things while continuing to endorse the status quo. (Even Levitt's most radical finding — that legalizing abortion cut crime rates in half — leads him to insist that the finding has no direct relevance for public policy.)

April 23, 2005

1. The stuff that Levitt is interested in — the reason why his book is interesting — is society, the field studied by sociology. In this sense, Freakonomics is really a sociology book. Yet its attitude toward sociologists could be parodied as "And thank goodness a sociologist risked his life by spending four years embedded with a drug gang because he managed to find a couple notebooks of business transactions that he could give to an economist!" One might expect that the picture of a drug gang resulting from four years of embedded research might be more interesting than a couple of notebooks, but apparently no.
2. http://delong.typepad.com/sdj/2005/03/freakonomics.html

THE IMMORALITY OF FREAKONOMICS

As the hype around the book Freakonomics reaches absurd proportions (now an "international bestseller", the authors have been signed for a monthly column in the *New York Times* Magazine), I think it's time to discuss some of the downsides that I mostly left out of my main review. The most important of which is that economist Stephen Levitt simply does not appear to care — or even notice — if his work involves doing evil things.

The 1960s, as is well-known, had a major civilizing effect on all areas of American life. Less well-known, however, was the immediate pushback from the powerful centers of society. The process involved a great number of things, notably the network of right-wing think tanks I've written about elsewhere, but in the field of education it led to a crackdown on "those institutions which have played the major role in the indoctrination of the young", as a contemporary report (*The Crisis of Democracy*) put it.

The indoctrination centers (notably schools) weren't doing their job properly and so a back-to-basics approach with more rote memorization of meaningless facts and less critical thinking and intellectual development was needed. This was mainly done under the guise of "accountability", for both students and teachers. Standardized tests, you see, would see how well students had memorized certain pointless facts and students would not be allowed to deviate from their assigned numbers. Teachers too would have their jobs depend on the test scores their students got. Teachers who decided to buck the system and actually have their students learn something worthwhile would get demoted or even fired.

Not surprisingly, as always happens when you make people's lives depend on an artificial test, teachers begun cheating. And it is here that Professor Levitt enters the story. He excitedly signed up with the Chicago Public School system to try to build a system that would catch cheating teachers. Levitt and his co-author write excitedly about this system and the clever patterns it discovers in the data, but mostly ignore the question of whether helping to get these teachers fired is a good idea. Apparently even rogue economists jump when the government asks them to.

Levitt has a few arguments — teachers were setting students up to fail in the higher grade they would be advanced to — but these are tacked on as afterthoughts. Levitt never stops to ask whether contributing to the indoctrination of the young or getting teachers fired might not be an acceptable area of work, despite being an economist, he never weighs any benefits or even considers the costs.

Levitt, by all appearances, was not, like some of his colleagues, a self-conscious participant in this regressive game. He was just a rube who got taken in. But surely preventing others from the same fate would be a more valuable contribution.

June 17, 2005

THE CONSERVATIVE NANNY STATE

For years, progressives have watched as both Democratic and Republican administrations have taken away what little remained of economic liberalism in this country. Bill Clinton, for example, took away what meager assistance the government paid to poor single mothers, signed NAFTA, and begun attempting to chip away at Social Security[1].

But even worse than these policy defeats are the conceptual defeats that underly them. As cognitive scientist George Lakoff has argued[2] people think about politics through conceptual moral frames, and the conservatives have been masterful at creating frames for their policies. If the left wants to fight back, they're going to have to create frames of their own.

Enter Dean Baker, co-director of the Center for Economic and Policy Research and one of the people instrumental in fighting back against the most recent attempt to privatize social security (as author *Social Security: The Phony Crisis* he had plenty of facts to demonstrate that the crisis was, in fact, phony). He has a new book out, *The Conservative Nanny State: How the Wealthy Use the Government to Stay Rich and Get Richer*, which takes decades of conservative frames and stands them on their head. (Disclosure: I liked the book so much I converted it to HTML for them and was sent a free paperback copy in return.)

His most fundamental point is that conservatives are *not* generally in favor of market outcomes. For far too long, he argues, the left has been content with the notion that conservatives want the market to do what it pleases while liberals want some government intervention to protect people from its excesses.

No way!, says Baker. Conservatives *love* big government — only they use it to give money to the rich instead of the poor. Thus the conservative nanny state of the title, always looking out for crybaby moneybags to help.

Take, for example, trade policy. The conservative nanny state is more than happy to sign free trade agreements that let manufacturing jobs in the United States flee offshore. And they're happy to let immigrant workers come into the country to replace dishwashers and day laborers. But when it comes to the professional class, like doctors, lawyers, economists, journalists, and other professionals, *oh no!*, the conservative nanny state does everything it can (through licensing and immigration policy) to keep foreign workers out.

This doesn't just help the doctors, it hurts all of us because it means we have to pay more for health care. NAFTA boosters estimate that the entire agreement saved us $8 billion dollars a year. Using competition to bring only doctor's salaries down the levels seen in Europe would save us *eighty* billion dollars — nearly $700 per family per year, just from improved prices for doctor's. You'd see similar amounts from other major professions.

Baker's book is also one of the few to reveal the shocking secret behind the Federal Reserve Board you always hear messing with interest rates on the news. This unaccountable technocracy, most of whose members are appointed by banks, uses its power over interest rates to drive the economy into a recession so that wages won't get too high. That's right, the government tries to slow down the economy so that you get paid less. (Full details are in the book.)

Baker's book is also chock-full of fascinating new policy ideas. He points out, for example, that corporations aren't part of the free market, but instead a gift offered by the government. (A very popular one too, since companies voluntarily pay $278B each year for it.) And because of this, there's absolutely no reason the government can't tweak its terms to make us all better off. For example, Baker points out that currently, corporate rules count shareholders who don't vote at all as voting in favor of whatever the director's of the corporation prefer. Baker suggests requiring that all CEO pay packages get approved by a majority of those actually voting, instead of letting major CEOs pick how much to pay themselves as they do now.

Or what about copyright and patents? Again, this isn't a law of nature, but a big government gift. People who really care about shrinking government would want to try to get rid of or shrink the laws that say the government gets to make rules about what songs and movies we can have on our personal computers.

Americans spend $220 billion on prescription drugs, largely because of government-granted patents. Instead of handing that money to big drug companies, the government could spend far less (only a couple hundred million) funding researchers itself and making the resulting drug discoveries free to the public. College students spend $12 billion. Again, the government could make free textbooks for one-thousandth that. And we spend $37 billion on music and movies. Why not create an "artistic freedom voucher" (vouchers — a conservative favorite!) that can only be spent on artists who place their work in the public domain?

None of these would require outlawing the existing system — they could work side-by-side, simply forcing the existing drug, textbook, and movie companies to compete with this alternate idea. If their version works better, then fine, they'll get the money. But if not, there'll be no conservative nanny state to protect them.

Similarly, the government could expand the social security program, allowing every to buy additional personal accounts from a system with amazingly low overhead (0.5% versus the 20% of private funds) and a 70-year track record of success. Or it could try to improve our pitifully-bad health care system by letting people buy into the government's Medicare program, which again has amazingly low administrative costs (did you know that, on a per person basis, we spend 80% of what Britain spends on health care altogether simply on administration?) and serious bargaining power to push down prices. Again, why not let the private companies try their best to compete?

The book itself also discusses bankruptcy laws, torts and takings, small businesses, and taxes. And it goes in to far more detail on each of these subjects. And it's all available for free on the Internet, so there's no excuse for not reading it. It's an fun read, the kind of book that turns the way you think about the economy upside-down.

May 22, 2006

1. http://www.pbs.org/newshour/bb/fedagencies/jan-june98/security_4-7a.html

WHAT IS ELITISM?

This week's Sunday Bonus Post comes from local genius Kragen Sitaker.

Upon reading an article that claimed:

[S]cience is hard. It is therefore inherently "elitist," merely in this obvious sense: as with skateboarding, some will be demonstrably better at it than others.

Kragen saw fit to ponder the meaning of elitism. Kragen thinks of himself as an anti-elitist, but he's also very pro-science. How to reconcile the two?

Kragen begins by defining "elite":

An "elite" is a small group of people who are distinguished from the majority in one of two ways: either they are better in some way, or they have more power. These are distinct meanings, although apologists for established orders like to conflate them, and sometimes one leads to the other. Sometimes an elite is distinguished by the mastery of a particular skill, such as skateboarding or mathematics, and sometimes by past accomplishments; but the much more common sense of the term today is to refer to a group of people who have power.

Elitism, then (according to Kragen) is the ideology that insists that the elite and non-elite reached their positions through intrinsic merit. (This belief might also be called meritocracy, but that is perhaps a less pejorative term.)

Ironically, the very article that begun this investigation appears to believe in this ideology. The article claims that textbooks, in trying to be "democratic", lower their standards so that even the dullest students can comprehend them. Instead, the article insists, textbooks must be more "elitist" and teach real science, which is hard.

Anti-elitists like Kragen and I would agree that textbooks should teach more real science, which is hard. But we do not consider this elitist, because we do not believe that only a small elite has the capability of comprehending physics.

To anti-elitists, egalitarianism does not require lowering standards, since we believe more people can reach higher standards with more resources. But to elitists, this seems an impossibility. The only reason they are in the club is because they deserve it; to let others in requires bringing the requirements down.

October 29, 2006

A TRIP TO THE COURTHOUSE
PART 1

The United State Court of Appeals for the Ninth Circuit is a federal-looking building nestled in among the offices and shops and business parks of San Francisco's downtown. Large marble walls and staircases try desperately to send the message that what goes on here is of paramount importance, that the decisions made in these halls will reverberate throughout a large part of the country: Alaska, Arizona, California, Hawaii, Idaho, Montana, Nevada, Oregon, and Washington — the largest of any appeals court.

But, this morning, the courtroom tells a different story. With people packed like Sardines into a room not much bigger than a bedroom in a San Francisco apartment, with one of the judges missing and replaced — without explanation — with a large television, and with hesitant, stammering public defenders arguing their cases against only slightly-less-hesitant civil servants, I briefly wondered if I was in the wrong room.

The first case I saw appeared to be a man requesting asylum in the US from his home country. I missed large portions of the case, but as I paid attention, the facts started coming out. He wanted asylum from persecution because he was gay. But the country he was hiding from didn't exactly have a record of persecution of gays. And the only evidence of persecution he could point to was that a couple people on the street once called him gay.

The next case seemed a little better for the non-government guy. It was about a man who accused of defrauding Medicare by double-billing. He noted that the Court had changed the law during the case; instead of just requiring the jury to find whether double-billing had occurred, it now required the jury to find how much. But they'd made that change after the trial, so he'd never had a chance to present any evidence on how much double-billing had occurred. His lawyer asked for a chance to hold a hearing to present the evidence.

"Do you have the evidence?" a judge asked. The lawyer responded that he didn't, because he was a public defender and needed to hire a professional accountant to look through the math, but couldn't afford to without a judge's permission, and the judge denied his request at the same time he denied the hearing on the subject. But, he explained, the government's accountant had admitted on the stand that there were mistakes in the math he presented, although he didn't know what impact they had. Couldn't he just get a trial to assess the math? The judges didn't seem to think so.

If the judges weren't going to give a victory on that case, they really weren't on the next one. A man who lived with his mom in Massachusetts was challenging the government's search of his storage locker in Arizona. His lawyer sparred with the judges for some time about the details of Fourth Amendment law. Then the government's lawyer took the stage. "Let me tell you about this man," he said. "As a condition of his parole, he wasn't permitted to have any guns. But he kept one gun, the machine gun he'd had since he was a kid — he called it his baby. The government got a tip and showed up on his doorstep and he practically handed them the gun and then told them to go away. It was raining outside and he wouldn't let them into his house. They searched the house and found another machine gun kit."

"In Court, he was asked if he had any more guns. His lawyer, acting on his client's behalf, insisted that the Court didn't have jurisdiction because all the other guns were in a storage locker in Arizona. After the lawyer said that, we had to search the locker in Arizona. There we found a huge shipping crate. To take the crate into evidence, the government had to inventory it. There we found 44 flamethrowers, 22 submachine guns, 5 hand grenades, and a handful of pistols. We had to call in the bomb squad and check over everything. And he's arguing that the Fourth Amendment doesn't permit us to open that crate."

Later, I heard some of the lawyers on a different case joking. "Once opposing counsel says flamethrowers, you've lost. Doesn't matter how good your case is. You're never going to recover from that."

It was into this environment that Larry Lessig stepped. Lessig has been thinking about the implications of copyright law for most of his career. He has spent months practicing to argue before the Supreme Court and other lesser courts. He spent the weekend practicing this case with other faculty members at the Stanford Law School. He spent the morning pacing the halls, going over his notes one last time. And as he strode into the Courtroom that morning and begun his argument before the Court, unlike every other lawyer who had presented, he didn't stumble over a single word.

In some ways, this should have been home territory for Lessig. It was his own

Court, right in his own town of San Francisco. And as he paced the halls, he was continually interrupted by former students of his at Stanford Law, who had gone on to careers as lawyers in the area, which had brought them here, to argue before the Court just like him. And, perhaps he figured, the judges would welcome a break from the endless parade of petty complaints to his arguments about the big issues — the First Amendment, the Progress clause, copyright. Weren't things like that why they became judges in the first place?

Perhaps not.

November 27, 2006

A TRIP TO THE COURTHOUSE
PART 2

"For a hundred and eighty-six years America had an opt-in system of copyright," Lessig began. "Copyright was not granted automatically but was limited to works that were published. And then only to those with notice. And then only to those published with notice that were deposited and registered promptly. And to those [published,] marked, deposited, and registered, the copyright still had to be renewed after 28 years. Under this system, nearly fifty percent of published work entered the public domain immediately and ninety-three percent within twenty-eight years."

"Following the 1976 Copyright Act, that all changed and copyright was granted automatically, for a full term, as soon as a work was fixed in a tangible form. No longer was it necessary to published, deposit, mark, or renew. Copyright moved from an opt-in system to an opt-out. And under this system, zero percent of published work will enter the public domain for at least a hundred years."

"This is a radical change — perhaps the most radical change — to copyright law, going from ninety-three percent of works going in the public domain to zero. And the result is a huge increase in 'orphaned works' — works whose copyright holder cannot even be located to ask permission."

"In Eldred v. Ashcroft, the Supreme Court ruled that copyright only needed judicial review when the 'traditional contours' of copyright law were changed. This is clearly a change to copyright's traditional contours and thus deserves a chance for judicial review."

The government's lawyer — slick, but not as slick as Lessig — argued that the Court was referring to only two traditional contours: the right to fair use (which allows things like the use of small snippets of copyrighted material and limited copies for educational use) and the "idea/expression dichotomy" (which says that you can't copyright ideas but only a particular way of expressing them).

Lessig responded that this was absurd. If the government ruled that cartoons featuring the prophet Mohammed could not receive copyrights, the law would clearly be subject to First Amendment review, even though neither fair use nor idea/expression were touched. Similarly, the change from opt-out to opt-in deserves review.

There were three judges, as required by law to hear all federal appeals. The one on the right, who was live via satellite, didn't say a word the entire time. The one on the left didn't ask more than a question or two. The judge in the middle was responsible for most of the questions. And she did not appear to get it.

"How is this different from Eldred?" she asked.

A quarter of the way in to the argument, she handed a slip of paper to her aide. Her aide scurried away and came back with a thick document. She looked down at it and then looked up.

"You were the lawyer in Eldred as well," she asked Lessig.

"Yes, your honor."

"How is this different from Eldred?"

"In Eldred," Lessig explained, trying again, "the issue was whether Congress could continue expanding the length of copyright in order to keep Mickey Mouse from going into the public domain. The Court — Justice Ginsburg channelling Justice Scalia — said that since Congress had been doing this forever they could keep doing it. But in this case, we're talking about a new change, one that effects orphaned works — works for who the copyright holder cannot be located."

"Which wouldn't include Mickey Mouse, because every can find Disney?" the judge asked.

"Precisely," Lessig replied.

During the government's rebuttal, the judge asked who was lobbying against this change in copyright law. "Well," the government's lawyer replied, "um, I suspect it was people very much like the ones you see here today." ("Yeah," Lessig scoffed later, "I was testifying in Congress against the bill back when I was fifteen!")

By the same token, the judge asked Lessig about what solutions to the problem he would expect were the law ruled unconstitutional. "There are many possible solutions," Lessig replied, drawing a picture of a network of people fighting this issue in all branches of government. There was this lawsuit, of course, but there was also a bill introduced by local Congresswoman Zoe Lofgren to require a one-dollar renewal fee (based, Lessig did not say, on a *New York Times* op-ed he had written), there was a series of hearings by the U.S. Copyright Office on the orphaned works problem, which concluded "The orphan works problem is real. ... Legislation is necessary to provide a meaningful solution to the orphan works problem as we know it today." and provided several proposals.

"Your time is up," the judge said, before the red light saying his time was up had gone on, and Lessig quietly packed up his papers and filed out, half the courtroom following behind him.

"Congratulations," Internet Archive founder Brewster Kahle (the man who Lessig is filing this lawsuit on behalf of) said to Lessig, shaking his hand and smiling broadly. Lessig smiled back, then posed politely for photos with Kahle and his associate Rick Prelinger. The well-wishers soon streamed out until it was just Lessig and his fellow law school lawyers. The smile disappeared from Lessig's face. "They didn't get it," Lessig said downcast.

"Oh, I think they were getting it towards the end there," one of the lawyers said, trying to cheer Lessig up. "No," he replied, "they weren't." "Well," another lawyer chimed in, "to write an opinion they'll have to read the briefs and then they'll see your argument." "No," he explained, "they can just tell a clerk which way to write the opinion and have them do it."

"Actually, our best hope now is that they won't write an opinion at all and then Golan [a related case in a different Circuit] will go the other way and then we'll have a circuit split." (A circuit split is when two different circuit courts rule different ways on the same issue. Usually the Supreme Court then has to step in to resolve the disagreement.)

"Well, at least your case didn't have any flamethrowers," someone said, trying to lighten the mood. But Lessig just wasn't in the mood.

November 28, 2006

FREE SPEECH
BECAUSE WE CAN

In the field of Constitutional Law, there are many pages spent trying to come up with a reason for free speech. It's about the "marketplace of ideas" some say: by putting all claims and points of view out in the open, the public can sort through and figure out the truth, leaving the untruths to fall by the wayside. Others argue that free speech is necessary for democracy, since voters must hear different opinions to decide how to use their votes, and that since even non-political speech can change people's views, all speech must then be protected.

There are many more justifications like this — a limit on government abuse, a policy to promote a more tolerant citizenship, etc. — but, like most justifications, they all say we should permit free speech because it allows us to do something else. And the frustrating thing about that is that it suggests that free speech should not be permitted when it doesn't achieve those goals.

Theorists of free speech are, in general, fans of the idea (or at least their market consists of fans) so they try to dance around this. "Oh no," the marketplace-of-ideas partisans say, "we weren't suggesting that obviously false statements could be prohibited because, after all, you really never know when false statements could turn out to be true!"

But, as something of a free speech absolutist, it troubles me that such a thing is even theoretically possible. And I worry that if others adopt this theory, they may not be so stringent about the practical requirements. The temptation to clamp down on free speech is always strong; it's probably not a sound idea to build the principle on such a shaky foundation.

So I have my own justification for freedom of speech: because we can. Human freedom is important, so we should try to protect it from encroachment wherever possible. With most freedoms — freedom of motion, freedom of exchange, freedom of action — permitting them in full would cause some problems. People shouldn't be free to walk into other people's bedrooms, take all their stuff, and then punch the poor victims in the face. But hurling a bunch of epithets at the guy really isn't so bad.

Freedom of speech is one place where we can draw the line and say: all of this is acceptable. There's no further logic to it than that; freedom of speech is not an instrumental value. Like all freedom, it's fundamental, and the only reason we happen to single it out is because it's more reasonable than all of the others.

Close readers will note that this theory doesn't quite live up to my own goals. By laying freedom of speech's provision on top of our reasonable ability to do so, I suggest that freedom of speech could be taken away if providing it became unreasonable. But I think this is the right choice: if people really, seriously started getting hurt because of freedom of speech, it seems right for people to take the privilege away. But, to be honest, I can't even imagine how that might be possible. Words just don't genuinely wound, they're always mediated by our listening.

I do worry that people might try to stretch this justification — say that continued free speech might destroy the war effort, or the government, or civil society. But I have no problem destroying all of those. It's only the destruction of actual people that I worry about.

So here's to free speech: because we can.

November 23, 2006

IDENTITY FETISHISM

Marx wrote incisively about commodity fetishism — the tendency of people to see only the results of production (commodities), ignoring the hours of human labor that actually created them. The humanities seems to suffer from something of the reverse problem: a tendency to be absorbed by the names of big people and not seeing beyond to the ideas they espouse.

The most extreme example is Leo Strauss, who encouraged his students to put aside their prejudices and fully imerse themselves in the worlds and minds of the greats. The greats were so great, Strauss suggested, that if you disagree with them, you probably just don't understand them well enough.

But even other teachers of philosophy have the same problem, presenting the views of X and Y even when X is pretty clearly wrong. Despite its absurdities, students must learn to understand X's view. This seems fairly universal; even books like *What is the Meaning of it All?*, which explains philosophy without the names or complex terminology, still presents clearly bogus ideas on the same footing as more reasonable ones.

In other fields, this pattern is less frequent, but still there for whole courses of research. In sociology, papers must cite long-dead patron theorists to lend their empirical research an air of legitimacy by presenting it as a member of a recognized family. Even more recent works, like Annette Lareau's brilliant *Unequal Childhoods*, are at pains to show how they adhere to a theoretical model (the recently-alive Bourdieu in that case). In most other fields, the theorists take pains to make sure their work is consistent with the evidence, not the other way around.

Even in most humanities classes, the course content consists of a series of papers making arguments. The goal of the class is to understand the view of the authors and determine (in the best ones) to what extent you agree or disagree.

This isn't particularly unreasonable, but is a far cry from life in the hard sciences, where usually there is an actual consensus on some subject and otherwise there are a couple of named theories, each being developed by a group of people.

Why the diference? First, is it perhaps hard science that's in the wrong? I don't think so. The goal of science is to discover the truth about the world. Truths remain true no matter who says them and it's unlikely that one person will discover the whole truth. Thus the pattern of letting multiple people develop a theory and try to find evidence for it to convince the others.

So why don't the softer sciences follow the same model? The problem gets worse the softer you get, which suggests the problem lies in the softness itself. The problem is that without identities, one has to judge the ideas themselves which, in a soft science is somewhat difficult to do.

It's easy in science to run an experiment and see if it proves a theory true or false, it's much harder to get consensus about a reasonable theory of morality in philosophy. But it is easy to pick out the famous in academy culture and assign their stuff.

Identity fetishism thrives in a world afraid to make its own judgments. It exalts the thinkers of the past and, in doing so, diminishes its own capacities. But science must march forward instead of backward and that requires the daring to distinguish true from false.

November 21, 2006

DRUGS AND GUNS

In movies, it's clear when the camera is drunk: blurred vision, shaky motions, everything becoming slightly less clear. It's similarly obvious when the camera is on acid: rainbow colors, things melting into each other, and a sort of dazed gaze. Yet, despite the prevalence of pot, I've never seen a film or TV show where the camera is high on marijuana.

Perhaps that's because there's nothing to show. Some deep breaths, a slight tingling sensation, and then an odd feeling as if something is pressing on part of your brain, lifting your head up, making you happy. An odd happiness, to be sure, but a happiness nonetheless. Friends are unable to distinguish between when I've just gone skinnydipping and when I'm simply high. It's hard to show a camera being happy.

Contrast this with Omega-3 fatty acids, the fish oil acids that various new studies are supposed to show have all sorts of positive effects for your brain. When I swallowed a stack of Omega-3 pills, I felt as if I was crawling up into my head, living in there instead of plotting the next moves for my body. It made it pretty hard to get anything done.

In San Francisco, medical marijuana is perfectly legal and health-food culture makes Omega-3 practically mandatory, but possessing a gun is actually outlawed within city limits (even for off-duty cops). To actually discharge one you have to drive south of the border, where shooting ranges allow deprived northerners to partake of this recreational craze.

Unlike the flowing, hippie vibe of drug culture, gun culture is strictly utilitarian: concrete walls, florescent lights, drab carpeting. Tough-looking guys take your license and hand you a gun. First-timers go into the training room for a quick primer on how to use it, then you take your weapon, ammo, and target into the shooting range.

Most of the targets are pretty bland — vague silhouettes or bullseyes — but there was one frightening option that featured a blatantly stereotypical illustration of a hooded bad guy character holding a gun to a cute young girl's head. Normally descriptions of such pictures are more evocative than the pictures themselves, but this drawing was just about perfect.

Naturally, this was the target our neighbors on the shooting range had chosen and were now shooting at with enormous shotguns whose blasts shook the entire room. Meanwhile, I had a small handgun with a little bit of a kick and a simple silhouette.

My gun jammed the first couple of times I tried to shoot; I had to go through the process of unloading and reloading it several times before I even shot a single bullet. It's amazing how comically fake the actual gun feels when you do this — it makes all the noises and motions you'd expect from a gun, but it seems to lack any internal mechanisms for doing the actual shooting, like a prop for a movie.

When I finally did manage to get the gun working, I relaxed, aimed my weapon, and took ten shots at where I thought the bullseye was. (My long-distance eyesight is really terrible and I hadn't thought to bring my glasses until now, so I gave it my best shot.) I shot again and again, the pattern of kicking and aiming becoming almost rhythmic. When the gun was finally empty, I pushed the little button to whirr my target back to me. To my amazement, nearly all ten bullets had gone in right by the bullseye. My partner looked frightened.

What's odd about shooting is how, well, relaxing it is. Something about the furious action of the gun seems to drain you of all your nervous energy. And while, if you think about it, the item you're holding is a weapon of terrible destruction, there's very little visual evidence of that fact. Just as the gun feels like a prop, the whole thing feels like a game: aim, press the trigger, and some dots appear in a piece of paper. But when you're done you don't feel hyped-up like after a video game. Instead you feel as if what you actually discharged was your nervous energy.

We rolled up the bullet-ridden silhouette to take home as a souvenir. "Maybe I'll mail this to my mom," I said. "I don't think that's a very good idea," came the reply.

December 19, 2006

MEDIUM STUPID

In July 1, 2004, Paul Krugman gave a talk about the state of the American economy. After the significant 2001 recession, the economy had begun growing again, with increasing growth in America's economic output, or GDP. But, unlike the growth in the Clinton years, the extra money being made in America wasn't going to the average person. Instead, as the economy grew, the wages for the average person stagnated or even declined. All the extra money was going to the people at the very top.

In the press, President Bush's supporters complained that the public wasn't more happy about the growing economy Bush had given them. After all, he'd pulled the country out of a recession; normally that's good for a boost in the polls. Sadly, Americans were just too dumb to notice, Bush's supporters concluded. If only they paid more attention to the news. But what these people "are really urging," Krugman explained in his talk, "is not that the public should be smart, but that the public should be medium stupid."[1]

If the public was really "stupid" (i.e. uneducated), it wouldn't watch the news at all. Instead, it would notice it was out of work, poorly-paid, or otherwise having trouble making ends meet, and conclude that the economy wasn't doing very well. On the other hand, if the public was really smart, it'd dig deep into the numbers to find that — surprise, surprise! — for most people, the economy wasn't doing as well as the headline numbers about GDP growth would suggest. The only way for the public to buy the Bush administration spin is to be medium stupid.

The medium stupid idea has much wider applicability. Most specifically, it explains the general state that the mainstream media tries to inculcate in the public. The uneducated American has a general idea that invading other countries is probably a bad idea. The overeducated American can point to dozens of examples of why this is going to be a bad idea. But the "medium stupid" American, the kind that gullibly reads the *New York Times* and watches the CBS Evening News, is convinced that Iraq is full of weapons of mass destruction that could blow our country to bits at any minute. A little education can be a dangerous thing.

(Along these lines, at one point I was working on a documentary film about the evening news that would demonstrate this point. The title, *Medium Stupid*, would also be a convenient homage to *Medium Cool*.)

The same is true in school. As Christopher Hayes points out in his genius article, Is A Little Economics A Dangerous Thing?[2], the uneducated American thinks raising the minimum wage is a pretty good idea — after all, people deserve to be paid more than $5 an hour. And the overeducated American feels the same way; like the dozens of Economics Prize winners who signed a petition to raise the minimum wage, they've seen the studies showing that raising the minimum wage has only a negligible effect on employment. But those who have only had Economics 101 buy the propaganda that government interference in the market will only make things worse. And, as Hayes shows[3], this leads to bad decisions in many areas — the minimum wage being only one prominent example.

The medium stupid idea has applicability in other areas of life. The uncultured person who knows nothing about fashion doesn't mind wandering around in jeans and a t-shirt. And the overcultured person knows exactly what to wear to be hip. But medium stupid ol' me looks bad and feels bad about it.

To work, propaganda, be it from the Bush administration or the fashion industry, requires you to be medium stupid. Know too little and you never hear the falsehoods. Know too much and you can spot it for a fraud. Which side of the line do you want to be on?

December 19, 2006

1.   http://www.americanprogress.org/kf/krugman-final.pdf
2.   http://www.inthesetimes.com/site/main/article/2897/
3.   http://www.inthesetimes.com/site/main/article/2897/

THE GOOG LIFE
HOW GOOGLE KEEPS EMPLOYEES BY TREATING THEM LIKE KIDS

I was talking with a friend the other day about that perennial subject of conversation in the Valley, Google. And finally she gave me the clue that made the whole place make sense. "It's about infantilizing people," she explained. "Give them free food, do their laundry, let them sit on bouncy brightly-colored balls. Do everything so that they never have to grow up and learn how to live life on their own."

And when you look at it that way, everything Google does makes a sick sort of sense.

Not a whole lot has changed since the last time I visited Google. The campus is bigger — the buildings across the street, instead of being reserved for lawyers and other lowlifes, are now being used by the engineering staff as well, to keep up with Google's nonstop growth. And the employees seem a little less excited about things than the last time I was there. Nobody says "We're on a mission to change the world!" anymore. Now they say, "Yeah, I'm just going to stick around here another six months until my options vest." and "I kind of want to transfer out of my group but I worry that all the other groups are worse."

But the two blatant changes to the campus are a large, terribly fake-looking replica of SpaceShipOne hanging in the middle of the main building and a replica dinosaur skeleton standing outside. "It's as if this place is being decorated by seven-year-olds," a friend comments. It also reminds me of Robert Reich's comment about Newt Gingrich: "His office is adorned with figurines of dinosaurs, as you might find in the bedrooms of little boys who dream of one day being huge and powerful."

The dinosaurs and spaceships certainly fit in with the infantilizing theme, as does the hot tub-sized ball pit that Googlers can jump into and throw ball fights. Everyone I know who works there either acts childish (the army of programmers), enthusiastically adolescent (their managers and overseers), or else is deeply cynical (the hot-shot programmers). But as much as they may want to leave Google, the infantilizing tactics have worked: they're afraid they wouldn't be able to survive anywhere else.

Google hires programmers straight out of college and tempts them with all the benefits of college life. Indeed, as the hiring brochures stress, the place was explicitly modeled upon college. At one point, I wondered why Google didn't just go all the way and build their own dormitories. After all, weren't the late-night dorm-room conversations with others who were smart like you one of the best parts of college life? But as the gleam wears off the Google, I can see why it's no place anyone would want to hang around for that long. Even the suburban desert of Mountain View is better.

Google's famed secrecy doesn't really do a very good job of keeping information from competitors. Those who are truly curious can pick up enough leaks and read enough articles to figure out how mostly everything works. But what it does do is create an aura of impossibility around the place. People read the airbrushed versions of Google technologies in talks and academic papers and think that Google has some amazingly large computer lab with amazingly powerful technology. But hang around a Googler long enough and you'll hear them complain about the unreliability of GFS and how they don't really have enough computers to keep up with the load.

"It's always frightening when you see how the sausage actually gets made," explains a product manager. "And that's exactly what the secrecy is supposed to prevent. The rest of the world sees Google as this impenetrable edifice with all the mysteries of the world inside ("I hear once you've worked there for 256 days they teach you the secret levitation," explains xkcd[1]) while the select few inside the walls know the truth — there is no there there — and are bound together by this burden.

Such a strategy may have worked in the early days, when Googlers were a select and special few, but as the company grows larger and employee's identification with it grows thinner, Google has to step up their efforts to acculturate. And that's where the life-size dinosaur replicas come in. Enjoy being huge and powerful while you can. Because, like the dinosaurs, this too will pass.

December 13, 2006

1.   http://xkcd.com/c192.html

COMPETITION OF EXPERIMENTATION?

It should be clear to anyone who has studied the topic that the way to drive innovation forward is to have lots of small groups of people each trying different things to succeed. In *Guns, Germs, and Steel,* for example, we see that certain societies succeed because geography breaks them up into chunks and prevents any one person with bad ideas from getting control of too much, while other societies fail because their whole territory can too easily be captured by an idiot.

It might at first seem more efficient to let the whole territory be captured by a genius, but a moment's reflection will show that there are few geniuses whose brainpower can match the combined results of many independent experiments. This has fairly obvious applications to business (see article "Google and the Gradient") and other fields, but for a moment let's just think about the concept itself.

This idea is often presented as a defense of competition and the capitalist market system that embraces it. Innovation only happens, such people say, when lots of people are competing against each other for the prizes of success. In a communist country, where Big State decides what will be worked on and how, there is no incentive to innovate. Only in a country like ours, where the victor gets the spoils, can new technology be developed.

And yet we also know that competition is a terrible way to get people do well. In *No Contest: The Case Against Competition* we see dozens of studies that show that, by all sorts of metrics, people's performance (and enjoyment) goes down when they are forced to compete. Even worse, it goes down most notably for creative tasks — precisely the kind of thing involved in innovation.

How do we resolve the contradiction? The key is to notice that competition, especially market competition, isn't the only way to encourage experimentation. And that's often hard to do, because typically market competition is treated as the only sensible form of competition and competition as the only sensible form of experimentation. But that's not at all the case.

Instead of providing a prize for winner, we could provide rewards to everyone who tries. And that actually makes sense — not only because prizes also decrease productivity and creativity — but also because, when it comes to experimentation, it's not really your fault if the experiment doesn't work. In fact, we want to encourage people to try crazy things that might not work, which is exactly why rewards are so counterproductive.

But even if you don't give an explicit prize, competition is still unhealthy. Contrary to what the apologists for market theology would like you to believe, people do not work better when they're terrified of the guy next to them finding the solution first. Which is why we should look at this as simply experimentation, not competition.

Experimentation can certainly be carried out cooperatively. Imagine many different scientists in a lab, each trying different ideas during the day, swapping notes and tips over lunch, perhaps joining together to form small groups for certain experiments, or perhaps helping with little pieces of other projects in which they have particular expertise. Each scientist may disagree on which is the right direction to pursue, but that doesn't make them enemies.

That's the way that science progresses. And, if you let it, other things too.

December 7, 2006

THE ENEMY TOO CLOSE TO HOME

How bizarre a book is *The Enemy At Home*, Dinesh D'Souza's new screed insisting the left is responsible for Islamic extremism? Pretty bizarre. The book's argument, according to the *Times*[1] is that "1) that the American left is allied to the Islamic radical movement to undermine the Bush White House and American foreign policy; and 2) that 'the left is the primary reason for Islamic anti-Americanism…' because 'liberals defend and promote values that are controversial in America and deeply revolting to people in traditional societies, especially in the Muslim world.'"

Follow that? The left is allies with Islamic extremists because the extremists hate the left. Just like Dinesh D'Souza. "[W]hen it comes to core beliefs," he writes, "I'd have to confess that I'm closer to the dignified fellow in the long robe and prayer beads than to the slovenly fellow with the baseball cap [Michael Moore]."

In other words, it sounds like the right is allied with Islamic extremists in hating the liberal elements of American culture. What to do about this is left as an exercise to the reader.

February 8, 2007

1.   http://www.nytimes.com/2007/02/06/books/06kaku.html

JOHN HOCKENBERRY
ON REPORTING THE WAR AT NBC

John Hockenberry is a long-time, well-known American journalist. He's won four Emmy awards and three Peabody awards. Now that, as he puts it, "mainstream media doesn't want John Hockenberry anymore," he's become a Distinguished Fellow at the MIT Media Lab, where he recently gave a talk which commented on some of his experiences covering the Iraq war while at NBC.

Here are some excerpts:

I was very happily employed at NBC. I wasn't like, running around, trying to stuff toilet paper into the plumbing and sabotage the place. […] But I was interested, because we had a lot of meetings at NBC about, you know, if you're doing a story and the person you're doing the story about offers to buy you a drink, you've gotta say no. If you're doing a story and they send you, after they see the story, some napkin rings — silver napkin rings that are monogrammed "Thank you, Jon, for the story," you've got not only to return those, you've got to report those to the standards people at NBC because there's a whole ethics and conflict-of-interest thing.

So at one of these ethics meetings — I called them the return-the-napkin-ring kinds of meetings — I raised my hand and said "You know, isn't it a problem that the contract that GE has with the Coalition Provisional Authority […] to rebuild the power generation system in Iraq [is] about the size of *the entire budget of NBC*? Is that kind of like the napkin rings thing?" And the standards people said "Huh. That's interesting. No one's brought that up before." Now I'm not saying that I'm smart or that I'm advanced or that I'm ahead of my colleagues or maybe I had a lot of free time to think about this or maybe I'm some pinko-proto-lefty like Richard Nixon. I don't know! But the fact that it drew a complete blank among the NBC standards people was interesting to me.

[Now] in fact what happens in the networks — and you can find this at ABC and other networks at well — is that this [conflict with the profit motive] manifests itself [as journalists saying] "Well, we are better reporters because we deal with these kinds of conflicts all the time. And because we deal with those and we *always* decide in favor of the audience, it sort of exercises our journalistic muscle." And this is the line you get from all of the entities.

You may or may not be aware that there was a real strong full-court press to sell the media — and I'm not pro- or against it at this particular point, but there was a process in place where individuals in the media got access to the individuals involved in the planning of the war. There were generals who came in, there were former secretaries of defense, Schwarzkopf spent a whole lot of time giving sort of off-the-record, quiet briefings. And the generals would sort of bring in a certain group of editors and reporters and I went to all of these briefings.

At one of them, Hockenberry explains, a well-known pollster told about a briefing he gave to all the senior officials at the White House about how the polling data from the Arab world showed that America's negatives were simply off-the-charts. Everyone was quiet. Condi asked a few technical questions and then finally Karl Rove spoke up. "Well, that's just until we start throwing our weight around over there," he said.

Hockenberry was stunned and thought they should do a piece on what this revealed into the mentality of the war's planners. But NBC News didn't think this was a very good idea. America wanted the war to happen; their job was just to wait and see how it turned out. "We're not particularly interested in the story," Hockenberry explains. "We're a process that's trying to maintain people in front of the set, so in a certain sense media at that point was doing its own kind of shock-and-awe that went right along with the war's shock-and-awe [because] the business is just to grab eyeballs."

Later, his team edited together a montage of clips about what it was like for reporters who were still in Iraq to experience the shock-and-awe campaign. Vibrant images, narrated by a tense reporter who was on the ground at the time.

We played this piece for the editors. And it was very moving, very powerful, and it was a very different perspective from what we were getting. And at the end […] there was quiet around the table, because it was kind of an emotional piece and certainly the emotion in this reporter's voice was detectable over a satellite phone line.

And the standards person goes — and again, this is his job, I don't begrudge him that — he goes, "Seems like, seems like she has a point of view here."

The table was silent. Just dead silent. And I was infuriated. But whenever I get this sort of infuriated feeling I think "You know, this is a career-ending moment here." There is something I could say that would be right. There is something I could say that would be wrong. And there is something that I could say that would be right — and also would be wrong.

And it was the beginning of the coverage of an event that would be extraordinary and I definitely wanted to be around to be a part of the next day's coverage, but I had to say something. And it seemed as though, if nobody said anything, people would go "well, I guess we'll have to tone her down."

So I said, "You mean, the war-is-bad point of view?"

The piece aired.

March 28, 2007

NEWSPEAK™

It started way back in the eighties, with the Stay Free maxi-pads. At least, that's what they said on this TV documentary I saw once. How could you tell people to protect their freedom when they thought you were talking about feminine hygiene products? I mean, you still had the words, of course, it wasn't Orwellian or anything, they didn't take away the words, they just "added" new meanings to them. Particular kinds of meanings. And who really wanted to use them after that? It made the whole idea of freedom seem kind of dirty.

We don't have freedom either, of course. Freedom lasted a little longer, before finally dying out in the late nineties when the name was taken by that pornography download software. I mean, try telling some guy in the street you're just trying to protect your freedom. I've tried! He laughs and then he makes some sort of obscene sexual pantomime. Makes it kind of hard to be an activist.

Activist took a little longer. Companies bought out the core concepts before they moved to the little stuff like us activists. Activist was what they called it when they privatized the sewer system in the late 2000s. "Activists are shit," you used to hear the right-wingers say. Now they don't even need to say it — it's in the dictionary.

So when I recruit kids I can't tell them what they'd be. Saying they'd be activists is straight out, obviously. But I can't even tell them we do protests. Protest is what they call it when you call AAA when your car breaks down. Kids don't want to go around fixing broken cars. They're not big on protests.

Liberty quickly became the leading brand of thong underwear. Control is the #2 online role-playing game. Rights are the new name for gift certificates. Democracy is the kind of M&Ms where you get to pick the color. ("Geez man, we all like chocolate, but you're taking things a bit too far," is what the kids say when I tell them we need to fight to protect democracy.)

It's like a nightmare version of *Intelligence* (or, as it used to be called, *Wheel of Fortune*). They bought up all my words.

March 25, 2007

THIS TELEVISION LIFE

Have you ever listened to that show on NPR, *This American Life*? I don't know about you, but as far as I'm concerned, it has to be one of the most amazing things to ever grace our country's airwaves. Back when it started, over a decade ago now, it was unlike just about anything you heard on public radio. This wasn't a show about news or music or comedy. It wasn't even, really, a show about people. It was a show about stories, stripped down to their pure essence, people talking to you with a little bit of music in the background.

Humans seem to have a natural craving for stories. Whatever the topic, it's more fun to hear a story about it. Everyone tells stories. Everyone tells stories, but some people love crafting them until they're perfect, like little pastries of information with curves in all the right places. And that's what *This American Life* did each week on the radio: it presented three or four perfectly-crafted stories, all tangentially related to one loose theme, to your car or home for one full hour.

A couple years ago the Showtime network called Ira Glass, the head and host of *This American Life* and asked him if he wanted to make a television version of his show. For most people, getting a call from a television network would be a fairly big deal. But not Glass. Every week, his radio show is heard by 1.6 million people. A hit show on Showtime gets half a million. So Glass said no, there was no way their show would work on television. Still, Showtime persisted, asking what it would take to make it work. So Glass thought of every crazy demand that came to mind. And Showtime met them all.

The result, which premieres tonight on the pay-cable Showtime network, has to be one of the most amazing things to grace American television. It is unlike just about anything you've ever seen on TV. The best way I can think to describe it is this: Have you ever seen one of those stock photo movies? You know, the kind with the lusciously oversaturated colors, weird landscapes, and slow-motion movements? The kind of footage that makes the normal world look magical? Now, take that, and imagine an entire television show made out of it. It's absolutely incredible.

To promote the show, since Showtime isn't exactly, *This American Life* went on a six-city tour. I caught them in Chicago, where a jam-packed crowd of dedicated fans (still pissed about the team moving to New York to film the TV show) came to hear "What I Learned From Television". We were in the Chicago Theater, a local landmark that holds thousands. And, I have to say, it's probably the most fun I've ever had in a theater.

You know how on the radio show, they do these incredibly moving stories that just send chills of emotion down your spine. Now imagine listening to that, in the middle of a crowd of thousands of people who all came out to hear the very same thing. I mean, these were people who cheered individual names in the credits at the end of the show. (We'll miss you Elizabeth Meister!) I've never felt a room so charged with emotion before.

So do these guys a favor. Do yourself a favor. Take your Nielsen box and switch it to Showtime tonight at 10:30. It'll be like nothing you've ever felt before.

March 23, 2007

REAGAN, STAR WARS, AND THE END OF THE COLD WAR

It's not hard to see why building technology to defend against nuclear missiles is tricky. First, there's the obvious difficulty of shooting at a moving target — like a bullet shooting a bullet. Then there's the fact that whatever device is defending you must itself be well defended, or else the enemy can simply take it out. And then there's the nasty fact that with nuclear war, near-perfect defense is necessary — even a single failure can cause enormous damage.

What is hard is explaining why, despite this, so many people took the idea so seriously. That's the question Frances FitzGerald takes up in *Way Out There In The Blue*, in which she uses the "Star Wars" initiative as a prism with which to understand the Reagan administration. Combined with Rick Perlstein's forthcoming *Nixonland*, the books provide allegorical insight into our current government: Bush II has combined the criminality of Nixon with the intellectual emptiness of Reagan.

Ronald Reagan was an actor. Even when off the set, he recited polished lines and played up a well-practiced demeanor. Indeed, he appears to have no inner life whatsoever. No one can be found to whom Ronald Reagan ever "opened up"; even his wife commented that "There's a wall around him ... even I feel that barrier." As president, he was given the equivalent of shooting instructions specifying exactly where he was supposed to be every hour of the day and when he attended public events toe marks were chalked on the ground to indicate where he should stand.

Considering the state of the American political system, having an actor for a President is perhaps not the worst idea. But what was problematic was that nobody — including Reagan's closest aides — seemed to realize that that was what they were getting. For months they were continually shocked that Reagan refused to ever make a decision or take an action on any issue whatsoever. Instead, they watched dumbly as he simply listened to what he was told and nodded politely. When two of his subordinates disagreed, he was uncomfortable, but he steadfastly refused to intervene.

The result was that decisions ended up getting made by whoever was around — Nancy Reagan, his wife; Michael Deaver, his aide in charge of public relations; etc. Reagan's top people, such as his cabinet officials, frightened that they were actually making policy without any supervision, kept this fact secret from their staffs and the public until they all published their kiss-and-tell memoirs after Reagan had left office. Even more shocking, Reagan didn't seem to mind when the members of this group changed. One day Reagan's inner circle informed him that they were leaving and bringing the Treasury Secretary in to take their place. Reagan simply thanked them for their service.

There was one thing Reagan did seem to care about (aside from politely answering his fan mail): speeches. Reagan would rewrite his own speeches, removing abstract verbiage and adding homespun stories. And it was out of this concern that he stumbled into launching the Star Wars initiative.

After many years of right-wing propaganda about a "window of vulnerability" in our arms race with the Soviet Union, the Pentagon developed the MX missile series to ensure American superiority. The problem was where to put them. The MX missiles were designed to protect against the Soviets simply destroying all of our missiles, so they could not simply be put out in the open or the Soviets would simply destroy them as well. A variety of Rube Goldberg-like ideas were proposed to solve the problem.

After a thorough investigation, the military concluded the best solution was what came to be called "the racetrack": the missiles would be put on huge underground circular tracks, with little launching stations cut sporadically in the track. There would be several times more launching stations than missiles, so the Soviets would not know which stations to attack. But, to verify compliance with arms treaties, the stations could be opened so that the Soviets could see which ones contained missiles from space.

The problem was that the racetracks would need to be huge and the only practical space for such a thing was in Utah. The Mormon Church was understandably unhappy about having a huge nuclear missile field being built near them and thus the powerful Republicans from that region of the country scuttled the plan.

Other ideas were tried — the racetrack was converted to a straight line system, then to a configuration known as "Dense Pack" in which the missiles were all placed close together, in the hopes that all the missiles coming to attack them would blow each other up and perhaps spare some of our missiles. Another plan, known as "Big Bird", had the missiles flying overhead on large transport planes, but it was scrapped when technicians raised concerns about the wings falling off. Another proposal involved hiding the missiles as normal luggage on cross-country passenger trains. It got to the point where the best idea was literally known as DUMB — deep underground missile basing — in which the missiles would be loaded on corkscrews which would drill down underground. Finally, they decided just to deploy the missiles in superficially-hardened housing, even though this meant they could be easily destroyed.

At the same time, a mass popular movement for a nuclear freeze was growing, encompassing college students, churches, and many unpoliticized citizens. Reagan's credibility on foreign policy was slipping away while books and movies and massive protests scared citizens into thinking about the unthinkable prospect of a nuclear holocaust. The Democrats were seizing power and mindshare and a nuclear freeze bill passed the House. Clearly something had to be done.

Missile defense seemed like the perfect alternative. It didn't require any diplomatic changes or sacrificing any weapons development — indeed, it allowed for more spending on research. But it allowed Reagan to use the language of the doves — a sincere desire to rid the world of the scourge of nuclear war. So when a Reagan aide proposed the idea (which the aide conceived of as a chip to be bargained away for with the Soviets), Reagan seized upon the idea and worked it into a speech at the next available opportunity.

There was just one problem: nobody had any idea how to make it work. The most prominent right-wing scientist, Edward Teller, was very excited about a new technology in which a high-powered X-ray could be sent along a rod to vaporize small objects. Teller proposed a large satellite with such rods sticking out of it, a device that came to be known as the "space-based sea urchin". What happens when the Soviets target the defense? he was asked. Teller didn't seem to have considered the question but, unfazed, came back the next day suggesting the defense weapons be stored underwater and "pop up" when missiles were overhead.

Such debates disguised the fact that no actual missile defense technology existed or was likely to for a long, long time. Tactics and costs for disintegration rays and sea urchins could be discussed endlessly, but such discussion was irrelevant, as nobody knew how to build the key components. But this fact was carefully kept from politicians and the press who, ignorant of the science, continued to discuss missile defense as if it was a serious proposal. Thus, a majority of Americans were convinced that scientific ingenuity would find a way to protect the country — indeed, they believed it already had.

But the sheen of a someday-to-be-developed missile defense system could not last forever — Reagan needed something more repeatable to boost his flagging poll numbers, especially in the wake of such scandals as Iran-contra. The result was an ongoing series of carefully-spun summits with the Soviets, in which the President claimed to be making good progress on negotiations for arms reduction. (That negotiated arms reduction could serve as a replacement for a missile defense initiative never seemed to occur to the Reagan administration; it was not exactly a group prone to analytical self-reflection.)

On the Russian side, Mikhail Gorbachev, a brilliant and daring new politician, had come to power. Gorbachev seemed more like an American figure than a Russian one — he spoke plainly, made daring moves toward peace, and played well for the cameras. For much of the following years, Gorbachev had higher poll numbers in the US than Reagan did. Washington was said to have been swept away with "Gorby fever" and "Gorbymania".

Gorbachev unilaterally made a series of striking reforms in both domestic and foreign policy. He offered the US a wide variety of concessions in disarmament talks, insisting only that the US stop the SDI program (the one principle which Reagan refused to concede). Then he begun the process of glasnost, increasing the freedom of the press and allowing a left-wing reform movement to develop. As part of this, he freed dissident physicist Andrei Sakharov, who proceeded to tell the media that SDI was a bluff that the US could never successfully develop. Shortly thereafter, Gorbachev was even willing to budge on that, allowing the US to continue SDI. Meanwhile, he begun the process of perestroika, reforming the Russian political and economic system to increase the scope of democracy.

Meanwhile, Reagan's side continued to bungle or misunderstand all of Gorbachev's moves, using his disarmament proposals for little more than PR victories at home and continuing to insist his reforms were merely cosmetic attempts to prop up the old system. Reagan and Gorbachev continued to hold summits with plentiful photo opportunities, but little in the way of actual agreement was ever reached.

Indeed, Reagan actually made Gorbachev's reforms much more difficult by doing things like giving speeches demanding the General Secretary "tear down this wall". Such speeches only lent credence to the conservatives who charged that Gorbachev was simply doing the West's dirty work from the inside.

Yet despite Reagan's ineptitude, Gorbachev's reforms took hold — perhaps even more strongly than he had intended — and the old Soviet system began to fall apart. Democratic parties were elected, troops were withdrawn, and the wall finally came down.

But Americans were reluctant to believe that the destruction of the Soviet system had come from the reformers within it. Instead, they retrospectively lionized Reagan as the man whose tough talk had made the system come apart.

March 13, 2007

WHY YOU SHOP AT WAL-MART
ECONOMICS EATS ITSELF

There is a theory (quite an elegant one, actually) that says that because we live in a marketplace of free choices we end up getting basically what we want — our dollars are like votes for the society we wish to live in. Many have challenged this view, from a variety of perspectives, but Tom Slee (who calls this notion MarketThink) has chosen to focus on just one: the economic subfield of "game theory".

In his elegant little book, the poorly-titled *No One Makes You Shop At Wal-Mart*, Slee walks through the major discoveries of game theory, explains them in simple language with reference to a fictional town of Whimsley, and discusses how they refute standard economic conclusions while still playing by basic economic assumptions with effects that appear to show up in the real world.

Take the problem of littering, for example. The town of Whimsley has a large park between its coffee shop and its office building. Residents can toss their empty coffee cups on the ground in the park, thereby saving themselves the trouble of carrying it but minutely spoiling the park, or they can carry it to the trash at the office, saving the park but bothering their hands. In the absence of anyone else, each resident is better off tossing their cup — the bother of carrying it is much more than the small amount of spoilage. But if everyone does this, the park is quickly full of litter. Each individual, acting perfectly rationally, creates a situation that none of them want.

A similar problem gives the book its title. Imagine you get some utility from having a vibrant downtown of independent shops. Then a Wal-Mart opens up on the outskirts of town. You begin shopping at the Wal-Mart because the prices are cheaper and you can still walk through the vibrant downtown when you like. But with everyone buying things at Wal-Mart, the downtown stores can no longer afford to stay open and the center of your city turns into an empty husk. You'd prefer to have the vibrant downtown to the Wal-Mart, but nobody ever gave you that choice.

The book is full of dozens of examples like this, each with careful analysis and clear writing. Perhaps the most odd feature of the book is its politics. On the one hand, Slee is plainly a committed leftist, with positive references to Naomi Klein and other capitalist critics. But on the other hand, he never gives up on the rational actor and methodological individualist assumptions of modern economics, and shows little patience for those (typically his political allies) who have more thorough-going critiques. Nonetheless, the book is a recommended read for anyone interested in these questions.

Online Bonus: Watch Tom Slee eviscerate Chris Anderson's inbox-stuffer, *The Long Tail* on his weblog[1], Whimsley. Because, remember folks, "Abundance, like growth itself, is a force that is changing our world in ways that we experience every day, whether we have an equation to describe it or not." (p. 146)

March 13, 2007

1. http://whimsley.typepad.com/whimsley/2007/03/the_long_tail_1.html

A CALL FOR SCIENCE THAT MATTERS

Ever see a study that makes you scratch your beard? Ever hear about a research result that makes you go "I wish everybody knew about this!"? Ever want to run into a congressman's office and hit them over the head with a journal article? In this era of technological complexity and postmodern fiction, sometimes brain scans can reveal more about the human condition than a new novel. And yet, while the novels get detailed reviews in the *New York Times*, the best a research study is likely to get is an inaccurate description and some ambiguous quotes from the study's authors.

Well, here's your chance to change that. In the comments, post your favorite study — the one that makes you sit up and say "wow, this result ought to change everything". If you don't mind, we'll take the best to help fill up a new website we're starting, collecting and sharing these new research results.

I'll go first:

In 1994, the RAND Corporation, a major US military think tank, conducted a massive study (with funding from the Office of National drug Control Policy, the US Army, and the Ford Foundation) to measure the effectiveness of various forms of preventing the use of illegal drugs, particularly cocaine.

They analyzed a variety of popular methods and calculated how much it would cost to use each method to reduce cocaine consumption in the US by 1%. Source-country control — military programs to destroy drug production in countries like Peru, Bolivia, and Colombia — are not just devastating to poor third-world citizens; they're also the least effective, costing $783 million for a 1% reduction. Interdiction — seizing the drugs at the border — is a much better deal, costing only $366 million. Domestic law enforcement — arresting drug dealers and such — is even better, at $246 million. But all of those are blown completely out of the water by the final option: funding treatment programs for drug addicts would reduce drug use by 1% at a cost of only $34 million.

In other words, for every dollar spent on trying to stop drugs through source-country control, we could get the equivalent of twenty dollars benefit by spending the same money on treatment. This isn't a bunch of hippy liberals saying this. This is a government think tank, sponsored by the US Army[1].

April 24, 2007

1.   http://www.rand.org/pubs/monograph_reports/MR331/index2.html

SECURED LEISURE

"When I was disengaged myself, as above mentioned, from private business, I flattered myself that, by the sufficient though moderate fortune I had acquired, had secured leisure during the rest of my life for philosophical studies and amusements. I purchased all Dr. Spence's apparatus, who had come from England to lecture in Philadelphia, and I proceeded in my electrical experiments with great alacrity; but the public, now considering me as a man of leisure, laid hold of me for their purposes; every part of our civil government — and almost at the same time — imposing some duty upon me. The Governor put me into the commission of the peace; the corporation of the city chose me one of the common council, and soon after alderman; and the citizens at large elected me a burgess to represent them in the Assembly."

(Benjamin Franklin, *Autobiography*)

April 22, 2007

THE HANDWRITING ON THE WALL

I recently attended a talk at Stanford by Walter Bradford Ellis, a too-little-known activist and writer on the issue of global poverty and world hunger. It's transcribed from a recording I made. The sound quality was lousy, so apologies if I've mangled some of the specifics.

Good evening. This is the first time I've spoken before a college audience, and therefore I would like to take advantage of your presence to ask you a few questions before I begin on my prepared speech. Basically I want to know how morally committed the students at a typical 'good' school are, and while I know an audience of several hundred from one school is neither large enough nor diverse enough to give an especially accurate picture, still the results should provide a rough indication of where the real truth lies. That's sort of an interesting juxtaposition of words. 'Truth lies' I mean.

Anyway, as I said, I'm interested in knowing how morally committed you are. I must say at the outset, I am pessimistic. At any rate, primarily what I want to find out tonight is how important it is to you for you to act according to your own definition of right and wrong. In other words I'm not interested in knowing what sort of behavior you think is right or wrong but merely how committed you are to living up to whatever standards of right and wrong you possess.

I was trying to think a few minutes ago what questions I could ask you to find out this information, and it is very difficult to come up with anything satisfactory simply because individual standards of right and wrong vary so markedly. I had to pick a situation which seems perhaps a little silly because it is so improbable, but that is because I wanted as pure a case as possible — one which is in no way connected with any existing world situation — so that your prejudices and preconceived notions about a particular situation will play no part in your answers.

My hypothetical circumstances are concerned with a person who murders innocent people, and I suspect that nearly every one of you will agree that that is wrong. So please now imagine yourself to be in an ancient country which is ruled over by an evil king who has absolute power of life or death over all his subjects — including yourself. Now this king is very bored, and so for his amusement he picks 10 of his subjects, men, women, and children, at random as well as an eleventh man who is separate from the rest. Now the king gives the eleventh man a choice: he will either hang the 10 people picked at random and let the eleventh go free, or he will hang the eleventh man and let the other 10 go free. And the eleventh man must decide which it is to be.

Now if death is bad, then on average 10 deaths must be 10 times as bad as one. So hopefully nearly all of you will agree that the eleventh man should give up his life in order that the other 10 might live. But that is not the question I am asking you. I'm asking whether you would in fact make that sacrifice if you were the eleventh man — if you really did have to decide whether you or they would die. And you knew the king meant business because he did this every year and sometimes killed the 10 people and other times the eleventh depending wholly upon what the eleventh had decided.

Now I am about to ask you for a show of hands, but of course I realize that few of you know yourselves so well that you can be certain of the correctness of your answer — especially if your answer is yes. So I will simply ask you to hold up your hand and answer yes if you are any more than 50% certain that you would make that sacrifice. Understand?

All right, all yes answers, please raise your hands. Let me see, that must be about a third of you. That's more than I would have guessed.

Now let me ask only those who are reasonably certain — say 95% certain — that they would make the sacrifice to please raise their hands.

Yes. That's more like what I expected. That's at most a tenth of you. I have a feeling that most of that tenth of you are kidding yourselves, but perhaps human beings aren't as selfish as I have always thought.

Now just two more quick questions. Same situation except that the king says he will let his 10 hostages go free if you will go to prison for 20 years, otherwise he kills them. That's an easier question to be sure of your answer about than the previous one, so this time answer yes only if you are quite certain — 95% or better. All right everybody hold up his hand if he is at least 95% sure he would go to prison for 20 years in order to save 10 people's lives.

Well that looks like about three-quarters of you. Again I think you have overly high opinions of yourselves, or maybe some of you are too embarrassed to tell the truth, but I sincerely hope you are correct in your self-assessments.

Just one question more now. The king says he will let his people go if you will agree to give him all the money you have and all the money you will make in the future, except of course enough for you to feed and house yourself and take care of all the absolute necessities. In other words he's asking you to be poor, but not so poor that it impairs your health in any way. Again I'm asking for at least 95% certainty. All in that category please hold up your hands.

Well that's nearly every one of you! I'm very pleased; I hope you mean it. Perhaps in fact you do this time. After all, since you have the power to decide whether 10 people die or whether you give up your money, if you made the other decision you would be killing 10 people in order to make money for yourself, and surely that is murder.

I see some head-shaking — it looks as though a few of you disagree. The king has said, kill these 10 people or I'll take your money. If you kill them, that is murder.

Look at it another way. If you are poor and kill 10 people in order to steal their money, that is surely murder. But morally speaking, that situation is exactly the same as this one. In both situations if the people die, you will be rich; if they live, you will be poor, and it is within your power to decide which it is to be. In either situation if you decide that they should die in order that you can be rich, you have put your happiness, or not actually even that, you have put material riches for yourself above 10 people's lives. That is the moral error you have made and it is exactly the same for both cases. One is as bad as the other and if one is murder so is the other.

Anyway, those are all the questions I wanted to ask you. I didn't mean to spend as much time on them as I did, but at least from my point of view it was well worth the time. Thanks for your indulgence, and also for your soul-searching — I guess those weren't easy questions to answer if you answered them honestly. Just be happy it was a make-believe situation and none of you is likely ever to really be forced to make any of those rather unpleasant decisions.

And now I'll get on to what is supposed to be my topic: world hunger.

In 1650 the population of the world was 500 million (500M). Within the next 50 years an absolute minimum of 500M people will starve to death. The UN reports that around 10M people starve to death every year and the problem is only going to get worse as the population increases.

Perhaps that figure of 500M is too large for you to grasp in abstract terms. Let me translate it into something more concrete: if those 500M people were all to join hands, then figuring at about 1,000 people per mile, they would form a line long enough to stretch to the moon and back — with enough left over to reach across the United States 6 times. Or if you prefer keeping things more down to earth, they would reach 20 times around the world.

The US Army's M-16 machine-gun fires 700 rounds per minute, or about 12 rounds per second. If you drove a car past the line of people at a little over 40 miles per hour, you would pass 700 people every minute. If you used poisoned bullets or some such deadly concoction, you might be able to kill 1 person with every shot as you drove past. If you kept your finger on the trigger for 10 hours a day, 7 days a week, killing 1 person with every shot, it would take you 3 years and 4 months to kill them all.

It is a rather gruesome picture, and yet all these people — and probably many more — are absolutely doomed to die in the next 25 to 50 years. And it won't be the quick, easy death of a bullet, but the slow, pitiful, wasting death of starvation.

There is one bright spot in all this, however — the legions of the doomed will not really reach quite 20 times around the world. Perhaps they'll really only reach 12 or 15 times around, for most of them are children and their arms are short.

Opposed to these ravaged peoples of the world are the gluttons of America. You yourselves are good examples. As future graduates of a good college, it is surely within the grasp of most of you to be making a salary, after taxes, of $50,000 or more within a few years. How much money is that? Well, you could easily take care of all the true necessities of life for $20,000, thus leaving you $30,000 for the luxuries. In America, anyone can stay healthy spending five dollars a day for food. It is not even hard to do. If one really skimps, he can stay alive and well for a dollar — for I have done it. If it can be done in America for a dollar a day, it can surely be done for that in the countries where people are starving. Thus your $30,000 of luxury money could be providing 82 people with a dollar worth of food a day — people who otherwise might starve. Since presumably if your $30,000 were donated to UNICEF, they would take care to pick out poorer than average people, I think it not unreasonable to state that $30,000 per year over a period of 40 years is enough to keep healthy 10 people who would otherwise starve to death — plus a good many more who would otherwise be malnourished.

So you see, I lied to you a little while ago when I said none of you would ever have to make any of those three unpleasant decisions. You will never have to make the first or the second — the two hardest choices — but you are this moment confronted with the third: for the 10 who would otherwise starve are the 10 hostages, you are the eleventh man, and hunger is the king. Thus if you decide to go on with the life you were probably planning to lead, you will be letting 10 people die rather than give up your flat-screen television and your cocktail parties. And that is more than gluttony, it is murder.

Good evening.

Aaron again. I'd like to make a few remarks about the speech, but before I do I should admit something. The speech was not given by Walter Bradford Ellis. Instead, it was written by a too-little-known philosopher named Louis Pascal. He published it in the 1980s under the same subterfuge in the journal Inquiry and it was reprinted in Peter Singer's collection Applied Ethics. (I have modified it to bring the numbers up to date and shortened it a little to make it more blog-sized.) He justifies the subterfuge as necessary to get readers to more seriously engage in the thought experiment. I do think it would be wonderful to have this talk given in person, however. If you are interested in pursuing this, please let me know.

If you do want to help needy people, you can donate to UNICEF or Oxfam.

December 6, 2007

JUDGMENT DAY

People don't like being told that they're bad. And they especially don't like it if it's going to cost them a lot to be good. Finding other ways out is preferable, even if it requires some violence to the truth. Today we look at some ways people try to evade responsibility.

[Please read the previous article "The Handwriting on the Wall" before continuing.]

A large number of people insist that "things aren't proven" or "aid doesn't work". In his 1996 book *Living High and Letting Die* Peter Unger reports a study where he found that, including in administrative expenses and other overhead, $200 could feed a malnourished child through the highest-risk childhood years. UNICEF just recently released a new report[1] finding that, for the first time, the number of children dying before 5 has fallen, thanks to their intervention. And Oxfam, to take just one example, through its development projects in Cambodia has helped over 35,000 people[2] come to support themselves. Doctors Without Borders reports[3] that they treated 10 million people last year, treating 26,000 people from cholera, for example, and treating 63,000 children for malnutrition. Even the most vocal critics of aid, like William Easterly, who has written many books and op-eds attacking government aid programs as unhelpful, has to concede that private projects like Oxfam and UNICEF are successful and positive. Nobody, of course, provides any real argument against these things. They just say it's "too unclear".

If that's the real issue, then donate to an organization like Poverty Action Lab[4] at MIT. PAL does controlled randomized trials of the success of aid interventions. Your money won't go directly to help people, but it will help to test other people's aid interventions and improve their effectiveness. A recent report finds that mass deworming programs dropped infections by 23 points and increased school participation by 25% (thanks, in part, to spillover effects), apparently caused children to grow taller and healthier, and cost only $5 for each disability-adjusted year of life saved.

Barry Kelly insists that he has no duty to help others and thus is not culpable for their suffering. Of course, this is an irrelevance. Nobody is trying to put him on trial — just arguing he should do more to help.

But Barry goes one step further: he says that he should not help because giving his money to starving people would lead to "lack of incentive to compete, lack of investment base for risky & experimental ventures, and congealing layers of bureaucracy feeding on income redistribution." Taking this at face value for a moment, it is not clear to me why why saving people from starvation would cause the first two — wouldn't there be a huge incentive to compete for saving lives and trying new experimental techniques in doing so? Perhaps Barry means that the first-world might have less competition in a field like, say, luxury watches. I don't see this as a tragedy. It amazes me that someone would admit that they prefer to have millions of people starve to death than to have a complicated bureaucracy.

In response, Barry explains that "there needs to be a cost-benefit analysis". He does not explain what he wants to analyze. Should we make a little chart with the benefits of competition in the luxury watch market on one side and the benefits of saving people from starvation on the other?

He also argues that we should do nothing about starvation because many people die in car accidents. I am not sure how this is relevant, but I deplore the deaths of people in car accidents and personally do not drive because of it.

Sohail provides the amazing argument that one shouldn't donate to UNICEF because "They have a business model that revolves around needy people. To keep the model going, you need needy people." It is not clear how this principle is supposed to work. Are the people at UNICEF supposed to be quietly sabotaging their efforts in order to preserve their jobs? Since non-profit employees generally take large salary cuts and do unusually-onerous work, this seems wildly unlikely. If they wanted a safe job they would surely join the for-profit sector. Sohail provides no evidence for this amazing claim.

MC argues that people will starve since he no longer purchases their products. But certainly fewer people will starve if he spends his money directly on keeping people from starving as opposed to having people not starve incidentally because he is purchasing TVs from them. Is he claiming that the people not starving right now somehow have a special right not to starve? It's hard to see why that would be the case.

That Hypothetical says that "Development economics is a complex subject." I'm not sure how this is relevant. Perhaps in the ancient society the King has a lot of scholars working for him making the issue of how to decide which person to choose into some complex subject. That doesn't change the moral issues.

Mike Bruce says that if we all spent our disposable income on helping starving people, we might face economic collapse. This seems absurd but also certainly isn't a question anyone is facing. Even if all the readers of this blog spent all their disposable income on preventing starvation, that would be inconsequential in economic terms.

There are actual arguments against the issues raised in the last article. These are not them.

December 10, 2007

1. http://www.unicef.org/progressforchildren/2007n6/index_41403.htm
2. http://www.oxfam.org/en/programs/development/easia/cambodia_development
3. http://www.doctorswithoutborders.org/publications/ar/i2006/index.cfm
4. http://www.povertyactionlab.org/
5. http://www.povertyactionlab.com/papers/J-PAL_briefcase04_web_01a.pdf

THE VISIBLE HAND
A SUMMARY

What follows is my summary of *The Visible Hand* by Alfred D. Chandler, Jr.

PART 1

It's difficult today to imagine what American companies were like before the 1840s. They were small concerns, owned and operated by the same person in one location, and focusing on a particular type of product (cotton, provisions, wheat, dry goods, hardware, drugs) and one piece of the distribution chain (retailing, wholesaling, importing, exporting). Their corporate structure (the partnership), accounting techniques (double-entry bookkeeping), and financial instruments (letters of credit) were essentially unchanged from those used by the Italians in the 1390s.

Bigger projects were pursued through personal relationships between small firms: family farms had their slaves grow crops, which they sold to the local merchant, who shipped it to his son or nephew in London, who sold it to the local merchants there, and thence to the customers. (At the same time, credit headed the other direction.) As time went on, the number of intermediaries only increased: factors and jobbers and brokers and dealers and commission agents. Coordination was handled through the market.

(The one exception was the Bank of the United States, which had branches in many locations and thus could coordinate on something of a national scale. But it was politically unpopular and both the First and Second banks were allowed to expire by Congress.)

There was incredible inefficiency, but it mattered little since the technology of the time did not allow for great speed or volume. Canal boats were still pulled by animals, for whom four miles an hour was an impressive speed, and most products (clothing, furniture, clocks, nails) were produced by hand in people's homes through the "putting-out" system. There were a handful of textile factories, but since they depended on water-power there was only room for a few of them.

PART 2

All this changed with the railroads, a technological improvement which allowed business to move their products vastly faster. Careful coordination was essential (one didn't want trains crashing into each other), market entry expensive (constructing a railroad line cost a great deal of money), and network effects powerful (a railroad was much more valuable if it could move things all the way across the country).

As a result, the railroads built big enterprises, with professional managers to operate them. The businesses were the first to be structured along largely modern lines (the line-and-staff system): a board of directors appointed a professional manager as president, who oversaw a series of vice presidents supervising various company-wide topics (finance, traffic, legal) as well as a general manager. The general manager oversaw a number of divisions, each with departmental managers with profit and loss responsibility and a staff of their own. Each department sent statistics back to headquarters, allowing senior management to improve overall efficiency.

In addition to consolidating various different roles into a single organization, the railroads consolidated different organizations into a cartel with a few large players who coordinated pricing schemes and extracted the maximum each merchant was able to pay. The quintessential player in this era of empire-building was the speculator Jay Gould and his nemesis Cornelius Vanderbilt.

Gould got his start in 1868 when Vanderbilt attempted to seize control of the Erie railroad, the nearest competitor to his New York Central. Gould succeeded in stopping him and became the Erie's largest stockholder and president. He then leased two additional lines and purchased shareholder proxies for two more lines, which he used to vote new directors into power, who then agreed to sell the lines to the Erie. (The courts and legislature quickly moved to stop him and the Pennsylvania seized control of the lines.) He merged with additional lines in Illinois, Ohio, and Michigan, before attempting to corner the market on gold, leading to a stock market crash. The crash forced other lines to sell, but Vanderbilt had more funds and bought them up.

Gould had more success in the telegraph industry, where consolidation came even more rapidly. Gould's railroads had contracts with Western Union allowing it to operate telegraph lines along the road. He canceled the contracts and signed agreements to partner with the lines attached to several other railroads. After he bought ocean lines to Latin America, Western Union was scared enough to purchase the competitor. (Gould sealed the deal by offering Vanderbilt, Western Union's largest stockholder, a controlling stake in one of his railroads if he persuaded the board to go through with the purchase.) After the sale, Gould started a new company with the telegraph lines of his remaining railroads, signed several additional deals, and announced plans to build a transatlantic cable. Western Union stock plummeted and Gould bought it up, becoming his competitor's largest shareholder. He used this position to persuade Western Union to purchase his competitor at an inflated price and become the controlling member of Western Union's board, a position he used to fend off any future competitors.

Theodore Vail played a similar role at AT&T, while local utilities (power, light, heat) ended up being operated by regulated "natural monopolies". Soon the nation's infrastructure was entirely owned by either public (e.g. the post office) or private (AT&T) monopolies. In each case, it was operated by professional managers who planned and controlled the entire system.

PART 3

The new national infrastructure (railroads, telegraph, steamships, post office) allowed for new national distributors (wholesalers, department stores, mail-order houses, chains) which were themselves organized and managed in the same ways. Department stores, for example, had a manager in charge of each department, with only things like janitors and delivery people shared across the entire store.

Such big stores moved to also take the place of wholesalers by building their own distribution networks and, in time, take control of manufacturing as well. Large mail-order houses like Sears Roebuck began building systems of conveyer belts and pneumatic tubes for ensuring orders got assembled promptly — along with systems for punishing those who held the line up. And the geographically-distributed chain stores organized themselves under regional managers who kept tabs on local performance with a team of inspectors.

Geographic centralization, automation, and employee monitoring allowed such national concerns to move goods faster, which made them more efficient than the numerous local stores they put out of business. It was economies of speed, not of scale.

A similar speeding-up happened in production. The opening of the coal mines provided cheap power for new factories with mass-production machines while railroads provided a market their output. The factories were set up as simple assembly lines operating continuous-process machines, like those built to cut wheat, solder cans, and roll cigarettes. Henry Ford extended this system into assembly with his "moving assembly line" in which continuous conveyor belts moved parts past the workers. In each factory, managers personally oversaw the line foremen who oversaw each part of the process. By the 1880 census, 80% of manufacturing employees worked in factories, with the putting-out system remaining only for clothing.

Fredrick W. Taylor encouraged factories to speed up even further by following his system of "scientific management". He proposed a company's lines be run by a planning department which would conduct careful time-and-motions studies to discover the optimal way to carry out each part of the process. Line-level managers would then be responsible for ensuring that individual employees kept producing at the optimal rate. Few followed Taylor's recommendations exactly, especially his suggestion to place the planning department in charge of the lines, but many companies adopted his ideas to accelerate their factories.

PART 4

The new speeds, in turn, produced so many products that the national stores couldn't sell them all, leading the manufacturers into distribution and marketing of their own. They began building a regional sales staff, doing national ad campaigns, and buying up competitors. The result was national brands like American Tobacco, Diamond Match, Quaker Oats, Pillsbury Flour, Campbell Soup, Heinz, Borden, Carnation, Libby, Procter & Gamble, and Kodak — most of which remain leaders today.

Why did these few leaders achieve such domination? It was not thru their superior technology — they leased the machines they use for assembly. Nor was it their marketing acumen — they all hired professional marketers for the job. And it could not be the power of their brands, for they all invented these brands from scratch. Instead, it was their superior organization that provided the main barrier to entry. Anyone who wanted to compete would have to build their own national network of managers, buyers, and salesmen.

And even this was made more difficult for competitors. The first-mover was able to start small, use profits to fund growth, and use the resulting economies of scale to lower prices while expanding nationally. But any competitor would have to start out by competing against this national, low-price network. They would either have much higher per-item costs since they were producing so much less or they would have to borrow enormous amounts of capital to build a high-volume network from the beginning. And who would want to fund such a risky endeavor? Newcomers did appear (Kellogg, Postum, Colgate, Babbitt) but they were rare and the industries remain oligopolies.

Industrial products (lumber, petroleum, metal, etc.) also began forming national oligopolies. It started with industry-wide trade associates, which quickly became cartels that conspired to fix prices. However, the incentive to cheat on the cartels by secretly lowering prices was too great and, since cartels were illegal, there was no legal way to prevent it. So companies moved to form trusts, in which one firm would hold in trust the shares of the other firms in exchange for shares of itself. When the Sherman Antitrust Act outlawed trusts, New Jersey stepped in to allow the creation of holding companies — easy-to-establish corporations which simply held the stock of other corporations. But in the early 1900s the courts ruled that even this form violated the law and the companies moved to merge outright, forming a single corporation.

But such horizontal integration was rarely very profitable. The real success always came from vertical integration: taking control of suppliers and distribution.

PART 5

Managers who oversaw the factories carefully measured their efficiency. They wanted to maximize the use of the expensive equipment they had purchased, so the repeatedly pushed to speed up the lines and use them more efficiency. This increased efficiency resulted in increased production which resulted in corporate growth which naturally required more lines.

At the same time corporations continued this within-industry expansion, higher-level managers saw the generic processes at work and pushed for between-industry expansion: reusing the same management structures and same tools to grow the company and brand into new businesses.

And thus, managerial capitalism — the corporate form in which professional managers ran large, national corporation whose owners had at most veto power over their efforts — spread across the country. Their administrative coordination allowed for greater productivity and lower costs, but required a managerial hierarchy which could carry out more functions. The managers also allowed them to increase volume, but also allowed the managers to ensure a permanent place for themselves. The task of management became more technical and specialized and management became separated from ownership. As a result, managers were able to direct the company in ways that favored stability over profits, and the resulting huge enterprises changed the shape of the economy.

March 2, 2008

SLAVES OF SOME DEAD SOCIOLOGIST

Imagine you were suddenly put in charge of Google. What would you spend your time doing? Branding? The Google brand is pretty important, but it's not really something you can control directly, it's more of a side-effect of the other decisions you make. (If your legal team decides to give up the names of Chinese dissidents to the secret police, that's going to hurt your brand.) Product design? Clearly this is also important, but at a company the size of Google it's too big a job for one person — most of Google's innovative new products are designed by rank-and-file engineers. Strategy? This is a good one, and probably what Google's current rulers spend most of their time on, but I'm skeptical as to how good anyone can really be at long-term strategy with such a huge company. Hiring? Obviously hiring is pretty important, but even the greatest group of people aren't going to save your company if they waste their time once their inside.

No, I think the most important thing a person in charge of a large company can work on is sociology — designing the social structure of the company. It's the sociology that determines who gets hired, what their life is like, how much freedom they have, what sorts of things they work on, etc. Clearly these structures determine an enormous amount about the corporation. And yet, strikingly, I've never heard of a single corporation that has a high-level group devoted to studying and improving them.

"Practical men," Keynes famously wrote at the end of his *General Theory*[1], "who believe themselves to be quite exempt from any intellectual influences, are usually the slaves of some defunct economist." And sociology seems to have worked out much the same way. Chandler claims[2] that the modern command-and-control corporation was worked out just about identically by several different people around the same time and its military methods have been with us ever since.

Despite enormous changes in the kinds of things big companies do as well as in the way that they do them, the actual structure of the large corporation (with very few exceptions) has hardly changed at all. It's gotten to the point where even tinkering with the cubicle seems radical.

Since such questions are so alien, let me give a sense of the questions I mean. For example, how do you hire? Right now, it appears that at Google each team gets to hire people for its projects and then once you're inside Google you get to switch to another project if you like. Why not have a team dedicated to hiring which tries to find the best way to pick the best people as well as making sure they match a particular company culture?

Also, how do projects get picked? Do you have a command-and-control structure deciding what things need to get worked on from the top? Do you let everybody work on what they like? Do you let the company vote on what its priorities should be?

What do you do with people who don't work out? Do you have performance reviews? Bonus pay? Three-strikes firing offenses? Or do all these systems just make working more frightening and problematic?

It seems to me any reasonable company ought to have a whole department dedicated to working on these issues, studying the systems that are in place, studying the kinds of things that others have tried, and doing their own experiments to see if they can do things better. And yet, to my knowledge, no one does. Even the handful of companies that do something innovative with their corporate structure did it as a one-off — they have no team dedicated to coming up with and trying new such innovations.

Now normally when you discover that everyone else is doing something wrong, there's an opportunity for you to get ahead by doing it right. But that's much more difficult here, because these questions only really make sense for large organizations and very few of us find ourselves in charge of large organizations. For example, its arguable that Fog Creek[3] has done some things along these lines, but it's pretty difficult to tell since they've never had more than a couple dozen people.

Instead, the real innovation hasn't come from companies, but the online peer-production projects, like GNU/Linux, that take contributions from a distributed set of volunteer contributors. But such groups solve the problem largely through eliminating it — they don't have to worry about who to hire and how to treat them because they don't hire anyone.

Instead, most of the people who work on GNU/Linux are hired by other companies where they must contend with the antiquated social structures that those companies provide. And since those are the brutal facts that most humans must contend with, it would be nice if more people were thinking about alternatives.

April 15, 2008

1. http://www.marxists.org/reference/subject/economics/keynes/general-theory/ch24.htm
2. see article "The Visible Hand: A Summary"
3. http://www.fogcreek.com/About.html

THE FALSE CONSCIOUSNESS FALSEHOOD

American intellectual life has a large number of ways of responding to an argument without actually addressing its substance — namecalling in other words. You can say that someone is "blaming the victim" or spinning a "conspiracy theory" or "assuming people are stupid" or that they're subject to "false consciousness".

Most of these are kind of transparently silly, but even otherwise smart people seem to think the false consciousness charge has some heft to it. The argument is never fully spelled-out, but the argument seems to be that to think that people are systematically mistaken about their own interests is the kind of crazy idea that only vulgar Marxists would believe and, furthermore, it requires assuming that people are stupid and explaining how you've been able to see past the illusion.

Well, I'm personally not under any illusion that providing a rational explanation is going to stop people from leveling this charge, but I figure one ought to, if only to set the record straight.

Let's begin with a parable — a simplified case that will at least establish whether some of these arguments are logically true. Imagine a new regime comes to power that decides to imprison everyone with red hair. They insist that there is nothing amiss about this — they were elected democratically, and furthermore, everyone imprisoned is still allowed to vote. But inside the prisons, they only permit limited contact with the outside world. Most prisoners only watch the one prison-provided news station which is systematically biased, constantly suggesting that the Purple Party is in favor of additional rights for red-haired people while their opponents, the Yellow Party, just used the red-haired issue for pandering. (Anyone who's watched, say, Fox News discuss black issues will know how this is possible.) The result is that when election time rolls around, the majority of red-haired prisoners vote for the Purple Party candidate who gets into power and provides no new rights for them.

Call it false consciousness or not, I think it's perfectly reasonable to look at this situation and say while the red-haired prisoners are not stupid, they are systematically mistaken, which is leading them to act against their own interests. If they knew the truth they would vote for the Yellow Party, the party which wants to take steps to get them out of prison, instead. Furthermore, it's possible to imagine that there are some prisoners who, through one means or another, have learned this and thus are able to see this situation while the other prisoners do not. (They try to tell the other prisoners what's going on, but they keep getting labeled conspiracy theorists.)

Now obviously vast portions of America are not imprisoned. But most people do get their news from a small number of sources and I think everyone would agree that, in one way or another, these sources are systematically biased. (You can argue about which way they're biased or whether it makes a difference, but I think it's pretty clear that all the major news sources share a general conception of what is "news" and what isn't.) So why is it so implausible that something similar is going on?

The major difference between the two scenarios is that in the first, people were basically forced to watch the biased news, while in the real world they have lots of other alternatives. But I'm not sure this matters as much as it might seem at first.

First, most people have busy lives that don't revolve around the news or politics and thus are going to get the news in the most convenient form they can. For most people, this is typically television or the newspaper. But starting a new television station or newspaper is very expensive, especially if you want it to have wide reach, and the only projects that can get funding and advertising are those that buy into at least some of the systematic biases. So for most people, there simply isn't a better alternative when it comes to the formats they want.

Second, even if someone gets their news from the Internet or another source where getting started is less expensive, they may not know about the alternatives. If you grew up with your parents reading the *New York Times* you may simply live your life checking in on nytimes.com, without ever stopping to wonder whether the news you were getting was systematically biased and whether there was some more preferable alternative.

Again, just as there was no way for the prisoners to know they were being lied to, it's not really reasonable for the average person to figure out that they're getting biased news if the only news they read comes from biased sources.

Now I'm not arguing here that this idea is true (that would require more real-world evidence), merely that it's possible. The fact is that we live in a world where most people get their information about what's going on from a very small number of sources which tend to report largely the same things in the same way. This seems like a rather important fact of life and I think we ought to stop dismissing suggestions that it might have some negative effects on people out of hand.

May 19, 2008

SIMPLISTIC SOCIOLOGICAL FUNCTIONALISM

Often sociologists notice a pattern in which certain attributes of a social system fits well with a particular social structure. To take an example I have at hand, Rosabeth Moss Kanter notes that because a secretary has access to facts that could embarrass her boss, it's convenient for the boss that the secretary is entirely dependent upon him for wages and status.

Unfortunately, these claims are often phrased as saying X causes Y. Here's how Kanter does it:

> The possibilities for blackmail inherent in [a secretary's] access … to the real story behind the boss's secrets … made it important that she identify her interest as running with, rather than against, his. Thus, forces were generated for the maintenance of a system in which the secretary … was to find her status and reward level dependent on the status and, hence, success of her boss. (*Men and Women of the Corporation*, 82)

Note that, although she is unusually careful to hedge her comments ("made it important", "forces were generated", "maintenance of a system") Kanter is making a particular historical claim here: the secretary could blackmail, which pushed the boss to tighten control. But this is not the type of claim that Kanter, who's research consisted mostly of direct observation of present-day offices, is likely to have any real evidence for.

Making such claims is problematic, both because most sociologists don't really know whether they are strictly true, and because they lead Jon Elster to show up at your house and yell at you for hours. But both problems can be easily avoided: simply rephrase such comments to describe the phenomena as *effects* rather than *causes*.

Instead of saying a secretary's ability to blackmail leads bosses to tighten their grip, simply note that the boss's tight grip has the effect of weakening the secretary's ability to blackmail. You get all the same points across and nobody gets hurt. See? Easy.

May 13, 2008

TECTONIC PLATES
AND MICROFOUNDATIONS

In 1915, Alfred Wegener argued that all the continents of Earth once used to fit together as one giant supercontinent, which he later named Pangea. As Wikipedia summarizes:

> In his work, Wegener presented a large amount of circumstantial evidence in support of continental drift, but he was unable to come up with a convincing mechanism. Thus, while his ideas attracted a few early supporters ... the hypothesis was generally met with skepticism. The one American edition of Wegener's work ... was received so poorly that the American Association of Petroleum Geologists organized a symposium specifically in opposition... ... By the 1930s, Wegener's geological work was almost universally dismissed by the scientific community and remained obscure for some thirty years.

Today, of course, every schoolchild knows about Pangea. But for a long time the theory was dismissed, not because it lacked evidence or predictive power — it explained why the shapes of the continents fit together, why mountain ranges and coal fields lined up, why similar fossil were found in places separated by oceans, and so on — but because Wegener had no plausible mechanism.

A similar problem happens in the social sciences. Paul Krugman recently noted[1] that while Larry Bartels (in his new book *Unequal Democracy*) provides solid, convincing evidence that Republican presidents systematically preside over slower growth and increasing inequality, most social scientists don't believe him because we haven't yet identified the mechanisms. Krugman:

> Now, I'm a big Bartels fan; I've known about this result for quite a while. But I've never written it up. Why? Because I can't figure out a plausible mechanism. Even though I believe that politics has a big effect on income distribution, this is just too strong — and too immediate — for me to see how it can be done. Sure, Republicans want an oligarchic society — but how can they do that?

Bartels, for his part, argues that[2] providing the mechanisms isn't his job — his goal is to highlight the phenomena and encourage many others to research the mechanisms: *How do presidents produce these substantial effects?*

One of my aims in writing Unequal Democracy was to prod economists and policy analysts to devote more attention to precisely that question. Douglas Hibbs did important work along these lines ... He found that Democrats favored expansionary policies ... while Republicans endured and sometimes prolonged recessions in order to keep inflation in check. (Not coincidentally, unemployment mostly affects income growth among relatively poor people, while inflation mostly affects income growth among relatively affluent people.) In recent decades taxes and transfers have probably been more important. Social spending. Business regulation or lack thereof. And don't forget the minimum wage. Over the past 60 years, the real value of the minimum wage has increased by 16 cents per year under Democratic presidents and declined by 6 cents per year under Republican presidents; that's a 3% difference in average income growth for minimum wage workers, with ramifications for many more workers higher up the wage scale. So, while I don't pretend to understand all the ways in which presidents' policy choices shape the income distribution, I see little reason to doubt that the effects are real and substantial.

When it comes to addressing such arguments more generally, the most famous commentator is Jon Elster. In his classic article "Marxism, Functionalism, and Game Theory[3]", he insists:

Without a firm knowledge about the mechanisms that operate at the individual level, the grand Marxist claims about macrostructures and long-term change are condemned to remain at the level of speculation.

(To be fair, Elster doesn't make this as a general argument, but his vehemence has led some of his followers to suggest that it is.)

To be clear, I think discovering mechanisms is important work. All I'm arguing is that it shouldn't be a necessity for believing in a theory. Instead, I believe it's an irrational side-effect of an emotional distaste for gaps in knowledge.

As evidence, let me note that such demands for mechanisms never go more than one level deep. Nobody has ever said, "Well, your theory that people are motivated by greed is all very nice, but I just can't believe it until you can explain how greed is manifested in the brain." Neuroscience is obviously the microfoundation of psychology, but psychological theories are regularly accepted without neuroscientific microfoundations.

In general, it seems like such commentators support a double-standard. Theories with mechanisms should be judged by their fit with the evidence and predictive power. Theories without mechanisms should be judged by the evidence and predictive power and whether you can think of any plausible mechanisms. I don't see how this can be justified. There's no reason mechanism should be privileged in the assessment of knowledge; things are true or false, even if we don't know *why* they are true or false.

Indeed, it we typically only investigate the causes of phenomena once we're convinced that they exist. (Elster admits as much in *Explaining Social Behavior*, noting that establishing a phenomena's existence is the first step towards explaining it.) So let's stop making the mistake of not believing things are true because we don't know how they happen.

May 14, 2008

1. http://krugman.blogs.nytimes.com/2008/04/02/bartels-alfred-wegener/
2. http://press.princeton.edu/releases/m8664.html
3. http://www.geocities.com/hmelberg/elster/AR82MFGT.HTM

HOWTO: FIX THE NEWS

Newspaper circulation continues to decline. The top-selling paper in the country, *USA Today*, distributes only 2 million copies a day (half, no doubt, placed outside hotel room doors). Around the same number, with an average age of 71, watch *The O'Reilly Factor* nightly, with the number decreasing as the audience dies off. Everyone quietly concedes the news industry is dying. It's the Internet's fault, they all assure us.

But what if it wasn't? The other day I heard a news program that was so good that I wanted to listen to it again. And I'm not alone — all my friends have been talking about it as well. And while I don't have exact numbers, it seems as popular as any one of those other news outlets. That show? The *This American Life* episode on The Global Pool of Money — a comprehensive explanation of the housing mess.

There were three things about the show that made it stand out from the rest of the news pack:

1. It believed in the intelligence of its audience. It didn't try to pander with sex or disasters or quick cuts. It took a serious news story and investigated it thoroughly for a full hour, with only one break. And it didn't try and dumb any of it down — it explained the whole thing, from top to bottom.

2. It didn't assume you already knew the subject. Most news stories on important topics are incomprehensible to the average person who doesn't know much about their topic. Here's a quote from a random news story about the housing crisis: "They said financial institutions have been unwilling to expose themselves to the mortgage market, and lenders are hesitant to lend to risky borrowers in a declining house price market after the subprime meltdown." Unless you've been following the story (like the reporter, presumably) do you really know what that means? *TAL* instead assumed you knew nothing and explained every component and term so that you actually had a picture of what was going on.

3. It was done in an entertaining and conversational tone. It didn't treat the

news as some important series of facts that had to be seriously conveyed to you. It treated it as something interesting they wanted to tell you about, a story that involved real people's lives (who you got to hear from at length) and was full of genuinely interesting pieces. Look at that news quote above one more time. Can you really imagine someone sitting down and saying that with a straight face?

At first these things may seem contradictory — how can you believe in the intelligence of your audience while assuming they don't know anything? how can you be entertaining and yet still explain a subject? — but the more you think about them you see how well they fit together. Being intelligent doesn't mean you're knowledgeable; it means you're curious. Which means you want to hear the whole story from beginning to end and which means you might actually find it entertaining. And being conversational prevents you from assuming the mask that lets you talk down to your audience while pretending they only need to hear the handful of new facts that you're providing.

In every other field, that kind of formality has been dropped. Even banks run advertisements these days about how their associates will be your friend. And yet the news chugs along with its arrogant formality, watching its audience get older and older, and wondering why its circulation is declining.

Together, these three points seem like the recipe for a genuine news show: intelligent, comprehensive, and entertaining. And yet, I can't think of a single thing that follows them. Surely in an era of desperation and experimentation, the wacky idea of actually respecting your audience has to be worth a try by *someone*. Anyone want to give it a shot?

May 12, 2008

A THEORY OF CHANGE

People want to make the world a better place. But how? Barack Obama says I can change the direction of the country by voting for him. Al Gore says I can solve the climate crisis with a letter to the editor. MoveOn says I can stop George W. Bush by signing their petition. Perhaps, but these requests ring hollow. How is writing a letter to my local paper going to stop the polar ice caps from melting?

Most groups have a couple steps at the end (switch to alternative energy, stopping carbon from being emitted, preventing global warming) and a couple steps at the beginning (write your congressman and send a letter to the paper) but in between they seem to expect that some kind of miracle will happen. They're missing the concrete steps in between, the actual way we get from here to there.

In the nonprofit world, such a plan is called a Theory of Change. And the reason they're so rare is because they're dreadfully hard to come by. The world has no shortage of big problems, but it's hard to think of ways we might realistically solve them. Instead, the same few things — vote, preach, march — get trotted out again and again.

For over a year now, I've been looking for theories of change for politics. And I've found a few that I think just might work. But I can't pull them off by myself. So here they are, in case someone out there wants to help.

THE NETROOTS CONGRESS

Here's how you get elected to Congress today: First, you make friends with a bunch of wealthy people, being sure to agree with them on all the important issues. Then you take their money and hire a well-connected Washington, D.C. campaign manager. The campaign manager shows you how to ask for more money and then gives it to his partner, who makes some TV and radio ads and runs them in your district. They keep doing this until your money runs out and then, if you're lucky, you get more votes than the other guy.

Because of the netroots, it's now possible to change the first part of this story. Instead of raising your money from conservative or centrist rich people, you can now raise money from progressive people over the Internet. So instead of candidates who all agree that telephone companies shouldn't be punished for spying on Americans, you can have candidates who think every American should have free health care.

Concretely, you'd ask people who want to do this to sign up to pay $X a month. Then you'd go around looking for candidates (or potential candidates) who genuinely believe in progressive principles. When you find them, you give them the money, and now they actually have a chance of getting elected.

Bonus: Get more money by fiercely promoting how bad the incumbent is or how good the challenger is.

This sort of thing has been done haphazardly and achieved some real successes. Donna Edwards, for example, is now a member of Congress. The idea here is to institutionalize it.

THE PLAIN-SPEAKING PARTY

The last plan changes the first part of the election process I mentioned. But you could also try changing the rest of it. Right now, if you want to run as a Democrat, your biggest source of funding will be the Democratic Party, especially the Democratic Congressional Campaign Committee (DCCC). To get their money, the DCCC requires you hire one of their friends. Their friends are all corrupt hacks who run the same failed campaigns again and again.

This is normally thought to be unavoidable because you can't win without money and you can't get money without the DCCC. What this misses is that you don't need as much money if you're running a radically innovative campaign.

Instead of raising money to run ads, do a PR stunt that will get lots of free media and word-of-mouth attention. Center your campaign around a clear proposal that most of the public will support but no other politician would dare touch. Be forceful and refuse to back down in the face of attacks from the press or your opponent. And, above all, always make it clear to people that you're an average person, not an average politician. No boring speeches, no political buzzwords, no meaningless cliches.

It's never been seriously tried outside of the movies, but I expect that the effect would be electrifying. The media would cover your every entertaining move and money would flow in from around the Internet. The 60% that doesn't vote in midterms would start to reconsider. Hell, Ron Paul attempted half this strategy while being completely nuts and he still received enough money and volunteers to win five House seats.

If you can actually win an election this way, you'll be able to get dozens more to follow your lead the next time around. Pretty soon, it'll be a movement.

SLATE CARDS

It's not just about the President and it's not just about Congress. (It's also not just about the US, but that's what we're focusing on today.) Local elections also have an impact, if only the people who win them often go on to even bigger positions. (Who in Wassila, Alaska thought they might be picking a future president?)

Most local races don't get a lot of attention and most people don't do much research on them. Which makes them much easier to influence that bigger races. Imagine a site where you gave it your email address and zip code and every time there was a local election, it'd send you the progressive candidates to vote for. You could print it out and take it to the polls and feel much better about your pick for "register of probate".

In San Francisco, the local papers issue endorsements on all the races and each of the candidates they endorse chip in some money to send a postcard with the whole endorsement list to every voter. This group could do the same thing. It could also ask folks to chip in a couple bucks to help pay for mailing post cards to their neighbors. (Or they could print some out at home.)

SHAREHOLDER DEMOCRACY

Supposedly, corporations aren't actually controlled by their CEOs. The CEOs are instead hired by the shareholders, to run the business that the shareholders actually own. A lot of these shares are held by people who aren't big fans of business as usual. If they got together they could use their shares to vote for reform.

Now voting on shares is complicated enough that most people don't bother, but increasingly votes are being moved onto the Internet. It's possible for an aspiring organization to build some software that could automatically vote for people if they wanted. So you could imagine, for example, a couple million MoveOn members letting a new progressive group vote their shares for them, allowing progressives to apply some real pressure to misbehaving corporations.

Combined with legal changes that are being considered that would further make corporate voting more fair, this is something that could make a real impact.

SERIOUSLY INTERESTING JOURNALISM

I've written about this before (see article "How to Fix the News"). The basic idea is simple: There's lots of fascinating stuff going on in the world. And yet, to become news, all the background and color is drained out of it. Worse, to be on TV, a story has to be so dumbed down that you feel stupid for watching it. And to be in the paper, a story has to have so little background that only an expert could understand it. A news show that covered interesting stories in a way that made them genuinely interesting would be quite popular and could have a tremendous impact.

More?

I'll try to remember to update this page as I learn more. Post your own ideas in the comments. (Remember: "Require all politicians to wear a lie detector" is not a theory of change — we're looking for ways to get there.)

September 10, 2008

CAPITAL AND ITS COMPLEMENTS
SUMMARY

The following is a non-technical summary of Brad DeLong's May 2008 paper "Capital and Its Complements"[1].

Adam Smith explained that in all countries with "security of property and tolerable administration of justice" citizens would spend all their money (capital), either on consumption or investment, causing the country's economy to grow. After some contention, later economic studies tended to bare this out: a shortage of capital wasn't always the bottleneck, but when it was, removing it could lead to extraordinarily rapid growth.

The problem for poor countries is that, because of high mortality rates (which require more children to have some survive) and low educational levels (which mean those children can find productive employment quickly), they have high population growth and thus low capital-to-labor ratios. Worse, trade allows you to spend your money buying manufactured goods from overseas, for which you have only your very cheap labor to provide in return. The result is that it requires an enormous amount of domestic investment to improve capital-to-labor ratios.

And so rich country economists made "the neoliberal bet" on behalf of poor countries: they hoped that loosening restrictions on international capital flows would send capital rushing in to poor countries and build their economies, the same way that Great Britain's massive investment in a young United States (in 1913 Britain's foreign assets equaled 60% of its domestic capital stock) built up that country.

But what ended up happening was exactly the opposite. Yes, NAFTA led US companies to invest the $20 to $30 billion a year on manufacturing in Mexico that its boosters predicted, but that investment was more than outweighed by the $30 to $40 billion a year fleeing the country from Mexico's wealthy wanting to invest it in the United States. Why? In part because the US was more politically stable, and thus a safer investment climate. And in part because the US treats its own workers so poorly — with productivity rising 35% since 2000 while real wages remain flat — it provides an excellent investment opportunity.

But meanwhile, all this investment in the US was dwarfed by the Chinese acquisition of our debt (and thus the political risk it represents). China needed to do this, since US purchase of their exports is the only thing funding the manufacturing-led industrialization of a massive portion of their economy; there would be massive dislocation if that funding dried up.

"Recognition of these facts came slowly." First, Larry Summers said it was our unsustainable current account deficit. (That was the 1990s; today that deficit is four times as large.) Later, economists thought it must have been our large budget deficits. Then they began thinking it was the run-up in housing prices. But that, it is now clear to most economists, was the result of a bubble. And yet the flow of capital to the US continues. But, perhaps even more frighteningly, it could stop at any moment.

June 30, 2008

1. http://www.j-bradford-delong.net/2008_pdf/20080521_capital.pdf

THE PERCENTAGE FALLACY

There's one bit of irrationality that seems like it ought to be in behavioral economics introduction but mysteriously isn't. For lack of a better term, let's call it *the percentage fallacy*. The idea is simple:

> One day I find I need a blender. I see a particularly nice one at the store for $40, so I purchase it and head home. But on the way home, I see the exact same blender on sale at a different store for $20. Now I feel ripped off, so I drive back to the first store, return the blender, drive back to the second store, and buy it for $20.

The next day I find I need a laptop. I see a particularly nice one at the store for $2500, so I purchase it and head home. But on the way home, I see the exact same laptop for $2480. "Pff, well, it's only $20," I say, and continue home with the original laptop.

I'm sure all of you have done something similar — maybe the issue wasn't having to return something, but spending more time looking for a cheaper model, or fiddling with coupons and rebates, or buying something of inferior quality. But the basic point is consistent: we'll do things to save 50% that we'd never do to save 1%.

At first this almost seems rational — of course we're going to do more to save more money! But you *aren't* saving more money. With both the blender and the laptop, you have the chance to save $20. Either way, you're going to have another twenty in your pocket, which you can spend on exactly the same things later on. Yet we behave differently depending on whether we got that twenty by skimping on a small purchase or skimping on a big one. Rationally, if driving back to the store isn't worth $20 when you're buying a laptop, it isn't worth $20 when you're buying a blender.

On the other hand, don't those small savings tend to add up after a while? If you start blowing $20 every time you buy a trinket, you're soon going to be out of disposable income. Meanwhile, spending several thousand dollars is much rarer, so isn't it OK to slack off a bit on such occasions?

If we work to save 50% on everything, big or small, that's the equivalent of saving 50% of our money altogether. Whereas if we only try to save fixed amounts on every purchase, how much we save is dependent on how many things we buy.

So which is the real irrationality? I'm not entirely sure of the answer.

July 21, 2008

RETHINKING HYPERBOLIC DISCOUNTING
OR, THE PERCENTAGE FALLACY, CONTINUED

In a famous experiment, some people are asked to choose between $100 today or $120 tomorrow. Many choose the first. Meanwhile, some people are asked to choose between $100 sixty days from now or $120 sixty-one days from now. Almost everyone choose the laster. The puzzle is this: why are people willing to sacrifice $20 to avoid waiting a day right now but not in the future?

The standard explanation is hyperbolic discounting: humans tend to weigh immediate effects much more strongly than distant ones. But I think the actual psychological effect at work here is just the percentage fallacy. If I ask for the money now, I may have to wait 60 seconds. But if I get it tomorrow I have to wait 143900%more. By contrast, waiting 61 days is only 1.6% worse than waiting 6 days. Why not wait an extra 2% when you get 16% more money for it?

Has anyone done a test confirming the percentage fallacy? A good test would be to show people treat the $100 vs. $120 tradeoff as equivalent to the $1000 to $1200 tradeoff.

October 7, 2010

HIGH GAS PRICES ARE REAGAN'S FAULT

A decade from now, when the seas begin to rise and the earth begins to boil, who will get blamed? Surely not George W. Bush, who spent 8 crucial years denying the problem, slowing the movement of other countries, and giving India and China an excuse for delay.

As evidence, look at what happen to Jimmy Carter. He called for a national investment in alternative energy so that gas-guzzling cars would be a thing of the past. Reagan scuttled all that and today as oil prices rise we have very little in the way of alternatives ready. But the sainted Reagan is never blamed.

September 18, 2008

WHAT COULD HAPPEN

My usual attitude is one of skepticism toward politicians. They routinely disappoint. But, for a moment, let's take the opposite scenario. What's the most that we could hope for?

Barack Obama grew up middle class and black. Obviously intelligent, he left school knowing he wanted to make a difference, but unsure how. Inspired by the civil rights movement and SNCC, he joined various progressive organizations like NYPIRG and worked as a community organizer.

He then entered law school and graduated highly, but instead of taking a clerkship went back to Chicago to write a book about race relations and, later, run a voter registration drive. He taught Constitutional Law and joined the board of various progressive foundations. He turned his sights toward politics, where he's spent the last ten years, representing largely progressive districts.

Throughout his political career, he has been criticized for being overly cautious and moderate. But he's been taken unusual pains to reach out to left-wing journals (including fairly obscure ones) who have leveled such criticisms, talked to them personally, and tried to defend himself.

In his presidential campaign, he's raised hundreds of millions of dollars, much of it coming from small-dollar donors. He's built a grassroots organization never seen before in this country, with millions of well-coordinated members. Through an incredibly well-executed campaign and a series of eloquent speeches, he seems poised to take the presidency with both houses of Congress, a solid majority, and a strong mandate.

This is unique. He hasn't spent enough time in politics to get chewed up by the system. He hasn't become dependent on a handful of big-money donors. He comes from a background of progressive politics. And he has an army of cash and people behind him.

Let's say he wanted to reform health care, an issue towards the top of Americans' minds and a task that's necessary to balance the budget and get real wages rising again. The majority of the country supports a single-payer program, like in every other industrialized nation, but because of the vast influence of money in politics, it's often been considered politically impossible to achieve.

But Obama could pull it off. With his eloquence, he could easily sell the plan to the country. The Democratic majority in both houses would get him most of the votes he needed. With his fundraising and volunteer network, he could threaten to have primary challengers replace any Congresspeople who disagree. (Obama personally has raised around $700M. The average Congressional campaign costs less than $1M.) With his tactical shrewdness, he could outwit industry lobbying groups.

Across a wide variety of such issues, it's possible to imagine a President Obama getting such things done. He has sufficient skill, background, and power to pull it off. It's hard to imagine a similar situation in history. (FDR, who Obama is often compared to, came from a very upper-class background and was strongly pulled by the far-left inspired by the Depression.)

Do I think it will happen? No. The far-right spent these final days shrieking that Obama is a closet socialist who will take this country into a new era of single-payer health care, strong financial regulation, revitalized unions, progressive taxation, a green economy, and universal voting rights. I wish it were so.

Instead, Obama has proposed the most moderate and cautious plan of all Democratic candidates, repeatedly refused to make ideological challenges out of fear of alienating voters, caved on even obvious questions like illegal wiretapping, surrounded himself with old centrist party hacks, and spent most of his campaign arguing for vague generalities like "change" rather than specific policy proposals. So all signs point to Obama being another cautious moderate.

But the striking thing is that none of these are dispositive. It's possible to imagine that, like W, Obama has run a quiet campaign focused on building an electoral majority which he plans to use to push through the policies he truly favors. It's implausible (the hardest thing to explain away is the FISA vote; even my most hopeful side can't think of any decent explanation for that) but it is possible. And it will only be more likely if we fight for it.

If we don't it seems Obama's most likely path is to become what the left's pundits call "a more competent steward of empire" — do a bunch of reasonable, sensible things that will probably have quite positive effects on the lives of most Americans, while leaving all the fundamentals untouched. But while that would be a welcome respite from the past eight years, let's not squander this rare opportunity for something more.

October 31, 2008

ECONOMIC *BS* DETECTOR

People are trying to lie to you. Or maybe they just don't know what they're talking about. Either way, you shouldn't listen to them. But how can you tell? Here's a guidebook of key phrases that indicate someone doesn't know what they're talking about when they talk about the economy:

Creates/destroys jobs. You often hear men of business saying that their company "created" 2000 new jobs. And in some sense that may be true, but it's probably less exciting if it turned out that they did it by destroying 2000 jobs somewhere else

The same is true for economic policy in general; it will typically create jobs in one place, but only at the expense of losing them somewhere else. That's because the number of jobs (i.e. the unemployment rate) isn't just a free-floating fact of life; it's specifically controlled by the Federal Reserve.

The Federal Reserve is a cadre of bankers and economists that, among other things, meets regularly to decide interest rates. When there are too few jobs, they lower interest rates, making it easier for people to borrow money and start new companies, hiring new people and creating jobs. (The current crisis is the rare exception — interest rates are at zero and there still aren't enough jobs. Thus the stimulus package.) When there are too many jobs, they raise interest rates, making it harder for businesses to start and expand, and cutting back on jobs.

Wait, too many jobs? The Federal Reserve worries that if unemployment gets too low, we'll hit a cycle of accelerating inflation where prices spiral up and up. Critics argue that they actually don't like low unemployment because then businesses have to compete for employees, which means they have to pay more and give out nicer benefits. So, critics argue, they try to leave some unemployment, so that employees are competing and can be pushed into taking lower wages.

If you really care about how many jobs there are — and obviously you should — then you shouldn't worry about particular policies or people, whose effects either won't matter or will be counteracted by the Fed. You should worry about the Fed and who controls it.

Helps/hurts competitiveness. Let's face facts: America isn't competing with anyone. Remember competition? You sell a widget for $5; I come along and sell it for $4; then you have to either lower your price or lose all your customers to me and go bankrupt. But America isn't going to go bankrupt. Countries don't really do that sort of thing.

Instead, what matters for how well a country is doing is (roughly speaking) its productivity, i.e. how much stuff it makes per person-hour of work. Sometimes you can increase this productivity by working with other countries — by, for example, trading some steel for some coffee. But this is just a way to up your own country's productivity; it has nothing to do with competition.

The competitiveness bogeyman is often trotted out when someone is trying to get you to do something you don't want. "Oh, sure," they say, "you may not want to do it, but the Chinese are and they're going to eat your lunch." It just isn't so. Nothing will stop us from chugging along, eating our lunch just fine; even if the Chinese are eating two lunches.

Sadly, a lot of "economic commentators" don't know what they're talking about, so you see these phrases everywhere. Now that you know they're bogus, it should save you a lot of time.

January 28, 2009

CASS SUNSTEIN, CONCERN TROLL

Remember when President Bush tried to put more arsenic in our drinking water? Lots of people got outraged — it seemed like a classic example of a deregulator-in-chief helping his corporate friends at our expense. Not Cass Sunstein, a prominent (and nominally-liberal) law professor.

Sunstein, working for and with right-wing deregulatory think tanks, published a piece called "The Arithmetic of Arsenic", arguing that everyone needs to stop being so *emotional* about these things. We can't decide whether arsenic should be in our water based on fuzzy-wuzzy arguments about not killing people. No, we need to be hard-headed realists and decide exactly how much a human life is worth and whether filtering arsenic is worth the cost. In short, we have to do *cost-benefit analysis*.

As fellow law prof Tom McGarity pointed out, Sunstein continued to hold this view despite the fact that Sunstein's own research into the subject showed that there was so much uncertainty around the issue that just using different previously-published estimates could result in whatever conclusion you like. And there was no obvious way to decide which estimate to trust.

All of this would be just another story in the annals of out-of-touch intellectuals — a law professor who gets off on killing people to save money, actual facts be damned — except for one frightening fact: Barack Obama just put this law professor in charge of cost-benefit analysis for the whole government.

The Office of Information and Regulatory Affairs (OIRA) was set up by Ronald Reagan to allow him veto power over any federal regulation. If the EPA wanted to stop companies from poisoning fish, if the DOJ wanted to stop businesses from discriminating, if OSHA wanted to protect miners' lungs, OIRA could intervene and double-check their cost-benefit analysis. They could rejigger the numbers to make it so that the regulation got killed or if they failed at that they could just demand more and more research from the agency, delaying the regulation it was finally abandoned.

OIRA was one of Reagan's most powerful tools for keeping the Federal Government from doing its job. And now someone who's a strong fan of its mission has been put in charge. It's a scary thought, especially as you're going to get a glass of drinking water.

January 16, 2009

HOW DEPRESSIONS WORK

On Capitol Hill sit many powerful people — Congressmen, Senators, Justices — but also numerous others who do the daily work of keeping government running. And, like anyone with such a weighty responsibility, they sometimes want a break: a chance to see a movie or eat out with their spouse.

Kids always make these things difficult, so in the late 1950s someone thought of starting a Capitol Hill Babysitting Coop. The idea was simple: a bunch of families would get together and dole out scrip — little fake money — amongst themselves. Anytime you wanted to go out, you could just hire another family in the coop to watch your kids: one piece of scrip per hour. Later, of course, you'd earn the money back by watching someone else's kids.

It was a brilliant system and much beloved, until sometime in the 1970s. See, when people left the babysitting coop, they got to keep the balance of their scrip. And so, over the years, the amount of scrip in circulation fell. Soon scrip was in short supply and people begun hoarding theirs for fear of losing it forever. There were few opportunities to babysit (and thus earn scrip) so people didn't want to lose the scrip they had by paying it to a sitter. Which, of course, meant even fewer babysitting opportunities, making more people want to hoard their scrip, and on and on in a downward spiral.

Since the coop consisted largely of lawmakers and lawyers, they attempted a legislative solution to the crisis, requiring everyone go out at least once every six months. The proposal just made things worse. Eventually, someone tried the idea of handing out more scrip to everyone, and soon, the coop's delicate balance was restored.

In the 2000s, house prices started rising and everyone started sinking their money into them. Average people would buy houses and mortgage them, banks would buy mortgages, investors would buy mortgage derivatives from banks, and so on. Pundits published books with titles like *Why the Real Estate Boom Will Not Bust* and many people just assumed housing prices would go up forever. At the peak of it, we had roughly $80 trillion in global financial assets.

Of course, it was clear to anyone who looked closely that this couldn't go on forever — and that when it stopped, it would bring a lot down with it. And, sure enough, today housing prices are almost back to their usual level and we now have only $60 trillion.

Just like people taking scrip out of the babysitting coop, an enormous amount of money has been taken out of the economy. So naturally people want to hold on to what's left. So they don't spend their money, which means there's less employment opportunities, which means more people want to hold on to their money, and on and on in a downward spiral.

Normally when this happens, as in a recession, the government has an easy solution: lower interest rates. What happens is the country's leading bankers meet at the Federal Reserve and vote to lower interest rates. Let's say they decide to lower them (as they've done a lot lately). Then the Federal Reserve Bank in New York starts buying up Treasury Bills (government IOUs) for cash, injecting money into the economy. This allows banks to lend out more money, lowering the interest rate at which money is lent out, and thus encouraging people to start spending again. (Later, when the economy is doing well, they'll raise the rates again, pulling money out and making sure things don't get out of hand.)

But this isn't simply a recession. The Fed's lowered the interest rate to zero — zero! they're giving money away — and unemployment just keeps rising. Losing a quarter of global financial assets hurts. But now the Fed has a problem: it can't lower the interest rate anymore. Interest rates don't go any lower than zero.

Which means, as J. M. Keynes foresaw back during the first Great Depression, we need another way of getting money into the economy. This isn't rocket science — Keynes suggested stuffing bills into bottles and burying them down mineshafts; Milton Friedman once proposed tossing cash out of helicopters. But as long as the government is spending money, we might as well spend it on something useful. And thus, fiscal stimulus.

We spend the money to build roads and trains and high-speed Internet connections. We give away health care and hand out welfare checks and mail people tax rebates. We do whatever it takes to get more money into the economy. Which people then turn around and spend on all the things they normally start spending money on and the engine of capitalism once again start to turn.

Keynes' genius came in seeing that the Depression wasn't a moral problem. We're not being punished for our exuberance or our stinginess, just as the folks on Capitol Hill weren't at fault for not wanting to go out. In both cases, the problem wasn't legislative, but merely technical: there just wasn't enough money to go around. And the technical problem has a technical solution: print more money.

The moralists insist it's irresponsible for us to just print more money. After all, they say, debt got us into this mess; is more debt really going to get us out? This is what they told FDR, causing him to hit the break on a recovery that was pulling us out of the Great Depression. This is what they told Japan, ending their recovery and plunging the country into a "lost decade" of unemployment.

It's not irresponsible to spend money; it's irresponsible not to. Factories are lying idle, people are sitting at home unemployed, and our economy is slowing. We can spend money to make use of it all, or we can just continue downward spiral. The choice is ours.

Further reading:
- Sweeney and Sweeney, "*Monetary Theory and the Great Capitol Hill Baby Sitting Co-op Crisis*[1]" [PDF]
- DeLong, "*The Financial Crisis of 2007-2009: Understanding Its Causes, Consequences — and Its Possible Cures*[2]" [scribd]
- Krugman, *The Return of Depression Economics*[3]
- Baker, *Why Stimulus Won't Increase the Debt*[4]

February 4, 2009

1. http://cda.morris.umn.edu/~kildegac/Courses/M&B/Sweeney%20&%20Sweeney.pdf
2. http://www.scribd.com/doc/9719227/null
3. http://www.amazon.com/Return-Depression-Economics-Crisis-2008/dp/0393071014
4. http://www.prospect.org/csnc/blogs/beat_the_press_archive?month=11&year=2008&base_name=mankiw_promulgates_confusion_o#111235

WHO REALLY RULES?

Who Really Rules?, by G. William Domhoff, is one of my very favorite books. But explaining why will take some background. In the 1950s and 60s researchers were looking at what they called the "power structure" in American cities — the people who really pulled the strings and called the shots. Foremost among them was Floyd Hunter, whose study of Atlanta practically invented the field. Naturally the whole notion that anyone was pulling the shots behind the scenes in America offended the deans of mainstream liberal political science and so their leader, Robert A. Dahl, set out to defend democracy's good name.

He argued that one could only figure out who was in charge by doing careful case studies — looking at controversial decisions and seeing who was involved in making them — that and only that could tell you where true power lay. And, in his most famous work, *Who Governs?: Democracy and Power in an American City* he aimed to do just such a case study in his hometown of New Haven, where his employer, Yale University, resides.

Dahl proposed a theory called pluralism in which no small elect is in charge but power is instead shared across conflicting groups, each marshaling its own resources on the issues it feels strongly about. Democracy, although perhaps in a more sophisticated form, is vindicated, and the ridiculous notions of a shadowy elite disproven. As Dahl writes:

> It is all the more improbable, then, that a secret cabal of Notables dominates the public life of New Haven through means so clandestine that not one of the fifty prominent citizens interviewed in the courts of this study — citizens who had participated extensively in various decisions — hinted at the existence of such a cabal; so clandestine, indeed, that no clues turned up in several years of investigation led to the door of such a group. (185)

Of course that wasn't quite true. Domhoff was skeptical of Dahl's results and decided to request access to his source material and reresearch the matter for himself. In going through Dahl's interview notes, Domhoff found these choice comments:

> First Informant said that [contacting the First National Bank] was essential, that they had to deal with what he called the "power structure" if they wanted to accomplish anything. First Informant kept emphasizing the "power structure."
>
> According to Second Informant, nothing gets done without the First National Bank saying so. According to him, it is "at the top of the power structure." ... I asked him why ... [and he] said, "Just look at who's on its board of directors." ... He said, "The bank's support is necessary for anything that is done in this town including redevelopment." (Sounds like a quote from Hunter.)

But, of course, Dahl wanted to disprove Hunter, not sound like him, so he never followed up on these leads. But Domhoff does. In the intellectual battle over which version of how cities work is more accurate, he scores a decisive victory over Dahl. He not only takes Dahl's method, he also takes Dahl's town and indeed his specific case study and shows how the decisions were made by a sinister cabal after all.

And his results are much more convincing. Dahl, after all, was trying to prove a negative: that there *wasn't* anyone pulling the strings. Whereas Domhoff can simply point out who was. Dahl's central case study is the question of New Haven urban renewal. A bold Democratic mayor, he claims, came into office and proposed a plan, dragging local businessmen and Federal officials along with him to get it done.

Nonsense, says Domhoff. The plan for urban renewal was drafted by the local chamber of commerce years before. And when the new mayor got elected, the Chamber of Commerce invited him to lunch and explained the whole thing. They even told the mayor who to hire to carry the plan out and, in the end, got exactly what they'd wanted all along.

But Domhoff doesn't simply prove Dahl wrong. He gives an engrossing case study of how powerful businessmen get things like this done, based on extensive archival research and contemporaneous notes. And he tells an entire alternative history of American urban renewal, showing how big business turned a plan to build housing for the poor into an excuse to expel them to make room for upscale businesses.

The result is a *tour de force*: a complete demolition of one of the most influential books of political science, an engrossing case study of how power really operates, and an example of how to do research into the people who, after all, really rule.

March 23, 2009

JOURNALISTIC CAPTURE AND FIXING CNBC

Sometimes the government will set up a new regulatory agency, like a Mine Safety and Health Administration or something to keep watch on the mining industry. And off they go, investigating the mining industry to make sure they're being safe.

Only something funny happens. It turns out all the people they talk to all day are mining industry officials. And whenever they hold meetings to ask for advice, the only people who show up are mining industry officials. When they make proposals and ask for public comment, all the comments are from mining industry officials. And pretty soon, they start thinking like mining industry officials.

Academics call this regulatory capture — an office was put in place to regulate an industry, but it ended up just being a tool of the industry.

But what's striking is that the problem isn't just limited to regulation; the same thing happens to journalists as well. Call it journalistic capture. And there are few examples of it more obvious than that of CNBC.

CNBC, a channel supposed to cover economic news, basically acts as a full-time cheerleader for the financial industry. When the market was booming, this wasn't so noticeable. Whole swaths of the country started daytrading and checking the CNBC ticker regularly to feed their buy-sell trigger fingers.

But now that the market's gone belly-up, it all seems a whole lot less appealing. Which is what Jon Stewart has been getting at with his critiques of the network.

Well, it's less satisfying to complain when you can actually do something about it, so some friends and I have started a new campaign: Fix CNBC! As HuffPo reported[1], we're demanding CNBC commit to holding Wall Street accountable, starting with hiring someone who was *right* about the economic crisis.

We'd really love for you to sign our open letter.

March 16, 2009

1. http://www.huffingtonpost.com/2009/03/16/economists-progresses-pet_n_175249.html

IN DEFENSE OF ELECTIONS

Traditional left-wing thought treats elections as epiphenomenal: build a strong enough social movement and politicians will be forced to do what you want. In this view, it doesn't really matter who gets elected since they're ultimately all subject to the same structural forces. Working to get someone "good" elected is really just a waste of time, since they'll turn out to be as bad as all the others once they get into office.

(Think Noam Chomsky's comments about the unimportance of electoral politics, or the Alinskyite theory that one should try to cultivate an attitude of "fear and loathing" among politicians.)

There's clearly a great deal of truth to this — structural forces are ultimately very powerful. But I think it misses a great deal as well. This model assumes politicians are this separate class of rational actors who respond purely to electoral incentives; if your grassroots movement gets them votes, they'll help you out, but they're just as happy to sell you out to a higher bidder.

But what if the politicians involved are actually activists themselves? What if the choice isn't between joining a electoral campaign and joining an issue campaign, but between starting a electoral campaign and starting an issue campaign? Here I think the calculus changes wildly.

For one thing, just at the campaign level, electoral campaigns have a lot of advantage over issue campaigns. They fit into a designated "news hole" so it's easier for the media to cover them, they have clear deadlines which spur people to action, and there's a clear existing model for how to do them (including fundraising, scheduling, volunteer management, etc.).

Furthermore, if you actually win, you can now continue the campaign from a much stronger institutional base: you'll have a full-time salaried staff, your pronouncements will be de facto news, and there will be strong social pressure preventing the whole thing from fizzling out as people decide to do other things with their lives.

Of course, there's also the positive impact you can make as an officeholder. Obviously you'll be able to help institutionalize your goals by passing laws and regulations you support (just as you would try to push as an outsider), but you'll also be able to promote things in innumerable smaller ways, just by meeting with other politicians and using the influence of your office. Take this story from Matt Taibbi about Bernie Sanders, the socialist Senator from Vermont:

> [He] kept coming back to a story about his very first meeting with the Health, Education, Labor, and Pensions Committee. At the meeting, the subject of the Head Start program had come up. Ted Kennedy, who runs the committee, had proposed a modest increase. Sanders wanted more — so he went and had a word with Kennedy after the meeting.
>
> "The end result is that we got a 6 percent increase, instead of a 4 percent increase," he said. "Over a three-year period, that's five hundred million dollars more. What I'm finding out is it's just a different world. Not saying it's better, it's just different. If you want something you just go talk to someone in the hall. […]"
>
> He tried to sound like it was a good thing, and it might very well have been, in terms of getting more money for a worthy-enough program. But the subtext of this story was Sanders expressing amazement that he could get $500 million just by talking to someone. As any human being would, he looked blown away by the reality of his situation.
>
> *(The Great Derangement, 127)*

Obviously there are few offices as powerful as United States Senator, but every job has opportunities for simple victories like these, if at a much smaller scale. Sure, outside groups can always try to push officials to do things like this, but if you actually are the elected official you can just do them. (Plus, how often do outside groups know about these simple things?)

The late Senator Paul Wellstone, who came to electoral politics from grassroots organizing himself, argued that political change had three parts: the intellectual work of discovering what's wrong and how to fix it (i.e. policy development), the organizing work of mobilizing citizens into activist groups, and the electoral work of running for office and getting elected. And it seems that the left seems to neglect the last of these.

For a young leftist, a career in academia or the think tanks is an easy choice, while those who are bolder go into full-time activism. But running for office never seems like a viable option. (When people ask Noam Chomsky how they can fix things, he never says they should run for office.) (We'll ignore for a moment the delusion the left seems to have that they should run for office as a third-party in a two-party system.) The result is a severe deficit of genuine leftist candidates. Which of course feeds their sense that politicians are just going to sell you out.

Leftists need to think more about running for office. Not as an alternative to advocacy or activism, but as an extension of it. Campaigns are an incredible opportunity to explain and fight for the issues you believe in, while elected offices are a great opportunity to achieve them. That's how the left took Santa Cruz, probably the only real city in the country with a leftist government, and that's how they'll take the country.

1. http://sociology.ucsc.edu/whorulesamerica/santacruz/progressive_
   politics.html

A 24 PUZZLE

Imagine you've kidnapped the President of the United States. You record her making a statement that, if published, will strengthen the international forces of evil. The military is about to blow up the building you're in, so you have to get the video out electronically, but they're monitoring your communications and will be able to put enormous pressure on anyone who receives a copy from you.

Here's the question: in the few minutes you have before the building is reduced to rubble, where do you upload the video to maximize the chance that it will get published?

Alright, so your first inclination is to upload it to your servers, but that's easy — they just seize your servers.

So you upload it to YouTube and have Google copy it to all of their servers. But then they just call Google and have them delete it.

Obviously if you had it on the front page of a popular website, that would solve things, but the front pages of popular websites are pretty closely guarded.

You could try mailing it to WikiLeaks, but although WikiLeaks is pretty openminded, they may not actually want to strengthen the international forces of evil. The same goes for any other particular free speech activist you could name — dst, Cryptome, etc.

Your best bet is probably to have a smart guy on the outside who keeps uploading it various places from behind Tor as older copies get deleted. But how many people have smart guys on the outside?

You could try spamming it to a bunch of blogs, wikis, and other sites (or even by email or IM for that matter), but that'll take too long — you only have a couple of minutes and probably a flaky connection to boot. There's no way you can hit very many servers.

You could publish it on a Tor hidden service, but then they'd probably just DOS the whole Tor network.

Freenet seems too small and unreliable. Other P2P systems don't even make copies except on request.

Usenet seems like it should be a promising option, but does anyone use Usenet anymore?

More promising options seem like emailing it to some kind of large mailing list. But which list has the most insane free speech activists? (cypherpunks? lkml?) And will it mail out all those copies before the Feds get it unplugged?

How else do you get stuff onto lots of people's machines? Web, Usenet, email, IM, HTTP access logs, DNS caches.

Can you think of anything better?

The current winner is Andy Baio with:

Upload it to Sharebee (which then sends it out to Megaupload, Rapidshare and a bunch of other anonymous hosting sites) and post the link to 4chan. They're big on evil over there.

March 4, 2009

INVESTIGATIVE STRIKE TEAMS

Journalists get mad at bloggers: "Without real reporting, they'd have nothing to comment on!" Bloggers get mad at journalists: "There's a reason nobody reads newspapers anymore. They're dry and dull and wrong." But the gap is shrinking: bloggers are doing more real reporting, journalists are getting more humanized (with all the digressions, opinions, and biases that entails).

So what if you paired an investigative reporter with a blogger? Reporters didn't used to write their own stories. (Why would a good investigator be a good writer?) The reporter would be out in the field, knocking on doors and taking notes, which they'd hand to a writer at a desk, who would turn them into a coherent, vivid story. (Newsweek still operates this way.)

Replace the writer with a blogger. They'd post the story as it unfolded, capturing the excitement of discovery: the big breaks, the wrong turns, the moment when it all comes together. Like any talented blogger, they'd keep people coming back: *What happens next? I want to know more!* They'd keep up a conversation with readers and other bloggers, sharing new leads with the reporter. It'd be a powerful duo.

But blogging isn't everything. You also want to recap the story so far: for those just tuning in, here are the characters, here's what's happened, here's why it's important. Keep a summary article alongside the blog and update it in tandem. It would lay out the whole story in one place, with links to particular posts or source documents for more information. That way everyone can always get an overview of the bigger picture — including the reporters.

You'll also want a tech person around to help out. Many stories involve databases; you need someone to work with the reporter to parse and process the data, then work with the blogger to put the results online. And there are plenty of other times where a small program or some tech knowledge comes in handy.

And you'll need a lawyer on staff. Getting information isn't easy. You'll need someone who can file FOIA lawsuits and respond to legal threats. Maybe you can even file lawsuits against corporate malefactors and obtain documents in discovery. Then work with pro bono lawyers or public interest law firms to win the lawsuit in its own right.

Lawsuits are needed because modern investigations can't stop at publication. If there was an era when a front page Times story could stop a scandal, that era is over. Ending abuses requires action. This makes traditional journalists uncomfortable. They see their job as reporting the facts, not changing them.

We may always need the detached journalist interested only in The Truth, but there's room for more. Just as journalism needs to become more humanized, it needs to become more activist. Journalists uncover outrageous things, which gets people outraged, but they seem to think channeling that outrage into something productive is someone else's responsibility.

Instead, a good investigative team needs a political organizer. They can build an email list of people who get outraged by their reporting and use it, along with blogs and the lists of other political groups, to put pressure on the bad guys, fundraise for further journalism, and collect a team of volunteers. The volunteers can help with aspects of the reporting — a modern investigation can get much further by crowdsourcing certain tricky aspects and depending on talented volunteers for particular tasks. A good political organizer knows how to get and manage volunteers.

But to make your organizing maximally effective, you'll need (gasp!) a lobbyist. They'll meet with representatives to encourage them to hold hearings based on stories you're working on, where they can subpoena documents and testimony. They'll ask representatives to introduce bills to address the abuses you've uncovered and work with them on legislative strategy to get those bills passed. And they'll team up with the political organizer to get constituents writing to their representatives in favor of these bills.

The only way to get good at something is deliberate practice: trying various things and seeing how they work. But when it comes to making change, that's very hard to do. Change requires so many people and takes so long that it's almost impossible to say for sure that your doing X helped accomplish Y. Which means that it becomes very easy to fool yourself into thinking you're more effective than you are.

But if you have one team — some reporters, a blogger/writer, a techie, a lawyer, an organizer, and a lobbyist — together, they form an investigative strike team: uncovering corruption, exposing it, and effecting change. They can watch the whole process unfold from a reporter's suspicion to a writer's story to a legislative fix. And they can get better at it. It'd be a powerful combination. That's the kind of future-of-news that I want to see.

April 28, 2009

TRANSPARENCY IS BUNK

Adapted from an impromptu rant I gave to some people interested in funding government transparency projects.

I've spent the past year and change working on a site, watchdog.net, that publishes government information online. In doing that, I've learned a lot: I've looked at everything from pollution records to voter registration databases and I've figured out a number of bureacratic tricks to get information out of the government. But I've also become increasingly skeptical of the transparency project in general, at least as it's carried out in the US.

The way a typical US transparency project works is pretty simple. You find a government database, work hard to get or parse a copy, and then put it online with some nice visualizations.

The problem is that reality doesn't live in the databases. Instead, the databases that are made available, even if grudgingly, form a kind of official cover story, a veil of lies over the real workings of government. If you visit a site like GovTrack, which publishes information on what Congresspeople are up to, you find that all of Congress's votes are on inane items like declaring holidays and naming post offices. The real action is buried in obscure subchapters of innocuous-sounding bills and voted on under emergency provisions that let everything happen without public disclosure.

So government transparency sites end up having three possible effects. The vast majority of them simply promote these official cover stories, misleading the public about what's really going on. The unusually cutting ones simply make plain the mindnumbing universality of waste and corruption, and thus promote apathy. And on very rare occasions you have a "success": an extreme case is located through your work, brought to justice, and then everyone goes home thinking the problem has been solved, as the real corruption continues on as before.

In short, the generous impulses behind transparency sites end up doing more harm than good.

But this is nothing new. The whole history of the "good government" movement[1] in the US is of "reformers" who, intentionally or otherwise, weakened the cause of democracy. They too were primarily supported by large foundations, mostly Ford and Rockefeller. They replaced democratically-elected mayors with professional city managers, which required a supermajority to overrule. They insisted on nonpartisan elections, making it difficult to organize people into political blocs. Arguing it would reduce corruption, they insisted city politicians serve without paying, ensuring the jobs were only open to the wealthy.

I worry that transparency groups may be making the same "mistake".

These are some dark thoughts, so I want to add a helpful alternative: journalism. Investigative journalism lives up to the promise that transparency sites make. Let me give three examples: Silverstein, Taibbi, Caro.

Ken Silverstein[2] regularly writes brilliant pieces about the influence of money in politics. And he uses these sorts of databases to do so. But the databases are always a small part of a larger picture, supplemented with interviews, documents, and even undercover investigation — he recently did a piece where he posted as a representative of the government of Turkmenistan and described how he was wined and dined by lobbyists eager to build support for that noxious regime. The story, and much more, is told in his book Turkmeniscam[3]. (His book *Washington Babylon*[4] is similarly indispensable.)

Matt Taibbi, in his book *The Great Derangement*,[5] describes how Congress really works. He goes to the capitol and lays out the whole scene: the Congressmen naming post offices on the House floor, the journalists typing in the press releases they're handed, the key actions going on behind the scenes and out of the public eye, the continual use of emergency procedures to evade disclosure laws.

And Robert Caro, in his incredible book *The Power Broker*[6] (one of the very best books ever published, I'm convinced) takes on this fundamental political question of "Who's actually responsible for what my government is doing?" For forty years, everyone in New York thought they knew the answer: power was held by the city council, the mayor, the state legislature, and the governor. After all, they run the government, right?

And for forty years, they were all wrong. Power was held — held, for the most part, *absolutely*, without any checks or outside influence — by one man: Parks Commissioner Robert Moses. All that time, everyone (especially the press) treated Robert Moses as merely the Parks Commissioner, a mere public servant serving his elected officials. In reality, he pulled the strings of all those elected officials.

These journalists tackled all the major questions supposedly addressed by US transparency sites — who's buying influence? what is Congress doing? who's in power in my neighborhood? — and not only tell a richer, more informative story, but come to strikingly different answers to the questions. In this era where investigative reporting budgets have been cut to the bone and newspapers are folding left and right, it's fallen to nonprofits like ProPublica and the Center for Independent Media and, from a previous era, the Center for Public Integrity, to pick up the slack. They've been using the Internet in innovative ways to supplement good old-fashioned narrative journalism, where transparency sites are a supplement, rather than an end-in-themselves.

For too long we've been funding transparency projects on the model of if-we-build-it-they-will-come: that we don't know what transparency will be useful for, but once it's done it will lead to all sorts of exciting possibilities. Well, we've built it. And they haven't come. The only success story its proponents can point to is that transparency projects have bred even more transparency projects. I'm done working on watchdog.net; I'm done hurting America. It's time to give old-fashioned narrative journalism a try.

April 23, 2009

1. http://sociology.ucsc.edu/whorulesamerica/power/local.html
2. http://www.harpers.org/subjects/KenSilverstein
3. http://www.amazon.com/Turkmeniscam-Washington-Lobbyists-Stalinist-Dictatorship/dp/140006743X
4. http://www.amazon.com/Washington-Babylon-Alexander-Cockburn/dp/1859840922
5. http://www.amazon.com/The-Great-Derangement-Terrifying-Politics/dp/038552062X
6. http://www.amazon.com/The-Power-Broker-Robert-Moses/dp/0394720245

KEYNES, EXPLAINED BRIEFLY

If you read the economic textbooks, you'll find that the job market is a market like any other. There's supply (workers) and demand (employers). And the incredible power of market competition pushes the price (wages) to where those two meet. Thus massive unemployment is about as likely as huge unsold piles of wheat: if people aren't buying, it's just because you're setting the price too high.

And yet, as I write, 17.5% of the country is unemployed. Are they all just insisting on being paid too much? Economists are forced into the most ridiculous explanations. Perhaps people just don't know where the jobs are, some say. (Maybe the government should run ads for Craigslist.) Or maybe it just takes time for all those former house-builders to learn new jobs. (This despite the fact that unemployment is up in all industries.) But they're typically forced back to the fundamental conclusion of the textbook: that people are just demanding to be paid too much. It might be for the most innocent of reasons, but facts are facts.

John Maynard Keynes' great insight was to see that all of this was nonsense. The job market is a very special market, because the people who get "bought" are also the people doing all the buying. After all, why is it that people are hired to farm wheat? It's because, at the end of the day, other people want to buy it. But if lots of people are out of a job, they're doing their best to save money, which means cutting back on purchases. And if they cut back on purchases, that means there are fewer people for business to sell to, which means businesses cut back on jobs.

Clearly something is badly wrong with the basic economic theory. So let's go through Keynes' masterpiece, *The General Theory of Employment, Interest, and Money*, and understand his theory of how the economy works.

When you get your paycheck at the end of the week, you spend it. But presumably you don't spend all of it — you put some money away to save, like you were told as a child. Saving is seen as a great national virtue — thus all those Public Service Announcements with talking piggy banks. Everyone knows why: put some money away today and it'll be worth more tomorrow.

But there's a kind of illusion involved in this. Money isn't worth anything on its own, it's only useful because it can buy things. And it buys things because it pays other people to make them for you. But you can't save people in your bank account — if fifteen million people are out of work, they can't put their time in a piggy bank for when things are looking up. The work they could have done is lost forever.

So yes, some people can save while others borrow from them — you can let your neighbor buy two iPods in exchange for letting you buy four next year — but the country, as a whole, cannot. At the end of the day, someone has to buy the things we can make. But if everyone's saving, that means people aren't buying. Which means the people making stuff are out of a job.

It's a vicious cycle: if people buy less, companies make less, which means people get paid less, which means people buy less. And so on, until we're all out of work. (Thankfully it doesn't get that bad — but only because some people are refusing to lower their wages. The thing that mainstream economists said was causing unemployment is actually preventing it!)

But this cycle can be run in reverse. Imagine Donald Trump hires unemployed people to build him a new skyscraper. They're suddenly getting paid again, which means they can start spending again. And each dollar they spend goes to a different business, which can start hiring people itself. And then those newly-hired people start spending the new money they make, and so on. This is the multiplier: each dollar that gets spent provides even more than one dollar's worth of boost to the economy.

Now let's look at things from the employer's side — say you run an truck factory. How do you decide how many trucks to make? Obviously, you make as many as you think you can profitably sell. But there's no way to calculate something like that — it's a question about what customers will do in the future. There's literally no way to know. And yet, obviously, trucks get made.

It used to be, Keynes says, that wealthy men just thought investing was the manly thing to do. They weren't going to sit around and calculate what kind of bonds yielded the greatest expected return. Bonds are for wusses. They were real men. They were going to take their money and build a railroad.

But they don't make rich people like that anymore. Nowadays, they put their money in the stock market. Instead of boldly picking one great enterprise to invest in, they shift their money around from week to week (or hire someone else to do it for them). So these days, it's the stock market that stimulates most new investment.

But how does the stock market figure out what profits are supposed to be? In truth, it has no more clue than you do. It's really just based around a convention. We all pretend that whatever the stock price is now is a pretty decent guess and then we only have to worry about the various factors that will cause the stock price to change. We forget about the most basic fact: that nobody has any clue what the stock price should be to begin with.

So instead of people trying their best to figure out which businesses will make money in the future, and investing in those, we have people who try to figure out which stock prices will change in the future, and trying to get there first. It's like a giant game of musical chairs — everybody's rushing not to be the one left standing when the music stops.

Or, you could say, it's like those newspaper competitions where you have to pick the six prettiest faces from a hundred photographs. The prize goes to the person who picks the faces that are most picked, so you don't pick the faces you find prettiest, but instead the faces you think everyone else will find prettiest. But it's not even that, since everyone else is doing the same thing — you're actually picking the faces you think everyone else will think everyone else will find prettiest! And no doubt there are some people who take this even further.

You might think this means that someone who actually did the work and tried to calculate expected profits would clean up, taking money from all the people playing musical chairs. But it's not so simple. Calculating expected profits is really quite hard. To make money, you'd have to be unusually good at it, and it seems much easier to just guess what everyone else will do.

And even if you were somehow good at guessing long-term profits, where would you get the money to invest? It's in the fundamental nature of your strategy that your investments seem crazy to everyone else. If you're successful, they'll write it off as a lucky fluke. And when your stocks aren't doing well (which is most of the time — they're long-term picks, remember), people will take this as evidence of your failures and pull their money out.

The scary thing is that the more open our markets get, the faster people can move their money around and the more trading is based on this kind of speculation instead of serious analysis. And that's scary because — recall — the whole point of the stock market is to decide the crucial question of what we, as a society, should build for the future. As Keynes says, "When the capital development of a country becomes a by-product of the activities of a casino, the job is likely to be ill-done."

The best solution is probably a small tax on each trade. Not only would this raise a ton of money (modern estimates suggest even a tiny tax could raise $100 billion a year), it would help redirect all the brains on Wall Street from these wasteful games of musical chairs to something actually useful.

But even if we solve the problem of the stock market, there's still some irreducible uncertainty. Because whether new investment makes sense always depends on whether the economy will be doing well in the future. And whether the economy is doing well depends on whether there's new investment. So, at the end of the day, investment doesn't depend simply on a careful calculation of future expected yield, but on our "animal spirits," our optimism about the future. It's this factor that exaggerates booms and deepens slumps and makes it hard to get out of a bad situation.

Even more perversely, it means economic performance depends in no small part on keeping businessmen happy. If electing Obama gets businessmen depressed, they might pull back their investments and send the economy into a slump. It doesn't even have to be intentional — they may very well believe that a President Obama is bad for the economy. But when you have a system that only works when businesspeople feel good, their fears become a self-fulfilling prophecy.

The result, Keynes suggests, is that the government will have to step in to prevent the economy from crashing every time rich people get a bit of indigestion.

So that's how we calculate the income side of things, now what about costs? Most costs are pretty clear — you need to buy equipment and hire people. But since you need to make stuff now that you can only sell in the future, one of your big costs is going to be money to use in the meantime. And the cost of money is just the interest rate. (If you get a loan for a million dollars at 5% interest, you're essentially paying $50,000 for the right to use the money now.)

Thus lowering interest rates increases investment — it reduces the cost of getting money, which reduces the cost of making stuff, which means more things can make a profit. And if more things can make a profit, more things get made, which means more people get hired. So what determines the interest rate?

Well, if the interest rate is the cost of money, the obvious answer is the amount of money in circulation. If there's a lot of money lying around, you can get some pretty cheap. Which means that, fundamentally, unemployment is caused by a lack of money: more money (assuming people don't hoard it all) means lower interest rates, lower interest rates (assuming expected profits don't crash) means higher investment, higher investment (assuming people don't stop buying) means more employment, and more employment means higher prices, which means we're going to need more money.

Money is created by the central bank (the Federal Reserve in the US), which decides what they want the interest rate to be and then prints new money (which they use to buy up government debt) until the interest rate is where they want. To get the economy back on track, all they have to do is keep lowering interest rates until investment picks up again and everyone has a job.

But there's one catch: the interest rate can't go below zero. (Keynes didn't think this problem was very likely, but in the US we're facing it right now.) What do you do if the interest rate is zero and people are still out of work?

Well, you can pray that billionaires will start hiring us all to build them giant mansions, but that's no way to run a country. The government has to step in. Instead of waiting for billionaires to build pleasure-domes, the government can hire people to build things we all need — roads, schools, houses, high-speed Internet connections. Although, honesty, it doesn't have to be things we all need. They could hire people to do anything. This is why inspecting the stimulus money for waste is so ridiculous — waste is perfectly fine, the important thing is to get the money into circulation so that the economy can get back on track.

Another good solution is redistributing income. Poor people are a lot more likely to spend money than billionaires. If we take some money from the billionaires and give it to the poor, the poor will use it to buy things they need and people will get jobs making those things.

Remember that money is just a kind of illusion. In reality, there are just people who want things and people who make things. But we're stuck in a completely ridiculous situation: there are lots of people who desperately want jobs making things — they're literally not doing anything else — while at the same time there are lots of people who desperately want things made. It seems ridiculous not to do something about this just because some people have all the little green sheets of paper!

Capitalism seems to go through frustrating cycles of booms and busts. Some people say the solution is just to prevent the booms — raise interest rates so the party doesn't get out of hand and we won't all be sorry the next morning. Keynes disagrees: the remedy "is not to be found in abolishing booms and thus keeping us permanently in a semi-slump; but in abolishing slumps and thus keeping us permanently in a quasi-boom."

Think back to the dot-com era, when venture capitalists were spending all their money laying fiber-optic cable under the street. The right solution wasn't for the Fed to raise interest rates until even punch-drunk venture capitalists could realize all this investment in fiber wouldn't be profitable. The right solution was to take their money away. Give it to the poor, who will spend it on something useful, like food and clothing.

So those are Keynes' prescriptions for a successful economy: low interest rates, government investment, and redistribution to the poor. And, for a time — from around the 1940s to the 1970s — that's kind of what we did. The results were magical: the economy grew strongly, inequality fell away, everyone had jobs.

But, starting in the 1970s, the rich staged a counterattack. They didn't like watching inequality — and their wealth — melt away. There was a resurgence in classical economics, Keynes was declared to have been debunked, and interest rates were raised drastically, throwing millions out of work. The economy tanked, inequality soared, and things have never been the same since. For a while people talked about levels of inequality that hadn't been seen since the 1920s. Then they talked about a recession the size of which hadn't been seen since the 1930s.

Once again, Keynes provides us with the instructions on how to get out of this mess. The question is whether we'll follow them.

September 24, 2009

HOW POLICY GETS MADE: A PRIMER

Barack Obama's campaign was a model of efficiency and foresightedness. Bill Clinton treated his campaign plans like marketing documents, poll-testing each proposed new idea, and forcing his administration to only begin seriously thinking about what to do once they were in office. Obama, by contrast, started early and put together a series of policy teams even before the campaign had begun in earnest.

Each policy team had a different subject — technology, health care, foreign policy — and was led by a top ally or fundraiser in the field. Let's take technology, since it's the case I'm most familiar with. Julius Genachowski was named Chairman of the Technology, Media and Telecommunications policy working group. Genachowski was a Harvard Law School classmate of Obama's who had gone on to become a chief executive at Barry Diller's IAC/InterActiveCorp (market cap: $2.1 billion). He went on to become a venture capitalist and sit on the board of numerous technology companies.

He used his wealth (annual income: $1.6 million) and influence to become the leading Silicon Valley fundraiser for his old classmate — indeed, one of Obama's top fundraisers nationally. As a result, he was the obvious pick to define Obama's technology policy. Genachowski canvassed his fellow Silicon Valley business leaders for policy suggestions and his team synthesized the results into proposed policy documents. These proposals were circulated among a wider circle for further comments before being published on the campaign website.

After the election was won, the teams were reassembled as transition teams. Genachowski was again leading the technology team, now named the Technology, Innovation & Government Reform Policy Working Group (TIGR). It was staffed by old government hands, like Thomas Kalil (Deputy Assistant to President Clinton for Technology and Economic Policy, rode out the Bush years as Special Assistant to the Chancellor for Science and Technology at UC Berkeley). Also brought out were business leaders, like Andrew McLaughlin (Head of Global Public Policy and Government Affairs for Google), and business-affiliated academic experts, like Susan Crawford (UMich law professor and a former partner at a DC law firm).

The teams worked on converting the policy documents from the campaign into instructions that would be given to federal agencies or executive orders the President could sign. They fleshed out campaign proposals, interviewed potential candidates for government positions, and held audiences with various interest groups. I visited DC during this period and got to see the aforementioned names at DC cocktail parties or the diner outside transition headquarters that became the informal meeting-place of the team. "It's the hardest I've ever worked in my life," Susan Crawford told me, clearly relishing the challenge.

After the inauguration, the teams disbanded and their members either returned to private life or were named to the administration. Genachowski, who obviously had his pick of positions, was named chairman of the Federal Communications Commission. Thomas Kalil became Associate Director of Science and Technology Policy. Susan Crawford became Special Assistant to the President for Science, Technology, and Innovation Policy. McLaughlin went back to work at Google, where his connections to the new administration are no doubt invaluable.

May 17, 2009

THE MEDIAN VOTER
AND THE MIXED VOTER

Our minds work by making models of the world and using them to predict how things will happen. These models are powerful because they're so deeply-ingrained we don't even realize we're using them. They just seem like "common sense." In politics, there are two major models for how voters think, which I'll call the median voter model and the mixed voter model.

The median voter model says that politics lives on a line from left to right. Voters are scattered across this line and vote for the politician that's closest to them on it. Politicians get elected by "positioning" themselves closest to the most voters, which usually means in the "center" of the line.

There are some complications, though. Because primary voters tend to be "more extreme" (i.e. Democratic primary voters are all on the left, Republicans on the right), politicians take a more extreme tack during the primaries, before heading back to the center for the general. And because they don't want to seem like flip-floppers, they're somewhat constrained by the primary positions they take.

But, in general, this model is pretty widely-accepted in politics. So widely that it's not even thought of as a model — it's implicitly assumed by all the things political commentators say. Comments like "He's moving to the center to pick up votes," "[X] couldn't get elected in that district, so how is someone more extreme going to make it?" only make sense because we all have this model in our heads.

But, while I haven't studied the question in detail, there doesn't seem to be much evidence for this model. Even intuitively, it doesn't make sense: does the average person really develop a location on a one-dimensional issue spectrum and then figure out where various politicians stand on that same spectrum? The notion seems almost ridiculous.

UPDATE: Andrew Gelman has studied the question in detail, and concludes that the median voter theorem doesn't seem to be true: "My research with Jonathan Katz suggests that being a moderate is worth about 2% of the vote in a congressional election: it ain't nuthin', but it certainly is not a paramount concern for most representatives. … Incumbent congressmembers almost always win reelection. And, when they don't, they're often losing as part of a national swing (as in the 1994 Republican sweep or the 2006/2008 Democratic shift). And when an incumbent does lose unexpectedly, it can be for something unrelated to their votes (remember the "check kiting scandal" of 1992?)."

The mixed voter model, promoted by George Lakoff and most prominently adopted by Howard Dean, says that voters aren't rational, coherent evaluators but a bundle of feelings, prejudices, and contradictions. Politicians get elected by playing on the feelings voters already have that would encourage a voter's' support. Thus, instead of moving to the center to get more votes, Lakoff argued politicians should actually become more extreme. Conservatives won votes by appealing to people's sense of order; liberals would have to respond by appealing to their sense of empathy. Moving to the center by promoting a compromise position that prevented rhetorical appeals of either type, was doomed. This model was used to explain why radical conservative politicians kept winning elections against moderate and centrist Democrats, when there was no evidence of a conservative electorate.

This model makes much more sense to me, although again I haven't seen too much specific evidence for it. But it's still pretty rare and seems deeply-counterintuitive to most practitioners of politics. But whether it's right on the details or not, it's clear that unless we evaluate and question these models and think about them critically instead of just assuming one is true, it'll be hard to make much political progress.

July 28, 2009

A POLITICAL STARTUP

"Politics is like the weather: everybody discusses it but nobody actually does anything about it."

The golden dome of the Massachusetts State House rises majestically over the grass of Boston Common. The sun glints off the dome while kids play on the grass, but on the State House steps there is nobody except for a couple of my friends — and me, holding a ridiculously-large stack of paper that threatened to blow away in the breeze. "This is what failure looks like," I thought.

Within half an hour, I found myself standing in the same place, surrounded by TV cameras and microphones on all sides, reporters throwing questions as fast as I could answer them. And the papers hadn't blown away. How did I get here?

At the beginning of the year, I cofounded a political action committee, the Progressive Change Campaign Committee[1]. We had no money and no members and not much of a plan for how to get them. We wrote up long proposals for big donors on why they should write us checks, and tried negotiating with electoral candidates on why they should send us members, but neither of these were particularly successful. Then Jon Stewart attacked Jim Cramer.

Cramer came to symbolize the foolishness and vapidity of the media in the face of the financial crisis. His blatantly buffoonish cluelessness (*"Don't move your money from Bear! That's just being silly! Don't be silly!"*) were the epitome of a press that championed the housing bubble and fumbled the crash. We were giddy about the press getting their day in scorn, but we wanted to accomplish positive change as well. So we hit upon the idea of starting a petition to demand CNBC hire someone who was right about the housing crisis.

We spread the word to friends and bloggers and before we knew it we had nearly 20,000 signatures — 20,000 new members. It was quite the start.

A couple months later, frustrated that Norm Coleman wouldn't drop his spurious legal challenges against Al Franken being named a Senator, we started NormDollar. com. We asked people to donate a dollar each day Norm Coleman didn't drop out of the race, money we'd spend electing progressive candidates. It was featured on *Hardball* and throughout the political press. We also videotaped Norm's donors' reactions when we told them about the program. But my favorite was when we presented Norm with a big novelty check for him to sign, representing all the money he'd raised for progressives.

Now we had money too.

I came back from my month offline to find we were raising money for TV ads — running ads in DC pressuring representatives to support the public health care option, asking whether they'd sold out to their insurance industry campaign contributors. And when Sen. Ben Nelson started a campaign to stall the health care bill, we filmed an ad with Mike Snider. Mike talked plainly to the camera about how, as owner of the local Syzzlyn Skillet, he received a call from his insurers saying they were raising his rates by 42%. "I can't afford that!" he exclaimed. And then to hear his own Senator was trying to prevent health care reform?

Mike was just an average guy who made a real political difference. After we started airing our ad, Ben Nelson's spokesperson tried to denounce him and the Senator himself called Mike and asked to see his health care bills. Mike was a guest on *The Rachel Maddow Show* and his restaurant has become a base of operations for the local political community. Mike's story was so powerful that Ben Nelson was forced to put up his own ads directly responding to it — even though Nelson isn't up for reelection in years — in which he (ridiculously) calls Mike a lying DC politician.

Mike's story really inspired me as to the difference just one person could make, but I never thought that person would be me. When my Senator, Ted Kennedy, passed away, I wanted to honor his memory by fighting for the causes he fought for. His last request had been a letter to the Massachusetts legislature asking them to change the law and let a replacement be appointed to his seat to continue his fight for universal health care. Without the change, the seat would stay vacant for five months while an election could be scheduled — and the next five months will be crucial.

With the rest of the (growing) PCCC team, we came up with a plan to launch a petition asking the legislature to honor that request. We sent out an email asking people to sign and tell their friends. Within a few days, we had 20,000 signatures. I was blown away — clearly people cared.

I'd promised to deliver the signatures on Monday, without really thinking about what that entailed. I called the office of the Senate President and Speaker of the House to ask when I could come by and film a short video of the petitions being dropped off. The President of the Senate's office blew me off, insisting that under no circumstances were cameras allowed in their office and saying that the President simply couldn't meet with me. So we decided to make the delivery something they couldn't ignore.

We emailed our list to ask people in the area to show up on the State House steps at 11am Monday. Then we emailed the press and asked them to get there at 11:15. I stayed up all night the night before, feeding paper into the printer trying to print out 20,000 names. Then I grabbed a stack and headed to the State House.

The stack — 600 sheets or so — kept trying to fall over and blow away and at the

State House there were only a couple friends who were loaning me their camera. We decided to go in and scope out President Murray's office. When we came back, our members started arriving: old ladies with their grandchildren, college students, and everyone in between. The media started pressing closer: a photographer for the *Herald*, a cameraman for Fox. Microphones kept being shoved in my face and people kept asking me to spell my name. I hefted the stack of petitions and kept repeating why I was here.

Local TV news isn't exactly known for its crack reporters, but I have to say I was impressed by Janet Wu. She didn't just ask me the standard questions, but kept pushing me on the hard stuff, barking responses at me, not letting me off the hook. The other reporters smelled blood and joined in. Soon I was at the center of a full scrum of cameras and microphones — surrounded on all sides, every local TV station there. I like to think I comported myself well: I didn't get angry or flustered, I refused to me taken off-message, I kept stressing that this was about doing what the people wanted.

(Later, away from the cameras, Wu was a completely different person. "Hey there, little guy," she cooed at a grandchild. "Hey, it's OK, you can talk to me." Actually, I thought the kid might have the right idea by staying quiet.)

At some point all the cameras dematerialized. "OK, go in," someone said. "Just pretend we're not here." They'd all rematerialized down the street, to film us marching into the capitol, stack of signatures in hand.

Believe it or not, it's not easy to walk into the state capitol holding 600 pieces of paper with TV cameras in front of you and a crowd of supporters behind. I kept wondering where to look and trying not to lose the rest of the crowd. Who knows how that footage came out. And when I got up the steps the reporters dematerialized again and rematerialized inside at the Senate President's office, to film us marching down the hallway. We entered her office and all crowded in — I didn't think we were all going to fit, but we just barely did. The receptionist — in the middle of a phone call — looked a bit flustered. We waited patiently. Soon a broad-shouldered man in a suit came out. "Thanks so much for the petitions," he said, taking them from me. "The proposal will go through the usual process. He turned to head out. I was dumbstruck.

But, bravely, one of the older women spoke up. "Wait," she said. "The normal process? Isn't this a matter of some urgency?" "All I can say is it will go through the usual process." Those women wouldn't let him go. But eventually he did, looking the perfect image of the arrogant unconcerned Boston pol, and Janet Wu stuck a microphone in my face. "Do you feel satisfied?" she asked. I started to speak but she interrupted. "Wait. OK, go again: Do you feel satisfied?"

Outside, a cameraman turned the bright lights on one of the older woman. She was saying, far more clearly and convincingly than me, that no, she wasn't satisfied. That this was an important issue and she wanted to be heard. I was so glad she came.

And then the press and the supporters dematerialized again. I was left, once again, alone with just my friends. We stood in the hallway trying to process what just happened. We caught the man who'd taken the petitions as he was coming out of the office. "So, what is your actual title?" I asked. "Director of Communications," he said.

"And where is the Senate President really?" asked a friend. "Oh, she's in Russia," he explained. "Russia?" "Yeah, she's helping with a nonprofit to assist orphaned children. Pre-scheduled trip. She does it every year." "You're saying she can't meet with us because she's in Russia saving orphans?" I asked. "That's a pretty incredible excuse." We all laughed. He headed off down the hallway.

"Wait, one more thing," a friend called after him. "Where's a good place around here we can get some lunch?"

Please, sign our petition.

September 8, 2009

1. http://boldprogressives.org/

THE TROUBLE WITH NONPROFITS

In the 1990s, a group of psychologists began studying what made experts expert. Their first task was to see whether experts really were expert — whether they were particularly good at their jobs.

What they found was that some were and some weren't. Champion chess players, obviously, are much better at playing chess than you and I. But political pundits, it turns out, aren't that much better at making predictions than a random guy off the street.

What distinguishes people who are great at what they do from those who are just mediocre? The answer, it seems, is feedback. If you lose a chess game, it's pretty obvious you lost. You know right away, you feel bad, and you start thinking about what you did wrong and how you can improve.

Making a bad prediction isn't like that. First, it's months or years before your prediction is proven wrong[1]. And then, you make yourself feel better by coming up with some explanation for why you were wrong: *well, nobody expected that to happen; it threw everything else off!* And so you keep on making predictions in the same way — which means you never get good at it.

The difference between chess and predictions is a lot like the difference between companies and nonprofits. If your company is losing money, it's pretty obvious. You know right away, you feel bad, and you start thinking about how to fix it. (And if you don't fix it, you go bankrupt.) But if your nonprofit isn't accomplishing its goals, it's much less obvious. You can point to various measurable signs of success (look at all the members we have, look at all the articles we've been quoted in) and come up with all sorts of explanations for why it's not your fault.

This isn't to say that we should have companies replace nonprofits, any more than we should have chess games replace predictions. The two serve completely different goals — nonprofits aim at improving the world, not making money. But it does mean that if you're involved in nonprofits (or predictions), you need to be much more careful about making sure you're doing a good job.

Unfortunately, few nonprofits do that. Take, for example, the Center for American Progress, widely believed to be one of the most effective political nonprofits. They say their goal is "improving the lives of Americans through ideas and action." But their "marketing brochure," while filled with glossy photos, doesn't even attempt to see whether they're accomplishing this goal. It touts that they've released "an economic strategy for the next administration," "convened a task force … to develop policy," and "developed a plan for the bulk transfer auction of at-risk mortgages." There's not a single attempt to demonstrate that any of these things has improved the lives of Americans, let alone estimate how much.

Measuring things is hard and expensive, even in the simplest cases. Measuring the effect of loaning money to Africans seems a lot easier than measuring the impact of of a think tank report. But when Peter Singer asked Oxfam to measure the effectiveness of giving microcredit to villages in West Africa, they declined, on the grounds that it would have taken up half the budget.

But not measuring is even more expensive. Imagine that Oxfam experimented with two microcredit programs and found that one did 10% better than the other. Even with this very modest improvement, it would only take helping five villages before the experiment paid for itself.

And, as anyone who's done these sorts of experiments knows, you often see improvements well in excess of 10%. To take a silly example, Dustin Curtis experimented[2] with getting more readers of his weblog to follow him on Twitter. After four experiments, he'd achieved a 173% improvement. And even this is probably underestimating things. I expect many nonprofits are not accomplishing their goals at *all*. Even if they made a little bit of progress, their improvement would be mathematically infinite. (It's also quite possible that many nonprofits are actually being *counter*-productive. After all, before we started measuring the effects of medical treatment, we were bleeding people with leeches.)

What can be done about this? I think that everyone who donates to a nonprofit should demand an accounting of results — not just the number of times they've been cited in the media or the number of policy discussions they've held, but an actual attempt to measure how much they're improving people's lives. For most nonprofits, I expect these numbers will be depressingly small. But that's much better than having no numbers at all. For feeling bad about failing is the first step to doing better next time.

September 7, 2009

1. http://wrongtomorrow.com/
2. http://dustincurtis.com/you_should_follow_me_on_twitter.html

SUBJECTIVISM

I have two friends — let's call them Q and R — whose political philosophy I find alien and fascinating. Like me, they genuinely want to help the poor but, like conservatives, they object to most typical solutions for doing so. (And yes, I know conservatives claim they want to help the poor, but it usually turns out that there are other things they think are more important. Not so with Q and R.)

Q thinks the most important thing is how it feels to be poor. The problem isn't so much that they don't have money, but that they're made to feel bad because of it. Welfare is thus a bad idea because it just makes the poor feel worse — not only can they not make money, but they have to come hat-in-hand to the government for help. My first reaction to this was that the poor were wrong: it wasn't their fault they were poor, they were just the losers in a rigged game. But, of course, they don't know the game is rigged and things they don't know can't make them feel better. By focusing on the objective facts, Q argues, we're ignoring the actual lived experiences of the poor.

Q is thus upset by socialist writers, like Orwell (*Down and Out in Paris and London, The Road to Wigan Pier*) and Ehrenreich (*Nickel and Dimed, Bait and Switch*), who attempt to get the reader to imagine what it would be like if they were poor. Because this is just another way of getting the reader to focus on the objective situation. In all probability, the reader will not be poor ands thus the question of what it would be like is irrelevant; what's important is what it would be like for the actual poor and that requires talking to them.

R also objects to welfare policies, but on rather different grounds. R starts from the premise that people are bad at making themselves happy. Well-to-do professionals, who seem so much better off than the poor, may not actually be doing that much better. To continue to live in the style to which they've become accustomed, they must work long hours at a job they dislike. Because of the endowment effect, getting off this treadmill would cause them even more pain. A few lucky people earn money at tasks they find fulfilling, but perhaps not many more than are happy being poor.

Welfare — or, indeed, any proposal to improve the objective situation of the poor — is a bad idea in R's view because it simply makes it harder for them to get off the treadmill. One might think the right response to this is what we might call (with apologies to Thaler) a kind of utilitarian paternalism, where the government steps in and shows people how to be happy. But why would the government know how to be happy? Having a satisfied life is a cultural problem, R argues, and the solution lies in non-governmental steps to reform culture.

I find these arguments interesting because they start from rather inarguable premises (what matters is how it feels to be poor, people don't know the best way to make themselves happy) to draw very frustrating conclusions.

Take Q. Corporate profits (and thus employee pay) depend on how much of a monopoly the company has. Even the secretary at Google is a millionaire, while even the owner of a farm is desperately poor. There's no way to make a company in a competitive market pay more because there just isn't more money to pay. But getting rid of competitive markets seems like a bad idea; competition has clearly made our lives better. But if we want to make things better for those who aren't paid well (and let's just say we do, since that's kind of the basic premise of this whole article), that just leaves transferring money from those who have it to those who don't. Which, according to Q, doesn't make anyone feel better.

Other countries seem to deal with this by designing the money so that money isn't transferred directly, but is spent on universally available public services. It's not that the French poor get given money they can spend on health care, it's that in France health care is free to everyone. Poor people don't feel singled out and aided — everyone uses government health care. (And the wealthy are much less likely to vote against programs they themselves use.)

This also goes some way to addressing R's objection: people aren't being given more money to spend how they see fit, they're being given access to services we expect to make them happy. And the access doesn't ever go away, so it doesn't contribute to the endowment effect.

Even so, R would argue, much of these universal services are things like education which make it so that a broader group of people can sign up to work at rat race jobs and thus get on the unhappy treadmill. Why support policies that bring more people into this unhappy system? (R also happens to think schooling is bad on its own terms, as is health care, but I don't think that's necessary for the argument.)

But a tax for service system compresses the whole wage structure. The wealthy earn less money, because they pay some of it in taxes, and thus don't have as far to fall. And the poor get more services, which means that even if the wealthy do lose their job and fall, they don't fall as far, since the floor has been raised. All of this would seem to make it easier to quit a job you don't like. (Egads, I'm mixing metaphors like Thomas Friedman. Falling off a treadmill to services on a higher floor?) Indeed, in the extreme case, services would be so high you wouldn't have to work at all unless you wanted to. (Whether this extreme is economically feasible is a separate discussion.)

So that's what I'm for: democracy within organizations, transfers between organizations, and structuring the rules of the market to maximize social benefit. Oh, and euthanasia of the rentier (see article "Keynes, Explained Briefly").

October 19, 2009

BECAUSE WE CAN

When I first started studying the First Amendment — nearly a decade ago; yikes, this is a very overdue blog post — I read about the different theories trying to make sense of it. Some scholars argued the First Amendment's goal was to create a robust marketplace of ideas: if everyone could share their opinion, the truth could come out through robust debate. Others concluded the First Amendment was a sort of logical safeguard: by protecting speech and assembly and petitions for redress of grievances, it guaranteed people the right to work against laws they disapprove of, kind of the way the Second Amendment is said to be a bulwark against totalitarianism.

These aren't just theoretical debates; the theories have practical consequences for how one interprets that key amendment. If you believe it's for a marketplace of ideas, then you will support regulation aimed at correcting market failures by suppressing certain kinds of problematic speech. If you believe it's a political safeguard, then you will not be too worried about speech regulation aimed at clearly nonpolitical speech.

Now, I'm not quite sure why such a theory is needed. The First Amendment always struck me as perfectly clear: "Congress shall make no law." No law meant no law (at least with regard to content; I'm more lenient when it comes to regulating other aspects). But if one has to have a theory, it struck me the right one was something completely different: Because We Can.

The Framers were very skeptical of government. The system they designed was full of checks and fetters, of which the First Amendment is probably the most extreme (unless you believe in a libertarian conception of the Tenth). They saw government as a necessary evil; they were willing to accept it, but they wanted to constrain it where they could.

And speech is a very obvious way to constrain it. A government needs to be able to stop violence and make war and so on or its people will get very badly hurt. But there's no reason it has to stop speech. As the old saying goes, sticks and stones may break my bones but words will never hurt me. Words do hurt, of course, but theirs is a tolerable pain. People, and society, march on even in the face of grievous insults. And so the Framers decided to exclude this class of regulation from the government's ambit. Not because speech is particularly good, but because it's not particularly bad. Because it's one thing they could safely exclude. Because we can.

The implications of this theory for interpretation are obvious: they lead to the most expansive conception of the First Amendment compatible with the other goals of government: a stable democratic body to promote the general welfare, and so on. That's certainly further than any court heretofore has gone and probably a bit further than I'd personally prefer, but isn't that what fetters are for?

October 20, 2009

GOOGLING FOR SOCIOPATHS

One of the best things about capitalism is the way it handles sociopaths. Major executives look up to Alexander the Great and apparently try to follow in his footsteps. But instead of leading a murderous campaign across Asia, they decide to make something people want: newspapers and movies and television shows. True, they're far from perfect, but you have to admit it's a lot better than mass slaughter.

Many books have been written about Google, even though we're all pretty familiar with the company to begin with, but what makes Ken Auletta's Googled interesting is that it's a history of the company as told by the incumbent sociopaths. These are the people Auletta has spent his life covering: the media moguls who tried to acquire and conquer their own empires of content and delivery. And to them what's most shocking and galling about Google's incredibly rapid rise is that instead of being engineered by a fellow sociopath, it was largely done by normal, decent people plainly applying the forces of new technology.

"What has Google ever done for the world?" ask the sociopaths at various points throughout the book. "All they do is steal other people's content!" To a normal human the question is ridiculous — it's almost impossible to imagine life without Googling for something, checking your Gmail, or watching videos on YouTube — but sociopaths aren't used to doing things that create value for people. They're just interested in conquering more and taking control. When Disney bought ABC for $19 billion, it didn't improve most people's lives in any real way, but it did let Michael Eisner regain control of the company he once ran.

So naturally the sociopaths are outraged that their control is being taken away. Newspapers, book publishers, television companies, ad agencies — their businesses are all failing, while Google's is on the rise. The sociopaths may be outraged, but this is exactly what's supposed to happen. Most people don't have a vested interest in whether ABC does well or even continues to exist. What they want are good television shows at a reasonable price, and if they can get those from Apple and Google instead of their local cable company, then bully for Apple and Google.

The thing that's hard for the sociopaths to get their head around is that this isn't because one of their rivals has outsmarted them — it's just the march of technology. When the only way to get most television shows to people's houses was over a wire or across airwaves that could only hold so many channels, their particular distribution model made sense. But when the same connection — whether cable, DSL, satellite, or WiFi — can let people download whatever video program they choose, an entirely new model can take hold. The shift isn't Google's fault any more than America should be blamed for breaking off from Pangea.

As a result, the closest people to moguls behind the recent shifts in media distribution are two computer science grad students: Larry and Sergey. These guys don't even have the decency to behave like real moguls — they wear t-shirts and sneakers, get bored during meetings, and like to travel around the world instead of around Manhattan. What's worse, they're constantly talking about "making the world a better place" (by, for example, donating 1% of their profits to charity) and "empowering the user" (by cutting out middlemen and not forcing choices down people's throats). Sociopaths don't talk like that! Who do these people think they are?

Google gets a lot of criticism (often deserved), but it's worth taking a moment to think of all the things they haven't done. If Microsoft had Google's market share in search, is there any doubt that they'd be systematically demoting or even banning their competitors in the search results? Demoting someone in Google is a virtual death sentence, and yet not only has Google never been accused of using this vast power, the idea itself is almost unimaginable.

Hearing things from the sociopaths' perspective, it's easy to get fooled. "Yeah!" you think. "Why should these Google guys get to control everything?" But for average people, this shift has been great: much more stuff is available, faster and freer than ever before, and the people making all the money off of it are actually decent human beings who feel some responsibility for the planet they inhabit. Sure, I don't agree with them on everything and there's a lot more they can do, but let's not lose sight of the basic point: at least they're not sociopaths.

December 14, 2009

FEWER REPRESENTATIVES OR MORE MONITORS?

Matt Yglesias saw Lawrence Lessig speak about the problem of money in politics concluded his concern on the influence of money in politics was "too narrow"[1]. I tend to agree that Lessig's focus is a bit too narrow — that's why I started the PCCC[2] — but I was shocked by Yglesias' "broader" solution: fewer elected officials.

Matt's focus on institutional reforms is definitely a well-needed antidote to most political journalists' tendency to focus on personalities and other small-picture details, but in this instance it's just crazy. In what sense is the number of elected officials broader than the influences that come to bear on them?

Matt seems to be arguing that countries with fewer elected officials are better run because voters can monitor the performance of those officials better. I don't see how this argument can possibly survive engagement with the details of our political system.

Let's take health care, since that's in the news lately. Health care has basically been talked about nonstop by every news outlet, yet even voters who follow these things in detail have no clue what's really in it. (This is true even of my friends who are political junkies; they know a public option isn't in the bill, but they basically have no idea what the exchanges are or how they would work.) When election season rolls around, campaigns will begin running lots of ads about the health care bill. None of these ads will help inform them what's in it. And the press will continue not to inform them about what's in it.

I don't see how having fewer elected officials will change any of this. The problem is not that voters try to monitor their elected officials but are simply overwhelmed; the problem is that voters have no tools for actually monitoring their elected officials in any meaningful sense. Yes, one can point to a Chris Hayes flowchart[3] here or an Alec MacGillis guide[4] there, but there's no way any significant number of voters know how to find those things. And even if you tell them about those, there's no system for finding similar documents about issues in the future.

And that's the biggest issue Congress is considering this session! And that's just its broadest outlines! The health care bill has thousands of pages of detailed provisions and it's just one of thousands of bills Congress is trying to pass. There's nobody who's even reading all of those provisions, let alone trying to figure out which ones are good ideas and which representatives are fighting for the good ideas.

Instead, there's a vast industry of lobbyists, each of which care really deeply about a handful of those tiny issues and are willing to spend vast amounts of money and effort persuading members of Congress to take their side. On most issues, they face no opposition. So naturally, the members take their side.

What's needed is not fewer representatives, but better monitoring systems and institutional incentives to make monitoring less necessary. Better monitoring systems is what I'm working on and better institutional incentives is what Lessig is fighting for. If Matt thinks that fewer representatives is a better or "broader" solution, I'd like to hear him explain how it's going to help.

Disclosure: I'm on the board of Lessig's group, Change Congress.

January 30, 2010

1. http://yglesias.thinkprogress.org/archives/2010/01/for-less-voting.php
2. http://boldprogressives.org/
3. http://www.donkeylicious.com/2009/09/improved-health-insurance-reform.html
4. http://www.washingtonpost.com/wp-dyn/content/article/2009/08/14/AR2009081401669.html

WHEN IS TRANSPARENCY USEFUL?

The following essay appears in the new O'Reilly book Open Government *and attempts to combine and clarify some of the points I made in previous essays. It was written in June 2009.*

Transparency is a slippery word; the kind of word that, like *reform*, sounds good and so ends up getting attached to any random political thing that someone wants to promote. But just as it's silly to talk about whether "reform" is useful (it depends on the reform), talking about transparency in general won't get us very far. Everything from holding public hearings to requiring police to videotape interrogations can be called "transparency" — there's not much that's useful to say about such a large category.

In general, you should be skeptical whenever someone tries to sell you on something like "reform" or "transparency." In general, you should be skeptical. But in particular, reactionary political movements have long had a history of cloaking themselves in nice words. Take the Good Government (goo-goo) movement early in the twentieth century. Funded by prominent major foundations, it claimed that it was going to clean up the corruption and political machines that were hindering city democracy. Instead, the reforms ended up choking democracy itself, a response to the left-wing candidates who were starting to get elected.

The goo-goo reformers moved elections to off-years. They claimed this was to keep city politics distinct from national politics, but the real effect was just to reduce turnout. They stopped paying politicians a salary. This was supposed to reduce corruption, but it just made sure that only the wealthy could run for office. They made the elections nonpartisan. Supposedly this was because city elections were about local issues, not national politics, but the effect was to increase the power of name recognition and make it harder for voters to tell which candidate was on their side. And they replaced mayors with unelected city managers, so winning elections was no longer enough to effect change.[1]

Of course, the modern transparency movement is very different from the Good Government movement of old. But the story illustrates that we should be wary of kind nonprofits promising to help. I want to focus on one particular strain of transparency thinking and show how it can go awry. It starts with something that's hard to disagree with.

SHARING DOCUMENTS WITH THE PUBLIC

Modern society is made of bureaucracies and modern bureaucracies run on paper: memos, reports, forms, filings. Sharing these internal documents with the public seems obviously good, and indeed, much good has come out of publishing these documents, whether it's the National Security Archive[2], whose Freedom of Information Act (FOIA) requests have revealed decades of government wrongdoing around the globe, or the indefatigable Carl Malamud and his scanning[3], which has put terabytes of useful government documents, from laws to movies, online for everyone to access freely.

I suspect few people would put "publishing government documents on the Web" high on their list of political priorities, but it's a fairly cheap project (just throw piles of stuff into scanners) and doesn't seem to have much downside. The biggest concern — privacy — seems mostly taken care of. In the United States, FOIA and the Privacy Act (PA) provide fairly clear guidelines for how to ensure disclosure while protecting people's privacy.

Perhaps even more useful than putting government documents online would be providing access to corporate and nonprofit records. A lot of political action takes place outside the formal government, and thus outside the scope of the existing FOIA laws. But such things seem totally off the radar of most transparency activists; instead, giant corporations that receive billions of dollars from the government are kept impenetrably secret.

GENERATING DATABASES FOR THE PUBLIC

Many policy questions are a battle of competing interests — drivers don't want cars that roll over and kill them when they make a turn, but car companies want to keep selling such cars. If you're a member of Congress, choosing between them is difficult. On the one hand are your constituents, who vote for you. But on the other hand are big corporations, which fund your reelection campaigns. You really can't afford to offend either one too badly.

So, there's a tendency for Congress to try a compromise. That's what happened with, for example, the Transportation Recall Enhancement, Accountability, and Documentation (TREAD) Act. Instead of requiring safer cars, Congress simply required car companies to report how likely their cars were to roll over. Transparency wins again!

Or, for a more famous example: after Watergate, people were upset about politicians receiving millions of dollars from large corporations. But, on the other hand, corporations seem to like paying off politicians. So instead of banning the practice, Congress simply required that politicians keep track of everyone who gives them money and file a report on it for public inspection.

I find such practices ridiculous. When you create a regulatory agency, you put together a group of people whose job is to solve some problem. They're given the power to investigate who's breaking the law and the authority to punish them. Transparency, on the other hand, simply shifts the work from the government to the average citizen, who has neither the time nor the ability to investigate these questions in any detail, let alone do anything about it. It's a farce: a way for Congress to look like it has done something on some pressing issue without actually endangering its corporate sponsors.

INTERPRETING DATABASES FOR THE PUBLIC

Here's where the technologists step in. "Something is too hard for people?" they hear. "We know how to fix that." So they download a copy of the database and pretty it up for public consumption — generating summary statistics, putting nice pictures around it, and giving it a snazzy search feature and some visualizations. Now inquiring citizen can find out who's funding their politicians and how dangerous their cars are just by going online.

The wonks love this. Still stinging from recent bouts of deregulation and antigovernment zealotry, many are now skeptical about government. "We can't trust the regulators," they say. "We need to be able to investigate the data for ourselves." Technology seems to provide the perfect solution. Just put it all online — people can go through the data while trusting no one.

There's just one problem: if you can't trust the regulators, what makes you think you can trust the data?

The problem with generating databases isn't that they're too hard to read; it's the lack of investigation and enforcement power, and websites do nothing to help with that. Since no one's in charge of verifying them, most of the things reported in transparency databases are simply lies. Sometimes they're blatant lies, like how some factories keep two sets of books on workplace injuries: one accurate one, reporting every injury, and one to show the government, reporting just 10% of them[4]. But they can easily be subtler: forms are misfiled or filled with typos, or the malfeasance is changed in such a way that it no longer appears on the form. Making these databases easier to read results only in easier-to-read lies.

Three examples:

1. Congress's operations are supposedly open to the public, but if you visit the House floor (or if you follow what they're up to on one of these transparency sites) you find that they appear to spend all their time naming post offices. All the real work is passed using emergency provisions and is tucked into subsections of innocuous bills. (The bank bailouts were put in the Paul Wellstone Mental Health Act.) Matt Taibbi's *The Great Derangement* tells the story.

2. Many of these sites tell you who your elected official is, but what impact does your elected official really have? For 40 years, people in New York thought they were governed by their elected officials — their city council, their mayor, their governor. But as Robert Caro revealed in *The Power Broker*, they were all wrong. Power in New York was controlled by one man, a man who had consistently lost every time he'd tried to run for office, a man nobody thought of as being in charge at all: Parks Commissioner Robert Moses.

3. Plenty of sites on the Internet will tell you who your representative receives money from, but disclosed contributions are just the tip of the iceberg. As Ken Silverstein points out in his series of pieces for Harper's[4] (some of which he covers in his book Turkmeniscam), being a member of Congress provides for endless ways to get perks and cash while hiding where it comes from.

Fans of transparency try to skirt around this. "OK," they say, "but surely *some* of the data will be accurate. And even if it isn't, won't we learn something from how people lie?" Perhaps that's true, although it's hard to think of any good examples. (In fact, it's hard to think of any good examples of transparency work accomplishing anything, except perhaps for more transparency.) But everything has a cost.

Hundreds of millions of dollars have been spent funding transparency projects around the globe. That money doesn't come from the sky. The question isn't whether some transparency is better than none; it's whether transparency is really the best way to spend these resources, whether they would have a bigger impact if spent someplace else.

I tend to think they would. All this money has been spent with the goal of getting a straight answer, not of doing anything about it. Without enforcement power, the most readable database in the world won't accomplish much — even if it's perfectly accurate. So people go online and see that all cars are dangerous and that all politicians are corrupt. What are they supposed to do then?

Sure, perhaps they can make small changes — this politician gets slightly less oil money than that one, so I'll vote for her (on the other hand, maybe she's just a better liar and gets her oil money funneled through PACs or foundations or lobbyists) — but unlike the government, they can't solve the bigger issue: a bunch of people reading a website can't force car companies to make a safe car. You've done nothing to solve the real problem; you've only made it seem more hopeless: all politicians are corrupt, all cars are dangerous. What can you do?

AN ALTERNATIVE

What's ironic is that the Internet does provide something you can do. It has made it vastly easier, easier than ever before, to form groups with people and work together on common tasks. And it's through people coming together — not websites analyzing data — that real political progress can be made.

So far we've seen baby steps — people copying what they see elsewhere and trying to apply it to politics. Wikis seem to work well, so you build a political wiki. Everyone loves social networks, so you build a political social network. But these tools worked in their original setting because they were trying to solve particular problems, not because they're magic. To make progress in politics, we need to think best about how to solve its problems, not simply copy technologies that have worked in other fields. Data analysis can be part of it, but it's part of a bigger picture. Imagine a team of people coming together to tackle some issue they care about — food safety, say. You can have technologists poring through safety records, investigative reporters making phone calls and sneaking into buildings, lawyers subpoenaing documents and filing lawsuits, political organizers building support for the project and coordinating volunteers, members of Congress pushing for hearings on your issues and passing laws to address the problems you uncover, and, of course, bloggers and writers to tell your stories as they unfold.

Imagine it: an investigative strike team, taking on an issue, uncovering the truth, and pushing for reform. They'd use technology, of course, but also politics and the law. At best, a transparency law gets you one more database you can look at. But a lawsuit (or congressional investigation)? You get to subpoena all the databases, as well as the source records behind them, then interview people under oath about what it all means. You get to ask for what you need, instead of trying to predict what you may someday want.

This is where data analysis can be really useful. Not in providing definitive answers over the Web to random surfers, but in finding anomalies and patterns and questions that can be seized upon and investigated by others. Not in building finished products, but by engaging in a process of discovery. But this can be done only when members of this investigative strike team work in association with others. They would do what it takes to accomplish their goals, not be hamstrung by arbitrary divisions between "technology" and "journalism" and "politics."

Right now, technologists insist that they're building neutral platforms for anyone to find data on any issue. Journalists insist that they're objective observers of the facts. And political types assume they already know the answers and don't need to investigate further questions. They're each in their own silo, unable to see the bigger picture.

I certainly was. I care passionately about these issues — I don't want politicians to be corrupt; I don't want cars to kill people — and as a technologist I'd love to be able to solve them. That's why I got swept up in the promise of transparency. It seemed like just by doing the things I knew how to do best — write code, sift through databases — I could change the world.

But it just doesn't work. Putting databases online isn't a silver bullet, as nice as the word *transparency* may sound. But it was easy to delude myself. All I had to do was keep putting things online and someone somewhere would find a use for them. After all, that's what technologists do, right? The World Wide Web wasn't designed for publishing the news — it was designed as a neutral platform that could support anything from scientific publications to pornography.

Politics doesn't work like that. Perhaps at some point putting things on the front page of the *New York Times* guaranteed that they would be fixed, but that day is long past. The pipeline of leak to investigation to revelation to report to reform has broken down. Technologists can't depend on journalists to use their stuff; journalists can't depend on political activists to fix the problems they uncover. Change doesn't come from thousands of people, all going their separate ways. Change requires bringing people together to work on a common goal. That's hard for technologists to do by themselves.

But if they do take that as their goal, they can apply all their talent and ingenuity to the problem. They can measure their success by the number of lives that have been improved by the changes they fought for, rather than the number of people who have visited their website. They can learn which technologies actually make a difference and which ones are merely indulgences. And they can iterate, improve, and scale.

Transparency can be a powerful thing, but not in isolation. So, let's stop passing the buck by saying our job is just to get the data out there and it's other people's job to figure out how to use it. Let's decide that our job is to fight for good in the world. I'd love to see all these amazing resources go to work on *that*.

Thanks to Andy Oram and Andy Eggers for their insightful comments on earlier versions of this essay.

February 11, 2010

1. For more, see http://sociology.ucsc.edu/whorulesamerica/power/local.html.
2. http://www.gwu.edu/~nsarchiv/
3. http://public.resource.org/
4. http://www.harpers.org/subjects/KenSilverstein
5. Fast Food Nation, Eric Schlosser, Houghton Mifflin, 2001. [p. 180]

THE REASON SO MANY PEOPLE ARE UNEMPLOYED

Around the time of the Great Depression, a man named John Maynard Keynes made an incredible discovery. The reason so many people were out of work was not really because of irresponsible banks or high taxes or reckless government policy. It was really much simpler than all that: there wasn't enough money.

Now, as individuals, we'd all like a little more money for ourselves. But pause for a moment and think about what it means if there isn't enough money in the economy as a *whole*. A good way to wrap your head around this is to think about a much smaller case: instead of the whole economy, let's think about a now-famous babysitting co-op on Capitol Hill. Instead of dollars, the co-op used its own scrip that was worth an hour of babysitting time. When you wanted to go out, you'd pay a couple hours to someone else to watch your kids; then when they wanted to go out, they'd pay you or someone else to do the same for them.

It all worked great for a while, until one day they found they had too few pieces of scrip. Every couple had only a couple hours left and, having so little, they didn't want to waste it. So they all decided to save it for a very special occasion. This was kind of an incredible situation — even though there were people who wanted someone to babysit their kids, and people who were willing to do just that, the deal didn't happen, simply because the co-op hadn't printed enough colored pieces of paper. Eventually the co-op learned their mistake, printed some more scrip and handed it out, and everybody went back to babysitting like before and were much happier for it.

The same thing happens in the real economy. When there aren't enough green-colored pieces of paper around, everybody gets worried and holds on to the little they have. Even if you'd like someone to build an extension on your house, and there's someone else out there who'd like to build an extension on your house, the deal doesn't happen, just because you don't have enough green pieces of paper (or, more realistically, dollars in your bank account). This is a total waste. You don't get the extension and the other guy doesn't get a job, all because we haven't run the printing presses enough (or added enough zeroes to the bank's computers).

Before the Great Depression, most countries wouldn't simply print more colored pieces of paper. They were on the "gold standard" and they would only print more currency when more gold was discovered. This led to the most bizarre series of booms and busts as more gold was discovered in strange places and then "used up" by population growth or other things. After Keynes, countries eventually stopped this silliness and just started printing their money directly. As soon as they abandoned the gold standard[1], they begun recovering from the Great Depression.

But the power to print more money is obviously a very special power and you wouldn't want it to fall into the wrong hands. So, in the United States, we've taken it away from elected politicians and given it (mostly) to the big banks. The banks select people to run their local Federal Reserve and then some of those people (along with some additional folks nominated by the President) are selected to be members of a group called the Federal Open Market Committee (FOMC). The FOMC, essentially, decides how much money there should be in circulation, which in turn decides how many people have jobs.

You might think this sounds crazy — a bunch of unelected bankers get to decide how many people have jobs? — and, in fact, it is crazy. But I'm not making it up. Ask a macroeconomist, like Paul Krugman, and this is exactly what he'll tell you. And if you look in the Federal Reserve Act or on the Fed's website, you'll find their mission[2] is to "promote effectively the goals of maximum employment, stable prices, and moderate long-term interest rates." These multiple goals are relatively recent; before 1978, the goal was simply "maximum employment, production, and purchasing power."

Now some people will claim that the Federal Reserve has done all it can to create more jobs but the recession is so deep this time that there's nothing else it can do. But that's just not true — even the chairman of the Federal Reserve, Ben Bernanke, says it's not true. He was asked about this in a Senate hearing. As the *Economist* summarized his response[3]: "Mr Bernanke does not want to risk a de-anchoring of inflation expectations. He is willing to accept 10% or greater unemployment and the resulting economic and political fall-out in order to avoid that risk."

Which brings us to the subject of inflation. Obviously if you print a lot of new money, it makes existing money worth a little less. This is annoying, but is it worse than having people out of work? Well, it depends who you are. If you have a lot of money, you're more worried about it becoming worth less. But if you work for a living, you're more worried about people being out of work. As you might expect, Mr. Bernanke has a lot of money, as do the other bankers on the committee and the people who selected them. So they've decided to let millions and millions of people be unemployed and the rest of us experience the resulting recession rather than risk the chance that some of their money might be worth a little less.

The biggest reason this is possible is because nobody realizes it. If it was conventional wisdom that a bunch of unelected bankers looking out for rich people were the reason everyone was out of work, politicians would be forced to explain to angry voters why we had this crazy system and might actually consider doing something about it. But, incredibly, it just seems like nobody has any idea. Voters don't realize it, politicians don't understand it, journalists don't cover it. And, in fact, they're so far from having any idea that it's really difficult to explain it to them. When you say a bunch of unelected bankers are the reason there are no jobs, they just look at you like you're crazy. I've just spent a page or two explaining it and you still probably think I'm crazy. But it's true! This isn't some Ron Paul-type crackpot idea; this is mainstream economics, from Paul Krugman to the head of George W. Bush's Council of Economic Advisors.

I feel a bit like the guy in one of those movies, going around and telling everyone that the murderer is standing right over there — right there, look! — but nobody believes him and people continue to die. It's incredibly frustrating, and I have no idea what to do about it.

One final point: How did we get into this mess in the first place? Why did we suddenly find ourselves without enough money? Well, there was a housing bubble: for many years, house prices kept going up and up for no other reason than everyone was betting that they were just going to keep going up. When house prices were unsustainably high, that was part of the money in circulation. But when the music stopped and the bubble popped, house prices cratered and nearly $8 trillion disappeared overnight. The government has printed a bunch of money since then, but nowhere near the $8 trillion we lost. Obviously a lot of other bad stuff happened during the financial crisis, but this is the reason everybody is out of work.

March 14, 2010

1. http://phoenixwoman.files.wordpress.com/2009/06/delong-march2009.jpg
2. http://www.federalreserve.gov/aboutthefed/section2a.htm
3. http://www.economist.com/blogs/freeexchange/2009/12/from_the_horses_mouth

THEORY OF CHANGE

I am increasingly convinced that the difference between effective and ineffective people is their skill at developing a theory of change. Theory of change is a funny phrase — I first heard it in the nonprofit community, but it's also widespread in politics and really applies to just about everything. Unfortunately, very few people seem to be very good at it.

Let's take a concrete example. Imagine you want to decrease the size of the defense budget. The typical way you might approach this is to look around at the things you know how to do and do them on the issue of decreasing the defense budget. So, if you have a blog, you might write a blog post about why the defense budget should be decreased and tell your friends about it on Facebook and Twitter. If you're a professional writer, you might write a book on the subject. If you're an academic, you might publish some papers. Let's call this strategy a "theory of action": you work *forwards* from what you know how to do to try to find things you can do that will accomplish your goal.

A theory of change is the opposite of a theory of action — it works backwards from the goal, in concrete steps, to figure out what you can do to achieve it. To develop a theory of change, you need to start at the end and repeatedly ask yourself, "Concretely, how does one achieve that?" A decrease in the defense budget: how does one achieve that? Yes, you.

AUDIENCE MEMBER: Congress passes a new budget with a smaller authorization for defense next year.

Yes, that's true — but let's get more concrete. How does that happen?

AUDIENCE: Uh, you get a majority of the House and Senate to vote for it and the President to sign it.

Great, great — so how do you get them to do that? Now we have to think about what motivates politicians to support something. This is a really tricky question, but it's totally crucial if we want to be effective. After all, if we don't eventually motivate the politicians, then what we've done is useless for achieving our goal. (Unless we can think of some other way to shrink the defense budget.)

But this is also not an insoluble problem. Put yourself in the shoes of a politician for a moment. What would motivate you? Well, on the one hand, there's what you think is right. Then there's what will help you get reelected. And finally there's peer pressure and other sort of psychological motivations that get people to do things that don't meet their own goals.

So the first would suggest a strategy of persuading politicians that cutting the defense budget was a good idea. The second would suggest organizing a constituency in their districts that would demand they cut the defense budget. And maybe one of you can figure out how to use the third — that's a little trickier.

But let's stick with the first, since that's the most standard. What convinces politicians that something is the right thing to do?

AUDIENCE: Their beliefs?

In a sense, I suppose. But those are going to be pretty hard to change. I'm thinking more, if you have a politician with a given set of beliefs, how do you convince them that cutting the defense budget advances those beliefs?

AUDIENCE: You outline why to them.

Well, OK, let's think about that. Do you think if you ran into Nancy Pelosi in the hallway here and you tried to explain to her why cutting the defense budget would accomplish her beliefs, that you'd convince her?

AUDIENCE: Probably not.

Why not?

AUDIENCE: Because she wouldn't really listen to me — she'd just smile and nod.

Yeah. Nancy Pelosi doesn't trust you. She's never met you. You're not particularly credible. So you need to find people the politicians trust and get them to convince the politicians.

Alright, well, we can continue down this road for a while — figuring out who politicians trust, figuring out how to persuade *them*, figuring out how to get them to, in turn, persuade the politicians, etc. Then, when the politicians are persuaded, there's the task of developing something they can vote for, getting it introduced so they can vote on it, then getting them to vote on the specific measure even when they agree with the overall idea. You can see that this can take quite a while.

It's not easy. It could take a while before you get to a concrete action that you can take. But do you see how this is entirely crucial if you want to be effective? Now maybe if you're only writing a blog post, it's not worth it. Not everything we do has to be maximally effective. But DC is filled with organizations that spend millions of dollars each year and have hardly even begun to think about these questions. I'm not saying their money is totally wasted — it certainly has some positive impacts — but it could do so much more if the people in charge thought, concretely, about how it was supposed to accomplish their goals.

I'll close with one more example, showing how this strategy can be used personally as well. I was at a party once and I told someone I was writing a book and that I wanted it to be a bestseller. They laughed at that and I think it's because they had a theory of action model in their head: you write the best book you can, and of course you want it to be a bestseller, but either it does or it doesn't.

But I was working backwards, I had a theory of change: I asked, What makes something a best seller? Well, lots of people buy it. OK, how do you get lots of people to buy something? Well, you have to persuade them it's something they want. OK, how do you persuade them it's something they want? Well, first it has to meet some desire or need they have and second you need to explain to them how it meets that need. So what are the desires or needs people have? (Looking at bestsellers: entertainment, escape, self-improvement, etc.) What are the ways of explaining your book meets their need? (Being popular early on, appearances in the media, persuading readers to tell other readers, etc.)

Again, we can keep going for quite a while until we get all the way back to something I can actually do. But because of this, I didn't have to simply have to hope that my book became a bestseller, like every other author. I could actually do something about it.

That's the power of a theory of change.

March 14, 2010

PHILOSOPHICAL PUZZLES RESOLVED

PUZZLE 1: EQUALITY AND DISABILITY

Daniel Wikler posed to me the following problem he encountered while Staff Ethicist at the WHO[1].The WHO recommends two principles: first, treat all citizens equally; second, aim to maximize overall quality of life. But imagine two citizens will die without a kidney transplant, one of whom is seriously disabled, but there is only one kidney. The first principle requires that both have an equal chance of getting the kidney. But the second principle requires we give it to the non-disabled person: if the disabled person dies, overall quality of life in the society will be higher, since it will have one less disabled person. (We accept, by definition, that disability lowers quality of life.) What to do?

Response: It seems pretty clear that the first value is simply wrong. We have no interest in promoting the health of the population; the population is simply an abstraction. Our interest is in promoting the health of (the sum of) individual people, who are conscious and therefore have moral interests.

One can see this clearly by looking at the cases where the population changes but people do not: birth, death, exile, and immigration:

Birth: The society has a controlled population growth program and assigns birth permits; birth permits are assigned to parents with the healthiest genes.

Death: The society has a limited number of organs; organs are given to the least-injured.

Exile: Sick people are tossed out of the society.

Immigration: Only healthy people are allowed to immigrate.

In all four such cases, it seems pretty clear to me that the population health position is wrong. (Exile seems particularly cruel.)

PUZZLE 2: THE REPUGNANT CONCLUSION

Derek Parfit poses[2] the following problem. 1: Imagine there are a group of happy people (A). 2: Now imagine that some other people are created in some other completely unconnected place that are happy, but less happy than the previous group (B). 3: Now imagine that both groups are adjusted to be at some equal, but intermediate point of happiness between A and A+. 4: Now imagine these two societies are connected, resulting in C: more people at a lesser degree of happiness.

2 is no worse than 1, since the additional people are happy and do not affect anyone. 3 is no worse than 2, since the people in B are made happier by more than the people in A are made unhappy. 4 is no worse than 3, since we are simply introducing folks to each other. But continue this and you reach the repugnant conclusion: a huge

swarm of people who are just barely happy is better than a handful of people who are extremely happy.

Response: The problem is step 2, which is in fact worse than 1. Parfit assumes that simply adding extra people whose lives are worth living cannot make things worse. But that's ridiculous. Imagine our society, then imagine our society with a bunch more feral people living on the huge island of garbage in the middle of the Pacific, unable to speak except in a growl, with none of the surrounding societies ever noticing. I think the people living in the garbage heap's lives would be worth living (I wouldn't want to kill them, nor would they want to be killed), but I distinctly prefer the former society.

PUZZLE 3: THE LOGIC OF THE LARDER

Many people say that we shouldn't eat animals, because that would mean killing them. But for many of these animals, if they aren't going to be killed and eaten, they would never be born in the first place. What if the animal preferred to have a short, pleasant existence before being consumed as food rather than having no existence at all? Wouldn't that mean we should breed the animal, give it a nice life, then kill and eat it?

Response: This is a ridiculous hypothetical — you're suggesting an animal that doesn't exist yet has a preference about existing. I don't respect hypothetical creatures' hypothetical desires to not be hypothetical. If I did, you could get me to do all sorts of absurd things just by hypothesizing them. You could, say, simply hypothesize a utility monster's very strong desire to exist and I would be morally bound to try to create one. Or perhaps my hypothetical children really want to exist, so I have to hurry to procreate. That's ridiculous.

I think we should maximize the actual interests of actual people.

PUZZLE 4: ADDITION VS. SUBTRACTION

As a consequentialist, if I support not adding people (as I do in my resolution to 2 and 3), then I must support removing people, since the consequences are identical. If I prefer a society with fewer, happier people, then I must support euthanizing some people to make the rest better off. Sure, there are practical questions with implementing this, but philosophically, I must be in favor of eliminationism.

Response: I am not a consequentialist about societies, I'm a utilitarian: I think we should work toward outcomes that maximize the interests of individuals.

There's a fundamental disanalogy between addition and contraction. Addition means creating new people with interests that didn't exist before the addition. Contraction, on the other hand, means getting rid of actually-existing people. I do not respect the hypothetical interests of hypothetical individuals to not be hypothetical, but I do respect real people with real interests right now, who presumably have an interest in not being gotten rid of. Thus, I support not getting rid of people and not arbitrarily creating new ones.

March 8, 2010

1. The problem is also discussed in F.M. Kamm, "Disability, Discrimination, and Irrelevant Goods"
2. http://en.wikipedia.org/wiki/Mere_addition_paradox

BROUGHT TO YOU BY THE LETTER 'S'

When you're writing laws, changing the smallest details can have huge effects. But I've never seen anything as big as what happened this week, when the White House gutted an entire section of financial regulation by removing the letter **s**.

Right now, shareholders of big companies vote to decide who will be on the board of directors by filling out a mail-in ballot called a proxy card. But currently the corporation's CEO gets to decide who's on the card! The result is a board hand-picked by the CEO — and they return the favor by providing CEOs with exorbitant salaries.

The current financial regulation bill — in a provision passed by both the House and Senate — would change that by allowing shareholders with 5% of the stock to come together and propose additional names for the ballot. But the White House is trying to gut this proposal at the last minute, and they've done it in an incredibly sneaky way — they removed the letter s from the end of the word shareholders.

Now instead of shareholders whose stock adds up to 3% coming together, you have to be a single shareholder with 5% of the stock all by yourself. And for most big companies, there just isn't anyone like that. Take GE, for example — its biggest shareholder only owns about 3.4% of the company.

So by removing a single letter, they managed to make this provision completely useless.

The White House is being barraged by major CEOs begging them to keep fighting for this provision — after all, no CEO wants to see their lavish salaries cut! As Barney Frank put it, "I think there are some people in the White House who think, 'Well, we're fighting the financial institutions, but why fight with some of the others, you know, the other corporations?'" Apparently they're so scared of a fight, they're willing to gut a provision passed by both the House and Senate.

If you're interested in fighting for real corporate reform, please sign our petition to the White House:

> "Stop lobbying against shareholder power in corporate decision-making — and against protections that would finally rein in CEO pay. That's not change we can believe in."

June 21, 2010

WHEN BRUTE FORCE FAILS

Liberals don't like talking about crime. The classic answer — fixing the root causes of crime — now seems hopelessly ambitious. And our natural sympathy for the millions ground down by an out-of-control prison system and a pointless war on drugs doesn't play well with voters, especially when most criminals can't vote. The general belief seems to be that the problem of crime has been solved — after all, crime levels have dropped dramatically since the law-and-order 80s — and that the real problem now is not too much crime, but too much punishment. If voters don't agree, it's because TV news continues to obsess over violent crime even as actual occurrences of it have cratered, leaving behind a population who wants to do even more to crack down on an army of bad guys who don't really exist. The smartest liberal position on crime seems to be changing the subject and talking about white-collar crime instead (which, as recent economic news has made clear, is a real epidemic).

Mark Kleiman, in his brilliant new book, When Brute Force Fails, takes a different view. Crime, aside from drug crimes (where his work persuasively argues that "the abuse of illicit drugs is a human tragedy but not a major threat to the social order"), is serious. (Presumably this only applies to classic violent crimes; it's obvious this logic doesn't work for violations of copyright law and civil disobedience.) Even where there's a small amount of actual crime, it's possible that's just because people are wasting so much time preventing it. There's a serious social cost to having to remember to lock our doors and carry our keys around all the time, let alone the money we waste on burglar alarms and car-tracking services and all the rest.

While I find the methodology he uses to show it wildly problematic[1], I agree with his point that crime really sucks. Even if a burglar only causes $400 worth of damage, I'd pay far more than $400 to prevent a burglary — the loss of privacy, the sense of violation, the disruption of my normal order, the distraction of having to deal with police and repairmen and insurance agents, etc. all add up to make burglary a nightmare well above the direct economic damage it causes.

Such things are a frustration for white suburbanites, but for poor people stuck in the ghetto, they're a nightmare. Crime is yet another disadvantage and a particularly noxious one at that. Even aside from all the other indignities suffered by the poor, just imagining life in a crime-ridden neighborhood is enough to make your skin crawl.

But, Kleiman insists, we also have to count the harm to the criminals! Going through lengthy court proceedings, spending years in abusive prisons, having to deal with officious parole officers and the loss of liberty they cause are all serious costs and we can't wave them away just because they happen to the bad guys. Law enforcement isn't a zero-sum game: both criminals and victims can benefit from less punishment.[2]

So there's the question: How can we have less crime with less punishment? The first thing to notice is that low-crime is an equilibrium state: if nobody is committing any crimes, all anti-crime resources can be focused on anyone who decides to break the law, making it irrational for them to even try. But high-crime is also an equilibrium (assuming reasonable levels of punishment): if everyone is breaking the law, the police can't possibly stop all of them, so it's not so risky to keep on breaking the law.

To reduce both crime and punishment, you just need to tip the society from one equilibrium to the other. And, Kleiman argues, we can do that with a technique he calls "dynamic concentration." Imagine there are three robbers (Alice, Bob, and Carol) and one policeman (Eve). Eve can only stop one robber at a crime, so if more than one person is committing a burglary at the same time, she decides to be fair and switch around who she arrests — sometimes she nabs Alice, sometimes Bob, sometimes Carol.

The problem is that the robbers know this and they know it means they only have a 1/3 chance of getting caught. A guaranteed arrest is bad news, but a 1/3 chance of getting arrested isn't worth quitting over. So the robbers keep on robbing and the cop keeps failing to keep up with them.

But now imagine Eve adopts a new policy: dynamic concentration. Instead of randomly deciding who to go after, she goes after people in alphabetical order. So if Alice is committing a crime, Eve always goes after her first if she's committing a crime — otherwise Bob, and then Carol. Now Alice knows that if she robs someone, she's guaranteed to get caught (instead of just having a one-third chance), so she decides to sit this one out. You might think this would just lead Bob to step into the breach, but now that Alice is out, Eve can turn her focus to Bob instead. So Bob also decides to call it quits. That just leaves Carol, who Eve now gets to watch like a hawk, and so Carol also gives up the game. And there you have it: dynamic concentration stops all the crime without adding any more police.

Obviously things aren't so clean in the real world, but I think this is the first game-theoretic argument I've read that seems to have some real force. Kleiman backs it up with some messier simulations and some real-life examples. Unfortunately, most are stories about cracking down on drugs or other unserious crimes like squeegee men, but the general point seems to work.

For twenty years, High Point, North Carolina had tried to fight the crack dealing in the city's African-American West End neighborhood. Any viewer of *The Wire* can guess the results: as soon as they made a case against one drug dealer, another would jump in to take his place. So with the help of crime scholar David Kennedy, they tried a new approach. First, they spent months building trust between the police and the community to build consensus that the drug trade was something worth stopping. Then they pushed extra resources into the neighborhood and started putting together cases against the dealers — but didn't make any arrests. Only when they had a case against every known dealer did they act.

Even then they didn't make arrests. They visited the dealer's homes with a neighborhood leader, who told them that the neighborhood had decided they had to go straight. Meanwhile a cop presented them with the legal case against them. The pair asked the dealer to quit and offered whatever services — tattoo removal, job training — would help them do that. Ten of the thirteen dealers took them up on the offer, leaving plenty of room for the justice system to lock up the remaining three, plus the one new dealer who tried to take over their old business. Five years later, the market is still closed, and the police have been able to direct their resources to pull the same trick on the other drug markets. Crime is down, and arrests are down too. Dynamic concentration works, with the city's different drug markets standing in for Alice, Carol, and Bob. (The other examples — especially Hawaii's HOPE program — are even more interesting, but take longer to tell.)

Dynamic concentration isn't a panacea. Obviously it only works where the costs of monitoring are much less than the costs of enforcement. But this still leaves lots of opportunities and clever selection of the population to concentrate on can significantly decrease the cost of monitoring.

While the big idea of dynamic concentration is at the center of the book, it's not one of those one-trick monographs where the author lays out one good idea and then spends the rest of the book repeating it. Instead, the book ranges over the whole theory and practice crime control in America and nearly every page is filled with interesting facts and a new perspective.

And in a brilliant final chapter, he turns his lens on himself and asks what could go wrong with his proposals. For an intellectual, the level of humility and self-criticism involved is truly impressive. (He confesses to probably all of the complaints that you're thinking about raising right now.)

For anyone interested in policy analysis, this book should be a classic. It shows how simple tools (calculating the scale of the problem, modeling it with game theory, and calculating the costs of a solution) can have radical implications.

1. Kleiman uses surveys asking people how much they would pay to achieve a ten percent reduction in a crime. Aside from all the usual problems with such willingness-to-pay metrics, this seems like a particularly meaningless question. I don't have a good sense of what the crime rate is, let alone what a 10% decrease in it would look like. I can't possibly assign a sensible monetary value to something so abstract. It'd be better to ask people what they'd pay to prevent one crime, assuming the crime rate is low enough that Karelis-type effects don't come into play.
2. Since a rational criminal would by definition be better off committing the crime, this mainly comes up in cases of information asymmetry. Unlike in playground games of Cops and Robbers, real police are better off warning the criminals away from doing crime than tricking them into doing it and then sneaking up and catching them.

October 18, 2010

THE REAL PROBLEM WITH WAITING FOR 'SUPERMAN'

Waiting for "Superman", in case you haven't heard, is the hot new film from *Inconvenient Truth* director Davis Guggenheim. While his last film capitalized on liberal guilt over destroying our planet (and maybe voting for Ralph Nader?), *"Superman"* (yes, the film is weirdly insistent on those unnecessary quotation marks) is for people who feel bad about sending their kids to private school while poor kids wallow in the slums.

"Teaching should be easy," Guggenheim declares as we watch a cartoon teacher rip open his students' skulls and pour what looks like blue Spaghetti-O's inside. (When he closes the skulls the kids sprout wings and fly out the open classroom window.) This is about as close as the film gets to depicting actual teaching. (I checked with the friend who paid for my ticket and he confirmed this scene was meant seriously, though thankfully not literally.)

Despite repeatedly insisting poor kids just need better teachers, the film never says what it is that better teachers actually do. Instead it highlights the voices of American Express pitchman Geoffrey Canada and Bill Gates, whose obsessions with higher standardized test scores have led their schools to cancel recess and art in favor of more hours of scripted memorization. Why bother with art if teaching is just about filling kids' heads with pre-determined facts?

The real crisis in American education isn't teachers' unions preventing incompetent teachers from getting fired (as awful as that may be), it's the single-minded focus on standardized test scores that underlies everything from Bush's No Child Left Behind to Obama's Race to the Top to the charter schools lionized in the film. Real education is about genuine understanding and the ability to figure things out on your own; not about making sure every 7th grader has memorized all the facts some bureaucrats have put in the 7th grade curriculum.

This would be obvious if the film dared to show real teaching in the schools it lauds. Instead of the rich engagement you imagine from progressive private schools, you find teachers who read from assigned scripts while enforcing a regime of zero-tolerance discipline. They're nightmarish gulags where children's innate creativity is beaten out of them and replaced with martial order. Because standardized behavior is what makes you do well on standardized tests.

Film is the perfect medium for showing what this life is like. Seeing terrified kids up on the big screen, you can't help but empathize with them. So we never see it. Instead, the film hides behind charts and graphs and interviews. "When you see a great teacher, you are seeing a work of art," Geoffrey Canada tells us, but this is something Guggenheim would rather tell than show.

The film has other flaws. It insists all of America's problems would be solved if only poor kids would memorize more: Pittsburgh is falling apart not because of deindustrialization, but because its schools are filled with bad teachers. American inequality isn't caused by decades of Reaganite tax cuts and deregulation, but because of too many failing schools. Our trade deficit isn't a result of structural economic factors but simply because Chinese kids get a better education. Make no mistake, I desperately want every kid to go to a school they love, but it seems far-fetched to claim this would solve all our country's other problems. At the end of the day, we have an economy that works for the rich by cheating the poor and unequal schools are the result of that, not the cause.

I'm glad a talented filmmaker has decided to draw attention to the horrible inequities in our nation's schools. But I'm terrified that the solutions put forth by its proponents will only make things worse. We know what happens when we fire teachers who don't do enough to raise their students' test scores, or when we adopt more stringent requirements for classroom curriculum: we squeeze out what little genuine education these schools have left. And that's something we should really feel guilty about.

October 8, 2010

GOODS, SERVICES, AND DELEGATIONS

Things you can buy are typically divided into tangible things (goods) and intangible actions (services). But recently I've realized there's a much more interesting type of thing to buy: delegations.

A delegation is like a service, except instead of asking someone to do a specific thing, you ask them to achieve some goal. Hiring someone to paint your wall white would be a service, hiring someone to make your house pretty is a delegation.

Delegations are a *lot* harder than services. In the same way you can be pretty sure that when you buy a pen it will write, you can be pretty sure that when you hire someone to paint your wall white, she'll actually do it. And if she doesn't, you can just not pay her.

But if you want to hire an interior designer, it's a mess. Let's say you pick one by looking through their portfolio and concluding that you like their work. But when they come to design your place, you hate the result. What can you do? You say that what you got looks nothing like the stuff in the portfolio and they'll just say that every space is different and so has a different result. There's no way to ever prove they did a bad job.

And that's something fairly inconsequential. Imagine you're wrongly charged with murder[1] or stricken with a potentially-fatal illness. Picking the right lawyer or doctor could make the difference between life and death.

But now there's not even a portfolio for you to look at. Sure, you can see if the lawyer's won a lot of cases or if the doctor's kept most of her patients alive, but that doesn't tell you much — it probably just means they're either very lucky or mostly choose easy cases.

Perhaps instead of looking at outcomes, you could look at the decisions they made along the way. But even if you could get your hands on those records, how could you possibly learn enough about law or medicine to evaluate them? And even if you somehow tried, there's probably all sorts of relevant specific details about the circumstances that could never make it into even the most detailed histories.

But it's not just hard for the delegator — for the same reason, it's hard for the delegatee. If you want to be great at painting walls white, it's easy to get pretty immediate feedback about whether you did the job correctly. But if you're a elementary school teacher, you'll really just never know. You hope you're helping your kids succeed in life, but there's no way for you to check that. And what are the chances that you started doing everything right just by intuition?

No, the expert performance movement has shown the only way to get really good at something is to practice, continually comparing what you did against the results it achieved. But in any sort of delegated job this is practically impossible: the uncertainties are too great, the feedback loops take too long, the opportunities to practice much too rare.

Traditionally, we solve these problems by having an academic discipline figure out the right thing to do using scale. If doctors were just on their own, they'd still be no better than witch doctors: people would come in with problems and they'd pick a random herb or spell to try and pray it made the patient feel better. They'd never really know whether they were helping or hurting. But they're not on their own: because medical schools can conduct randomized trials with hundreds of people, they can just read the results and learn what actually works.

A lot is still left to individual judgment — there's not a medical study for every scenario and even if there was, you'd still have to choose how to interpret the results — but there is definitely a trend toward knowing more. And some of the most exciting developments in medicine come from replacing human judgment with checklists and decision trees.

But medicine is probably the best-case scenario. I've never heard of lawyers reading up on the results of statistical trials[2] and aesthetics is so subjective and fashion so temporary that I doubt anything like this could ever be possible for interior designers. (Education is probably somewhere in the middle.) How do people ever get good at these things?

Part of why running a nonprofit is so hard is that pretty much all nonprofits are delegation. Donors aren't buying a particular thing they know they want, they're buying a chance to help others, without knowing exactly what it is *they* want. And that's why randomized controlled trials[3] have been transformational for the nonprofit sector — they've converted a delegation into a service. Great nonprofits[4] don't have to guess at what will help people the most; they just need to look up the most helpful service and then purchase more of it.

Poor Economics[5] is a remarkable book if only because it shows how crucial this is. It's full of tales of small-scale experiments where well-intentioned do-gooders try hard to help some people and fail catastrophically. But they only notice because there are academics there collecting data; in the typical nonprofit, where the decisionmakers are far removed from the evidence on the ground, they'd probably never know that much was going wrong (assuming that they even cared[6]).

But "political" nonprofits don't get off so easily. It's fairly impractical to do randomized controlled trials of things like lobbying, public campaigning, white papers, investigative journalism, public relations, strategic litigation, electoral campaigns, and the rest. There are brave and noble efforts[7] to try to improve some of the details most amenable to testing, but while you can test which direct mail flyer makes people more likely to vote, it's hard to test whether GOTV mail is a good use of campaign funds at all.

Now you can get a lot out of combining all these things[8] so you can make big-picture decisions about how to allocate resources. And you can get a lot out of having the same team do them over and over so they can build up institutional expertise. But there's also a lot of room for learning within each one as well. Just as randomized controlled trials have revolutionized development nonprofits, I think political nonprofits will be revolutionized by developing institutional structures to formalize the process of learning from campaigns.

What would this look like? A good first step would be developing a series of case studies of major campaigns, successful or unsuccessful, to get some sense of big picture stories. From this, you could distill a toolbook of various tactics, with some notes on which seem to be more and less effective and some open questions or avenues of exploration for each. Then within each tactic, you could bring together practitioners to swap best practices and try to improve the state of the art.

Interviewing people right after campaigns also seems like a fruitful avenue. As they look back on what happened, what do they see as the big mistakes? The big successes? What do they wish they'd had?

These might all seem like minor, parochial concerns, but when you stop to realize that the world is full of huge problems that can only be solved by collective action, figuring out how to inspire coordinated action most effectively doesn't just seem interesting — it seems essential.

July 18, 2011

1. http://www.newyorker.com/reporting/2009/09/07/090907fa_fact_grann
2. http://blogs.discovermagazine.com/notrocketscience/2011/04/11/justice-is-served-but-more-so-after-lunch-how-food-breaks-sway-the-decisions-of-judges/
3. http://www.povertyactionlab.org/about-j-pal
4. http://www.givewell.org/
5. http://pooreconomics.com/
6. http://byliner.com/originals/three-cups-of-deceit
7. http://www.nytimes.com/2010/10/31/magazine/31politics-t.

PROFESSIONAL POLITICIANS BEWARE!

The government of a republic, James Madison wrote in Federalist No.39 (Conformity of the Plan to Republican Principles, 1788), must "be derived from the great body of the society, not from an inconsiderable proportion, or a favored class of it; otherwise a handful of tyrannical nobles, exercising their oppressions by a delegation of their powers, might aspire to the rank of republicans, and claim for their government the honorable title of republic."

Looking at our government today — a House of professional politicians, a Senate filled with multimillionaires, a string of presidential family dynasties — it seems hard to maintain that our officials are in fact "derived from the great body of the society" and not "a favored class" merely posing as representatives of the people.

Unless politics is a tradition in your family, your odds of getting elected to federal office are slim. And unless you're a white male lawyer, you rarely get to vote for someone like yourself in a national race. Nor, in reality, do we have an opportunity to choose policy positions: no major candidates support important proposals that most voters agree with, like single-payer health care.

Instead, national elections have been boiled down to simple binary choices, which advertising men and public relations teams reduce to pure emotions: Fear. (A bear prowls through the woods.) Hope. (The sun rises over a hill.) Vote Smith. Or maybe Jones.

Nor does the major media elevate the level of debate. Instead of substantive discussions about policy proposals and their effects, they spend their time on horse-race coverage (who's raised the most money? who's polling well in Ohio?) and petty scandals (how much did that haircut cost? was someone somewhere offended by that remark?)

The result after all this dumbing down? In 2004, voters who said they chose a presidential candidate based on the candidate's agendas, ideas, platforms, or goals comprised a whopping 10% of the electorate. So it's not too surprising when political scientists find that voters' decisions can be explained by such random factors as whether they like red or blue, whether the economy is good or bad, or whether the current party has been in office for long or not.

Aside from the occasional telephone poll, the opinions of "the great body of the society" have been edited out of the picture. Way back in Federalist No. 10 (The Utility of the Union as a Safeguard Against Domestic Faction and Insurrection (continued), 1787), Madison put his finger on the reason. "However small the republic may be," he noted, "the representatives must be raised to a certain number, in order to guard against the cabals of a few." But similarly, "however large it may be, they must be limited to a certain number, in order to guard against the confusion of a multitude."

The result is that the population grows while the number of representatives stays fixed, leaving each politician to represent more and more people. The first Congress had a House of 65 members representing 40,000 voters and three million citizens (they had a whopping 1.3% voter turnout back then). That's a representative for around every 600 voters or 46,000 citizens (the size of the average baseball stadium). A baseball stadium may be a bit of an unruly mob, but it's not unimaginably large.

Today, by contrast, we have 435 representatives and 300 million citizens — one for roughly every 700,000 citizens. There isn't a stadium in the world big enough to hold that many people. It's a number more akin to a television audience (it's about how many people tune in to watch Keith Olbermann each night).

Which is exactly what the modern constituency has become: the TV audience following along at home. Even if you wanted to, you can't have a real conversation with a TV audience. It is too big to convey a sense of what each individual is thinking. Instead of a group to represent, it's a mob to be managed.

I agree with Madison that there is roughly a right size for a group of representatives "on both sides of which inconveniences will be found to lie. By enlarging too much the number of electors, you render the representatives too little acquainted with all their local circumstances and lesser interests; as by reducing it too much, you render him unduly attached to these, and too little fit to comprehend and pursue great and national objects."

But what Madison missed is that there is no similar limit on the number of such groups. To take a technological analogy, the Internet is, at bottom, an enormous collection of wires. Yet nobody would ever think of it this way. Instead, we group the wires into chips and the chips into computers and the computers into networks and the networks into the Internet. And people only deal with things at each level: when the computer breaks, we can't identify which wire failed; we take the whole thing into the shop.

One of the most compelling visions for rebooting democracy adopts this system of abstraction for politics. Parpolity, developed by the political scientist Stephen Shalom, would build a legislature out of a hierarchical series of nested councils. Agreeing with Madison, he says each council should be small enough that everyone can engage in face-to-face discussion but large enough that there is a diversity of opinion and the number of councils is minimized. He estimates the right size is 25 to 50 people.

So, to begin with, let us imagine a council of you and your 40 closest neighbors — perhaps the other people in your apartment building or on your block. You get together every so often to discuss the issues that concern you and your neighborhood. And you may vote to set policy for the area which the council covers.

But your council has another function: it selects one of its own to send as a representative to the next council up. There the process repeats itself: the representative from your block and its 40 closest neighbors meet every so often to discuss the political issues that concern the area. And, of course, your representative reports back to the group, gets your recommendations on difficult questions, and takes suggestions for issues to raise at the next area council meeting.

By the power of exponents, just five levels of councils, each consisting of only fifty people, is enough to cover over three hundred million people. But — and this is the truly clever bit — at the area council the whole process repeats itself. Just as each block council nominates a representative to the area council, each area council nominates a representative to the city council, and each city council to the state council, each state council to the national council, and so on.

Shalom discusses a number of further details — provisions for voting, recalls, and delegation — but it's the idea of nesting that's key. Under such a system, there are only four representatives who stand between you and the people setting national policy, each of whom is forced to account to their constituents in regular, small face-to-face meetings. Politicians in such a system could not be elected through empty appeals to mass emotions. Instead, they would have to sit down, face-to-face, with a council of their peers and persuade them that they are best suited to represent their interests and positions.

There is something rather old-fashioned about this notion of sitting down with one's fellow citizens and rationally discussing the issues of the day. But there is also something exciting and new about it. In the same way that blogs have given everyone a chance to be a publisher, Wikipedia lets everyone be an encyclopedia author, and YouTube lets anyone be a television producer, Parpolity would let everyone be a politician.

The Internet has shown us that the pool of people with talent far outnumbers the few with the background, connections, and wealth to get to a place in society where they can practice their talents professionally. (It also shows us that many people with those connections aren't particularly talented.)

The democratic power of the Net means you don't need connections to succeed. In a world where kids can be television stars just by finding a video camera and an Internet connection, citizens may begin to wonder why getting into politics is so much harder.

For many years, politicians had a ready excuse: politics was a difficult job, which required carefully weighing and evaluating evidence and making difficult decisions. Only a select few could be trusted to perform it; the vast majority of the population was woefully underqualified.

And perhaps in the era of a cozy relationship between politicians and the press, this illusion could be sustained. But as netroots activists and blogs push our national conversation ever closer to the real world, this excuse is becoming laughable. After all, these men and women of supposedly sober judgment voted overwhelmingly for disasters like the Iraq War. "No one could have ever predicted this," TV's talking heads all insist. No one, that is, except the great body of society, whose insistence that Iraq did not pose a threat and that an occupation would be long and brutal went ignored.

New online tools for interaction and collaboration have let people come together across space and time to build amazing things. As the Internet breaks down the last justifications for a professional class of politicians, it also builds up the tools for replacing them. For the most part, their efforts have so far been focused on education and entertainment, but it's only a matter of time before they turn to politics. And when they do, professional politicians beware!

April 18, 2012

AMERICA AFTER MERITOCRACY
CHRIS HAYES' THE TWILIGHT OF THE ELITES

In his new book, *The Twilight of the Elites: America After Meritocracy*, Chris Hayes manages the impossible trifecta: the book is compellingly readable, impossibly erudite, and — most stunningly of all — correct. At the end, I was left with just two quibbles: first, the book's chapter on "pop epistemology" thoroughly explicated how elites got stuff wrong without bothering to mention the non-elites who got things right, leaving the reader with the all-too-common impression that getting it right was impossible; and second, the book never assembled its (surprisingly sophisticated) argument into a single summary. To discuss it, I feel we have to start with remedying the latter flaw:

Our nation's institutions have crumbled, Hayes argues. From 2000–2010 (the "Fail Decade"), every major societal institution failed. Big businesses collapsed with Enron and Worldcom, their auditors failed to catch it, the Supreme Court got partisan in *Bush v. Gore*, our intelligence apparatus failed to catch 9/11, the media lied us into wars, the military failed to win them, professional sports was all on steroids, the church engaged in and covered up sex abuse, the government compounded disaster upon disaster in Katrina, and the banks crashed our economy. How did it all go so wrong?

Hayes pins the blame on an unlikely suspect: meritocracy. We thought we would just simply pick out the best and raise them to the top, but once they got there they inevitably used their privilege to entrench themselves and their kids (inequality is, Hayes says, "autocatalytic"). Opening up the elite to more efficient competition didn't make things more fair, it just legitimated a more intense scramble. The result was an arms race among the elite, pushing all of them to embrace the most unscrupulous forms of cheating and fraud to secure their coveted positions. As competition takes over at the high end, personal worth resolves into exchange value, and the elite power accumulated in one sector can be traded for elite power in another: a regulator can become a bank VP, a modern TV host can use their stardom to become a bestselling author (try to imagine Edward R. Murrow using the nightly news to flog his books the way Bill O'Reilly does). This creates a unitary elite, detached from the bulk of society, yet at the same time even more insecure. You can never reach the pinnacle of the elite in this new world; even if you have the most successful TV show, are you also making blockbuster movies? bestselling books? winning Nobel Prizes? When your peers are the elite at large, you can never clearly best them.

The result is that our elites are trapped in a bubble, where the usual pointers toward accuracy (unanimity, proximity, good faith) only lead them astray. And their distance from the way the rest of the country really lives makes it impossible for them to do their jobs justly — they just don't get the necessary feedback. The only cure is to reduce economic inequality, a view that has surprisingly support among the population (clear majorities want to close the deficit by raising taxes on the rich, which is more than can be said for any other plan). And while Hayes is not a fan of heightening the contradictions, it is possible that the next crisis will bring with it the opportunity to win this change.

This is just a skeletal summary — the book itself is filled with luscious texture to demonstrate each point and more in-depth discussion of the mechanics of each mechanism (I would call it Elster meets Gladwell if I thought that would be taken as praise). So buy the book already[1]. Now, as I said, I think Hayes is broadly correct in his analysis. And I think his proposed solution is spot on as well — when we were fellows together at the Harvard Center for Ethics, I think we annoyed everyone else with our repeated insistence that reducing economic inequality was somehow always the appropriate solution to each of the many social ills the group identified.

But when talking to other elites about this proposal, I notice a confusion that's worth clarifying, about the *structural* results of inequality, rather than the merely quantitative ones. Class hangs over the book like a haunting spectre (there's a brief comment on p. 148 that "Mills [had] a more nuanced theory of elite power than Marx's concept of a ruling class") but I think it's hard to see how the solution relates to the problem without it. After all, we started by claiming the problem is meritocracy, but somehow the solution is taxing the rich?

The clue comes in thinking clearly about the alternative to meritocracy. It's not picking surgeons by lottery, Hayes clarifies, but then what is it? It's about ameliorating power relationships altogether. Meritocracy says "there must be one who rules, so let it be the best"; egalitarianism responds "why must there?" It's the power imbalance, rather than inequality itself, that's the problem.

Imagine a sci-fi world in which productivity has reached such impressive heights that everyone can have every good they desire just from the work young kids do for fun. By twiddling the knobs on their local MakerBot, the kids produce enough food, clothing, and iPhones to satisfy everyone. So instead of working, most people spend their days doing yoga or fishing. But scarcity hasn't completely faded away — there's still competition for the best spots at the fishing hole. So we continue to let those be allocated by the market: the fishing hole spot is charged for and the people who really want it earn the money to pay for it by helping people with various chores.

In this sort of world, inequality doesn't seem like much of a problem. Sure, some people get the best fishing hole spots, but that's because they did the most chores. If you want the spot more than they do, you can do more work. But the inequality doesn't come with power — the guy with the best fishing hole spot can't say "fuck me or you're fired"[2].

This sci-fi world may sound ridiculous, but it's basically the one Keynes predicted[3] we'd soon be living in:

> Now it is true that the needs of human beings may seem to be insatiable. But they fall into two classes – those needs which are absolute in the sense that we feel them whatever the situation of our fellow human beings may be, and those which are relative in the sense that we feel them only if their satisfaction lifts us above, makes us feel superior to, our fellows. Needs of the second class, those which satisfy the desire for superiority, may indeed be insatiable; for the higher the general level, the higher still are they. But this is not so true of the absolute needs – a point may soon be reached, much sooner perhaps than we are all of us aware of, when these needs are satisfied in the sense that we prefer to devote our further energies to non-economic purposes.
>
> [...] But, of course, it will all happen gradually, not as a catastrophe. Indeed, it has already begun. The course of affairs will simply be that there will be ever larger and larger classes and groups of people from whom problems of economic necessity have been practically removed.

And that's what a reduction in economic inequality could achieve. The trend in recent decades (since the fall of the Soviet Union and the ruling class's relief that "There Is No Alternative") has been for the people at the top to seize all the economic gains, leaving everyone else increasing insecure and dependent on their largesse. (Calling themselves "job creators", on this view, is not so much a brag as a threat.) But with less inequality, it could be otherwise. Instead of a world in which there are a handful of big networks with the money to run television shows, everyone could afford to have their Sunday morning conversations[4] filmed and livestreamed. Instead of only huge conglomerates having the capital and distribution to launch new product lines, everyone could make and market their own line of underwear[5] or video games (instead of just elite Red Sox pitchers[6]).

Even on strict efficiency grounds, this strikes me as a more alluring view than the usual meritocracy. Why put all your eggs in one basket, even if it's the best basket? Surely you'd get better results by giving more baskets a try.

You can argue that this is exactly where technology is bringing us — popular kids on YouTube get made into huge pop sensations, right? — and the genius of Hayes' book is to show us why this is not enough. The egaliatarian demand shouldn't be that we need more black pop stars or female pop stars or YouTube sensation pop stars, but to question why we need elite superstars at all. I hope Hayes' next book shows us what the world without them is like.

1. http://www.chrishayes.org/about/bio/
2. http://crookedtimber.org/2012/06/11/lizardbreath-meet-charter-cities/
3. http://www.marxists.org/reference/subject/economics/keynes/1930/our-grandchildren.htm
4. http://up.msnbc.com/
5. http://blogs.reuters.com/felix-salmon/2012/04/26/kickstarter-of-the-day-flint-and-tinder-edition/
6. http://www.slate.com/articles/business/moneybox/2012/06/_38_studios_and_kingdoms_of_amalur_how_curt_schilling_s_video_game_company_duped_rhode_island_out_of_75_million_.html

THINKING CLEARLY ABOUT PIECE-WORK

My friend Jonathan Zittrain has been working on a book about how the return of piece-work will destroy America. As someone who kind of misses piece-work, it made me want to think through the issues involved.

Because, in the real world, competition is imperfect, when a company sells something it earns a surplus. That surplus then must be divided between capital and labor, or more concretely, the company and the employee. The terms of distribution are determined by the employment agreement (i.e. how much the employee will get paid).

If labor has all the power, it will want almost all of the surplus, so it'd demand an employee agreement where it gets paid a big chunk per good produced — this is basically piece-work. If capital has all the power, it will want to pay employees barely enough to stay alive and be able to show up for work — this is basically wages. So, to a first approximation, wages are what you get when capital is in charge and piece-work is what you get when labor is in charge.

But there are some additional considerations. The transaction costs for capital are relatively low — you can invest in a whole bunch of companies at a time, whereas you can really only do a couple jobs at a time (or usually just one) and it's quite painful to find another one. So employees also want insurance — they want to guarantee they'll keep getting paid even when the market for the stuff they produce declines. Again, we can imagine two extremes: if labor is in charge, it'll want a job for life, where getting downsized is inconceivable; if capital is in charge, it'll want to employ people for exactly as long as their marginal product is profitable — which means staffing up in booms and downsizing freely in busts (and not just business cycle booms and busts — companies want to hire lots of temporary workers for Christmas, for example).

Now obviously a job for life doesn't make a ton of sense in a piece-work world. If AT&T has guaranteed you a job for life with steady wages, then it makes sense for it to invest in retraining you for some different part of the business when mechanical telephone switches get replaced by computer servers. It's less clear how this would work in a piece-work deal. But the fact is there's no reason the insurance part should be tied to the wages. In Denmark, for example, if your job disappears the government simply pays you 90% of your old salary until you find a new one (up to some cap, of course). There's no reason piece-work can't coexist with this kind of social insurance system, which would seem to be the choice of our all-powerful labor.

But that's treating labor as a monolithic entity. The third thing wages do is collapse differences in pay between workers. For example, it's well established that programmer productivity varies by an order of magnitude — the best programmers at a company can be ten times as productive as the worst programmers — but I've never heard of a company where programmer pay varies by anywhere near that much. Really great programmers might be paid double or perhaps even triple the worst programmers, but I've never heard of anything close to a 10x difference.

The one place where you do see these really huge differences is in CEO pay, but even this isn't really a counterexample since CEO is a job with no intra-company reference class. That is, it's not like companies will have one CEO getting paid $1.2M and a another getting paid $12M (indeed, I'd guess companies with co-CEOs find them getting paid the same amount) — instead, the order-of-magnitude differences are all found across companies.

But order-of-magnitude differences are totally possible with piece-work, especially the kind of intellectual piece-work that Zittrain is concerned with. Krugman has bragged that he "writes faster than anyone in journalism" and it's quite possible to imagine him turning out columns in a tenth the time of Barbara Ehrenreich (who turned down the NYT op-ed columnist job because it was too time-consuming). So wages might be a way of quietly redistributing money from the speedy Krugmans to the dawdling Ehrenreichs. But just as with social insurance, you can imagine this role being taken up by the government instead: through progressive taxation.

Now according to classic economic theory, these changes wouldn't just be details of style, but would increase the size of the overall pie. And, on the squishy side, they'd provide much greater scope for human freedom. Assuming I was guaranteed a decent wage either way, I'd far rather be able to stay up late working one night in exchange for blowing off work the next. Not to mention getting to work the hours I want, from the place I want, in the way I want, etc.

Now the practical fact is that most jobs don't have a concrete enough product to be amenable to piece-work. They're a mixture of all sorts of different tasks, require interaction with a specific group of other people, and have all sorts of other features that kind of force them to be your usual office job. But none of that applies to Zittrain — he's talking about jobs that are *already* piece-work and arguing that they shouldn't be. But it seems to me like, if you're on the side of labor, your preferred solution should be more social insurance and progressive taxation instead.

July 5, 2012

IS AWKWARDNESS AVOIDABLE?

In his brilliant book *Awkwardness*, Adam Kotsko analyzes the US version of the television show *The Office*, concluding it, unlike its British counterpart, shies away from the emancipatory potential of awkwardness by concluding it's ultimately the result of inherently awkward individuals.

As his key example, he cites the arc of Charles Miner (*The Wire*'s Idris Elba), a high-powered Dunder Mifflin executive who visits the Scranton branch for a short while as part of his attempts to improve northeast sales. Miner's arrival forces Jim into a series of awkward comic mishaps, thus suggesting Jim's normal level of cool isn't just because he's a naturally cool person but only because he's particularly well-suited to his normal situation. But Miner ultimately reveals himself to be overly aggressive, thereby, Kotsko argues, showing Jim's awkwardness was merely a result of Miner being a fundamentally awkward person and thus withdrawing the tentative suggestion that awkwardness might actually be situational.

I think this is a misreading that shows the limits of a theory of awkwardness that lacks a notion of competence. For this arc shows precisely the opposite of what Kotsko says it does: it shows that awkwardness is fundamentally situational.

Miner's addition to the series marks the rare appearance of a character that is more competent than Jim. However much Jim may feel himself above the petty stressors of the Scranton office, Miner is far above that, executing with a similar level of suave at a much higher rung in the organization. When Jim comes face-to-face with a superior talent, it immediately reduces him to the level of gibbering awkwardness his coworkers are always finding themselves in, thereby demonstrating Jim's level of comfort isn't an innate character trait, but simply the result of being well-adapted to his absurd environment.

The reveal of Miner's aggression is not an undercutting but an emphasis of this theme. How did Miner get to be so cool? Was he just born with even more innate coolness than Jim and thus is able to be awkward in fewer situations? On the contrary, this coda reveals. Miner got to where he is through an aggressive ambition. His relentless striving has forced him to be competent in more and more business situations so he can move up the corporate ladder.

The Office operates under a sort of Peter Principle[1] of awkwardness. The Peter Principle says employees are promoted to the level of their incompetence (since as long as they remain competent, they keep getting promoted). *The Office* demonstrates that being incompetent is awkward, so people are thereby promoted to the level of their awkwardness. Thus Michael Scott (Steve Carrell), who is actually a quite talented and thoroughly comfortable salesman, gets promoted to regional manager, where he is an awkward and incompetent dolt. We can only assume that Miner is normally at the level of his awkwardness as well; he only seems cool when slumming it in Scranton, the same way that Jim only gets to seem cool by being unambitious enough to persist in a job he is obviously too good for. It is our ambition that makes us awkward, the show argues.

This is emphasized in the later plot where David Wallace (Andy Buckley), who appears as a confident corporate CFO in earlier seasons, gets made redundant in Dunder Mifflin's acquisition by Sabre and is forced to retire to his suburban mansion with his generous severance package. Without a corporate ladder to climb but with his ambition intact, he now finds himself working on a startup (producing a vacuum for children's toys called "Suck It"). But his competence as an upper executive is worthless as a startup founder and makes him so painfully awkward that even Michael can't stomach it. (Later, when Wallace returns to the corporate world, he's immediately unawkward again.)

The clear message is the opposite of Kotsko's reading: we are all awkward when we're out of our depth; our only escape from awkwardness is to develop a competence for a particular situation. But even that is short-lived: our ambition will drive us to leave such non-awkward comforts for the next challenge — and even if we don't, the vagaries of economic forces may still push us into a role we are ill-suited for. The only refuge from this pervasive awkwardness is the pervasive boredom of unambition.

P.S. Kotsko's followup, *Why We Love Sociopaths* is even better.

July 23, 2012

1.   https://en.wikipedia.org/wiki/Peter_Principle

WHAT HAPPENS IN BATMAN BEGINS

Warning: Naturally, spoilers follow — for both Batman Begins *and* The Dark Knight Rises.[1]

We begin in the 1980s, when the global forces of evil have decided to institute a new economic policy on the world. Their nefarious plan dramatically exacerbates inequality, making the rich filthy rich while the poor suffer terrible levels of unemployment.

The difference is that in the Batman universe, Gotham's leading billionaire (Thomas Wayne) can't stand the suffering and begins investing in the city when the government won't. He builds a giant Keynesian supertrain in a desperate attempt to get the city back to work. But, in an ironic twist, he ends up murdered by one of the desperate poverty-stricken citizens he's trying so hard to help.

The murder of the billionaire shocks the surviving billionaires, leading them to reverse their neoliberal policies. Instead of getting tough on crime, they decide to indulge criminals, with a deep willingness to treat criminality as merely a mental health problem.

As the billionaires retreat from power, organized crime steps in, taking their place in buying off judges and unions and cops. Instead of being run by Wayne Enterprises, the city ends up being run by mob boss Carmine Falcone.

But a few rogue elements in the police and DA's office refuse to be bought off. They free the man who murdered Thomas Wayne in exchange for his testimony against Falcone. Bruce Wayne, the billionaire's son, is so haunted by his personal demons that he can't stand this trade-off. When his childhood-friend-turned-rogue-ADA points out the selfishness of his position, he confronts Falcone. When Falcone explains that Bruce will always live in fear of what he does not understand, Bruce sets off on a quest to understand criminals.

His search concludes in a far eastern terrorist training camp, which turns out to be backed by the same global forces of evil that invented neoliberalism. It's the year 2000 and they have a new plan: attacking Gotham with the hope of inspiring enough fear that the city will destroy itself.[2]

Bruce, still haunted by the execution of his parents, refuses to become an executioner himself and, instead of joining the plot, sets fire to the camp before returning to clean up Gotham his own way. He begins by putting together a case against Falcone and re-seizing control of Wayne Enterprises by buying up its shares on the public market.

In doing so, he begins a reversal of history that eventually culminates in The Dark Knight Rises. His attack on Falcone leads to a new era of tough-on-crime, which dethrones the organized criminals and allows the wealthy to seize power again. The wealthy quickly reinstitute neoliberalism and buy back Bruce's shares on the public market, putting Wayne Enterprises back in their hands. But the global forces of evil step in once again to "restore balance" by letting Bane to release the organized criminals.[3] Bruce Wayne goes back to being an innocent child of privilege and the trilogy ends exactly where it started.[4]

August 22, 2012

1. Batman Begins is very clearly the mirror image of The Dark Knight Rises (some scenes are almost word-for-word the same), so understanding one can help us understand the other.
2. Yes, in this trilogy 9/11 really was an inside job, from the same folks who brought you Reaganomics.
3. Democrats, Republicans, organized crime, or billionaire financiers — whoever tries to seize power, the global forces of evil continue to hold the reins from behind-the-scenes, making sure nobody changes the system too much.
4. Exactly, right down to how Robin (who see as a small boy in the first film, the same way we see Bruce in flashbacks) ends the film frustrated by the system (the same way Bruce was frustrated by Rachel) and is about to head out in a quest of his own, following the same path Bruce Wayne took. Thus the cycle continues.

WHAT HAPPENS IN THE DARK KNIGHT

Spoilers, obviously.

As we've discussed, in *Batman Begins*[1] 1960s-style full employment and antipoverty programs lead to skyrocketing crime while in *The Dark Knight Rises* 1980s-style tough-on-crime policies and neoliberal economics lead to a revolt of the economic underclass. The films are mirror images, one about the failure of liberal policies; the other about the failure of conservative policies. In this sense, The Dark Knight is truly the final film in this nihilistic trilogy, documenting the hopelessness of anything outside that usual left-right struggle.

From the start, the city is torn about how to handle the Batman, who has inspired a wave of second-rate imitators. Some believe it's wrong to be idolizing a masked vigilante, but most (including the new DA, Harvey Dent) approve of his results.

Dent is doing his own part to lock up the criminals, working inside the system. He's arrested all the mob bankers (except Lau) and is now going after the gangsters themselves, starting with mob boss Maroni (who took over for mob boss Falcone). But while the prosecutions bring him a great deal of political attention, they don't seem to achieve much in the way of concrete results — new gangsters spring up to take the place of whoever Dent arrests.

Dent decides the only way to win is to go big — really big. He arrests everyone at once, on charges that are unlikely to stick. Dent doesn't care that he's breaking the rules, as long as it solves the problem. He cites the Romans who suspended democracy to protect their city. (Although, as Rachel points out, they ended up losing democracy.) "You either die a hero or you live long enough to see yourself become the villain," Dent explains. He hopes to take up Batman's mantle, but do it from inside the system.

But, as the mayor explains, Dent isn't just taking on his own sense of ethics, he's taking on the entire system: "the mob, politicians, journalists, cops — anyone whose wallet's about to get lighter". If he fails, both of their careers are over.

Just as Dent is frustrated with the justice system, the Joker is frustrated with the criminals. He tells them they need to go big: they need to kill the Batman. He offers to do it for a sizable sum of money, which the gangsters eventually agree to. The Joker is obsessed with the *homo economicus* of game theory (from whence his name?): when the gangsters ask why he needs the money to kill the Batman, he explains "Like my mother used to tell me: if you're good at something, never do it for free."

The film opens with the Joker hiring five men to rob a mob bank: Dopey silences the alarm, Happy shoots him and drills through the vault, Grumpy shoots him and empties the cash into duffel bags, a bus runs him over, Bozo shoots the bus driver. Finally, Bozo pulls off his mask to reveal he's the Joker. This is a classic pirate game and, just as in the theory, the Joker gets to keep almost all the cash.

Batman eventually tries to track down the Joker by threatening the gangster Maroni.

But it's no use, as Maroni explains: "No one's gonna tell you anything — they're wise to your act — you got rules. The Joker, he's got no rules. No one's gonna cross him for you." This is a straightforward application of game theory's Davies-Folk theorem: the rational thing is to seem irrational so your opponents can't count on you doing the rational thing.

Alfred sees this quickly, because it reminds him of a story from his own past:

I was in Burma. A long time ago. My friends and I were working for the local government. They were trying to buy the loyalty of tribal leaders, bribing them with precious stones. But their caravans were being raided in a forest north of Rangoon by a bandit. We were asked to take care of the problem, so we started looking for the stones. But after six months, we couldn't find anyone who had traded with him. … One day I found a child playing with a ruby as big as a tangerine. … The bandit had been throwing the stones away. … Some men just want to watch the world burn.

Note the parallels. In Alfred's story the entire status quo (including the local government and tribal leaders) is totally corrupt: *the official plan* is to bribe people. But the plan is defeated by someone even crazier, someone willing to steal the money but not interested in keeping it for himself.

Sure enough, when the Joker finally does get his hands on the money, he merely lights it on fire.

Meanwhile, Dent's ethical compromises begin to grow and grow. When he kidnaps one of the Joker's thugs, he tries to threaten information out of him. This is something Batman does routinely, but Batman reminds Dent that Dent can't get away with that sort of thing — it'd destroy his credibility as an insider.

In a climactic scene, the Batman finally confronts the Joker in the middle of the street. The Joker knows Batman lives by just one rule ("I will not be an executioner") and encourages him to break it and kill him. But Batman can't bring himself to do it, he swerves at a key moment and ends up smashed while the Joker survives. (Yep: the Joker has just won the game of chicken.)

When he comes to, the Joker tells Batman that despite nominally working outside the system, he's actually just the system's pawn:

To them you're a freak like me. They just need you right now. … But as soon as they don't, they'll cast you out like a leper. … Their morals, their code… it's a bad joke. Dropped at the first sign of trouble. They're only as good as the world allows them to be. You'll see — I'll show you…

You have these rules. And you think they'll save you. … [But t]he only sensible way to live in this world is without rules.

Gordon arrests the Joker and takes him to the major crimes unit, only to find the Joker claiming Gordon does not actually control the unit — his people actually working for mob boss Maroni. "Does it depress you, Lieutenant, to know how alone you are?" he asks (a classic principal-agent problem[1]).

AARON SWARTZ

The Joker has kidnapped both Dent and Rachel and set them both to blow so that Batman can only rescue one (opportunity cost[2]). Batman goes to rescue Rachel but the Joker has switched their addresses and he actually ends up rescuing Dent[3]. Rachel dies and Dent loses half his face, becoming Two-Face.

Reese, one of Bruce Wayne's employees goes on TV and threatens to reveal the identity of the Batman, but the Joker calls in and asks him to stop. "I had a vision," he says. "Of a world without Batman. The mob ground out a little profit and the police tried to shut them down, one block at a time… and it was so… boring. I've had a change of heart." He threatens to blow up a hospital unless someone kills Reese. (He has thus constructed a trolley problem[4]: people must decide whether it's better to let the 100 die or kill the 1.)

At the hospital, the Joker explains things to Dent:

Do I really look like a guy with a plan, Harvey? I don't have a plan… The mob has plans, the cops have plans. … Maroni has plans. Gordon has plans. Schemers trying to control their worlds. I'm not a schemer, I show the schemers how pathetic their attempts to control things really are.

It's the schemers who put you where you are. You were a schemer. You had plans. Look where it got you. … Nobody panics when the expected people get killed. Nobody panics when things go according to plan, even if the plan is horrifying. If I tell the press that tomorrow a gangbanger will get shot, or a truckload of soldiers will be blown up, nobody panics. Because it's all part of the plan. But when I say that one little old mayor will die, everybody loses their minds! Introduce a little anarchy, you upset the established order and everything becomes chaos. I'm an agent of chaos. And you know the thing about chaos, Harvey? … It's fair.

This pushes Dent over the edge. He starts going after everyone responsible for killing Rachel: He starts with Weurtz, who kidnapped him. Weurtz gives up Maroni, who points to Ramirez, who helps him get Gordon's family, who naturally gets Gordon.

Batman, meanwhile, is also crossing lines. In his attempt to find the Joker, he has turned every cell phone into a spy device. Even he admits this might be too much power for one man to have.

The Joker scares the city onto its two ferries. Once the ferries are in the middle of the water, he cuts their power and gives them both a button to blow up the other ferry, thereby constructing a prisoner's dilemma[5] (one boat is filled with real prisoners). The passengers discuss and vote. One of the prisoners makes a Ulysses pact[6] and credibly commits[7] by tossing the detonator overboard.

The Joker also took a busload of people from the hospital to the Prewitt Building where, through the window, you can see Joker's thugs with guns holding hospital people hostage. Gordon rushes in to get the thugs, but Batman discovers the thugs are hostages and the hostages are the thugs. (The Joker is illustrating "The Market for Lemons"[8]: if the Joker is making it easy for you to kill his henchmen, why should you believe they're actually his henchmen?)

(Batman saves the hostages (dressed as thugs) and stops the SWAT team and takes out the thugs (dressed as hostages). Neither of the boats decides to blow up the other and Batman prevents the Joker from triggering the failsafe.)

He then goes to rescue Gordon, who is trying to stop Dent from killing his family. Dent explains his new philosophy:

> You thought we could be decent men in an indecent time. You thought we could lead by example. You thought the rules could be bent but not break…[9] you were wrong. The world is cruel. And the only morality in a cruel world is chance. Unbiased. Unprejudiced. Fair.

Throughout the film, we've seen various desperate attempts to change the system by ignoring the usual rules: Batman originally thought he could inspire change by being a cultural exemplar, but only ended up causing a bunch of kids to get themselves hurt by dressing up as him. Dent thought he could clean up the system by pushing righteously from the inside, but ended up cutting more and more ethical corners until his own personal obsessions ended up making him a monster. The Joker had by far the most interesting plan: he hoped to out-corrupt the corrupters, to take their place and give the city "a better class of criminal".

And the crazy thing is that it works! At the end of the movie, the Joker is alive, the gangsters and their money launderers are mostly dead, and their money has been redistributed (albeit though the deflationary method of setting it on fire). And, as we see from the beginning of the third movie, this is a fairly stable equilibrium: with politicians no longer living in fear of the gangsters, they're free to adopt tough anti-crime policies that keep them from rising again.[10]

The movie concludes by emphasizing that Batman must become the villain, but as usual it never stops to notice that the Joker is actually the hero. But even though his various games only have one innocent casualty, he's much too crazy to be a viable role model for Batman. His inspired chaos destroys the criminals, but it also terrorizes the population. Thanks to Batman, society doesn't devolve into a self-interested war of all-against-all, as he apparently expects it to, but that doesn't mean anyone enjoys the trials.

Thus Master Wayne is left without solutions. Out of options, it's no wonder the series ends with his staged suicide.

November 1, 2012

1. I'm actually not sure which game this is supposed to be. It's a bit like the poisoned goblets game in The Princess Bride, but I can't find a name for it in the literature.
2. http://en.wikipedia.org/wiki/Principal-agent_problem
3. http://en.wikipedia.org/wiki/Opportunity_cost
4. These two sentences are in the shooting script but got cut from the film version: "You thought we could lead by example. You thought the rules could be bent but not break…"
5. http://en.wikipedia.org/wiki/Trolley_problem

6. http://en.wikipedia.org/wiki/Prisoner's_dilemma
7. http://en.wikipedia.org/wiki/Ulysses_pact
8. http://en.wikipedia.org/wiki/Dynamic_inconsistency
9. http://en.wikipedia.org/wiki/The_Market_for_Lemons
10. This also explains why the law-and-order crowd seems so miffed about succeeding — it wasn't actually their policies that succeeded.

SCIENCE & STUFF

FRAUD IN SCIENCE

It can't happen here. That's what most scientists will tell you about fraud in science. Science is magically self-correcting, fraudsters are isolated incidents, fraud is something that happens in those other professions. Well, they're all wrong, as Horace Freeland Judson shows in his new book *The Great Betrayal: Fraud in Science*. While estimates of fraud — faking evidence, omitting or distorting evidence, and plagiarism — are naturally hard to come by, even very conservative studies place it as high as 10% — a staggering number to those who place their trust in Science.

Judson is at various times a historian, philosopher, sociologist, journalist, and student of science, but he combines all this into a detailed book that combines the best of each field — the journalism is thrilling and readable, the science accurate, the history and social causes analyzed, and so on. Judson seems to know everything about the subject — he's at every major event, he interviews every major figure at their home, and so on. The result is a through book.

The book traces the cultural context of fraud, analyzes the history of fraud (Mendel, Darwin, Pasteur, Freud — all committed fraud to some extent), gives a very detailed description of many modern cases of fraud (including a whole chapter on the famed "Baltimore affair"), then discusses the problems of peer review and authorship, which most people think prevent fraud, then onto the future of science with open access publications on the Internet, and closing with how institutions can respond to end fraud.

Judson paints a picture of a scientific community that is trapped in its own sense of infallibility. Whistleblowers brings evidence fraud to the university president and he (almost always a he) brushes them off saying "it doesn't happen here." And anyway, science is self-correcting. The whistleblower goes public and gets fired — they're inventing a fuss, tarnishing the name of the university. The government's Office of Research Integrity investigates and concludes it is fraud but the case is appealed to a board of lawyers who don't understand the science, are not allowed to look at the scientific evidence, and almost always overturn the case, making specious arguments like "if this data was fraudulent, it wouldn't look so messy". Even in the rare case when fraud is generally conceded, all the usual figures trot out the usual "few bad apples" claim — the rest of science is just fine, they say. When Congress dares hold hearings on the matter, the scientists being questioned rile up their colleagues by claiming that government is attacking scientific freedom.

So, in the end, the whistleblower ends up disgraced and unemployed, usually viciously attacked in public. The fraudster might have to go to another university or even retire early if it's really bad. And the department head who let it happen under him gets no blame and so has no incentive to change things. And so fraud goes on, uninvestigated, unimpeded.

What's the fraud like? A few examples:

- William T. Summerlin (chief of transplantation immunology at Sloan-Kettering) claimed he could transplant onto animals corneas, glands, and skin that would normally be rejected — sometimes even across species. He was discovered only after three years of this when a lab assistant noticed that the black "skin graphs" were drawn on with a marker (all the rest of his work turned out to be fake as well).

- John Long (a resident) studied Hodgkins's cell lines at Mass General in collaboration with MIT. A year later, a junior colleague charge fraud and it was discovered that the cell lines were from monkeys and healthy people.

- Elias A. K. Alsabti (a researcher at Boston University) had published sixty papers by his mid-twenties, when it turned out that most of them were papers published in obscure foreign journals with only slight changes (like a new title).

- Vijay Soman, an assistant professor at Yale, was asked to peer review a paper by Helena Wachslicht-Rodbard. He sent back a negative review, delaying publication, then turned around and submitted the same paper to another journal. He was found out when, in an amazing twist of fate, Helena Wachslicht-Rodbard was asked to peer review Soman's paper and recognized it as her own.

- John Darsee had published dozens of papers with completely made up data — and done an incredibly bad job making up the data. (One paper claimed a father had four children — conceived when he was 8, 9, 11, and 12 years old, respectively.) To cover up this fact, Darsee had practiced "gift authorship" — adding people as co-authors even when they didn't do any work. Darsee had been at Harvard for three years before he was discovered by some postdocs, even then it took the university five months to admit the fraud.

- Stephen Breuning (University of Pittsburgh) studied the long-term effects of certain tranquilizers on mentally ill patients. His research found they were seriously damaging the patients and it causes mental hospitals to change procedures. Two years later, Breuning's mentor at the University of Illinois began to suspect that Breuning couldn't possibly have time to do all the work he claimed to be doing. — and sure enough he made it up. Sparague (the senior of the two, remember) sent a report to the National Institute of Mental Health (NIMH), which funded Breuning. Breuning was forced to resign and NIMH appointed an investigator — who proceed to investigate Sprague. Seeing that Breuning's work was not being investigated and corrected, Sprague went public. His federal funding was cancelled. Sprague was asked to testify before Congress, in response the University of Pittsburgh threatened a libel suit.

That's a small sample — the cases go on and on. Kudos to Judson for shedding light on a topic few know even exists.

March 14, 2005

DAVID M. CLARK
ON COGNITIVE THERAPY

David M. Clark, head of psychology at King's College in the UK, has come to talk to us about anxiety disorders. Unlike the stuff from the normal introductory psychology lectures, Clark seems very smart and science-minded. He's done research developing "cognitive therapy" for anxiety, which means using discussion and experiments to get people to stop feeling anxious, as opposed to drugs or other more "direct" methods.

The specific technique, it turns out, basically involves proving to the patient that their fears are irrational. People who suffer from panic attacks, it turns out, are actually more sensitive to their heart beats than other people. They notice perfectly normal phenomena, like the heart skipping a beat, and interpret it as the beginning of a heart attack, which then of course makes them anxious. They behave in various "safety behaviors", like lying down or breathing deeply, to stave off the heart attack, which of course goes away (because it isn't real).

The therapy consists of proving to the patient that these aren't really heart attacks. First, you point out that no one can survive 40,000 heart attacks (the number of panic attacks the patient may have had) — at most they get one or two. Then you ask them to think of times they thought they were having an attack and they got distracted — say, the phone rang with important news. Recall how the panic attack went away? Heart attacks don't just go away. After showing the attacks can be eliminated, you show the attacks can be induced, by asking the patient to read a series of trigger words ("breathless, chest tight, dying, suffocate, heart attack"). Finally, you gradually have the patient bring on the attacks without doing their safety behaviors. Eventually, they realize the attacks aren't real.

The technique above is specific to panic disorders, but the same principles can be applied to any sort of anxiety. It's sort of surprising how common sense it all seems. Indeed, Clark's "tips for dealing with anxiety" are exactly the ones my mother used when I was scared or shy:

1. Identify the fear. What am I afraid will happen? What's the worst that could happen?" [My mother was always asking this; it did help.]
2. Challenge negative thoughts. How likely is it? What would be so bad about that? Is there an alternative explanation? How would someone else think? How will I be in X months time?
3. Prepare.
4. Repeated practice.

Is this technique effective? Clark tells an incredible story. There is a standard psychological treatment for post-traumatic stress syndrome: you have the person who suffered some sort of stress discuss the incident with a therapist. After 9/11, for example, thousands of therapists discussed the incident with victims. And if you measure the number of traumatic flashbacks the patients have, they go down after the debriefing (from about 36 to about 32, according to Clark's slide, which cites "Mayou, Ehlers & Hobbs, 2000"). And the patients love it — the thank the therapists, send flowers, gush about how helpful they've been, etc.

But is that enough? I am reminded of a story, quoted by Edward Tufte, from Dr. E. E. Peacock, Jr.:

One day when I was a junior medical student, a very important Boston surgeon visited the school and delivered a great treatise on a large number of patients who had undergone successful operations for vascular reconstruction. At the end of the lecture, a young student at the back of the room timidly asked, "Do you have any controls?" Well, the great surgeon drew himself up to his full height, hit the desk, and said, "Do you mean did I not operate on half the patients?" The hall grew very quiet then. The voice at the back of the room very hesitantly replied, "Yes, that's what I had in mind." Then the visitor's fist really came down as he thundered, "Of course not. That would have doomed half of them to their death." God, it was quiet then, and one could scarcely hear the small voice ask, "Which half?"

(Dr. E. E. Peacock, Jr., University of Arizona College of Medicine; quoted in *Medical World News* (September 1, 1972), p. 45, as quoted by Tufte)

So, you may now ask, what about the other half — the people who suffered traumatic incidents but were not debriefed. Well, their number of traumatic flashbacks fell too. But while those who were debriefed fell from 36 to 32, those who were not debriefed fell from 31 to 9. 9.

In other words, for decades we've been dooming people who have suffered traumatic incidents to relive them over and over under the guise of helping them. I mean, [I knew psychology was bad], but still…

So how do Clark's treatments stack up under the gold standard — randomized controlled trials (where you decide which half gets help randomly)?

Well, one typical solution — a Swedish deep breathing exercise — works in 25% of cases. Another, pills, works in 40% of cases. But the problem with pills is that they stop working as soon as you stop taking them. Cognitive therapy is a relatively quick series of five one-hour sessions and then it's over. So even if it did worse that pills, it might still be a worthwhile treatment.

But it does better than pills — much better. Cognitive therapy essentially cures people in 80% of cases. It does this with panic disorders, social phobias (extreme shyness), etc. And the cures last for years.

All in all, Clark's talk was an exciting vindication for the field — it showed how a scientific approach can really help people in concrete ways. And it was heartening to see there were some hardworking, rational people out there. Which is why it's sort of ironic that at the core of Clark's method is teaching people to be more rational — helping them overcome irrational fears through logic and experiment. It's almost as if science itself were the cure.

March 26, 2005

THE DISAPPEARANCE OF THOUGHT

Neil Postman is generally considered a thoughtful liberal critic of technology and its deleterious effect on our culture. My friends praise his attacks on television and rethinking of education. But it's hard for me to take him seriously after reading his *The Disappearance of Childhood*, in which he argues (p. 87) that television is bad because it teaches children homosexuality is normal and praises the Moral Majority as being the only group to realize this important truth. And true, he admits it's an exaggeration to say "such a situation necessarily and categorically signifies cultural degeneration", he does insist it clearly "poses dangers".

Postman's argument is that childhood is the creation of the printing press, which led to a culture in which learning to read was necessary to become an adult, and thus children became a separate group. In the same way, he argues, the emergence of television, which requires no special training to view, is destroying the distinction between children and adults and bringing us back to that pre-literate age.

Not once does Postman ever explain why this should be considered a bad thing. Instead, his book simply assumes it's obvious that we need to pretend to keep kids from naughty words (even though they know them anyway), that we need to make it hard for kids to learn about sex, that we need to pretend for them that political leaders are infallible, etc.

One is almost tempted to believe the book is tounge-in-cheek, an impression assisted by the preface to the second edition — the only place where actual children are ever considered — which quotes letters Postman has received from students who have read portions of the book and disagree completely with his argument that childhood is disappearing. They don't, however, criticize childhood itself, so Postman assumes they are in favor of it and praises them as "a force in preserving childhood", a sort of "moral majority".

And this, in miniature, is the problem with the whole book. Postman investigates the history of childhood and modern thought, finding it a creation of the printing press, and thus a social and not a biological entity. But instead of investigating whether the result was good or bad, he simply ignores his own work and proceeds directly to assuming it must be good. What we are witnessing here is not the disappearance of childhood, but the disappearance of thought.

January 28, 2006

DO FACES CAUSE DEPRESSION?
SELF-EXPERIMENTATION IN SCIENCE

It all started, Seth Roberts says, when he wanted more practice doing experiments. The closest thing at hand was himself. He was trying to treat his acne and, although convinced that the pills were effective and the cream was not, he decided to chart their effectiveness anyway for practice. The results were the exact opposite of what he expected — the cream helped and the pills did not. His acne went away and Roberts went looking for bigger problems to solve.

It's obvious that sleep follows some sort of circular rhythm, an inner biological clock that makes us tired at the end of the day and refreshed at the beginning. This is the clock that gets thrown off when we travel and thus causes jet lag, for example. But what if other things mess with the clock than simply when we go to sleep?

It wasn't simply academic for Roberts, who frustrated from a serious bout of "early awakening", in which he'd wake up around 4am feeling tired but unable to get back to sleep for another couple of hours. Roberts searched for a way to cure his problem but none of the standard methods seemed appropriate. So he decided to research the subject.

A 1979 study of people in caves suggested that contact with other people affected when we fell asleep and a 1985 survey of daily activities in 12 countries led to another clue: Americans were much more often awake around midnight than people in any other country and the only distinguishing factor seemed to be late-night television. Perhaps, Roberts thought, watching television could influence sleeping rhythm?

The most popular late-night television show at the time the study was done was the *The Tonight Show*, with its person-heavy monologue. So one morning Roberts decided to watch Jay Leno and David Letterman's monologues. It seemed to have no impact; an otherwise normal day. But the next morning he woke up feeling great.

It was hard to believe that the television show could be responsible, so Roberts decided to formalize the study. Every hour he'd write down three numbers between 0 and 100 to measure how unhappy/happy, irritable/serene, and reluctant/eager he was. And then he tried turning the TV watching on and off again to see if it impacted his mood. It did — he always felt better the next day. So he tried adjusting the show and television set, finding that, despite his love for *The Simpsons*, life-size human faces at about a meter away for 30 minutes worked best.

I have to concede, at this point, that the results sound fairly absurd and unbelievable. But reading Roberts's papers on the subject, what's striking is how careful he is about the subject. An actual psychologist, publishing in psychology journals, he's taken into account every objection. The results cannot be, as one would first expect, simply self-induced by his own wishes. For one, Roberts took quantitative notes, so his memory couldn't be playing tricks on him. For another, the size of the difference was too large to be explained through normal explanations. If Roberts could simply will himself into waking up happy, why hadn't he done it before? Nor could such an explanation explain the numbers's careful sensitivity to how similar the TV watching was to human face contact, especially since Roberts was originally hoping to be able to watch his favorite shows, not face-heavy ones like Charlie Rose.

He also began noticing something he wasn't expecting — his mood wasn't just raised the next morning, it was lowered that night. This graph shows the pattern:

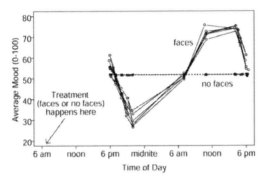

Graph of mood over the course of 48 hours based on whether faces were seen or not

Mood spikes up from 6am to noon, stays high during the day, and then takes a dive around 6pm. (When not seeing faces, mood stays flat.)

And what about all those people who watched TV at night? Roberts found that watching TV after 6pm also reduced mood, with the effect more pronounced the later it was watched.

So what's going on? If you look at faces in the morning, you feel worse 12 hours later but better 24 hours later. But the effect is muted if you see faces in the evening. Roberts theorizes that your body is using the faces to set its inner mood clock, which works similarly to its inner tiredness clock. You want to be happy during the day (as opposed to the night), but how do you tell when the day starts? The body assumes that you gab with people when you wake up, so it uses seeing other faces as a way to synchronize the clock. Of course, you want to make sure you've got the timing right on the nighttime side as well, so if you see faces late in the evening it tries to tweak the clock then as well.

This is consistent with what we know from other sources about depression. Depression is highly correlated with insomnia as well as social isolation and is often treated by disturbing sleep. The Amish, who eat breakfast communally and go to bed very early, have 1/100th the rate of depression as other Americans. And depression rates increased by 10 times in the 1900s, around the same time radio/TV, electric lighting, and other such things became common.

I'm hoping to get a chance to test this myself, but it sure appears that one easy way to improve mood is to look at faces in the morning.

Of course, even more than mood (which is generally considered difficult to tweak)

people want to improve their look. And Roberts has done research on this as well, concluding that the body uses a similar internal system to measure the ideal weight. The result is his *Shangri-La Diet* which uses similar techniques to trick the body's internal system to cut down on appetite. His book on the subject, The Shangri-La Diet, comes out this week. It's been hailed as a diet book unlike any other. More on that next time.

April 23, 2006

1. http://sethroberts.net/self-experiment/
2. http://books.theinfo.org/go/0399153640

SCIENCE SUMMARIES

Anybody who's ever read so much as a Malcolm Gladwell article or an Alfie Kohn book knows that science can be fascinating, that its attempts at answering our questions not only can have a real impact on our lives but are interesting in their own right. Wouldn't it be great if there was a place that reported these things?

If this exists, please tell me — I'd love to read it. But if it doesn't, I'd like to start one. Here's the idea:

We have a bunch of contributors, each of whom reads a variety of journals or journal summaries. When they come across an article that seems particularly interesting, they write up a one or two paragraph summary of the experiment and the findings aimed at an intelligent but generalist audience along with a link to the actual article.

So here's an example of what this might look like:

Economists at Cornell and Indiana University tried to see if television causes autism. Thinking that rainfall could cause kids to watch more TV and thus induce autism, they looked at county-level data in California, Oregon, and Washington — states with high variability in rainfall — and found that autism was was correlated with rainfall (R^2=.77). Thinking that the use of cable TV was another random variable that increased autism, they looked at similar data in California and Pennsylvania and found the use of cable TV correlated with autism (R^2=.21). [Paper]

(I probably screwed up the R^2 bit, but that's why I'm looking for other people to write these.) Of course, this particular study got lots of media attention (that's why I knew about it), but I'm hoping that with enough contributors we'll uncover interesting studies that don't make it into the general news.

So the contributors write a paragraph like this and send it in to an editor, who posts it to a blog, where people can subscribe and comment and so on like any other blog.

I'm happy to set up the blog and serve as the initial editor, so what I really need are contributors. Do you read journals or other reports of new science?

October 18, 2006

1. http://www.johnson.cornell.edu/faculty/profiles/waldman/autpaper.html

THAT ISN'T SCIENCE!

Larry Wall once noted that the scientificness of a field is inversely correlated to how much the word "science" appears in its name. Physics, of course, doesn't have science in the name and is the most scientific of all sciences. Then comes biology and and ethology and so on. Then come the non-sciences like Computer Science and Poultry Science. And worst of all is Scientology.

In general, whenever someone tells you that "science" has decreed that you should do one thing or another that doesn't seem reasonable, it's probably because they're trying to pull one over on you, whether it's the "scientific" medicines you see on late-night TV or the science of the behaviorists who say you shouldn't love your kids.

But nowhere is this more evident than when people try to tell you what science itself is. This field of meta-science seems to attract more charlatans and malintents than any other. If you control how the very notion of what's scientific is defined — well, then that's real power. Even if the very idea is patently absurd. (A real scientist would never tell you that doing X isn't really science; their goal is to get the truth, not sit around making rules about who's in and who's out.)

For much of the outside world, the test for a real science is "falsifiability" — the possibility that there could be evidence proving the claim wrong. This notion was invented by Karl Popper, who was himself an enemy of science who tried to insist that science never actually made any progress, that we never learned anything more about the world.

But even if we put aside this noxious pedigree, Popper's definition is still absurd. Take the distinction between astronomy and astrology. We would all agree, I think, that the first is a science but the second isn't. But both of their predictions are equally falsifiable — astrology makes a dozen falsifiable predictions in the newspaper five times a week. Popper's criteria isn't of much help to us, even on such a basic case.

Sadly, like many American intellectuals, the Supreme Court assumed that falsifiability was a standard scientific test. In the *Daubert* case it, as Chris Mooney summarizes the view of the *American Journal of Public Health*, "blundered miserably" and set judges the task of using this "deeply confused philosophy of science" to act as gatekeepers in keeping scientific claims from juries. Actual scientists like DefendingScience.org is working to undo this these mistakes, but you wouldn't know it from the rhetoric — after all, *Daubert*'s defenders claim their just trying to uphold sound scientific standards. (Chris Mooney's book *The Republican War on Science*, among others, has a fascinating exposé of the junk science/sound science notions cooked up by the PR industry to trash actual science. But that's another subject.)

What are the real effects, though? Daubert was a parent whose child was born with birth defects they believed were caused by the drug Benedictin which, in animal studies, appeared to cause the defects they were suffering. By making it harder for science to be presented in Court, these kinds of rulings make it easier for drug companies to claim there's no "sound science" that they're hurting anyone.

America isn't alone, however. In Britain a group supporting what they call "evidence-based medicine" is trying to tighten restrictions on what experiments can be examined when approving drugs. Evidence-based medicine? Who could be against that! But again, they're playing the same games. Behind evidence-based science are a bunch of very bizarre claims about what science is and isn't, taken not from doctors or scientists, but from econometricians (the subspecialty of economics that has to do with calculating things), which have quite a few problems of their own when it comes to the subject of evidence.

Under "evidence-based medicine" rules, doctors aren't allowed to prescribe drugs on the basis of case studies and other reports; instead, the only real evidence are large double-blind random controlled trials whose results have a less than 5% probability of being due to chance. (Why 5%? No good reason. But according to the EBM people anything more than that isn't evidence.)

Again, you have the same negative effects: when someone tries to claim in court that a certain drug destroyed their life, the drug company can claim that there's no "evidence" to support this if the studies just happen to be 94% likely instead of 95%, or if there's only a series of case studies instead of a controlled trial.

This isn't evidence, this isn't rationality, this isn't science. Science is about trying to get the truth about the world, using whatever mechanisms are most effective at the job, whether you're studying the nature of planets in space or the nature of other cultures. When someone tells you otherwise, tries to insist that technique X or subject Y doesn't deserve the name science, it's probably because they're trying to pull a fast one on you.

October 18, 2006

THE HARD SCIENCES

If we say that science is the goal of trying to figure things out about the world, then we see the sciences broadly classified into two categories: "hard" and "soft". In the former are subjects like physics, biology, and perhaps the honorary inclusion of mathematics. The "soft" sciences, by contrast, include fields like history, psychology, sociology, and economics.

As you might gather from the terms involved, partisans of the hard sciences often look down upon the softer sciences, considering them barely worthy of the term science at all. Indeed, the soft sciences rarely formulate general laws or clear predictions, as the harder sciences sometimes do. But why is that?

The reason is, because the "soft" sciences are, in fact, harder. Humans are far more complicated than atoms, trying to figure out how they work is a great deal more difficult than coming up with the rules of mechanics. As a result, the social sciences are less well developed, which means there's less to study, which means the fields are easier to learn.

Nonetheless, since the field is so much harder, the people who make progress in it should get more respect. Physicists can isolate atoms and run an experiment; historians have to try to find clever ways to make a "natural experiment".

Obviously, the progress has to be actual, rather than simply perceived, which is indeed a common confusion in the social sciences, but real observers of science should reconsider who they esteem.

July 11, 2006

THE SEXUAL LIFE OF SAVAGES

In the early 1900s, anthropologist Bronislaw Malinowski did his field work in the Trobriand Islands of the Western Pacific. After getting himself ashore, he dropped himself into their culture and begun having to learn their language and understand their customs. The result were a series of groundbreaking books in the field of anthropology, much of which is still entertaining to read today.

In *The Sexual Life of Savages* (savages, Malinowski assures us, is a technical term and not meant to cause offense) he describes the customs of Trobriand's intimate life, which is fascinating both for how it is different and how it is the same.

To a certain degree, it seems like the culture of the islanders presages our own. Back when Malinowski was doing his field work, he was amazed that islanders could freely have premarital sex and yet still found it desirable to get married. The same question would prove no puzzle to any American today.

And, indeed, the islanders seem like a case study in the ultimate consequences of the sexual revolution: girls want sex just as much as guys, kids start having sex at a very young age — 6-8 for the girls and 10-12 for the guys — with no social stigma, there are few customs about dating to inhibit "hooking up", and, of course, revealing clothing has been taken to its limit, with girls actually going topless.

Of course, much of the story of a Trobriand's intimate life is the same: initial attractions budding into lasting relationships, etc. And then, out of nowhere, Malinowski drops in something totally bizarre. The islanders don't kiss, he explains. Instead, they scratch. The girls scratch the guys so hard that they draw blood and, if the guys can withstand the pain, then they move forward to having sex. The ethnographer (as Malinowski calls himself) verified this by noting that just about everyone on the island had noticeable scratches. And while everybody is having sex whenever they want, premarital meal-sharing is a big no-no. You're not supposed to go out for dinner together until after you get married.

But the most fascinating and strange part about the islanders are their beliefs on the subject of pregnancy, also described in Malinowski's classic article "Baloma: The Spirits of the Dead in the Trobriand Islands"[1]. When people die, you see, their spirit takes a canoe to the island of Tuma, which works very much like the normal island except everybody is a spirit of the dead. When the spirit gets old and wrinkled it shrugs off its skin and turns back into an embryo, which a spirit then takes back to the island and inserts into a woman. This, you see, is how women get pregnant.

That's right. The islanders do not believe that sex causes pregnancy. They don't believe in physiological fatherhood. Malinowski was incredibly skeptical about this, so he tried all sorts of ways to see if this was simply a story they told, while they actually the real deal. But no, they assured him that it was really true, that all the white people who insisted otherwise were being silly, that the spirits caused pregnancy, not sex.

They argued the case quite logically. After all, they noted, one fellow went on an expedition for a year or two and when he came back, he had a new son. He obviously wasn't having sex with her while he was away, so where did the kid come from? (Cough.) And, they note, there are some really hideous people on the island who nobody would dare have sex with, yet they manage to become pregnant. (Malinowski spies some kids looking sheepish when this subject is raised.)

They also argue the other way: people on the island are having sex all the time from a very early age and yet they very rarely get pregnant. (Naturally, the islanders don't practice any form of contraception; the very idea doesn't make sense when sex doesn't cause pregnancy.) The white man's argument just doesn't make sense. Indeed, recent visitors[2] report, the islanders still believe that sex doesn't cause pregnancy, despite the best efforts of health workers.

It is speculated that the yams that form the basis of the island diet have a contraceptive agent in them (The Pill was originally made by looking at chemicals in wild yams), which conveniently explains quite a bit, including the low birthrate despite the high level of sexual activity. Indeed, the whole idea lends quite a bit of support to the idea that material factors shape culture — after all, our own sexual revolution didn't happen until we got the yam's chemicals in pill form in 1960.

The notion has some other interesting consequences. For example, the society is necessarily matrilineal, since fathers have no technical lineage. Yet sociological fathers (the mother's husband), Malinowski notes, show more love and care for their children than most he's seen in Europe.

Furthermore, they believe the same rules apply to the rest of the animal kingdom. This is what clinches it for Malinowski — despite all the effort they go to to raise pigs, they insist that pigs also reproduce asexually. They never attempt to breed pigs; indeed, they castrate all the male pigs they have. (To them this is further proof — we castrated all the pigs and yet they keep having children! Malinowski notes that the domestic pigs often sneak off to canoodle with those in the wild.)

When I told a friend of mine about this odd state of affairs, he wondered if the islanders were just stupid. After all, he noted, sex and childbirth aren't exactly two physically unconnected human activities. But as he reflected on it further, he considered that this belief wasn't that much different from what passes for religion in our country. Smart people believe strange things.

October 16, 2006

1. http://www.aaronsw.com/weblog/static/baloma.pdf
2. http://www.travelintelligence.net/wsd/articles/art4print_520.html

SOCIOLOGY OR ANTHROPOLOGY

Sometimes people ask me what the difference is between sociology and anthropology. There are the surface ones, of course — sociology typically studies first-world societies, whereas anthropology has a rep for studying so-called "primitive" cultures. But the fundamental difference is a philosophical one: sociologists study society, while anthropologists study culture.

What's the difference? Let's do a case study. It's easy to notice a subtle sort of sexism in American textbooks. For example, studies have found that in biology textbooks sperm are seen as competitive creatures while eggs are passive receptacles they aim to penetrate. But the actual science on the subject is much less clear: eggs seem to do a fair bit of selection themselves, etc.

I saw a paper by an anthropologist on this fact; their argument was that these textbooks were a result of the sexism of American culture, a culture which sees men as competing for access to women, and those notions are naturally transported onto our writing about conception. Sexist culture, sexist output.

A sociologist would dig a little deeper. They'd see who writes the textbooks, perhaps notice a disproportionate number of males. They'd look into why it was that males got these jobs, find the sexism inherent in the relevant institutions. They'd argue it was the structures of society that end up with sexist textbooks, not some magical force known as "American culture".

As you might guess, I'm on the side of the sociologists. Blaming things on culture — as if it were a natural property of a group of people or a mystical life force with its own mind — seems too facile. It also seems wrong.

I've mostly been talking about the cultural anthropologists, but there are also a subset of racist anthropologists (sometimes called "anthropological science," in accordance with Wall's Law — see article "That Isn't Science!"). These anthropologists tried to measure different properties of people, see if they could quantify the differences between the races and predict criminality from the shape of the head.

Cultural anthropologists disdain all that and prefer to endorse a very left-wing notion of cultural relativism. (One shouldn't make judgments about other cultures!) But in doing so, they end up pushing the judgments off onto the peoples involved. Just like the racist anthropologists, they end up suggesting that the reason people over here believe act differently from the people over there is because they're different people.

But if there's one thing we've learned from psychology, it's that — for the most part — people are people, wherever you go. As Zimbardo's Stanford Prison Experiment showed, put normal people into the wrong situation and they turn into devious enforcement machines. And put the same people into a different society and they'll change just as fast.

It isn't culture — whatever that is — that causes these things; it's institutions. Institutions create environments which force a course of action. And that's why I'm a sociologist.

Bonus recommendation: I've been watching *The Wire* lately; perhaps the most sociologically-inclined show on television. And that's what makes it interesting, unlike all the other good-evil cop dramas.

December 23, 2006

HOW QUANTUM MECHANICS IS COMPATIBLE WITH FREE WILL

The actions of almost everything in this world are causally determined by the state of the world that precedes them. Once you start a machine, if no one touches it, its behavior can be predicted entirely in advance from the laws of physics. When you drop a pen down a well, it is physically necessary that it fall.

But our behavior doesn't feel that way. When we stick out our tongue it feels as if we had to specifically choose to stick it out, that this was our own action and not a predetermined consequence of the existing state of the world.

Some people argue that because the evidence for determinism is so overwhelming, free will must simply be an illusion. But if so, it is a very odd kind of illusion. Most illusions result from a naive interpretation of our senses. For example, in a classic illusion, two drawings of equal size appear to be of different size. But when we are told this is an illusion, we can correct for it, and behave under the new (more accurate) impression that the drawings are in fact of equal size.

This simply isn't possible with free will. If someone tells you that you do not actually have free will but have actually been acting under an illusion, you cannot sit back and let determinism take over. When the waiter asks you whether you like soup or salad, you cannot say "Oh, well I've just learned that free will is an illusion and all my actions are completely determined by the previous state of the world, so I'll just let them play themselves out." I mean, you can say that, but the waiter will look at you like you're crazy and you will get neither soup nor salad.

It seems overwhelmingly bizarre that evolution would have given us this strangest of illusions. This is not a spandrel, a small place evolution never had time to be concerned about. The illusion of free will affects all aspects of our lives and takes an enormous amount of work. One would think evolution would have eliminated it were it genuinely false.

So what is the other possibility? The other possibility is that not all actions are entirely determined by the preexisting state of the world. And, in fact, recent advances in physics seem to show this is somewhat the case. Quantum mechanics suggests that at some fundamental level there is randomness involved in the laws of the world. And chaos theory shows us that small amounts of randomness in a system can have real large-scale effects.

So, although it seems extremely improbable, if we have to avoid the improbability of evolution not breeding out an illusory free will, then we're forced to look to the randomness of quantum mechanics for an explanation.

But, some argue, this is insufficient. Quantum mechanics only gives us randomness — but free will isn't just the pursuit of random behavior, it's the pursuit of particular behaviors. While quantum mechanics can't predict each individual bit, it does give overall probability distributions. Volitional behaviors would wreak havoc with those even distributions.

Not true. Imagine the simple case where we have one quantum bitstream: a series of zeroes and ones, in which each individual number cannot be predicted, but there's an overall law saying that roughly half of them will be one and half will be zero. And let us simplify the system to say that if the result of the quantum effect is 0 then the person moves left, and if it's 1 they move right. In the naive scenario, free will affects this quantum bitstream so that when the person wants to move left the randomness keeps coming up zeroes. But that would violate the laws of physics — the results would no longer be half ones and half zeroes.

So here's the trick: first, the system gets a random bit from some other source. Then it adds the bit from the other source with the bit from the quantum bitstream and uses the result to decide if you move left or right. Now, when you want to continually move left, half the time you'll have to make the quantum bitstream return zeroes and the other half the time ones — exactly what the laws of quantum mechanics require.

With a little additional mathematical complexity, the scenario is generalizable to much more complicated quantum functions and human results. But the basic principle is the same: one can use quantum randomness to exercise free will without violating any statistical laws.

Of course, this still leaves one key problem. What is picking the results of this quantum bitstream? And how does it do it? I have to admit I cannot really think of a sensible way. But this seems like a problem for neurobiology to figure out and report back to us. I merely aim to prove that its doing so is consistent with what we know about the laws of physics.

March 18, 2007

A VERY SPECULATIVE THEORY OF FREE WILL

Attention conservation notice: I am well aware that this post will get me called all sorts of silly names and insults (Penrosian apparently the worst among them). For once, I am not going to respond. I just think the theory ought to be published and if you are not inclined to believe it, then feel free to ignore it.

The big mystery of the mind is reconciling two things: what we know about the physical structures of the brain and what we experience from day to day as conscious people. The first tells us that our brain is made up of a series of interconnected neurons which fire in response to certain inputs. The second tells us that people have subjective unified experiences and at least the appearance of free will. It seems hard to explain how the first can lead to the second, although they're obviously connected somehow.

So, for example, if we're looking at certain visual illusions, we can choose to see them one way or to see them another way. And obviously this choice has some impact on the rest of the brain, especially the part that processes vision. But nobody's been able to find the place in the brain from which such choices originate.

I don't know enough about the subject to vouch for it, but this article[1] claims that neurons are small enough that we could see quantum effects in their high-level behavior:

The juncture between two neurons is called the synapse. Each of the perhaps 100 billion neurons in the brain is connected to about 1,000 other neurons. At the synapse, a firing neuron either passes a neurochemical signal to the next neuron, or it does not pass a signal, with the passing or not passing depending on the complex neurochemistry of the synapse. If, within a millisecond, a certain number of signals are passed on to a neuron, then that neuron will fire. Otherwise it will not fire. Thus what happens at the various synapses — signal passed on or not passed on — is the sole determinant of the firing pattern of the neurons in the brain. The synapses are the control points for our flow of thoughts.

The synaptic gap, the gap between one neuron and the next, is quite small, 3.5 nanometers, which is about 35 (hydrogen) atoms. The sizes of the adjacent parts of the synapse, where much of the neurochemistry goes on, are also small, on the order of 3,500 atoms wide. Now one of the peculiar effects of quantum mechanics is that if the volume where an atom might be located (the place where the wave function is non-zero) is initially small, it will spread out in time. One can use Heisenberg's uncertainty principle to show that a calcium ion, for example, will spread out to the size of the synapses (not just the synaptic gap) in about .1 milliseconds (see 8 below). Neural processes in the brain occur on a time scale of a millisecond, ten times slower than the spread of a calcium ion over the whole synapse.

So here's the proposal: a series of entangled quantum particles at the synaptic level allow for coordinated firing patterns which occur in response to choices by our conscious free will. Just as my previous post reconciled free will with statistical randomness, this would seem to reconcile free will with the neuroanatomy.

It still seems incredible that there is some high-level coordinated process with its fingers in the quantum effects of our synapses. But we know something incredible is going on because we have subjective experience. So this doesn't seem like much of a stretch to me.

January 28, 2008

1.   http://www.quantummechanicsandreality.com/Primer/iia8_brain.htm

DISCRIMINATION AND CAUSATION

First, let's imagine that tomorrow scientists announced the discovery of rock-solid, unimpeachable, 100% convincing evidence of differences in mental function between men and women. Let's say, for example, they notice that there's a tiny hole where the "math center" of the brain should be. No wonder they do worse at math!

No doubt, *The Times* would respond with a handwringing article[1] about the important scientific implications and David Brooks would throw a party[2] and denounce closed-minded liberals. George Bush would cancel programs aimed at helping girls learn math and Harvard University would shut down their task force on getting women tenure.

But are these really appropriate responses? Showing genetic differences is only the first in a long line of things that need to be shown to prove that gender-based disparities in tenure are unavoidable. As Jeremy Freese[3] has pointed out, it's a long line from genes to social outcomes. To make the case, you need to go a lot further.

Second, you have to show the genetic differences are relevant. It's possible the hole in the math center could be completely insignificant, that women do just as well at math irrespective. So you need to show that the hole *causes* differences in functioning. One way to do this is to find different people with differing sizes of holes, control for as many other factors as possible, and see if the size of hole is correlated with some test of math functioning.

Third, you need to prove that the differences are unavoidable. The brain has amazing levels of neuroplasticity. Perhaps with the right environment, women can be taught to do math with another part of their brain. Perhaps, as a result, they might even do better than men at math. Again, Freese has pointed out[4] that the same genetic differences (or genetic similarities) can go all sorts of different places in different environments. If there's an easy environmental change that makes even genetically different women equally good at math, we ought to make it.

Fourth, you need to show a causal link from the genetic difference to the tenure disparity. Why is it that doing worse at math causes you to do worse at tenure? Are speed-math-tests used as a relevant factor in tenure decisions? If so, maybe you guys should really cut that out, because that's a pretty stupid test.

Fifth, you need to show that it's the only cause of discrimination. Even if genetic differences cause some of the disparity, it's still morally required for us to remove the rest. Do guys with holes in their math center do just as bad as women at getting tenure? Do women with no holes do just as well as men?

Right now, there's only even arguable evidence for the very first of these. Those of us who want to shove discrimination under the rug need to do a lot more work on the other four.

May 23, 2007

1. http://itre.cis.upenn.edu/~myl/languagelog/archives/003894.html
2. http://itre.cis.upenn.edu/~myl/languagelog/archives/003246.html
3. http://jeremyfreese.blogspot.com/2006/11/twenty-four-stories-of-internal.html
4. http://jeremyfreese.blogspot.com/2006/11/eight-plots-revised.html

AREA SCIENTIST'S STUDY CONFIRMS OWN PREJUDICES

CAMBRIDGE, MA — In a study published today in the prestigious journal *Nature*, Harvard professor Dr. Thomas Jacobson, an expert in the field of physical neuroscience, finds that the gangly cortex, the area of the brain associated with stumbling, fumbling, and general klutziness, is smaller in members of the Red Sox sports team than in other major league baseball players.

The study, entitled "Differential Size Analysis of the Gangly Cortex In Professional Sports", was conducted using a technique called Functional Magnetic Resonance Imaging, or fMRI, in which brain activity is observed on a computer monitor while subjects perform a mental activity. In his fMRI studies, Dr. Jacobson noted significantly less mental activity in the gangy cortex of Red Sox players when he asked them to visualize various aspects of a baseball game.

"Obviously far more research needs to be done," explained Dr. Jacobson, "but this evidence does appear to support the popular belief that Red Sox players are just better than everyone else."

The study could have major implications for the entire field of physical neuroscience, which examines how differences in the brain can affect performance in various types of strenuous physical activity, including baseball, American football, running the mile, hockey, and the biathlon.

"I haven't seen the study but I think it's extremely brave work," said former Harvard President Lawrence Summers when asked to comment. "There's an academic orthodoxy of political correctness that says you shouldn't inquire too much into the differences between sports teams. Well, Dr. Jacobson has thrown that out the window and science is better off for it."

The study appears in the July 27th issue of *Nature*, along with new research showing that eating chocolate is good for your heart[1], Jews are just smarter than everyone else[2], semen makes women happier[3], and all women are bisexual[4]. A new study showing that having sex with[5] scientists is associated with a 20-point increase in IQ[6] is expected to be released soon.

October 22, 2007

1. http://news.bbc.co.uk/2/hi/in_depth/sci_tech/2001/glasgow_2001/1521982.stm
2. http://www.seedmagazine.com/news/2005/12/jews_on_jews_jews_are_great.php
3. http://news.bbc.co.uk/1/hi/health/2067223.stm
4. http://www.sciencedaily.com/releases/2003/06/030613075252.htm
5. http://cr.yp.to/postpropter.html
6. http://bactra.org/weblog/523.html

SCIENCE OR PHILOSOPHY?
JON ELSTER AND JOHN SEARLE

As the name suggests, the social sciences have often seen themselves as an analogue or extension of the natural sciences and have from the beginning aspired to their successes. Like many who want to duplicate success they do not understand, social sciences has been obsessed with duplicating the form of the natural sciences and not its motivations. Just as rival music player manufacturers have tried to copy the look of the iPod without understanding why it takes that look, the social sciences have copied the structure of the natural sciences without understanding why they take that structure.

The greatest success of the natural sciences is undoubtedly the laws of physics. Here, an handful of simple equations can accurately predict the motion of a vast variety of everyday objects under common actions. Seeing this, social scientists have aspired to derive similar laws that predict the behavior of whole societies. (Others, meanwhile insist the entire project is impossible because the society will respond to the creation of the law, making the law invalid — reflexivity.)

But reflection upon the history of the natural sciences will see that this notion is insane. Physics did not develop thru attempts to discover the laws that explained all of motion. Instead, various kinds of motion (like falling objects) were described, rules for their behavior deduced, and commonalities in those rules discovered. Eventually it was the case that the commonalities were so great and the rules so few that a handful of laws could explain most of the phenomena, but this assumption was not made a priori.

Jon Elster argues that the social sciences should proceed in a similar way: various social phenomena should be described, the mechanisms that give rise to them explained, and the commonalities among mechanisms discovered. Most of his work consists of practicing social science in this way, with a few attempts at laying out a toolbox of these common mechanisms.

Modern social science is so split between attempts at grand law-like theories and modest essays of careful description that Elster's third way seems alien and hard to comprehend. But there is a clear model that social scientists can look to: analytical philosophy.

Analytical philosophers do not take as their task grand law-like explanations for the world. Instead, they set upon a particular piece of conception — language, free will, ethics — and try to discover its logical structure. In doing so they often develop tools they shared in common with other philosophical projects.

This similarity can perhaps be best seen in the work of the man who is Jon Elster's closest equivalent in the world of analytical philosophy, John Searle. In his career, Searle has addressed a number of topics: language, intentionality, consciousness, social reality, and rationality. Throughout he has taken has his task providing a clear description of the phenomena and explaining the pieces it consists of. And in explaining those pieces, he frequently develops tools that he reuses in his other explanations.

Take the notion of *direction of fit*. Searle argues that all statements have a direction of fit, which can be either up, down, both, or null. If we imagine (by convention) that statements float above the world pointing down at the things they represent, then statements like "John and Jill are married", in which it is the job of the statement to change to accurately represent the world, have a downward direction of fit. By contrast, statements like "I want to marry him", in which it is the world must change to match the statement, have an upward direction of fit.

This notion, which Searle and Austin developed for describing language, Searle later reused for describing mental states. Love, for example, has an upward direction of fit, belief downward, and joy null. And in my own everyday life, I have found the same tool useful in thinking about various phenomena I've encountered.

Social scientists don't seem to read much philosophy. I suspect most of them see it as an alien culture consisting of, as Paul Graham put it, "either highly technical stuff that doesn't matter much, or vague concatenations of abstractions their own authors didn't fully understand." But perhaps they should, because even if the technical stuff lacks interest (and considering some of the topics involved, I'm skeptical that this is always the case), the tools, and the way they're wielded, should be a lesson.

May 12, 2008

THE TRUE STORY OF THE TELEPHONE

I grew up in Highland Park, Illinois, just down the street from where the telephone was invented. I now live in Cambridge, Massachusetts, just down the street from where it was stolen. Seth Shulman's recent book The Telephone Gambit *lays out the clearest case yet of how it all happened. Here's the summary:*

Alexander Graham Bell (or Aleck Bell, as he was then called) was the son of Alexander Melville Bell, the inventor of a system of phonic notation called Visible Speech. The elder Bell would use Aleck as an assistant in his demonstrations: After sending Aleck to wait in another room, Mr. Bell would ask the audience for a word or strange noise then write it in Visible Speech. Aleck would return and reproduce the sound from the writing alone. Voila.

As a child growing up like this, he played at inventing machines that could talk and telegraphs that could listen. But he found his career in tutoring the deaf — by teaching them to pronounce the phonemes of Visible Speech, he eventually succeeded in teaching them to talk and read lips.

One of his students was Mabel Hubbard, daughter of prominent Boston lawyer Gardiner Greene Hubbard. Son of a Massachusetts Supreme Court Justice, Hubbard established water and gas and trolley utilities for Cambridge, Mass. — some of the first in the nation. He also fervently lobbied Congress to replace Western Union's monopoly on the telegraph with a new corporation, the US Postal Telegraph Company, that would contract with the government Post Office.

At the time, telegraph wires blanketed the skies of Boston, hanging in a dense web above the buildings. Many desperately wished for someone to develop a telegraph that could send multiple messages over the same wire, so that many wires could be replaced with just one. The theory was that if one could transmit the messages using different tones, they would "harmonize" instead of interfere, leading the idea to be called the "harmonic telegraph". Naturally, Alexander Graham Bell turned his tinkering to this problem and persuaded Hubbard (as well as Thomas Sanders, another father of a Bell student) to finance his research in exchange for a share of any future US profits. Further complicating matters, Bell had fallen in love with his student, Mabel Hubbard. Mr. Hubbard made it clear he did not approve of such a marriage unless Bell made a profitable discovery.

But Bell was simply a hobbyist, the real research was being done by a man named Elisha Gray. Gray ran Western Electric, the leading supplier of technical expertise to telegraph monopoly Western Union. From his lab in Highland Park, Illinois, he and his assistants worked feverishly at new discoveries. Bell was well aware of this and considered himself to be in a race with Gray to invent the harmonic telegraph first.

In 1875, Bell made a breakthrough in his work on the harmonic telegraph. But he was a crafty fellow — his deal with Gardiner and Sanders was only about splitting US profits; it said nothing about profits overseas. British law at the time granted patents only to inventions not patented elsewhere first, so Bell drew up several copies of his harmonic telegraph patent and sent some to be filed in Britain first. The rest were sent to DC to be filed as soon as word got back from Britain.

On February 14, 1876, while the lawyers were waiting in DC to file Bell's patent, Gray filed a patent of his own. Bell's lawyers were close to the patent officers and had asked to be tipped off if Gray tried to file something, so they could file Bell's patent first. When Gray's patent was placed in the patent office's inbox, Bell's lawyers hand-delivered Bell's patent to the examiner, so they could claim he'd received Bell's first.

The patent examiner, Zenas Fisk Wilber, had fought in the civil war with Bell's attorney, Marcellus Bailey. Wilber was an alcoholic and owed Bailey money (a serious Patent Office ethics violation). To pay his friend back, he showed him Gray's application. Bailey was startled to find it wasn't a patent on a harmonic telegraph at all — it was a patent for a telephone, capable of transmitting all the sounds of human speech and music. He called for Bell to come to DC at once.

Bell did, and examiner Wilber showed him Gray's patent as well, taking time to explain how it worked. Bell thanked him and returned that afternoon with $100 for his trouble. Bell then quickly scribbled an addition to his patent in the margin, adding that it should also cover "transmitting vocal or other sounds telegraphically" (this addition does not appear in any of the other copies).

Contravening much standard practice at the time, Bell's (modified) patent was quickly granted, while Gray's was denied. It was issued the same day Bell returned home from DC, March 7, 1876. The following day, Bell drew in his lab notebook a copy of the diagram he had seen in Elisha Gray's patent:

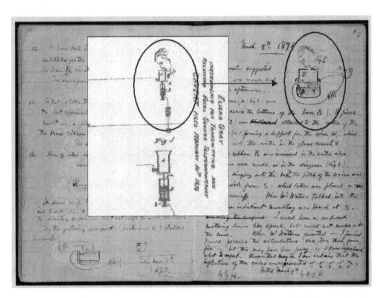

Diagram showing the similarity between Gray's patent and Bell's notebook

It took Bell several days of tinkering, but soon he was able to replicate Gray's device. On March 10, he made that now-famous call: "Watson — come here — I want to see you." Both Bell and his assistant Watson recorded the event that night in their notebooks.

But Bell didn't want to simply duplicate Gray's work; he wanted to invent a telephone of his own. He spent many months trying to develop a telephone that worked on a different principle, but never succeeded in getting it to clearly transmit audible speech. Bell was always extraordinarily reluctant to demonstrate his telephone, for fear that Gray would learn it was a simple copy. Mabel had to trick him into attending the Centennial Exposition, where he was supposed to demonstrate his work to a group of engineers, including Elisha Gray. On one occasion, Bell's telephone patent was set to be annulled unless Bell would swear under oath that the invention was truly his. Bell fled the country, testifying only at the last minute after desperate pleading from Mabel.

The legal conniving a success, Bell and Mabel were soon married. Feeling guilty, Bell gave all but ten of his shares in the Bell Telephone Company to her and swore to never work in telephony again. The company was operated by Gardiner and others while Bell went back to working with the deaf. He always said he was more proud of his work for the deaf than of the telephone.

It took Gray a long time to realize that Bell's patent was a fraud. For one thing, he was still focused on the harmonic telegraph; his customers at Western Union couldn't imagine running telephone wires to every house and thus couldn't see how talking over wires was particularly useful. For another, it took years for the story to leak out, through numerous court battles and Congressional hearings. Zenas Fisk Wilber's affidavit[1] confessing to what he'd done did not appear until 1886, a decade later. Bell's notebooks, making clear the blatant copy, were not made public until the 1990s.

Bell's biographers have gone to heroic lengths to explain away all the evidence. Refusing credit for the telephone just showed Bell's humility; not being involved in the corporation showed his dedication to pure research. The fact that both patents were filed on the same day is a grand historic coincidence — or perhaps *Gray* stole the idea from Bell.

As a result, Gray is forgotten and Bell is remembered as one of history's great inventors — not as he should be: a hobbyist and a fraud, forced by love into stealing one of the greatest inventions of all time.

January 5, 2009

1. http://upload.wikimedia.org/wikipedia/commons/c/c8/Zenas-fisk-wilber-affidavit.png

THE LOGIC OF LOSS

Imagine someone offered you a 1% chance of winning a million dollars. How much would you pay for it? The natural inclination would be to say you break even at 1% of a million, which is $10,000. Even if you could scrape together the cash, this doesn't seem like a very good deal. After all, there's a 99% chance that you'll have just thrown away ten grand.

Where did we go wrong? The problem is that calculating the average value this way only makes sense if you get to take the deal enough times to expect an average result. If you bought a couple thousand of these chances at $9000 each, then you might start to come out ahead. But buying just one doesn't seem very bright.

Of course, the same logic applies to more pedestrian examples of risk. It probably doesn't make sense to invest in just one startup, even if the returns on startups are huge. That's why VCs invest in large numbers of startups; the returns from the wins balance out the flops.

This should seem pretty obvious, but some people seem to forget it a lot. Take the St. Petersburg paradox. Imagine this game: A dollar is placed on the table and a coin is flipped. If the coin comes up heads, the money is doubled and the coin is flipped again. Tails, the game ends and you take the money. How much would you pay to play?

The paradox comes about because the naive answer here is infinite. There's a 50% chance you get a dollar (=fifty cents), a 25% chance you get 2 (another fifty cents), a 12.5% chance you get 4 (again), and so on infinitely. But, naturally, it seems insane to pay a fortune to play this game. Thus the paradox.

Folks seem to be genuinely stumped about this, but it's just the first offer taken to the limit: instead of a 1% chance of making a million, you have an infinitesimal chance of making an infinity. If you got to play the game an infinite number of times, shelling out cash might begin to make sense, but if you only play it once it's not worth much.

Keep that in mind next time someone offers you a game.

April 13, 2009

THE NEW SCIENCE OF CAUSATION

It seems like each new day brings another one of those headlines: regular sleep "linked to" life expectancy, playing video games "associated with" surgical prowess, bullies "at risk" of becoming criminals, and "does breastfeeding reduce a baby's blood pressure?" (the old rhetorical question gambit). Sometimes the articles are clear: the research has only found a correlation between two variables — breastfeeding and low blood pressure were found together. But more often, they imply that causation is at work — that breastfeeding *causes* lower blood pressure.

You've surely heard that old statistics adage: correlation does not imply causation. Just because breastfeeding and low blood pressure are found together doesn't mean the first caused the second. Perhaps the second caused the first (moms might prefer to keep breastfeeding calmer babies) or some other thing caused both of them (maybe moms who don't work both tend to breastfeed and stress their kids less). You can't tell from correlation alone.

Indeed, the philosopher David Hume argued that we could never know whether causation was at work. "Solidity, extension, motion; these qualities are all complete in themselves, and never point out any other event which may result from them," he wrote. But not causation: "One event follows another; but we never can observe any tie between them. They seem conjoined, but never connected."

And, as philosophers since Plato and Sextus Empiricus have argued, such evidence can deceive us. Imagine finding a button and, each time you press it, a beep is heard. Normally, we'd assume that the button always causes the beep. But we'd be wrong — one day the power goes out and the button does nothing.

Which is why, centuries later, Karl Pearson, the founder of mathematical statistics, banned the notion of causality from the discipline, calling it "a fetish amidst the inscrutable arcana of modern science" and insisting that just by understanding simple correlation one "grasped the essence of the conception of association between cause and effect."

His followers have kept it banished ever since. "Considerations of causality should be treated as they have always been in statistics: preferably not at all," wrote a former president of the Biometric Society. "It would be very healthy if more researchers abandon thinking of and using terms such as cause and effect," insisted another prominent social scientist.

And there the matter has stayed. Causality is a concept as meaningless as "the soul" and just as inappropriate for modern mathematical science. And yet, somehow, this doesn't seem quite right. If causation is nothing but a meaningless word that laypeople have layered over correlation, then why the ceaseless insistence that "correlation does not imply causation"? Why are our thoughts filled with causal comments (he made me do it!) and never correlational ones?

The result is exceptionally strange. Statistics has no mathematical way to express the notion "mud does not cause rain". It can say mud is correlated with rain (i.e. that there's a high probability of seeing mud if you see rain), no problem, but expressing the simple causal concept — the kind of thing any five-year-old would know — is impossible.

Statisticians may have never had to confront this problem but, luckily for us, Artificial Intelligence researchers have. It turns out if you're making a robot, having a notion of causality is essential — not just because it's the only way to understand the humans, but because it's the only way to get anything done! How are you supposed to turn the lights on if you don't know that it's the light-switch and not the clicking noise that causes it?

The result is that in recent years several teams of AI researchers have turned their focus from building robots to building mathematical tools for dealing with causality. At the forefront is Judea Pearl (author of the book *Causality*, Cambridge University Press) and his group at UCLA and Clark Glymour (author of *The Mind's Arrows*, MIT Press), Peter Spirtes, and their colleagues at Carnegie Mellon. The result is a quiet revolution in the field of statistics — one most practicing statisticians are still unaware of.

They started by dismissing Plato's skepticism about the problem. Granted, they say, we may never know for sure whether the button *always* causes the beep, but that's too stringent a demand. Science never knows anything for sure — the best we can hope for is extracting the most knowledge from the evidence we have. Or, as William James put it, "To know is one thing, and to know for certain that we know is another."

Next, they created a new mathematical function to formalize our notion of causality: $do(\ldots)$. do expresses the notion of intervening and actually trying something. Thus, to mathematically express the notion that mud does not cause rain, we can say $P(rain \mid do(mud=true)) = P(rain)$ — in other words, the chance of rain given that you made it muddy is the same as the chance of rain in general.

But causes rarely comes in pairs like these — more often it comes in complicated chains: clouds cause rain which causes both mud and wet clothing and the latter causes people to find a change of clothes. And so the researchers express these as networks, usually called causal Bayes nets or graphical causal models, which show each thing (clouds, rain, mud) as a node and the causal relationships as arrows between them:

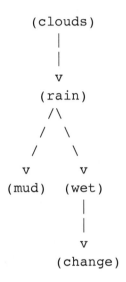

```
                (clouds)
                   |
                   |
                   v
                (rain)
                 /\
                /  \
               /    \
          v          v
       (mud)      (wet)
                     |
                     |
                     v
                (change)
```

And all this was just the warm-up act. Their real breakthrough was this: just as kids can discover causes by observation, computers can discern causes from data. Now obviously the easiest way to do this is just to measure what happens when you do($X=x$) directly — this, for example, is what randomized controlled trials do. Kids do it by dropping a fork on the floor and seeing if this causes Mom to pick it up; scientists do it by randomly giving some people a real drug and others just a placebo. The result is that we can be sure of the cause — after all, it was *we* who dropped the fork and gave out the drug; nothing else could be sneaking in and causing it.

But in most cases we don't have this luxury. We'd like to know whether a new tax policy will cause the economy to tank *before* we enact it; we'd like to know whether smoking causes cancer without forcing kids to smoke; and even in randomized controlled trials, we can give half the patients the real drug, but we can't make them take it. If the drug being tested makes someone so horribly sick that they stop taking it and then get better, drug trials still count that as a victory for the drug!

Obviously we can't always know such things just from observing, but in a surprising number of cases we can. And the researchers have developed a mathematical method — called the *do*-calculus — for determining just when you can. Feed it a Bayes network of variables, their relationships, and their values, and it will return back what it knows and with what certainty.

Thus, in an example Pearl frequently uses, tobacco companies used to argue that the correlation between smoking and cancer was simply because there were certain genes that made people both more likely to smoke *and* more likely to get cancer. It didn't matter if they quit smoking — their genes would lead cancer to get them anyway. Pearl shows that if we assume only smoking causes tar deposits on the lungs and the tar deposits are the only way smoking causes cancer, we can simply measure the tar deposits and calculate whether the tobacco companies are right.

Or, in another example in his book *Causality*, he analyzes data from a study on a cholesterol-reducing drug. Since whether people got the placebo or not is unassociated with any other variables (because it was randomly assigned) if we merely assume that receiving the real drug has *some* influence on whether people take it, we can calculate the effectiveness of the drug even with imperfect compliance. Indeed, we can even estimate how effective the drug would have been for people who were assigned it but didn't take it!

And that's not all — Peter Spirtes and Clark Glymour have developed an algorithm (known as PC, for Peter-Clark) that, given just the data, will do its best to calculate the causal network behind it. You can download the software implementing it, called TETRAD IV, for free from their department's website — it even has a nice graphical interface for drawing and displaying the networks.

As an experiment, I fed it some data from the IRS about 2005 income tax returns. It informed me that the percentage people donate to charity is correlated with the number of dependents they have, which in turn correlates with how much people receive from EITC. That amount, along with average income, causes how many people are on EITC. Average income is correlated with the tax burden which is correlated with inequality. All interesting and reasonable — and the result of just a few minutes' work.

The applications for such tools are endless. As Pearl points out, they have the possibility to radically improved how statistics are used in medicine, epidemiology, economics, sociology, and law. And, as Glymour observes, it lets us better understand results in neuroscience and psychology. Take *The Bell Curve*, the 1992 bestseller that argued blacks had lower IQs, causing poorer performance in school and thus lower-paying jobs and more crime. Glymour shows, by applying the do-calculus, these results only hold if you assume that there are no other interactions between the variables (e.g. that parental attitude toward learning doesn't affect both IQ and performance in school). But the PC algorithm and TETRAD IV can demonstrate otherwise.

Such results may be a revolution in social science, but compared to building human-like robots, they're child's play. That's certainly the impression one gets from Pearl. Discussing his work at a conference of Artificial Intelligence researchers, he said:

> One of the reasons I find these areas to be fertile grounds to try out new ideas is that, unlike AI, tangible rewards can be reaped from solving relative small problems. Problems involving barely 4 to 5 variables, which we in AI regard as toy-problems, carry tremendous payoffs in public health and social science.

Billions of dollars are invested each year on various public-health studies: Is chocolate ice-cream good for you or bad for you? Would red wine increase or decrease your heart rate? etc. etc.

The same applies to the social sciences. Would increasing police budget decrease or increase crime rates? Is the Colorado school incident due to TV violence or failure of public education? The Inter-university Consortium for Political and Social Research has distributed about 800 gigabytes worth of such studies in 1993 alone.

Unfortunately the causal-analytical methodology currently available to researchers in these fields is rather primitive, and every innovation can make a tremendous difference. […] This has been changing recently as new techniques are beginning to emerge from AI laboratories. I predict that a quiet revolution will take place in the next decade in the way causality is handled in statistics, epidemiology, social science, economics, and business. While news of this revolution will never make it to DARPA's newsletter, and even NSF is not equipped to appreciate or support it, it will nevertheless have enormous intellectual and technological impact on our society.

For science's sake, I hope he's right.

September 21, 2009

SHOULD OUR COGNITIVE BIASES HAVE MORAL WEIGHT?

In a classic piece of psychology[1], Kahneman and Tversky ask people what to do about a fatal disease that 600 people have caught. One group is asked whether they would administer a treatment that would definitely save 200 people's lives or one with a 33% chance of saving 600 people. The other group is asked whether they would administer a treatment under which 400 people would definitely die or one where there's a 33% chance that no one will die.

The two questions are the same: saving 600 people means no one will die, saving just 200 means the other 400 will die. But people's responses were radically different. The vast majority of people chose to save 200 people for sure. But an equally large majority chose to take the chance that no one will die. In other words, just changing how you describe the option — saying that it saves lives rather than saying it leaves people to die — changes which option most people will pick.

In the same way that Festinger, et. al. showed that our intuitions are biased by our social situation, Kahneman and Tversky demonstrated that humans suffer from consistent cognitive biases as well. In a whole host of examples, they showed people behaving in a way we wouldn't hesitate to think was irrational — like changing their position on whether to administer a treatment based on what it was called. (I think a similar problem affects our intuitions about killing versus letting die.)

This is a major problem for people like Frances Kamm, who think our moral philosophy must rely on our intuitions. If people consistently and repeatedly treat things differently based on what they're called, are we forced to give that moral weight? Is it OK to administer a treatment when it's described as saving people, but not when it's described as not saving enough? Surely moral rules should meet some minimal standard of rationality.

This problem affects a question close to Kamm's work: what she calls the Problem of Distance in Morality (PDM). Kamm says that her intuition consistently finds that moral obligations attach to things that are close to us, but not to thinks that are far away. According to her, if we see a child drowning in a pond and there's a machine nearby which, for a dollar, will scoop him out, we're morally obligated to give the machine a dollar. But if the machine is here but the scoop and child are on the other side of the globe, we don't have to put a dollar in the machine.

But, just as with how things are called, our intuitions about distance suffer from cognitive biases. Numerous studies have shown that the way we think about things nearby is radically different from the way we think about things far away. In one study[2], Indiana University students did better on a creativity test when they were told the test was devised by IU students studying in Greece than when they were told it was devised by IU students studying in Indiana.

It's a silly example, but it makes the point. If our creativity depends on whether someone mentions Greece or Purdue, it's no surprise our answers to moral dilemmas depend on whether they take place in the US or China. But surely these differences have no more moral validity than the ones that result from Tversky's experiment — they're just an unfortunate quirk of how we're wired. Rational reflection — not faulty intuitions — should be the test of a moral theory.

January 8, 2010

1. http://scholar.google.com/scholar?cluster=15957198663841029024
2. http://www.scribd.com/doc/24928678/Lessons-from-a-Faraway-land-The-effect-of-spatial-distance-on-creative-cognition

THE PERILS OF PARFIT 1: CREDIBLE COMMITMENTS

On the advice of several people, I started reading Derek Parfit's *Reasons and Persons*. I haven't gotten very far, but it seems to me to be a horribly muddled book, wrong on just about every point. So perhaps this will be an ongoing series where I debunk the book in sequence. I apologize to my readers if these posts seem obvious and not very interesting. That's because I think the situations Parfit discusses are actually quite simple and it's only his muddled terminology that makes them seem tricky.

Let's clarify Parfit's discussion of self-defeating theories, which really comes down to a discussion about credible commitments. For simplicity, imagine there is no interest or inflation and your only goal in life is to maximize how much money you have. Thus an act is rational iff it contributes to that goal.

Case 1: There are two buttons. SUBTRACT removes $1000 from your bank account, ADD adds $5000 to your bank account. Obviously it is rational to press ADD and irrational to press SUBTRACT.

Case 2: There is one button, BOTH, which does both at the same time. Obviously it is rational to press BOTH, since it results in a net gain of $4000.

Case 3: There is a different button, DELAY, which adds $5000 to your bank account today and then removes $1000 in exactly one week. (DELAY is a weird button — to prevent you from using it twice at the same time, it stays down for the whole week and only pops back up once the $1000 is removed.) Obviously it is rational to press DELAY since it too results in a net gain of $4000.

Case 4: There are two buttons: DELAY, which is the same as before, and EVADE, which changes your bank account number so that none of the other buttons work. You can only press each button once and they have no other consequences. It is rational to press DELAY and then EVADE, for a net gain of $5000.

When is it rational to press EVADE? Only when you don't expect to be able to press DELAY ever again. (EVADE gains you at most $1000, while DELAY gains you at least $4000.) If you could press DELAY twice, would it be rational to hit EVADE after the first press? Of course not, it'd cost you at least $4000. But Parfit seems to suggest one is acting rationally irrationally by not pressing it. The notion seems nonsensical.

Case 5: Same two buttons, except after you press the DELAY button it engages a little impenetrable metal cover that physically prevents you from pressing EVADE. It's rational to press DELAY. Then it's rational to press EVADE, but that's kind of irrelevant, because it's also impossible.

Case 6: Same as 5, except it injects you with a serum that prevents you from pressing EVADE. Again, it's rational to press DELAY and then rational but impossible to press EVADE.

I don't see a big difference between these two cases, but Parfit seems to think the difference is vital.

Perhaps it's the fact that another person is involved that leads to the complications? Case 7: Same as 4, except the $1000 goes into Bob's account and only Bob can press DELAY. Bob has the same notion of rationality as you and thus will only press DELAY if he believes you will not press EVADE. You could promise not to press it, but it would be irrational for you to keep that promise so Bob rightly does not believe it. However, it would be rational for you to engage the impenetrable cover or take the serum that prevents you from pressing EVADE.

There is no rational irrationality. Your goal of maximizing your money is not self-defeating. This all seems like the most obvious, unarguable stuff in the world. So I don't see why Parfit is so confused about it.

July 1, 2010

INDIVIDUALS IN A WORLD OF SCIENCE

We are all the same, we are all different — this is the great modern dilemma. At the same time science and technology lets us see our patterns (guess what books we'll like without ever meeting us, predict the probability with which a certain drug will have a certain side effect) our social independence encourages us to believe we cannot be so easily controlled (thus millions of people watching the same TV ad insisting they "think different").

The tension can be felt most acutely in medicine, where a long and storied tradition of individualism (each patient is unique, with their own symptoms and history and makeup) confronts the most expensive products of modern megascience (every pill of a drug is the same, its workings validated through a test on thousands of people). And then you have doctors, caught in the middle: what are they to be — brilliant individuals, cunningly solving problems on their own (or, more realistically, with a small team) or dutiful cogs, administering the treatments shown most effective by large experiments?

For every individual person, you can come up with a story about why the larger results may not apply (most of the people in that study were young and healthy, but you are old and frail). But that just replaces hard science with educated suspicion. On the whole what was proven true on the whole must work better, right?

This is the position of evidence-based medicine, which says that doctors can't be trusted to make these decisions by themselves. Unduly swayed by whim and bias, bribed in endless ways by the manufacturers of expensive drugs and tools, incentivized to give themselves more business, EBM proponents say we must take these choices out of their hands and give them to a panel of experts, who can review with time and distance what solid scientific studies say actually works and does not.

I've made it sound like I'm on the side of the scientific mass, but I'm really not. Is there any evidence that evidence-based medicine really works? Everything I've seen is shockingly inconclusive.

There have been big benefits from smaller interventions — giving doctors tools to encourage them to do the right things. Atul Gawande has been the greatest chronicler of such programs, from forceful reminders to wash your hands[1] to careful checklists before surgery.[2] But for the most part such programs aid doctors, not overrule them. This is good politics, but it's also good science: everyone rebels against direct instruction.

I think we have a choice to make. Doctors can be simply told what to do — in which case, why require all those years of med school? why not write down all the rules and instructions and let any random nurse follow them? — or they can be taught the lessons of the science but allowed to practice it on their own. They can be show their own human frailties and biases, the huge value that comes from following the proven rules, trained in the common fallacies of probability andstatistics, but in the end, allowed to make the final judgment for themselves. We can screen out those who fail to learn these lessons, but if we can't, at the end of the process, trust them to make their own decisions, why even bother to have doctors at all?

Medicine is the field where this is clearest, but the same tension has come to teaching as well — every student is the same, every student is different. We once allowed each teacher to direct their classroom in their own way, but high-stakes tests and "value-added" measurements now force all of them into the same mold.

Isn't this a good thing, demands Matt Yglesias? We have science that shows good teaching can make a huge difference in people's lives — doesn't everyone deserve the benefits that come from having a good teacher? He dismisses the stories of the individual horrors that result from this process as mere anecdote — inevitably in imposing a one-size-fits-all solution there will be some negative side effects for a few, but the benefits for the many outweigh the costs. Again, I have tried to put this position in its most favorable light (I hope Matt will correct me if I've failed) but I'm flabbergasted by its callous naiveté. The problem with allowing hard incentive systems to squeeze out individual judgment is inevitably that people begin trying to game the system — they cheat on the tests, they coach students on the answers, they cut recess and art for more drill-and-skill. To dismiss the on-the-ground evidence[3] of how badly these tests hurt kids, in favor of some Olympian view of the benefits of rising test scores, is ludicrous when the on-the-ground view is telling you *the test scores are actually bogus*.

Fine, Matt says, that just means we need to crack down on cheating. (This is always the first response of the incentive designer — we just need to improve the incentive system!) The fact that a couple teachers cheat on their students' tests is no reason to give up on all the benefits better teachers can being. And that's true, but blatant cheating is just the tip of the iceberg.

In medicine, we can at least measure whether people get healthy. A doctor with some radical new treatment can prove she's right by testing it against the previous best answer and showing it works better. And we want brilliant teachers to do the same: to come up with innovative new ways of teaching students and prove they work better than the old stale system. But the ultimate goal of school is much less clear and more disputed — is it to create orderly little capitalist worker bees or curious independent thinkers?

Matt *says please, we don't need to enter into this debate. I'm only talking about the fundamentals — basic literacy and arithmetic.* But I don't think that really helps. What good is learning to read if, by the end, you hate doing it?

One solution is to measure students by real results, rather than artificial tests. Can a child read and understand? Ask them to tell you about the books they've read lately. (This was how my library's summer reading program tested whether you actually read the books you claimed. Apparently I didn't understand most of Snow Crash as a kid, but I loved reading it anyway.) Or, better yet, ask them a question that involves doing some research and see if they can look up and read the answer.

For math, ask them to build something that involves a little calculation, or make change, or any of the real-world activities these isolated skills are supposed to be actually useful for. What you learn from that will be much more revealing than which bubbles kids fill in on a sheet.

The other alternative is to put your trust in teachers, to assume they can tell the difference between a class that's learning and a class that isn't, and then give them a chance to do better. Take them to some of the best-run classes in the world and let them absorb the lessons for themselves. Have them meet regularly with their fellow teachers and discuss how they can make their teaching better. This is the humane response to those who want to reduce teaching to a rote question of merely reading off a script (no joke — this is literally what happens in the most test-driven schools... because, after all, science shows the script is best for test scores).

In both cases, I sympathize with the humane aims: I don't want doctors to become shills for pharmaceutical companies, I don't want poor kids to grow up unable to read. But I blanch at the inhumane means proposed to carry them out. As Seeing Like a State describes, the history of high modernist utopian projects has not been a pretty one. The quest for policy designers, then, is how to promote huge positive changes without crushing the individuals involved underfoot.

April 6, 2011

1. http://www.amazon.com/Better-A-Surgeons-Notes-Performance/dp/0312427654
2. http://www.amazon.com/The-Checklist-Manifesto-Things-Right/dp/0312430000
3. http://www.amazon.com/Tested-American-School-Struggles-Grade/dp/0805088024
4. http://www.amazon.com/Seeing-Like-State-Institution-University/dp/0300078153

DO I HAVE TOO MUCH FAITH IN SCIENCE?

We live in a society where it's almost impossible to give science too much credit. Ever since the atom bomb and the space race, it's just been taken for granted that civilization advances through the progress of science. Science — we are told — grows our food, cures our diseases, creates our new technologies, and just generally propels the human race forward.

If science is the engine of progress, then those who have not been captured under its spell must be dusty relics of prejudice and caprice. Fields under the sway of hidebound tradition must be bulldozed and renovated in the image of science. Thus doctors, instead of making decisions by random whim, must be forced to practice "evidence-based medicine" where all their prescriptions are backed by randomized controlled trials. Policymakers, instead of just being bleeding-heart do-gooders, must temper their enthusiasm for regulation by doing cost-benefit analyses to see if their proposals make sense. Managers, instead of following their intuition, must subject their strategies to rigorous experiment — through A/B tests in the market.

But what's weird about this mania for science is how unscientific it all is. As far as I know, no studies have shown that evidence-based medicine leads to better patient outcomes or that companies which practice comprehensive A/B testing are more profitable than those which follow their intuition. And the evidence that science is responsible for stuff like increased life expectancy is surprisingly weak.

But there's such a mania for science that even asking these questions seems absurd. How could there possibly be evidence against evidence-based medicine? The whole idea seems like a contradiction in terms. But it is not.

Recent decades have seen science encroach on the kitchen, with scientific approaches to cooking and cuisine. Where other chefs might simply follow instructions they found on a yellowing scrap of paper, the new modernists seek to understand the physics behind their actions. This approach has led to some interesting new techniques, but it's also led us to understand that some of those silly traditions aren't so silly after all.

Eggs, for example, were often beaten in copper bowls. Why copper bowls? Chefs might have been able to give you some kind of reason, but it would have sounded silly to scientific ears. But the modernists discovered that the ions in the copper ended up forming complex bonds with the conalbumin in the eggs.

This was not something that chefs had ever established as scientific knowledge — no aproned Isaac Newton ever discovered this was the right way to cook the eggs — but it was knowledge chefs had nonetheless. It was, in Polyani's phrase, tacit knowledge, part of the things society genuinely knew but was never able to write down or clearly prove.

Scientism systematically destroys tacit knowledge. If chefs were forced to follow "evidence-based cooking", not using anything special like a copper bowl until their was a peer-reviewed double-blind randomized controlled trial proving its effectiveness, the result surely would be worse food. So why is it crazy to believe the same attitude leads to worse medicine?

In business, too, scientism could be quite destructive. Can Steve Jobs provide a proof for the rightness of every iPhone feature? Can Doug Bowman do a scientific experiment to justify his every shade of blue[1]? Forcing them to could well make their work far worse instead of better.

Scientism even fails just within our own heads. If you're struggling with a decision, we're taught to approach it more "scientifically", by systematically enumerating pros and cons and trying to weight and balance them. That's what Richard Feynman would do, right? Well, studies have shown that this sort of explicit approach repeatable leads to *worse* decisions than just going with your gut. Why? Presumably for the same reason: your gut is full of tacit knowledge that it's tough to articulate and write down. Just focusing on the stuff you can make explicit means throwing away everything else you know — destroying your tacit knowledge.

Of course, there's no guarantee that just trusting your gut will work either. Intuition and tradition are often just as wrong as scientific cluelessness. And in the cases where they genuinely have little to contribute, throwing them away (or quarantining it until it's proven by scientific test) might not be such a bad idea. But I've always just assumed that this was *always* true — that tradition and intuition had nothing to contribute, unless carefully coached by scientific practice. That science was the only way to get knowledge, rather than just another way of codifying it. Now, instead of throwing it all away, I'm now thinking I ought to spend more time finding ways to harness all that tacit knowledge.

August 10, 2012

1.   http://stopdesign.com/archive/2009/03/20/goodbye-google.html

WORK & TECH

AARON JOINS CREATIVE COMMONS
AS RDF ADVISOR

SF Gate: *All Hail Creative Commons: Stanford professor and author Lawrence Lessig plans a legal insurrection*[1].

Today I've been given permission to announce that I'm working on the Creative Commons project as an RDF Advisor. I can't say what I'm doing except that it involves RDF and I'm advising them on it. Details on what the project is about are in the article above. They're very kindly flying me to *O'Reilly's Emerging Technology Conference*[2] (what the P2P hackers bitterly call "Emerging Fads") where the project will be making its debut splash[3]. BTW, it looks to be a very exciting conference. I put together a long list of people I'm looking forward to seeing[4].

Some choice quotes:

Stanford law professor Lawrence Lessig's Creative Commons intends to produce "flexible, customizable intellectual-property licenses that artists, writers, programmers and others can obtain free of charge to legally define what constitutes acceptable uses of their work."

Technical Architect, Lisa Rein, discusses and demonstrates how the project uses JavaScript, Perl, HTML, and XML to create a web-based application for generating metadata, associated with digital works in a machine-readable format. The metadata corresponds to innovative and flexible licenses designed to help creators of intellectual works share their work with the public on generous terms. Search engines, file sharing applications, digital rights management tools, and other emerging technologies recognize the terms on which those works may be used.

March 05, 2002

1. http://www.sfgate.com/news/article/All-Hail-Creative-Commons-Stanford-professor-2874018.php
2. http://conferences.oreillynet.com/etcon2002/
3. http://conferences.oreillynet.com/cs/et2002/view/e_sess/2376
4. http://blogspace.com/swhack/weblog/2002/03/05/#i1015313089.384566

COPYRIGHT IS UNCONSTITUTIONAL!

I just read a wonderful article by Jed Rubenfeld[1]: The Freedom of Imagination: Copyright's Constitutionality[2] [via Felten[3]].

Imagine a country where reciting a poem in public could get you thrown in jail, the article suggests. You live in that country. Copyright law, of course, prevents public performance of a copyrighted work like a poem.

The article convincingly argues that copyright's restriction on derivative works is a clear violation of the First Amendment. It shoots down the five common arguments to the contrary:

- "Copyright is an enumerated power, so it is immune from the bill of rights." Rights trump powers, not vice versa. Outlawing interstate Bible sales would be unconstitutional, even though interstate commerce is an enumerated power.
- "Copyright only regulates the expression, not the idea." The idea behind "Fuck The Draft" can also be expressed in different ways, but the court ruled that the expression (even though it used profanity when it was unnecessary to communicate the idea) was protected.
- "Fair use prevents copyright from violating the First Amendment." Fair use does exactly the opposite. A law prohibiting all speech except that criticizing the government would clearly be unconstitutional, but fair use only protects derivative works that parody the original (and some other exceptions).
- "Copyright creates more speech overall, so it is in the First Amendment's interest." We don't make First Amendment judgements on these terms. Banning books creates more speech (from the uproar about the ban) but that's no excuse to ban books.
- "Copyright is just another form of property. You have no First Amendment right to trample on my property." Trampling on your property is illegal not for expressive reasons but for practical ones. (It's not allowed even when it's not expressive.) Infringing on your copyright is aimed at preventing certain forms of expression. Were you to do the same infringing activity (say, publishing a book) but with different content, it would be permitted.

The author goes on to suggest a form of copyright that would be constitutionally-permissible. Instead of preventing or punishing those who express derivative works, it could require that they pay a portion of their profits to the author. This wouldn't prevent anyone speaking (by definition, profit is a gain; taking it away would make you no worse off than if you had never done the thing at all) and would allow people to give away modified works for free, but would give authors what many feel is a just return for their work.

In this world, anyone could make *Harry Potter* into a movie or stage show, as long as they paid J. K. Rowling a portion of the money the make. Different adaptations and interpretation of the works would flourish; the public would get a chance to experience all sorts of new creative expression, here-to-fore impossible. This makes sound policy sense to me: the public gets the right to express it self, and creators of intellectual works get paid. But, as the author points out, it's irrelevant what you think of it as policy; it's required by our Constitution.

Finally, the author presents a unified theory of the First Amendment: it protects the freedom to imagine, express what you've imagined, and listen to that expression. It doesn't protect the right to misrepresent what you've imagined as fact (thus libel, perjury, and false advertising laws), nor does it protect the right to act out your imagination (you can't break someone's nose to express what you imagine a broken nose feels like). However, it does protect the freedom to imagine alternate beliefs (thus freedom of religion) or alternate governments (thus petitioning for a redress of grievances).

Back to the subject of copyright, it doesn't protect those who copy others works verbatim (that requires no imagination) but it does protect those who perform it, rework it, or express it — those who add their own spark of creativity to that which has come before. It's time for copyright law to stop suffocating the resulting flame and let it grow, as the First Amendment requires.

[I'm sure I cannot do justice to the cogent and well-expressed arguments of this fifty-page paper, but I hope I've given you some idea of them. If you're interested, I recommend you read it for yourself.]

December 07, 2002

1. http://www.law.yale.edu/outside/html/faculty/jr73/profile.htm
2. http://www.yale.edu/yalelj/112/112-1ab1.html
3. http://www.freedom-to-tinker.com/archives/000212.html

COPYRIGHT LAW EXISTS TO ENLARGE THE PUBLIC DOMAIN

Over on Doc Searls' DG, Timothy Philips makes a really profound statement[1]: "Copyright law exists to enlarge the public domain. That's all."

On its face it seemed false to me, which is why it's so interesting. Copyright law is certainly counter-intuitive — we lock things up so that more things will be free? It's very close to the GPL in fact — the GPL adds more restrictions so that other works will have less.

Certainly current copyright law hasn't lived up to these goals. The public domain hasn't gotten much larger since 1929! This statement is a concise way of explaining why copyright must serve the public and protect progress and it certainly makes you think. Thanks, Timothy.

It seems clear to me that this is the next battle. Once we've stopped the absurd regulations like the DMCA and Coble's bill, we need to go back and remove all the crud that's been added to copyright law over the years. I'd love to see it pushed back to fourteen years, renewable once. Even retroactively — that'd show them! Stay tuned.

[For crying out loud Dave[2], [the Berman-Coble bill] is super simple. If I build a house and people try to sleep in it I can kick them out.]

August 28, 2002

1. http://doc.weblogs.com/discuss/msgReader$2267?mode=day
2. http://scriptingnews.userland.com/backissues/2002/08/28#When:2:54:00PM

THE CASE FOR SOURCE CODE ESCROW

Lessig's latest post, *please, no philosophy*[1], explains why he thinks source code escrow is important. Here's a reformulation of the argument:

- 1. Copyright law restricted copies, but in return required that the government hold onto a copy and let others make copies when that copyright expired.
- 2. Now copyright law restricts modifications too. In return, it should require that the government let others make copies when the copyright expires.
- 3. With books, it's not so difficult to make modifications from the printed copy. But with software, it's nearly impossible: you'll probably end up rewriting much of the source code to get things to work right.
- [3a. Some have suggested this is analogous to making writers give their brains to the public. This is wrong: writers already distribute their work in a form that's easy to modify — a form that's rarely different from what the writer used themselves.
- 3b. A better analogy is that of an architect's plans: you can "reverse-engineer" a building (take pictures, walk around, maybe punch some holes in the walls) but if you want to modify it and make a derivative building, you'll probably end up recreating the plans and adding your modifications.]
- 4. To best let others make modifications of software, the government must ensure that the source code is made available when the copyright is up. The best way to do this is with source code escrow.

November 07, 2002

1. http://cyberlaw.stanford.edu/lessig/blog/archives/2002_11.shtml#000597

CHARGING SOCIETY

Mark Bernstein, who should know better, argues that software should be charged for[1]. I hear this a lot, but it ignores the underlying reality of how software is made. (In fact, it reminds me of the people who argue that the Internet should be pay-per-bit because, hey, look at all those bits being used up!) Producing software only costs a bunch of time, once.

There are a number of ways you can get that time: the author could already have a living (a lot of the best software is written this way, by professors or by programmers in their free time), his salary can be paid by some or all of the users who commission the software, or the software can be written speculatively and the cost can be paid back slowly by individual users.

All of these are perfectly valid ways of getting to write software, yet Mark (and others) imply that the first two (free time and commissioned) are somehow less valid than others.

I would argue (rather controversially) that the last might be less valid. It allows authors of popular things to make far more money than those who make less popular ones, even if they put in the same amount of work.

We don't see this outside of the creative world: the man who paves the LA freeway makes roughly the same as the man who paves the little dead-end street outside my house, even though the LA freeway is used a great deal more often.

What's the benefit of society paying all this extra money? The traditional one seems to be to offset the costs of speculation. The author of speculative software takes the risk that no one will buy it, and he'll lose everything he spent creating it. In exchange, he gets the reward that if it's really popular he'll make far more then he spent to create it, hopefully enough to subsidize his failures.

This seems like a realy stupid and inefficient system to me, and while I'm not sure how to replace it in every case, it seems like it should be avoided when possible. That's why I don't understand it when Mark denigrates the systems we've come up with for replacing it. If anything, it's the system of speculation (and its high costs to society) that should be denigrated.

Mark, as someone developing software speculatively, may not want to call attention to the money he could be unfairly taking from society through this system. But Mark's software seems to be exactly the niche product which would benefit from an alternate system. So what keeps him attached to this one? Is it the dream of writing the Great American Program and striking it rich?

May 26, 2003

1. http://markbernstein.org/May0301.html#note_34865

THE EARLY DAYS OF A BETTER WEBSITE

A reporter asked me to describe what the early days of our startup were like. Here's my response.

In the early days of Reddit, there were four of us crammed into a dingy little three-bedroom apartment (I slept in a kitchen cabinet). Every morning we'd wake up and stumble into the small space that I think was supposed to be a living room, where we'd placed desks along all four walls (Steve's wall had a small window, with a beautiful view of the wall of the next building over, just a couple feet away). The sky would be gray, the floor would be filthy, and we'd be three feet floors away from the rest of the world. Looking back, it's hard to see how we got any work done. Actually, looking back, I'm not sure we did.

Aside from the filth, my memories of those days mostly consist of an unending series of petty annoyances and frustrations. It's hard spending your working days in such close quarters with other people. It's even harder when you spend your nights there too. And it's almost impossible when you're all high-strung socially-awkward geeks. Tensions frequently flared.

Not that there wasn't a lot to get flared about. There were always bugs or complaints or new features you just couldn't get to work. And when you finally got the site working fine, a new storm of traffic would overwhelm things and you'd be back to picking up the pieces, making it run faster and more reliably.

There were lots of problems, but somehow we got over them. Take a nap, walk the fifteen minutes into town to get some food, go across the street to the abandoned playground, or, when things got really bad, just look at that ever-growing traffic graph. We must be doing something right, we figured, or at least not doing much that's particularly wrong.

While behind the scenes work was a disaster, in public things were going great. Every time we went out, more people seemed to know what Reddit was. We started selling Reddit t-shirts and people wearing them and recognizing started to pop up over town. One fan, on a short trip to Boston, even made a pilgrimage to our apartment and stole the Reddit sticker off our door. (We only found out where the missing sticker had gone when he bragged about it on his blog.) Reddit heads started appearing on more and more weblogs and sites I read started talking about Reddit as if they assumed everyone already knew what it was.

At parties, the awkwardness of trying to tell people what we did for a living ("We, uh, build a website. You know, it's kind of a news-type website.") gave way to recognition ("Oh yeah, I've heard of that site."), and then to profuse thanks for a great time-waster. Towards the end, actual introductions became unnecessary — people started recognizing us and coming up to say hi.

When I went home to visit my family, my dad insisted on setting up a meeting for me with a magazine publisher he knew. I was sure the visit would be a disaster — why would a magazine publisher take a punk kid like me seriously? — but once she heard our monthly visitor numbers, she was eager to start a partnership. The same scene repeated itself over and over.

Even when people had no idea what we did, the traffic gave us confidence. Once we won a free meal at a restaurant (actually, we won at least three different times) in exchange for suffering through a short lecture about financial planning opportunities. As the man talked about being sure to put money away for a safe day, we looked at each other knowingly. Either we'd sell big or blow up entirely. Staying safe just wasn't in our vocabulary.

November 7, 2006

PRIVACY, ACCURACY, SECURITY: PICK TWO

THE PROBLEMS WITH COMPULSORY LICENSING

Millions of people want to download music for, essentially, free. The record companies don't want them to do this, and claim that they're losing money and threaten to sue you into oblivion. How do we reconcile these two? One proposal is compulsory licensing.

The basic idea is that a large portion of the population pays a relatively small tax to the government who then gives it to the artists whose work is downloaded. Terry Fisher says that with a small tax on CD burners, DVD burners, DSL, and cable modems (costing the average family ~$50, less than they spend on DVDs and CDs) could pay for all the music and movies plus a 20% bureaucratic overhead.

Assuming this could be made to work, people could be convinced to accept it, and Congress could pass it, there are still three problems which can't all be solved.

PRIVACY

Some proposals suggest that we simply monitor everyone's Internet connection (or, usually, get the ISPs to do it) and send the results to the government. I think this is an unacceptable invasion on privacy. It's bad enough we have to have Carnivore watching our packets and describing our emails when law enforcement gets a warrant, but now you want the government to keep track of all the music and movies we download, all the time? I don't think that's going to fly.

ACCURACY

OK, they say, we won't watch everyone's computers. We'll just use sampling. This has worked well in other media. TV networks, for example, make money off of advertising. They charge for ads based on how many people watch the shows. They figure out how many people watch the shows using Nielsen ratings. Nielsen ratings are calculated by getting a small percentage of the population to install a set-top box which monitors what they watch and when and sends the results back to Nielsen.

(This has some interesting effects, among which is the fact that boycotts of shows only have a real effect insofar as the boycotters are Nielsen homes. This means that as long as you're not a Nielsen home, you can boycott a show and still watch it.)

("Sweeps week" is a similar phenomenon but on a somewhat smaller scale. Each individual TV station (like our local NBC affiliate, WMAQ) sells advertising also, so they need to know how many people locally watch the shows. But each little station can't afford to do the Nielsen thing, so they do something similar with paper diaries that they send out one week of the year. But they all do it on the same week (sweeps week) so the networks purposely introduce big guest stars and major cliffhangers that week to get more people to watch the show.)

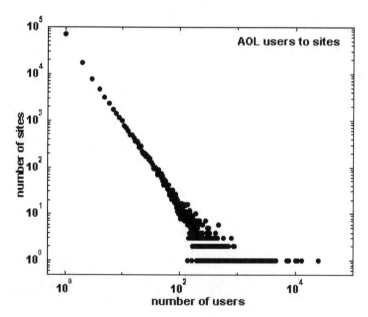

graph from Zipf, Power-laws, and Pareto — a ranking tutorial

This sounds good, and it works reasonably well for TV, but it won't work on the Internet. Popularity on the Internet doesn't follow the old rules, it follows something called a power law. (Thanks to Kevin Marks for pointing out this issue to me.) For example, the number of visitors to web pages follows a power law:

A graph of number of sites against number of users in log-log, showing a practically straight line.

The point of this graph (see next page) is that there are hundreds of thousands of sites with tens of users and tens of sites with hundreds of thousands of users. And there are tens of thousands of sites with hundreds of users, and thousands of sites with thousands of users and so on.

Sampling can't cope with this kind of disparity. It can deal when there are a small number of known groups who make up a very small amount of the population (just seek out those groups specifically). But it can't deal when there's a large number of unknown groups who each make up a very small amount of the population (like the tons of small websites, each with a small but loyal fanbase).

Who cares about these people? you may say. But while each of these groups have small fanbases individually, collectively they make up a significant portion, if not a majority, of the overall system. In other words, if you count these guys out you'll be doubling the amount of money folks like Britney Spears get over what they deserve.

Britney Spears seems to be doing just fine with the current system. If all we're doing is helping her, why are we going to all this trouble. And furthermore, if you're going to tax me to pay the artists I listen to, it's a little unfair if none of that money goes to the ones I actually care about.

SECURITY

Fine, fine, they say, if they read this far. How about we just have people submit the songs they listen to anonymously? People want their favorite artists to be paid, so they'll be happy to.

Yeah, but that's exactly the problem. People want their favorite artists to be paid, especially when those artists are themselves. What stops me from anonymously submitting that 1M people listened to my band and waiting for the money to roll in? Small things like that will get lost in the noise.

Even if the system isn't anonymous (so we're forgetting about privacy) you still have this problem. An enterprising MIT student, taking advantage of the fact that MIT has 16.5M IP addresses to themselves, writes a little program to pretend to be a whole bunch of MIT students who all have decided that his band is their new favorite. Again, it'll get lost in the noise of MIT and the money will roll in.

It doesn't seem right to tax Americans and give their money to fraudsters, no matter how clever the fraudsters are. It'll be really hard to eliminate fraud, and when it's so easy and anonymous, it'll be more widespread than anything we've seen before.

CONCLUSION

I've gone through all the compulsory licensing scenarios, and I always seem to get stuck on one (or more) of these issues. If anyone's found a way to eliminate all of them, please let me know!

July 29, 2003

SECRETS OF STANDARDS

In mjd's[1] talk "Mailing List Judo" (removed from the Web due to its evil content), he gives several strategies for getting your changes into Perl. The key point is that you only need to convince one person to accept your patch: the patch pumpkin. (The patch pumpkin is the one who folds patches into the official distribution of Perl.) Everyone else can be reasonably ignored.

With many standards projects, the process is reasonably similar. The group's output takes the form of a set of documents, each of which is controlled by one or two people (the Editors) who fold in changes and maintain the official version. There's sometimes also a dispute-resolution process (voting, consensus, etc.) if the editor doesn't know what to put in or the group disagrees with the editor.

The genius of Sam's wiki[2] was that there was no editor. Thought something was ugly? Change it. Think the text needed clarification? Clarify it. Sometimes disputes spilled out into separate pages but for the most part the process worked amazingly well.

But the process failed when it came to the big unresolved disputes. What should we name it? Should we encode HTML? There were polls but people didn't trust them. There were discussions but they never came to consensus. And often the loudest or most persistent voice would win by pushing their opponent to exhaustion. Unfortunately the most persistent voice is often the least experienced.

As we've begun to write actual specs, things have gotten even worse. Joe Gregorio and Mark Nottingham have become traditional editors of the API and feed format respectively. Sam Ruby and Mark Pilgrim took control of the spec by declaring milestones and updating their validator accordingly. The Wiki was turned into a unavigable swamp of a discussion forum for the drafts edited by other people. It's less than clear how to be a real part of the core group.

It's not too late to turn things around. Specs could be moved back into the wiki until they're nearly done. Editors, instead of being gatekeepers, could be helpful moderators. A clear process for making controvertial decisions could be decided on. And the validator could follow consensus instead of leading it. But do the people running the show want this?

Standards bodies tread a fine line between organizations for the public good and shelters for protecting collusion that would be otherwise illegal under antitrust law. For the dominent vendors involved, the goal is to give the illusion of openness while giving themselves full control to enforce their will behind the scenes.

The IETF is a good example of this. Often lauded by the public as a model of openness and and and freedom, the reality is that working group chairs, appointed by a self-elected ruling board, get away with declaring whatever they want (usually an inferior and difficult to implement alternative) as "rough consensus", routinely ignoring comments from the public and objections from working group members. One working group (in charge of DNS extentsions) went so far as to censor mail from working group members[3]. The dictators running the IETF, when informed, didn't seem to mind.

Is the same sort of thing at work in the Pie/Echo/Atom Project? It appears so at first glance: Sam running the show from behind the scenes, putting friends in charge of the specs (although that isn't what actually happened). The lack of a dispute-resolution process only makes things worse: when there's no clear guide on how to make decisions or contributions, it's far from obvious how to challenge a decision Sam has made.

There's no question that the group takes contributions from outsiders but they need to make it clearer that you can be part of the development process. I think moving specs onto the wiki will reinvigorate work and setting up a dispute resolution process will help us start moving forward, instead of stuck here where no decisions have been "final". The group seems to have fallen into a rut. I want to help them get out of it.

August 20, 2003

1. http://perl.plover.com/
2. http://intertwingly.net/wiki/pie/
3. http://cr.yp.to/djbdns/namedroppers.html

INTRODUCING INFOGAMI

Yay, Infogami is finally out. (If you don't know what Infogami is, go check out the front page.)

I began working on Infogami last summer, as part of the first batch of Y Combinator startups. At the end of the summer we had a working prototype and a number of offers for funding. Things were going so well I took a leave of absence from college to work on it.

But getting funding, as I hope to describe in later posts, wasn't as easy as I thought. I spent the next few months working full-time chasing funding offers, but eventually they all fell apart. I found myself stuck without any money, any partners, or any place to live. The whole experience was incredibly trying. There were many days when I felt like my head was going to literally explode.

One Sunday I decided I'd finally had enough of it. I went to talk to Paul Graham, the only person who had kept me going through these months. "This is it," I told him. "If I don't get either funding, a partner, or an apartment by the end of this week, I'm giving up." Paul did his best to talk me out of it and come up with solutions, but I still couldn't see any way out.

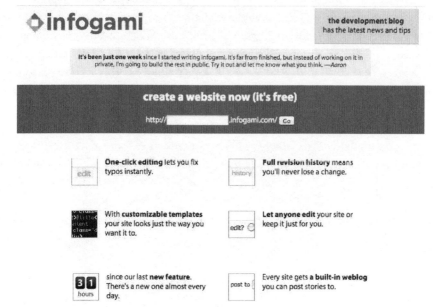

The next night I had dinner with Paul and his friends. They noted my birthday was tomorrow and asked me what I wanted. I thought for a moment about what I wanted most. "A cofounder," I finally said. We all laughed.

The next morning was my birthday and I was awakened by a knock on the door from Paul. "I thought of a solution to your problem," he exclaimed with his inimitable energy. "Merge with Reddit!" "That's an interesting idea," I said, still picking the sleep out of my eyes. As we discussed it, we just got more and more excited — it seemed like such a perfect fit. I still can't even imagine a better solution.

Steve "spez" Huffman and Alexis "kn0thing" Ohanian, the team behind Reddit, also liked the idea and we began working together that very day. Immediately, we could see things were going to work out great. We also got Steve and Alexis's housemate, Chris "KeyserSosa" Slowe, a Harvard physics Ph.D. student, to join the team. Together, we felt unstoppable.

Last month, when we got back from winter break, we began working on Infogami in earnest. It was clear that the prototype I'd built would never work for any serious site, so Steve built an amazing new industrial-strength database system while I built the software to talk to it. Unfortunately this amazing system is pretty much invisible to the outside world, but it's going to allow us to quickly build software that's more advanced than anything else out there.

Last week we moved over reddit.com to the new system, proving that it can handle a lot of users. With that finally finished, I decided I had to get Infogami up as soon as possible. Normally, we'd spend another couple months working on the software before we'd show it to the public, but I just couldn't wait much longer. So we decided to work like crazy for a week and launch whatever we had after seven days.

Obviously there's lots more work to do — right now we only have the most basic of features. But instead of continuing to work on it behind closed doors, we're going to try something different: we're going to build it in public.

There's tons of stuff left to build, including lots of things we can copy over from my original prototype. But more importantly, we want to hear what you want. Send us feedback and if you have an idea for Infogami, post it to our reddit where other users can vote it up and down. We'll try to implement the most popular requests.

Here's my goal: something new for Infogami every weekday. Some days it'll just be a blog post or a bug fix. But most days, we'll try to add a whole new feature. I hope you'll stay tuned.

March 1, 2004

REWRITING REDDIT

2012 note: This article was first published in 2005. After it was published, Django launched a RemovingTheMagic project to address some of my criticisms (though personally I still find it unusable), web.py inspired FriendFeed's tornado.web and Google's gae.webapp and others (though I still prefer web.py), and this article led to a permanent surge in Reddit traffic that still hasn't really stopped growing.

Over at reddit.com, we rewrote the site from Lisp to Python in the past week. It was pretty much done in one weekend. (Disclosure: We used my web.py library.) The others knew Lisp (they wrote their whole site in it) and they knew Python (they rewrote their whole site in it) and yet they decided liked Python better for this project. The Python version had less code that ran faster and was far easier to read and maintain.

The idea that there is something better than Lisp is apparently inconceivable to some, judging from comments on the reddit blog. The Lispers instead quickly set about trying to find the real reason behind the switch.

One assumed it must have been divine intervention, since "there seems to be no other reason for switching to an inferior language." Another figured something else must be going on: "Could this be…a lie? To throw off competition? It's not as though Paul Graham hasn't hinted at this tactic in his essays…" Another chimed in: "I decided it was a prank." Another suggested the authors simply wanted more "cut corners, hacks, and faked artisanship."

These were, of course, extreme cases. Others assumed there must have been outside pressure. "Either libraries or hiring new programmers I guess." Another concluded: "some vc suit wants a maintainable-by-joe-programmer product. I hope he pays you millions."

The Lisp newsgroup, comp.lang.lisp, was upset about the switch that they're currently planning to write a competitor to reddit in Lisp, to show how right they are or something.

The more sane argued along the lines of saying Lisp's value lies in being able to create new linguistic constructs and that for something like a simple web app, this isn't necessary, since the constructs have been already built. But even this isn't true. web.py was built pretty much from scratch and uses all sorts of "new linguistic constructs" and — even better — these constructs have syntax that goes along with them and makes them reasonably readable. Sure, Python isn't Perl 6, so you can't add arbitrary syntax, but you can often find a clever way to get the job done.

Python, on the other hand, has problems of its own. The biggest is that it has dozens of web application frameworks, but none of them are any good. Pythonists are well aware of the first part but apparently not of the second, since when I tell them that I'm using my own library, the universal response is "I don't think Python needs another web application framework". Yes, Python needs fewer web application frameworks. But it also needs one that doesn't suck.

The framework that seems most promising is Django and indeed we initially attempted to rewrite Reddit in it. As the most experienced Python programmer, I tried my best to help the others out.

Django seemed great from the outside: a nice-looking website, intelligent and talented developers, and a seeming surplus of nice features. The developers and community are extremely helpful and responsive to patches and suggestions. And all the right goals are espoused in their philosophy documents and FAQs. Unfortunately, however, they seem completely incapable of living up to them.

While Django claims that it's "loosely coupled", using it pretty much requires fitting your code into Django's worldview. Django insists on executing your code itself, either through its command-line utility or a specialized server handler called with the appropriate environment variables and Python path. When you start a project, by default Django creates folders nested four levels deep for your code and while you can move around some files, I had trouble figuring out which ones and how.

Django's philosophy says "Explicit is better than implicit", but Django has all sorts of magic. Database models you create in one file magically appear someplace else deep inside the Django module with a different name. When your model function is called, new things have been added to its variable-space and old ones removed. (I'm told they're currently working on fixing both of these, though.)

Another Django goal is "less code", at least for you. But Django is simply full of code. Inside the django module are 10 different folders and inside each of those are a few more. By the time you actually build a site in the Django tutorial, you've imported

`django.core.meta`, `django.models.polls`, `django.conf.urls.defaults.*`, `django.`
`utils.httpwrappers.HttpResponse`, and `django.core.extensions.render_to_response`.
It's not clear how anyone is supposed to remember all that, especially since there appear to be no guiding principles for what goes where or how it's named. Three of these are inserted automatically by the start scripts, but you still need to memorize such names for every other function you want to use.

But Django's most important problem is that its developers seem incapable of designing a decent API. They're clearly capable Python programmers — their code uses all sorts of bizarre tricks. And they're clearly able to write code that works — they have all sorts of interesting features. But they can't seem to shape this code into something that other people can use.

Their APIs are ugly and regularly missing key features: the database API figures out queries by counting underscores but has no special syntax for JOINs, the template system requires four curly braces around every variable and can't do any sort of computation, the form API requires 15 lines to process a form and can't automatically generate the template.

I tried my best to fix things — and the Django community was extremely supportive — but the task simply dwarfed me. I just couldn't do it mentally, let alone with the time constraints of having to actually build my own application for my own startup.

And so, Lisp and Django found wanting, we're left with web.py. I'd like to say that web.py learned from these mistakes and was designed to avoid them, but the truth is that web.py was written long before all this and managed to avoid them anyway.

The way I wrote web.py was simple: I imagined how things should work and then I made that happen. Sometimes making things just work takes a lot of code. Sometimes it only takes a little. But either way, that fact is hidden from the user — they just get the ideal API.

So how should things work? The first principle is that code should be clear and simple. If you want to output some text, you call web.output. If you want to get form input, you call web.input. There's nothing particularly hard to remember.

The second principle is that web.py should fit your code, not the other way around. Every function in web.py is completely independent, you can use whichever ones you want. You can put your files wherever you like, and web.py will happily follow along. If you want a piece of code to be run as a web app, you call web.run, you don't put your code in the magical place so that web.py can run you.

The third principle is that web.py should, by default, do the right thing by the Web. This means distinguishing between GET and POST properly. It means simple, canonical URLs which synonyms redirect to. It means readable HTML with the proper HTTP headers.

And that, as far as I'm concerned, are pretty much all the principles you need. They seem pretty simple and obvious to me and I'm even willing to fudge on some of them, but no other Python web app framework seems to even come close. (If you know of one, tell me and I'll happily recant. I don't want to be in this business.) Until then, it looks like I'm forced to do that horrible thing I'd rather not do: release one more Python web application framework into the world.

December 6, 2005

A BRIEF HISTORY OF AJAX

New technology quickly becomes so pervasive that it's sometimes hard to remember what things were like before it. The latest example of this in miniature is the technique known as Ajax, which has become so widespread that it's often thought that the technique has been around practically forever.

In some ways it has. During the first big stretch of browser innovation, Netscape added a feature known as LiveScript, which allowed people to put small scripts in web pages so that they could continue to do things after you'd downloaded them. One early example was the Netscape form system, which would tell you if you'd entered an invalid value for a field as soon as you entered it, instead of after you tried to submit the form to the server.

LiveScript became JavaScript and grew more powerful, leading to a technique known as Dynamic HTML, which was typically used to make things fly around the screen and change around in response to user input. Doing anything serious with Dynamic HTML was painful, however, because all the major browsers implemented its pieces slightly differently.

Shortly before web development died out, in early versions of Mozilla, Netscape showed a new kind of technique. I don't think it ever had a name, but we could call it Dynamic XML. The most vivid example I remember seeing was a mockup of an Amazon.com search result. The webpage looked just like a typical Amazon.com search result page, but instead of being written in HTML it was a piece of XML data which was then rendered for the user by a piece of JavaScript. The cool part was that this meant the rendering could be changed on the fly — there were a bunch of buttons that would allow you to sort the books in different ways and have them display using different schemes.

Shortly thereafter the bubble burst and web development crashed. Not, however, before Microsoft added a little-known function call named XMLHttpRequest to IE5. Mozilla quickly followed suit and, while nobody I know used it, the function stayed there, just waiting to be taken advantage of.

XMLHttpRequest allowed the JavaScript inside web pages to do something they could never really do before: get more data.[1] Before, all the data either had to be sent with the web page. If you wanted more data or new data, you had to grab another web page. The JavaScript inside web pages couldn't talk to the outside world. XMLHttpRequest changed that, allowing web pages to get more data from the server whenever they pleased.

Google was apparently the first to realize what a sea change this was. With Gmail and Google Maps, they built applications that took advantage of this to provide a user interface that was much more like a web application. (The startup Oddpost, bought by Yahoo, actually predated this but their software was for-pay and so they didn't receive as much attention.)

With Gmail, for example, the application is continually asking the server if there's new email. If there is, then it live updates the page, it doesn't make you download a new one. And Google Maps lets you drag a map around and, as you do so, automatically downloads the parts of it you want to look at inline, without making you wait for a whole new page to download.

Jesse James Garrett of Adaptive Path described this new tactic as Ajax (Asynchronous Javascript And XML) in an essay and the term immediately took off. Everyone began using the technique in their own software and JavaScript toolkits sprung up to make doing so even easier.

And the rest is future history.

Both systems were relatively ill-supported by browsers in my experience. They were, after all, hacks. So while they both seemed extremely cool (KnowNow, in particular, had an awesome demo that allowed for a WYSIWYG SubEthaEdit-style live collaboration session in a browser), they never really took off.

Now apparently there is another technique, which I was unaware of, that involved changing the URL of an iframe to load new JavaScript. I'm not sure why this technique didn't quite take off. While Google Maps apparently used it (and Oddpost probably did as well), I don't know of any other major users.

December 22, 2005

1.   As my commenters point out — and as I well knew, but momentarily
      forgotten — this isn't really true. Before XMLHttpRequest, people used
      a trick of not closing the connection to the server. The server would
      keep adding more and more to the page, never saying it had finished
      downloading. Ka-Ping Yee used this technique to make a real-time chat
      system based on an animated GIF. And the ill-fated startup KnowNow used
      a similar technique with JavaScript to allow for live-updating pages.

RELEASE LATE, RELEASE RARELY

When you look at something you're working on, no matter what it is, you can't help but see past the actual thing to the ideas that inspired it, your plans for extending it, the emotions you've tied to it. But when others look at it, all they see is a piece of junk.

You only get one chance to make a first impression; why have it be "junk"? Once that's associated with your name or project, it's tough to scrape off. Even people who didn't see it themselves may have heard about it second-hand. And once they hear about it, they're not likely to see for themselves. Life's too short to waste it on junk.

But when you release late, after everything has been carefully polished, you can share something of genuine quality. Apple, for example, sometimes releases stupid stuff, but it always looks good. Even when they flub, people give them the benefit of the doubt. "Well, it looks great but I don't really like it" is a lot better then "it's a piece of junk".

Still, you can do better. Releasing means showing it to the world. There's nothing wrong with showing it to friends or experts or even random people in a coffee shop. The friends will give you the emotional support you would have gotten from actual users, without the stress. The experts will point out most of the errors the world would have found, without the insults. And random people will not only give you most of the complaints the public would, they'll also tell you why the public gave up even before bothering to complain.

This is why "release early, release often" works in "open source": you're releasing to a community of insiders. Programmers know what it's like to write programs and they don't mind using things that are unpolished. They can see what you're going to do next and maybe help you get there.

The public isn't like that. Don't treat them like they are.

July 5, 2006

THE FRUITS OF MASS COLLABORATION

I often think that the world needs to be a lot more organized. Lots of people write reviews of television shows, but nobody seems to collect and organize them all. Good introductory guides to subjects are essential for learning, yet I only stumble upon them by chance. The cumulative knowledge of science is one of our most valuable cultural products, yet it can only be found scattered across thousands of short articles in hundreds of different journals.

I suspect the same thoughts occur to many of a similar cast of mind, since there's so much effort put into discouraging them. The arbiters of respectable opinion are frequently found to mock such grand projects or point out deficiencies in them. And a friend of mine explained to me that soon out of school he nearly killed himself by trying to embark on such a grand project and now tries to prevent his friends from making the same mistake.

One can, of course, make the reverse argument: since there is so much need for such organization projects, they must be pretty impossible. But upon closer inspection, that isn't true. Is there a project more grand than an encyclopedia or a dictionary? Who dares to compress all human knowledge or an entire language into a single book? And yet, there's not just one but several brands of each!

It seems that when the audience is large enough (and just about everyone has use for encyclopedias and dictionaries), it is possible to take on grand projects. This suggests that the hold-up is not practical, but economic. The funding simply isn't there to do the same for other things.

But all this is only true for the era of the book, where such a project means gathering together a group of experts and having them work full-time to build a Reference Work which can be published and sold expensively to libraries. I tend to avoid net triumphalism, but the Internet, it would seem, changes that. Wikipedia was created not by dedicated experts but by random strangers and while we can complain about its deficiencies, all admit that it's a useful service.

The Internet is the first medium to make such projects of mass collaboration possible. Certainly numerous people send quotes to Oxford for compilation in the Oxford English Dictionary, but a full-time staff is necessary sort and edit these notes to build the actual book (not to mention all the other work that must be done). On the Internet, however, the entire job — collection, summarization, organization, and editing — can be done in spare time by mutual strangers.

An even more striking, but less remarked-upon, example is Napster. Within only months, almost as a by-product, the world created the most complete library of music and music catalog data ever seen. The contributors to this project didn't even realize they were doing this! They all thought they were simply grabbing music for their own personal use. Yet the outcome far surpassed anything consciously attempted.

The Internet fundamentally changes the practicalities of large organization projects. Things that previously seemed silly and impossible, like building a detailed guide to every television show are now being done as a matter of course. It seems like we're in for an explosion of such modern reference works, perhaps with new experiments into tools for making them.

July 18, 2006

THE TECHNIQUES OF MASS COLLABORATION
A THIRD WAY OUT

I'm not the first to suggest that the Internet could be used for bringing users together to build grand databases (see article on previous page). The most famous example is the Semantic Web project (where, in full disclosure, I worked for several years). The project, spearheaded by Tim Berners-Lee, inventor of the Web, proposed to extend the working model of the Web to more structured data, so that instead of simply publishing text web pages, users could publish their own databases, which could be aggregated by search engines like Google into major resources.

The Semantic Web project has received an enormous amount of criticism, much (in my view) rooted in misunderstandings, but much legitimate as well. In the news today is just the most recent example, in which famed computer scientist turned Google executive Peter Norvig challenged Tim Berners-Lee[1] on the subject at a conference.

The confrontation symbolizes the (at least imagined) standard debate on the subject, which Mark Pilgrim termed million dollar markup versus million dollar code[2]. Berners-Lee's W3C, the supposed proponent of million dollar markup, argues that users should publish documents that state in special languages that computers can process exactly what they want to say. Meanwhile Google, the supposed proponent of million dollar code, thinks this is an impractical fantasy, and that the only way forward is to write more advanced software to try to extract the meaning from the messes that users will inevitably create.[3]

But yesterday I suggested what might be thought of as a third way out; one Pilgrim might call million dollar users. Both the code and the markup positions make the assumption that users will be publishing their own work on their own websites and thus we'll need some way of reconciling it. But Wikipedia points to a different model, where all the users come to one website, where the interface for inputting data in the proper format is clear and unambiguous, and the users can work together to resolve any conflicts that may come up.

Indeed, this method strikes me as so superior that I'm surprised I don't see it discussed in this context more often. Ignorance doesn't seem plausible; even if Wikipedia was a late-comer, sites like ChefMoz[4] and MusicBrainz[5] followed this model and were Semantic Web case studies. (Full disclosure: I worked on the Semantic Web portions of MusicBrainz.) Perhaps the reason is simply that both sides — W3C and Google — have the existing Web as the foundation for their work, so it's not surprising that they assume future work will follow from the same basic model.

One possible criticism of the million dollar users proposal is that it's somehow less free than the individualist approach. One site will end up being in charge of all the data and thus will be able to control its formation. This is perhaps not ideal, certainly, but if the data is made available under a free license it's no worse than things are now with free software. Those angry with the policies can always exercise their right to "fork" the project if they don't like the direction things are going. Not ideal, certainly, but we can try to dampen such problems by making sure the central sites are run as democratically as possible.

Another argument is that innovation will be hampered: under the individualist model, any person can start doing a new thing with their data, and hope that others will pick up the technique. In the centralized model, users are limited by the functionality of the centralized site. This too can be ameliorated by making the centralized site as open to innovation as possible, but even if it's closed, other people can still do new things by downloading the data and building additional services on top of it (as indeed many have done with Wikipedia[6]).

It's been eight years since Tim Berners-Lee published his Semantic Web Roadmap[7] and it's difficult to deny that things aren't exactly going as planned. Actual adoption of Semantic Web technologies has been negligible and nothing that promises to change that appears on the horizon. Meanwhile, the million dollar code people have not fared much better. Google has been able to launch a handful of very targeted features, like music search and answers to very specific kinds of questions but these are mere conveniences, far from changing the way we use the Web.

By contrast, Wikipedia has seen explosive growth, Amazon.com has become the premier site for product information, and when people these days talk about user-generated content, they don't even consider the individualized sense that the W3C and Google assume. Perhaps it's time to try the third way out.

July 19, 2006

1. http://news.com.com/Google+exec+challenges+Berners-Lee/2100-1025_3-6095705.html
2. http://diveintomark.org/archives/2002/12/29/million_dollar_markup
3. I say supposed because although this is typically how the debate is seen, I don't think either the W3C or Google actually hold the strict positions on the subject typically ascribed to them. Nonetheless, the question is real and it's convenient to consider the strongest forms of the positions.
4. http://chefmoz.org/
5. http://musicbrainz.org/
6. http://en.wikipedia.org/wiki/Wikipedia:Tools
7. http://www.w3.org/DesignIssues/Semantic.html

WHAT DOES BLOGSPACE LOOK LIKE?

I've been analyzing the content of blogs lately, looking for patterns. It's a huge amount of data, which makes for some tricky technical problems. Finally, tonight, thanks to some help from friends and the Large Graph Layout package, I've finally got some results. And they're stunning. Ladies and gentlemen, the blogosphere:

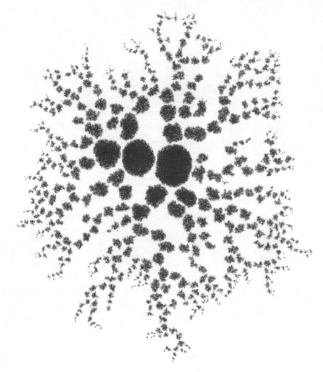

graph of blogspace

And, for fun, let's zoom in one of those small splotches:

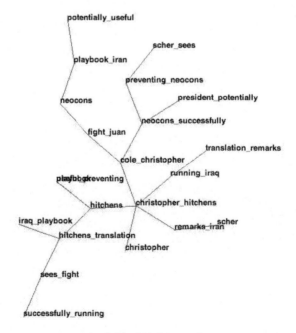

graph of the hitchens node

July 26, 2006

1. http://lgl.sourceforge.net/

WIKIMEDIA AT THE CROSSROADS

A couple weeks ago I had the great privilege of attending Wikimania, the international Wikimedia conference. Hundreds from all over the world gathered there to discuss the magic that is Wikipedia, thinking hard about what it means and why it works. It was an amazing intellectual and emotional experience.

The main attraction was seeing the vibrant Wikipedia community. There were the hardcore Wikipedians, who spend their days reviewing changes and fixing pages. And there were the elder statesmen, like Larry Lessig and Brewster Kahle, who came to meet the first group and tell them how their work fits into a bigger picture. Spending time with all these people was amazing fun — they're all incredibly bright, enthusiastic and, most shockingly, completely dedicated to a cause greater than themselves.

At most "technology" conferences I've been to, the participants generally talk about technology for its own sake. If use ever gets discussed, it's only about using it to make vast sums of money. But at Wikimania, the primary concern was doing the most good for the world, with technology as the tool to help us get there. It was an incredible gust of fresh air, one that knocked me off my feet.

There was another group attending, however: the people holding up the platform on which this whole community stands. I spent the first few days with the mostly-volunteer crew of hackers who keep the websites up and running. In later days, I talked to the site administrators who exercise the power that the software gives them. And I heard much about the Wikimedia Foundation, the not-for-profit that controls and runs the sites.

Much to my surprise, this second group was almost the opposite of the first. With a few notable exceptions, when they were off-stage they talked gossip and details: how do we make the code stop doing this, how do we get people to stop complaining about that, how can we get this other group to like us more. Larger goals or grander visions didn't come up in their private conversations; instead they seemed absorbed by the issues of the present.

Of course, they have plenty to be absorbed by. Since January, Wikipedia's traffic has more than doubled and this group is beginning to strain under the load. At the technical level, the software development and server systems are both managed by just one person, Brion Vibber, who appears to have his hands more-than-full just keeping everything running. The entire system has been cobbled together as the site has grown, a messy mix of different kinds of computers and code, and keeping it all running sounds like a daily nightmare. As a result, actual software development goes rather slowly, which cannot help but affect the development of the larger project.

The small coterie of site administrators, meanwhile, are busy dealing with the ever-increasing stream of complaints from the public. The recent Seigenthaler affair, in which the founding editor of USA Today noisily attacked Wikipedia for containing an grievous error in its article on him, has made people very cautious about how Wikipedia treats living people. (Although to judge just from the traffic numbers, one might think more such affairs might be a good idea…) One administrator told me how he spends his time scrubbing Wikipedia clean of unflattering facts about people who call the head office to complain.

Finally, the Wikimedia Foundation Board seems to have devolved into inaction and infighting. Just four people have been actually hired by the Foundation, and even they seem unsure of their role in a largely-volunteer community. Little about this group — which, quite literally, controls Wikipedia — is known by the public. Even when they were talking to dedicated Wikipedians at the conference, they put a public face on things, saying little more than "don't you folks worry, we'll straighten everything out".

The plain fact is that Wikipedia's gotten too big to be run by just a couple of people. One way or another, it's going to have to become an organization; the question is what kind. Organizational structures are far from neutral: whose input gets included decides what actions get taken, the positions that get filled decide what things get focused on, the vision at the top sets the path that will be followed.

I worry that Wikipedia, as we know it, might not last. That its feisty democracy might ossify into staid bureaucracy, that its innovation might stagnate into conservatism, that its growth might slow to stasis. Were such things to happen, I know I could not just stand by and watch the tragedy. Wikipedia is just too important — both as a resource and as a model — to see fail.

That is why, after much consideration, I've decided to run for a seat on the Wikimedia Foundation's Board. I've been a fairly dedicated Wikipedian since 2003, adding and editing pages whenever I came across them. I've gone to a handful of Wikipedia meetups and even got my photo on the front page of the *Boston Globe* as an example Wikipedian. But I've never gotten particularly involved in Wikipedia politics — I'm not an administrator, I don't get involved in policy debates, I hardly even argue on the "talk pages". Mostly, I just edit.

And, to be honest, I wish I could stay that way. When people at Wikimania suggested I run for a Board seat, I shrugged off the idea. But since then, I've become increasingly convinced that I should run, if only to bring attention to these issues. Nobody else seems to be seriously discussing this challenge.

The election begins today and lasts three weeks. As it rolls on, I plan to regularly publish essays like this one, examining the questions that face Wikipedia in depth. Whether I win or not, I hope we can use this opportunity for a grand discussion about where we should be heading and what we can do to get there. That said, if you're an eligible Wikipedian, I hope that you'll please vote for me.

August 31, 2006

WHO WRITES WIKIPEDIA?

I first met Jimbo Wales, the face of Wikipedia, when he came to speak at Stanford. Wales told us about Wikipedia's history, technology, and culture, but one thing he said stands out. "The idea that a lot of people have of Wikipedia," he noted, "is that it's some emergent phenomenon — the wisdom of mobs, swarm intelligence, that sort of thing — thousands and thousands of individual users each adding a little bit of content and out of this emerges a coherent body of work." But, he insisted, the truth was rather different: Wikipedia was actually written by "a community … a dedicated group of a few hundred volunteers" where "I know all of them and they all know each other". Really, "it's much like any traditional organization."

The difference, of course, is crucial. Not just for the public, who wants to know how a grand thing like Wikipedia actually gets written, but also for Wales, who wants to know how to run the site. "For me this is really important, because I spend a lot of time listening to those four or five hundred and if … those people were just a bunch of people talking … maybe I can just safely ignore them when setting policy" and instead worry about "the million people writing a sentence each".

So did the Gang of 500 actually write Wikipedia? Wales decided to run a simple study to find out: he counted who made the most edits to the site. "I expected to find something like an 80-20 rule: 80% of the work being done by 20% of the users, just because that seems to come up a lot. But it's actually much, much tighter than that: it turns out over 50% of all the edits are done by just 0.7% of the users … 524 people. … And in fact the most active 2%, which is 1400 people, have done 73.4% of all the edits." The remaining 25% of edits, he said, were from "people who [are] contributing … a minor change of a fact or a minor spelling fix … or something like that."

Stanford wasn't the only place he's made such a claim; it's part of the standard talk he gives all over the world. "This is the group of around a thousand people who really matter", he told us at Stanford. "There is this tight community that is actually doing the bulk of all the editing", he explained at the Oxford Internet Institute. "It's a group of around a thousand to two thousand people," he informed the crowd at GEL 2005. These are just the three talks I watched, but Wales has given hundreds more like them.

At Stanford the students were skeptical. Wales was just counting the number of edits — the number of times a user changed something and clicked save. Wouldn't things be different if he counted the amount of text each user contributed? Wales said he planned to do that in "the next revision", but was sure "my results are going to be even stronger", because he'd no longer be counting vandalism and other changes that later got removed.

Wales presents these claims as comforting. Don't worry, he tells the world, Wikipedia isn't as shocking as you think. In fact, it's just like any other project: a small group of colleagues working together toward a common goal. But if you think about it, Wales's view of things is actually much more shocking: around a thousand people wrote the world's largest encyclopedia in four years for free? Could this really be true?

Curious and skeptical, I decided to investigate. I picked an article at random ("Alan Alda") to see how it was written. Today the Alan Alda page is a pretty standard Wikipedia page: it has a couple photos, several pages of facts and background, and a handful of links. But when it was first created, it was just two sentences: "Alan Alda is a male actor most famous for his role of Hawkeye Pierce in the television series MASH. Or recent work, he plays sensitive male characters in drama movies." How did it get from there to here?

Edit by edit, I watched the page evolve. The changes I saw largely fell into three groups. A tiny handful — probably around 5 out of nearly 400 — were "vandalism": confused or malicious people adding things that simply didn't fit, followed by someone undoing their change. The vast majority, by far, were small changes: people fixing typos, formatting, links, categories, and so on, making the article a little nicer but not adding much in the way of substance. Finally, a much smaller amount were genuine additions: a couple sentences or even paragraphs of new information added to the page.

Wales seems to think that the vast majority of users are just doing the first two (vandalizing or contributing small fixes) while the core group of Wikipedians writes the actual bulk of the article. But that's not at all what I found. Almost every time I saw a substantive edit, I found the user who had contributed it was not an active user of the site. They generally had made less than 50 edits (typically around 10), usually on related pages. Most never even bothered to create an account.

To investigate more formally, I purchased some time on a computer cluster and downloaded a copy of the Wikipedia archives. I wrote a little program to go through each edit and count how much of it remained in the latest version. Instead of counting edits, as Wales did, I counted the number of letters a user actually contributed to the present article.

If you just count edits, it appears the biggest contributors to the Alan Alda article (7 of the top 10) are registered users who (all but 2) have made thousands of edits to the site. Indeed, #4 has made over 7,000 edits while #7 has over 25,000. In other words, if you use Wales's methods, you get Wales's results: most of the content seems to be written by heavy editors.

But when you count letters, the picture dramatically changes: few of the contributors (2 out of the top 10) are even registered and most (6 out of the top 10) have made less than 25 edits to the entire site. In fact, #9 has made exactly one edit — this one!

With the more reasonable metric — indeed, the one Wales himself said he planned to use in the next revision of his study — the result completely reverses.

I don't have the resources to run this calculation across all of Wikipedia (there are over 60 million edits!), but I ran it on several more randomly-selected articles and the results were much the same. For example, the largest portion of the Anaconda article was written by a user who only made 2 edits to it (and only 100 on the entire site). By contrast, the largest number of edits were made by a user who appears to have contributed no text to the final article (the edits were all deleting things and moving things around).

When you put it all together, the story become clear: an outsider makes one edit to add a chunk of information, then insiders make several edits tweaking and reformatting it. In addition, insiders rack up thousands of edits doing things like changing the name of a category across the entire site — the kind of thing only insiders deeply care about. As a result, insiders account for the vast majority of the edits. But it's the outsiders who provide nearly all of the content.

And when you think about it, this makes perfect sense. Writing an encyclopedia is hard. To do anywhere near a decent job, you have to know a great deal of information about an incredibly wide variety of subjects. Writing so much text is difficult, but doing all the background research seems impossible.

On the other hand, everyone has a bunch of obscure things that, for one reason or another, they've come to know well. So they share them, clicking the edit link and adding a paragraph or two to Wikipedia. At the same time, a small number of people have become particularly involved in Wikipedia itself, learning its policies and special syntax, and spending their time tweaking the contributions of everybody else.

Other encyclopedias work similarly, just on a much smaller scale: a large group of people write articles on topics they know well, while a small staff formats them into a single work. This second group is clearly very important — it's thanks to them encyclopedias have a consistent look and tone — but it's a severe exaggeration to say that they wrote the encyclopedia. One imagines the people running Britannica worry more about their contributors than their formatters.

And Wikipedia should too. Even if all the formatters quit the project tomorrow, Wikipedia would still be immensely valuable. For the most part, people read Wikipedia because it has the information they need, not because it has a consistent look. It certainly wouldn't be as nice without one, but the people who (like me) care about such things would probably step up to take the place of those who had left. The formatters aid the contributors, not the other way around.

Wales is right about one thing, though. This fact does have enormous policy implications. If Wikipedia is written by occasional contributors, then growing it requires making it easier and more rewarding to contribute occasionally. Instead of trying to squeeze more work out of those who spend their life on Wikipedia, we need to broaden the base of those who contribute just a little bit.

Unfortunately, precisely because such people are only occasional contributors, their opinions aren't heard by the current Wikipedia process. They don't get involved in policy debates, they don't go to meetups, and they don't hang out with Jimbo Wales. And so things that might help them get pushed on the backburner, assuming they're even proposed.

Out of sight is out of mind, so it's a short hop to thinking these invisible people aren't particularly important. Thus Wales's belief that 500 people wrote half an encyclopedia. Thus his assumption that outsiders contribute mostly vandalism and nonsense. And thus the comments you sometimes hear that making it hard to edit the site might be a good thing.

"I'm not a wiki person who happened to go into encyclopedias," Wales told the crowd at Oxford. "I'm an encyclopedia person who happened to use a wiki." So perhaps his belief that Wikipedia was written in the traditional way isn't surprising. Unfortunately, it is dangerous. If Wikipedia continues down this path of focusing on the encyclopedia at the expense of the wiki, it might end up not being much of either.

September 4, 2006

WHO WRITES WIKIPEDIA? — RESPONSES

First, on a personal note, let me simply say thanks. I probably put more work yesterday's post than anything else I've ever written. In addition to the research I describe, I've spent my free time the past few weeks going over the text of the article again and again, agonizing about the proper phrasing, getting everything just right. It was definitely worth it. My sincere thanks to everyone who made it possible.

FURTHER RESEARCH IS NEEDED

Getting down to business, many are interested in pursuing this line of quantitative research. The work I did was intended for an article, not a formal paper, and while I'm fairly confident the basic principles are correct there's plenty more work to be done.

I was heartened to discover research by Seth Anthony which, independently and more formally, came to largely the same conclusions. As he explained on Reddit[1]: "Only about 10% of all edits on Wikipedia actually add substantive content. Roughly a third of those edits are made by someone without an account, half of someone without a userpage (a minimal threshhold for considering whether someone is part of the "community"). The average content-adder has less than 200 edits: much less, in many cases."

One of the more interesting things Anthony did was look at the work of admins in detail. In his sample, he noticed that none of the genuinely substantive edits were done by official site admins. He found that when admins originally joined the site, they contributed a lot less frequently and consistently but created a lot more substantive content. After they became admins, however, they turned into what Anthony calls "janitors".

One of the wonderful things about Wikipedia is that literally all of the data — every single edit and practically every discussion made on or about the site — is easily available. So there's an enormous amount more to learn about how it gets written. (In addition to nailing down what we know so far a little better.) If you're interested to contributing to further research on this and related topics, send me an email and I'll try to coordinate something.

WHO GETS TO VOTE?

Another response was to think about the implications on who gets to vote in Wikipedia elections. 'I tried to vote,' commented Eric*, 'but since I am one of your "occasional contributors" (I've edited only one article to make content changes), I am not eligible[ ]. It appears that the opinions of "occasional contributors" will not be heard.' Others, including William Loughborough and Jason Clark, expressed similar sentiments. 'HURRAH, I am DISENFRANCHISED', complained Bill Coderre*.

ALIENATING THE WORLD

But by far the most common response was people sharing their experience trying to contribute to Wikipedia, only to see their contributions be quickly reverted or rewritten.

'You can definately tell the "regulars" on Wikipedia', joshd* noted. 'They're the ones who ... delete your newly reate[d] article without hesitation, or revert your changes and accuse you of vandalis[m] without even checking the changes you made.' 'Every modification I made was deleted without any comment', complained CafeCafe*. 'I know there are a lot of people like me willing to help, but unless there is a real discussion behind, I won't waste my time to help anymore which is a sad thing.'

Bowerbird* complained that 'my contributions ... have been warped by people who merely want to "make it sound like an encyclopedia" without having any knowledge of the topic' while Ian* 'got fed up of the self-appointed officious jobsworths who [rewrite your] things [to] fit "their vision" .... My time is too valuable to argue with these people...'

Bill Coderre* told of how he wrote entire articles from scratch, only to see them ruined 'by some super-editors, who removed content, and turned what I thought was gosh-darn good writing into crap. .... These people, by and large, "edited" thousands of articles. In most cases, these edits were to remove material that they found unsuitable. Indeed, some of the people-history pages contained little "awards" that people gave each other — for removing content from Wikipedia.'

And it seems like half of all the people I meet have a story about being listed for deletion and the nasty insults that ensued. Seriously, there have been numerous times I've said something about Wikipedia to a relatively well-known person and they responded back with a story about how someone insulted and deleted them. '[T]here are culture vultures overlooking Wkidpedia waiting to kill anything that doesn't fit the norm', wrote Mediangler[*].

Why does this matter? Why should we listen to the angry complaints of random people on the Internet? If occasional contributors are the lifeblood of Wikipedia, as the evidence suggests, then alienating such people just can't be healthy for the project. As Ian wrote, 'if we are to invest our valuable time contributing some expert knowledge on some subject, we want to know that our work will remain there for others, and not just keep getting reverted out in seconds by some control freak that knows nothing about the actual subject. ... your article proves the exist[e]nce of this "inner gang" that I feel are actually holding Wikipedia back. To allow Wikipedia to grow and really pick the brains of the experts around the world, you need to do something to break up this inner gang and the mini empires they are building for themselves.'

Perhaps we can improve things with new rules (not only should you not bite[2] the newcomers, you shouldn't even bark at them) and new software (making it easier to discuss changes and defend contributions), but most importantly, it's going to require a cultural shift. Larry Sanger famously suggested that Wikipedia must jettison its anti-elitism so that experts could feel more comfortable contributing. I think the real solution is the opposite: Wikipedians must jettison their elitism and welcome the newbie masses as genuine contributors to the project, as people to respect, not filter out.

September 5, 2006

References & Notes:

1. http://reddit.com/info/g9si/comments/cgc62
2. http://en.wikipedia.org/wiki/WP:BITE
* username

FALSE OUTLIERS

So far my Wikipedia script has churned through about 200 articles, calculating who wrote what in each. This morning I looked through them to see if there were any that didn't match my theory. It printed out a couple and I decided to investigate.

The first it found was Alkane[1], a long technical article about acyclic saturated hydrocarbons that it said was largely written by Physchim62[2]. Yesterday a good friend was telling me that he thought long technical articles were likely written by a single person, so I immediately thought that here was the proof that he was right. But, just to check, I decided to look in the edit history to make sure my script hadn't made an error.

It hadn't, I found, but once again simply looking at the numbers missed the larger point. Physchim62 had indeed contributed most of the article, but according to the edit comments, it was by translating the German version! I don't have the German data, but presumably it was written in the same incremental way as most of the articles in my study.

The next serious case was Characters in Atlas Shrugged[3], which the script said was written by CatherineMunro. Again, it seemed plausible that one person could have written all those character bios. But again, an investigation into the actual edit history found that Munro hadn't written them, instead she'd copied them from a bunch of subpages, merging them into one bigger page.

The final serious example was Anchorage, Alaska[4], which appeared to have been written by JeffreyAllen1975[5]. Here the contributions seemed quite genuine; JeffreyAllen1975 made tons of edits each contributing a paragraph at a time. The work seemed to take quite a toll on him; at his user page he noted "I just got burned-out and tired of the online encyclopedia. My time is being taken away from me by being with Wikipedia." He lasted about four months.

Still, something seemed fishy about JeffreyAllen1975, so I decided to investigate further. Currently, the Anchorage page has a tag noting that "The current version of the article or section reads like an advertisement." A bit of Googling revealed why: JeffreyAllen1975's contributions had been copied-and-pasted from other websites, like the Anchorage Chamber of Commerce[6] ("Anchorage's public school system is ranked among the best in the nation. … The district's average SAT and ACT College entrance exam scores are consistently above the national average and Advanced Placement courses are offered at each of the district's larger high schools.").

I suspect JeffreyAllen1975 didn't know what he was doing; his writing style suggests he's just a kid: "In my free time, I am very proud of my-self by how much I've learned by making good edits on Wikipedia articles." I'm pretty sure he just thought he was helping the project: "Wikipedia is like the real encyclopedia books (A thru Z) that you see in the library, but better." But his plagiarism will still have to be removed.

When I started, just looking at the numbers these seemed to be several cases that strongly contradicted my theory. And had I just stuck to looking at the numbers, I would have believed that to be the case as well. But, once again, investigation shows the picture to be far more interesting: translation, reorganization, and plagiarism. Exciting stuff!

September 5, 2006

1.   http://en.wikipedia.org/wiki/Alkane

2. http://en.wikipedia.org/wiki/User:Physchim62
3. http://en.wikipedia.org/wiki/Characters_in_Atlas_Shrugged
4. http://en.wikipedia.org/wiki/Anchorage%2C_Alaska
5. http://en.wikipedia.org/wiki/User:JeffreyAllen1975
6. http://www.anchoragechamber.org/info/relocation.htm

WHO RUNS WIKIPEDIA?

During Wikimania, I gave a short talk proposing some new features for Wikipedia. The audience, which consisted mostly of programmers and other high-level Wikipedians, immediately begun suggesting problems with the idea. "Won't bad thing X happen?" "How will you prevent Y?" "Do you really think people are going to do Z?" For a while I tried to answer them, explaining technical ways to fix the problem, but after a couple rounds I finally said:

Stop.

If I had come here five years ago and told you I was going to make an entire encyclopedia by putting up a bunch of web pages that anyone could edit, you would have been able to raise a thousand objections: It will get filled with vandalism! The content will be unreliable! No one will do that work for free!

And you would have been right to. These were completely reasonable expectations at the time. But here's the funny thing: it worked anyway.

At the time, I was just happy this quieted them down. But later I started thinking more about it. Why did Wikipedia work anyway?

It wasn't because its programmers were so far-sighted that the software solved all the problems. And it wasn't because the people running it put clear rules in place to prevent misbehavior. We know this because when Wikipedia started it didn't have any programmers (it used off-the-shelf wiki software) and it didn't have clear rules (one of the first major rules was apparently Ignore all rules[1]).

No, the reason Wikipedia works is because of the community, a group of people that took the project as their own and threw themselves into making it succeed.

People are constantly trying to vandalize Wikipedia, replacing articles with random text. It doesn't work; their edits are undone within minutes, even seconds. But why? It's not magic — it's a bunch of incredibly dedicated people who sit at their computers watching every change that gets made. These days they call themselves the "recent changes patrol" and have special software that makes it easy to undo bad changes and block malicious users with a couple clicks.

Why does anyone do such a thing? It's not particularly fascinating work, they're not being paid to do it, and nobody in charge asked them to volunteer. They do it because they care about the site enough to feel responsible. They get upset when someone tries to mess it up.

It's hard to imagine anyone feeling this way about Britannica. There are people who love that encyclopedia, but have any of them shown up at their offices offering to help out? It's hard even to imagine. Average people just don't feel responsible for Britannica; there are professionals to do that.

Everybody knows Wikipedia as the site anyone can edit. The article about tree frogs wasn't written because someone in charge decided they needed one and assigned it to someone; it was written because someone, somewhere just went ahead and started writing it. And a chorus of others decided to help out.

But what's less well-known is that it's also the site that anyone can run. The vandals aren't stopped because someone is in charge of stopping them; it was simply something people started doing. And it's not just vandalism: a "welcoming committee" says hi to every new user, a "cleanup taskforce" goes around doing factchecking. The site's rules are made by rough consensus. Even the servers are largely run this way — a group of volunteer sysadmins hang out on IRC, keeping an eye on things. Until quite recently, the Foundation that supposedly runs Wikipedia had no actual employees.

This is so unusual, we don't even have a word for it. It's tempting to say "democracy", but that's woefully inadequate. Wikipedia doesn't hold a vote and elect someone to be in charge of vandal-fighting. Indeed, "Wikipedia" doesn't do anything at all. Someone simply sees that there are vandals to be fought and steps up to do the job.

This is so radically different that it's tempting to see it as a mistake: Sure, perhaps things have worked so far on this model, but when the real problems hit, things are going to have to change: certain people must have clear authority, important tasks must be carefully assigned, everyone else must understand that they are simply volunteers.

But Wikipedia's openness isn't a mistake; it's the source of its success. A dedicated community solves problems that official leaders wouldn't even know were there. Meanwhile, their volunteerism largely eliminates infighting about who gets to be what. Instead, tasks get done by the people who genuinely want to do them, who just happen to be the people who care enough to do them right.

Wikipedia's biggest problems have come when it's strayed from this path, when it's given some people official titles and specified tasks. Whenever that happens, real work slows down and squabbling speeds up. But it's an easy mistake to make, so it gets made again and again.

Of course, that's not the only reason this mistake is made, it's just the most polite. The more frightening problem is that people love to get power and hate to give it up. Especially with a project as big and important as Wikipedia, with the constant swarm of praise and attention, it takes tremendous strength to turn down the opportunity to be its official X, to say instead "it's a community project, I'm just another community member".

Indeed, the opposite is far more common. People who have poured vast amounts of time into the project begin to feel they should be getting something in return. They insist that, with all their work, they deserve an official job or a special title. After all, won't clearly assigning tasks be better for everyone?

And so, the trend is clear: more power, more people, more problems. It's not just a series of mistakes, it's the tendency of the system.

It would be absurd for me to say that I'm immune to such pressures. After all, I'm currently running for a seat on the Wikimedia Board. But I also lie awake at night worrying that I might abuse my power.

A systemic tendency like this is not going to be solved by electing the right person to the right place and then going to back to sleep while they solve the problem. If the community wants to remain in charge, it's going to have to fight for it. I'm writing these essays to help people understand that this is something worth fighting for. And if I'm elected to the Board, I plan to keep on writing.

Just as Wikipedia's success as an encyclopedia requires a world of volunteers to write it, Wikipedia's success as an organization requires the community of volunteers to run it. On the one hand, this means opening up the Board's inner workings for the community to see and get involved in. But it also means opening up the actions of the community so the wider world can get involved. Whoever wins this next election, I hope we all take on this task.

September 7, 2006

1. http://en.wikipedia.org/wiki/Wikipedia:Ignore_all_rules

MAKING MORE WIKIPEDIANS

Wikipedia, the Vice President of the *World Book* told us, is now recognized by ten percent of Americans. He presented this in a tone of congratulation: with no marketing budget or formal organization, a free online-only encyclopedia written by volunteers had achieved a vast amount of attention. But I took it a different way. "Only ten percent?" I thought. "That means we have ninety percent to go!"

Wikipedia is one of the few things that pretty much everyone finds useful. So how do we get all of them to use it? The first task, it appears, is telling them it exists. An ad campaign or PR blitz doesn't quite seem appropriate for the job, though. Instead, our promotion should work the same way way the rest of Wikipedia works: let the community do it.

Wikipedia's users come from all over society: different cultures, different countries, different places, different fields of study. The physics grad students who contribute heavily to physics articles are in a much better position to promote it to physicists than a promotional flack from the head office. The Pokemon fan maintaining the Pokemon articles probably knows how to reach other Pokemaniacs than any marketing expert.

Sure, you might say, but isn't the whole question of marketing Wikipedia somewhat silly? After all, you obviously know about Wikipedia, and your friends probably all seem to as well. But things are a lot thinner than you might expect: as noted above, only one in ten Americans even knows what Wikipedia is, and most of those don't truly understand it.

It's shocking to discover how even smart, technically-minded people can't figure out how to actually edit Wikipedia. Dave Winer wrote some of the first software to have an "Edit This Page" button (indeed, he operated editthispage.com for many years) and yet he at first complained that he couldn't figure out how to edit a page on Wikipedia. Michael Arrington reviews advanced Web 2.0 websites daily, yet he noted[1] that "Many people don't realize how easy it is for anyone to add content to wikipedia (I've done it several times)". If prominent technologists have trouble, imagine the rest of the world.

Obviously, this has implications for the software side: we need to work hard on making Wikipedia's interface clearer and more usable. But there's also a task here for the community: giving talks and tutorials to groups that you know about, explaining the core ideas behind Wikipedia, and giving demonstrations of how to get involved in it. The best interface in the world is no substitute for real instruction and even the clearest document explaining our principles will be ignored in a way that a personal presentation won't.

But beyond simply giving people the ability to contribute, we need to work to make contributing more rewarding. As I previously noted, many people decide to dive into writing for Wikipedia, only to watch their contributions be summarily reverted. Many people create a new article, only to see it get deleted after an AfD discussion where random Wikipedians try to think up negative things to say about it. For someone who thought they were donating their time to help the project, neither response is particularly encouraging.

I'm not saying that we should change our policies or automatically keep everything a newcomer decides to add so we don't hurt their feelings. But we do need to think more about how to enforce policies without turning valuable newcomers away, how we can educate them instead of alienating them.

At Wikimania, no less an authority than Richard Stallman (who himself long ago suggested the idea[2] of a free online encyclopedia) wandered around the conference complaining about a problem he'd discovered with a particular Wikipedia article. He could try to fix it himself, he noted, but it would take an enormous amount of his time and the word would probably just get reverted. He's not the only one — I constantly hear tales from experts about problems they encounter on Wikipedia, but are too complicated for them to fix alone. What if we could collect these complaints on the site, instead of having these people make them at parties?

One way to do that would be to have some sort of complaint-tracking system for articles, like the discussion system of talk pages. Instead of simply complaining about an article in public, Stallman could follow a link from it to file a complaint. The complaint would be tracked and stored with the article. More dedicated Wikipedians would go through the list of complaints, trying to address them and letting the submitter know when they were done. Things like POV allegations could be handled in a similar way: a notice saying neutrality was disputed could appear on the top of the page until the complaint was properly closed.

This is just one idea, of course, but it's an example of the kinds of things we need to think about. Wikipedia is visited by millions each day; how do get them to contribute back their thoughts on the article instead of muttering them under their breath or airing them to their friends?

September 11, 2006

1. http://www.techcrunch.com/2005/07/12/profile-wikipedia/
2. http://www.gnu.org/encyclopedia/

MAKING MORE WIKIPEDIAS

Maybe it's just me, but it seems like everywhere you look people are trying to get a piece of Wikipedia. Wikis sites have been started in every field from the Muppets[1] to the law[3]. The domain Wiki.com recently was sold for 3 million dollars[3]. Professor Cass Sunstein, previously seen[4] arguing the Internet could tear apart the republic, just published a new book arguing tools like wikis will lead us to "Infotopia". So is it possible to replicate Wikipedia's success? What's the key that made it work?

Unfortunately, this question hasn't gotten the attention it deserves. For the most part, people have simply assumed that Wikipedia is as simple as the name suggests: install some wiki software, say that it's for writing an encyclopedia, and *voila!* — problem solved. But as pretty much everyone who has tried has discovered, it isn't as simple as that.

Technology industry people tend to reduce web sites down to their technology: Wikipedia is simply an instance of wiki software, DailyKos just blog software, and Reddit just voting software. But these sites aren't just installations of software, there also communities of people.

Building a community is pretty tough; it requires just the right combination of technology and rules and people. And while it's been clear that communities are at the core of many of the most interesting things on the Internet, we're still at the very early stages of understanding what it is that makes them work.

But Wikipedia isn't even a typical community. Usually Internet communities are groups of people who come together to discuss something, like cryptography or the writing of a technical specification. Perhaps they meet in an IRC channel, a web forum, a newsgroup, or on a mailing list, but the focus is always something "out there", something outside the discussion itself.

But with Wikipedia, the goal is building Wikipedia. It's not a community set up to make some other thing, it's a community set up to make itself. And since Wikipedia was one of the first sites to do it, we know hardly anything about building communities like that.

Indeed, we know hardly anything about building software for that. Wiki software has been around for years — the first wiki was launched in 1995; Wikipedia wasn't started until 2001 — but it was always used like any other community, for discussing something else. It wasn't generally used for building wikis in themselves; indeed, it wasn't very good at doing that.

Wikipedia's real innovation was much more than simply starting a community to build an encyclopedia or using wiki software to do it. Wikipedia's real innovation was the idea of radical collaboration. Instead of having a small group of people work together, it invited the entire world to take part. Instead of assigning tasks, it let anyone work on whatever they wanted, whenever they felt like it. Instead of having someone be in charge, it let people sort things out for themselves. And yet it did all this towards creating a very specific product.

Even now, it's hard to think of anything else quite like it. Books have been co-authored, but usually only by two people. Large groups have written encyclopedias, but usually only by being assigned tasks. Software has been written by communities, but typically someone is in charge.

But if we take this definition, rather than wiki software, as the core of Wikipedia, then we see that other types of software are also forms of radical collaboration. Reddit, for example, is radical collaboration to build a news site: anyone can add or edit, nobody is in charge, and yet an interesting news site results. Freed from the notion that Wikipedia is simply about wiki software, one can even imagine new kinds of sites. What about a "debate wiki", where people argue about a question, but the outcome is a carefully-constructed discussion for others to read later, rather than a morass of bickering messages.

If we take radical collaboration as our core, then it becomes clear that extending Wikipedia's success doesn't simply mean installing more copies of wiki software for different tasks. It means figuring out the key principles that make radical collaboration work. What kinds of projects is it good for? How do you get them started? How do you keep them growing? What rules do you put in place? What software do you use?

These questions can't be answered from the armchair, of course. They require experimentation and study. And that, in turn, requires building a community around strong collaboration itself. It doesn't help us much if each person goes off and tries to start a wiki on their own. To learn what works and what doesn't, we need to share our experiences and be willing to test new things — new goals, new social structures, new software.

September 14, 2006

1. http://muppet.wikia.com/wiki/Muppet_Wiki
2. http://lii.law.cornell.edu/wex/index.php/Main_Page
3. http://www.wired.com/news/technology/internet/0,71591-0.html?tw=wn_
technology_1
4. http://www.amazon.com/Republic-com-Cass-R-Sunstein/dp/0691095892

CODE, AND OTHER LAWS OF WIKIPEDIA

Code is law, Lawrence Lessig famously said years ago, and time has not robbed the idea of any of its force. The point, so eloquently defended in his book *Code, and Other Laws of Cyberspace*, is that in the worlds created by software, the design of the software regulates behavior just as strongly as any formal law does; more effectively, in fact.

The point is obvious in some contexts. In the online 3D universe of Second Life, if the software prevents you from typing a certain word, that's a far more effective restraint on speech in that world than any US law could ever be in ours. But the point is far more subtle than that; it applies with equal force to the world of Wikipedia, the thriving community and culture that our wiki software creates.

For one thing, the software decides who gets to be part of the community. If using it is clear and simple, then lots of people can use it. But, if it's complicated, then only those who take the time to learn it are able to take part. And, as we've seen, lots of intelligent people don't even understand how to edit Wikipedia, let alone do any of the other things on the site.

For another, the software decides how the community operates. Features like administrative controls privilege some users over others. Support for things like stable revisions decide what sorts of things get published. The structure of talk pages help decide what and how things get discussed.

The page design the site uses encourages specific actions by making some links clear and prominent. Software functions like categories make certain kinds of features possible. The formatting codes used for things like infoboxes and links determine how easy it is for newcomers to edit those pieces of the site.

All of these things are political choices, not technical ones. It's not like there's a right answer that's obvious to any intelligent programmer. And these choices can have huge effects on the community. That's why it's essential the community be involved in making these decisions.

The current team of Wikipedia programmers is a volunteer group (although a couple of them were recently hired by the Wikimedia Foundation so they could live a little more comfortably) working much like a standard free software community, discussing things on mailing lists and IRC channels. They got together in person in the days before Wikimania to discuss some of the current hot topics in the software.

One presentation was by a usability expert who told us about a study done on how hard people found it to add a photo to a Wikipedia page. The discussion after the presentation turned into a debate over whether Wikipedia should be easy to to use. Some suggested that confused users should just add their contributions in the wrong way and a more experienced users would come along to clean their contributions up. Others questioned whether confused users should be allowed to edit the site at all — were their contributions even valuable?

As a programmer, I have a great deal of respect for the members of my trade. But with all due respect, are these really decisions that the programmers should be making?

Meanwhile, Jimbo Wales also has a for-profit company, Wikia, which recently received $4 million in venture capital funding. Wales has said, including in his keynote speech at Wikimania, that one of the things he hopes to spend it on is hiring programmers to improve the Wikipedia software.

This is the kind of thing that seems like a thoughtful gesture if you think of the software as neutral — after all, improvements are improvements — but becomes rather more problematic if technical choices have political effects. Should executives and venture capitalists be calling the shots on some of these issues?

The Wikipedia community is enormously vibrant and I have no doubt that the site will manage to survive many software changes. But if we're concerned about more than mere survival, about how to make Wikipedia the best that it can be, we need to start thinking about software design as much as we think about the rest of our policy choices.

September 18, 2006

(THE DANDY WARHOLS) COME DOWN

Well, the Wikipedia election has finally ended. The good news is that I can now talk about other things again. (For example, did you know that Erik Möller eats babies?) I have a backlog of about 20 posts that I built up over the course of the election. But instead of springing them on you all at once, I'll try to do daily posting again starting Monday. (Oooh.)

The actual results haven't been announced yet (and probably won't be for another couple days, while they check the list of voters for people who voted twice) but my impression is that I probably lost. Many wags have commented on how my campaign was almost destined to lose: I argued that the hard-core Wikipedia contributors weren't very important, but those were precisely the people who could vote for me — in other words, I alienated my only constituency.

"Aaron Swartz: Why is he getting so much attention?[1]"wrote fellow candidate Kelly Martin. "The community has long known that edit count is a poor measure of contributions". Others, meanwhile, insisted my claims were so obviously wrong as to not be even worth discussing.

Jimbo Wales, on the other hand, finally sent me a nice message the other day letting me know that he'd removed the offending section from his talk and looked forward to sitting down with me and investigating the topic more carefully.

And for my part, I hope to be able to take up some of the offers I've received for computer time and run my algorithm across all of Wikipedia and publish the results in more detailed form. (I'd also like to use the results to put up a little website where you can type in the name of a page and see who wrote what, color-coded or something like that.)

As for the election itself, it's much harder to draw firm conclusions. It's difficult in any election, this one even more so because we have so little data — no exit polls or phone surveys or even TV pundits to rely upon. Still, I'm fairly content seeing the kind words of all the incredible people I respect. Their support means a great deal to me.

The same is true of the old friends who wrote in during my essays along with all the new people who encouraged me to keep on writing. Writing the essays on a regular schedule was hard work — at one point, after sleeping overnight at my mother's bedside in the hospital, I trundled down at seven in the morning to find an Internet connection so I could write and post one — but your support made it worth the effort.

I hope that whoever wins takes what I've written into consideration. I'm not sure who that is yet, but there are some hints. I was reading an irreverent site critical of Wikipedia when I came across its claim that Jimbo Wales had sent an email to the Wikipedia community telling them who they should vote for. I assumed the site had simply made it up to attack Jimbo, but when I searched I found it really was genuine[2]:

> I personally strongly strongly support the candidacies of Oscar and Mindspillage.
>
> [...]
>
> There are other candidates, some good, but at least some of them are entirely unacceptable because they have proven themselves repeatedly unable to work well with the community.

For those reading the tea leaves, this suggests that the results will be something like: Eloquence, Oscar, Mindspillage. But we'll see.

The let-down after the election is probably not the best time to make plans but, if I had to, I'd probably decide to stay out of Wikipedia business for a while. It's a great and important project, but not the one for me.

Anyway, now everyone can go back to vandalizing my Wikipedia page[3].

Laters.

September 22, 2006

1. http://nonbovine-ruminations.blogspot.com/2006/09/aaron-swartz-why-is-he-getting-so-much.html
2. http://mail.wikipedia.org/pipermail/foundation-l/2006-September/009964.html
3. http://en.wikipedia.org/wiki/Aaron_Swartz

A UNIFIED THEORY OF MAGAZINES

For as long as I've been building web apps, it's been apparent that most successful websites are *communities* — not just interactive pages, but places where groups of like minded people can congregate and do things together. Our knowledge of how to make and cultivate communities is still at a very early stage, but most agree on their importance.

A magazine, we may imagine, is like a one-way web site. It doesn't really allow the readers to talk back (with the small exception of the letters page), it doesn't even have any sort of interactivity. But I still think communities are the key for magazines; the difference is that magazines *export* communities.

In other words, instead of providing a place for a group of like-minded people to come together, magazines provide a sampling of what a group of like-minded people might say in such an instance so that you can pretend you're part of them. Go down the list and you'll see.

The magazines of Condé Nast, for example, export "lifestyles". Most readers probably aren't the "hip scene" the magazines supposedly cover, but by reading these things they learn what to wear and what to buy and what these people are talking about. Even their high-brow magazines, like the New Yorker, serve the same purpose, only this time it's books instead of clothes.

The late, great *Lingua Franca* exported the university. Academemphiles, sitting at home, probably taking care of the kids, read it so they could imagine themselves part of the life of the mind. Similarly, the new SEED magazine is trying to export the culture of science, so people who aren't themselves scientists can get a piece of the lab coat life.

Alumni magazines similarly export college life, so that graying former college students can relive some of their old glory days, reading pieces about library renovations as they recall having sex in the stacks. And house organs export a particular kind of politics, telling you what a party or organization's take is on the issues of the day, giving you a sense of the party line.

Run down the list and in pretty much every case you scratch a magazine, you find an exported community. Magazines that want to succeed will have to find one of their own.

September 28, 2006

AND NOW, THE NEWS

My company was acquired today. *Friends in Cambridge*: we'll be hanging out at Border Cafe tonight.

- TechCrunch[1] (reddit): "always played second fiddle to Digg"
- Reddit Blog[2]: "you all have made it everything that it is. A number of you even stuck with us after we switched away from Lisp."
- E-Consultancy.com[3]: "suggest[s] that we're in a serious period of inflation, though let's stop short of calling this a bubble."
- Matthew Roche[4]: "the Avis Rent-a-car of the content voting sites."
- David Weinberger[5]: " a very very smart move by CondeNet…if they let the Reddit folks heavily influence how the service is developed."
- Blake Killian[6]: "Conde Nast, the unlikely Disruptor."
- Bivings Report[7]: "just sort of scratched at the surface of what might be possible if traditional publishers embrace social technologies."
- Digg[8]: "Reddit is where you go when you need someone to explain to you why North Korea is heaven on earth and America is the devil"
- Wired News[9]: Users can also append negative votes to stories that are of poor quality or that fail to capture their interest."
- Mark Pilgrim[10]: "a new form of online scam in which you make all the content, and we keep all the money."
- Media Wire Daily[11]: "a clear sign that Charles Townsend is making sure that Conde's digital dick is solid enough to swing with the big boys."
- Matthew Ingram[12]: "No word so far on whether the rumoured price of $65-million has any relationship to reality"
- Gawker[13]: "merging with the ickle kiddies … the Nasties decided they needed more of that Reddit magic."
- GigaOm[14]: "Reddit received 16 percent of about 300 votes cast, following Boing Boing and Gawker."
- Valleywag[15]: I went to their Boston pad, we played some video games."
- Webomatica[16]: "digg gone through a Craigslist filter."
- Slashdot[17]: "the great big Web 2.0 bubble continues to inflate towards the popping point"
- The Register[18]: "the price is many heaps smaller than the $150m that Kevin Rose reportedly wants for Digg"
- Joey DeVilla[19]: "I see that Aaron's been keeping track of what they've written about the acquisition on his blog."
- ReadWriteWeb[20]: "Reddit is another to have been extensively profiled by [us].
- Press Release[21]: "Reddit achieves our objectives on both counts, and we are

confident that other companies will find Reddit to be a partner that can bring tremendous value to their Web efforts."

- Marketing Shif[22]t: "The obvious question to ask is if Conde Nast will allow Reddit's rankings to remain neutral and not benefit the company's properties."
- CNET[23] / MEDIAWEEK[24]

October 31, 2006

1. http://www.techcrunch.com/2006/10/31/breaking-news-conde-nastwired-acquires-reddit/
2. http://reddit.com/blog/trickortreat
3. http://www.e-consultancy.com/news-blog/362018/reddit-acquired-by-conde-nast-to-join-wired-digital.html
4. http://www.landingpageoptimization.com/2006/10/the_medium_is_t.html
5. http://www.hyperorg.com/blogger/mtarchive/reddit_acquired.html
6. http://www.voodooventures.com/2006/10/31/conde-nast-buys-redditcom-but-have-you-seen-lipstickcom/
7. http://www.bivingsreport.com/2006/cond-nast-buys-reddit/
8. http://www.digg.com/tech_news/Breaking_News_Reddit_has_been_acquired
9. http://www.wired.com/news/technology/internet/0,72038-0.html?tw=wn_index_5
10. http://diveintomark.org/archives/2006/10/31/ugc
11. http://www.mediawiredaily.com/2006/10/creddit-condenast-reportedly-snapping.html
12. http://www.mathewingram.com/work/2006/10/31/reddit-gets-to-digg-ify-conde-nast/
13. http://www.gawker.com/news/reddit/conde-nast-buys-reddit-211371.php
14. http://gigaom.com/2006/10/31/wired-buys-reddit-extended-version/
15. http://www.valleywag.com/tech/reddit/behind-the-deal-volume-iii-wired-buys-reddit-211400.php
16. http://www.webomatica.com/wordpress/2006/10/31/reddit-acquired/
17. http://slashdot.org/articles/06/10/31/1910231.shtml
18. http://www.theregister.co.uk/2006/10/31/wired_buys_reddit/
19. http://www.globalnerdy.com/blog/_archives/2006/10/31/2463082.html
20. http://www.readwriteweb.com/archives/wired_acquires_reddit.php
21. http://biz.yahoo.com/bw/061031/20061031005974.html?.v=1
22. http://www.marketingshift.com/2006/10/wired-bookmarks-reddit.cfm
23. http://news.com.com/2061-10802_3-6131232.html
24. http://www.mediaweek.com/mw/news/interactive/article_display.jsp?vnu_content_id=1003319448

OFFICE SPACE

People are always asking me how I manage to get so much done. For a while I tried to impress them with my pearls of wisdom (see article "How to be more productive") but soon I just sort of gave up. I don't really feel like I do anything special — I worry about getting stuff done a lot, but mostly I just sort of do it.

It wasn't until I started working in an office that the question begun to make sense. Since I moved to San Francisco I literally haven't gotten anything done. I haven't finished a book (I finished three on the plane out here), I haven't answered many emails (I used to answer hundreds a day), I've written only a couple blog posts (I used to do one a day), and I haven't written a line of code (I used to write whole programs in the evenings). It's a pretty incredible state of affairs.

You wake up in the morning, take some crushing public transit system or dodge oncoming traffic to get to work, grab some food, and then sit down at your desk. If you're like most people, you sit at a cube in the middle of the office, with white noise buzzing around on every side. We're lucky enough to get our own shared office, but it's not much better since it's huge windows overlook a freeway and the resulting white noise is equally deadening.

Wired has tried to make the offices look exciting by painting the walls bright pink but the gray office monotony sneaks through all the same. Gray walls, gray desks, gray noise. The first day I showed up here, I simply couldn't take it. By lunch time I had literally locked myself in a bathroom stall and started crying. I can't imagine staying sane with someone buzzing in my ear all day, let alone getting any actual work done.

Nobody else seems to get work done here either. Everybody's always coming into our room to hang out and chat or invite us to play the new video game system that Wired is testing. The upside is that while we haven't gotten much of our work done, we have managed to do many other people's. Various folks from around the office have shown up to have us help them with their technical problems, which we usually solve fairly quickly. We joked that we should get transferred to their IT department instead of Web development.

We've been spared most of the brunt of it, but their IT policy is pretty scary. There's a company Internet connection, which routes everything through the IT HQ in Delaware, presumably the better to spy on us on. On Day 1 they took our laptops and "backed up" the drives to ensure they had a copy of all our data. (We scurried to get our MP3 collections and worse off first.)

Then they issued us company-approved laptops: terribly-slow iBook G4s complete with Conde Nast desktop and screensaver with spy software pre-installed. When they gave us the machines we didn't even have administrator access on them. The clock was set to the Eastern time zone; I needed an IT department person to change it to show me California time.

The company laptop is necessary to read our company email which, being on a Microsoft Exchange server, requires a special Microsoft email client to read. You also need to be on a company laptop to access the company network, where you can log into a maze of PeopleSoft web sites to file expense reports and change your health benefits.

I feel wiped after dealing with this non-work for a couple hours, but I can't get any rest from lying on our couch because it too is surrounded by the white noise.

Finally at 5 the office empties out and I can go home where, to compensate for the dullness of the days, I brighten up the nights. Life-threatening bicycle rides, dinners and movies with friends, museums, running along the beach, navigating the nightmare of public transit to visit the new hot spot. And if I get home early there are the roommates eager to chat about their days. By the time I break away it's midnight, if not 3am. I had to spend much of the weekend sleeping just to catch up.

And then it's back to the grind once again. A carousel that never stops to let you get off.

November 15, 2006

LIFE AT THE OFFICE

It started when he stopped going home. The rent in San Francisco was so expensive and the commutes so painful that it just seemed easier not to leave. Nobody really noticed at first — the cleaning crew came in around 7 and just assumed he was staying late, while the other employees just assumed he was an early riser. And really, who's going to complain about an employee who puts in too much time at the office? Especially when he wasn't using it to get additional work done.

Then he started wondering if he could eliminate the trip for food too. He found a website that sold nutritionally-balanced diet bars and ordered a whole tub, which he placed under his desk. All day he'd be munching on one bar or another, no longer feeling hungry around lunch or dinner. So he just sat at his desk munching instead. Strangely, this didn't seem to make him any more productive.

Between the lack of exercise and nonstop eating, he began growing fat. Nobody really said anything to him about it. He was rail-thin when he started so many co-workers were secretly happy to see him put on a few pounds. But it quickly got out of hand, with rolls of fat oozing between the cracks in his Aeron chair. Still, nobody wants to insult a fat man, so he just continued to grow. He never really needed to leave his chair anymore, so he didn't mind it much.

Soon he began — I'm not quite sure how to describe it, I guess he was sort of fusing with the chair. The rolls of fat would sneak through a crack and then continue growing, like vines crawling through a gate. It quickly got to the point where he couldn't even get out of the chair if he wanted too, the fat had locked him in. He could still roll around the office on it but that movement quickly became tiring and as he grew fatter the wheels snapped off.

Nobody really seemed to mind, though. He had become an office fixture — people came to him now. He'd chat with them about their day or keep an eye on things for them. Since he was always there he knew everything that went on in the office and people could always rely on him for gossip or signing for their packages.

Soon it seemed like he was part of the office itself, like some sort of roboreceptionist you read about in Negroponte novels. Desks began subtly organizing themselves around him and employees began treating him as just another office fixture. There's the bathroom and there's the kitchen and there's, well, you know…

And then, one day, they left. Some corporate restructuring or something; they were all being moved to a different building. People packed their stuff in boxes, cleaners cleaned one more time, and then suddenly they were all gone. He was all that was left, keeper of an office without any officers.

November 10, 2006

PRODUCTS THAT SHOULD EXIST

A free Gmail clone. A lot of people I know use Gmail for email. It's not because they don't have access to servers or can't afford a couple gigabytes of disk space. It's because Gmail is simply the best interface for email out there right now. It'd be even better if it was free software, though.

The biggest problem with Gmail is that you can't run it offline. But if it was free software, you could run it on your local machine and use it even when not connected to the net. This would also have the nice benefit of making it much faster for the user. Some synchronization code would be necessary, but it'd be worth it.

Gmail isn't all that complicated; this really shouldn't be that hard.

A nice OS X Tor interface. I've talked to a bunch of people who would like to use Tor, but find it just too complicated. Ideally, the interface should be very simple. You download the Tor binary and double-click it to start using Tor and quit out to stop. And so that you know it's working, it'll have a little window that will show you the names of servers you're connected to.

OS X has APIs for changing the system preferences; just use those to set the SOCKS server properly. Tor has APIs for finding out when you connect to a server, use those to set the display. For a decent Mac programmer, this can't be more than a day's worth of work, but it'd make Tor vastly more usable.

Decent backup software. I've already written about this. It still hasn't happened.

If anyone's interested in building any of these, let me know and perhaps we can work something out.

December 29, 2006

EIGHT REASONS (SOME) WIKIS WORK

The stunning success of Wikipedia in creating an encyclopedia from scratch has led many to believe that they can achieve similar results. (Want to get rich? Easy! Just install the MediaWiki software, title it "how to get rich", and wait for the answers to start flowing in.)

Clearly the wiki approach does not solve every problem. So what made Wikipedia work so well? We can't say for certain, but by looking at similar sites that haven't taken off — as well as those that have (like TV IV — http://tviv.org/) — we can spot some patterns.

1. **Clear goal**. Wikipedia is an encyclopedia. It's an understandable task with a clear end result. When you want to know something, you know whether it's the kind of thing that might be in Wikipedia or not. And when you want to contribute, you know what kinds of things to add. By contrast simply adding a wiki to your existing website has no clear purpose.

2. **Worth doing**. Collecting the sum of human knowledge in one place is just the kind of grand goal that inspires their people to sink their time into a big, collective effort. There are people on Wikipedia who spend their time going down long lists of computer-generated format and style errors, fixing each one by hand. It's hard to imagine people putting the same amount of effort into cleaning up a wiki about the greatness of Tide laundry detergent. But people are willing to do it for something only a few people care a lot about (like a very specialized technical topic) or something a lot of people care a little about (like a piece of popular culture).

3. **Objective standards**. It's pretty clear what an encyclopedia article should be. It needs to contain an explanation of what it is and why it's important, the history, the uses (or actions), criticism, and pointers to more information. And the whole thing needs to be written in a plain, dry style. The result is that it's pretty clear what needs to be done, which means everyone can work together to do it. Contrast this with a novel, where the book's success depends on the author's creativity and, well, novelty.

4. **Made from small pieces**. Encyclopedias are huge projects, but they're made up of manageably-sized articles. If an article ever grows too long, it can be split into parts (see Al Gore Controversies). When a page is small enough that the whole thing can fit comfortably in your head, it's much easier to work with: you can write it in one sitting, you can read it relatively quickly, and you can remember the whole thing. Contrast this with books, which are so big that working seriously on them requires special dedication.

5. **Each piece is useful**. Each article in an encyclopedia is useful in its own right. Even if Wikipedia had just started and all it had was an article about

the Striped Burrowing Tree Frog, that page would still be useful, just like every other page on the Internet about an obscure topic. The page, if it was good enough, would show up on the right Google searches and more Tree Frog fans would begin contributing to it. And if that page worked well, it could easily lead to others. Contrast this with a dictionary, which you're probably only going to use if it has a high percentage of the words you want to look up.

6. **Segmented subjects**. Few people are passionate about learning all human knowledge. But many more people are passionate about some subset of that. Encyclopedias allow the people who really care about French social theorists to spend all their time on that, without ever caring about the rest of the site. And the same is true of readers. The result is that lots of different people can work on lots of different parts, with the whole project getting done as a result, even though nobody worked on that explicitly. Contrast this with coming up with a theory, where the work requires understanding all the data and thinking about it as a whole.

7. **Personally useful**. The best way to understand something is to write about it and the best thing to write is a layman's explanation. An encyclopedia provides a opportunity to do just that. At the same time, it captures what you've learned in case you forget it later and gives the concept more form so that you're more likely to remember. By contrast, writing guides for children doesn't teach you much.

8. **Enjoyable work**. An encyclopedia mostly consists of people trying to explain things and explaining things can be quite fun. At parties, if you as someone about the problem they've dedicated their life to, they'll gladly talk your ear off about it for hours. Wikipedia capitalizes on this tendency while also magnifying it — now it's not just one partygoer, it's the whole world listening. Contrast this with a project like categorizing all the pages on the Internet, which most people would find quite boring.

I came up with these principles just by thinking about why I use Wikipedia and not about specific examples of people who have violated them. So it's a little surprising that it turns out to mostly be a list of wiki sites that haven't exactly taken off: SourceWatch fails 1, vanity projects fail 2, Wikitorial failed 3, Wikibooks fails 4, Wiktionary fails 5, the over-specialized sites fail 6, Wikijunior fails 7, and Wikispecies fails 8 (at least as far as I'm concerned).

Of course, even if you get all these things right, that says nothing about whether your site will succeed. Success requires more than just a good idea, it requires doing the hard work of actually making things happen. But that's a topic for another article.

December 12, 2006

7 HABITS OF HIGHLY SUCCESSFUL WEBSITES

I got a phone call from my father the other day. "Oh," I thought immediately, "he's probably calling to finally apologize for failing to attend that basketball game I played at in fourth grade." But no, I was once again wrong. He was calling to pitch his web startup.

They're at the racquetball court, the grocery store, the venture capitalists' offices — you can't avoid this new crowd of so-called "Web 2.0" startups. And every time they meet you, if they're not asking for angel funding, they're asking for suggestions on how they should run their company.

For a long time, I'd simply tell them they should ask a real expert, like Dr. Paulson Graham of the Institute of Advances Startup Studies, but the number of queries has become so great that I've decided to conduct some research of my own.

I picked out seven recent extremely popular websites. While perhaps not having the mindshare of a "Basecamp" or a "Ning", these websites do have the benefit of having tons of actual users. Here they are, ranked roughly in order of popularity:

- MySpace
- Wikipedia (basically tied)
- Facebook
- Flickr (pronounced flick-her)
- Digg
- Del.icio.us (pronounced dell-dot-icky-oh-dot-you-ess)
- Google Maps (no popularity data available but I bet it's pretty popular)

I looked at all these websites to see what they have in common. Here's what I discovered.

BE UGLY

With the single exception of Flickr, all these websites are hideous. Facebook and Wikipedia redesigned late in the game, upgrading their web design from "hideous" to "barely tolerable", but MySpace has continued on, its name becoming synonymous with design so atrocious it has actually been known to induce vomiting in epileptic Japanese children. Not surprisingly, it's the most popular site on the list.

Unlike most of Google, Google Maps actually isn't such a bad looking website in itself, but most of its Web 2.0 "cred" comes from its ability to make "mashups" in which people stick a Google Map with several hundred thousand different little red blurble icons sticking all over it onto a webpage whose design sense can best be described as "MySpace knockoff". Normally I don't go in for guilt by association, but in this case

I think it's deserved.

Del.icio.us and Digg both attempted redesigns at one point but due to a tragic mixup in communication, the web design teams they hired misheard their instructions and thought their job was actually to try to make the site look worse instead of better. Having blown several thousand dollars of their VC's money on this enterprise, they had no choice but to launch the resulting look.

DON'T HAVE FEATURES

Let's start with MySpace. Again, just as it's a leader in traffic, it's a leader in this category. MySpace has so few features, I don't even know what it does. Neither, apparently, do its users, who in fact create MySpace accounts simply to impress their friends and annoy their teachers. (Personal communication)

The last time Wikipedia added a substantive new feature was the addition of categories a couple years ago and, frankly, that was a pretty bad idea because it was so poorly implemented. Otherwise it's basically just been a big box you edit text in with a bunch of kluges on top. That's how it got to be number two.

Facebook, Flickr, and Digg all add features occasionally, but they're more than counteracted by Del.icio.us and Google Maps, which in fact have actively taken features away. Del.icio.us decided that tag intersections (finding links that are tagged with two words) was just too hard to get back online after they were purchased by Yahoo! and so they simply took the feature down without notice. The site spiked in popularity until they added them back the other day and traffic went down once again.

Google Maps, meanwhile, has just removed everything else from the page except for the map and the search box, ensuring no features get in between the user and their mapping experience. Like most Google software, though, features are definitely not going to be added.

LET USERS DO YOUR JOB

None of the content on any of these sites is provided by the people who made the site. In every case, the content is provided by the users. The only exception is Google Maps, where the content is provided NAVTEQ.

Combined with the last principle, you might begin to suspect that this is simply because the developers of these sites are extremely lazy. But I don't believe that; I think there's a more complicated principle at work.

I believe in a theory I'll call "The Stupidity of Crowds". Here's the basic idea: if just one person or a small group of people builds a website, they have to be at least moderately intelligent. Buying servers and writing programs is somewhat hard and takes a little bit of brainpower. This means that the content for their site will be similarly intelligent and thus it won't be of interest to the vast majority of Internet users.

The glorious thing about the Internet, however, is that it allows us to aggregate the combined stupidity of literally millions of people. No longer do you have to try to play towards the lowest common denominator — now you can actually have the lowest common denominator build your site for you. No single mortal could possibly come up with the content you find on the average MySpace, let alone the hideous color scheme, garish backgrounds, and awful auto-playing background music. No, something like that takes The Stupidity of Crowds.

IGNORE STANDARDS

Like 99.999999% of all websites on the Internet, none of these websites supports web standards, the documents that explain the proper way to use the Web. Enough said.

BUILD TO FLIP

MySpace, Flickr, Del.icio.us, and Google Maps all sold out to larger companies. (Google Maps didn't even launch until after it was acquired.) Wikipedia is apparently some sort bizarre legal construction called a "donation-funded non-profit" and this apparently has made it hard to sell. (Note to future founders: make sure not to incorporate your company as one of these as it can severely hamper your options later on.)

Facebook and Digg haven't sold out yet, but I bet they want to. (Another tip: taking large quantities of VC money also makes it hard to sell your company, both because it gives you a swelled head but also because it gives the VCs control over when you can sell, and their heads are really big.)

December 12, 2006

THE POLITICS OF WIKIPEDIANS

A film director named Jaron Lanier recently published an essay titled "Digital Maoism". The essay is a dreadful mishmash of name-calling, whining, and downright incoherence, but insofar as Lanier has a point, it is this: people often attribute facts and claims to "Wikipedia", as if it was some giant hive mind that combined all our individual thoughts into one group opinion. But, in reality, Wikipedia is simply written by people, people with individual voices and ideas. And technology is making us lose sight of that.

(I maybe doing Lanier too great a service by attributing such a coherent view to him as nothing quite so clear is ever actually expressed in the article. Nonetheless, I will continue as if this is Lanier's view.)

It is an interesting point, but what Lanier finds so frightening is precisely what I find so exciting about these technologies. I still remember the light bulb that went off in my head when my friend Dan Connolly answered a question by saying "According to Google, X is the case." "Google" had said no such thing, of course, but the Google algorithm had processed all the links on the Web and send Dan the page it thought most relevant to his query. It was this particular page that said X, of course, but the notion that Google itself was answering questions in this way was a revelation.

The same is true of Wikipedia. There are individual people, obviously, but what makes Wikipedia so fascinating are the technical and social processes that combine their work, turning it into something no individual person is responsible for or would necessarily endorse.

I often find myself wondering what Wikipedia would say about such-and-such a subject or how important Wikipedia thinks something else is. I refuse to edit my Wikipedia page, not only because it's bad form, but because I'm genuinely curious about how Wikipedia sees me. It's an odd thing, to think a site that anyone can edit actually has opinions or concerns or a point of view on the world, but it does, and it's a fascinating one.

December 12, 2006

THE POLITICS OF WIKIS

Anarchism has a pretty bad rap. Put aside all the people who think it's about smashing windows and shooting presidents and just focus on the idea (*an arch* — without rulers). If someone told you that you should start a business where basically no one is in charge of anything and everyone shares ownership of everything and all decisions are made by consensus, you'd think they were a hopeless utopian about to get a large dose of reality. Yet that's pretty much what Wikipedia is.

There's the obvious anarchism of wikis: namely, "anyone can edit". No intelligence tests or approval rules or even a temporary probation. Anyone can just wander up and hit that edit button and get started. Where in the world can a random person get a larger audience? That's pretty radical in itself, but things go much deeper. There's no ownership over text. If you write something, as soon as you post it to Wikipedia, it's no longer "yours" in any real sense. Others will modify and mangle it without a second thought and anyone who quotes those words in the future will attribute them to "Wikipedia" and not to you. In a culture where directors are suing people for fastforwarding over the smutty scenes in their movies, that's pretty wild.

And while there are a few technical tricks to give some people more software features than others, for the most part the Wikipedia community is pretty flat. Every non-edit decision, from which pages get deleted to what the logo in the corner is, gets made by consensus with everyone getting a chance to have their say.

In real life, few people are willing to take such a radical stand. Even the farthest reaches of the far left hold back from proposing such extreme ideas, suggesting that not only that such extreme freedom wouldn't fly in a capitalist culture like ours, but that perhaps some of these restrictions are just necessary because of human nature. But it's humans who edit Wikipedia, and mostly humans raised in capitalist culture as well. Perhaps it's time to give more extremism a chance.

December 11, 2006

ANNOUNCING THE OPEN LIBRARY

Early this year, when I left my job at Wired Digital, I thought I could look forward to months of lounging around San Francisco, reading books on the beach and drinking fine champagne and eating *foie gras*. Then I got a phone call. Brewster Kahle of the Internet Archive was thinking of pursuing a project that I'd been trying to do literally for years. I thought long and hard about it and realized I couldn't pass this opportunity up. So I put aside my dreams of lavish living and once again threw myself into my work. Just as well, I suppose, since San Francisco's beaches are freezing cold, champagne has a disgusting taste, and *foie gras* is even worse.

I thought of the smartest programmers and designers I knew and gave them a ring, sat down for coffee with them, threatened to fly out to their homes and knock on their doors. In the end, we got together an amazing group of people — all sworn to secrecy of course — and in the past few months we've put together what's probably the biggest project I ever worked on.

So today I'm extraordinarily proud to announce the Open Library project. Our goal is to build the world's greatest library, then put it up on the Internet free for all to use and edit. Books are the place you go when you have something you want to share with the world — our planet's cultural legacy. And never has there been a bigger attempt to bring them all together.

Visit the Open Library site: https://openlibrary.org/about

July 16, 2007

THE JOY OF PUBLIC SPEAKING

A few months ago I was asked if I wanted to give a talk (via video-conference) to a technology conference in India. Being extraordinarily bad at saying no, I said yes. I asked what they wanted me to talk about and they said I could speak about whatever I liked. I thought about it for a while and concluded that I should talk about my life and how I got out of a small town in the middle of the country and ended up working with famous people. Due to a timing screw up, I didn't get to spend as much time on it as I liked, but I did my best. I can put the draft up if anyone wants it.

(My hope was that talking about all these things would give people lots of different subjects to ask questions on, and then I could go into more detail about whatever interested people. But oddly, the questions were instead mostly about the few things I'd left out of the narrative. I wonder if that means I addressed everything in enough detail that I answered all their questions or whether I didn't talk about the things they actually cared about.)

Giving a talk via videoconference is a painful thing. First, your disembodied head is looming six feet tall over a room of people. It's hard to imagine that's attractive to anyone other than Big Brother's most ardent fan. Second, you have only the blurriest view of the audience you're speaking to. Third, you can't hear whether they're laughing or not, because if you get an audio channel then all you hear is the delayed sound of your own voice repeated back to you — which is incredibly distracting — so instead all you get is silence. It's incredibly difficult to connect with an audience under these conditions.

Still, I did my best, and I'm told it went reasonably well. I sure had fun — there's a real buzz you get from speaking before an audience, whether it's on the radio or via videocast or in person. Suddenly your depression and thirst and hunger melt away and you just light up with enthusiasm and energy. The students who filled the room I was addressing applauded and thanked me; but in truth I really owe a debt to them.

September 27, 2007

HOWTO: GET A JOB LIKE MINE I

Talk, as prepared, for the Tathva 2007 computer conference at NIT Calicut.

The American writer Kurt Vonnegut used to always title his talks "How to Get a Job Like Mine" and then proceed to talk about whatever he felt like. I'm in a bit of the opposite situation. I was told I could talk about whatever I felt like and I decided that, instead of pontificating for a while about the future of the Internet or the power of mass collaboration, the most interesting thing I could talk about was probably "How to Get a Job Like Mine".

So how did I get a job like mine? Undoubtedly, the first step is to choose the right genes: I was born white, male, American. My family was fairly well-off and my father worked in the computer industry. Unfortunately, I don't know of any way of choosing these things, so that probably isn't much help to you.

But, on the other hand, when I started I was a very young kid stuck in a small town in the middle of the country. So I did have to figure out some tricks for getting out of that. In the hopes of making life a little less unfair, I thought I'd share them with you.

STEP 1: LEARN

The first thing I did, which presumably all of you have already got covered, was to learn about computers, the Internet, and Internet culture. I read a bunch of books, I read enormous numbers of web pages, and I tried stuff. First I joined mailing lists and tried to understand the discussions until I felt comfortable jumping in and trying to participate for myself. Then I looked at web sites and tried to build my own. And finally I learned how to build web applications and I started building them. I was thirteen.

STEP 2: TRY

The first site I built was called get.info. The idea was to have a free, online encyclopedia that anyone could edit or add things to or reorganize, right through their web browser. I built the whole thing, added lots of cool features, tested it on all sorts of browsers, and was very proud of it. It actually won even a prize for one of the best new web applications that year. Unfortunately, the only people I knew at the time were other kids in my school, so I didn't really have anyone writing a lot of encyclopedia articles. (Luckily, several years later, my mother pointed me to this new site called "Wikipedia" that was doing the same thing.)

The second site I built was called my.info. The idea was that instead of having to scrounge around the Internet for news from all sorts of different web pages, why not just have one program that went and grabbed news from all those web pages and put them in one place. I built it and got it working, but it turned out I wasn't the only one who had that sort of idea at the time — lots of people were working on this new technique, then called "syndication". A group of them split off and decided to work on a specification for this thing called RSS 1.0 and I joined them.

STEP 3: GAB

It was summer and I was out of school and didn't have a job, so I had a lot of free time on my hands. And I spent all of it obsessively reading the RSS 1.0 mailing list and doing all sorts of odd jobs and whatever else they needed someone to do. Soon enough, they asked me if I wanted to become a member of the group, and I ended up becoming a co-author and then a co-editor of the RSS 1.0 specification.

RSS 1.0 was built on top of this technology called RDF, which was a bit of a source of heated debate on the RSS lists, so I started looking more into RDF, joining the RDF mailing lists, reading things and asking stupid questions and slowly starting to figure things out. Soon enough, I was becoming known in the RDF world and when they announced a new working group to develop the next RDF spec, I decided to sneak on.

First I asked the working group members if I could join. They said no. But I really wanted to be on that working group, so I tried to find another way. I read the rules of the W3C, which was the standards body that operated the Working Group. The rules said that while they could reject any requests to join from an individual, if an organization that was an official member of the W3C asked to put someone on the working group, they couldn't say no. So I looked down the list of W3C member organizations, found the one that seemed friendliest, and asked them to put me on the Working Group. They did.

Being a Working Group member meant weekly phone calls with all the other members, lots of mailing list and IRC discussion, occasionally flying off to odd cities to meet in person, and lots of all-around getting-to-know people.

I was also a true believer on the subject of RDF, so I worked hard to get other people to adopt it. When I saw that professor Lawrence Lessig was starting a new organization called Creative Commons, I sent him an email saying he should use RDF for his project and explaining why. A few days later he wrote back saying "Good idea. Why don't you do that for us?"

So I ended up joining Creative Commons which ended up flying me out to all sorts of conferences and parties and so on where I ended up meeting even more people. Between all of this people were starting to know who I was and I was starting to have friends in lots of different places and fields.

STEP 4: BUILD

And then I left it all and went to college for a year. I attended Stanford University, an idyllic little school in California where the sun is always shining and the grass is always green and the kids are always out getting a tan. It's got some great professors and I certainly learned a bunch, but I didn't find it a very intellectual atmosphere, since most of the other kids seemed profoundly unconcerned with their studies.

But towards the end of the year, I got an email from a writer named Paul Graham who said that he was starting up a new project, Y Combinator. The idea behind Y Combinator is that you find a bunch of really smart programmers, fly them out to Boston for the summer, and give them a little bit of money and the paperwork to start a company. They work really really hard on building something while you teach them everything they need to know about business and hook them up with investors and acquirers and so on. And Paul suggested I apply.

So I did and I got in and after lots of pain and toil and struggle I found myself working on a little site called Reddit.com. The first thing to know about Reddit was that we had no clue what we were doing. We had no experience in business. We had hardly any real experience in building production software. And we had no idea whether or why what we were doing was working. Every morning we woke up and made sure the server wasn't down and that our site hadn't been overrun by spammers and that all our users hadn't left.

When I first started at Reddit, growth was slow. The site was put online very early — within weeks of starting work on it — but for the first three months it hardly got above three thousand visitors a day, which is about baseline for a useful RSS feed. Then, in a couple weeks of marathon coding sessions, we moved the site from Lisp to Python and I wrote an article about it for my blog. It got a lot of attention — Hell hath no fury like a Lisp fan scorned — and even today I still run into people at parties who, when I mention that I worked at Reddit, say "Oh, the site that switched from Lisp."

Around that time traffic really started taking off. In the next three months, our traffic doubled twice. Every morning we'd wake up to check our traffic graphs and see how we were doing — whether the new feature we'd launched had gotten us more attention, whether word of mouth was still spreading our site, whether all our users had abandoned us yet. And every day the number grew higher. Although we couldn't shake the impression that we seemed to grow faster whenever we took a break from doing actual work on the site.

We still had no idea how to make money. We sold t-shirts on the site, but every time we made a little bit of money on those we spent it on ordering more t-shirts. We signed up with a major Web ad representative to sell ads on our site, but they never seemed to be able to sell any ads for us and we rarely made more than, literally, a couple of dollars a month. Another idea we had was licensing the "Reddit technology" to let other people build sites that worked like Reddit. But we couldn't find anyone who wanted to license it from us.

Soon, Reddit was getting millions of users every month — a number that far surpassed the average American magazine. I know that, because I was talking to a lot of magazine publishers at the time. They all wondered how Reddit's magic could work for them. @@ At first, we just said yes to everything they suggested. And, fortunately for us, that worked out, since we could program faster than they could write up an official contract for what they wanted.

In addition, online news sites started noticing that Reddit could send them vast amounts of traffic. They somehow thought they could encourage this by adding "reddit this" links to all of their articles. As far as I know, adding such links doesn't actually improve your chances of being popular on Reddit (although it does make your site look more ugly), but it did give us lots of free advertising.

Soon enough, the partnership talks turned to talks of acquisition. Acquisition: the thing we'd always dreamed of! No longer would he have to worry about making money. Some company out there would take over that responsibility in exchange for just making us all rich. We dropped everything to negotiate with our acquirers. And then it stayed dropped.

We negotiated for months. First, we argued over the price. We prepared plans and spreadsheets and went to headquarters to make presentations and had endless meetings and phone calls. Finally, they refused our price, and we walked away. Then they changed their tune and we finally shook hands and agreed on the deal — only to begin negotiating on some other key point, only to walk away again. We must have walked away three or four times before we finally got a contract we could agree to. We must have stopped doing real work for six months.

I started going crazy from having to think so much about money. We all started getting touchy from the stress and lack of productive work. We begun screaming at each other and then not talking to each other and then launching renewed efforts to work together only to have the screaming begin again. The company almost fell apart before the deal went through.

But eventually, we went into the offices of our lawyers to actually sign all the documents and the next morning the money was in our bank accounts. It was done.

We all flew out to San Francisco and begun working at the offices of Wired News (we were purchased by Condé Nast, a big publishing company which owns Wired, along with many other magazines).

I was miserable. I couldn't stand San Francisco. I couldn't stand office life. I couldn't stand Wired. I took a long Christmas vacation. I got sick. I thought of suicide. I ran from the police. And when I got back on Monday morning, I was asked to resign.

STEP 5: FREEDOM

The first couple days without a job were odd. I hung around the house. I took advantage of the San Francisco sunshine. I read some books. But soon I felt like I needed a project again. I started writing a book. I wanted to collect together all the interesting studies I'd found in the field of psychology and tell them, not as research results, but as stories. Every day I went down to Stanford to do research in their library. (Stanford is a great school for psychologists.)

But one day I got a call from Brewster Kahle. Brewster founded the Internet Archive, an incredible organization which tries to digitize everything it can get its hands on and put it all up on the Web. He said he wanted to get started on a project we'd talked about in the past. The idea was to collect information on all the books in the world in one place — a free wiki. I got right to work and over the next couple months I began calling libraries, roping in programmers, working with a designer, and doing all sorts of other odd jobs to get the site online. That project ended up becoming Open Library and a demo version is now up at demo.openlibrary.org. Much of it was built by a very talented Indian programmer: Anand Chitipothu.

Another friend, Seth Roberts, suggested we try to find some way to reform the higher education system. We couldn't really agree on a good solution, but we did agree on another good idea: a wiki to tell students what different jobs are like. That site should be launching soon.

Then another old friend, Simon Carstensen, sent me an email saying he was graduating college and wanted to start a company with me. Well, I'd been keeping a list of companies I thought were good ideas and pulled the top one off the list. The idea was this: make building a web site as easy as filling in a textbox. Over the next few months we worked and worked to make things simpler and simpler (and a little more complex as well). The result, which launched a couple weeks ago, is Jottit.com.

I also signed up to mentor two Summer of Code projects, both of which were stunningly ambitious and with much luck should be launching soon.

I also decided I wanted to get into journalism. My first print article got published the other week. I also started a couple blogs about science and begun working on an academic paper of my own. It builds upon a study I did a while back about who actually wrote Wikipedia. Some people, including Jimmy Wales, the kind of public spokesman of Wikipedia, claimed that Wikipedia wasn't such a big distributed project after all but instead was only written by around 500 or so people, many of whom he knew. He had done some simple studies to back this up, but I ran the numbers more carefully and found the opposite: the vast majority of Wikipedia was created by new editors, mostly people who didn't even bother to create accounts, adding a couple sentences here and there. How did Wales make such a big mistake? He looked at the number of changes each user made to Wikipedia, but didn't look at the size of the change. It turns out there is this group of 500 who makes an enormous number of changes to Wikipedia, but all of their changes are quite small: they do things like fix spelling and change formatting. It seems much more reasonable to believe that 500 people went around editing much of an encyclopedia than it does to think they wrote it.

WORDS OF ADVICE

What's the secret? How can I boil down things I do into pithy sentences that make myself sound as good as possible? Here goes:

Be curious. Read widely. Try new things. I think a lot of what people call intelligence just boils down to curiosity.

Say yes to everything. I have a lot of trouble saying no, to an pathological degree — whether to projects or to interviews or to friends. As a result, I attempt a lot and even if most of it fails, I've still done something.

Assume nobody else has any idea what they're doing either. A lot of people refuse to try something because they feel they don't know enough about it or they assume other people must have already tried everything they could have thought of. Well, few people really have any idea how to do things right and even fewer are to try new things, so usually if you give your best shot at something you'll do pretty well.

I followed these rules. And here I am today, with a dozen projects on my plate and my stress level through the roof once again.

Every morning I wake up and check my email to see which one of my projects has imploded today, which deadlines I'm behind on, which talks I need to write, and which articles I need to edit.

Maybe, one day, you too can be in the same position. If so, I hope I've done something to help.

30 September 2007

HOWTO: BUILD DECENT PRODUCTIVITY SOFTWARE

These days it seems like everyone is making productivity software — software that helps you manage all the the things you need to get done. Yet all of them seem to be missing some basic pieces. A productivity application has two jobs: remembering everything you need to do and getting you to do it. The second is necessary because without it, you'll put all your tasks in the application and then never do them. The first is necessary because otherwise the application will have no idea what to tell you to do.

I think the ideal piece of productivity software would be like having a great assistant or a campaign manager: someone who intimately knows all aspects of your life's todo lists and schedules and wasn't afraid of saying you had to wrap this meeting up because you promised the kids you'd be home at 5 to take them to the game. Judged against this standard, present productivity software is woefully lacking — it's usually not much more than a glorified todo list.

Remembering everything: Most software lets you store the classical todo list items: call Jon back, finish report, buy toy for kids.[1] Some systems even branch out into vaguer life goal stuff: spend time with family, become accomplished novelist, learn more about history. But that's about it.

But most people also have tasks in their project management software (fix this bug), various calendar-style events (lunch with Jon, catch plane), and a vast quantity of email (answer Jon's question, fix the frobnitz and report back to Bob, etc.) Yet no one seems to have dared to integrate their software with a calendar, email client, or even bug tracking software.

Since it's unlikely anyone writing productivity software is also going to write an email client, a calendar, and a bug tracker (although it would be nice), I'll settle for having support for plugins that import tasks and events from these various other apps. It has to be very simple to upload your whole life to your todo app.

Getting you to do stuff: The best I've seen is some kind of filtering in which the software lets you only look at tasks that can be done in 5 minutes while on a train. But if you're the kind of person who's dysfunctional enough to need productivity software, simply having a big list of tasks probably isn't going to help you much. (I can write a big list of tasks in Notepad.) Instead, the software should be proactive about getting you to do stuff, like telling you to quit goofing off and get ready for that big deadline you have tomorrow or to hurry up and answer that urgent email from yesterday.

How does it do this? First, it needs to know what's important. After you import your life it should let you walk through and triage it all: look at each one and decide how important it is (or whether it's already done). I've written a program to do this just for my mail and it's been invaluable — within a couple hours a morass of three thousand messages turned into a neatly labeled set of piles ordered by importance. Similarly, it can turn a tall pile of assorted todos into the beginnings of an action plan.

Then comes the crucial part: it tells you what to do. I'm not demanding anything fancy, like a robot dog that follows you around and barks orders (although that might be nice). I'm just saying provide a little pop-up window with a suggested next task. Psychologically, it's easy to ignore a long todo list. In fact, long todo lists are depressing and make you want to look away. But a simple suggestion about one particular thing to do next is much harder to dismiss.

Of course, the suggestions have to be good. The software would generate them by taking into account everything it knows about your tasks and calendar today. And if you still don't like the suggestion, you tell the program you can't do it because...:

- that'll take too long (adds a time estimate to the task; used to make sure the task can be done before the next event on the calendar)
- that's not very important (adds a priority to the task; used to sort by importance)
- I can't do that here (adds a physical context to the task, like being in a certain place; used to find tasks you can do in your current context)
- I can't do that yet (adds a dependency; dependencies can then be checked occasionally to see if they've been finished yet)
- I already did that (marks as done)
- that's not due for a while (adds a due date; used to make sure things get done before their deadlines)

and so on. Ideally, the system would be well-informed and smart enough that you could trust its predictions. But even if it wasn't perfect, just suggesting tasks in order of priority would likely be a vast improvement over the whimsical system used by most people in need of productivity software. It's hard to imagine such a tool wouldn't be a godsend.

Most of the classical productivity guides are aimed at middle managers whose lives, as far as we can tell from the examples, consist of calling people, finishing reports, and placating their families. Who am I to break with tradition?

October 29, 2007

INTRODUCING THEINFO.ORG

A lot of the work I've been doing on Open Library for the past few months has to do with handling large quantities of data. Either I'm writing crawlers to download them from various public web sites, or I'm meeting with librarians to persuade them to give me copies, or I'm evaluating algorithms for processing them, or building tools for viewing it all.

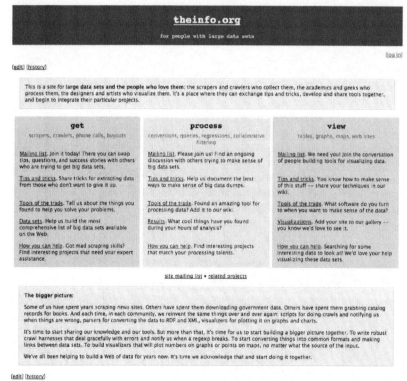

And while I've been doing this for information about books, I've noticed my friends doing similar things in other fields. Reporters try to get large data sets to write stories. Programmers get large data sets to add features to their sites. Friends are trying to make available data about the inner workings of the government.

And while each community has ways of talking to each other — reporters talking to other reporters, RDF people talking to other RDF people, library hackers talking to other library hackers — there's no community that cuts across these topical lines. And that's too bad, because there's a lot there we could share, from tips on how not to get caught when crawling to tools to make it easier to build big charts and maps.

So that's why I've started a new community site for people who work with large data sets. It's called theinfo.org and I'd really appreciate it if you joined the mailing lists and spread the word.

January 15, 2008

WELCOME, WATCHDOG.NET

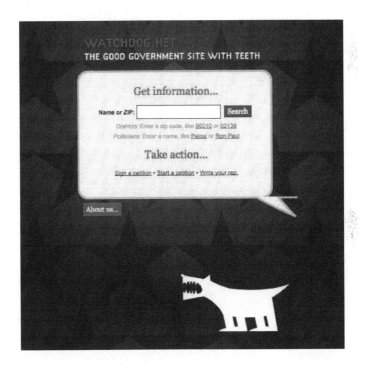

As you've probably noticed, it's political insanity season in the US. I can hardly go outside these days without running into someone complaining about the latest piece of campaign gossip. I've mostly tried to keep it off this blog, but it's hard to not get swept up in the fever. As someone who wants to make a difference in the world, I've long wondered whether there was an effective way for a programmer to get involved in politics, but I've never been able to quite figure it out.

Well, recent events and Larry Lessig got me thinking about it again and I've spent the past few months working with and talking to some amazing people about the problem. I've learned a lot and must have gone through a dozen different project ideas, but I finally think I've found something. It's not so much a finished solution as a direction, where I hope to figure more of it along the way.

So the site is called watchdog.net and the plan has three parts. First, pull in data sources from all over — district demographics, votes, lobbying records, campaign finance reports, etc. — and let people explore them in one elegant, unified interface. I want this to be one of the most powerful, compelling interfaces for exploring a large data set out there.

But just giving people information isn't enough; unless you give them an opportunity to do something about it, it will just make them more apathetic. So the second part of the site is building tools to let people take action: write or call your representative, send a note to local papers, post a story about something interesting you've found, generate a scorecard for the next election.

And tying these two pieces together will be a collaborative database of political causes. So on the page about global warming, you'll be able to learn more about the problem and proposed solutions, research the donors and votes on the issue, and see or start a letter-writing campaign.

All of it, of course, is free software and free data. And it's all got a dozen different APIs to make it easy for others to build on what we've done in their own work. The goal is to be a hub, connecting citizens, activists, organizations, politicians, programmers, and everybody else who's interested in politics.

The hope is to make it as interesting and easy as possible to pull people into politics. It's an ambitious goal with many pieces and possibilities, but with all the excitement right now we want to get something up as fast as possible. So we'll be developing live on watchdog.net, releasing pieces as soon as we finish them. Our first goal is to put up data about every representative and a way to write them.

I've managed to find an amazing group of people willing to help out with building it so far. And the Sunlight Network has encouraged me and graciously agreed to fund it. But we still need many more hands, especially programmers. If you're interested in working on it, whether as a volunteer or for pay, please send me an email telling me what you'd like to help with.

We only officially started work yesterday, so there's not much up yet, but hopefully it'll give you a sense of where we're going.

April 14, 2008

HOWTO: PROMOTE STARTUPS

When people talk about how government can promote startups, there seems to be a fairly standard consensus: we need more economic inequality. Lower income[1] and capital gains[2] taxes provide more incentive to work, looser labor laws make it easier to fire non-performers, and large private wealth funds provide investment capital.

But having been through a startup myself, I think there's much more you can do in the other direction: decreasing economic inequality. People love starting companies. You get to be your own boss, work on something you love, do something new and exciting, and get lots of attention. As Daniel Brook points out in *The Trap*, 28% of Americans have considered starting their own business. And yet only 7% actually do.

What holds them back? The lack of a social safety net. A friend of mine, a brilliant young technologist who's been featured everywhere from PBS to Salon, stayed in academia and the corporate world while all of her friends were starting companies and getting rich. Why? Because she couldn't afford to lose her health insurance. Between skyrocketing prices and preexisting condition exclusions, it's almost impossible for anyone who isn't in perfect health to quit their job. (I only managed because I was on a government plan.)

Anyone with children is also straight out. Startup founders tend to be quite young, in no small part because no one can afford to support a family on a startup founder's salary. But if we had universal child care, that would be much less of an issue. Parents would be free to pursue their dreams, knowing that their children were taken care of. And universal higher education could let parents spend their savings on getting a business started, instead of their children's tuition. Plus, it'd give many more kids the training and confidence they needed to start a company.

And those large private wealth funds that result from growing inequality? A real problem for startup founders is that they're too large. It used to be that you could borrow a couple thousand dollars from friends and neighbors to get your business off the ground. Nowadays, they're too busy trying to make ends meet to be able to afford anything like that. Meanwhile, those large wealth funds I mentioned are now so big they can only afford to invest in multi-million dollar chunks — much more than the average founder needs, or can even justify. And the large investments come with large amounts of scrutiny, further narrowing the recipient pool.

But imagine if the government provided a basic minimum income, like Richard Nixon once proposed. Instead of having to save up (increasingly difficult in a world in which the only way to survive is on credit card debt) or borrow money to stay afloat, you could live off the government-provided income as you got things started. Suddenly having to quit your job would no longer be such a huge leap — there'd be a real social safety net to catch you. (Not to mention if those labor laws some people want to loosen required your old job to take you back if things didn't work out.)

Of course, there is some truth to the standard proposals. Some startup founders are encouraged by dreams of financial security, and high taxes can make that dream more elusive. And complex labor regulations can make it difficult to get new companies off the ground. But it's not an issue of whether we should have taxes or labor laws — it's an issue of how they're targeted.

Estate taxes on inherited fortunes would have basically no impact on startup founders, but could go a long way to funding a social safety net. And since most startups are acquired as stock, income taxes are basically irrelevant — it's really capital gains tax that gets applied. There's no reason the government couldn't apply a lower capital gains tax to startups that get acquired than they do to the shares of publicly-traded companies that large investors trade.

The same is true for labor laws: preventing large companies from firing people at random can provide some much-needed stability to their lives, especially if they're saving up money in the hopes of going into business themselves. But there's no reason such laws also have to be applied to small startups, where the company is more likely to go out of business than to fire you.

Look at social democratic Europe, where these policy prescriptions have been tried. While there's much less of a culture of entrepreneurship and only 15% of Europeans think about starting their own company, nearly all (14.7%) of them actually go ahead and do it.

The fact is, if governments really want to promote startups and the economic innovation they bring, they shouldn't listen to the standard refrain of cut taxes and deregulate. They need to start rebuilding the social safety net, so that their citizens know that if they go out on a limb and try something risky, someone will be there to catch them if things don't work out.

Thanks to Daniel Brook's book The Trap: Selling Out to Stay Afloat in Winner-Take-All America *for suggesting this line of argument and providing the statistics.*

June 9, 2008

1. http://www.paulgraham.com/inequality.html
2. http://www.paulgraham.com/america.html

GUERILLA OPEN ACCESS MANIFESTO

Information is power. But like all power, there are those who want to keep it for themselves. The world's entire scientific and cultural heritage, published over centuries in books and journals, is increasingly being digitized and locked up by a handful of private corporations. Want to read the papers featuring the most famous results of the sciences? You'll need to send enormous amounts to publishers like Reed Elsevier.

There are those struggling to change this. The Open Access Movement has fought valiantly to ensure that scientists do not sign their copyrights away but instead ensure their work is published on the Internet, under terms that allow anyone to access it. But even under the best scenarios, their work will only apply to things published in the future. Everything up until now will have been lost.

That is too high a price to pay. Forcing academics to pay money to read the work of their colleagues? Scanning entire libraries but only allowing the folks at Google to read them? Providing scientific articles to those at elite universities in the First World, but not to children in the Global South? It's outrageous and unacceptable.

"I agree," many say, "but what can we do? The companies hold the copyrights, they make enormous amounts of money by charging for access, and it's perfectly legal — there's nothing we can do to stop them." But there is something we can, something that's already being done: we can fight back.

Those with access to these resources — students, librarians, scientists — you have been given a privilege. You get to feed at this banquet of knowledge while the rest of the world is locked out. But you need not — indeed, morally, you cannot — keep this privilege for yourselves. You have a duty to share it with the world. And you have: trading passwords with colleagues, filling download requests for friends.

Meanwhile, those who have been locked out are not standing idly by. You have been sneaking through holes and climbing over fences, liberating the information locked up by the publishers and sharing them with your friends.

But all of this action goes on in the dark, hidden underground. It's called stealing or piracy, as if sharing a wealth of knowledge were the moral equivalent of plundering a ship and murdering its crew. But sharing isn't immoral — it's a moral imperative. Only those blinded by greed would refuse to let a friend make a copy.

Large corporations, of course, are blinded by greed. The laws under which they operate require it — their shareholders would revolt at anything less. And the politicians they have bought off back them, passing laws giving them the exclusive power to decide who can make copies.

There is no justice in following unjust laws. It's time to come into the light and, in the grand tradition of civil disobedience, declare our opposition to this private theft of public culture.

We need to take information, wherever it is stored, make our copies and share them with the world. We need to take stuff that's out of copyright and add it to the archive. We need to buy secret databases and put them on the Web. We need to download scientific journals and upload them to file sharing networks. We need to fight for Guerilla Open Access.

With enough of us, around the world, we'll not just send a strong message opposing the privatization of knowledge — we'll make it a thing of the past. Will you join us?

Aaron Swartz

1. Source: https://archive.org/stream/GuerillaOpenAccessManifesto/
    Goamjuly2008_djvu.txt

HOWTO: LAUNCH SOFTWARE

37signals recommends that software developers pursue what they call the Hollywood Launch[1]. They don't give any argument for this method, except perhaps the title (as if Hollywood was a business you should try to imitate?) — I guess the idea is that you're supposed to do it since 37signals says to.

The basic idea behind the Hollywood Launch is simple: you release a few hints about your product to build buzz, slowly revealing more and more until the big day, when you throw open the doors and people flood your site, sent there by all the blog coverage and email alerts.

This may work well for Hollywood — if your movie is a big hit at the box-office on opening weekend, then the movie theaters are more likely to keep showing it in the weeks to come and you get credit for being "one of the weekend's biggest films". But for software developers, it's moronic. Your software isn't being released in theaters, it's available over the Web. You don't have to worry about the theater no longer showing after week one; you can keep pushing it for years, growing your userbase.

Instead what happens when software developers try the Hollywood Launch, and I've seen this many times, is that users indeed do flood to your site on launch day but…

1. They bring the site down from the load. You scramble to get it back up and succeed by coding like a mad man, only to find…

2. They discover some big bug that you never quite noticed before, which makes the whole thing look like embarrassing hackwork. (*What? You forgot to test that last-minute JavaScript change in IE6 1/2?*) So you're desperately rushing to fix the bug before the traffic dies down, rush-patching things and restarting the server when…

3. You bring the site down for everyone because there was a syntax error in your patch that keeps the server from coming back up. You fix it while cursing yourself madly. Finally everything seems to work. You take a breath and decide to see what people are saying about you on the Web, only to discover…

4. Everyone misunderstood what your product does because your front page wasn't clear enough. Now they all think it's stupid and wonder aloud how you even know how to breathe. So you reply in all the comment threads and fix your front page to ensure no one could possibly misunderstand what it is you're doing just in time to find…

5. All the traffic is gone.

Tomorrow, hardly any of those users come back. Your traffic graphs look like the sharpest mountain you've ever seen: a huge climb up and then, almost immediately, a similarly-sized crash back down.

So what do you do then? Well, you do what you should have done all along: you grow the site.

I'll call this technique the Gmail Launch, since it's based on what Gmail did. Gmail is probably one of the biggest Web 2.0 success stories, so there's an argument in its favor right there. Here's how it works:

1. Have users from day one. Obviously at the very beginning it'll just be yourself and your co-workers, but as soon as you have something that you don't cringe while using, you give it to your friends and family. Keep improving it based on their feedback and once you have something that's tolerable, let them invite their friends to use it too.

2. Try to get lots of feedback from these new invitees, figuring out what doesn't make sense, what needs to be fixed, and what things don't work on their bizarre use case combination. Once these are all straightened out, and they're using it happily, you let them invite their friends. Repeat until things get big enough that you need to...

3. Automate the process, giving everyone some invite codes to share. By requiring codes, you protect against a premature slashdotting and force your users to think carefully about who actually would want to use it (getting them to do your marketing for you). Plus, you make everyone feel special for using your product. (You can also start (slowly!) sending invite codes to any email lists you might have.)

4. Iterate: give out invite codes, fix bugs, make sure things are stable. Stay in this phase until the number of users you're willing to invite is about the same as the number you expect will initially sign up if you make the site public. For Gmail, this was a long time, since a lot of people wanted invites. You can probably safely do it sooner.

5. Take off the invite code requirement, so that people can use the product just by visiting its front page. Soon enough, random people will come across it from Google or various blogs and become real users.

6. If all this works — if random people are actually happy with your product and you're ready to grow even larger — then you can start building buzz and getting press and blog attention. The best way to do this is to have some kind of news hook — some gimmick or controversial thing that everyone will want to talk about. (With reddit, the big thing was that we switched from Lisp to Python, which was discussed endlessly in the Lisp and Python communities and gave us our first big userbase.)

7. Start marketing. Once you start using up all the growth you can get by word-of-mouth (and this can take a while — Google is only getting to this stage

now), you can start doing advertising and other marketing-type things to provide the next big boost in growth.

The result will be a graph that just keeps accelerating and climbing up. That's the graph that everyone loves to see: solid growth, not a one-day wonder. Good luck.

Since 37signals quotes from people who followed their advice, I thought I might as well do the same. mojombo[2]:

- I find this to be excellent advice. This is exactly the approach we took at GitHub almost down to the letter. It took about 2 months until the site was good enough to use to host the GitHub source, another month until we started private beta with invites, and three more months until public launch.
- Artificial scarcity is a great technique to generate excitement for a product while also limiting growth to a rate that won't melt your servers. We worked through a huge number of problems and early users gave us some of the ideas that have defined GitHub. By doing a Hollywood launch, things would have been very different and I am convinced, very much worse.
- Do not, I repeat, DO NOT underestimate how much your users will help you to define your product. If you launch without having significant user feedback time, you've essentially thrown away a massive (and free) focus group study.
- Let me also say that when we finally did our public launch, there was plenty of buzz, and all of it was the RIGHT kind of buzz. The buzz that attracts real, lasting customers (and no, we weren't on TechCrunch, that traffic is garbage).

August 22, 2008

1. http://gettingreal.37signals.com/ch13_Hollywood_Launch.php
2. http://news.ycombinator.com/item?id=284057

IN DEFENSE OF ANONYMITY

In 1787, when America's framers wanted to argue for its Constitution, they published their arguments (the Federalist Papers) anonymously. Whistleblowers have released everything from the Pentagon Papers to the Downing Street Memos. Anonymous speech is a First Amendment right.

And yet, on the supposedly Wild West frontier of the Internet, publishing anonymously is not so easy. Hosting providers require a name and credit card, which they have to hand over to the FBi at the drop of a National Security Letter. Free hosting sites zealously obey takedown requests and require publishers to reveal their identity if they want their stuff put back up (a tactic Scientologists have used). Luckily there are now services like Wikileaks[1], but they only publish a very narrow range of content.

But, talking with Virgil Griffith and others, I hit upon a new way of allowing for anonymous publishing. The amazing Tor project[2] lets you use the Internet anonymously, by disguising your traffic thru a long series of relays. Less well-known is that it also allows for anonymous publishing, by running the system in reverse. Unfortunately, you need the Tor software to visit anonymously-published sites, but we realized there's no reason this need be so.

So I dusted off some work I'd begun years and years ago and build a tor2web proxy. Now anyone with a web browser can visit an anonymous Tor URL like `http://sexy36iscapohm7b.onion/` from any Web browser, without any special software, just by going to: `http://sexy36iscapohm7b.tor.theinfo.org/`.

Which means that publishing an anonymous website is now also fairly easy. (There are instructions on the Tor site[3] — just replace the .onion when you hand out the URL. If that's too tricky, you could use an existing provider like Freedom Hosting.)

tor2web proxies act like any other sort of proxy or router; they just route traffic from a client to a server and don't get involved themselves, so they can't be held legally responsible for the content that passes thru them. But to prevent against a single point of failure, I'm asking others to set up tor2web nodes[4] to distribute the load. The next step, of course, is to support mirroring[5] so that people can still find interesting files, even if one hidden server goes down.

Here's to anonymity — and more tools protecting it.

October 24, 2008

1. http://wikileaks.org/
2. http://www.torproject.org/
3. https://www.torproject.org/docs/tor-hidden-service.html.en
4. http://tor.theinfo.org/config
5. http://tor.theinfo.org/mirror

OCLC ON THE RUN

OCLC is running scared. My comments on their attempt to monopolize library records has been Slashdotted, our petition has received hundreds of signatures, and they're starting to feel the heat.

At a talk I gave this morning to area librarians, an OCLC rep stood up and attempted to assure the crowd that what I was saying "wasn't entirely true". "What wasn't true?" I asked. "I'd love to correct things." She declined to say, insisting she "didn't want to get into an argument."

This evening, OCLC's Vice President for WorldCat and Metadata, provides more details. In a blog comment (which, I understand, was sent to OCLC members), she tries to downplay the issue, continuing the OCLC trend of doublespeak about this serious change.

She tries to claim we're on the same side ("We are likely in solid agreement") and insists they are just updating "the principles ... which have been in place since 1987" and absurdly claiming that the new rules are just a "clarification". (This is just one of a number of black-is-white falsehoods in her post.)

But never once does she defend the actual changes. And they're right there in black-and-white: the records aren't allowed to be used in anything that "substantially replicates the function, purpose, and/or size of WorldCat." I'm not sure how much clearer they can get; these new rules prohibit anyone from building anything that gets anywhere close to WorldCat.

My fundamental point stands: As servers have gotten cheaper, it's become easy to do for free the things OCLC charges such outrageous amounts for. But OCLC can't have that — they'd have to give up their huge office complex and high salaries (Ms. Calhoun was recently hired away from academia, so her salary isn't available yet, but her fellow VPs make around $300,000/year). So they're trying to stamp out the competition.

Karen insists that "OCLC welcomes collaboration with Open Library", which seems a funny way of putting it. As I said last time, they've played hardball: trying to cut off our funding, hurt our reputation, and pressured libraries not to cooperate. When we tried to make a deal with them, they dragged their feet for months, pretended to come to terms, and then had their lawyers send us an "agreement" to sign that would require we take all OCLC-related records off our site.

Karen, if you really want to "increas[e] information access to users around the globe", like you say, here's an easy first step: put the 2 million WorldCat web pages you shared with Google and Yahoo up for download on your website. It's only a small portion of your catalog and you've already shared it with others. Until you take even a baby step like that, it's hard to take your protestations of good intent seriously.

November 15, 2008

NON-HIERARCHICAL MANAGEMENT

You want to get something done. But it's too big to do it by yourself, so you bring in some friends to help out. In your dreams, all your friends just "click", understand exactly what it is they're all supposed to do, and do it quickly and effective. In reality, this almost never happens.

In order for any team to succeed, they need someone helping them all stay on track — someone who we will call a "manager".

The word manager makes many people uncomfortable. It calls up the image of a bossman telling you what to do and forcing you to slave away at doing it. That is not effective management.

A better way to think of a manager is as a servant, like an editor or a personal assistant. Everyone wants to be effective; a manager's job is to do everything they can to make that happen. The ideal manager is someone everyone would want to have.

Instead of the standard "org chart" with a CEO at the top and employees growing down like roots, turn the whole thing upside down. Employees are at the top — they're the ones who actually get stuff done   and managers are underneath them, helping them to be more effective. (The CEO, who really does nothing, is of course at the bottom.)

Most guides on management are written for big bosses at big companies, not people starting something new who want their team to be as effective as possible. (Hi, startup founders!) So herewith, a guide to effective non-hierarchical management.

POINT 1: MANAGEMENT IS A JOB

Management is not a typical job. People who manage programmers don't spend their day programming. Nor do they spend their day writing memos. In fact, from the outside, it may appear like they don't spend their day doing very much at all. Don't be fooled.

Management is a serious job. It is incredibly difficult and wildly consuming. As an employee, if you miss a day off work, it's no big deal: some work doesn't get done and you (or someone else) has to catch up on it later. As a manager, it can become a serious problem — if you're not working, then the dozen people you serve aren't working effectively as well. It makes knocking off work to go to the fair a stressful proposition.

On the other hand, it can be incredibly rewarding. If you do your job right, you turn a group of individuals into a team, a group that's more effective than the sum of its parts. Together, you and your team can achieve amazing things. As a manager, your task is to serve the team — to make it as effective as it can possibly be, even if that means stepping on the toes of a few individuals.

One incredibly popular misconception is that managers are just there to provide "leadership" — you set everyone up, get them pointed in the right direction, and then let them go while you go back to the "real" stuff, whether it's building things yourself, meeting with funders, or going on the road and talking up your organization. Those are all perfectly valid jobs, but they are not management. You have to pick one. You cannot do both.

POINT 1A: STAY ORGANIZED

As the manager, it's your job to make sure things get done. This means you need a system for making sure things get done. This doesn't have to be anything fancy or complicated — a simple todo list will do — but simply trying to remember or writing yourself a note is not a system.

One of the nice things about having a system is it actually makes you less stressed out. Most people just keep their todo list somewhere in the back of their head. As things pile up, they become harder and harder to keep track of, and you become more stressed out about getting them all done or forgetting about them.

Simply writing them down on a list makes everything seem more manageable. You can see the things you have to do — really, there's not quite as many important ones as you thought — and you can put them in order and get that nice burst of satisfaction that comes from crossing them off.

Yes, it all sounds like silly, basic stuff, but it's important. Just having a list with all the stuff you need to do — and taking it seriously, actually going down it and checking stuff off every single day — is the difference between being a black hole of action items and being someone who actually Gets Stuff Done.

POINT 2: KNOW YOUR TEAM

As a servant, it's crucial you know your masters well. You need to know what they're good at and what gives them trouble. You need to be able to tell when they're feeling good and when they're in a rut. And you need to have a safe enough relationship with them that they can be honest with you and come to you when they're in trouble. This is not easy. (You have to be willing to hear bad news about yourself.)

The most important piece is understanding what people are good at and what they like doing. A good first step is to just ask them, but often people are wrong or don't know. So you try giving them different things, seeing how they do at them, and adjusting accordingly.

But in addition to your team's professional skills, it's important to understand their personal goals. However much you may care about the work, at bottom it's still a job. You need to understand why your team members took it. Was it because it seemed interesting? Because it seemed worthwhile? Because it would give them valuable experience and help them get a better job down the road? It's important that you know, so you can make sure your tasks and expectations are in line with their goals.

POINT 2A: HIRE PEOPLE SMARTER THAN YOU

You want the best working for you. People who aren't just good at their job, but people who are also good at your job. People you can trust to not just do something right but tell you that the way you suggested doing it was wrong. People you can rely on to get things done if you just stay out of their way. At least, that's the ideal. In practice, it's hard to find people like that and even when you do, they still need help.

I have never found the traditional methods of hiring — resumés, interviews, quizzes — to be helpful at all. Instead, I look at two things: what someone has done and whether I enjoy spending time with them. The first shows not just their talent but also their ability to execute. If they haven't made something interesting, whether as a side project or at a previous job, then they're probably not worth hiring. It's not *that* hard to sit down and accomplish something; be wary of people who haven't.

Similarly, you need to keep in mind that you're not just hiring a robot — you're hiring a flesh-and-blood human who you're going to need to spend a lot of time with during the day. That means they need to be someone you not just get along with, but enjoy being around. A formal interview, with all its stress and structure and contrivance, is a pretty bad environment for seeing if you like someone. Instead, just go get coffee and chat.

POINT 2B: BE CAREFUL WHEN HIRING FRIENDS

Everyone wants to work with their friends. After all, you have so much fun hanging out after work, why not hang out during work too? So they recruit their friends to work with them. (Or, even worse, they recruit their lovers.) But being friends is very different from being colleagues. All friends learn ways to adjust themselves to each other — which tones to use, which subjects to avoid, when to give each other space.

These go out the window when you're working together. You can't just not say things because they'll get your friend upset. So you say them, and they get upset, and you realize you have no way of dealing with each other when you're like this. It makes working together difficult, to say the least.

The situation is the same, but vastly worse, with couples. Plus, you're really screwed when your relationship falls apart under the stress.

If you do decide to work with people you're close with, you need to find a way to put your other relationship "on hold" while you work together. Which means you both need to be strong enough to be able to blow up at each other at work and then go out for drinks like nothing ever happened. If you can't do this (and few can), then either give up on the relationship or give up on the job.

The most extreme form of this, of course, is that you need to be able to fire your friend. Just because you like them doesn't mean they'll automatically be a good employee. And, sadly, there's really no way for you to know in advance. Bad employees are no less disastrous because they're your friends. Which means that if you hire a friend, you need to be able to fire them.

POINT 2C: SET BOUNDARIES

Conversely, don't become close friends with the people you work with. You have to set some personal boundaries: you're their manager, not their friend. Naturally, part of being a manager means that you have to talk to people about their personal problems and possibly even offer advice. After all, it's your job to make your team effective and if personal problems are distracting from that, you are going to have to face someone's personal problems.

But be sure to keep these problems at arm's length. Actually getting involved in someone's personal life or otherwise establishing a close personal relationship them is asking for trouble.

POINT 3: GO OVER THE GOALS TOGETHER

Your first job as a manager is to make sure everyone's on the same page. The team needs to understand what they're expected to do, why they're doing it, and who else is involved (funding it, using it, counting on it). If you picked a good team (point 2a), they'll hear this and find holes in your plan and catch things you hadn't thought of. (Which is good! Together, you can fix it.)

But real work can't begin until everyone's on board with the plan.

POINT 3A: BUILD A COMMUNITY

You're not managing a bunch of individual employees; you're managing a team. You're all trying to accomplish the same goal. It's the manager's job to make sure everyone's comfortable with each other. (Hint: Those dumb break-the-ice games do not make people *more* comfortable.) And while there's obviously a lot of feedback you need to give people one-on-one (never chew people out in front of a group), you should try to do a lot in front of the team as well.

It's easy to fall into a trap where you're just giving feedback individually. The result is that everyone feels isolated, not knowing where their work fits in to the bigger picture. Providing opportunities for everyone to see what everyone else is up to is crucial to making your team actually feel like it's a community, instead of just a group of your friends. (First law of friendship drift: Just because you like two people doesn't mean they'll automatically like each other.)

It's also a good opportunity to set a tone. You want people to treat each other like friends and colleagues, not backstabbing assholes or bickering siblings. As my friend Clay comments:

> I have a "no asshole rule" which is really simple: I really don't want to work with assholes. So if you're an asshole and you work on my team, I'm going to fire you. Now, if the whole team says "gosh, that's awful. We want to work with as many assholes as we can!" then we have a simple solution. I'll fire me! (FYI: The "No Asshole Rule" is a book. I thought it was actually a pretty good book as far as Business books go. As far as I'm concerned, anybody could stand to read 100 pages giving them the MBA Book cover they need to say to their boss: let's get the assholes out of here.)

But a community is about more than just tone, there's process as well. You need to figure out how your team members work and how you can get them to work together.

Some people like constant human feedback; others like locking themselves in a room for a couple hours and just getting something done. Everyone has their own habits and styles. Your job is to find an appropriate mix that makes everyone as productive they can be.

POINT 4: ASSIGN RESPONSIBILITY

First, break the plan up into parts. Make sure everybody understands the parts.

Second, find a team member who wants to do each part. The key word here is *wants* — some things just have to get done, it's true, but things will get done much better by people who want to do them.

One of the weird facts of life is that for just about everything you hate doing, there is someone out there who loves doing it. (There are even people who get a real kick out of cleaning toilets.) You may not currently employ them and you may not be able to hire them, but the is the goal worth striving toward.

It's also important to realize that a lot of what makes a task attractive or unattractive is outside the task itself. Managing the company's accounting books at first seems like a pretty uninteresting job. But when you realize it makes you indispensable and gives you authority over how all the money is spent, it suddenly seems a little more exciting. Use your knowledge from point 2 to structure tasks in a way that's attractive to your team members.

POINT 4A: VARY RESPONSIBILITIES

Another thing to keep in mind is that most people like variety in their work. It's very tempting to think of someone as "the finance guy" and just give them all the finance-related tasks. But in any organization there's lots of different kinds of things to do and a wide mix of people to do it. Many people will appreciate the opportunity to switch up the kinds of things they do.

It's tempting to think that this is inefficient, that by having one guy do all the finance tasks they'll become an expert in it and the finance tasks will get done more effectively. And there's definitely some truth in it. But one of the best ways to be inefficient is to make your team unhappy. If doing something new makes someone enjoy their job more, it'll be well worth the cost in time of them having to learn how to do it.

Even better, their fresh perspective might just help you make improvements you'd never thought of before.

POINT 4B: DELEGATE RESPONSIBILITY

As the manager, it's a continual temptation to keep important jobs for yourself. After all, they're usually fun to do and doggone-it they're *important*, you can't risk them on somebody else! Resist the temptation.

For one thing, taking jobs for yourself is one way of distracting yourself from having to do actual management (point 1). But more importantly, you'll never be able to develop your team if you keep all the real responsibility for yourself. Sure, Jony may not be as good at meeting funders as you, but a lot of that's because she's never gotten a chance to practice. If it's something she wants to do (point 2), take her along and give him a chance to learn.

POINT 5: CLEAR OBSTACLES

This is the bulk of what non-hierarchical management is about. You've got good people, they've got good responsibilities. Now it's your job to do everything in your power to help them get them done.

A good way to start is just by asking people what they need. Is their office too noisy? Did they get confused about something you said? Are they stuck on a particular problem? Are they overwhelmed with work? It's your job to help them out: get them a quieter office, clarify things, find them advice or answers, shift some stuff off their plate. They shouldn't be wasting time with things that annoy them; that's your job.

But you have to be proactive as well. People tend to suffer quietly, both because they don't want to come whining to you and just because when you're stuck in a rut all your attention is focused on the rut. A key part of being a manager is checking in with people, pointing out that they're stuck in a rut, and gently helping them out.

POINT 5A: PRIORITIZE

At any given time, there's lots of stuff that needs to be done. Part of your job is helping people decide what to tackle first. You don't want to be *too* didactic about it — people like choice and variety, they're not always so happy when you just give them one instruction after another — but even that's usually far preferable to being overwhelmed with stuff.

The best prioritization relationship is a dialogue: "OK, what's next?" someone asks. "Well, what about building the new sprocket management engine?" "Ugh, I'm too tired for that today." "OK, how about cleaning the frobnitz?" "Bo-ring." "Oh, I know! We need someone to document the doohickey." "Ooh, perfect — thanks!"

POINT 5B: FIGHT PROCRASTINATION

Procrastination is the crop blight of the office-work world. It affects just about everyone and it's very hard to fight alone. The single best way to stop procrastination is to sit down with someone and come up with the next concrete step they have to take and then start doing it together. There's something magical about having another person sit down with you and do something that can overcome procrastination's natural resistance. And once you get someone started, momentum can often carry them through the rest of the day.

Even if all you do is help people overcome procrastination, you will be well worth it.

POINT 6: GIVE FEEDBACK

White-collar work is lonely. You sit at a desk, staring at a screen, poking at buttons. It's easy to get lost and off-track and depressed. That's why it's important to check in and see how things are doing. Not only does it give you a chance to see how people are doing (point 5), it gives you a chance to see how things are coming and gently steer them back on course if they've drifted from what you've intended.

POINT 6A: DON'T MICROMANAGE

Remember, your job isn't to tell people *how* to do things; it's to help them get it done. Sometimes this means helping them figure out how to do it, but in general you should assume that you work with smart people and they'll be able to handle it themselves. Again, be a servant, not a boss.

Studies consistently show that people are much happier and more productive when they have control over the way they work. Never take that away.

POINT 7: DON'T MAKE DECISIONS (UNLESS YOU *REALLY* HAVE TO)

As manager, people will often come to you to make decisions or resolve disputes. It's very tempting, with people looking up at you for guidance, to want to give your sage advice. But the fact is, even if (or especially if) as a manager you're held up on a pedestal, you probably know less about the question than anyone else on the team.

The worst managers don't just make decisions when people come to them, they parachute in and start dictating tiny details. The urge to do this can be overwhelming, but there are few things more disastrous to morale. If you really have to give input, couch it as such. And if people fight back, know when to step back and say "look, you're the expert. I was just giving my two cents." (Hint: It's right after they start fighting back.)

The best managers use these opportunities not to dictate an answer, but to have a Socratic dialogue to help figure out what the best answer is. Often when people are stuck on something, they really just need someone else to talk things over with, either for assistance or validation. Here's your chance to help.

POINT 8: FIRE INEFFECTIVE PEOPLE

Firing people is hard. It's probably the hardest thing you'll ever do. People go to absurd lengths to try and make it easier ("we'll just try him out for a month and see how it goes" is a common one) but they never really help. You just have to bite the bullet and let people go. It's your job. If you can't do it, find someone else.

Firing people isn't just about saving money, or petty things like that. It's the difference between a great organization and a failure. Ineffective people drag everyone else down to their level. They make it so that you can't take pride in what you're doing, so that you dread going into work in the morning, so that you can't rely on the other pieces of the project getting done. And assholes, no matter how talented they may be, are even worse. Conversely, there are few things more fun than working hard with a really nice, talented group of people.

You are never going to be able to tell whether someone is going to work out in advance. Assholes are sometimes easy to spot, but people can have great resumes, solid references, a charming interview style, and still be total failures. And the worst part is, there will always be excuses for their failures. "I know, I know," they'll say, "it's just that I've been really sick this week. I've been distracted with family things. I've been traveling. Look, I'm sorry. I promise I'll do better this week." I've said them all myself.

If you're not getting things done, you can always come up with excuses for why. Competent people get things done anyway. Ineffective ones let the excuses pile up. They're not going to leave themselves. You have to pull the trigger.

POINT 9: GIVE AWAY THE CREDIT

As the team's manager, there will be many opportunities where people will want to give you credit. And getting credit is nice, it makes you feel good. So you start coming up with excuses for why you deserve it, even though you didn't do any of the work. "Well, it was my vision," you will say. "I was the one who made it all happen."

But think of all those talented people slaving away at desks. They were the ones who actually made it happen. Make sure they get the credit. And not in a facetious, "thanks to all the little people way". No, you need to own up. You are the assistant. They did all the work. As Clay says, "A manager's worst enemy is his or her own ego."

POINT 10: YOU'RE PROBABLY NOT CUT OUT FOR THIS

Spending your days doing grunt work for people who are smarter than you. Obsessing over their mood and personal problems. Turning down all opportunities to take credit or get attention so you can continue to work as a servant. Does this really sound like a job you want?

Probably not. Few people are cut out for it. It's really hard. It's incredibly stressful. It's not at all glamorous. But it's vitally important. A team without a manager is doomed to be an ineffective team. So if you can't do it, find somebody else.

Thanks *to* Clay Johnson[1] *and* Emmett Shear[2] *for their comments on drafts of this essay.*

February 16, 2009

1. http://www.sunlightfoundation.com/people/cjohnson/
2. http://blog.emmettshear.com/

A NON-LOCAL REVOLUTION

Paul Graham has recently argued for two points: first, that tech startups will continue to collect in Silicon Valley[1]. Second, that startups may represent a new economic phase[2], replacing the corporate ladder of old[3]. Now he's suggesting that these two effects combined might lead to a very local economic revolution[4].

The first point — that tech startups collect in Silicon Valley — is certainly true, just like car companies all tend to cluster in Detroit. This is because of a feedback effect set off by some random initial condition: Shockley Semiconductor was started in Silicon Valley, so when its employees left to start their own companies they did so there, and so on. Now everyone in the industry moves to Silicon Valley because that's where everyone else is.

This isn't a new idea; it was a central topic in Paul Krugman's research, for example, and even before that you can see similar ideas expressed by social theorists like Jane Jacobs. (For more information, see the Wikipedia article Business cluster[5], Krugman's Geography and Trade, and Jacobs' brilliant book *The Economy of Cities*.) Industries tend to cluster together.

The second — that startups represent a new economic phase — may also be true. It's a rather more extreme claim, but it would be pretty cool.

But I don't think it combines with the first to create a local revolution. It's true, tech startups have generated a lot of wealth, but they're far from the only kind of startup to do so. The amazing thing about the Internet is that it makes all sorts of startups possible.

Previously, if you wanted to start a newspaper, you had to buy a building and hire a staff and get some printing presses and a delivery service and an ad sales team and access to the wire services. Now you just start a blog, read the wire services online, and link to the stories you like.

Previously, if you wanted to sell a new kind of soap, you had to build warehouses and a distribution network and a shipping infrastructure and make deals with retail outlets. Now you have Amazon Fulfillment Services[6] handle all the physical details and just advertise your product on the Web.

And new startups are helping this process along all the time. One Y Combinator startup tries to make things easier for food producers, another helps you run an online magazine. More are surely close behind.

It's tempting to think that a soap company which only sold through the Internet would always be a small concern. But why should it be any different from Internet companies? Reddit was small when it started, but it quickly grew through word-of-mouth. Sure, we had some tough nights making things scale, but in the end we were able to ramp up to a site with millions of users.

Similarly, I met some folks in Brooklyn who started a small salsa company[7] in their apartment. At first they made the salsa in their kitchen and sold jars through their bedroom window. As business picked up, they got a bigger space and started selling more. Now they're manufacturing in scale and you can find them at Whole Foods. This worked because New York City was a big enough audience that they had room to scale up. The Internet is big in exactly the same way.

As the Internet is everywhere and everyone knows how to use it, why won't we see online startups in every industry? And then why not all across the globe? It may make sense for tech startups to move to Silicon Valley, but does it really make sense for soap startups? For food startups? No, it seems more likely that each industry will cluster the way tech companies and car companies have.

Silicon Valley may have had the first wave, but the next one belongs to the world.

April 15, 2009

1. http://www.paulgraham.com/startuphubs.html
2. http://www.paulgraham.com/highres.html
3. http://www.paulgraham.com/ladder.html
4. http://www.paulgraham.com/revolution.html
5. http://en.wikipedia.org/wiki/Business_cluster
6. http://www.amazonservices.com/content/fulfillment-by-amazon.htm
7. http://bksalsa.com/

REDESIGN

I was going through my weblog archives the other day and found an early post I'd written *nine years ago* (in yet another piece of blogging software I'd written myself…). But what was even more shocking than the notion that I'd been blogging for over a decade was that my web design back then was better than it was today.

This really kept nagging at me, so I took a couple hours tonight to do a redesign. I still have very little in the way of positive artistic talent (see article "Two Conceptions of Taste"), so it's nothing impressive, but I do hope that it will keep me from recoiling in horror from my own weblog. My apologies to everyone I borrowed design features from.

Feel free to use this thread to comment on the redesign.

September 23, 2009

djb

I think it's time to remind people that D. J. Bernstein is the greatest programmer in the history of the world.

First, look only at the objective facts. djb has written two major pieces of system software: a mail server and a DNS server. Both are run by millions of Internet domains. They accomplish all sorts of complicated functions, work under incredibly high loads, and confront no end of unusual situations. And they both run pretty much exactly has Bernstein first wrote them. One bug — one bug! — was found in qmail. A second bug was recently found in djbdns, but you can get a sense of how important it is by the fact that it took people nearly a decade to find it.

No other programmer has this kind of track record. Donald Knuth probably comes closest, but his diary about writing TeX (printed in *Literate Programming*[1]) shows how he kept finding bugs for years and never expected to be finished, only to get closer and closer (thus the odd version numbering scheme). Not only does no one else have djb's track record, no one else even comes close.

But far more important are the subjective factors. djb's programs are some of the greatest works of beauty to be comprehended by the human mind. As with great art, the outline of the code is somehow visually pleasing — there is balance and rhythm and meter that rivals even the best typography. As with great poetry, every character counts — every single one is there because it needs to be. But these programs are not just for being seen or read — like a graceful dancer, they move! And not just as a single dancer either, but a whole choreographed number — processes splitting and moving and recombining at great speeds, around and around again.

But, unlike a dance, this movement has a purpose. They accomplish things that need accomplishing — they find your websites, they ferry your email from place to place. In the most fantastic movies, the routing and sorting of the post office is imagined as a giant endless choreographed dance number. (Imagine, perhaps, "The Office" from Brazil.) But this is no one-time fantasy, this is how your email gets sorted *every day*.

And the dance is not just there to please human eyes — it is a dance with a purpose. Each of its inner mechanisms is perfectly crafted, using the fewest number of moving parts, accomplishing its task with the most minimal energy. The way jobs are divided and assigned is nothing short of brilliant. The brilliance is not merely linguistic, although it is that too, but contains a kind of elegant mathematical effectiveness, backed by a stream of numbers and equations that show, through pure reason alone, that the movements are provably perfect, a better solution is guaranteed not to exist.

But even all this does not capture his software's incredible beauty. For djb's programs are not great machines to be admired from a distance, vast powerhouses of elegant accomplishment. They are also tools meant to be used by man, perfectly fitted to one's hand. Like a great piece of industrial design, they bring joy to the user every time they are used.

What other field combines all these arts? Language, math, art, design, function. Programming is clearly in a class of its own. And, when it comes to programmers, who even competes with djb? Who else has worked to realize these amazing possibilities? Who else even knows they are there?

Oddly, there are many people who profess to hate djb. Some of this is just the general distaste of genius: djb clearly has a forceful, uncompromising vision, which many misinterpret as arrogance and rudeness. And some of it is the practical man's disregard for great design: djb's programs do not work like most programs, for the simple reason that the way most programs work is wrong. But the animosity goes much deeper than that. I do not profess to understand it, but I do honestly suspect at some level it's people without taste angry and frustrated at the plaudits showered on what they cannot see. Great art always generates its share of mocking detractors.

This is not to say that djb's work is perfect. There are the bugs, as mentioned before, and the log files, which are nothing if not inelegant, and no doubt djb would make numerous changes were he to write the software again today. But who else is even trying? Who else even knows this is possible? I did not realize what great art in software could be until I read djb. And now I feel dirty reading anything else.

October 19, 2009

1.   http://www.amazon.com/Literate-Programming-Center-Language-Information/dp/0937073806

HOW I HIRE PROGRAMMERS

There are three questions you have when you're hiring a programmer (or anyone, for that matter): Are they smart? Can they get stuff done? Can you work with them? Someone who's smart but doesn't get stuff done should be your friend, not your employee. You can talk your problems over with them while they procrastinate on their actual job. Someone who gets stuff done but isn't smart is inefficient: non-smart people get stuff done by doing it the hard way and working with them is slow and frustrating. Someone you can't work with, you can't work with.

The traditional programmer hiring process consists of: a) reading a resume, b) asking some hard questions on the phone, and c) giving them a programming problem in person. I think this is a terrible system for hiring people. You learn very little from a resume and people get real nervous when you ask them tough questions in an interview. Programming isn't typically a job done under pressure, so seeing how people perform when nervous is pretty useless. And the interview questions usually asked seem chosen just to be cruel. I think I'm a pretty good programmer, but I've never passed one of these interviews and I doubt I ever could.

So when I hire people, I just try to answer the three questions. To find out if they can get stuff done, I just ask what they've done. If someone can actually get stuff done they should have done so by now. It's hard to be a good programmer without some previous experience and these days anyone can get some experience by starting or contributing to a free software project. So I just request a code sample and a demo and see whether it looks good. You learn an enormous amount really quickly, because you're not watching them answer a contrived interview question, you're seeing their actual production code. Is it concise? clear? elegant? usable? Is it something you'd want in your product?

To find out whether someone's smart, I just have a casual conversation with them. I do everything I can to take off any pressure off: I meet at a cafe, I make it clear it's not an interview, I do my best to be casual and friendly. Under no circumstances do I ask them any standard "interview questions" — I just chat with them like I would with someone I met at a party. (If you ask people at parties to name their greatest strengths and weaknesses or to estimate the number of piano tuners in Chicago, you've got bigger problems.) I think it's pretty easy to tell whether someone's smart in casual conversation. I constantly make judgments about whether people I meet are smart, just like I constantly make judgments about whether people I see are attractive.

But if I had to write down what it is that makes someone seem smart, I'd emphasize three things. First, do they know stuff? Ask them what they've been thinking about and probe them about it. Do they seem to understand it in detail? Can they explain it clearly? (Clear explanations are a sign of genuine understanding.) Do they know stuff about the subject that you don't?

Second, are they curious? Do they reciprocate by asking questions about you? Are they genuinely interested or just being polite? Do they ask follow-up questions about what you're saying? Do their questions make you think?

Third, do they learn? At some point in the conversation, you'll probably be explaining something to them. Do they actually understand it or do they just nod and smile? There are people who know stuff about some small area but aren't curious about others. And there are people who are curious but don't learn, they ask lots of questions but don't really listen. You want someone who does all three.

Finally, I figure out whether I can work with someone just by hanging out with them for a bit. Many brilliant people can seem delightful in a one-hour conversation, but their eccentricities become grating after a couple hours. So after you're done chatting, invite them along for a meal with the rest of the team or a game at the office. Again, keep things as casual as possible. The point is just to see whether they get on your nerves.

If all that looks good and I'm ready to hire someone, there's a final sanity check to make sure I haven't been fooled somehow: I ask them to do part of the job. Usually this means picking some fairly separable piece we need and asking them to write it. (If you really insist on seeing someone working under pressure, give them a deadline.) If necessary, you can offer to pay them for the work, but I find most programmers don't mind being given a small task like this as long as they can open source the work when they're done. This test doesn't work on its own, but if someone's passed the first three parts, it should be enough to prove they didn't trick you, they can actually do the work.

(I've known some people who say "OK, well why don't we try hiring you for a month and see how it goes." This doesn't seem to work. If you can't make up your mind after a small project you also can't make it up after a month and you end up hiring people who aren't good enough. Better to just say no and err on the side of getting better people.)

I'm fairly happy with this method. When I've skipped parts, I've ended up with bad hires who eventually had to be let go. But when I've followed it, I've ended up with people I like so much so that I actually feel bad I don't get to work with them anymore. I'm amazed that so many companies use such silly hiring methods instead.

November 29, 2009

THE LOGIC OF GOOGLE ADS

When should you buy ads? Let's assume your goal is for people to click on the ads and give you money. (Reasons this may not be true: persuasion, brand-building, budget-maximizing.) The return from a block of ads is thus revenue — marginal_costs — ad_costs. Ads are an investment like any other; you keep buying them until your return on investment (revenue — marginal_costs / ad_costs) equals your cost of capital (usually the interest rate).

For simplicity, we'll assume your marginal cost is zero. (My marginal cost is almost always zero, so this doesn't strike me as too unrealistic.) So how do you estimate revenue? You can track how much money people who click on your ad give you, but this has two flaws. First, customers often give you more money over time. Maybe they buy level one of your video game when they click on the ad, but then they may buy levels two and three the next day after they beat level one. The future is always in the future, so revenue-per-user numbers may be too small.

Second, they might have given you money anyway. Your video game ads probably run on video game review sites, where readers might buy your game just from the review, even if you hadn't bought an ad. So your revenue numbers may be too big.

But these problems aren't so serious. In the first case, the worst that happens is you don't buy as many ads as you should. In the second, you don't actually lose money, it's just that some extra profit you could have kept has gone into ads.

Let's turn to the ad seller. They probably want to maximize how much they charge per ad impression (CPM). (Reasons this may not be true: unseemly ads.) A good way to do this is to hold an auction. It's impractical to have everyone bid live, so Google auctions work like eBay auctions: you enter the maximum you're willing to pay and get charged just enough to beat the other bidders. (One can think of this as a computer-simulated auction where everyone keeps bidding up the price by pennies until they hit the maximum they're willing to spend.)

But what are you bidding on? Ad sellers want to maximize revenue per impression, but ad buyers want to maximize profit per expense. In an ideal world, ad sellers auction off impressions (this is what Google Ad Manager does) while ad buyers bid per dollar of profit (entering their cost of capital).

Determining how much profit you make from an ad is hard. Can we just trust you? Let's say you make $2 in profit per 1000 impressions and everyone else makes $1. Now you can lie and say you make $1 in profit and then pay twice as much per profit-dollar. Now you pay the same amount as before, but you win all the profit-dollar auctions. Now that's not wrong — you're clearly making more money than the other bidders, so you should win — but your bid isn't cost-per-profit anymore, it's cost-per-impression.

What if you paid based on revenue? Verifying revenue is difficult, but Google could do it if everyone was using Google Checkout. (If you sent some of your users to a non-Google Checkout system, Google could catch you and fine you.) Google offers nicer ads to Checkout users, but they still don't have much market share, making this system impractical at present.

Some search engines apparently had cost-per-action (CPA) auctions, where you paid based on how many people actually bought things. I have no idea how they made that work, since lying about how many people took an action seems really profitable and easy. Maybe that's why no one does this anymore.

That just leaves cost-per-click (CPC). Cost-per-click seems ideal, since it's verifiable by both the ad seller (who uses a redirect link to track clicks) and the ad buyer (who sees the users show up on their page). It's a nice half-way point between buyer and seller.

So the ad seller holds an auction for CPC and multiplies CPC by click-thru-rate (CTR) to calculate CPM. They shows the highest CPM ads, charging each the bidder below them's CPC, times their relative CTRs. (In reality, Google doesn't just use CTR; they also factor in the relevance of the ad and the quality of the page it goes to.) And, voila: we've derived the basics of an online ad system.

This works out great for the ad seller — they maximize CPM, just like they wanted — but the ad buyer is still stuck converting their ROI into CPC. The ad buyer, recall, wants to increase their spending on ads (now determined to be CPC) until their return on investment equals their cost of capital.

It seems like this should be pretty easy, and indeed Google does provide tools to calculate ROI, but apparently not to optimize it. What they do provide is a tool to optimize your cost-per-action. Does anyone know why this is?

It seems like an automatic ROI optimizer would lead many people to spend more money on ads. It's hard to believe Google is leaving all that money on the table.

But Google does intelligently optimize the ads themselves. The variance in click-thru rates between different ads is huge — it's not uncommon to see two very similar ads, but one gets ten times as many clicks as the others. Google lets you put in as many ads as you like and automatically rotates them, showing ads with better CTRs more often.

So far we've just had a single ad seller. In the real world, lots of people want to sell ads and lots of people want to buy them. How do you match them up?

One option is make the buyer choose. This is how Google Search works: Google holds an auction for each search query and buyers pick which ones they want to compete in. Another is to group related websites together and run ads evenly across all of them. This is how most smaller ad networks work. And then there's AdSense. AdSense scans a page for relevant keywords, then runs the Google Search ads that won auctions for those keywords.

Google also knows a lot about ad viewers. By tracking what web pages you visit, they know what topics you're interested in. I'm apparently interested in Unix, the environment, elections, government, and social science, so Google prefers to show ads on those subjects to me.

But there's another way to think about ad matching: as a giant optimization problem. Which combinations of user, ad placement, and advertisement optimize click-thru rates (or, ultimately, ROI)?

For each of these, there are lots of variables. For each user, you know their history, geographical location, computer (browser, operating system, screen size), ISP, etc. For each ad placement, you know time of day, hosting website, page content, etc. And for each ad, there are numerous possible variations in phrasing and design that can be tested, as mentioned before.

The possible combinations are infinite. You can't test all of them, so you need to come up with ones that are plausible. You can look at which combinations worked in the past: has this ad done significantly better in some cities than others, or at some times than others? And you can look for patterns across ads: do ads that do well on CNN also do well on MSNBC? These hypotheses can then be tested and, if they work, you start running ads more there.

Netflix claims they've made millions from slight improvements in their movie recommendations.[1] When they offered a prize for more, researchers found thousands of tiny patterns and came up with all sorts of innovative algorithms to try to get an edge. After 32 months, researchers doubled the algorithm's effectiveness.

Imagine how much more is at stake for Google. Last year, they received $21 billion in ad revenue, of which 60% was apparently profit. Even tiny improvements would be worth the highest salaries — a 0.004% improvement would make $500,000. Doubling it would create unspeakable wealth.

Yet Google has no contest for improving ad click-thru rates. Indeed, press reports suggest they don't even have an internal team working on it. The AdWords user-interface (recently redesigned from jaw-droppingly wretched to just wretched) would seem to suggest they don't do this kind of optimization at all. Their blog asks people to optimize things manually. No doubt there are some things humans (even ad purchase reps) can do better than computers, but surely there's a lot more they can do together — with humans giving the machine additional hints and hypotheses to test. But there doesn't seem to be anything like that.

It's hard to believe this is true. It's hard to believe this can last.

Google's chief economist claims that Google's sewn up the ad market by being better than everyone else. What if you made an ad network that was better than Google?

Right now Google takes a 20% cut of every auction price. What if you were willing to take just 10%? You could give ad sellers a slightly higher CPM — they'd gladly run your ads when they paid more and Google's the rest of the time. Then you can offer ad buyers a slightly lower CPC. As long as the money people made was more than the cost of setting things up, they'd switch. I'm actually not sure why this hasn't happened.

Now imagine that you were a genius CS student who could come up with a better ad optimization algorithm. Your system would have a higher overall CTR, since it presented users with better ads. This means that, again, you can pay higher CPMs (since more people click per impression). And you can redirect some of the money you would spend on higher CPMs into lower CPCs, to attract advertisers.

But to develop the algorithms and do the optimization you need the data. Lots of it — lots of users, lots of advertisers, lots of ad spots. No startup will ever have that; it's only left to Google (or whichever giant eventually replaces them).

I'm not normally one to be too concerned about improving Google's bottom line (they seem to be doing alright), but as an ad buyer I'm frustrated I have to do this work myself. I'd rather solve the problem for everyone. And if Google wants to pay me for that, I certainly wouldn't mind.

It's weird that Netflix is so much more interested in this than, say, Amazon. Amazon makes money on every sale, whereas Netflix loses money every time they send a DVD out. Netflix claims they make up for this in higher customer retention rates, but why didn't Amazon think of this first?

November 3, 2009

---

1.   It's weird that Netflix is so much more interested in this than, say,
     Amazon. Amazon makes money on every sale, whereas Netflix loses money
     every time they send a DVD out. Netflix claims they make up for this in
     higher customer retention rates, but why didn't Amazon think of this
     first?

RESEARCHER JOB

I'm looking for a researcher to work with on a couple projects. The research will mostly be into questions of United States government policy and the relevant factual basis. For example, you might be asked to look up things about cap-and-trade legislation and the evidence for anthropogenic global warming. You can do it part-time. You can work from anywhere. I think the work will be interesting and I'll be doing it too. I think the work will be important, which is why I'm doing it.

The requirements are:

- generally lefty politics
- the ability to figure out the answers to complicated and politically controversial questions and find primary sources supporting those answers
- the ability to write clear summaries of those answers

The ideal person is probably someone who's contributed to Wikipedia, but that's not a requirement.

If you're interested, send a paragraph you wrote explaining or summarizing something to me with "researcher" in the subject. If you have ideas for how to find people like this, post them in the comments. (Or email them. Whatever.) I'll probably end up hiring a bunch of researchers so the more people and ideas the better.

December 27, 2009

IS APPLE EVIL?

Today's iPad introduction has to be about the most depressing Apple product launch I've ever watched. As has been noted, Jobs' Reality Distortion Field only works when he believes in what he's selling and he didn't seem to really believe in this. The audience must have further added to the disappointment, expecting a revolutionary product and only getting an oversized iPhone (iPod touch, actually).

That's not to say the iPad won't sell, or that I don't want one. The scariest thing is that I think it probably will. It's clear that Apple plans for the iPhone OS to be the future of its product line. And that's scary because the iPhone OS is designed for Apple's total control.

A lot of people have argued that requiring Apple to approve every application for the iPhone OS is some kind of "mistake", something they'll remedy as soon as they realize how bad things have gotten. But recent events — Phil Schiller's personal interventions, comments on their call to analysts, etc. — have made it clear it's not a mistake at all. It's their plan.

The iPad is their attempt to extend this total control to what's traditionally been thought of as the computer space. This is just the first step, but it's not hard to imagine Apple doing their best to phase out the Macintosh in the next decade, just as they phased out OS 9. In their ideal world, all computing will be done on the iPhone OS.

And the iPhone OS will only run software that they specifically approve. No Flash or other alternate runtimes, no one-off apps or open source customizations. Just total control by Apple. It's a frightening future.

I don't know why they're doing it. It's hard to see how it makes them more money. (Curating all those apps must be expensive, not to mention the lost sales from the unapproved ones.) I can only presume it's a result of Jobs' megalomaniacal need for control — not only does the hardware have to be flawless, the software must be too. And the only way to ensure that is to have Apple approve every inch of it.

I love Apple products. I'm a huge Apple fan. I'd buy an iPad right now if I could. But, for the first time, I've got a real sinking feeling in my stomach.

January 27, 2010

1. http://daringfireball.net/linked/2009/09/18/siegler-jobs

DO IT NOW

A year or two ago, I came up with a brilliant scheme for handling my email. The problem, I decided, was that there was just too much of it. Spam was mixed in with notes from friends along with important things from work and todo items I'd written to myself. What I needed to do was go thru and sort it — pick out the really important stuff to handle right away and move the junk to the bottom. So I wrote a little program that would let me go through and sort my email into neat little folders ordered by priority.

Well, here's what happened: I sorted all my email, and then I didn't answer any of it. I told myself that I shouldn't answer the unimportant stuff until the important stuff was taken care of, then when I looked at the important stuff it seemed hard, so I decided to go read some blogs first. To this day, all those important emails are just sitting there.

Recently, I came up with a really dumb system for handling my email: just do it. I'd start at the top of my inbox, answer the most recent email, and move on to the next one. No excuses. No matter what the email at the top was — no matter how difficult or awkward or unimportant, I had to answer it. I couldn't move on to another email and come back to it later. I had to answer the most recent email, no matter what it was.

By the end of the day, I'd answered a month's worth of email.

We procrastinate because we are afraid. We're afraid it's too much work and that it will drain us. We're afraid we'll screw it up and get in trouble. We're afraid we don't know how to do it. We're afraid because, well, we've been putting it off forever and every time we put it off it seems a little more fearsome in our minds. That's why not putting things off is so liberating. We're forced to confront our fears, not let them grow bigger by repeatedly running away. And when we confront them, we find they're not so scary after all.

This doesn't just apply to email, of course — it works for any todo list. But only if you say no to reordering, prioritizing, estimating deadlines, and doing the most important things first. Forget all that. Do it now.

January 8, 2010

HOWTO: GET A JOB LIKE MINE II

Apparently a lot of people have gotten the mistaken impression from my blog that I sit around and think about abstract philosophy all day. Well, I guess I do kind of do that, but my day job is actually much more exciting. I'm a cofounder of the Progressive Change Campaign Committee[1] and I spend my days experimenting with new ways to get progressive policies enacted and progressive politicians elected.

Like a lot of people, I grew up feeling frustrated with the world — extremes of wealth and poverty, insane and bloody wars, outdated intellectual monopoly laws, big corporations run amok. But I had no idea what to do about it. Writing just felt like preaching to the choir, marching in the streets felt like the protest of the powerless, working with people on the ground just didn't seem to scale.

But when my friend Larry Lessig decided to run for Congress, I begun to see that there was something I could do. During the short-lived campaign, we were besieged with offers of help from consultants, software companies, and services firms. Their technology was invariably outdated and incompetent (the leading tools are built on SQL Server), uncoordinated and poorly-designed. The advice they gave was horrendous, their incompetence bordered on sabotage, and the prices they charged would bankrupt us.

We started the Progressive Change Campaign Committee in January 2009 with the notion that we could fix all that. We would help filter the good consultants from the bad, write up best practices and conduct experiments to learn what works. Along the way, we got pulled into issue campaigns as well — at first going after CNBC for their terrible coverage of the economic crisis[2], then spending most of the last year getting Congress to pass a public option in the health care bill[3]. Along the way, we've gotten over 400,000 members and raised over a million dollars for our various tactics. Not bad for our first year!

But now, as the 2010 campaigns ramp up, we're getting back to our original mission. We've been working with campaigns to help them find talented staff, competent consultants, and money-saving techniques. But we also need some talented programmers to build the next generation of campaign tools. We've got some really exciting ideas, but we need your help.

So here's the ask: Want to work with me on building some amazing tools for some amazing campaigns? If so, just send me an email at aaron@boldprogressives.org or just fill out this form.

Then, tell your friends. Your country needs you.

April 7, 2010

1. http://boldprogressives.org/
2. http://fixcnbc.com/
3. http://whipcongress.com/

MANAGEMENT, ORGANIZING, MOBILIZING

Management is art of getting people who work for you to accomplish things. It's a subtle and fascinating art, the applied version of my great intellectual love, sociology. It's usually practiced badly, but even when done badly it can accomplish incredible things. One person can only do so much on their own — their time, their powers, their creativity are all limited. But even an incompetent manager, who uses only a fraction of the powers of her employees, is capable of accomplishing tasks far beyond the range of any single person.

Organizing is the art of getting people who don't work for you to accomplish things. Many of the underlying concepts are the same but the execution is vastly more difficult. You don't really get to pick your people. The people you get don't simply follow instructions, they must be persuaded and cajoled and made to understand your vision. But when it works, they accomplish great things you never would have allowed them to try.

Organizing has many forms. The obvious one is where you take a batch of volunteers and try to shape them into a manageable force. The best are selected, developed, promoted, and taught to do the same. It is like traditional management in reverse: instead of starting with the top of a hierarchy and building down through hiring, you start with a bunch of people at the bottom and try to build them up through training and promotion.

But organizing also means finding other leaders, people embedded in management structures (organizations) of their own, and using them toward a common goal. Sometimes this means explicit direction of their efforts, as in a coalition, where you get the heads of various groups to all work on a common project, or sometimes it's simply having them lend their name or knowledge to the cause. A great organizer of this sort develops rich networks they can quickly call upon in need. (Journalists can be good organizers in this sense, developing connections with sources and experts they can leverage to create a story.)

Organizing is most prevalent in my own field of politics, where the work I tend to do is often called "online organizing." This term usually means the kind of stuff you see on the MoveOn mailing list: emails asking you to call your senator, host a house party, attend a vigil — but mostly tell your friends and give us money. Since I got into this business, cranky old-timers have been yelling at me that organizing people over the Internet is impossible, that you have to organize people face-to-face. This struck me as a ridiculous claim (and still does), but I think I now see the truth these critics are reacting to.

Online organizing is a huge misnomer. Sending emails to millions isn't organizing, any more than writing company wide memos is managing. It does not teach people new skills or persuade them of a larger vision or get them to continue the work themselves. It takes people where they are and gives them small things they can do from there.

Mobilizing can be done thru any medium. The folks who knock on your door to ask for your vote (or donation) are face-to-face mobilizers. You can do the same by telephone or television (call now to contribute!). It is, however, a one-way relationship. You are simply a number on a list.

But this doesn't mean online organizing is impossible, just that it isn't often done. Obviously it's much harder than mere mobilization — and much more complicated — but it's much more rewarding as well. It is what makes for a successful open source project, or a thriving online community. The problem is one of scale — and that's true when it's done through any medium. IAF and ACORN never had five million members. Still, this seems to be the genuinely important question: whether the scaling power of the Internet allows for a revolution in the scale of real organizing. I don't know, but the first step toward answering it is being clear about what it means.

June 29, 2010

A CENSORSHIP-RESISTANT WEB

Imagine someone put a document up at http://pentagonpapers.com/volumes/1.html that a) some people want to read and b) some people want to keep you from reading.

STEP ONE: HOW IT WORKS NOW

On the current Web, the way you request such a document is like this:

1. You ask one of your pre-programmed root servers who is in charge of .com
2. They respond with VeriSign, so you ask VeriSign who is in charge of pentagonpapers.com
3. They respond with Acme ISP, so you ask ACME ISP where to find pentagonpapers.com
4. It responds with an IP address, so you request the page from that IP

The censors can ask VeriSign to give them control of pentagonpapers.com, they can try to shut down Acme ISP, they can try to prevent you from getting hosting, and they can try to shut down your IP. All of these have been used recently, with some success. You need a backup plan.

Let's imagine we want this URL to resolve in an uncensorable way. How would we do it?

STEP ONE: DOMAIN NAME OWNERSHIP

First we would have a certificate authority (CA) which would sign statements of the form: "As of [DATE], [DOMAIN NAME] is owned by the holder of [PUBLIC KEY]." (Let's call this a *certificate*.) Conveniently, there's already a whole industry of trusted businesses that make these statements — they're called SSL certificates.

The problem is that CAs are presumably just as subject to attack as the registrars (in fact, in some cases they are the registrars!). One possibility is to set up a certificate authority that will not sign such statements for people attempting to engage in censorship. It seems probable that such a policy would be protected by the First Amendment in the US. However, "people engaging in censorship" is a somewhat subjective notion. Also, it's always possible a court could order the certificate authority to turn over the private signing key (or the key could be obtained in some other way).

Another possibility is some kind of "rollback UI". If you know vaguely when the censorship attempts started, you can only trust certifications made before that date. This is a somewhat difficult feature to implement in a way that makes sense to users, though. The best case scenario is one in which the user can clearly distinguish between a censored and uncensored page. In that case, if the page appears censored they can hit a "go back a month" button and the system will only trust certifications made more than a month prior to the certification it's currently using. The user can hit this button repeatedly until they get an uncensored version of the page.

STEP TWO: WEB PAGE AUTHENTICATION

Next the owner of the website will need to sign statements of the form "The content of [URL] had the hash [HASH] on [DATE]." (Let's call this an authenticator.) Now given a page, a corresponding valid authenticator, and a corresponding valid certificate (call this trio an authentic page), browsers can safely display a page even if it can't access the actual web server. The digital signatures work together to prove that the page is what the website owner wanted to publish. If a browser gets back multiple authentic pages, it can display the latest one (modulo the effects of the "go back a month" button).

STEP THREE: GETTING AUTHENTIC PAGES

Set up a series of domain-to-certificate servers. These servers take a domain names (e.g. pentagonpapers.com) and returns back any certificates for it. Certificates can be obtained by crawling the Web or by being submitted by website owners or by being submitted by the CAs themselves.

Set up a series of URL-to-hash servers. These servers take a URL and return back any valid authenticators for that URL. Authenticators are very small, so each URL-to-hash server can probably store all of them. If spam becomes a problem, a little bit of hashcash could be required for storage. Website owners submit their authenticators to the URL-to-hash servers.

Set up a series of hash-to-URL servers. These servers take a hash and return a series of URLs which can be dereferenced in the normal way to obtain a file with that hash. People can submit hash-to-URL mappings to these servers and they can attempt to automatically verify them by downloading the file and seeing if the hash matches.[1,2] Again, these mappings are very small so each server can probably store all of them.[3]

Then there are a series of servers that host controversial files. Perhaps they saved a copy before the site was censored, perhaps they received it thru some out-of-band channel[4]. However they got it, they put them up on their website and then submit the URL to the hash-to-URL servers. Meanwhile, the site publisher submits an authenticator to the URL-to-hash servers.

Now, if a browser cannot obtain the pentagonpapers page through normal means it can:

1. Ask each domain-to-cetificate server it knows for certificates for pentagonpapers.com
2. Ask each URL-to-hash server it knows for authenticators for the URL
3. Ask each hash-to-URL server it knows for alternative URLs
4. Download from the alternative URLs[5]

This can be implemented through a browser plugin that you click when a page appears to be unavailable. If it takes off, maybe it can be built in to browsers. (While

I've been assuming the worst-case-scenario of censorship here, the system would be equally useful for sites that are just down because their servers couldn't handle the load or some other innocent failure.)

This system should work unless our adversary can censor every well-known CA, every well-known URL-to-hash server, every well-known hash-to-URL server, or every alternative URL.

STEP FOUR: BEYOND THE WEB

We can help ensure this by operating at least one of each as a Tor hidden service. Because the operator of the service is anonymous, they are immune to legal threats.[6] If the user doesn't have Tor, they can access them through tor2web.org.

Similarly, if you know your document is going to get censored, you can skip steps 1 and 2. Instead of distributing a pentagonpapers.com URL which is going to go down, you can just distribute the hash. For users whose browsers don't support this system, you can embed the hash in a URL like:

`https://hash2url.org/sha1/284219ea93827cdd26f5a697112a029b515dc9a4` where hash2url.org is a hash-to-URL server that redirects you to a valid URL.

And, of course, if you somehow have access to a working P2P system, you can just it to obtain authentic pages.

CONCLUSION

What's nice about this system is that it gets you censorship resistance without introducing anything wildly new. There are already certificate authorities. There are already hash-to-URL servers. There are already mirrors. There's already Tor. (There's already tor2web.) The only really new thing specific to censorship resistance is URL-to-hash servers of the form I described, but they're very simple and hopefully uncontroversial.

There is some work to be done stitching all of these together and improving the UI, but unlike with some other censorship-resistance systems, there's nothing you can point to as having no good purpose except for helping bad guys. It's all pretty basic and generally useful stuff, just put together in a new way.

If you're interested in helping build something like this, please send me an email.

1. Any server will have finite bandwidth, so an attacker could try to fool the hash-to-URL server by submitting a URL which when dereferenced never stops sending the data. The hash-to-URL servers should stop after a certain limit and mark the URL as unverified due to max file size. If the server ever obtains a file whose size is under the limit with that hash, it can toss all such URLs.
2. URLs can go out of date so perhaps upon receiving sufficient complaints about a URL being "bad", the server should attempt to

reverify. Again, hashcash can be used throughout to avoid spam.
3. A possible protocol for the above two servers is provided in RFC 2169.
4. I have ideas on how to automate this, naturally, but this essay is already far too long.
5. Optional bonus: Use HTTP Range headers to download 1/n of the file from each of the n URLs. There are some circumstances where this could speed things up. Or maybe it's just annoying.
6. This moves the censorship weak link to the distribution of introduction points to hidden services.[7] But instead of being published by a DHT, introduction points can be distributed through a flood protocol[8]. Or maybe the DHT can be modified so that there's no obvious censorship point?
7. The introduction points themselves can't be censored because they don't know who they're talking to. (I think they do in the current implementation of Tor, but this doesn't seem necessary. The hidden service can generate a new keypair for each introduction point and send the public key to the introduction point and to Alice.)
8. Is this too chatty? Probably. But remember, it's a last-case resort in some kind of insane police-state world where every country prevents people from running servers that give out the IP addresses of other servers that let you talk to a third server which will give you illegal content.

December 21, 2010

SQUARING THE TRIANGLE
SECURE, DECENTRALIZED, HUMAN-READABLE NAMES

When using computers, we like to refer to things with names. For example, this website is known as "www.aaronsw.com". You can type that into your browser and read these words. There are three big properties we might want from such names:

1. **secure**: that when you type the name in you actually get my website and not the website of an imposter
2. **decentralized**: that no central authority controls all the names
3. **human-readable**: that the name is something you can actually remember instead of some long string of randomness

In a classic paper, my friend Zooko argued that you can get at most two of these properties at any one time.

Recently, DNS legend Dan Kaminsky used this to argue that since electronic cash was pretty much the same as naming, Zooko's triangle applied to it as well. He used this to argue that BitCoin, the secure, decentralized, human-meaningful electronic cash system was impossible. I have my problems with BitCoin, but it's manifestly not impossible, so I just assumed Kaminsky had gone wrong somewhere.

But tonight I realized that you can indeed use BitCoin to square Zooko's triangle. Here's how it works:

Let there be a document called the scroll. The scroll consists of a series of lines and each line consists of a tuple (name, key, nonce) such that the first N bits of the hash of the scroll from the beginning to the end of a line are all zero. As a result, to add a line to the scroll, you need to do enough computation to discover an appropriate nonce that causes the bits of the hash to be zero.

To look up a name, you ask everyone you know for the scroll, trust whichever scroll is the longest, and then start from the beginning and take the key for the first line with the name you're looking up. To publish a name, you find an appropriate nonce and then send the new line to everyone you know.

OK, let's pause there for a second. How do you steal names in such a system? First, you need to need to calculate a new nonce for the line you want to steal and every subsequent line. Second, you need to get your replacement scroll to the user. The first is difficult, but perhaps not impossible, depending on how many lines ago the name you want to steal is. It requires having some large multiple of the rest of the network's combined CPU power. This seems like a fairly strong constraint to me, but apparently not to Dan. Luckily, we're saved by the second question.

Let there be a group of machines called the network. Each remembers the last scroll it trusted. When a new valid line is created it's sent to everyone in the network and they add it to their scroll.[1] Now stealing an old name is impossible, since machines in the network only add new names, they don't accept replacements for old ones.

That's fine for machines already in the network, but how do you join? Well, as a physical law, to join a network you need the identity of at least one machine already in the network. Now when you join, that machine can give you a fabricated scroll where they've stolen all the names. I don't think there's any way to avoid this — if you don't know anyone willing to tell you the correct answer, you can't will the correct answer out of thin air. Even a centralized system depends on knowing at least one honest root.

You can ameliorate this problem by knowing several nodes when you connect and asking each of them for their scroll. It seems like the best theoretically-possible case would be requiring only one node to be honest. That would correspond to trusting whichever node had the longest scroll. But this would leave you vulnerable to an attacker who a) has enough CPU power to fabricate the longest scroll, and b) can co-opt at least one of your initial nodes. The alternative is to trust only scrolls you receive from a majority of your list of nodes. This leaves you vulnerable to an attacker who can co-opt a majority of your initial nodes. Which tradeoff you pick presumably depends on how much you trust your initial nodes.

Publishing a false scroll is equivalent to fragmenting the namespace and starting a separate network. (We can enforce this by requiring nodes to sign each latest scroll and publish their signature to be considered members-in-good-standing of the network. Any node that attempts to sign two contradictory scroll is obviously duplicitous and can be discounted.) So another way of describing scenario (b) is to say that to join a network, you need a list of nodes where at least a majority are actually nodes in the network. This doesn't seem like an overly strenuous requirement.

And we're actually slightly safer than that, since the majority needs a fair amount of CPU to stay plausible. If we assume that you hear new names from some out-of-band source, for them to work on the attacker's network, the attacker must have enough CPU to generate lines for each name you might use. Otherwise you realize that the names you type in on your computer are returning 404s while they work on other people's computers and begin to realize you've been had by an attacker.

So there you have it. The names are secure: they're identifiable by a key of arbitrary length and cannot be stolen. They're human-meaningful: the name can be whatever string you like. And they're decentralized: no centralized authority determines who gets what name and yet they're available to everyone in the network.

Zooko's triangle has been squared.

UPDATE: I'm gratified by all the feedback and I've put up a Frequently Asked Questions[2] page in response to comments here and elsewhere.

January 6, 2011

1. What happens if two people create a new line at the same time? The debate should be resolved by the creation of the next new line — whichever line is previous in its scroll is the one to trust
2. https://squaretriangle.jottit.com/faq

HOW APPLE WORKS

Who takes over for Steve Jobs?[1] John Gruber recently posted[2] his argument for thinking it will be COO Tim Cook. The biggest point in Cook's favor is simple: "He's already run the company while Jobs has been on leave." That's true, but it's less meaningful than it sounds. But to understand why, you need to understand how Apple works.

In the same way that Google is a company driven by engineering or Amazon is driven by operations, Apple is driven by taste. Here's how Apple products are created: a team of designers decide exactly what a product should do and how it should look and feel, their work is ruthlessly edited by Steve until he approves, and then the entire rest of the company is given the task of moving mountains to make that dream real.

Tim Cook is in charge of that third step. And he's done a masterful job of it, accomplishing endless miracles never been seen by the public. Apple engineers have invented entirely new chips to fit the specified processing power into the tiny cases required by the spec; they build entirely new factories with entirely new production processes just to perfectly match the shade of pink in the original design; they've created a revolution in logistics to ensure these amazing products get into customers' hands on launch day. Cook runs this process, and there's no doubt he's brilliant at it.

But it's about fulfilling Jobs' dreams, not forging new ones. He can continue to run the company while Jobs is away because he's continuing to ensure the execution of designs that Jobs has already approved. But Apple can't run indefinitely on old plans. The only reason it works for Cook to be in charge while Steve is away is because Steve is still around, doing ruthless critiques of yet-to-be-invented products from his sickbed.

The only person with the credibility to helm Apple in the long run is a person who can do those critiques. And for all Cook's brilliance, I've seen no evidence he's a master of great taste. His creativity is at achieving a predetermined goal, not about deciding what goal to achieve.

As Gruber says, whoever takes Steve's place will be someone already at Apple. Not just because all the other options are absurd, but because Steve has spent the past decade or so carefully training his top lieutenants about how to do every aspect of his job. It makes no sense to hire from outside that elite group. But within that group, there's only one person who makes any sense as tastemaker-in-chief: Jony Ive.

This becomes obvious if you just watch the keynotes. Steve Jobs is well known for raising the product keynote to an art form. But the others who have taken over the speaking job in recent years — Scott Forstall, Phil Schiller, Tim Cook — seem like clumsy kids trying to fill the shoes of the master. There's only one person at Apple who gives talks with the elegance and style of Steve: Jony Ive.

Now the big criticism of Ive is that while he is clearly one of the most brilliant industrial designers in the world, he's shown no aptitude for software design. It's hard to know whether this is true. The Mobile Design Awards credited Ive[3] with the iPhone's user interface, but the patent credits Jobs and Forstall and a dozen others, but not Ive.

But even if Ive never designed a piece of software in his life, it'd be beside the point. I can't imagine Jobs has either. What's needed atop Apple is not creative brilliance — they have a design department full of that — but editorial taste. Like the director of a film[4], Apple's CEO needs to go through the thousands of creative ideas developed within Apple and decide which ones should be approved for production and which ones need to sent back for more work.

It's impossible to imagine Apple functioning without this role. (Would Apple splinter and start developing all sorts of random unapproved products like Google under Eric Schmidt?) It's impossible to imagine Tim Cook filling this role. (How can he be tastemaker for the whole company if he can't even pull off a decent keynote?) And it's impossible to imagine this role being anywhere but at the top of the org chart. (It'd be like crediting a film to the producer instead of the director.)

No, if Apple is to continue, it will be with a tastemaker at the top. And there are no serious candidates besides Ive.

July 22, 2011

1. This piece was written before Steve stepped down as CEO, but I think it

still stands. I mean when Steve really leaves: it seems obvious that
even as "Chairman of the Board" rather than CEO, he's still tastemaker-
in-chief at Apple.
2. http://daringfireball.net/2011/07/succeeding_steve_jobs
3. http://arstechnica.com/apple/news/2008/07/jonathan-ive-takes-home-mda-
    award-for-iconic-iphone-design.ars
4. http://kottke.org/11/07/a-day-in-the-life-of-john-lasseter

WHAT DOES GOOGLE MEAN BY 'EVIL'?

Pretty much ever since Paul Buchheit suggested "Don't be evil" as a corporate values statement (and Amit Patel begun writing it on whiteboards around the office), any time Google does something people don't like, they begin calling it "evil" and complaining that Google is violating its prime directive.

But surely "evil" means something more than just "wrong" or "bad". If the girl across the street peers through your window to watch you undress, we might say that was bad and wrong and awful, but I don't think anyone would try to claim it was evil. Evil is a really strong term!

Now part of the joke is that Google seems to be using it rather loosely. If you look at their examples of evil deeds[1], they seem rather mundane compared to cackling supervillains and mass murderers. They specifically name three: showing irrelevant ads, using pop-ups or other annoying gimmicks, and selling off actual search results.

Hardly the stuff of comic books. But what do these three have in common? **They're all instances of refusing to make things worse for your users in order to make more money**. Perhaps that still seems like a mundane conception of evil, but I think it gets at something important. Evil isn't just about doing terrible things — it's about doing terrible things for bad reasons. The evil villain cackles and brags about how they're on the side of evil — they explicitly oppose doing good. And this definition of evil is all about that: if you're working against your own users, you must have crossed the line and joined the other side.

When you stop to think about it, it's wild how many companies have done just that: Printer manufacturers who put chips on their ink cartridges, so you can't refill or recycle them but instead have to buy a new full-price cartridge. Apple preventing the Kindle app from having any sort of ebook buying functionality. Web publishers who break articles up into 20 pages so that you have to load 20 different ads just to read one article. These are pretty banal evils, but it's striking that I can't think of any example where Google has done anything like that. (Perhaps someone will name one I've missed in the comments.)

There are lots of things I disagree with Google about — the most recent being their refusal to let my friends with chosen names[2] use Google+ — but those things aren't evil by this definition. For example, Google defends[3] their real names policy by saying it'll lead to better conversations. They still claim to be fighting for the user.

So if you want to argue with Google, that's the way to do it: don't say that they're hurting someone out there in the world or violating some rule or principle, say that what they're doing isn't serving their users. Because that's the line Google's afraid to cross.

Thanks to Kragen Sitaker for discussions[4] that inspired this post.

UPDATE: Chris Soghoian observes[5] Google refuses to add Do-Not-Track support to its browsers or servers in order to maximize ad profits. Scott Teresi suggests[6] Google's refusal to provide customer support (in order to save money) qualifies. Tom Slee reminds me[7] of their infamous net neutrality deal with Verizon. John Gruber argues[8] that having ads at all is evil in this sense. Mark Heath points to[9] those infuriating YouTube ads.

August 22, 2011

1. http://www.google.com/about/corporate/company/tenthings.html
2. http://my.nameis.me/
3. http://www.jwz.org/blog/2011/08/nym-wars/
4. http://lists.canonical.org/pipermail/kragen-discuss/2011-August/001176.html
5. http://www.aaronsw.com/weblog/googevil#c8
6. http://www.aaronsw.com/weblog/googevil#c10
7. http://www.aaronsw.com/weblog/googevil#c19
8. http://daringfireball.net/linked/2011/08/23/swartz-google-evil
9. http://www.aaronsw.com/weblog/googevil#c33

STEVE JOBS AND THE FOUNDER'S PAIN

After reading the new biography Steve Jobs, the person I most identify with is Jony Ive. Ive and Jobs became close friends and collaborators, but Ive, "so instinctively nice," found himself puzzled about how his good friend could be so mean:

He's a very, very sensitive guy. That's one of the things that makes his antisocial behavior, his rudeness, so unconscionable. I can understand why people who are thick-skinned and unfeeling can be rude, but not sensitive people. [...And] because of how very sensitive he is, he knows exactly how to efficiently and effectively hurt someone. And he does do that. (462)

Steve's fits are legendary. "He would shout at a meeting, 'You asshole, you never do anything right,'" recalls his director of finance, Debi Coleman. "It was like an hourly occurrence." (124) "This is shit!" he yelled after seeing the first draft of the "Here's to the crazy ones" ad. "It's advertising agency shit and I hate it." (329)

Something was either "the best thing ever," or it was shitty, brain-dead, inedible. ...Any perceived flaw could set off a rant. The finish on a piece of metal, the curve on the head of a screw, the shade of blue on a box, the intuitiveness of a navigation screen — he would declare them to "completely suck" until that moment when he suddenly pronounced them "absolutely perfect." (561)

One way of reading this is that Steve Jobs is just a sociopath, someone who knows exactly where people's weaknesses are and plays on them masterfully until they do exactly, precisely what he wants, without little concern about human consequences.

But there's another, more sympathetic reading. I think Jobs really did feel this way. He had such an intense aesthetic sense that even something as minor as the curve on the head of the screw could cause him enormous pain. And, like anyone in pain, he responded by lashing out at the people around him. There are some people who, when they're insulted, can't resist punching the person who insulted them. Steve wasn't much for physical violence, but when something looked off to him, he couldn't help screaming.

I sympathize because I can see this in myself. Something that's perfect just feels much, much better than something that's almost right. When I'm doing something myself, I can just sit there and work at it until it's *exactly* right. It's embarrassing to launch a product with a bug in it! It physically hurts when I realize that's what I've done. But as projects and companies grow, there are more and more people in between me and those tiny details. And then I face a choice: do I keep complaining until something's perfect or do I just let go and consider it somebody else's problem?

Steve never let go. He continued to feel that founder's pain about everything in his life. When it was his project, he'd make people stay late until they got it right. When it was his company, he'd go right to the person responsible, even if they were 5 levels down in the org chart, and make them fix it. ("After looking at a bunch of screenshots, Jobs jumped up, grabbed a marker, and drew a simple rectangle on a whiteboard. 'Here's the new application,' he said. 'It's got one window. You drag your video into the window. Then you click the button that says "Burn." That's it.'" (382))

In fact, it didn't matter whose company it was. He once sent his fresh-squeezed juice back to the kitchen three times in a row until they got it right (527); when his cable box was frustrating him, he called the CEO of Comcast. ("I thought he was calling to say something nice about it," the CEO recalled. "Instead, he told me 'It sucks.'" (489))

And that's why I like Jony Ive. He too clearly feels that pain (he once insisted they hold up an entire product launch because he didn't like the polish on the screws) but he doesn't lash out at people about it. Instead, he sits down with the people involved and works to fix the problem until they get it just right.

Ask Jobs about his viciousness and he insisted it was all for the best: "I've learned over the years that when you have really good people you don't have to baby them… A-plus players like to work together, and they don't like it if you tolerate B work. Ask any member of that Mac team. They will tell you it was worth the pain." Even Debi Coleman agreed: "I consider myself the absolute luckiest person in the world to have worked with him."

But does it require so much pain? My hope is that I can be just as exacting, demand work just as good, without emotionally destroying people in the process. I want to be a perfectionist and a nice guy. I want to be Jony Ive. I hope it works—for my sake, and Apple's.

November 3, 2011

APPLE AND THE KINDLE

The Amazon Kindle is full of all sorts of amazing, delightful touches — the sort of thing you'd expect from an Apple product. For example, when you first take your Kindle out of its (gorgeous!) box, it boots right up knowing your name and logged into your account. This is actually out-Apple-ing Apple: it's possible because Amazon not only controls the hardware and the software, but the entire distribution channel; they know exactly who is going to get each Kindle.

And think about how the original Kindle came with a *lifetime unlimited worldwide* data plan. Imagine how much that must have cost! All so that you never had to think about syncing again: your Kindle was automatically synced, no matter where it was in the world.

Bezos must have spent tons of energy getting this stuff right. And he must be sitting there, pissed, that Steve Jobs gets all these laurels while no one ever recognizes the stuff he's done. But I don't think that's because Jobs is a better marketer and showman than Bezos (that's the easy way out); it's because the small details that delight get buried under small details that annoy.

For example, if you download a sample of a book and get to the end and decide to purchase the whole thing, the sample doesn't expand to download the remainder of the book — instead the full book downloads completely separately and you have to manually copy over all your highlights and annotations to the full one. (You can't just keep them in the sample because sample's don't even sync; you have to download a sample manually to each of your devices and hand-synchronize the page numbers.)

Or (and this is incredibly aggravating) when you select a word in the Kindle, depending on how common a word it is, the option that comes up highlighted by default is either "full definition" or "start highlight". Since e-ink's refresh rate is so slow, you typically don't see what's actually come up until you've pressed the button for the second time. So I often "double click" on words to highlight them, but some percentage of the time this kicks me over into the dictionary and I have to hit back twice to get out.

And this is all before I've even got to the disastrous incompatibilities between the Kindle device, the Kindle for Mac app, the Kindle for iOS app, the Kindle Online Reader (read.amazon.com), and the kindle.amazon.com social network — all of which are full of gruesome interface annoyances of their own.

That's the thing about delightful details: they're not just another thing you can add on top. Unless you sweat the details all the way through the user experience, the ones that delight quickly get drowned out by the ones that constantly annoy. I hope someone at Amazon will take that to heart.

November 3, 2011

REVOLUTIONS ON THE INTERNET

I hate to wade into such a sterile debate as whether social media helps revolutions, but I made a point about it recently at a conference and people seemed to like it, so I thought I'd put it up here for posterity.

Jon Elster has a four-phase theory of revolutions:[1]

1. A hard-core of committed activists get together to do something completely crazy.
2. The regime cracks down, attracting people who are sympathetic to the cause to rally to the support of the crazy ones.
3. As the protests grow, it seems like they might have a reasonable chance of succeeding and it seems worth it even for just normal reasonable people to start joining in.
4. The protests become so overwhelmingly large that even their opponents pretend to be part of them, so as not to be on the wrong side of history.

It seems pretty clear that the Internet helps with 1 — after all, it's brought together groups of crazy committed people about every other topic, from *Smallville* slash fiction to high-energy astrophysics. It'd be very surprising if it didn't bring committed activists together too.

It's clearly helped with 2 — YouTube videos of protestors being mistreated by police have been a staple of the #occupy movement, even though they haven't gotten much coverage on traditional TV; We are all Khaled Said presumably reached some people in Egypt.

3 and 4 are when the cable news and satellite television stations start joining in and when people support the protest just because it's such a huge physical presence in their lives. Here, I agree, the Internet probably has less effect.

The problem is that you never get to 3 and 4 without 1 and 2 — I don't think it's a total accident that all of these protests are happening now. I think they're happening because 1 and 2 have been made much easier thanks to the Internet. It's just that most people don't hear about them until steps 3 and 4, which are carried much more by traditional media. They suffer from the understandable fallacy that just because they heard about it on TV, that must be how everyone else did.

November 1, 2011

HOW PYTHON 3 SHOULD HAVE WORKED

As a workaday Python developer, it's hard to shake the feeling that the Python 2 to 3 transition isn't working. I get occasional requests to make my libraries work in 3 but it's far from clear how to and when I try to look it up I find all sorts of conflicting advice, none of which sounds very practical.

Indeed, when you see new 3.x versions rolling off the line and no one using them, it's hard to shake the feeling that Python might die in this transition. How will we ever make it across the chasm?

It seems to me that in all the talk about Python 3000 being a new, radical, blue-sky vision of the future, we neglected the proven methods of getting there. In the Python 2 era, we had a clear method for adding language changes:

- In Python 2.a, support for from future import new feature was added so you could use the new feature if you explicitly declared you wanted it.
- In Python 2.b, support was added by default so you could just use it without the future declaration.
- In Python 2.c, warnings begun being issued when you tried to use the old way, explaining you needed to change or your code would stop working.
- In Python 2.d, it actually did stop working.

It seems to me this process worked pretty well. And I don't see why it couldn't work for the Python 3 transition. This would mean mainly just:

A Python 2.x release that added support for from future import python3.

Putting this at the top of a file would declare it to be a Python3 file and allow the interpreter to parse it accordingly. (I realize behind the scenes this would mean a lot of work to merge tr 2 and 3 interpreters, but honestly it would always have been better to have a unified codebase to maintain.)

Then if I wanted my Python 2 program to use some 3 modules, I just need to make sure those modules have the import line at the top. If I want to do a new release of my module that works on Python 3, I just need to declare that it only works in Python 2.x and higher and release a version that's been run through 2to3 (with the new import statement). If my project is big, I can even port files to 3 one at a time, leaving the rest as 2 until someone gets around to fixing the rest. Most importantly, I can start porting to Puhon 3 without waiting for all my dependencies to do the same, parallelizing what until now has been a rather serial process.

Users know they can safely upgrade to 2.x since it won't break any existing code. Developers know everyone will eventually upgrade to 2.x so they can drop support for earlier versions. But since 2.x supports code that also runs in 3, they can start writing and releasing code that's future-compatible as well. Eventually the vast major code will work in 3 and users can upgrade to 3. (2.x will issue warnings to the remaining stragglers.) Finally, we can drop support for 2.x and all live happily having crossed the bridge together.

This isn't a radical idea. It's how Python upgrades have always worked. And unless we use it again, I don't see how we're ever going to cross this chasm.

March 9, 2012

THE POKAYOKE GUIDE
TO DEVELOPING SOFTWARE

NEED

A good project starts with a *need*. It's nice if it's a big need – that way you have a lot of potential customers – but much more important than that is that it's an *acute* need. Users should be *hungering* to fill this need – it should be so that when they find out about your product, they're compelled to use it. If you fill a desperate need of one person, you have at least one dedicated customer; if you fill a kind of theoretical need for 6 billion, you could easily end up with none. And since people are often alike, filling a need for one person usually fills a need for many others – or can easily be adapted to do so.

It's important that you feel this need yourself. Ideally, it's a need that you have, borne of your own experience. For example, you might be desperately searching for someone to date you. Second-best is if you can go out and try living the lifestyle that inspires that need. For example, if you're happily married, you might try asking your spouse for a pass so that you can go out and desperately try to find a date. It's not really the same, but at least it's something. At the very least, you should sit and watch people who have this need and be able to empathize with them. Go be your single friend's wing-person and watch them try to find someone.

Of course, it is possible for your need to be too idiosyncratic. Sometimes people will be so in love with an idea that they'll pretend to have a need for it. You want to make sure it's a genuine need you're filling and one good way to do that is to make sure you can find at least one stranger who feels the need as acutely as you do.

Example time: I worked on a site that provided people with a list of interesting and funny things to look at. For most office workers, this is a pretty acute need – offices are boring and you really can only sit at your computer and look at things, so you're desperate for something interesting to look at to break the tedium. By contrast, my friend worked on a site that let you look up various government things that were happening around you (new liquor permits getting approved, people getting arrested, cars getting towed, etc.). You can come up with lots of stories about why this is interesting or why people might want to know this sort of thing, but there's no real acute need that this site fills. Despite the fact that my friend did a much better job than I did, the site I was working on became vastly more popular than his.

IDEA

But a need is not enough – you also need an *idea* to meet the need. Look at your idea objectively for a second. Does it really seem like it will really meet the need? Most bad ideas are bad because they don't really do that. You want to work forwards from the need to the idea, not backwards from your idea toward some sort of justification. The government data site I mentioned suffered from this problem – government data is really cool and providing people with an easy way to search through it seems like a really cool idea. And once you're in love with that idea, it's easy to come up with needs that it might fill. But you're just coming up with justifications. It's not a direct way of addressing any one need. And it's always better to nail one need than to kind of fill two.

This isn't to say that one idea can't solve multiple needs. Great ideas do. But they genuinely solve them. They're direct and sensible solutions to the problem, not just ways to shoehorn different needs into justifying an idea you're already fond of.

Take the iPhone for example. You might say "What need does the iPhone solve? Steve Jobs just came up with a really good generic idea and then it happened to be useful to fill all sorts of needs." But that's not true at all. When the iPhone was launched, Jobs insisted it filled three needs: it was a widescreen video iPod, a vibrant Internet communicator, and a phone that's fun to use. Let's take the one of these that seems least like the iPhone. What would you need to just make a great widescreen video iPod? Well, you'd need a big, wide screen that takes up the whole device and a long-lasting battery. You'd also need some kind of input mechanism, but how do you do that when the screen takes up the whole device? Well, you have to make the screen the input mechanism. But now you have a brick about the size of your phone sitting in your pocket. You really ought to combine them. So why not use the touchscreen to provide the interface to a phone that's fun to use? And now that you have a big touchscreen and a wireless connection, it seems silly not to be able to use it to access the Internet... and you're back at the iPhone. Even Steve Jobs wasn't good enough to sell a good idea that doesn't fill a real need.

Once you have a basic idea, you don't need to go into a ton of detail about it. But since you're the kind of creative person that likes coming up with ideas, you will anyway. You'll constantly come up with all sorts of cool features or add-ons or uses and whatnot. These are not important, which means that they'll distract you unless you do something with them. So put them all in a Lenin Document. A Lenin Document is just a description of what the maximalist version of your idea will look like, starting from the core features (it will be able to make phone calls) and working out toward the more obscure (it'll have an app that will let you control your toaster from bed!).

You'll probably never look at this document again, but all the good ideas you and your colleagues come up with will stop harrassing you so much once you have a safe place to write them down in.

HIRING

Oh wait, what colleagues? You'll also need to put together a team. When hiring someone, you want to ask three key questions:

- Are they smart?
- Can they get things done?
- Can you work with them?

It's tempting to skimp on these, e.g. by hiring someone who meets two out of three. But it's a big mistake. Someone who's smart but doesn't get stuff done should be your friend, not your employee. Even if you don't hire them, you can still talk your problems over with them while they procrastinate on their existing job. Someone who gets stuff done but isn't smart is inefficient: non-smart people are always doing things the hard way and smart people can't bear to watch them do it and are always taking time off of their real jobs to go over and help. Someone you can't work with, you really can't work with. It's always tempting to say "well, it's just work, we don't have to be friends", but work is hard and if you don't feel like you can honestly communicate with someone, they end up doing the wrong thing and you don't correct them and then they just end up sitting in a corner somewhere not doing anything useful.

The traditional programmer hiring process consists of: a) reading a resume, b) asking some hard questions on the phone, and c) giving them a programming problem in person. I think this is a terrible system for hiring people. You learn very little from a resume and people get real nervous when you ask them tough questions in an interview. Programming isn't typically a job done under pressure, so seeing how people perform when nervous is pretty useless. And the interview questions usually asked seem chosen just to be cruel. How many of the people asking these questions could actually answer them the first time they heard them?

Instead, just try to answer the three questions. To find out if they can get stuff done, ask what they've done. If someone can actually get stuff done, they should have done so by now. If someone's really good at getting stuff done, they wouldn't have been able to avoid it. It's hard to be a good programmer without some previous experience and these days anyone can get some experience by starting or contributing to a free software project. So just request a code sample and a demo and see whether it looks good. You learn an enormous amount really quickly, because you're not watching them answer a contrived interview question, you're seeing their actual production code. Is it concise? clear? elegant? usable? Is it something you'd want in your product?

To find out whether someone's smart, just have a casual conversation with them. Do everything you can to take the pressure off: meet at a cafe, make it clear it's not an interview, do your best to be casual and friendly. Under no circumstances should you ask them any standard "interview questions" – just chat with them like you would with someone you met at a party. (If you ask people at parties to name their greatest strengths and weaknesses or to estimate the number of piano tuners in Chicago, you've got bigger problems.) It's pretty easy to tell whether someone's smart in casual conversation. We constantly make judgments about whether the people we meet are smart, just like we constantly make judgments about whether the people we see are attractive.

But if you're still not sure, look at three things. First, do they know stuff? Ask them what they've been thinking about and probe them about it. Do they seem to understand it in detail? Can they explain it clearly? (Clear explanations, ala Feynman, are a sign of genuine understanding.) Do they know stuff about the subject that you don't? Second, are they curious? Do they reciprocate by asking questions about you? Are they genuinely interested or just being polite? Do they ask follow-up questions about what you're saying? Do their questions make you think? Third, do they learn? At some point in the conversation, you'll probably be explaining something to them. Do they actually understand it or do they just nod and smile? There are people who know stuff about some small area but aren't curious about others. And there are people who are curious but don't learn, they ask lots of questions but don't really listen. You want someone who does all three.

Finally, figure out if you can work with them by just hanging out with them for a bit. Many brilliant people can seem delightful in a one-hour conversation, but their eccentricities become grating after a couple hours. So after you're done chatting, invite them along for a meal with the rest of the team or a game at the office. Again, keep things as casual as possible. The point is just to see whether they get on your nerves.

If all that looks good and you're ready to hire someone, do one last sanity check to make sure you haven't been fooled somehow: ask them to do part of the job. Usually this means picking some small and separable component you expect to need and asking them to write it. (If you really insist on seeing someone working under pressure, give them a deadline.) If necessary, you can offer to pay them for the work, but most programmers don't mind being given a small task like this as long as they can open source whatever they did when they're done. This test doesn't work on its own, but if someone's passed the first three parts, it should be enough to prove they didn't trick you, they can actually do the work they say they can.

Now it's tempting to say "OK, well why don't we try hiring you for a month and see how it goes." This doesn't work. First, it makes the person you hire feel like they're on eggshells the whole time, constantly having to prove themselves, which is cruel and counterproductive (the stress and fear makes them less productive). Second, if you can't bear to say no after a small project, you also won't be able to after a month and then you've just ended up hiring someone who isn't good enough. Better to just say no and err on the side of getting better people.

HYPOTHESIS

Now that you have your team, it's time to actually do some work. It's tempting to just dive in and start building your big dream (complete with the part that lets you make toast from bed). But this is a huge waste. You don't want to do the most you can, you want to do the least you can. Here's how.

To work, every idea depends on certain hypotheses about the world; if the hypotheses aren't true, our idea won't succeed. Let's say you work at an airline and the need you've identified is that people hate waiting in line to board and your idea for solving it is that they can buy a $5 "Early Board" ticket when they check in to get called to board the plane first. Now this idea depends on several hypotheses:

- Our customers want to board the plane early
- Our customers will pay $5 to do so
- Our customers will want to do this at check in
- But not so many of them will buy it that they all end up waiting in line again
- …and so on

You'll want to write out these hypotheses and pick the most important. Let's say that "Our customers want to board the plane early" is the most important. Now remember, if this hypothesis is false, all the work we've done will be wasted. So let's do as little work as we can until we've proven that it's true.

So what's the minimum necessary to test it? The original term for this is Minimum Viable Product or MVP, but this term has become a buzzword hijacked by people who don't really understand it. Most people would say the minimum viable product for this idea is a real bare-bones system that just lets you pay an extra $5 at checkout and maybe writes an extra letter on your boarding pass and then instructing all the gate agents to call people with that letter up first. Pretty easy, right?

Maybe, but it could be *way* easier. The truly minimal way to test this hypothesis is just to add a button to one of the checkout screens that says "Click here to board first." When someone clicks it, an error message pops up saying "Sorry, our 'Early Board' program isn't available." And you measure how many people press the button. If a lot of people press it, then clearly people do want to board early. If nobody presses it, then there's no demand for the product.

But how many presses are enough? It's very easy to come up with justifications for any number after the fact. "Oh, a thousand people pressed the button," you'll say. "That's huge! That's ten times as many use our deluxe bag check service!"

"No it's not," replies your arch-enemy. "That's a huge flop. That's half as many people used the elite pre-screen service."

You can avoid these arguments by just picking a number in advance that you and your arch-enemy agree on. You both sign off on it, saying that if it's above the number you'll agree the hypothesis will have been proven and if it's below the number it will have been disproven.

But what sort of number should you pick? Actually counting the literal number of button-presses isn't a very good idea. It's known as a *vanity* metric. Let's say only one out of a hundred people actually want to board the plane early, but your test happens to run during Christmas break, when three times as many people are flying as normally. Well, your button easily vaults over the two-thousand-person goal you set for it, but that's not because the button is so popular – it's because so many extra people were flying that week.

Instead, you want to measure an *innovation metric*, a number that's independent of everything except the thing you're testing. In this case, we'd want to measure the *percentage* of people who clicked the button. Let's say your goal is that 3% of everyone who saw the button clicked it. That's a number that won't shoot up just because a lot of extra people are traveling that week.

Of course, it might go down because Christmas travelers are less savvy than your usual travelers. So you might want to adjust your metric further and say your goal is for 3% of all *frequent travelers* to click the button. That's a metric that will stay stable even if a lot of occasional travelers happen to be flying that week.

You can even go further and develop *cohorts*. A cohort is a group of people chosen in advance. For example, you might pick out a group of specific frequent travelers in advance and only show them the button. That way, there's no way an influx of new customers can possibly affect your test – they'll never see it, since you've already picked out the specific existing customers who will.

You may also want to develop a *control*. Perhaps adding another button makes people less likely to buy a (much more expensive) seat upgrade. So take your pool of people picked in advance and randomly divide them in half. Half will get the button and the other half won't. Then you can compare metrics between the two halves to see if adding the button changed anything. Perhaps 4% of the experiment group bought an upgrade but 8% of the control group did – that would be a difference you could factor into your future planning.

TEAM

Once you've identified a hypothesis, a minimal way to test it, and a clear set of metrics for evaluating it, it's time to actually build it. You should start by picking a product owner. This is the "Steve Jobs" of your product – they're empowered to sign off on every detail to make sure the whole thing coheres.

You should write a card (this can be a physical 3x5 card or a task in some kind of task management system like Asana) describing your proposed experiment and the metrics you'll use for evaluating it:

- Select a cohort of frequent travelers and divide them into an experiment and a control group.
- As a member of the experiment group, when I check in for my flight I should see a button offering me a chance to board the plane first. If I click it, I should get an error saying this service isn't currently available.
- This is to test the hypothesis that our customers want to board early. We'll consider the hypothesis proven if more than 2% of the experimental group presses the button. We'll also monitor their purchase of other upgrades and their check-in completion rate to make sure introducing the button doesn't have any severe adverse effects.

Note that the first paragraph decides who gets experimented on. The second is a story about a change to a user's experience. And the third paragraph explains why we're testing and what metrics we'll look at.

This will go into a stack of cards (or an online todo list) sorted by priority, with the most important hypotheses to test at the top. Your designer, when they're done with their current task, will pull a card from the top of the pile. They will then work with the product owner to design what this experience should look like (where do you put the button? what exactly does it say?). Once the product owner has signed off on it, they'll hand the card to a programmer and work with them to implement the design.

Practical problems with implementation or experience with actually using it once implemented may cause them to revise the design a couple times, and maybe they bring the product owner in for more feedback on their revisions.

DEVELOPMENT

It's good practice to write automated tests for your software as you're developing it, so that people can easily know if they've broken part of it later. When you think you're finished, you can run the automated tests to make sure they all pass. You want to make sure the automated tests run against both the control and all the experiment arms, of course.

Programming is a mentally strenuous job, so it's often more efficient to have programmers work in pairs, with one typing and another observing and commenting. (Sometimes it's fun to have one person in the pair writing the tests, then sliding the keyboard over and having the other person write the code that makes them pass and the next round of tests.)

If you don't have a pair working with you the whole time, you should at least make sure you pull someone over to evaluate the changes you made. You should always read the diff before committing code to the project (for example, by running git diff HEAD).

ARCHITECTURE

If you're building a network service (e.g. a web application), you should design it as a Twelve-Factor Application[1]. A Twelve-Factor Application follows twelve principles:

1. The entire application's code is stored in a single revision control repository. If you have multiple repositories for different parts of the software, you should consider them to be separate applications that treat each other as services. If you have multiple applications in a single repository, you should factor out whatever they both use as a library they both depend on and then split them into two codebases.

   For your revision control system, you will probably want to use git, because it's the most featureful and most popular.

2. All your dependencies should be explicitly declared. In Ruby you can do this with a Gemfile, in Python with requirements.txt, etc. Locally, you should use a tool like bundler or virtualenv to isolate your environment to make sure you aren't using any undeclared dependencies.

3. All configuration values should be stored as environment variables. This includes anything you'd be afraid of making public, like passwords or secret keys, as well as anything that might be different from deploy to deploy, including the locations of databases or the administrator email address.

4. All backing services (like databases or in-memory caches) are treated as services. No distinction is made between local and third-party services; they're all accessed over the network.

5. Code is deployed in three separate stages: build (in which the software is compiled and built), release (in which it's combined with the configuration environment and put onto the appropriate servers), and run (in which it's executed). These stages should be completely isolated – the server can't change its configuration at runtime, since the release stage has already been passed. And the release process can't edit the software, since the build stage has already passed.

6. The application should execute as a series of stateless processes that share nothing – any process should be able to be killed at any time. This means any state needs to be stored in one of the backing services.

7. The application should be completely self-contained and contact the outside world through an IP port (designated by the $PORT environment variable). It shouldn't be expecting to live inside some sort of larger process.

8. The application should be made up of various process types and be able to scale by starting more instances of these process types. For example, if there's a lot of web traffic, you should be able to handle it by starting more instances of the web process type.

9. Processes should be *disposable* – you should be able to start them and stop

them at a moment's notice, without any harm.

10. The gap between development and production should be kept small – the same backing services, dependencies, and team should be used in both places. Development is just another deploy of the application with a slightly different config.

11. Logs are just a stream of events written unbuffered to stdout. It's not the application's job to make sure they get to the right place; that's the job of the infrastructure.

12. Administration tasks should be run as one-off processes.

You should also use a 12-factor hosting system, like Heroku[2], since it will force you to obey these constraints.

You should also introduce a *Chaos Monkey* to further ensure the robustness of your system. A Chaos Monkey is an automated process that deactivates different elements of a system to ensure they are robust in response to outages. For example, processes are meant to be disposable, so a Chaos Monkey would automatically kill randomly-selected production processes. This both provides an incentive for developers to avoid depending on processes being persistent and, if they make a mistake and do it anyway, catches the mistake early rather than later when it compounds with others and causes a catastrophic failure.

DEPLOYMENT

Developers commit their code to the revision control repository once the changes are made and all the tests pass.

If their code requires changes to one of the backing services (e.g. a change to the database schema), this should be done through *migrations*. A migration describes how to make and rollback such a change. When a new version of the software is deployed, any un-run migrations are run, synchronizing its version of the backing service to the one the code depends on. Upon rolling back, the migrations are also rolled back. This makes sure the backing services and the code are always in sync.

Almost all new code is committed to the main line of development (aka trunk or HEAD). This avoids the painful task of merging different branches of development later. Since any big change should be implemented as an experiment, if a change is unfinished or unready, it can be easily turned off by keeping most users out of the experiment. When the code is ready, more people can be added to the experimental group and the toggle can be eventually removed.

Once a commit is made to the repository, the repository should automatically build, release, and run the code in a fresh testing environment and run the automated tests against it. It should then try running the code and the migrations against a full copy of the production backing services (read: database) and try applying and rolling back the migrations, making sure the tests pass either way.

If they all pass, it should be pushed forward to production. To make sure that broken code that somehow got passed the tests doesn't make it into production, you should have an *immune system* to monitor the deploy. The immune system will watch your key innovation metrics (looking at new revenue, new users, etc.) to make sure they haven't been adversely affected by the deploy. If they are, it will automatically roll back and alert the team.

To make sure that code that hasn't been reviewed by the product owner doesn't make it into production, you give them control over launching the experiments. New features will initially make it into production with no one in the experiment. The product owner can then either add themselves to the experiment or turn the experiment on for everyone on a preview server to test it. QAs can also test it there as well. When everyone is happy, more people can be added to the experiment. If the metrics look good, even more can be added, until eventually 100% of users are in the experiment and the control arm can be removed from the codebase.

LAUNCH

Some people will encourage you to have a big Hollywood-style launch, hyping the release date for months in advance before throwing it open to an appreciative world. This may work well for Hollywood – if your movie is a big hit at the box-office on opening weekend, then the movie theaters are more likely to keep showing it in the weeks to come and you get credit for being "one of the weekend's biggest films". But for software developers, it's nonsensical. Your software isn't being released in theaters, it's available over the Web. You don't have to worry about the theater no longer showing after week one; you can keep pushing it for years, growing your userbase.

The problem with a big launch is that, unless you are perfect, launch day always reveals bugs and conceptual errors you hadn't noticed before. Now millions of people are visiting your product and experiencing those mistakes. (Perhaps one of your mistakes is that you didn't properly load test the service and now they're experiencing a downed website.)

Instead, you should treat your launch as another experiment, slowly ramping up the number of people allowed inside as long as the metrics are peforming well. Follow Gmail's example: give invitations to a handful of people, test your hypotheses against their usage and feedback, and when they like it let them invite a few more. Slowly ramp up until everyone that wants an invitation has one and the whole world is inside your big experiment.

Good luck!

June 26, 2012

ACKNOWLEDGEMENTS

This document was originally written by Aaron Swartz and is an assemblage of many different ideas, his and others. The need and idea discussions were probably influenced by discussions with Paul Graham. Hiring was adapted from Aaron's "How I Hire Programmers" which written in response to Joel Spolsky's writing (his book on hiring is called Smart and Gets Things Done). Hypothesis is adapted from *The Lean Startup*[3] and the Toyota Production System. Team and Development are based upon ideas from Extreme Programming[4]. Architecture is obviously based around the 12-factor application[1]. The Chaos Monkey is from Netflix[5]. Migrations is a term from Rails. Continuous deployment with an immune system comes from IMVU via Timothy Fitz[6]. The launch section is adapted from How to Launch Software[7].

1. http://12factor.net/
2. http://heroku.com/
3. http://theleanstartup.com/
4. http://www.extremeprogramming.org/
5. http://techblog.netflix.com/2010/12/5-lessons-weve-learned-using-aws.html
6. https://timothyfitz.wordpress.com/2009/02/10/continuous-deployment-at-imvu-doing-the-impossible-fifty-times-a-day/
7. see article "How To Launch Software"

EDUCATION
& PARODY

NOAM ON TERRORISM

Noam Chomsky: *The New War Against Terrorism*[1]. Chomsky is the kind of person who is so eminently reasonable that you can't help but agree with what he writes. But then you realize how far he is from the rest of the population and you wonder what's happened to the world today.

Also check out Bad News: Noam Chomsky Archive[2].

March 21, 2002

1. http://www.zmag.org/GlobalWatch/chomskymit.htm
2. http://monkeyfist.com/ChomskyArchive

LIKE FATHER LIKE SON

Son: Father, can I get this video game.
Father: Not now, I'm in the middle of something.
Son: But why not?
Father: I'm in the middle of something!
Son: Please! I'll pay for it.
Father: *Hold on!*
Son: But you haven't even looked at it!

...later, to Mother...

Father: Son is being such a brat lately. He always insists on getting his way.
Mother: I know, we'll just have to stand firm and show him that whining doesn't work.

...enough time later that the hypocrisy isn't immediately evident...

Father: Son, help me build this bookcase.
Son: I'm in the middle of something!
Father: I said help me! Do it right now or I'll take away your bed.
Son: I'm in the middle of something!
Father: Fine, I'll take away your bed!
Son: *Hold on!*

June 01, 2003

MEETING JUSTICE KENNEDY

I saw Justice Anthony Kennedy tonight at Northwestern Law School. He gave a short talk on ethics and the Constitution, answered questions, and then spoke individually with people at a reception afterwards. I got to ask him a question then (about the libertarian ramifications of his decision in *Lawrence v. Texas*) and hear him speak to others.

I thought the most interesting part was him describing the life of a Supreme Court Justice in DC. He talked about how one day he was late for work and driving down Pensylvania Avenue, but was stopped by a large line of people outside the National Archives. He asked a policeman what was going on, and was told that the Constitution was being taken down for new preservation measures[1] and all the people were there to wish it well.

He also talked about how powerless he was, even as a Justice. He discussed seeing homeless people sitting out in the cold DC winters. He joked that he'd take out his pocket constitution (he did) and say "I can make sure you have a fair trial but I can't give you food and shelter." On the other hand, he said it would probably be a mistake logistically for the Constitution to *require* that everyone have food, shelter, and health care (even though he wanted to government to ensure all these things) because the court was only good at preventing the government from doing things, not forcing it to do them.

But the real reason he came seemed to be that he really cares about students, and passing on the tradition of the Constitution. He longed for the days where every citizen also knew about the law, and discussed programs for getting high schoolers and other students interested in our important freedoms. He got really engaged in a discussion with our Constitutional Law teacher, recommending books and techniques for getting kids interested in the subject.

All in all, he seemed like a relatively normal guy (with a vast knowledge of the law) who was just trying to do what seemed right and fair. He talked about how he never wanted to lose touch with the actual people behind all of his cases, and how he really wants to be a trial judge so he can be listening to people's actual problems (he says he never had the political power to get the job). I think this is why he's often the "swing vote" — he doesn't care so much about political battles or overarching doctrines, but just doing what's right by the law and what's fair for the people.

A full report on his talk and the event follows.

My class on American Constitutional Law decided to take a field trip to come hear him speak. We drove downtown to the Chicago campus of Northwestern's Law School and sat in Lincoln Hall. He was introduced as the justice with the least dissents. (From now on I'll speak as Justice Kennedy.)

We live an amazing era. I never thought I'd see constitutions being formed, but now they're being created in Europe, and South Africa, and South America. But we have the oldest constitution, and more than an ethnic or geographic connection, the constitution is the thing that ties us together.

It's funny that while our constitution was created to deal with a lack of sovreignty, Europe is creating constitutions to deal with too much sovreignty.

The constitution is really part of our country's history. All over Europe, law is an undergraduate degree, but not here. In the days of the colonies, Blackstone was the #2 bestseller after the bible. Law schools have an important function in maintaining that legal literacy. The common language of the law allows us to communicate with others across space and time.

After 9/11, I was concerned about a lack of moral orientation in the young. The Constitution believes in moral absolutes, and has a moral component. I created something he called The Dialogue of Freedom², a program for high school students: Imagine being in a repressive country that didn't give many rights to women. What would they do to convince the people to give the women more equality?

I was scared to discover that most kids felt it was wrong to tell them how to run their country, even when just trying to persuade them. And even when the stakes were raised and I introduced a hypothetical genocide, 5-10% of the class still refused to intervene.

People are confusing tolerance with relativism. Tolerance is based in absolutes — human rights — relativism is the opposite. Students feel intolerant proposing a morality. That's wrong.

150,000 high schools did the program, and I watched tapes of some of them. I was concerned that even though most of the kids wanted to intervene in a genocide, they had no framework for justifying that.

I see the same thing with lawyers. You're a trial lawyer. You see your adversary is moving and has all his stuff packed up. Do you try to move up the date of depositions to throw him off? Most would. What if his son just died? Again, 5-10% still would. Your duty isn't just to your client. Ethics are universal principles to be respected.

Now societal attitudes are pendular, but this generation (and he hears this from those in other countries too) seems to have a great civic comittment right now. We need to teach this to the next generation. We need to tell them that the Constitution has an element of "inspiring and beautiful spirituality". We need to teach them to pay attention to not only the big-C Constitution but the little-C constitution, the social rules of what's right and wrong. We need to continue our history of great things like saving people from the depression and going on humanitarian missions.

Q: What's the difference between being on the Appeals Court and the Supreme Court?

I wanted and still want to be a trial judge. I never had the political power to achieve that. (Laughs.) That's the closest you get to touching real people. When I was in the appeals court, I didn't want to burn out and get crochety. There are still real people involved. In a social security case, you have to remember that you're talking about a real person's aching back.

In the appeals court I tried to write decisions with enough generality to be useful to other cases, but not so general so that I could distinguish a later case if I made a mistake. I can't really do that now. You've got to get it right, the Court can't zigzag. I used to think stare decisis was an uninteresting, backwards-looking principle. But it has "a forward thrust of tremendous force". You have to think carefully about the effects of your decisions. You're bound by what you write.

Q: You esteem the Constitution, but it hurts us too. The right to bear arms and protection from self-incrimination have caused real problems for society.

I disagree. The Constitution is the "single most brilliant and inspiring document in the history of western civilization". These people who had only known monarchies managed to protect our rights and human dignities. The rule of law has three parts: 1) The Government is bound by the law. 2) All people are equal. 3) The individual has a core personality that cannot be violated.

I don't lose sleep at night thinking about how to protect the Second Amendment. But protection from self-incrimination is important. We can't let people be tortured.

Q: Should we be looking toward other nations?

As I said, this is something new to this generation. There are two parts to this: a) should we look at what other constitutions provide? and b) should we look at how similar provisions are interpreted? Students say the Constitution should guarantee the right to food, shelter, and medical care. In DC winters I see homeless people with the right to a jury trial but unable to eat. But that shouldn't be in our Constitution. The Bill of Rights are negative things (the government can't do this); these entitlements are positive acts that have to be taken. It's easier to enforce the ten commandment's prohibition on stealing than the exhortation to love your neighbor. It's difficult to enforce things that require so much money. I think they should be aspirational or preforatory text — not something that's enforcable. As for (b), we'll be citing other courts as their standing improves.

Q: I've read every opinion of yours and your fidelity to law is consistent. What do you think about the distance between law and politics or personal preference? Do you feel that law is being challenged by the preferences of individuals in high positions?

Thanks for an easy question, professor. (Laughs.) Often I have to go back to square one. We make up our minds about what's right or wrong fast, and there's nothing wrong with that. But then we have to convert that into legal principle. If doing this creates doubts, then you have to go back and rethink. It's important to remember that I'm not the only one whose not results-oriented.

(Imitates a senator during nominations questioning:) Are you going to create the law? (Imitates the questioned judge trying hard to please:) No, no! (Back to normal:) Of course I'm going to create the law. I mean, where do they think the law comes from? The stork? But I strive to be fact-based and neutral.

Q: Does the Supreme Court play a role in setting social mores? What about *Lawrence v. Texas?*

Believing in the Constitution is taught. If we don't transmit our traditions consciously, we'll lose them. So the court needs to take high-profile, widely-publicized cases. The court shouldn't make political decisions — society needs to be able to make decisions to survive — but we need to protect basic rights from nonsensical government intrusion.

(Back to me now.) After his talk, we filed out for a reception with food and drinks in the atrium. There was a line of people waiting to talk to Justice Kennedy that I got in.

I had read Randy Barnett's take on the *Lawrence v. Texas* decision[3], and asked him if he thought the liberty reasoning could be extended to things beyond sexual liberty.

He didn't answer the question directly (he was very good at this) but he said that he felt the First Amendment, and the large quantity of jurisprudence built up around it protected the most important parts our liberty — the right to define our own personality, which he had previously said was one of the key protections required of a constitutional democracy — but that at the frontiers there were still aspects of liberty that needed protection.

Another student asked him what he thought about Canada's drug decriminalization. He also said Canada isn't in our consciousness enough and that it was important that different states and countries get to experiment, and we learn from their example.

When we introduced him to our Constitutional Law professor, he got very excited that there was an undergraduate constitutional law course. He talked about a book at the Supreme Court bookstore about cases that had to do with high schools, and suggested we talk similarly about college-related cases. He recommended a newspaper case at UVA. (He noted that he couldn't remember recent case names well — in the chambers they always talked about cases generally, such as "the UVA newspaper case".) (UPDATE: Jerry Goldman suggests the case is *Rosenberger v. Virginia*[4] which looks right and interesting.) He also suggested students study a particular justice's decisions and try to get inside their mind and predict how they would decide (he suggested Justice Stevens and Justice O'Connor, I think).

I took a few photos of the class with him and then we went back.

October 01, 2003

1. http://www.archives.gov/national_archives_experience/visit_renovation_details.html
2. http://www.cnn.com/2002/US/01/27/scotus.morals/
3. http://www.cato.org/dailys/07-26-03.html
4. http://www.oyez.org/oyez/resource/case/640/

STANFORD
PSYCHOLOGY IS A FRAUD

Today's psychology lecture is on individual differences, what distinguishes between people's personalities. The primary theory of the field, which admittedly has some initial plausibility, is called "dispositionism" — different people have different dispositions (honest, selfish, aggressive, etc.) which decide how they react in different situations.

So, in the 1920s, they did some experiments to see if this was the case. For example, they put people in situations where they could steal cookies or cheat on a test or something and measured whether the two activities were correlated (i.e. people either did both or neither). The correlation was really weak. They did an experiment where they asked camp counsellors to rate whether they thought a student was extroverted or introverted every day and then compared the ratings for odd and even days. Again, no connection.

In other words, they could find no evidence for this dispositionism — the same people behaved differently on different days and in different circumstances. A sane person would junk the theory at this point and try something else. Psychologists apparently are not very sane. Instead of dropping the theory, they decided to just ignore the experiments and keep on pushing dispositionism.

To give a sense of the absurdity, the slide on this is called "The Consistency Paradox". The paradox? That the psychologists really, really want to prove people are consistent, but they just can't do it. I don't think that's called a paradox; I think that's called dishonesty.

Psychologists continued promoting this bogus view up until the late sixties, when Walter Mischel published a book (Personality and Assessment) pointing out that they were all frauds. (You can almost hear the anger in the professor's voice at the guy's audacity to expose the field.)

It's worth noting that while dispositionists continued pushing their theory without evidence, the contrary position, while apparently not taken very seriously by the psychology community, was racking up stunning results. Stanley Milgram found that you could make over 90% of people electrocute someone, sometimes to the point of a heart attack, just by putting them in the right situation. And Dr. Zimbardo found that you could make average college students into sadistic guards and submissive prisoners, just by putting them in a fake prison.

Again, sane people might drop the dispositionism nonsense and adopt situationism. The psychologists instead decided to make their experiments less rigorous, which allowed them to get slightly better results for a much weaker theory. And so, to this day apparently, psychologists continue to support dispositionism despite the evidence.

Finally, I want to apologize to Dr. Zimbardo. I previously suggested that the evidence for his time perspective trait idea was a little weak and this was probably why psychologists didn't take it seriously. On the contrary, time perspective has more evidence than any of the traits supposed by "serious" psychologists and apparently is the only one to have some demonstrable effects. I think it's generally a bad sign for your field when the crazy guy who makes stuff up routinely outperforms all the serious scientists.

February 27, 2005

INTELLECTUAL DIVERSITY AT STANFORD

A shocking recent study[1] has discovered that only 13% of Stanford professors are Republicans. The authors compare this to the 51% of 2004 voters who selected a Republican for President and argue this is "evidence of discrimination" and that "academic Republicans are being eradicated by academic Democrats".

Scary as this is, my preliminary research has discovered some even more shocking facts. I have found that only 1% of Stanford professors believe in telepathy (defined as "communication between minds without using the traditional five senses"), compared with 36% of the general population. And less than half a percent believe "people on this earth are sometimes possessed by the devil", compared with 49% of those outside the ivory tower. And while 25% of Americans believe in astrology ("the position of the stars and planets can affect people's lives"), I could only find one Stanford professor who would agree. (All numbers are from mainstream polls, as reported by Sokal[2].)

This dreadful lack of intellectual diversity is a serious threat to our nation's youth, who are quietly being propagandized by anti-astrology radicals instead of educated with different points of view. Were I to discover that there were no blacks on the Stanford faculty, the Politically Correct community would be all up in arms. But they have no problem squeezing out prospective faculty members whose views they disagree with.

Sure, some might say, but the color of a person's skin is irrelevant to their duties as a professor while beliefs are at the core of the job. And to these critics, one can only say: you "knowledge" elitists have ignored the devastating critique of factual knowledge put together by the postmodernists! Objective reality is unknowable; our beliefs about it are merely "local truths", cultural whims we could change at a moment's notice. The only fair way to decide what gets taught is by what is believed!

But these far-left academics just ignore these devastating critiques[3]. They continue to pretend their job is to investigate "reality" and believe things based on "evidence", when everyone can see that these are merely absurd justifications for them to maintain their positions power and status over society. And, as has widely been conceded[4], their advanced "search committees" and "hiring requirements" are just ways to prevent nonconformists from challenging their orthodoxies.

The party of McCarthy must save academic freedom. Wealthy businessmen must pool their resources to fight elitism. Racists and sexists must tout the values of diversity. Conservatives must embrace postmodernism. Hard work? No doubt. But they are bravely willing to sacrifice all credibility to protect our nation's youth. We should salute their courage.

February 26, 2005

1. http://www.paloaltoonline.com/weekly/morgue/2005/2005_02_23.
   guest23blues.shtml
2. http://www.physics.nyu.edu/faculty/sokal/afterword_v1a/afterword_v1a_
   singlefile.html#167
3. http://www.crookedtimber.org/archives/002420.html
4. http://www.michaelberube.com/index.php/weblog/keeping_conservatives_out_
   of_academe/

FOUNDERS UNITE FOR STARTUP SCHOOL

[The following article was originally intended for Wired News, but was rejected for not being about any of its advertisers.]

Experts agree that it smells like a new startup age is beginning to boom. This time, however, it's being led by geeks themselves instead of business guys. At the center of this democratizing force is the new funding firm Y Combinator, led by Internet entrepreneur and essayist Paul Graham.

Y Combinator burst onto the scene by offering small grants to promising graduates (average age: 23) to pursue their ambitions in startup form over the summer. And this past weekend, the people behind Y Combinator, in association with the Harvard Computer Society, took their show to the masses, inviting 500 of the most promising startup founders to Harvard University for an intense one-day lecture series on all aspects of starting a company.

The weekend was kicked off with a smaller reception at Y Combinator's offices the night before. The room pulsed with networking between the various would-be founders, as well as some interesting meeting with some of the guests of honor.

"Last night was the first time I met my lawyer," said Steve Huffman, Lord Ruler and Supreme Leade[1]* of Reddit, one of the companies Y Combinator has funded. "The first thing I said was 'Am I getting charged for this?' 'No,' she told me. 'There are rules preventing us from charging for parties.'"

Meanwhile, clusters of people formed around the night's VIPs, including blogger Joel Spolsky, scientist Stephen Wolfram, and, of course, the Reddit developers themselves, who found themselves deluged by excited fans.

The startup school itself was a similarly star-studded event, with Apple Computer co-founder Steve Wozniak telling the story of how his company got started. Michael Mandel, chief economist for BusinessWeek touted the virtues of America's entrepreneurial culture to the assembled crowd. "People starting companies and risking failure are what makes America so great. The people in this room are doing God's work," he said to applause.

Senior officials from Google and Yahoo both espoused the virtues of their respective companies. Lawyers from top-tier law firms provided advice on protecting a company's intellectual property and navigating some of the complex legal waters of the modern business world. Founders Langley Steinert, Marc Hedlund, and Olin Shivers tried to share some of their assembled experience.

Because space was limited, people who wanted to attend simply needed to fill out a simple questionnaire about their background, but the event was entirely free of charge. It might seem unusual for a company interested in helping hackers start companies to try to give some of that value away but Paul Graham had an explanation. "There's a concept in venture capital known as 'deal flow'," he said in an interview. "The deal flow is all the interesting startups to fund flowing by. And venture capitalists just try to grab the best ones for themselves. Well, we think the real solution to this is to increase the total deal flow for everyone."

Paul Graham himself gave a very well-received talk on how to come up with ideas for startups. The thing that trips people up, he suggested, was mistakenly thinking that a good startup idea needed to be a million-dollar idea. Instead, he proposed prospective founders simply look around for things that are broken with the world and try to fix them.

Video of the talks will be available on the startup school website shortly.

Jessica Livingston contributed to this report. Sigh and Wrinkle contributed additional style tips from California.

October 16, 2005

1.   An earlier version of this article incorrectly referred to Steve Huffman
     as CEO of Reddit. Aaron Swartz: The Weblog regrets the error.

I LOVE THE UNIVERSITY

I went to visit a friend today at MIT. The past few days I'd been reading more stuff from academia and just that morning I was reading responses to my old posts at Stanford, so academia's siren song had been on my mind. But getting off the subway at MIT, with me full of energy after a morning jog, the sun shining brightly down, I couldn't help but feel like I was missing something, seeing smiles on the faces of the young geniuses who were everywhere around me.

Perhaps it's natural, when doing something so greedy and practical as a startup, to pine for the idealized world of academia. Its image as a place in an idyllic location filled with smart people has always been attractive; even more so with the sense that by being there one can get smarter simply through osmosis. People describe a place of continual geekiness, of throwing chemicals into the river and building robots in free time. A magical place for hackers to just enjoy themselves.

It's not that I don't enjoy my work; it's just that I feel like I'm getting dumber doing it. Or, at least, that I'm not getting as smart as I should.

This academaphilia isn't new. It's clearly what drove magazines like Lingua Franca and makes saying obscure names and words so impressive. But for some reason it feels stronger now. I've started downloading class syllabuses off the Web and doing the reading assignments at night; I've started thinking about how to sneak into courses and hang out with academics. In Cambridge, this paradise seems so close, so accessible.

And yet, it's hardly paradise at all. When I was actually there I was turned off by the conformism, the lack of interest in real work, the politics, the pointless assignments. My lunch date is a grad student and he tells me of the internecine squabbles, the overspecialization, the abandonment, the insecurity.

I go back to the W3C's offices and stand at the balcony. Down below, Tim Berners-Lee discusses details of a project with a group of kids who presumably took this on as summer job. I was once one of those kids, working there, and I think about why I left and why I miss it. I marvel at the pointlessness, the impracticality, the waste.

The sky is overcast now, the crowds of students have thinned out, and those that remain scurry from place to place with their heads down. I'm tired now, I feel sadder, and I wonder how I lost so much so quickly.

I want to feel nostalgic, I want to feel like there's this place, just a couple subway stops away, where everything will be alright. A better place, a place I should be in, a place I can go back to. But even just visiting it, the facts are plain. It doesn't exist, it never has. I'm nostalgic for a place that never existed.

July 26, 2006

TAKE THE EASY WAY OUT

When I was a kid, people were always telling me that there was no substitute for hard work. If I wanted to be smart, I had to sit and force myself to read hard books. If I wanted to lose weight, I had to force myself to exercise. If I wanted to play piano, I had to force myself away from the computer to practice. Cheating, they explained, would only cheat myself in the end.

And yet today I eagerly ran to the library to grab five large books (and return seven more), felt an itch to go jogging, and walked away from web surfing so I could go practice a musical instrument. The adults were completely wrong.

Your body's resistance to an activity isn't an obstacle to be overcome, it's a message that you're being an idiot, just like when your hand hurts after you punch a wall. The right solution isn't to start punching the wall harder, it's to look around for a tool to help you do the job.

In the case of books, the key is that you need to be sure to read books that are at your level. If you read books about subjects you don't know enough to understand or that use a dialect you're not familiar with, it's going to be hard and it's going to be a waste of time. With losing weight, the key is things like the *Shangri-La Diet*. And with learning an instrument, the key is using Bemani games[1] that actually make music fun.

I've discussed the other two in other places, but why do Bemani games work? First, you're playing real music. Normally when you play piano, you have to start on baby songs which are both infantilizing and uninteresting, with real music not even on the horizon. Bemani games start you on real songs from the beginning. Since the reason many people get excited about musical instruments in the first place is the chance to play their favorite song, this is a pretty compelling difference. And the fact that the computer simplifies the song and fills in the notes you don't play for you makes it possible.

Second, Bemani games provide clear additional results in proportion to additional effort. This is what makes them so much fun. I don't know about the real science, but in Barbara Ehrenreich's novel *Kipper's Game* the plot revolves around some research showing that games like that stimulate the pleasure centers of the brain. You get the high of achievement, but it quickly wears off as you get used to your new skill level, and so you want to do better so you can get another high.

This is also what makes these games so educational. Research on experts has found such immediate feedback is essential to learning, calling the general process "deliberate practice". In deliberate practice, "subjects should receive immediate informative feedback and knowledge of results of their performance. The subjects should repeatedly perform the same or similar tasks. When these conditions are met, practice improves accuracy and speed of performance on cognitive, perceptual, and motor tasks (Fitts & Posner, 1967; Gibson, 1969; Welford, 1968)." (K. Anders Ericsson, et. al, "The Role of Deliberate Practice", Psychological Review) Your attempts aren't random — it's very clear what works and what doesn't and you can adjust your strategies accordingly.

Third, you can do them in small chunks. When you normally play an instrument, if you hit a wrong note you often keep trying until you get it right. But with Bemani games, the music just keeps marching on without you. This might at first seem a disadvantage, but it means you don't get hung up on a mistake, each attempt takes at most as long the song does. With real music, if you hit a difficult part of the song you can easily get stuck trying over and over to get it right, before getting frustrated and giving up on the whole thing. Keeping the music moving forces you to look at the bigger picture.

The flip side of this is that playing the games gives you a continuous sense of motion and progress. In the mid-1980s — the heyday of video game research — some psychologists were trying to find out what video games quite so much fun. They took the classic Wozniak/Atari game Breakout[2] and started removing components to see if kids stopped playing it. What they found was you could remove just about everything — the levels, the score, the bouncing off the paddle — everything except for the animations of the bricks disappearing. It was making the bricks disappear, somehow, that made the game fun. (*Mind at Play*, Loftus and Loftus)

I doubt Bemani games were made with these kind of principles in mind — considering the history, it was probably just a coincidence. But it shows that you could have created Bemani from them. All you needed to do was pay attention to the fact that learning an instrument was frustrating and tried to eliminate the frustrating part. Good designers, when they see people having trouble using something they designed, don't tell the user to try harder. They fix the design. We should take the same attitude when we design our life as well.

Thanks to Emmett Shear for suggesting pieces of this writing.

September 29, 2006

1. http://en.wikipedia.org/wiki/Bemani
2. http://en.wikipedia.org/wiki/Breakout

THE AWFULNESS OF COLLEGE LECTURES

What do the children of privilege do when not engaging in conspicuous consumption while wearing fashionable clothes? Why attend class, of course! This bizarre, yet widespread, affectation seemed intriguing enough that I decided to pursue a further investigation in my inimitable "first-person snob" style.

The Harvard students sit patiently outside the lecture hall as they wait for the previous class to end. Many simply sit, but others, showing the go-get-it-ness that got them into Harvard, begin attempting conversation with their neighbors. The awkward situation shows through in the awkward conversation (which, no doubt, they will learn to smooth over as they get older) about superficial topics of schoolwork (never school content, of course).

As the previous class exits, we file in and take our seats. Gabbing continues somewhat for a while until, all of a sudden, as if by some mysterious consensus, it completely silences. The professor seems surprised too. "Well, uh, it got quiet all of a sudden," he says haltingly, "so I guess I better start talking." For a professor in social psychology, you think he'd show a little more interest.

He begins the lecture in the standard way since PowerPoint: a title slide (with a cute illustration), a table of contents slide (which he walks through interminably slowly), and then a series of chunks of text and illustrations, which he walks through one by one. It's so bad it makes we want to tear my hair out. The content is largely superficial; the presentation is unnaturally slow. (We literally spend a good five minutes talking about a specific gross-out gag.)

But while this may be an extreme version of it, at its essence, this is the college lecture. Someone who (we'll give them the benefit of the doubt) is quite smart appearing stupid for fifty minutes so that they can communicate basic facts to kids "at their level". Edward Tufte teaches us to always ask about the information density of a method of communication. The information communicated in this lecture could have fit on one side of a single piece of paper.

There was a camera in the back of the hall, presumably recording the proceedings. But had this been available online, I doubt I could have forced myself to watch it. (The other day someone asked me why more people don't watch the recordings of MIT lectures made available for free online. This is why.) The only reason the lecture is tolerable at all is because there's something captivating about being in the presence of another human being, regardless of what they're saying. But it doesn't seem like that communicates anything additional — whether you see the guy in person or watch him at home, he's still saying the same stuff. And so when you watch him at home, there's just not much there.

So if what he's saying isn't very interesting, why do we subject ourselves to it? How did this become the primary method of education? Why do kids paid tens of thousands of dollars, in large part to fly someplace else to see someone say something they would have been bored to watch at home?

Back at Harvard, as I walk out of the class I hear the students gabbing. "Wow, I'm so glad I took this class," one says. "That was the best lecture I've ever been in."

October 3, 2006

THE GREATNESS OF COLLEGE LECTURES

The other week I saw Scott McCloud give a presentation at a local college. Although he is not a professor himself, McCloud is a theorist of comics. Edward Tufte (among countless others) calls his guide Understanding Comics the best book on the medium. McCloud breaks comics down to its essential: the use of sequential art to tell a story — we see one thing, we see another, we imagine what happens in between. And watching McCloud speak, I realized that his talk was a vivid form of comics. The images weren't just illustrations, they drove the story along, with McCloud simply filling in the words to connect them together.

After his talk, someone commented that McCloud's presentation was the best he'd ever seen. McCloud explained that there are two kinds of presentations: "monkey bars", where a presenter swings from slide to slide, explaining each one in turn, and "magic carpet rides", where the presenter simply keeps talking, confident the slides will appear underneath him to illustrate a point. McCloud gives a masterful magic carpet ride.

Tufte himself is professor emeritus at Yale. These days he goes on tour, rock-star style, teaching classes on presenting information. Tufte is a brilliant presenter — his energy keeps the audience spell-bound for an entire day. At one point, as I recall, he jumped up on a table and asked us to imagine the information density of various media as charted from one side of the room to the other. But what, I couldn't help but wonder, was the information density of this presentation? After all, hadn't he written four books on the subject? (Copies of which are given to each participant to take home.)

Then there's Lawrence Lessig, who's presentations are so powerful and influential that an entire style of presentation has been named after him. At his peak, I saw him give a talk at the O'Reilly Open Source Conference that had the audience, as Wes Felter put it, looking to start a riot afterwards. Lessig's rhythmic, almost hypnotic, presentation, invariably blows people away.

Does these people's talks communicate more information than their books? I doubt it. But does a comic book communicate more information than a novel? No way. And yet McCloud (and Tufte) endorse it anyway. It's not because of the medium's informational density, it's because of its emotional density. The same is true of these presentations.

Reading Lessig's books, you'll probably learn more about the history of copyright law and the other things he discusses in his talk. But you won't feel his righteous indignation against those "extremists on the right and left" who are trying to distort its intentions and, in the process, hurt our culture.

Writing is quite effective at communicating facts, but to become a professional you need much more than a vast store of facts; you need to learn ways of thinking. These are what lectures, at their best, can provide. They show you how the speakers think about problems, how they feel about them, and, in doing so, provide a more fleshed-out notion than writing ever could.

October 4, 2006

COLLEGE: COMMODITY OR COMMUNITY?

When it was time for me to pick colleges, our family flew to Cambridge, Mass. and went on the tour of Harvard University. It's a grand, elegant campus, the school has a singular reputation, the neighborhood is one of the most interesting in the world. And yet, on the college tour, this isn't what they told us. They mentioned a bit about John Harvard and the 1700s but spent most of their time telling us how great it was they had "shopping week", where you could try out different courses for a couple classes.

The other month, I visited the University of Chicago. Chicago has a worldwide reputation as a tough-minded school. It seems like every field has a "Chicago School" of thought and the University's former presidents are responsible for things like the Great Books. But you wouldn't know that from the tour — the only time actually studying was mentioned was when one kid said he'd heard the University had a nose-to-the-grindstone reputation. "Well," the tour guide said, "you can work hard if you want," and then went back to talking about the sports program. ("Whenever I feel like exercise," the University's president once said, "I lie down until the feeling passes.")

It was as if the entire admissions program had been through a focus group, every bit of individuality shorn off. They put their self-description through a series of tests and only the generic things that every student finds themselves agreeing with survived the ordeal. "Oh no," they now insist, "we're just like every university. We want to let you be you." But why go to a University for that? I can be me at home just fine.

No, the real reason I want to go to a University — and the reason, when you get right down to it, everybody else seems to be interested in as well — is the people. I want to go to a place filled with people like me, but smarter; a place where you can't help but learn.

The key phrase there is "people like me". What I want to know is what the culture is like. To unfairly overgeneralize, people at Harvard are snobbish, people at Stanford are lazy, and people at MIT are nerds. But (with the possible exception of MIT which actually sells "nerd pride" clothing) none of these places advertise this fact. After all, advertising your individuality alienates some of the focus group. In fact, that's exactly the point!

And yet, somehow, the cultures remain. It's not clear to me whether the university itself has a culture (perhaps passed down by the older students and professors) and whoever attends simply learns to conform or whether there's a secret bulletin I'm not getting about which university each kind of person should go to. I suspect the former, since I've heard that even houses at Harvard, to which students are assigned randomly when they arrive, manage to develop a culture of their own.

So how to decide where to go?

There are some people who say that if you go to a large enough university, you'll be able to find a subculture of people you can get along with. At MIT, for example, a complicated "rush" system at the beginning of the school year allows incoming freshman to sample a variety of dorms and then floors within that dorm to find the place they belong. The dorms apparently put on lavish shows to communicate their culture to the incoming students and people seem fairly happy with where they end up.

MIT is a bit of a special case, of course, but some insists that similar subcultures exist at every college, you just have to seek them out. Perhaps that's true, but even so, what's the point of the university then? There's a subculture of people I can get along with right here; I want to go to school for something a little more concentrated.

Colleges need to drop the focus-group-enforced blandness. As Malcolm Gladwell would put it[1], people don't want ten varieties of bland tomato sauce to choose from. Some people love mild and some love extra-chunky. Trying to appeal to both only makes the experience worse for everyone. It doesn't seem like you should have to go to college to realize that.

October 6, 2006

1.   http://www.ted.com/search?q=malcolm+gladwell

IZ R CHILDRENS LRNNG?

Some of our most formative years are spent in schools, odd places whose ostensible goal is adult-directed education but in reality are controlled by student-culture peer groups of which adults have little actual understanding. Adults run examinations and programs, try to be "hip" to teen culture, but ultimately, we must admit, we have little idea what really goes on, making it easy for rumors to run wild.

Jeremy Iversen and Rebekah Nathan decided to see for themselves what school life was really like, by going undercover and experiencing it themselves. While they went to different places, in different guises, in entirely different situations (Iversen was a senior in high school, while Nathan was a freshman in college), the pictures they draw are startlingly similar: a world where genuine education is absolutely the last thing on everyone's mind.

Jeremy Iversen grew up in New York, attended a prestigious boarding school, and went to college at Stanford. But, he says, life after school didn't have the same appeal. So he decided to go back and get the typical high school education he never had. The result — *High School Confidential* — is a gripping memoir of what life is actually like for the cool kids in a southern California high school.

The general outlines are perhaps less than shocking to those who have been paying attention. High school kids routinely have casual sex with each other, for example. ("There's nothing else to do in this town," one student comments, "except start drama with everybody.") They take drugs — marijuana, cocaine, ecstasy, speed — right under their parents noses. (In one scene, Travis, the class's drug dealer, and Alexis, his sister, are confronted by their father. "I'm going to give you a drug test," he warns them. "But I've been clean since nursery!" Travis replies. "Oh, it's only your sister I'm worried about," explains the father.) The kids cheat, not just by copying on tests, but by taking copious steroids and human growth hormone to compete in sports. ("I read an article about high school steroid use in *Sports Illustrated*", comments the team coach, as the kids who are using look away. "Good thing that's not a problem in our school.")

Despite living in a very diverse community, many of the kids are full of casual racism and right-wing politics (white people need to stand up for their heritage, nuke all the Arabs), although they're far more liberal in practice (doing drugs with their Middle Eastern friends). When they get mad at each other, they aren't afraid to take it out in violent brawls. And when the school throws parties, everybody gets totally hammered. (There's a brilliant scene where some kids throw up on Richard Nixon's grave.)

However, the novel is gripping in its details, with more amusing characters and fascinating stories than any television show imitation of high school life. The teachers are such characters that were this fiction you might accuse them of being overwritten. School events are so lavish (a band performs every day at lunch, large coordinated dance-and-light shows are done for spirit rallies) that they seem like TV exaggerations. School assignments are so inane (cut apart this cat) that you might think the kid telling you this was exaggerating. But Iversen was there, the dialogue in the book is copied down verbatim, the description of events was taken first-hand.[1]

And, indeed, the most shocking components are not the tales of the kids, but of the schools. Iversen draws a picture of an institution that is not just failing at learning, but antithetical to it. Thea, the only girl in the book with any academic passion, is routinely discouraged by the actions of both peers and adults. But no other student even gets that far. The school's student culture makes caring about class unthinkable; the school's classes make learning near-impossible.

But the grandest component of Iversen's tale is how he dismantles our previous methods for trying to understand how schools operate. First, there is Derrick, the school board's secret weapon. Derrick is an articulate and popular student, admired by all, and elected class president. But it slowly becomes clear that student government, including him, is nothing but the administration's pawn. The regulations are designed to make genuine complaints impossible to bring before the administration, while the administration uses Derrick at every opportunity as a mouthpiece for their lies about what the children really think. Thus the only student representative most outside adults see is no representative at all.

Then there are the standards regulations, around which the curriculum is supposedly organized. The state school accreditation team is coming to verify that it is, and the adults worry that they're quite likely to fail. So the principal goes all-out, bribing, threatening, and faking the school into appearing good. Any kid who ever caused a problem is locked away in a hidden trailer for the duration of the inspector's visit, every class is replaced with fake, scripted, standards-compliant material. Every child puts on fake happy faces under severe duress. And the school passes with flying colors. "I wish every kid in the state could have an education this good", insists the lead inspector.

The reality is that between adult and student, there is a vast gulf in mentality. Iversen's genius is that he can get us inside the heads of both sides.

Around the same time, Rebekah Nathan, an anthropology professor at AnyU (both psuedonyms), was sitting in on some classes herself. She noticed that simply by acting like a student — sitting in class, taking notes, etc. — her fellow students began treating her like one, sharing gossip and trading facts she never got to see as a professor. Eager to cross that same mental gulf, she decided to spend her sabbatical the following year doing an undercover anthropological study of her own university.

Nathan enrolled as a freshman, lived in a dorm, and took a full load of courses. Despite looking like a mom, the other students accepted her as their own. She probably couldn't get involved in the party scene and didn't try — she stuck to studying the academic and intellectual side of college life — but pretty much everything she says fits with my impressions as a freshman Stanford student around the same time and I can even confirm a couple of her more surprising specific points.

After confining her focus to the intellectual, Nathan discovers that there simply isn't much there. Students have their own culture with regard to class, a language known as "Undergraduate Cynical", where actually caring about the material is deeply frowned upon, and the only questions you're permitted to ask of a teacher are about the details of grading and assignments:

> A good question, I learned, is one that voices a concern shared by other students or that asks for clarifications of upcoming work. "Will there be more questions on the test from the text or the lecture?" "Should the paper be double- or single-spaced?" [...]
>
> [...] "What does that mean?" is, incredibly, just not the kind of question that an American college student would ask.

This isn't just show; students genuinely aren't engaged in classes. They don't do the required reading, they dash off assignments, they ditch classes, they cheat on tests. Some go up and talk to the teacher about things, but they do so with ulterior motives in mind. Signs and talks geared to incoming students explain that one must "work the teachers" by talking to them, getting them to recognize you so they will give you hints about tests and go easy on you when you need exceptions. "I take the information I need from the professor", one highly-successful student tells Nathan, explaining what that consists of: "how they're going to grade you and what they think is important". Everything is seen as part of the game, not worthwhile for its own sake.

But it's all too easy to lament this sad state of student affairs, perhaps complain about the laziness of modern students. But Nathan goes one step further: she shows *why* it is happening. For even she, a professor with a Ph.D, finds herself doing the exact same things. "We don't need to study those things, they won't be on the test", she tells her study partner Rob. It takes Rob, a fellow student, to ask her whether she just cares about learning for its own sake.

The culture of Undergraduate Cynical, you see, is not created by student laziness or a lack of concern for intellectual life. It's created by the necessities of the schedule. Students simply don't have time to care. They take three to five classes, each with separate sections and lab assignments, each with its own schedule of papers and readings and adults to suck up to. That alone is enough to drive Rebekah crazy, despite her thinking she had pretty good time management skills juggling all her commitments as a professor. But on top of that most students go to activities and clubs, work an on- or off-campus job, party in the evenings, and try to maintain relationships. When you run the math, there just isn't enough time to care.

So students instead focus on doing what's required of them: just scraping by. Anything that won't impact their grade much is tossed and a desire to learn becomes a desire to pass. It's hard to imagine any sincere desire to learn surviving such a harried schedule. As soon as you get engrossed or a book or topic, you have to dash off to your next meeting.

Again, this is all something completely invisible to the professors. They spend their days worrying about tomorrow's lecture and are shocked when students don't do the same. But the students haven't had time: they've had two more classes and who knows how many assignments in the interim. And, anyway, they only picked this course because it filled a convenient hole in their schedule, they're not even sure what it's about.

So the students simply don't get engrossed, student discussion groups don't actually discuss things, but instead each student simply makes up a point of view and shares it so they don't get a zero on their in-class participation grade. There is no "meeting of the minds" on any subject; there are hardly any minds.

Both books, their research being conducted undercover, will no doubt lead some to raise ethical questions. Jeremy Iversen had to deceive and mislead his fellow students — including creating a fake backstory — in order to experience life with them. Rebekah Nathan, while not explicitly lying, led students to believe she was just an older woman going back to school, and certainly not one of their professors.

But deception alone is not an ethical violation. Psychology studies routinely deceive subjects into thinking the experiment is about X, when actually it is about Y. (I myself have been so deceived.) The key difference, and in my opinion the only possible ethical lapse on Iversen and Nathan's part, is that after the study is over, the psychologists explain what was really going on. Neither Nathan nor Iversen told their friends afterwards, leaving them only to discover it after the project had gone public.

(By contrast, Barbara Ehrenreich, in *Nickeled and Dimed*, her study of low-wage work, told her fellow workers at the end that she was working on a book about the experience. They were "remarkably blasé" about it, she found.)

But more generally, important scientific projects like these might have to step on a few ethical toes. Some of the greatest experiments in psychology — the Milgram experiments on obedience to authority and Zimbardo's Stanford Prison Experiment — were easy fodder for armchair ethicists. But while people may have their feelings ruffled, in all of these experiments there was little lasting hurt to the participants, while the educational consequences of the studies themselves have been immense.

The real ethical question is how we can justify forcing our children into such institutions of anti-intellectualism. Iversen found that high school students were quite conservative politically, even more so than their parents, and perhaps it's not surprising that Bush's anti-intellectual charm appeals to kids who daily experience education as a form of torture.

Perhaps students learn something by going through the necessary motions required to get a degree, but I defy anyone to read both of these accounts and continue to insist that schools are teaching kids to be "critical thinkers" with a "life-long love of learning". If anything, the real education is in the opposite.

Instead of critical thinkers, we have kids willing to accept any requirement, no matter how absurd, without question. "If you write what you want to that prof," explains a successful senior, "you're gonna end up with a bad grade. Whereas, if you write to them, you win — you can still have your own mindset and say, hell, I know this isn't the way I feel, but I'll give them what they want." But, as experiments in cognitive dissonance have shown us, if one continues saying what one doesn't feel, one begins feeling it before too long. It's easy to see how this is effective training for professionalism, which actually means doing what you're told, despite what you believe. But it's hard to see how this system is going to generate students who will buck a trend.

Instead of life-long learners, we have kids who learn that genuine learning is a joke. "Education" becomes that stupid thing in classrooms that you have to do to get a decent job, an entirely mercenary perspective that's unhelpfully encouraged by the mercenary pressures of student loans. If the only education you've ever experienced is doing what's necessary to get a good grade, why would you do it when the grades weren't around?

Our public high schools were supposed to make every child a good citizen of the democracy. Our great universities were supposed to show young people our grandest achievements. One could say that these institutions are failing at their jobs, but it might be more accurate to say that they're being all too successful.

October 11, 2006

1. Some of the more verbal students at the school, upset at being hoodwinked by an undercover writer and disappointed at their portrayal, have taken to posting nasty comments on web sites and in the school paper suggesting that Iversen's book is fictionalized. But, as far as I can see, everything they claim that he left out, he actually included (with a single exception: one person on the Internet claimed kids called him "Plasticface") and they have failed to dispute any details he included. So, while no doubt Iversen's book contains errors (every book does, especially one as difficult to write as this), I'm compelled to believe it is largely accurate.

GETTING IT WRONG

Anyone who's spent any time around little kids in school, or even read books about people who have, knows that they're terrified of getting the answer wrong. Geez, you don't even need to hang around little kids. When you're out chatting with a bunch of people and you say something that shows you didn't know something, you look embarrassed. When you're playing a video game and not doing well, you try to come up with an excuse. People hate failing, so much so that they're afraid to try.

Which is a problem, because failing is most of what we do, most of the time. The only way to stretch your abilities is to try to do things a little bit beyond them, which means you're going to fail some of the time. Even weirder are the competitive situations. If I'm playing a game that relies solely on practice against someone who's practiced more than me, I'm probably going to lose, no matter how good a person I am. Yet I still feel degraded when I do.

Anyone who wants to build a decent educational environment is going to need to solve this problem. And there seem to be two ways of doing it: try and fix the people so that they don't feel embarrassed at failing or try to fix the environment so that people don't fail. Which option to pick sometimes gets people into philopolitical debates (trying to improve kids self-esteem means they won't be able to handle the real world! preventing kids from experiencing failure is just childish coddling!), but for now let's just be concerned with what works.

Getting people to be OK with being wrong seems tough, if only because everybody I know has this problem to a greater or lesser degree. There are occasional exceptions — mavericks like Richard Feynman (why do you care what other people think?) often seem fearless, although it's hard to gauge how much of that was staged — but these just seem random, with no patterns suggesting *why*.

It seems quite likely that a lot of the fear is induced by a goal-oriented educational system, obsessed with grades for work (A, B, C) and grades for students (1st, 2nd, 3rd). And perhaps the fear of being wrong you see in older people stems from having been through such experiences in childhood. If this is the case, then simply building a decent non-coercive environment for children will solve the problem, but that seems like too much to hope for.

Perhaps the solution is in, as some suggest, building self-esteem, so that when kids are wrong on one thing, they have other things to fall back on. I certainly see this process operating in my own mind: "pff, sure they can beat me in *Guitar Hero*, but at least I can go back to writing blog entries". But self-esteem is like a cushion: it prevents the fall from being too damaging, but it doesn't prevent the fall.

The real piece, it would seem, is finding some way to detach a student's actions from their worth. The reason failing hurts is because we think it reflects badly on us. I failed, therefore I'm a failure. But if that's not the case, then there's nothing to feel hurt about.

Detaching a self from your actions might seem like a silly thing, but lots of different pieces of psychology point to it. Richard Layard, in his survey *Happiness: Lessons from a New Science*[1], notes that studies consistently find that people who are detached from their surroundings — whether through Buddhist meditation, Christian belief in God, or cognitive therapy — are happier people. "All feelings of joy and even physical pain are observed to fluctuate, and we see ourselves as like a wave of the sea — where the sea is eternal and the wave is just its present form." (p. 191)

Similarly Alfie Kohn, who looks more specifically at the studies about children, finds that it's essential for a child's mental health that parents communicate that they love their child for who they are, no matter what it is they do. This concept can lead to some nasty philosophical debates — what are people, if not collections of things done? — but the practical implications are clear. Children, indeed all people, need unconditional love and support to be able to survive in this world. Attachment parenting studies find that even infants are afraid to explore a room unless their mother is close by to support them, and the same findings have been found in monkeys.

The flip side is: how do we build educational institutions that discourage these ways of thinking. Obviously we'll want to get rid of competition as well as grades, but even so, as we saw with Mission Hill, kids are scared of failure.

While I'm loathe to introduce more individualism into American schools, it seems clear that one solution is to have people do work on their own. Kids are embarrassed in front of the class, shy people get bullied in small groups, so all that really leaves is to do it on your own.

And this does seem effective. People seem more likely to ask "stupid" questions if they get to write them down on anonymous cards. When people fail in a video game, it only makes them want to try again right away so they can finally beat it. Apparently when nobody knows you're getting it wrong, it's a lot easier to handle it. Maybe because you know it can't affect the way people see you.

Schools can also work to discourage this kind of conditional seeing by making it completely unimportant. Even Mission Hill, which ensured every classroom was mixed-age, still had a notion of age and clear requirements for graduating. What if school, instead of a bunch of activities you had to march through, was a bunch of activities students could pick and choose from. When people are no longer marching, it's hard to be worried about your place in line.

But can we take the next step? Can schools not just see their students unconditionally, but actually encourage them to see themselves that way? Clearly we could teach everybody Buddhist meditation or something (which, studies apparently show, is effective), but even better would be if there was something in the structure of the school that encouraged this way of thinking.

Removing deadlines and requirements should help students live more fully in the moment. Providing basic care to every student should help them feel valued as people. Creating a safe and trusting environment should free them from having to keep track of how much they can trust everyone else. And, of course, all the same things would be positive in the larger society.

Too often, people think of schools as systems for building good people. Perhaps it's time to think of them as places to let people be good.

Tomorrow: Getting it Right.

October 12, 2006

1. http://www.amazon.com/Happiness-Lessons-Science-Richard-Layard/dp/0143037013

GETTING IT RIGHT

There's an interesting little experiment you can do. If you have a classroom of kids and you give them a bunch of tasks they can work on of varying difficulty, the kids will pick the tasks that are just outside their level, that stretch them to do a little bit more. (This is, of course, if they aren't getting graded on this. If they're getting graded, they'll always pick the easy ones.)

When I first heard about this experiment, I just assumed it was because they were good kids. But now I think there's a different explanation. It's because doing this is fun.

Working on something that's too easy for you isn't enjoyable, it's just mindless. (There's a reason few people play 50K Racewalker[1].) But doing something that's too hard for you isn't fun either. It's just like trying to run through a wall: you're not going to succeed and you're not going to learn much from it. So, like Goldilocks, the kids pick the task that's just right.

But it's not simply by default either. There's something actively enjoyable in itself about learning to achieve more. (I've come to call this the "Kipper effect", after the novel Kipper's Game which revolves around this idea.) There's a definite high to achievement, the rush of accomplishment, just as there's a corresponding low when you fail.

I'm looking for more research on this idea — and I'd be very grateful if anyone could point me to it. What kinds of things trigger the Kipper effect? Does it wear off? etc.

October 13, 2006

1. http://www.hrwiki.org/index.php/50K_Racewalker

DROP OUT

I was wondering what I was going to find for today's Sunday Bonus Post. Luckily, at the last minute, the San Francisco Chronicle stepped in to save me:

> Aaron Swartz dropped out of high school after one year to study on his own. Then he dropped out of college after one year to seek his high-tech fortune. He was still in his teens a year later when he hit the jackpot, selling his startup in October to Wired Digital for an undisclosed but lottery-like payout.
>
> With his boyish mien and more geek credentials than engineers twice his age, the suddenly wealthy Swartz belongs to a new generation of young, brainy geeks who began booting up and logging on when their friends were still watching "Sesame Street." Before they were old enough to drive, they landed paying gigs. Now that another high-tech boom is heating up Silicon Valley, more of these technologically developed but underage techies are dropping out and starting up.
>
> [...]
>
> "Everything that would get you detention at school will get you funding in Silicon Valley," said Paul Saffo, a valley forecaster and essayist who has been exploring technological change and its impact on business and society for more than two decades.
>
> [...]
>
> Fancy new car? "I don't know how to drive," Swartz wrote on his blog, Raw Thought. Big house in the suburbs? "I like living in small apartments." Expensive clothes? "I've worn a T-shirt and jeans practically every day of my life." Hanging with the cool kids? "I'm so shy I don't even hang out with the people I know now."

(Jessica Guynn, Log on, drop out, cash in: These top techies weren't leery about leaving school[1])

Excuse my self-indulgence.

December 3, 2006

1. http://www.sfgate.com/business/article/Log-on-drop-out-cash-in-These-top-techies-2483834.php

NEVER BACK TO SCHOOL

When guests came to visit us at Stanford, they'd always comment on the beauty of our campus — the copious greenery, the modern decorations, the classic architecture. I used to take them at their word. I always thought Stanford was a very pretty campus. Now I realize that it was merely bright.

Coming back to Stanford after living in San Francisco is an odd experience, because the place seems so obviously much more fake. You don't notice when you're in it, but Stanford is a real wonder of a bubble. Surrounded by a moat of trees, it pretends to be its own self-sufficient city, complete with its own name (Stanford, California is not technically a city, but only a "census-designated place"; it has its own zip code, nonetheless). It has its own food, housing, public transit system, gas station (this is California), police force, job openings, newspaper, and events calendar. Most large universities have such things, of course, but they mesh with and supplement the outside world. At Stanford, despite being in the center of Silicon Valley, you'd hardly know the outside world existed.

Everything here is immaculately clean. There is rarely weather, just constant sun from a cloudless sky (the sky kindly rains only at night so as not to disturb anyone). There are no outsiders, just scrupulously examined teachers, carefully selected students, and well-behaved maintenance staff (who are not paid a living wage, despitee the proteests of generous-minded students).

Coming back to Stanford, wandering its august halls once again, it feels so strange. I lived here for a full year; this should feel like coming home. But while I recognize it all — not much changed while I was gone — it doesn't feel like home at all. Everything seems, well, smaller.

Part of that, obviously, is literally true: I'm physically bigger now, so things seem smaller in comparison. But it also feels psychologically smaller, like after living in San Francisco I can no longer accept this simulated city as a reality. Instead, I'm constantly seeing it in its context in the wider world.

The result is that everything feels like a bizarre show, played out on this phony stage. Beautiful guys in pajamas, talking to beautiful girls in less. Party music blaring. Kids scooting elegantly by on bicycles. Before I just thought this was the strange reality of the world I was dropped into. Now I see it as just another act.

I went to the top of the large tower in the middle of the Stanford campus, something I'd never found the time to do while I was a student. And looking out, the school splayed before me, I noticed something odd. The beaultiful Stanford buildings, so varied and complex at ground level, all look like big red rectangles from the sky. Perhaps Stanford is one of those things you really have to be in to genuinely see.

December 2, 2006

OUR UNDERACHIEVING COLLEGE PRESIDENTS

It would seem absurd to claim that nobody cares about the quality of higher education. After all, anyone paying attention can name a dozen bestselling polemics off the top of their head — *The Closing of the American Mind, The University in Ruins, Tenured Radicals, Higher Superstitions*. But as Derek Bok points out in his quietly subversive new book, *Our Underachieving Colleges*, these commentators have treated universities largely as a punching bag for their political and professional views, rather than out of any genuine concern for the education of the students.

A classic example are the heated debates about what should be in the core curriculum. Should the humanities be required? Should things be focused around the great books? What about classes in writing and public speaking? Professors will happily argue about the proper allocation of required classes for hours, but you'll never once hear them comment about the *way* in which these classes are taught. And without decent technique, it doesn't matter what the topic of the class is.

Bok shows deep familiarity with a largely-hidden literature about the effectiveness of college teaching. Nearly 80 percent of all college courses are simply lectures by professors, a stunningly ineffective form of teaching. By the end of a lecture, a student remembers less than half of what was taught. Only a week later, that number is down to 20%. At such stunning rates, it's hard to imagine much is left after a month, let alone by the time the student gets out of college.

And yet nobody seems to care one whit. Bok is hardly to be excepted from this criticism. After the Larry Summers scandal, he was appointed acting president of Harvard University (and before that he was president from 1971 to 1991). Bok expects to only have the job for a year and no doubt his hands are tied in many ways — but rumor about campus is that he wants to make his year count. Yet Bok's biggest changes have been a recommendation for more hands-on activities and the elimination of early admissions. Not bad moves, by any means, but hardly anything like the deep rethinking Bok's book suggests is necessary.

But if Bok — a thoughtful and intelligent figure who has written eloquently about these problems — can't use his position — the most prominent spot in the entire field, with the deadline already on his head freeing him from any accountability — can't do anything about these problems, what hope do we possibly have? Opportunities like this come around once a century and it appears that Bok is going to blow it.

February 9, 2007

DISCIPLINARY BUBBLES

Here's another blog post that's long overdue. There seems to be a surge of interest in the topic lately, so I thought I'd write up my longstanding thoughts.

The academy is often thought of as the ideal for developing knowledge: select the brightest minds in the country, guarantee them jobs, allow them all the resources they need to research anything, don't interfere with any of their conclusions. On some issues, these independent-minded academics form a consensus and we tend to give their consensus very heavy weight. They can't all be wrong, can they?

And yet, in my empirical research, I find they very often are. A short blog post is no place to do a careful study, but I can mention some examples. The classic works in industrial relations turn out to be complete hoaxes, yet they've dominated the teach of the field for over half a century. (See Alex Carey's book[1] for details.) In political science, the most respected practioner's most famous work shades and distorts his own findings to support a theory wildly at odds with the facts. (See Who Really Rules?[2]) The whole field of fMRI studies are so flat-out ridiculous that journal articles are even making jokes about them[3]. And, maybe most blatantly today, economics was dominated by a paradigm that believed substantive unemployment was impossible, despite that notion having been famously and thoroughly debunked by Keynes and, of course, reality.

How is this possible? I think the key, as in most institutional studies, is that of the filter. To become a professor of X, one must first spend several years receiving an undergraduate major in X, then several more years going to graduate school in X, then perhaps work as a postdoc or adjunct for a bit, before getting a tenure-track position and working like mad to make enough of a dent in the field of X to be seen as deserving of a prominent permanent position. When your time is called, a panel of existing professors of X passes judgment on your work to decide if it passes muster. Can you imagine a better procedure for forcing impressionable young minds to believe crazy things?

And so this process forms what I call disciplinary bubbles. Take the case of industrial relations for a moment. The field was largely created by the Rockefellers, who wanted research into how they could get rid of their unions. They paid lavishly and, not surprisingly, found people who told them what they wanted to hear: that treating workers nicely made unions unnecessary and companies more efficient. The studies were completely bogus but the people who conducted them were hailed as heroes, and provided with lavish funding to continue their research. The funding started new departments which trained new proteges, each of whom was taught that the founding studies as gospel. They were told to work on expanding and refining the results, not results, not questioning then, and so they did, becoming industrial relations professors in their own right and continuing the cycle.

Like other bubbles, disciplinary bubbles are difficult to pop. Imagine you do research outside their incorrect assumptions. Your research will simply be marginalized and ignored — you don't get into the conferences or the journals, it's just not seen as valid work. And even if you try to disprove the bogus assumptions, you get ignored. Everyone already in the field has built their careers on those assumptions. They've long rationalized them to themselves; nobody is going to support someone who argues their life's work is built on sand.

Thus ignorance marches on.

October 20, 2009

1. http://www.amazon.com/Taking-Risk-Democracy-Alex-Carey/dp/086840358X

A READING MACHINE

One of the things that has long puzzled me is why children, who so incredibly pick up spoken language without formal instruction, encounter so much trouble when learning to read. Perhaps, I thought for a while, it is because there is a "language organ" that has specifically evolved to let them learn speech while reading has to be learned with more general portions of the brain. But the more I learn about neurology, the more ridiculous that seems.

In retrospect, the answer is rather obvious. Children learn a language because they are surrounded by it. It's unavoidable. Their world is full of people speaking it and the pattern matchers in their brains go to town, figuring out the structures underlying its grammar and associated its vocabulary with the other things they see around them.

It's impossible for there to be anything similar with words. Sure, some words appear in fairly regular positions (MEN on bathroom doors, perhaps) and children may learn to recognize them, but for the most part words are rather avoidable and their patterns hard to spot. How are children to draw a connection between the words in the newspaper and any sentences that they can understand? The only clues are the pictures and anyone who's read picturebooks to a kid knows that kids make valiant use of those few clues, but it's simply not enough to let them learn to read.

What's needed is a way to give children the additional clues they require, but at their own pace. An adult can read books but only reads linearly and soon gets bored of reading the same thing over and over again. (I've often thought that children were being stupid by reading the same things over and over and over again. Now I realize I'm the stupid one; it's the kids who are being smart. Only through repetition can your brain see the patterns!) It's very difficult for children to pick up a pattern under such conditions.

But devices never get tired, so I would propose a device. Here is what I imagine: Give the child an iPad with a special program for reading books. The program provides a selection of nice picture books with words in large type underneath. Switching pages can be done the usual way; kids seem pretty good at figuring out gestural interfaces. But the big innovation is simply this: when you touch a word, it turns red while the speakers say it out loud.

In this way, the child can have the machine read the book to them. Tap the words in sequence and the book pronounces them. If a word is somehow unclear, just tap it again. When you finish the page, just go to the next one. When you finish a book, read another, or start over.

Soon, I imagine, the child will make some basic associations. They will learn that tapping the word "the" makes the sound "thuh" and means "the". They will no longer need to tap it every time to find this out — they can save time by saying it out loud themselves. Eventually, they can just say it in their heads.

Pretty quickly, more and more common words can be handled this way. Then the child begins noticing patterns between common words. All the words beginning with k have a kuh sound! With such patterns recognized, some words can be sounded out. Eventually, only strange words need to be tapped — the rest the child can read by themselves.

People who have not spent much time around children might claim such a device will make children lazy — why learn to read when a device will do it for them? But children are desperate to read; those who cannot will often try to memorize the shorter books their parents read to them so they can pretend to read those books themselves. This device would simply give them the tools they need. It would lead their brains to make the same associations that the software makes occur physically: point at this word, hear this sound. And there's nothing are brains are better at than recognizing such simple patterns and being able to predict them in the future.

Perhaps this software already exists. If so, please tell me. If not, I'd like to work with someone to make it. Will it work? There's only one way to find out, but I think it's got a pretty good shot.

March 29, 2010

LIFE & PARODY

ETHICS BY ANALOGY

For some reason I really learn a lot about things by analogy. I'm not sure if this is because my brain is poorly wired or that there's valuable information I've developed for other situations that I'm just moving over. Does anyone else think this way? (Additionally, my memory is indexed based on space/location, not time like many of my friends.)

As an example, I was able to think about free software licensing by thinking about my toaster. And why ICANN sucks is clear if you think of them as the dictators of a new planet (cyberspace). Just now I think I solve the challenge in a post by Glenn Reynolds by thinking about playground bullies.

Hm, the common theme seems to be moral/ethical questions and outrage. I'd be angry if someone locked me out of my own toaster, why shouldn't I feel the same way about my operating system? I'd revolt if ICANN tried to pass laws to govern the entire planet, why not when they try to govern all domain names? And I'm not too upset when the little guy teaches the playground bully a lesson, isn't the US similar?

I suppose we develop a sense of morals from context and situations. Perhaps by making the connection between seemingly abstract areas of technology to these everyday situations clear, the morally right choice comes into focus.

August 05, 2002

TO THE COURTHOUSE

I guess it's time to reveal the incredibly kind invitation I received. As many of you may have found out or guessed, I will be attending oral argument for the Eldred case before the Supreme Court.

I'm incredibly excited, as you might imagine. Visiting the Supreme Court would be quite enough, but seeing such an important case…Dayenu! When Lessig asked me if I was free that day to come, I laughed because I couldn't (and still can't) think of anything I'd rather do than attend. I am eternally grateful to Lessig for the chance to attend. On the other hand, I'm sort of embarassed to have the opportunity, when there are surely others who deserve it far more than me. Luckily, it seems that such deserving others will be able to get seats by camping in line with us.

So, I'll be arriving in D.C. on Tuesday, attending an Eldred/Duke/EPIC/Bookmobile superparty, and then camping in line with Seth Schoen, Lisa Rein, Jace Cooke but unfortunately not Cory Doctorow. If you'd like to come with us, let me know.

I was hoping I'd be able to take notes and post them to my weblog for those who couldn't make it, but as I read in today's Times, only lawyers and those with official press credentials are allowed to take notes! I think this is outrageous, but hopefully I will be able to remember enough to provide an interesting account.

In a related irony, today was "Disney Day" at Borders, where they played Disney rock songs with the volume turned up too loud, disturbing my usual habit of reading a book there. However, I did manage to skim through *The Practice of Programming*.

In an unrelated note, if you haven't been electrocuted by a Model T spark plug, I highly recommend it.

October 05, 2002

TODAY IS MY BIRTHDAY

It is now my birthday. In the US, we have a tradition that when you blow out the candles on your birthday cake, you should make a wish. Every year, as far back as I can remember, I've wished that I would see another birthday. It's not that I'm afraid of dying, I just liked living.

Living is definitely harder now than it was then, but it's also more rewarding. It's been incredible to work with so many interesting people on so many great things. It's also been difficult, stressful, and painful. But I press on, and continue looking for ways to improve.

On the bright side, my food, clothing, and shelter are taken care of so I'm not a starving artist programmer nor do I want to drive fork-lifts because my family doesn't appreciate my work.

So thanks, to my family and friends. Wes, who has taught me more than I can remember, punched me (in a friendly way) and Lessig, who has given me far more than I could possibly deserve, reminded me that it's my birthday where he is "but remember, not yet in california. forgive them for their slowness." I do.

November 08, 2002

BOOK CONNECTIONS
DEATH AND LIFE, FUTURE OF IDEAS, ELEMENTS OF TYPOGRAPHY

Last week, I began reading *The Death and Life of Great American Cities*[1]. It's a powerful tirade against the vision of America becoming one giant suburb, with green and parks surrounding everything, with the stores carefully separated off from the people. With brilliant prose and volumes of anecdotes and statistics, Jacobs shows why this leads to a life filled with boredom and fraught with danger.

One example: Charles Guggenheim, a documentary filmmaker watched kids in St. Louis at a daycare facility. Half couldn't wait to get home, the other half refused to. The half that refused lived at a project, filled with parks and green but separated from business. There were no people to watch them walk home or business that they could run to in danger, so they were always bullied by kids waiting for them. The kids who lived in the "slum" cities, where there were streets with interesting things to do and people to watch them didn't have this problem.

This week, the library got in Lessig's book, *The Future of Ideas*[2]. (I buy only beautiful books and reference books, the rest I check out from the library or read at the bookstore without purchasing. I guess that makes me a book pirate.) It's an interesting book, showing that commons we depend on are being depleted and how creativity and innovation are being stifled as a result.

The book is trying to make a point and, as a result, seems to ignore technology that could solve these problems. It mentions Wi-Fi, but not as a system where community networks could give themselves real IP service. Napster is discussed, but the possibility of an attack-resistant system is not. Of course, these are two things I'm working on. (Lessig says I'm wrong; details and corrections are appreciated, as always.)

One example: "Davis Guggenheim is a film director. [...] His passion, like is father's before, is documentaries." He has to do tons of work to make sure no copyrighted pictures, buildings, or chairs get into his films. Otherwise, the copyright holder will sue him, as some have sued over a number of other movies and won (at least) preliminary injunctions. Davis can't express himself the way he wants; he has to stay bland instead.

Hm, is Charles the father of Davis? Indeed, he is![3] A surprising coincidence.

Finally, as I was casting about for another book to read yesterday, a package comes. rillian[4] sent me a copy of *The Elements of Typographic Style*[5] for my birthday! Wow, a thousand thanks! It's a beautiful book and a joy to read. The only problem is that, like the Tufte books, I'm afraid I will harm it while reading. I think I'm going to go buy some latex gloves to use.

November 10, 2002

1. http://www.amazon.com/Death-Life-Great-American-Cities/dp/067974195X
2. http://the-future-of-ideas.com/
3. http://www.pbs.org/firstyear/production/
4. http://www.advogato.org/person/rillian/
5. http://www.amazon.com/Elements-Typographic-Style-Robert-Bringhurst/dp/0881791326

WHAT SHOULD I DO WITH MY LIFE?

The "holidays" have given me some time to relax and think about what to do next. What should I do next? Things don't seem as clear cut as they did before. Here are the things that seem interesting:

1. Use wireless to bring back the community-run Internet
2. Write software to make non-commercial copying easier
3. Learn new subjects and read lots of books
4. Answer email (I have 3069 messages to handle) and chat on IRC

1 would be the most fulfilling, but it's extremely difficult and involves a lot of talking to people who live in California and who I'm too nervous to talk to. 2 is eminently doable, but getting users will be hard. 3 is what I've been doing the past few weeks; it's enjoyable but it doesn't seem productive. 4 is what I used to do; it's enjoyable and productive but it didn't seem fulfilling.

To some extent, I guess, I need to do all of them, but I'm very bad at balancing my time. To get 1 or 2 done, I need to throw away all my other comittments, which is difficult. To do 3 or 4, I have to mute the dreams of 1 or 2 which is painful. (I get feelings of being overworked and out-of-control.)

Argh, what should I do?

December 29, 2002

NOTES TO SELF

1. Invent "Next Big Thing" so you can go to Foo Camp[1] (to paraphrase Seth Schoen[2], "You are in a field in Sebastapol. This field has better Internet access than most universities. You are surrounded by 100 of the smartest geeks."). Alternately, sneak in and pose as someone's son. (Reports: Sam Ruby[3], Tim Bray[4].)
2. Follow in the footsteps of Blake Ross[5] and look for "a professional athlete, renowned author, company CEO, leader of a country larger than Alabama, or otherwise someone very important, or [someone] adept at impersonating one of the above" to vouch for me on my Stanford application. (Hey, it worked for him[6].)

October 12, 2003

1. http://wiki.oreillynet.com/foo-camp/csp?HomePage
2. http://vitanuova.loyalty.org/2003-08-07.html
3. http://www.intertwingly.net/blog/1610.html
4. http://www.tbray.org/ongoing/When/200x/2003/10/11/FooNotes
5. http://www.blakeross.com/archives/2002_08_18_index.html#80443703
6. http://blakeross.com/

CHANGE OF COURSE

On my Interblog, anyone can write whatever they feel like. Unconstrained by standards and practices, bloggers feel free to write anything that's fair and accurate. For the past ten years, I've played this sorry game — telling you when I thought my friends books sucked, noting exactly which major media figures offered Schedule III Controlled Substances to teenagers, and speaking frankly about sex. I have finally seen the error of my ways. I plan to become an online magazine.

No more will I defend saying something simply because it is "the truth". No, from now on, I am adopting the rigorous standards of professional journalists. I've been convinced that telling people the truth will just hurt them and, frankly, I'm a little tired of being mocked and shunned for my honesty, which goes completely unappreciated by you people.

So, here's the new regime.

- Like all major newspapers, there will be no factchecking.
- Like *Newsweek*, I will run any possibly unflattering stories by my subjects before publishing them.[1]
- Like Bob Woodward, I will totally adopt the point of view of my sources in a piece, even if this means contradicting a previous piece.
- Like Judith Miller, I will go to jail in order to protect a source who committed a crime.
- Like Judith Miller, I will continue to insist my stories are true even when they obviously aren't.
- Like Ceci Connolly of the *Washington Post* and Chris Vlasto of *ABC News*, I will fabricate quotes and doctor audiotapes if it will help my political cause.
- Like Elizabeth Bumiller of the *New York Times*, I will write complete puff pieces about people in power.
- Like practically everyone famous, I will provide glowing blurbs for books I've never read.
- Like most news outlets, I will no longer try to provide facts about things and instead focus on personality.
- Like Robert Novak, I will promote products from my friends and family without disclosing my association.

The fun starts tomorrow, with a glowing profile of Seth Finkelstein (assuming he approves it, of course). But the first thing I plan to do as a journalist is convene a panel on blogger ethics. Somebody really needs to stop those guys before things get out of hand.

July 16, 2005

Notes:

1. I remember seeing a more detailed piece about this that included quotes from major media figures saying that Newsweek did the right thing in this case. I can't seem to find it but if anybody else can, please let me know.

THE BOOK THAT CHANGED MY LIFE

Two years ago this summer I read a book that changed the entire way I see the world. I had been researching various topics — law, politics, the media — and become more and more convinced that something was seriously wrong. Politicians, I was shocked to discover, weren't actually doing what the people wanted. And the media, my research found, didn't really care much about that, preferring to focus on such things as posters and polls.

As I thought about this more, its implications struck me as larger and larger. But I still had no bigger picture to fit them in. The media was simply doing a bad job, leading people to be confused. We just had to pressure them to do better and democracy would be restored.

Then, one night, I watched the film *Manufacturing Consent: Noam Chomsky and the Media* (I think it had come up in my Netflix queue). First off, it's simply an amazingly-good film. I've watched it several times now and each time I'm utterly entranced. It's undoubtedly the best documentary I've seen, weaving together all sorts of clever tricks to enlighten and entertain.

Second, it makes shocking points. I didn't understand all of what it was saying at the time, but I understood enough to realize that something was severely amiss. The core of the film is a case study of Indonesia's brutal invasion of the country of East Timor. The US personally gave the green light to the invasion and provided the weapons, which allowed Indonesia to massacre the population in an occupation that, per capita, ranks with the Holocaust. And the US media ignores it and when they do cover it, inevitably distorts it.

Shocked and puzzled by the film, I was eager to learn more. Noam Chomsky has dozens of books but I was fortunate to choose to read *Understanding Power*, a thick paperback I picked up at the library. Edited by Peter Mitchell and John Schoeffel, two public defenders in New York, the book is a collection of transcripts of group discussions with Chomsky.

Chomsky lays out the facts in a conversational style, telling stories and explaining things in response to questions from the groups, covering an incredibly wide range of topics. And on every single one, what he tells you is completely shocking, at odds with everything you know, turning the way you see things upside-down. Mitchell and Schoeffel know you're unlikely to believe these things, so they've carefully footnoted and documented every claim, providing blockquote excerpts from the original sources to establish them.

Each story, individually, can be dismissed as some weird oddity, like what I'd learned about the media focusing more on posters than on policy. But seeing them all together, you can't help but begin to tease out the larger picture, to ask yourself what's behind all these disparate things, and what that means for the way we see the world.

Reading the book, I felt as if my mind was rocked by explosions. At times the ideas were too much that I literally had to lie down. (I'm not the only one to feel this way — Norman Finkelstein noted that when he went through a similar experience, "It was a totally crushing experience for me. ... My world literally caved in. And there were quite a number of weeks where ... I just was in bed, totally devastated.") I remember vividly clutching at the door to my room, trying to hold on to something while the world spun around.

For weeks afterwards, everything I saw was in a different light. Every time I saw a newspaper or magazine or person on TV, I questioned what I thought knew about them, wondered how they fit into this new picture. Questions that had puzzled me for years suddenly began making sense in this new world. I reconsidered everyone I knew, everything I thought I'd learned. And I found I didn't have much company.

It's taken me two years to write about this experience, not without reason. One terrifying side effect of learning the world isn't the way you think is that it leaves you all alone. And when you try to describe your new worldview to people, it either comes out sounding unsurprising ("yeah, sure, everyone knows the media's got problems") or like pure lunacy and people slowly back away.

Ever since then, I've realized that I need to spend my life working to fix the shocking brokenness I'd discovered. And the best way to do that, I concluded, was to try to share what I'd discovered with others. I couldn't just tell them it straight out, I knew, so I had to provide the hard evidence. So I started working on a book to do just that. (I'm looking for people to help, if you're interested.)

It's been two years now and my mind has settled down some. I've learned a bunch more but, despite my best efforts, haven't found any problems with this frightening new world view. After all this time, I'm finally ready to talk about what happened with some distance and I hope I'm now able to begin work on my book in earnest.

May 15, 2006

HOWTO: BE MORE PRODUCTIVE

"With all the time you spend watching TV," he tells me, "you could have written a novel by now." It's hard to disagree with the sentiment — writing a novel is undoubtedly a better use of time than watching TV — but what about the hidden assumption? Such comments imply that time is "fungible" — that time spent watching TV can just as easily be spent writing a novel. And sadly, that's just not the case.

Time has various levels of quality. If I'm walking to the subway station and I've forgotten my notebook, then it's pretty hard for me to write more than a couple paragraphs. And it's tough to focus when you keep getting interrupted. There's also a mental component: sometimes I feel happy and motivated and ready to work on something, but other times I feel so sad and tired I can only watch TV.

If you want to be more productive then, you have to recognize this fact and deal with it. First, you have to make the best of each kind of time. And second, you have to try to make your time higher-quality.

SPEND TIME EFFICIENTLY

Choose good problems

Life is short (or so I'm told) so why waste it doing something dumb? It's easy to start working on something because it's convenient, but you should always be questioning yourself about it. Is there something more important you can work on? Why don't you do that instead? Such questions are hard to face up to (eventually, if you follow this rule, you'll have to ask yourself why you're not working on the most important problem in the world) but each little step makes you more productive.

This isn't to say that all your time should be spent on the most important problem in the world. Mine certainly isn't (after all, I'm writing this essay). But it's definitely the standard against which I measure my life.

Have a bunch of them

Another common myth is that you'll get more done if you pick one problem and focus on it exclusively. I find this is hardly ever true. Just this moment for example, I'm trying to fix my posture, exercise some muscles, drink some fluids, clean off my desk, IM with my brother, and write this essay. Over the course the day, I've worked on this essay, read a book, had some food, answered some email, chatted with friends, done some shopping, worked on a couple other essays, backed up my hard drive, and organized my book list. In the past week I've worked on several different software projects, read several different books, studied a couple different programming languages, moved some of my stuff, and so on.

Having a lot of different projects gives you work for different qualities of time. Plus, you'll have other things to work on if you get stuck or bored (and that can give your mind time to unstick yourself).

It also makes you more creative. Creativity comes from applying things you learn in other fields to the field you work in. If you have a bunch of different projects going in different fields, then you have many more ideas you can apply.

Make a list

Coming up with a bunch of different things to work on shouldn't be hard — most people have tons of stuff they want to get done. But if you try to keep it all in your head it quickly gets overwhelming. The psychic pressure of having to remember all of it can make you crazy. The solution is again simple: write it down.

Once you have a list of all the things you want to do, you can organize it by kind. For example, my list is programming, writing, thinking, errands, reading, listening, and watching (in that order).

Most major projects involve a bunch of these different tasks. Writing this, for example, involves reading about other procrastination systems, thinking up new sections of the article, cleaning up sentences, emailing people with questions, and so on, all in addition to the actual work of writing the text. Each task can go under the appropriate section, so that you can do it when you have the right kind of time.

Integrate the list with your life

Once you have this list, the problem becomes remembering to look at it. And the best way to remember to look at it is to make looking at it what you would do anyway. For example, I keep a stack of books on my desk, with the ones I'm currently reading on top. When I need a book to read, I just grab the top one off the stack.

I do the same thing with TV/movies. Whenever I hear about a movie I should watch, I put it in a special folder on my computer. Now whenever I feel like watching TV, I just open up that folder.

I've also thought about some more intrusive ways of doing this. For example, a web page that pops up with a list of articles in my "to read" folder whenever I try to check some weblogs. Or maybe even a window that pops up with work suggestions occasionally for me to see when I'm goofing off.

Make your time higher quality

Making the best use of the time you have can only get you so far. The much more important problem is making more higher quality time for yourself. Most people's time is eaten up by things like school and work. Obviously if you attend one of these, you should stop. But what else can you do?

EASE PHYSICAL CONSTRAINTS

Carry pen and paper

Pretty much everyone interesting I know has some sort of pocket notebook they carry at all times. Pen and paper is immediately useful in all kinds of circumstances — if you need to write something down for somebody, take notes on something, scratch down an idea, and so on. I've even written whole articles in the subway.[1]

(I used to do this, but now I just carry my computerphone everywhere. It doesn't let me give people information physically, but it makes up for it by giving me something to read all the time (email) and pushing my notes straight into my email inbox, where I'm forced to deal with them right away.)

Avoid being interrupted

For tasks that require serious focus, you should avoid getting interrupted. One simple way is to go somewhere interrupters can't find you. Another is to set up an agreement with the people around you: "don't bother me when the door is closed" or "IM me if I have headphones on" (and then you can ignore the IMs until you're free).

You don't want to overdo it. Sometimes if you're really wasting time you should be distracted. It's a much better use of time to help someone else with their problem than it is to sit and read the news. That's why setting up specific agreements is a good idea: you can be interrupted when you're not really focusing.

EASE MENTAL CONSTRAINTS

Eat, sleep, exercise

Time when you're hungry or tired or twitchy is low-quality time. Improving it is simple: eat, sleep, and exercise. Yet I somehow manage to screw up even this. I don't like going to get food, so I'll often work right through being hungry and end up so tired out that I can't bring myself to go get food.[2]

It's tempting to say to yourself, "I know I'm tired but I can't take a nap — I have work to do". In fact, you'll be much more productive if you do take that nap, since you'll improve the quality of the day's remaining time and you were going to have to sleep sometime anyway.

I don't really exercise much so I'm probably not the best person to give advice on that bit, but I do try to work it in where I can. While I'm lying down reading, I do situps. And when I need to go somewhere on foot, I run.

Talk to cheerful people

Easing mental constraints is much harder. One thing that helps is having friends who are cheerful. For example, I always find myself much more inclined to work after talking to Paul Graham or Dan Connolly — they just radiate energy. It's tempting to think that you need to get away from people and shut yourself off in your room to do any real work, but this can be so demoralizing that it's actually less efficient.

Share the load

Even if your friends aren't cheerful, just working on a hard problem with someone else makes it much easier. For one thing, the mental weight gets spread across both people. For another, having someone else there forces you to work instead of getting distracted.

Procrastination and the mental force field

But all of this is sort of dodging the issue. The real productivity problem people have is procrastination. It's something of a dirty little secret, but everyone procrastinates — severely. It's not just you. But that doesn't mean you shouldn't try to stop it.

What is procrastination? To the outside observer, it looks like you're just doing something "fun" (like playing a game or reading the news) instead of doing your actual work. (This usually causes the outside observer to think you're lazy and bad.) But the real question is: what's going on inside your head?

I've spent a bunch of time trying to explore this and the best way I can describe it is that your brain puts up a sort of mental force field around a task. Ever play with two magnets? If you orient the magnets properly and try to push them towards each other, they'll repel fiercely. As you move them around, you can sort of feel out the edges of the magnetic field. And as you try to bring the magnets together, the field will push you back or off in another direction.

The mental block seems to work in the same way. It's not particularly solid or visible, but you can sort of feel it around the edges. And the more you try to go towards it the more it pushes you away. And so, not surprisingly, you end up going in another direction.[3]

And just as you can't get two repelling magnets to sit together just by pushing real hard — they'll fling back as soon as you stop pushing — I've never been able to overcome this mental force field through sheer willpower. Instead, you have to be sneaky about it — you have to rotate a magnet.

So what causes the mental force field? There appear to be two major factors: whether the task is hard and whether it's assigned.

HARD PROBLEMS

Break it down

The first kind of hard problem is the problem that's too big. Say you want to build a recipe organizing program. Nobody can really just sit down and build a recipe organizer. That's a goal, not a task. A task is a specific concrete step you can take towards your goal. A good first task might be something like "draw a mockup of the screen that displays a recipe". Now that's something you can do.[4]

And when you do that, the next steps become clearer. You have to decide what a recipe consists of, what kind of search features are needed, how to structure the recipe database, and so on. You build up a momentum, each task leading to the next. And as your brain gets crunching on the subject, it becomes easier to solve that subject's problems.

For each of my big projects, I think of all the tasks I can do next for them and add them to my categorized todo list (see above). And when I stop working on something, I add its next possible tasks to the todo list.

Simplify it

Another kind of hard problem is the one that's too complicated or audacious. Writing a book seems daunting, so start by doing an essay. If an essay is too much, start by writing a paragraph summary. The important thing is to have something done right away.

Once you have something, you can judge it more accurately and understand the problem better. It's also much easier to improve something that already exists than to work at a blank page. If your paragraph goes well, then maybe it can grow into an essay and then into a book, little by little, a perfectly reasonable piece of writing all the way through..

Think about it

Often the key to solving a hard problem will be getting some piece of inspiration. If you don't know much about the field, you should obviously start by researching it — see how other people did things, get a sense of the terrain. Sit and try and understand the field fully. Do some smaller problems to see if you have a handle on it.

ASSIGNED PROBLEMS

Assigned problems are problems you're told to work on. Numerous psychology experiments have found that when you try to "incentivize" people to do something, they're less likely to do it and do a worse job. External incentives, like rewards and punishments, kills what psychologists call your "intrinsic motivation" — your natural interest in the problem. (This is one of the most thoroughly replicated findings of social psychology — over 70 studies have found that rewards undermine interest in the task.)[5] People's heads seem to have a deep avoidance of being told what to do.[6]

The weird thing is that this phenomenon isn't just limited to other people — it even happens when you try to tell yourself what to do! If you say to yourself, "I should really work on X, that's the most important thing to do right now" then all of the sudden X becomes the toughest thing in the world to make yourself work on. But as soon as Y becomes the most important thing, the exact same X becomes much easier.

Create a false assignment

This presents a rather obvious solution: if you want to work on X, tell yourself to do Y. Unfortunately, it's sort of difficult to trick yourself intentionally, because you know you're doing it.[7] So you've got to be sneaky about it.

One way is to get someone else to assign something to you. The most famous instance of this is grad students who are required to write a dissertation, a monumentally difficult task that they need to do to graduate. And so, to avoid doing this, grad students end up doing all sorts of other hard stuff.

The task has to both seem important (you have to do this to graduate!) and big (hundreds of pages of your best work!) but not actually be so important that putting it off is going to be a disaster.

Don't assign problems to yourself

It's very tempting to say "alright, I need to put all this aside, hunker down and finish this essay". Even worse is to try to bribe yourself into doing something, like saying "alright, if I just finish this essay then I'll go and eat some candy". But the absolute worst of all is to get someone else to try to force you to do something.

All of these are very tempting — I've done them all myself — but they're completely counterproductive. In all three cases, you've basically assigned yourself a task. Now your brain is going to do everything it can to escape it.

Make things fun

Hard work isn't supposed to be pleasant, we're told. But in fact it's probably the most enjoyable thing I do. Not only does a tough problem completely absorb you while you're trying to solve it, but afterwards you feel wonderful having accomplished something so serious.

So the secret to getting yourself to do something is not to convince yourself you have to do it, but to convince yourself that it's fun. And if it isn't, then you need to make it fun.

I first got serious about this when I had to write essays for college. Writing essays isn't a particularly hard task, but it sure is assigned. Who would voluntarily write a couple pages connecting the observations of two random books? So I started making the essays into my own little jokes. For one, I decided to write each paragraph in its own little style, trying my best to imitate various forms of speech. (This had the added benefit of padding things out.)[8]

Another way to make things more fun is to solve the meta-problem. Instead of building a web application, try building a web application framework with this as the example app. Not only will the task be more enjoyable, but the result will probably be more useful.

CONCLUSION

There are a lot of myths about productivity — that time is fungible, that focusing is good, that bribing yourself is effective, that hard work is unpleasant, that procrastinating is unnatural — but they all have a common theme: a conception of real work as something that goes against your natural inclinations.

And for most people, in most jobs, this may be the case. There's no reason you should be inclined to write boring essays or file pointless memos. And if society is going to force you to do so anyway, then you need to learn to shut out the voices in your head telling you to stop.

But if you're trying to do something worthwhile and creative, then shutting down your brain is entirely the wrong way to go. The real secret to productivity is the reverse: to listen to your body. To eat when you're hungry, to sleep when you're tired, to take a break when you're bored, to work on projects that seem fun and interesting.

It seems all too simple. It doesn't involve any fancy acronyms or self-determination or personal testimonials from successful businessmen. It almost seems like common sense. But society's conception of work has pushed us in the opposite direction. If we want to be more productive, all we need to do is turn around.

FURTHER READING

If you want to learn more about the pscyhology of motivation, there is nothing better than Alfie Kohn. He's written many articles on the subject and an entire book, Punished by Rewards, which I highly recommend.

I hope to address how to quit school in a future essay, but you should really just go out and pick up The Teenage Liberation Handbook. If you're a computer person, one way to quit your job is by applying for funding from Y Combinator. Meanwhile, Mickey Z's book The Murdering of My Years features artists and activists describing how they manage to make ends meet while still doing what they want.

December 28, 2005

1. Believe it or not, I actually have written in subways. It's easy to come up with excuses as to why you're not actually working — you don't have enough time before your next appointment, people are making noise downstairs, etc. — but I find that when the inspiration strikes me, I can actually write stuff down on a subway car, where it's absurdly loud and I only have a couple minutes before I have to get out and start walking.
2. The same problem exists for sleep. There's nothing worse than being too tired to go to bed — you just feel like a zombie.
3. Now it turns out I experience this same phenomenon in another area: shyness. I often don't want to call a stranger up on the phone or go talk to someone at a party and I have the exact same mental field pushing me off in some other direction. I suspect this might be because shyness is also a trait that results from a problematic childhood. (See "Assigned problems".) Of course, this is all very speculative.

4. While the terminology I use here ("next concrete step") is derived from David Allen's Getting Things Done, a lot of the principles here are (perhaps even unconsciously) applied in Extreme Programming (XP). Extreme Programming is presented as this system for keeping programs organized, but I find that a lot of it is actually good advice for avoid procrastination.

   For example, pair programming automatically spreads the mental weight of the task across two people as well as giving people something useful to do during lower-quality time. Breaking a project down into concrete steps is another key part of XP, as is getting something that works done right away and improving on it ("Simplify it" infra). And these are just the things that aren't programming-specific.

5. For a fantastic overview of the literature, see Alfie Kohn, Punished By Rewards. This specific claim is drawn from his article Challenging Behaviorist Dogma: Myths About Money and Motivation.

6. I originally simply assumed this was somehow biological, but Paul Graham pointed out it's more likely learned. When you're little, your parents try their best to manipulate you. They say do your homework and your mind tries to wriggle free and think about something else. Soon enough the wriggling becomes habit. Either way, it's going to be a tough problem to fix. I've given up trying to change this; now I try to work around it.

7. Richard Feynman tells a story about how he was trying to explore his own dreams, much the way I've tried to explore my own procrastination. Each night, he'd try to observe what happened to himself as he fell asleep:

   I'm dreaming one night as usual, making observations, … and then I realize I've been sleeping with the back of my head against a brass rod. I put my hand behind my head and I feel that the back of my head is soft. I think, "Aha! That's why I've been able to make all these observations in my dreams: the brass rod has disturbed my visual cortex. All I have to do is sleep with a brass rod under my head and I can make these observations any time I want. So I think I'll stop making observations on this one and go into deeper sleep."

   When I woke up later, there was no brass rod, nor was the back of my head soft. Somehow … my brain had invented false reasons as to why I shouldn't [observe my dreams] any more. (Surely You're Joking, Mr. Feynman!, 50)

   Your brain is a lot more powerful than you are.

8. So, for example, instead of writing "By contrast, Riis doesn't quote many people.", I wrote: "Riis, however, whether because of a personal deficit in the skill-based capacity required for collecting aurally-transmitted person-centered contemporaneous ethnographies into published paper-based informative accounts or simply a lack of preference for the reportage of community-located informational correspondents, demonstrates a total failure in producing a comparable result." The professor, apparently seriously desensitized to bad writing, never seemed to realize I was joking (despite going over the paper with me one-on-one!).

THE INTENTIONALITY OF EVIL

As children we're fed a steady diet of comic books (and now, movies based off of them) in which brave heros save the planet from evil people. It's become practically conventional wisdom that such stories wrongly make the line between good and evil too clear — the world is more nuanced than that, we're told — but this isn't actually the problem with these stories. The problem is that the villains know they're evil.

And people really grow up thinking things work this way: evil people intentionally do evil things. But this just doesn't happen. Nobody thinks they're doing evil — maybe because it's just impossible to be intentionally evil, maybe because it's easier and more effective to convince yourself you're good — but every major villain had some justification to explain why what they were doing was good. Everybody thinks they're good.

And if that's the case, then intentionality doesn't really matter. It's no defense to say (to take a recently famous example) that New York bankers were just doing their jobs, convinced that they were helping the poor or something, because everybody thinks they're just doing their jobs; Eichmann thought he was just doing his job.

Eichmann, of course, is the right example because it was Hannah Arendt's book Eichmann in Jerusalem: A Report on the Banality of Evil that is famously cited for this thesis. Eichmann, like almost all terrorists and killers, was by our standards a perfectly normal and healthy guy doing what he thought were perfectly reasonable things. And if that normal guy could do it, so could we. And while we could argue who's worse — them or us — it's a pointless game since its our actions that we're responsible for. And looking around, there's no shortage of monstrous crimes that we've committed.

So the next time you mention one to someone and they reply "yes, but we did with a good intent" explain to them that's no defense; the only people who don't are characters in comic books.

June 23, 2005

SERIOUS SOCIAL SCIENCE

I once attended a psychology lecture in which the speaker argued that Freud was really a brilliant psychologist, but the field had passed him by because of its "physics envy". His specific example is perhaps easy to mock, but it has resonance because the problem is a real one. As Paul Graham shows, in general physicists are smarter than social scientists. But (to use a Grahamism), like kids trying to act adult, the social scientists end up emulating the form of these fields but not the content. In other words, instead of getting smarter, they play make-believe.

The first thing that comes is the numbers. Real science papers are filled with tables and graphs and regressions on piles of data, so the social scientists decide to do all that. In economics, they even go so far as to start coming up with equations and proving theorems. Then comes the technical language. Physics papers discuss the "gravitational wave perturbations about a brane cosmology embedded in a five-dimensional anti-de Sitter bulk" so the cult studs decide they should be just as incomprehensible.

And then, in the headiness of this newfound power of science, grand claims are made. As J. K. Galbraith writes (Annals of an Abiding Liberal, p. 4): "It is the great desire of nearly all economists to see their subject as a science too. Accordingly, and without much thought, they hold that its matter is also fixed. The business firm, the market, the behavior of the consumer, like the oxygen molecule or the geologist's granite, are given."

This is not to say that there is anything intrinsically wrong with using math or jargon or making grand claims. But to adopt these habits reflexively is to put the means before the ends. Scientists do not use math because it is complicated but because, for what they are doing, it is effective. Their grand pronouncements become accepted because (sometimes, at least) they are true.

Such complaints, among a certain sector, are truisms. But the conclusion typically drawn with them is pure pessimism. Social behavior, they argue, is simply too complex for us to ever make real progress in the field. The topic is studied by idiots and charlatans because the intelligent and honest can immediately see its impossibility. I do not agree with such a view. In fact, I think it is only possible to maintain it thru abject ignorance of what science really knows.

The vulgar postmodern critique of science argued that scientists had become our modern priesthood: deified as "experts" they would make claims about how the world worked, claims with just as much authority as those made by religion in earlier times. And while such comparisons were wrong, they did betray a truth: society has, for largely selfish reasons, inflated the accomplishments of science beyond their actual existence. (See R. C. Lewontin's fabulous Biology as Ideology for evidence of this theme, from a respected scientist.)

Scientists — even the hardest of scientists — fabricate data, fabricate studies, fall prey to fads, and otherwise get things wrong. But more relevantly, they just don't know that much. We have very little idea of how the body works; the pills we take are made through the bluntest of means. We don't know how to calculate very simple things, like the dispersion of milk in a cup of coffee. The illusion that social science is ineffective can only be sustained by ignorance of such ineffectiveness of hard science. The upside of all this is that there is hope for social science.

So what is to be done? For reasons beyond the scope of this article, its unlikely that the existing disciplines can be reformed. Instead what is needed is a culture of serious social science built outside the existing systems of academia. Its work should be primarily outwardly-facing, because that's the important audience. This means clear writing (unlike this article, perhaps) for public consumption. And it means compilations of broad scope, instead of obscure monographs.

We can already see the beginnings of such a thing in the work by people like Doug Henwood and Christian Parenti. But there is certainly much more to do, including building structures to do the work in.

So that's the other thing I'm thinking about.

July 21, 2005

EAT AND CODE

Life seems so incredibly overworked and overcomplicated that you pare it down to the bare essentials: eat and code. Surely you should be able to handle this without distraction. Unfortunately, it's not so easy.

Let's take eating.

To be honest, I've always had a problematic relationship with food. I always liked plain things — the year before college I lived mostly off of eating plain, microwaved bagels. At oriental restaurants I would always just order steamed white rice. Wes Felter, noting I would apparently only eat white food joked, referencing a Science Fiction novel, that I would eat light bulbs, but "only the white ones". This reached its extremes at a World Wide Web conference where all the food was white, even the plate it was on. Tim Berners-Lee later pulled my mother aside to share his concerns about this diet.

Finally, one day at an oriental restaurant by Stanford (years before I went to school there), we had the typical discussion except this time Cory Doctorow spoke up: 'are you sure you're not a supertaster?' he asked. I had heard the They Might Be Giants song but never considered the possibility. I thought about it as the conversation continued and it seemed to make sense to me. [At this point I imagine a crane shot lifting up and up over the conversation at the restaurant. Fade to:] I did some research on the Internet and did the test (which formally consists of putting blue food coloring on your tongue, taking a piece of paper with a three-hole punch, placing it over the tongue and counting the number of taste buds in it) and indeed, I am a supertaster. This hasn't eliminated the discussions about my eating habits, but it does shift the blame.

In any event, I'm not one for the fine arts of cooking. So it's always seemed attractive to me to have a simple food that tastes decent that I can just pull out and eat whenever I want. And, lo, it appeared that I had found it: Cheerios. Cheerios claimed on the box to be healthy, they had little in the way of taste, I could eat them whenever I want, they had big boxes of them at the corner grocery store — everything seemed great. Cheerio boxes piled up in the corner.

There were some problems, though. I didn't eat them with water or milk, which meant that a fine Cheerio dust went everywhere. This dust was so fine that it got into invisible cracks in my laptop's surface and apparently bonded with the metal and had to be scraped out each time I ate. And then I begun to discover that the Cheerio dust was also into my system, possibly even my lungs and giving me some Cheerio form of silicosis; they made it difficult to breathe deeply. 'Wouldn't it be ironic if I died of pneumonoultramicroscopicsilicovolcanoconiosis?' I asked Simon. (I chose pneumonoultramicroscopicsilicovolcanoconiosis as a spelling word in 6th grade.)

At the same time, I was suffering from bouts of acid reflux which continued to grow in frequency and severity. First just some acid. Then, one night walking back from a Noam Chomsky lecture, I began to cough of what felt like my stomach lining. I gave up the Cheerios but it didn't help. Last night I threw up my entire dinner.

And then what do I eat instead? We go for regular meals at 12 and 6 but I'm only sporadically hungry and the food is getting boring. In Science Fiction stories, we imagine small packets of food that are healthy but taste like whatever we enjoy. Forget that, I'd be happy with just packets of food that are healthy. I'm sick of having to worry about food.

And then there's programming. When I'm feeling good, I'll have bouts of just amazing productivity, doing everything that needs to be done in hours. The only problem is that these good days are followed by a week of bad ones, where I feel tired or depressed or scared and can't quite force myself to sit and face the code.

I used to think this was just cowardice, that I just needed to sit down and program and I'd get the same level of productivity again. But what if this is some serious limit in my brain? What if programming takes so much out of me that it takes days to recharge? I've never seriously considered this possibility before, but it's not just fatalism — it has real implications for how I should structure my days.

The last time I was fighting procrastination I was watching a bunch of good television shows. And as part of this, I would read Tim Goodman, the Roger Ebert of television critics. I was struck to learn one day that even Tim Goodman, whose job was to literally sit down and watch TV, could not bring himself to accomplish this task. I mean, I knew all about Structured Procrastination but surely it had its limits. How could someone procrastinate sitting down and watching TV? And yet, here it was before my eyes — my favorite television critic, a hardworking and thoughtful man who had even spent a column answering a question I sent him, even though I lived in Chicago at the time.

The lesson I drew from this is that the human mind is such that whatever you do, it will try to avoid it. So you might as well aim high. Now the question is: what do you do with the rest of time?

August 2, 2005

THE MIRACLE DIET

You eat food that has calories. And you do things that burn calories. The calories left over get stored as fat. And thus, the typical advice for losing weight: eat less, exercise more. Fewer calories are eaten and more are burned and so the result is less fat. There's just one problem: that's really hard. To burn enough calories to lose a lot of weight, you really have to put an awful lot of time into it. And if you try to eat less, your body just feels hungry all the time, because it wants more.

So what if instead of forcing your body to eat less, you teach your body to want less. After all, it's clear that it's obesity, not lack of fat, that's the health problem. So getting your body to want less food would be a good thing. And it would make dieting incredibly easy too — instead of fighting to count calories or avoid eating certain foods, you do nothing at all; you're just not interested in eating.

It sounds like a pipe dream, but Seth Roberts argues that it's possible. Drawing on the results of a number of studies with rats, his own experiments on himself, and the best research on nutrition and weight loss, he's developed a theory of how the body decides what it feels like eating.

Our body's weight, he says, is regulated by a "set point", like the setting on a thermostat. If our weight is lower than our internal set point, we feel hungry; higher, we feel full. So if you want to weigh less, all you need to do is lower your body's set point. Your body will stop being hungry, you'll burn the fat you already have, and your weight will go down.

But how would you do that? Roberts argues that a person's set point isn't fixed, instead it goes up and down based on what they eat. After all, the whole reason the body stores up calories when food is abundant is so it can use them in "lean years", when food is scarce. So it would make sense for a person's set point to go up when food is abundant (allowing them to build up fat) and down when it's scarce (so they don't feel hungry all the time).

The problem, of course, is that food is never scarce anymore. You can always just go to McDonald's. The body is storing up for an eventuality that will never come. So how do you get it to stop? Maybe you could trick it into thinking food was scarce.

This is where Roberts's big insight comes — he argues that we use a Pavlovian sort of flavor-conditioning system to see whether food is scarce. If we eat foods frequently, we grow to like their taste, and thus our brain realizes we're eating them out of choice and raises the set point. On the other hand, if we eat new foods or foods with little taste, our brain assumes we're eating them because there's nothing else around and the set point is lowered.

And thus, the way to lower your set point: eat foods with no taste. Of course, they have to have calories as well, so Roberts's preferred suggestion is extra-light olive oil (ELOO), which is basically just oil with absolutely no taste. Your body gets the calories but it doesn't get the taste, so the set point goes lower every time you eat it.

It all seems crazy, but Roberts is sort of a crazy guy, so he decided to test it. He started taking a couple hundred tasteless calories every day. Almost immediately, he begun feeling less hungry. He started eating one meal every other day, even while still exercising, and felt great. He lost a pound of weight a week with no effort. He lost so much weight that his friends started telling him that he looked too thin, so he started taking less tasteless calories and put some weight back on. It was amazing; a diet plan unlike any other.

He told friends about it and it worked for them too. It was written up in The *New York Times* and readers wrote in with letters saying it was working for them. Blogs started to keep track of people's stories — almost all successful. And now he has a new book yesterday, The Shangri-La Diet, which explains how you can do it to.

The book is odd, in that it looks pretty much like any other silly diet book, but the contents are rather different. Although clearly rushed, the book has an appendix of scientific studies using rats to back up its arguments about theory and happily features the stories of people who tried the diet and found it didn't work along with those who tried the diet and found it did.

Obviously, such anecdotal evidence isn't enough to prove the system works, but it does make it intriguing enough to try. I've started taking a couple tablespoons of extra light olive oil and already I found myself skipping a meal, something I've never been able to do before. We'll see how it goes.

April 26, 2006

A FUTURE WITHOUT FAT

I've been on the Shangri-La diet long enough to convince myself that there's definitely something to it. Yesterday, for example, I spent all morning moving furniture (we're moving to a new apartment) and around lunch time I got invited to lunch at a favorite pizza place with a friend and I jogged all the way there. Normally, at this point, I'd be famished and devour half a pizza. This time, I wasn't hungry at all (but I had a slice out of politeness).

Of course, there's no reason my particular anecdotes should be more convincing than any others, but they are convincing to me, so I'd like to move from discussing the diet to discussing its implications. Weight and trying to lose it is a huge part of American culture and a system that makes doing it trivially easy will have far-reaching effects.

The most basic, it would seem, is more thin people. There's clearly an enormous number of people who want to lose weight. A lot are so desperate that they will try any number of painful and crazy tactics, from Slim-Fast shakes to Atkins meals, that are touted as helping. Obviously these people will try the diet.

But also a large number of people (like myself) who see themselves as too skeptical to fall for a fad diet or too lazy to jump through its hoops will try this diet, since it's both scientifically proven (or will be, after further clinical trials) and super-easy. And unlike Atkins, there are few concerns about nutritional dangers — the diet doesn't require you to change the balance of foods you eat, just the quantity — so a bunch more reasons not to do it disappear.

As it takes off, commercial products will soon follow — branded pocket-sized flasks of ELOO, for example. The media will do stories on this latest craze and the ideas behind it. Clinical trials will demonstrate its effectiveness and suggest areas for further research, which will lead to it being refined. And popular culture will likely try to deal with the results.

Among those results: lots of people you know getting thin. It's difficult to imagine what this is going to be like. The fat guy at the office won't be fat anymore. That cute-but-slightly-overweight girl you've had your eye on won't be slightly overweight anymore. Social dynamics will be seriously disrupted in a way that, to my knowledge, has no analog. People have gotten taller, and thinner, and prettier over time, to be sure, but never quite this fast.

The flip side of the drive to be thinner is the discrimination against those who are fat. American culture is simply vicious towards the less fortunate. You're poor because you're lazy, it says, and you're fat for the same reason. If only you got some exercise or ate better, you'd look fine. It's your own damn fault and there's nothing wrong with me looking down on you for it.

If the theory behind the diet is correct, however, this just isn't so. Fat people are that way simply because their body's set point is too high. That's not really anything you can blame them for and it's also something that, before the diet, was really hard to fix. They live with a burden of wanting to eat that thin people, with their lower set point, never have to deal with. And the entire time they've been struggling, they've been told it's simply their own damn fault. (As I noted, their situation mirrors that of the poor.)

Of course, it's unlikely our culture will ever notice the horrors its committed against fat people. Instead, the diet is likely to make it even more vicious. Now that there's a simple easy way to get thin, anyone who refuses to use it will be turned against with serious scorn. Being fat may become as much of a social rudity as being a smoker, with strangers feeling that they can lecture you about your unhealthy lifestyle in public. It'll be pure torture.

But, I have no doubt, it'll work. Sipping ELOO is much easier than quitting smoking and tons of people are doing the latter. And so the last few overweight people will be pushed to join the pack. While it's unlikely that obesity will be entirely eradicated, it's hard to imagine the last few hangers-on (perhaps those for whom the diet doesn't work or who can't do it for some reason) making up a significant sect of the population.

The diet book itself saves most of its vision for future generations who, it suggests, will never have to think about obesity at all because the new science behind the diet will allow us to build it right into our foods, so that we will simply never get fat in the first place. Certainly, at a minimum, children's set points will be regulated from a very early age (what parent wouldn't want to spare their child from fat-kid teasing?) and they'll likely never even consider another possibility.

To our children, obesity will probably seem like just another relatively-rare disease, like a learning disability or a speech impediment. They'll look back at movies from our time and think — well, actually, they won't notice anything because we've already removed the fat people from them.

April 28, 2006

FAT BACKLASH

They told me exercise and diet
If I would try it, would cure my ills
But though I'm already past my quota
I want another load o' those magic pills
— They Might Be Giants, "Renew My Subscription"[1]

The response to my suggestion that there might be a simple and painless way to lose weight brought some interesting responses. Many people who wrote in were excited about it or were actually trying it. But some of the rest were downright hostile.

Tuomov wrote:

No pain, no loss. Forget all these bullshit weight-loss manuals. Those four words above summarise all that you need to know. The rest is just pain management and scheduling. If you don't feel hungry occasionally, you're not losing weight.

And Martijn commented:

But how is this healthy? This diet sounds like a trick to fool your body. […] Why not just eat well? […] Somehow people want to lose weight the easy way, pff.. just prooves how lazy this 'McDonalds' generation has become.

Such comments strike me as slightly odd. "Eat better" has been the diet advice for as long as I can remember and undoubtedly everyone overweight has heard it by now. And yet, as these writers clearly know, obesity is, as I understand it, an epidemic in this country. So this supposed solution clearly isn't working. Yes, it might work in the sense that if everyone followed it they'd be fine (although even that is somewhat unclear), but plainly it's too hard to follow. If our goal is to actually stop obesity, then we're failing.

But I suspect for some people, that isn't the goal. And Martijn's last sentence hints at this. In my last piece I drew an analogy between being poor and being fat. And I think this rage at an easy way to lose weight parallels the rage we see at "government handouts" that provide an "easy way out" of being poor.

(To be clear, I'm talking about people who are opposed to easy ways to lose weight in general; not the people who were skeptical about this diet in particular or sick of fad diets altogether. Such reactions are perfectly right and reasonable.)

This is one thing I didn't really predict in my last piece on the subject, but undoubtedly such far-reaching changes will also have their backlash. People who have spent their whole lives putting themselves through the pain of starvation and strenuous exercise to maintain their physique are undoubtedly going to be a little upset to figure out it was all unnecessary. It would be bad enough if it was some new invention that made fat disappear — after all, it hadn't been invented yet when they'd gone through all that so there was no way they could take advantage of it. But olive oil and sugar water? That's been around forever! How could they have missed it?

Ronald Reagan got elected campaigning against imaginary "welfare queens" in supposed-Cadillacs. Will right-wing politicians of the future rail against those who take the easy way out of being fat?

One major difference is that economics is at least thought to be a zero-sum game. Those welfare queens are taking "*your money*", in the form of taxes. But you lose nothing if more people get thin. By the same token, there's not a whole lot the government can do about this problem. The welfare payments were theirs, so they could cut them (as Clinton savagely did) but what's the government going to do about the diet? Ban olive oil?

Perhaps instead we'll see social pressure. The major visible difference between someone on the diet and someone who isn't (considering that the olive oil can be taken in private) is that someone who's on the diet simply doesn't eat much. But eating is a major social function, around which much business and friendship is conducted. Perhaps backlash members will heap scorn on those who skip lunch or eat little, perhaps even ostracizing them until they start eating like normal (and thus weakening the effects of the diet).

I've seen a little bit of this myself — as a supertaster, my tastes are sufficiently strange that when eating with new people I'm often asked about my choice of food and then queried and lightly mocked for my explanation. It's not so bad and I'm sure people mean perfectly well by it, but it is a cost and if people are actually angry about the diet, it may get worse.

So while actually being fat may go away easily, the stigma might be a little harder to erase.

May 7, 2006

1. http://www.tmbw.net/wiki/index.php/Renew_My_Subscription

ON LOSING WEIGHT

Exactly three months ago, I wrote about the *Shangri-La Diet*. While I started on it basically immediately, it wasn't until exactly two months ago that I got a scale to measure my weight with (so some data has been lost). Since I got the scale, however, I've lost over twenty pounds.

Shockingly, losing weight has to be one of the easiest things I've ever done. I simply don't eat unless I'm really hungry and then I eat as little as possible (a couple crackers, for example). Most days I just have a couple crackers in the evening. It saves time and money and hassle (and makes it easy to eat healthy) and while I do get some weird looks from friends at restaurants, always being a fussy eater that's nothing new. (Furthermore, there's some evidence that not eating significantly prolongs lifespan.)

The one thing that really did surprise me is that while I predicted there would be strong social pressures to lose weight, in reality all the pressure seemed to go the other way. Friends and acquaintances urge me to eat more, doctors think I'm sick, family members suggest I have an eating disorder. Part of this is probably just due to novelty: While "eat less" is standard advice for losing weight, because we all have set points no one is actually able to pull it off. Thus when someone actually does losing weight by eating less, it's usually because they really are sick or something like that. But in my darker moments, I wonder if part of it is selfish. The extraordinarily thin people encouraging me to eat more, I darkly wonder, don't want me to be like them. The people who need to lose some weight don't like the example of my success. I don't like thinking this way, and I have no evidence for it, but it's hard to resist.

There's not much more to say; food is even less a part of my life than it was before. I still plan to lose more weight and will provide further updates accordingly. Still, since many people seem to be interested in the topic (and in keeping with the theme of my blog), a diary of my three months follows.

The first thing I noticed was the burping. When losing weight, it seems you burp quite a bit. But even worse is the feeling of wanting to burp. The olive oil, it seems, has inflated my stomach with gas, making me desperately want to burp, but I can't. In fact, it was so painful that I decided to stop taking the olive oil. I still ate less — it seems like once the olive oil lowered my set point, it was easy to keep things off from there. There were a couple days after eating lots where I would feel hungry for long periods of time and had to ignore it, but if I did that for a whole day, my set point went down, just like with the olive oil.

I went back home and saw some old friends at my high school's graduation. Many of them commented on how thin I was. I was kind of surprised, because I didn't think I was noticeably thinner yet, but I have to say I enjoyed the compliment. While on this vacation I told myself I'd forget the diet and would eat all the good home foods I missed. But even doing this, I couldn't gain weight while on vacation. I was taken out to a nice restaurant downtown but couldn't finish my hamburger (which I typically had no problem doing) — when I was half way through if I took another bite I felt like I was going to throw up, so I just stopped. When I got back, I weighed basically the same as when I'd left.

As I lost more weight I began to feel better. I'd look in the mirror and notice the fat that had disappeared from my chest, or when lying down I'd notice my legs were thinner. I felt like I had more energy. I felt happier. I felt more mobile, more able to move around and do things now that there was less of me. It felt wonderful.

One week I lost seven pounds in almost as many days and friends began to look at me with concern. But I didn't mind; I thought it was great. I had started eating significantly less, hardly anything at all really. When I moved into this new apartment (just as I was starting the diet), I thought I would have a hard time finding novel places to eat each day. But it hasn't been hard at all; I've hardly gone out to eat by myself once since I started the diet, except to treat myself to a food I already knew I loved.

Writing about a gastric bypass (a surgery in which the stomach is shrunk to help those who are extremely overweight lose weight) patient, surgeon Atul Gawande describes a sensation I found extremely familiar:

> [...] She [lost so much weight that] was unrecognizable to anyone who had known her before, and even to herself. "I went to bars to see if I could get picked up — and I did," she said. "I always said no," she quickly added, laughing. "But I did it anyway."
>
> The changes weren't just physical, though. She had slowly found herself to have a profound and unfamiliar sense of willpower over food. She no longer had to eat anything: "Whenever I eat, somewhere in the course of that time I end up asking myself, 'Is this good for you? Are you going to put on weight if you eat too much of this?' And I can just stop." The feeling baffled her. She knew, intellectually, that the surgery was why she no longer ate as much as she used to. Yet she felt as if she were choosing not to do it.
>
> Studies report this to be a typical experience of successful gastric bypass patients. [...]

(Atul Gawande, Complications, 174)

The newfound willpower allowed me to be more conscious about my diet. I started thinking about what foods I wanted to eat and researching the topic of nutrition. I read Walter Willett's book about the results of his epidemiological nutrition studies and begun looking at the labels of boxes I ate. I begun ordering different things at restaurants when I did eat and buying different things at the supermarket. But most of all I found myself eating less.

When this proved not to be enough, I found myself exercising. I seemed to be more out-of-shape now than it did when I started — I suspect with all the weight loss I lost some other things too — but exercising was probably easier to find the motivation for now. I fixed up my watch and started timing myself, trying to make sure I lost the weight I wanted to; this, of course, after I already lost twenty pounds and had stopped eating almost entirely.

Losing weight had other effects too, some that saved further time. Although I feel I have more energy overall, I still get tired. Sometimes I just lie in bed thinking, when I feel little pops in my thighs as my body breaks into the fat it has stored up over the years to find energy to fuel me with. And at those moments I can only smile.

July 26, 2006

NUTRITION BASICS

As part of changing my eating habits, I've become quite interested on the subject of nutrition. I can't seem to find a good guide to the subject online, so in the spirit of flailing in public until someone comes to my aid, I thought I'd write up what I think I know.

Calories are the basis of eating; they're a measure of the amount of energy a food provides. Your body gets calories from the food you eat and spends them to keep you moving. If you get more calories than you spend, your body stores the excess as fat. If you spend more than you get, your body burns some of the fat it's stored up (for just such an occasion).

Thus the standard advice for losing weight: eat less, exercise more. Eating less brings fewer calories in, while exercising more uses up more of them. Unfortunately, both of these things are quite hard to achieve, because the body seems to regulate them through the use of "set points": your body keeps track of how much fat you have through a chemical called leptin and makes you hungry if you're starting to lose weight. Thus, if you skip a meal in the morning, it'll be sure to make you extra hungry in the evening, so that your overall weight doesn't change.

A similar setpoint seems to operate for exercise. In one experiment, doctors measured how much children moved around with pedometers. Then they tried forcing the children to exercise by giving them a PE class. They found that when kids were forced to exercise at school, they exercised less at home, and ended up doing the same amount of exercise overall. So just as your body seems to make you hungry when you're losing weight and full when you're gaining it, it seems to make you tired when you've burned too many calories and antsy when you haven't burned enough. Of course, we're not total slaves to such motivations — we can force ourselves when to eat when full or not to eat when hungry, to exercise when tired or to stay still when antsy — but it's worth keeping in mind what we're up against.

Fats have gotten a bad rap, most likely because they share a name with body fat but also, some argue, because they seem lower-class. In truth, however, they're largely just one way to get calories, and a calorie is a calorie no matter where it comes from.

Fats also have effects on **cholesterol**, a key building block for your body's cells. There are two types of cholesterol — known informally as good and bad cholesterol. Good cholesterol consists of tightly-packed proteins of cholesterol in your blood stream, allowing cholesterol to be efficiently transported where it needs to go. Bad cholesterol is less densely packed and its cholesterol ends up sticking in the walls of arteries, clogging them and leading to heart disease. Fats have varying effects on cholesterol. Saturated fats should be avoided: they increase levels of bad cholesterol (although they also increase good cholesterol). Unsaturated fats, however, whether monounsaturated or polyunsaturated, are good: they lower bad cholesterol and raising good cholesterol. Trans fats are just the reverse: they increase bad cholesterol levels and decrease good ones; it's recommended they be avoided as much as possible.

Often nutrition labels only break out unsaturated fats and trans fats; you have to calculate the amount of saturated fat by subtracting these from the amount of total fat. The goal, remember, is to avoid trans fats whenever possible, avoid saturated fats, and go for unsaturated fats.

Carbohydrates are another source of calories, the kind found in white wheat products, like bread and pasta. **Sugars** are a form of carbohydrate and, in fact, the body breaks down other carbohydrates into simple sugars. The problem with sugars is that they go directly into the bloodstream, spiking your blood sugar level. This in itself is unhealthy, but it's even worse when the level inevitably crashes and you begin to feel hungry again and eat even more.

The exception is with fiber, which the body can't break down. Foods made from whole wheat are high in fiber, so your body takes longer to digest them and the sugar intake is spread out over a longer period of time. Thus while carbohydrates might generally be avoided, whole wheat products (along with fruits and vegetables), include additional nutrients as well as having a safe impact on blood sugar, and are the foundation of a healthy diet.

Protein is a similar essential nutrient, allowing the body to make essential components of muscle and hair and so on. If you don't get enough (about 9 grams of protein for every 20 pounds), the body begins breaking down its tissues. (Eating far too much protein, however, as people in low-carb diets do, can be unhealthy as it absorbs calcium from your bones.) While protein can be found in animal products, whole wheat bread is a also an excellent source — a single slice contains five grams of protein. Unfortunately, the proteins found in grains and vegetables are incomplete, so you either need to get some (complete) animal protein or eat a variety of them.

Calcium is necessary for building bones and teeth, maintaining the heart's rhythmym, and more. Deficiency can lead to weakened bones and fractures. While dairy products contain significant amounts of calcium, they also contain a lot of saturated fat and has been linked to some cancers. Many other foods are fortified with calcium and some vegetables (kale and collard greens, dried beans, and legumes) are also a good source.

Vitamins do all sorts of good things, as well as warding off diseases like scurvy and rickets. They're often added to juices and cereals and can be taken by themselves in a daily multivitamin as well.

For additional information, check out: Nutrition Source[1], Harvard School of Public Health.

July 28, 2006

1. http://www.hsph.harvard.edu/nutritionsource/

SIMPLE TIPS FOR LONGER LIVING

Understanding the human body and food's effects on it over long periods of time is hard. Counting, by contrast, is easy. This, at least, is the premise behind the Nurses Health Study, a multi decade project by Harvard to gather empirical information about nutrition. The idea behind the study is simple: collect a reasonably large group of people all in a rather similar situation (nurses) and have them fill out a yearly survey with two questions: "what did you eat?" and "are you dead yet?" They've been doing this since 1976.

Then you simply punch the information into a computer and figure out what foods kill people. The results, as described in the associated book *Eat, Drink, and Be Healthy* provide some simple tips for living longer.

Replace white bread with whole wheat. White bread is simply whole wheat bread shorn of all its nutritional value. Whole wheat has more nutrients, more protein, etc. Plus, white bread is metabolized quickly by your body so it leads to huge spikes in blood sugar which have unhealthy effects on your body and make you hungry after you crash; whole wheat bread is digested more evenly.

Replace burgers with chicken. Dark meat when grilled can lead to potential carcinogens, whereas white meat is overall healthier. Chicken contains less saturated (bad) fat while dark meat may give you too much iron.

Replace soft drinks with water. These results are from the same study[1] but weren't featured in the book. Drinking a soda makes you 85% more likely to develop diabetes and can cause you to gain up to ten pounds. "It's probably that high amounts of sugar in the bloodstream put an increased demand for insulin on the pancreas," the study's author explains.

I'm about the fussiest eater I know and even I can handle these changes. Whole wheat bread even tastes better than white.

July 31, 2006

1.   http://www.usatoday.com/news/health/2004-06-08-diabetes-soda_x.htm

SAY GOODBYE TO EMBARRASSMENT

I've decided to stop being embarrassed. I'm saying goodbye to the whole thing: that growing suspicion as the moment approaches, that sense of realization when it comes, that rush of blood reddening your cheeks, that brief but powerful desire to jump out of your own skin, and then finally that attempt big fake smile trying to cover it all. Sure, it was fun for a while, but I think it's outlived its usefulness. It's time for embarrassment to go.

Turning off an emotion is always a tough decision. I remember how a couple years ago I decided to say goodbye to anger. Sure, anger has its bright moments — you haven't really lived until you've known that special joy of hurling a chair across the room — but it's also quite time-consuming. Every time someone comes up and hits you, you have to run around chasing after them. And once you start getting angry it's hard to stop — an angry person doesn't really want to calm down, it sort of enjoys being angry. So I finally decided to get rid of the whole thing. And you know what? I haven't regretted the decision one bit.

Regret — that's another interesting emotion. I mean, what purpose does it really serve? "There's no use crying over spilled milk," my mom once told me when I started sobbing after I got milk all over the floor while trying to make cereal. "I suppose that's true," I replied between sobs. "Although maybe my tears will dilute the milk and make it stick to the floor less." But I was wrong — the milk stayed just as sticky. So maybe regret should be the next one to go.

But actually, I think it's going to be frustration. It's not discussed much, but frustration is really quite distracting. You're trying to solve some difficult problem but it's just not working. Instead of taking a moment to try and think of the solution, you just keep getting more and more frustrated until you start jumping up and down and smashing various things. So not only do you waste time jumping, but you also have to pay to replace the stuff you smashed. It's really a net loss.

But that's a decision for another time. Today it's time for embarrassment to join anger in the wastebasket of deactivated emotions. It might take some getting used to at first — when friends try to tease me about something I'll probably start to react before realizing there's just no need for it anymore — but before long I'm sure it will seem normal. Even if I'm a less normal person for it.

January 8, 2006

TIPS FOR BETTER THINKING

Go to the library and you'll find whole bookcases full of books on how to write better. But look for a book on how to think better and you'll be busy for a while. (The only major book I could find — *Crimes Against Logic* — was a dreadful little series of basic logical fallacies dressed up in political polemic.)

It can't be that writing is more important than thinking. While I've met many people who can't exactly write, it seems that just about everyone has to think — even writers. Nor do I think it's that the task is really harder. We know very little about the internal process of writing, so writing guides consist mostly of good and bad examples, along with some general rules. Surely one could do the same for thought.

Perhaps the answer is that there isn't such a thing as good thinking. But the case for it seems even stronger than the case for good writing. Good thinking is that which better helps us approximate reality — avoiding fallacies, missteps of judgment, faulty assumptions, misunderstandings, and needless fillips and loops.

And yet the subject's plain importance, I can find scarcely an article that takes up the topic. Where is the piece that savages bad thinking the way Mark Twain savaged Fenimore Cooper's aimless writing[1] or the way Orwell went after political abuses of English[2] or, for more modern readers, Matt Taibbi's dissection of Thomas Friedman's latest book[3]? It seems like it would be just as fun — if not more — to watch a gifted writer slice and dice up a convoluted thought until it becomes apparent that it's actually meaningless.

The closest I can think of is Chomsky's review of B.F. Skinner[4] (an unfair match-up if there ever was one — a bit like using a blow torch to clear off a dust mite). But Chomsky's attacking Skinner's ideas rather specifically (and, more generally, exposing the political implications behind bogus science); the essay is certainly not one in a series of examples of how to think better.

As one gets more skilled, the opportunities for improvement become less available — apparently because fewer people are interested in improving. The library gives free courses in how to read better, but these are for people who have trouble reading long books, not for those who already can but want to continue to improve. And there are courses in improving your writing, but they generally only get you from awful to serviceable, and not from serviceable to great. The same seems true of thinking — there are many books on fairly blatant logical fallacies to avoid, but few on more subtle improvements to thought.

And yet, at least with writing, people try. There are English courses in schools, taught by some of the greatest writers of the generation[5]. And journalists can semi-apprentice themselves by freelancing before great editors, who slice and dice their prose until it shines. Yet I've never seen a class or an apprenticeship in thinking, except perhaps incidentally.

The reason, I think, is because no one is thinking bigger. But that means there's plenty of opportunity. The field's wide open, folks.

December 15, 2006

1. http://www.pbs.org/marktwain/learnmore/writings_fenimore.html
2. http://www.orwell.ru/library/essays/politics/english/e_polit
3. http://www.alternet.org/columnists/story/21856/
4. http://www.chomsky.info/articles/19711230.htm
5. http://english.syr.edu/cwp/saunders.htm

THINK BIGGER
A GENERALIST MANIFESTO

Our world is full of forces pushing us towards specificity. Open a newspaper and it's divided into topic sections. Go to the bookstore and it's divided into subject categories. Go to school and the classes are all in separate fields. Get a degree and you have to study in a particular major. Get a job and you have to work at a particular task.

The world needs specificists, of course, but it also needs generalists. And we see precious few of those. It's not hard to see why: try to do something big and everyone will try to talk you out of it.

"That's impossible," they'll say. "Do that and you'll only drive yourself crazy."

"If that worked, don't you think someone else would have done it?"

"With all due respect, what makes you the expert on that subject?"

Tell someone you're working on a dissertation about the mating dance of the East African dung beetle and they won't bat an eye. It would be the height of impoliteness to ask "Is that really worth spending three years on?" — even if that's exactly what you're thinking. But set your sights a little bit higher and people have no problem knocking you down. "Come on," they'll say, furrowing their brow, "do you really think you're going to be able to pull something like that off?"

Don't listen to them. People are afraid of grandeur; it challenges the status quo. But you shouldn't be. "Look up more" should be your motto; "Think bigger" your mantra.

The first step is to recognize your place in things. If you study beetle mating habits, look at the larger mating patterns your studies fall into, look at the big picture of animal behavior, ask where you fit in the bigger question of what it means for an animal to behave. This is what I mean by "Look up more."

But if you do this — and I believe you will — then you'll find it hard to stay satisfied with your dung beetle project. You'll start wondering if you could move on to bigger things. Perhaps just a little bit bigger at first — analyzing a few more types, discussing a few more implications — but soon you'll notice that others have left the field wide open for the truly big picture stuff and you'll start wondering why it's not there that you should stake your claim. This is what I mean by "Think bigger."

Sure, at first it'll be frightening biting off more than you've ever had to chew. But the fear will soon give way to exhilaration and the extra work involved will be paid for in the additional notoriety, in the joy of knowing that you've made a real difference. After all, do you really want to spend the rest of your life studying dung beetles?

December 14, 2006

WHAT IT MEANS TO BE AN INTELLECTUAL

A friend sent me an email this morning and at the end of it, almost as an afterthought, he responded to a quote I'd sent him from an author praising books. "He would say that," my friend replied, "he's a writer."

I want to quibble with this statement — how is it that we can dismiss someone's argument simply because of their job? — but doing so would seem bizarre. There's a social norm that how much we discuss something should be roughly proportional to its importance. Mountains of print may be spilled on the issues of international relations but spending a couple emails discussing punctuation would seem dreadfully bizarre.

There's just one problem: I enjoy deep discussions of punctuation and other trivialities. I could try to justify this taste — some argument that we should think about everything we do so that we don't do everything we think about — but why bother? Do I have to justify enjoying certain television shows as well? At some point, isn't pure enjoyment just enough? After all, time isn't fungible.

But of course, the same drive that leads me to question punctuation leads me to question the drive itself, and thus this essay.

What is "this drive"? It's the tendency to not simply accept things as they are but to want to think about them, to understand them. To not be content to simply feel sad but to ask what sadness means. To not just get a bus pass but to think about the economic reasons getting a bus pass makes sense. I call this tendency the intellectual.

The word "intellectual" has a bit of a bad rap. When I think of the word I hear a man with a southern accent sneering at it. But this stain seems appropriate — the idea has a bad rap.

And why is that? One reason is that many people simply don't like to think about things. Perhaps it reminds them of school, which they didn't enjoy, and they don't want to go back there. Another is that they're busy people — men of action — and they don't have time to sit and think about every little detail. But mostly it's just because they think it's a waste of time. What's the point? What difference does it make what you think about punctuation? It's not going to affect anything.

This is the argument that's often used when demonizing intellectuals. As Thomas Frank summarizes the argument:

> The same bunch of sneaking intellectuals are responsible for the content of Hollywood movies and for the income tax, by which they steal from the rest of us. They do no useful work, producing nothing but movies and newspaper columns while they freeload on the labor of others. (116)

When I think of intellectuals, though, I don't really think of Hollywood producers or politicians or even newspaper columnists. But the people I do think of seem to have something else in common. They don't just love thinking, they love language. They love its tricks and intricacies, its games, the way it gets written down, the books it gets written into, the libraries those books are in, and the typography those books use.

Upon reflection this makes perfect sense. Language is the medium of thought and so it's no surprise that someone who spends a lot of time thinking spends a lot of time thinking about how to communicate their thoughts as well. And indeed, all the intellectuals that come to mind write, not because they have to or get paid to, but simply for its own sake. What good is thinking if you can't share?

This contrasts with how intellectuals are commonly thought of — namely as pretentious elitist snobs. But real intellectuals, at least in the sense I'm using the term, are anything but. They love nothing more than explaining their ideas so that anyone who's interested can understand them. They only seem pretentious because discussing such things is so bizarre.

This stereotype actually seems more like the caricature of the academic than the intellectual. (It's perhaps worth noting that most of the intellectuals I can think of aren't academics or at least have left the academy.) Far from being intellectuals, academics are encouraged to be almost the opposite. Instead of trying to explain things simply, they're rewarded for making them seem more complicated. Instead of trying to learn about everything, they're forced to focus in on their little subdiscipline. Instead of loving books, they have to love gabbing — up in front of class or at office hour with students or at professional conferences or faculty meetings.

Not that there's anything wrong with that. At the beginning I declined to justify my being an intellectual on any grounds other than pure personal enjoyment. And here, at the end, I can't think of any better justification. Certainly people should think deeply about their actions and the world's problems and other important topics. But the other ones? That's little more than personal preference.

April 17, 2006

A NON-PROGRAMMER'S APOLOGY

In his classic *A Mathematicians Apology*, published 65 years ago, the great mathematician G. H. Hardy wrote that "A man who sets out to justify his existence and his activities" has only one real defense, namely that "I do what I do because it is the one and only thing that I can do at all well." "I am not suggesting," he added, "that this is a defence which can be made by most people, since most people can do nothing at all well. But it is impregnable when it can be made without absurdity … If a man has any genuine talent he should be ready to make almost any sacrifice in order to cultivate it to the full.

Reading such comments one cannot help but apply them to oneself, and so I did. Let us eschew humility for the sake of argument and suppose that I am a great programmer. By Hardy's suggestion, the responsible thing for me to do would be to cultivate and use my talents in that field, to spend my life being a great programmer. And that, I have to say, is a prospect I look upon with no small amount of dread.

It was not always quite this way. For quite a while programming was basically my life. And then, somehow, I drifted away. At first it was small steps — discussing programming instead of doing it, then discussing things *for* programmers, and then discussing other topics altogether. By the time I reached the end of my first year in college, when people were asking me to program for them over the summer, I hadn't programmed in so long that I wasn't even sure I really could. I certainly did not think of myself as a particularly good programmer.

Ironic, considering Hardy writes that

"Good work is not done by 'humble' men. It is one of the first duties of a professor, for example, in any subject, to exaggerate a little both the importance of his subject and his own importance in it. A man who is always asking 'Is what I do worthwhile?' and 'Am I the right person to do it?' will always be ineffective himself and a discouragement to others. He must shut his eyes a little and think a little more of his subject and himself than they deserve. This is not too difficult: it is harder not to make his subject and himself ridiculous by shutting his eyes too tightly."

Perhaps, after spending so much time not programming, the blinders had worn off. Or perhaps it was the reverse: that I had to convince myself that I was good at what I was doing now, and, since that thing was not programming, by extension, that I was not very good at programming.

Whatever the reason, I looked upon the task of actually having to program for three months with uncertainty and trepidation. For days, if I recall correctly, I dithered. Thinking myself incapable of serious programming, I thought to wait until my partner arrived and instead spend my time assisting him. But days passed and I realized it would be weeks before he would appear, and I finally decided to try to program something in the meantime.

To my shock, it went amazingly well and I have since become convinced that I'm a pretty good programmer, if lacking in most other areas. But now I find myself faced with this dilemma: it is those other areas I would much prefer to work in.

The summer before college I learned something (see "The Book That Changed My Life" in Part II) that struck me as incredibly important and yet known by very few. It seemed clear to me that the only responsible way to live my life would be to do something that would only be done by someone who knew this thing — after all, there were few who did and many who didn't, so it seemed logical to leave most other tasks to the majority.

I concluded that the best thing to do would be to attempt to explain this thing I'd learned to others. Any specific task I could do with the knowledge would be far outweighed by the tasks done by those I'd explained the knowledge to.[1] It was only after I'd decided on this course of action (and perhaps this is the blinders once again) that it struck me that explaining complicated ideas was actually something I'd always loved doing and was really pretty good at.

That aside, having spent the morning reading David Foster Wallace[2], it is plain that I am no great writer. And so, reading Hardy, I am left wondering whether my decision is somehow irresponsible.

I am saved, I think, because it appears that Hardy's logic to some extent parallels mine. Why is it important for the man who "can bat unusually well" to become "a professional cricketer"? It is, presumably, because those who can bat unusually well are in short supply and so the few who are gifted with that talent should do us all the favor of making use of it. If those whose "judgment of the markets is quick and sound" become cricketers, while the good batters become stockbrokers, we will end up with mediocre cricketers and mediocre stockbrokers. Better for all of us if the reverse is the case.

But this, of course, is awfully similar to the logic I myself employed. It is important for me to spend my life explaining what I'd learned because people who had learned it are in short supply — much shorter supply, in fact (or so it appears), than people who can bat well.

However, there is also an assumption hidden in that statement. It only makes sense to decide what to become based on what you can presently do if you believe that abilities are somehow granted innately and can merely be cultivated, not created in themselves. This is a fairly common view, although rarely consciously articulated (as indeed Hardy takes it for granted), but not one that I subscribe to.

Instead, it seems plausible that talent is made through practice, that those who are good batters are that way after spending enormous quantities of time batting as a kid.[3] Mozart, for example, was the son of "one of Europe's leading musical teachers"[4] and said teacher began music instruction at age three. While I am plainly no Mozart, several similarities do seem apparent. My father had a computer programming company and he began showing me how to use the computer as far back as I can remember.

The extreme conclusion from the theory that there is no innate talent is that there is no difference between people and thus, as much as possible, we should get people to do the most important tasks (writing, as opposed to cricket, let's say). But in fact this does not follow.

Learning is like compound interest. A little bit of knowledge makes it easier to pick up more. Knowing what addition is and how to do it, you can then read a wide variety of things that use addition, thus knowing even more and being able to use that knowledge in a similar manner.[5] And so, the growth in knowledge accelerates.[6] This is why children who get started on something at a young age, as Mozart did, grow up to have such an advantage.

And even if (highly implausibly) we were able to control the circumstances in which all children grew up so as to maximize their ability to perform the most important tasks, that still would not be enough, since in addition to aptitude there is also interest.

AARON SWARTZ

Imagine the three sons of a famous football player. All three are raised similarly, with athletic activity from their earliest days, and thus have an equal aptitude for playing football. Two of them pick up this task excitedly, while one, despite being good at it, is uninterested[7] and prefers to read books.[8] It would not only be unfair to force him to use his aptitude and play football, it would also be unwise. Someone whose heart isn't in it is unlikely to spend the time necessary to excel.

And this, in short[9], is the position I find myself in. I don't want to be a programmer. When I look at programming books, I am more tempted to mock them than to read them. When I go to programmer conferences, I'd rather skip out and talk politics than programming. And writing code, although it can be enjoyable, is hardly something I want to spend my life doing.

Perhaps, I fear, this decision deprives society of one great programmer in favor of one mediocre writer. And let's not hide behind the cloak of uncertainty, let's say we know that it does. Even so, I would make it. The writing is too important, the programming too unenjoyable.

And for that, I apologize.

1. Explaining what that knowledge is, naturally, a larger project and must wait for another time.
2. You can probably see DFW's influence on this piece, not least of which in these footnotes.
3. Indeed, this apparently parallels the views of the psychologists who have studied the question. Anders Ericsson, a psychology professor who studies "expert performance", told the New York Times Magazine that "the most general claim" in his work "is that a lot of people believe there are some inherent limits they were born with. But there is surprisingly little hard evidence … ." The conclusion that follows, the NYTM notes, is that "when it comes to choosing a life path, you should do what you love — because if you don't love it, you are unlikely to work hard enough to get very good. Most people naturally don't like to do things they aren't 'good' at. So they often give up, telling themselves they simply don't possess the talent for math or skiing or the violin. But what they really lack is the desire to be good and to undertake the deliberate practice that would make them better." (see http://www.nytimes.com/2006/05/07/magazine/07wwln_freak.html?ex=1148875200&en=61175 1da74b96d1b&ei=5070)
4. The quote is from Wikipedia where, indeed, the other facts are drawn from as well, the idea having been suggested by Stephen Jay Gould's essay "Mozart and Modularity", collected in his book Eight Little Piggies.
5. I've always thought that this was the reason kids (or maybe just me) especially disliked history. Every other field — biology, math, art — had at least some connection to the present and thus kids had some foundational knowledge to build on. But history? We simply weren't there and thus know absolutely nothing of it.
6. It was tempting to write that "the rate of growth" accelerates, but that would mean something rather different.
7. Many people, of course, are uninterested in such things precisely because they aren't very good at them. There's nothing like repeated failures to turn you way from an activity. Perhaps this is another reason to start young — young children might be less stung by failure, as little is expected from them.
8. I apologize for the clichédness of this example.
9. Well, shorter than most DFW.

May 27, 2006

A CLARIFICATION

A lot of people seem to have misunderstood my piece *A Non-Programmer's Apology* and my blog more generally. Let me explain:

I am 19 and live in Cambridge, Massachusetts, in an apartment with two others. The three of us together work full-time on the site reddit.com and I spend most of my days working on programming and various related tasks for it.

In the nights and weekends I read and think and write. I'm working on a large book project, which I expect to take years, and which I don't discuss much on the Web.

I also think about lots of things, many of which don't relate to either reddit or the book project. When a thought crystalizes I type it up and post it to my blog. I don't read it before I post it, I don't show it to anyone, and I don't edit it. I literally sit down and type one word after another and hit save and hit upload. (Obviously, there are some exceptions, but this is standard practice.)

If you think the writing here is poor, that's probably why. Real writing takes editing. But I don't consider this writing, I consider this thinking. I like sharing my thoughts and I like hearing yours and I like practicing expressing ideas, but fundamentally this blog is not for you, it's for me. I'm sorry. Maybe that isn't how it should be, but at least for now that's how it is. In my defense, nobody's making you come here.

I plan to keep doing this until the company fails or becomes a huge success.

Afterwards, I hope to work on the book project (and a related project) full time.

I hope that clears things up.

June 20, 2006

LIFE IN SUBURBIA
LAND OF CLICHE

From my desk in my apartment in Cambridge, I see the green leaves of trees out the window and, when I step closer, winding streets with quirky shops and interesting people stretching out below them. From my desk in my old home in suburban Chicago, you see the same trees, but behind them is asphalt and McMansion and long twisting driveways.

No one here uses public transportation. The city does have a train station, but one gets the sense that its purpose is mostly decorative — train stations remind people of the imaginary small town life that suburbs attempt to imitate. To get out to your house, you instead drive down long stretches of drab gray highway, besotted by hideous billboards and lined with ugly office parks.

The weather is certainly nice. On most days, if you go for a walk it's quite beautiful — as long as you keep your head pointed at the sky, where the bright green leaves interweave with the brilliant blue. But as soon as you look down there are SUVs driving the wealthy to their half-hidden palazzos — just enough visible to be bragging, just enough hidden to be private.

Whereas in Cambridge the ambitious try to fill their houses with books, in suburbia you go for art and interior decorating. The tasteless fill their houses with large marble staircases and glistening chandeliers; the more tasteful prefer bright white rooms accented with sculptures and pictures — specific enough not to be intellectual, but abstract enough to be art.

You came back here to raise a family, but you wouldn't even consider sending them to public school. Why would you, when there's a perfectly good private school just twenty minutes away? There the kids are white and wealthy. After all, how could they be anything else at these tuition prices? The school does give out scholarships, but only based on "merit": "interviews, teacher recommendations, examination results and current school records". The school is in the wealthiest zip code in America, surrounded by trees and houses, like everything else in suburbia.

The school is preparing for graduation. You see a slide show of those about to receive their diplomas, seen when they're so young that the smiles leap off their faces. How could anything so precious be unhappy here, with everything in its right place? Afterwards the families mingle in the courtyards, surrounded by the gleaming metal of the newly-built extensions.

Not too far, another group of kids hides behind trees by the parking lot, protecting a cooler full of water balloons they use to pelt their fellow students as they try to reach their cars. One kid, his yellow country-club sweater tied around his neck, complimenting his finessed blond hair, hides behind a glass door, fear visible in his eyes as he looks at his newly-purchased convertible and prays it won't get hit. (He bought it, the kids explain, to match his new girlfriend. Then they turn and pelt two girls walking by.)

Despite their brazen acts, the kids are quite afraid — afraid of getting caught. They hide at the sight of parents or teachers and they restrain themselves from hitting the head of school's daughter. But they needn't worry. Parents see right through the charade and laugh it off. Oh kids, oh kids and their water balloons. How delightful! they say to themselves as they scurry to their cars.

The kids were right to guard the parking lots; not only is suburbia unmanageable without a car, driving cars is a central part of the culture: what kind, at what age, and where to? The funny thing is that there simply aren't that many places to go. There's your house, and your friends, and the shops uptown or at the mall.

Not that there's much difference between the two anymore. The malls have become open-air and the town centers have become so desiccated that they're little different, just chain shops surrounded by fake walkways to other chain shops. The difference, I suppose, is that in town centers no one uses the walkways — why bother when you can drive?

While the kids enjoy their eating and shopping, the mothers get down to business at the grocery store, a menagerie of food and drink and color. Huge carts are filled and paid for and then passed off to low-wage Mexicans, who load them in your car as you drive out of the parking lot.

In between the malls and downtown, even the fakery disappears and the raw commercialism that pervades the suburb is left naked, assuming its default form of ugly highway signs and strip malls, all in an almost nausea inducing gray, stretching out in all directions, leaving little escape.

Not all the people of the suburbs are cold and vicious as their surroundings. For the most part, they're "liberals", the kind who are deeply affected by the plight of the homeless as they head back to their minivan. A small sign at the menagerie of a grocery store draws attention to the plight of the hungry. No, you don't have to feed them; just feel bad: the sign advertises "national hunger awareness day" (sponsored, the web site says, "by many prominent organizations" — organizations like Macy's, Southwest Airlines, and the Food Marketing Institute).

After all, this is the generation of the New Left. 25 miles south, Chicago was rocked by the '68 Democratic Convention, where kids charged the city while filmed by newscameras, before the Chicago police decided to start beating up on both. The suburbanites didn't participate, of course, but they watched it on the news and felt sympathy for their brethren and invited the indicted Chicago 7 up to give a talk.

The war is now Iraq, not Vietnam, and the protest is more muted. A sculpture in the town center draws attention to our dead servicemen, while old ladies occasionally stage protests with large signs. Now the antiestablishment kids have become establishment parents, Mayor Daleys of their own households, full of tensions no less visible than those which engulfed Chicago.

Son one plays music too loud for son two who insists that right this minute he needs to play a video game. And when these fighting factions are supposed to come together, as in a graduation, the tensions boil over, parents screeching at kids who scream at each other, dragged down to the car where they argue about which windows to open and settings for the AC, until, realizing that they're all stuck there together, tensions cool down somewhat. Still, it doesn't seem like much fun for anyone.

At the graduation, everyone has a camera to immortalize this precious moment. They force everyone into straightening their rarely-worn suits and dresses and smiling in rarely-seen ways so that the camera can "capture the moment", an instant of artifice, entirely yanked from time, its history completely erased so that the fake smiles may be preserved.

The graduation itself is a whole event of such artifice: the students are trained to walk down the aisles absurdly slowly (while the organist stretches Pomp and Circumstance far, far beyond the breaking point) so that every parent may get copious photos of them standing in the aisle. Once on stage they fake their love for teachers they hated only days ago, while dressed in fake costumes and standing in front of a fake set. The parents are given programs whose professional typography hides the normal disarray of school, makes them think this place is Professional.

Oh, the absurdity of it all: putting all that effort into making memories they won't remember of good times they never had. But I guess that's suburbia — the fake coat of paint that lets you pretend your unhappy life is just as nice as everyone else's, even if it easily flakes off.

June 16, 2006

LEGACY

Ambitious people want to leave legacies, but what sort of legacies do they want to leave? The traditional criterion is that your importance is measured by the effect of what you do. Thus the most important lawyers are the Supreme Court justices, since their decisions affect the entire nation. And the greatest mathematicians are those that make important discoveries, since their discoveries end up being used by many who follow.

This seems quite reasonable. One's legacy depends on one's impact and what better way to measure impact than by the effect of what you've done. But this is measuring against the wrong baseline. The real question is not what effect your work had, but what things would be like had you never done it.

The two are not at all the same. It is rather commonly accepted that there are "ideas whose time has come" and history tends to bear this out. When Newton invented the calculus, so did Leibniz. When Darwin discovered evolution through natural selection, so did Alfred Russel Wallace. When Alexander Graham Bell invented the telephone, so did Elisha Gray (before him, arguably).

In these cases the facts are plain: had Newton, Darwin, and Bell never done their work, the result would have been largely the same — we'd still have calculus, evolution, and the telephone. And yet such people are hailed as major heroes, their legacies immortalized.

Perhaps, if one only cares about such things, this is enough. (Although this seems a rather dangerous game, since the future could wake up at any moment and realize its adulation is misplaced.) But if one genuinely cares about their impact, instead of simply how their impact is perceived, more careful thought is in order.

I once spent time with a well-known academic, who had published several works widely recognized as classics even outside his field, and he offered some career advice in the sciences. (Actually, come to think of it, there are two people of whom this is true, suggesting the phenomenon has broader significance.) Such-and-such a field is very hot right now, he said, you could really make a name for yourself by getting into it. The idea being that major discoveries were sure to follow soon and that if I picked that field I could be the one to make them.

By my test, such a thing would leave a poor legacy. (For what it's worth, I don't think either person's works fall into this category; that is to say, their reputation is still deserved even by these standards.) Even worse, you'd know it. Presumably Darwin and Newton didn't begin their investigations because they thought the field was "hot". They thought through doing it they would have a significant impact, even though that turned out to be wrong. But someone who joined a field simply because they thought a major discovery would come from it soon could never enjoy such a delusion. Instead, they would know that their work would make little difference, and would have to labor under such impressions.

The same is true of other professions we misconceive of as being important. Take being a Supreme Court justice, for example. Traditionally, this is thought of as a majestic job in which one gets to make decisions of great import. In fact, it seems to me that one has little impact at all. Most of your impact was made by the politics of the President who appointed you. Had you not been around for the job, he would have found someone else who would take similar positions. The only way one could have a real impact as Supreme Court justice would be to change your politics once appointed to the bench and the only way you could prepare for such a thing would be to spend the majority of your career doing things you thought were wrong in the hopes that one day you might get picked for the Supreme Court. That seems a rather hard lot to swallow.

So what jobs do leave a real legacy? It's hard to think of most of them, since by their very nature they require doing things that other people aren't trying to do, and thus include the things that people haven't thought of. But one good source of them is trying to do things that change the system instead of following it. For example, the university system encourages people to become professors who do research in certain areas (and thus many people do this); it discourages people from trying to change the nature of the university itself.

Naturally, doing things like changing the university are much harder than simply becoming yet another professor. But for those who genuinely care about their legacies, it doesn't seem like there's much choice.

June 1, 2006

WHAT MAKES A PERSONALITY SCARY?

I've noticed recently that I sometimes find myself a little afraid of people's personalities. It's kind of a weird experience: it makes sense to be afraid of people and other things that can hurt you, but being afraid of a personality? It doesn't make a lot of sense. Personalities can seem quirky or interesting, but scary?

At first, I thought this was simply an odd personal tic, since you don't exactly hear anyone else talking about it. But on reflection, you sometimes do. Imagine a movie, the heroine character learning about some shocking evil deed the brave male lead has committed. "I don't even know who you are anymore," she sobs. "You're starting to scare me."

What's frightening, it would seem, is that people aren't the way we expected. They seemed to be brave and kind-hearted, but when the moment was right they were capable of being crafty and manipulative. We're shocked, at first, because it's not what we expected. "But he seemed so nice... How could he do that?" Then we're upset, because at some level it seems like dishonesty. "He made me think he was a good person, yet he's capable of so much bad." And finally, we're scared, because if we were wrong about him, then our view of the world seems a little bit off.[1]

Having the world be off is frightening. I remember once I found myself at Caltrain's Milbrae station late at night. Milbrae is a huge new station, a sprawling complex complete with a subway, 10 bus stops, a train, and a huge parking garage. There's nothing really around it for quite a bit and it's all open-air, with the cold night air chilling me in my shirt, as I was transferring between the subway and the train. On the way to the train tracks, I checked the schedule. The next train was at 10:47 it said; it was 10:40, so I hurried downstairs to wait for the train. I sat down and got out my book, waiting, and waiting, while the train never came. I checked the clock — it was past 10:47, well past. So I checked the downstairs schedule. There was no 10:47 train. I ran upstairs to see if the schedule I'd read was simply out-of-date. It had no 10:47 train either, nothing even close. I was certain I had read it saying 10:47 — the memory was clear in my mind, and I'd followed the line with my finger to make sure I had the right station.

I suddenly got quite scared. What was going on? Was I in a dream? Was someone sneaking around the schedules on me? Was I the victim of some practical joke? The fabric of my reality was being torn — something clearly impossible had happened: a time had disappeared off a train schedule. Things weren't working the way I expected.

I later figured out, of course, that nothing so devious had happened. In my hurry to catch the subway, I'd read the wrong side of the schedule — the train was at 10:47am, not 10:47pm, and when I went back to look for the time I looked at the right side of the schedule and, naturally, the train wasn't there. But my larger point is that tears in the way we think things work are scary. If things are this bad when a piece of paper doesn't say what we expect, it's not surprising that it's worse when people we know don't behave the way we thought.

I say we here, but as I mentioned at the start, I seem to be a bit alone on this. One possibility is that I'm hypersensitive to such emotions. Other people might simply feel a prick at such a scheduling anomaly, but I feel it as full-blown fear. Another (more flattering) possibility is that I'm more perceptive about people than others; since others don't notice the duplicity, they don't feel the associated fear.

The latter makes some sense to me, as the things that make me scared of people are often very subtle, and others don't seem to recognize them at all, even when I ask them about it specifically. Even I can't quite put my finger on what it is sometime, it's just a subtle signal that the person isn't being straight with you, that what they're saying sounds honest and friendly, but is actually manipulative. It's not a pleasant feeling.

July 17, 2006

1. In talking about this sequence of emotions (shocked, upset, scared), I'm referring to a logical progression, not an actual one. I don't really feel all of these things in order upon seeing someone scary, just the last. But the other emotions are what gets you to the last.

THE SMALLTALK QUESTION

One of the minor puzzles of American life is what question to ask people at parties and suchly to get to know them.

"How ya doin'?" is of course mere formality, only the most troubled would answer honestly for anything but the positive.

"What do you do?" is somewhat offensive. First, it really means "what occupation do you hold?" and thus implies you do little outside your occupation. Second, it implies that one's occupation is the most salient fact about them. Third, it rarely leads to further useful inquiry. For only a handful of occupations, you will be able to say something somewhat relevant, but even this will no doubt be slightly annoying or offensive. ("Oh yeah, I always thought about studying history.")

"Where are you from?" is even less fruitful.

"What's your major?" (in the case of college students) turns sour when, as is tragically all too often the case, students feel no real passion for their major.

"What book have you read recently?" will cause the majority of Americans who don't read to flail, while at best only getting an off-the-cuff garbled summary of a random book.

"What's something cool you've learned recently?" puts the person on the spot and inevitably leads to hemming and hawing and then something not all that cool.

I propose instead that one asks "What have you been thinking about lately?"

First, the question is extremely open-ended. The answer could be a book, a movie, a relationship, a class, a job, a hobby, etc. Even better, it will be whichever of these is most interesting at the moment. Second, it sends the message that thinking, and thinking about thinking, is a fundamental human activity, and thus encourages it. Third, it's easiest to answer, since by its nature its asking about what's already on the person's mind. Fourth, it's likely to lead to productive dialog, as you can discuss the topic together and hopefully make progress. Fifth, the answer is quite likely to be novel. Unlike books and occupations, people's thoughts seem to be endlessly varied. Sixth, it helps capture a person's essence. A job can be forced by circumstance and parentage, but our thoughts are all our own. I can think of little better way to quickly gauge what a person is really like.

"What have you been working on lately?" can be seen, in this context, to be clearly inferior, although similar.

So, what have you been thinking about lately?

August 16, 2006

OF THE MBTA

It was night, and Central Square was largely empty. A few cars drove down the street, a few guys loitered outside the bars, a few lights were on in windows, but the city was quietly shutting down. I walked down the steps into the subway, paid my fare, and began looking for a place to sit and read.

I found a bench, another kid sitting at the opposite side, and took my seat. "Spare a dollar?" the kid asked. "Sorry," I said, "spent everything I have to get in here." "Man, wish I had five bucks," he said. "If I had that I'd be out there grabbing a meal. I haven't eaten in like two days."

I tried to read my book but he wanted to talk. "You just come back from school?" he asked. "No," I said, "I was visiting a friend." "Oh, I thought you were at school 'cause of the book." "Oh, I've been carrying this around all day," I said. "What is it?" he asked. "It's a book about books," I said. He laughed. "I thought it was a bible or something."

"You heading to Alewife?" I asked. "No," he said, laughing. "I'm staying right here." I blinked twice and began to realize what he meant. He wasn't asking for money because he'd been out all night and spent the cash his parents gave him. He was asking for money because he was homeless. And with fits and starts, he told me a little of his story as I waited for the train.

He grew up with his family in New Hampshire. They were "rich" then, at least by comparison, lived in a real "mansion". Inspectors started coming around to check out the house, three in one month. Finally a man came to tell them the bad news. "You have to move out," he said. "The house is infested with termites; it'll collapse within months." "What are you talking about?" his mom responded. "This place is fine; inspectors have been looking it all over." The man picked up a large hammer, lifted it above his head and struck a mighty blow — at the wall. The drywall broke away to reveal termites filling the insides, eating away at the wood.

They had to leave fast, didn't even have time to pack stuff. The bulldozers came the next day, turned the whole thing into rubble. They also bulldozed his mom's car, where she kept all the money. They were homeless and penniless. The Department of Social Services picked up his five-year-old brother, insisted on $100 fee if they wanted to regain custody. "If I had that kind of money," he explained, "I'd be eating with it."

So he decided to start hitchhiking, head to Cambridge where he had some family. Caught a ride in the back of a UPS truck, then after that dropped him off, waited for another hour or two in the middle of nowhere before he could find someone else. Finally he found his way to part of the Boston subway system, where he managed to sneak his way through the turnstiles. Now he could ride all around town, get to Cambridge, where he set up base in Central Square.

"Mostly I just sit here," he explained. "Sometimes I just ride the trains all day, Braintree to Alewife and back. Found a violin some guy had lost — hey, I'm homeless and you're not — and started playing it for money, but the cops picked me up for performing without a license and threw me in jail for the night. Just because I'm a homeless kid you're going to throw me in jail? Anyway, I make more money than that just telling jokes."

"Pretty absurd, actually. Spent all day here asking folks for spare change, nobody could spare a thing. Here I am, homeless kid in Cambridge, and nobody even has a couple spare pennies!"

To outward appearances he seems like a normal kid with a bit of an army look. His hair is buzzed, he wears a wifebeater shirt with an army jacket and baggy army pants. At first I thought this was just a style, but actually it's utilitarian — everything he owns is in the pockets of those pants. He showed me what he had.

"Stole this from a friend today," he said, pulling something out from under his jacket. "Brand new CD player, awesome headphones, full batteries, great CD inside." He began playing it for me; it was rap songs: Ridin' and Eminem. "And check out this he said," before pulling out a PSP. "Got this when we were rich, but can't use it for much now; had to sell all our games so we could try to find a house." He popped it open. "See, no cartridges. Still, I borrow some from friends sometimes."

There was a pause, as Eminem came out of his headphones, which he'd cranked all the way up so I could listen. "Man, imagine if Eminem were right here now, all those girls shaking their asses by him. Wouldn't that be crazy?" "Crazier things have happened," I said. "Lots of famous people go to Harvard Square." "Yeah," he said,

"Beyonce was there the other week — came in for a wedding or something — it was like a mob scene, people jumping all over her."

He often took the conversation in the direction of such imaginations — what if a celebrity popped up here? He talked about how he used to play *Grand Theft Auto: San Andreas* with a cheat code to make celebrities appear in the game. But aside from these discursions, he was remarkably cogent, pretty sane for someone in such a screwed-up situation.

"Man, my life sucks," he said after a pause. "If you could do anything, what would you do?" I asked. "If I could do anything?" he said. "Yeah." "Man, I'd be back at home with my mom and brothers and family and stuff."

He begun telling me something about his mom — how she'd managed to recover one of her debit cards from the rubble of her car and bought a new house, but never told him about it, he'd only heard rumor of it third-hand, how she'd put her own child out on the street to fend for himself, but I couldn't quite hear him because the train pulled up as he was talking. He finally stopped talking, but I strained, waiting for more. "That's your train," he finally said, "you better catch it." "Sorry," I said, walking towards it.

I grabbed a seat, hearing "Spare change? Spare change?" as the doors closed and we pulled away. I started trying to read my book, but found I wasn't really capable of reading anything at all.

September 25, 2006

ALONE IN THE HOSPITAL

Going to the hospital has never been particularly safe, but hospitals have tried to do what they can. In the early part of the 1900s, hospitals became fanatical about sterility, to prevent infection. Each infant in their care, for example, had its own white coat for doctors to wear as they visited that infant, hung on hooks inside out for the next doctor to don. Holding babies was considered dangerous (as signage emphasized), so they were fed without being held — bottles were simply propped up where the infants could get at them. Needless to say, parents were denied visits.

And yet mortality rates for infants in hospital care ranged from 30 to 75 percent. The babies were cared for and nourished, they had no outward physical problems, they simply succumbed to a mysterious phenomenon the doctors labeled "failure to thrive". Some thought it might be a hidden infection.

So the nurses wore masks and hoods, carefully scrubbed up before they handled infants. Some hospitals put infants in boxes with glove-valves — the kinds you see in movies when scientists are handling radioactive material — so that they'd never have to touch the infant at all. But the problem just got worse.

Henry Bakwin, pediatric director of New York's Bellevue Hospital, saw this and thought that perhaps they were going about things exactly wrong. The infants weren't dying of infection, he believed, they were dying of loneliness — a loneliness that made it easier for them to succumb to infection. He took down the signs about washing hands and put up signs requiring everyone to pick up and fondle a baby. And infection rates went down.

Harold Skeels and a team at the Iowa Child Research Welfare Station decided to try an experiment. They took thirteen girls out of institutionalized care and had them "adopted" by older girls in "a home for the feeble-minded". Within nineteen months, the average IQs of the adopted kids jumped from 64 to 92.

But these folks were the radicals. The mainstream scientific community refused to believe there was anything wrong — people were blowing things out of proportion, they insisted, and anyway, everyone knows children that young can't suffer from depression. The studies were flawed.

John Bowlby came at it from a different perspective. Interviewing severely disturbed kids, he discovered they all shared a traumatic separation from their parents when they were young. He concluded the mother-infant relationship was essential to development and issued recommendations much like Skeels and Spitz. "The mothering of a child is not something which can be arranged by roster," he wrote in reports for the World Health Organization. But still the hospitals didn't change.

Bowlby's student John Robertson begun doing observation at hospitals. He noticed that babies screamed painfully as they were admitted. The nurses explained that this was normal and they'd soon settle down. He noticed that these "settled" babies returned to violent fits when they were taken home, attacking her as if they blamed her. The nurses said that was normal too, mothers weren't just as good at taking care of kids as the nurses. Robertson had a different explanation.

He decided to make a movie to prove it. Unlike the last, this one would be completely scientific. He would pick a name at random from the list of babies, then always film them at a specific hour, clock in the background, so you could tell he wasn't cheating. The name he picked was Laura.

When he went to find her he was devastated: Laura was the one girl in a hundred who wasn't crying; her parents had reared her so strictly that she quietly restrained all her emotions. "I saw immediately [she] was going to be the one child in a hundred who was not going to demonstrate what I had been shouting my head off [about]," Robertson said. But he couldn't pick another child — that would be cheating. The project continued.

The first day, Laura jumped out of her bath to the door in an attempt to escape. Her smiles disappear and sometimes she quietly sobs while clutching her teddy. "Where's my mummy?" she asks repeatedly, while trying hard to hold back tears. Each day she grows grayer until on the fifth, when she appears unsmiling and resentful. Her mother comes to visit (thanks to a special exception to the rules Robertson negotiated), but she wipes away her mother's kiss. When her mother waves goodbye, she looks away. When her mother finally comes to take her home on the eight day, she begins shaking with sobs. She gathers up all of her stuff, but refuses to take her mother's hand as they walk out.

They presented the film to the Royal Society of Medicine in London. The audience was outraged. It was false, it was slander, it was a trick, it was an atypical child, it was filmed selectively, it was edited dishonestly. "People stood up and said that their children's wards were not like that, two-year-olds were all happy," Robertson recalls. Robertson was banned from some of the wards he was observing, pediatricians walked across the street when they encountered him. The hospital claimed that Robertson had interfered with the nurses trying to care for Laura. As Robertson toured Britain with the film, the reaction was always the same.

When Laura finally saw the film, six months later, she burst into tears. "Where were you all that time?" she asked her mother.

Reviews in the medical journals, however, were all positive. And younger nurses and doctors begun telling Robertson how they agreed with him and would do things differently, if only they were in charge. And a few higher-ups quietly sent some votes of support. So Robertson kept going. He took the film to the United States, hoping for a similarly positive reception. But the Americans insisted that while it was a great film about Britain, it had no relevance in their country. And nobody was willing to take the obvious step of letting mothers stay with their children on the wards.

Not until 1955 were there signs of change. Fred Stone, a doctor at the Royal Hospital in Glasgow, decided to do a pilot study. "I would drive up the hill to come here," he recalled, "and there would be two hundred parents queueing up in the rain to get in for their half hour's visiting." A colleague who had control of two pediatric wards decided to offer one of them to Stone to prove that his suggestions wouldn't work.

When the nurses heard about this, they threatened to resign together. To placate them, Stone set up a series of meetings. "The aggression after the first meetings was unbelievable, truly unbelievable," he explained. But the aggression soon turned to tears. "They said, 'You don't understand what you are asking of us. [You mean] a parent can just walk in and see how we're neglecting these poor kids[?]' [...] And, of course, at that point we had to say, 'But what on earth makes you think that we're criticizing you? You're doing an impossible job remarkably well.' And, of course, then the tears came as you can imagine." Finally they agreed the experiment should at least be tried.

"I never heard any more about the issue at all. Nobody ever came back to me and said, 'The six months are up.' Nobody ever reported that it had been a success or a failure; all I knew was that somehow I heard that two wards were doing it, four wards were doing it, the whole hospital was doing it. And since then we've had almost unrestricted visiting in the whole hospital."

Similar experiments were conducted in London, although changes on the Continent didn't happen until the late 1970s. In 1959, the British minister of health made it official policy. And in the early 1960s, Robertson told BBC Radio parents that they should sit-in by their children's cot and force the hospital to try to evict them. Slowly the tide began to turn.

This article is based on Robert Karen's tour de force book *Becoming Attached*.

September 26, 2006

A FEMINIST GOES TO THE HOSPITAL

In *A Pattern Language*, Christopher Alexander comments on the idiocy of trying to nurse people to health by locking them up in the land of the sick, but a visit to an actual hospital makes the point more vividly than logical argument ever could. The modern hospital is a place of nightmares, even visiting I cannot manage to spend more than an hour here without beginning to go insane. I cannot imagine how anyone ever escapes.

An island of white in an ocean of green, the modern hospital's landscaping dangles the promise of verdant beauty while its insides are all white sterility. The hallways of identical doors twist and turn around so much that it's impossible to find any room that isn't carefully numbered, even after several attempts to try to discern the building's layout. The muted colors and dreary duplication do not reward such attempts at investigation, or even mere attempts at life.

It seems like the building itself is ill. Odd pieces are blocked off with white sheets, larger ones with completely opaque walls. Bizarre machines with large tubes line the hallways, apparently standing in for broken parts of the building's innards, while workmen wander around attempting to treat the other symptoms.

The rooms themselves are monstrous cells, tiny boxes with doors that stay open and walls that fight any attempts at individuality or privacy. The size makes entertaining guests awkward, while the lack of activities makes loneliness unbearable.

Were the large sign reading "Hospital" to go missing, one might easily mistake the facility as one for torture: men whose clothes have been replaced by dreary gowns slowly wander the halls in dreary stupor, their battered faces making them appear as if they have been badly beaten. They are not permitted to escape.

Were one, under such amazing conditions, to try to mount an attempt at fruitful work, it would quickly fail. Even assuming one was able to muster the energy to focus, the noises through the thin walls and unclosed doors would quickly distract. The beeps and buzzes from the assorted machinery would frustrate to no end. The screeching announcements from the loudspeakers would fast derail any trains of thought. And if one manages to get past all these things, well, it will only be a short while until a nurse or orderly comes to insert another needle or run some other humiliating and invasive task.

And so one simply watches the seconds tick away, as in some odd form of Chinese water torture. Sometimes the pain is made more vivid by the combination of very real physical discomfort, which incapacity makes difficult to alleviate. Itchiness, dirtiness, and restlessness are the orders of the day, with powerlessness coming in to make sure the others don't escape.

Ostensibly this place is meant to cure things, the unimpeachable knowledge of science and the clean sterility of the building meant to combine to induce health. But, as before in history, the cure may be worse than the disease. Robert Karen has documented how early concerns about antisepsis led hospitals to keep children far away from their parents. The result, as was plain to anyone paying attention, was severe psychological trauma for the children, who assumed their parents had abandoned them, leading to mental problems that last a lifetime.

While modern hospitals induce problems apparently less severe, they are still problems. Again, the doctors that are supposed to help the patients seem less concerned about the patients as people than bodies, things to be measured and operated upon, puzzles to solve, problems to fix. They do not tell the patient what is being done to them, do not reap the benefits that could be received by engaging them in the search for the solution, but instead only share knowledge when forced by law and precedent, preferring to keep the real details private among the priesthood of doctors and nurses.

Barbara Ehrenreich and Deidre English note how well-off women of the pre-feminist era suffered from mysterious symptoms of inactivity, a condition they diagnose as the psychological result of their inactivity and powerlessness; society entrusted them with no responsibility and so their minds collapsed from lack of active use.

While women have made great strides in the years since, for many the problem is still quite real. And laid up in a hospital, with domestic and childrearing tasks undoable, they may find the responsibilities they had fade away, their condition stripped back to that of their afflicted forebearers.

And so patriarchical society and patriarchical medicine combine to strip all vestiges of humanity away. No freedom, no responsibility; no movements, no tasks; no privacy, no thought. The person becomes the body that the doctors treat them as.

Friends and family may try to visit, in an attempt to bring a bit of their outside world into this sterile place, but the awkward situation strains even the best relationships. Friendly conversations become hard when one party is lying in bed moaning, while strained family relationships are stretched further, surfacing their most disgustingly dysfunctional aspects. Family members, whatever else they may accomplish, somehow learn the remarkable skill of knowing just what to do to drive you up the wall. And as the hospital environment (along with the psychological stress of seeing you trapped in it) drives them insane as well, their presence quickly becomes more curse than blessing.

I've never seen an environment so effective at inducing such severe psychological pain. After just an hour, I feel like screaming, tearing, pounding, killing. I go "out of my mind" and yearn to get out of my body as well, running around in circles, pounding against the floor, with not even exhaustion appearing to cure me.

It needn't be this way, for there is a cure: the joy of life. Sanity can be restored through attempts at music, channeling the fundamental disorder into form and elegance, focusing the energy toward good. Art, especially the art of nature, as Alexander suggested, is likely another cure. But hospitals aren't built for that.

September 27, 2006

LIFE IN THE HOSPITAL

From an extra-special guest:

The very walls of the hospital seemed to suck the life out of me — painted in puke yellow — and the window, which did look out at some trees, unfortunately framed a week's worth of grey, rainy weather. The floors and walls were filthy (I won't even mention the bathroom); the furniture old, chipped and stained; the framed artwork (like an old puzzle drawing out of Boy's Life magazine with faces and animals and broomsticks hiding in the trees) faded; the food rancid, stinky and inedibly heavy and overly sweet. I seldom saw the doctors wash their hands or use the Purell dispenser on the wall (I began to fear catching some super hospital germ infection). When I could finally walk the halls in my hideous hospital gowns and infantilizing slipper socks, I was tethered to a top-heavy pole with bad wheels, which made dragging it over any bumps or turning corners an exercise in futility. I begged to be let out, to be sent home where it was clean, where I could have simple healthy food and take a shower; I begged the residents, the doctors (when they came on rounds) to take the tubes out of me. And they just made me feel idiotic, patronized, weak and helpless.

Finally, in the middle of one sleepless, endless night spent staring at the walls, being sure the clock was actually moving backwards, it occurred to me with perfect clarity that the patient is never going to win the battle with the doctors… because the doctors have all the weapons. Just then the door slammed open, yet another nurse threw on all the lights and jabbed me with a needle, filling me with some other substance she refused to identify. Oh god, it was the most horrible hospital experience I have ever been through. And the scariest part of it is that this hospital is on the list of the 100 Best Hospitals in Illinois. Imagine what the others not on the list are like.

[…]

My brother has a theory. You go into a hospital to have something fixed but they immediately take you totally out of your normal environment: off your normal food and caffeine, off all your regular medications, etc. They do the surgery (or whatever) and invade your body with all sorts of foreign substances (IVs, narcotics, oxygen, TPNs, blood thinners, insulin, etc.) Then, as they gradually withdraw the foreign substances they have assaulted you with, they declare you "cured." Then you are eventually allowed to go back home and resume your normal routine. Odd.

October 1, 2006

EVERYBODY TELLS ME SO

I remember when I was in fourth grade, while we were eating our snack (graham crackers and milk) in the kitchen, my classmates began discussing the effects of wealth. "Money doesn't make you happy," I insisted. I tried to argue the point, but no one else believed me. (The same class was later adamant that Clinton should be impeached, although they did spontaneously throw an anti-fur-coat demonstration.) "Of course money makes you happy," they insisted. "Just wait, when you're rich, you'll change your mind." I haven't.

On TV, whenever a kid is given a to-him-large sum of money, the fatherly adult handing it out says "Don't spend it all in one place." Don't want the kid blowing it on a single movie and then feeling bad that he spent it all. Someone emailed me the same thing the other day, and I had to laugh. I don't really know how to spend the money period. How could I possibly spend it all in one place? Donate it to the UN?[1]

A friend told me to be sure not to let the money change me. "How could it possibly do that?" I asked. "Well, first you'd buy a fancy new car." "I don't know how to drive." "Then you'd buy a big house in the suburbs." "I like living in small apartments." "And you'd start wearing expensive clothes." "I've worn a t-shirt and jeans practically every day of my life." "And you'd start hanging out with different people." "I'm so shy I don't even hang out with the people I know now!"

For months, every time we thought we'd really gotten somewhere on the Condé Nast deal, we'd get a call from Paul Graham. "Don't get your hopes up," he'd say. "Deals fall through." Whenever we passed him on the street, "Deals fall through." In emails, "Deals fall through." It got to the point that Alexis put up a photo of Paul Graham and captioned it "Deals fall through."

I got an email from Paul Graham the other day. "Ok," he wrote. "Now you can get your hopes up."

November 3, 2006

---

1. http://edition.cnn.com/US/9709/18/turner.gift/

MEETING PETER SINGER

I remember watching an episode of *Penn & Teller* about animal rights. As usual, the show mostly consisted of a long series of clips relating to animal rights, followed by comments from Penn making fun of the idea. This show, I recall, was particularly weak. They didn't even pretend to make an argument; it was entirely mockery.

Watching this, I couldn't help but realize there was a powerful logical argument at the core of the animal rights groups: animals should be treated much the same way humans are — their lives should be respected, their pain minimized, etc. Make this one simple change to your system of morality and everything else falls into place. PETA actually seems kind of measured when they refer to "the Holocaust on your plate".

Peter Singer is the moral philosopher who has probably done the most to promote this idea. With a wide-ranging career spanning from Marx to meat, his book *Animal Liberation*, which quietly and thoughtfully makes this case, is widely-regarded as launching the animal liberation movement.

I was recently dragged to the Boston Vegetarian Festival to see Singer speak about his new book, *The Way We Eat*, and was deeply impressed by his thoughtfulness and clarity of mind. An aging fellow with thoughtful glasses, he looks like Noam Chomsky, another plainspoken professor. He is not a passionate activist who has taken on the cause of animals, but simply what he appears: a moral philosopher who started thinking about the issue one day and drew the logical conclusions.

After his talk, a woman in the audience asked a question about the rumors that he would sometimes eat non-vegan food. The audience was scandalized. "Let me address that," Singer said. "I don't believe in veganism as a religion. I simply believe that refraining from eating animal products is the most effective way of putting pressure on producers to stop abusing and killing animals. Sometimes, if a host misunderstands my request and makes non-vegan food, instead of throwing it away, I will eat it. I don't think this is a problem, because I don't think this does any moral harm."

Another person asked how he could say good things about Whole Foods when they were still serving numerous animal products. "Whole Foods has the best standards for animal treatment of any major organization," he replied. "That's simply a fact. And, I think it's a good thing. Do I think not using animals at all would be even better? Of course. But I praise people for the good things they do and condemn them for the bad ones."

A final question raised the incrementalism versus revolutionism debate common to all left-wing social movements. Should one really worry about animal treatment when the animals were still going to be killed? Pinger said the answer was undoubtedly yes. "Look, I thought that when *Animal Liberation* came out everyone would read it and become a vegan. But it's been thirty years and vegans are still less than 10% of the population. If you genuinely care about animal suffering, you have to admit that, and say, 'what else can we do to ease animal suffering?'"

After Singer's talk, I began thinking through the consequences of his morality. A question occurred to me: "Should we also stop animals from eating each other?" I was sure others had made such arguments as *reductio ad absurdums* of vegetarianism, but I thought I might be the first to be genuinely interested in it from a moral perspective.

"Of course not," said my friend. "It's not our fault if the animals kill each other." "You mean," I said, "that you think it's perfectly moral to let that guy" — I pointed at a random guy nearby — "go around killing people?" "Well, OK," he said. "But it's different with animals, because they don't know any better." "You mean it would be OK to let him go around killing people if he was mentally ill and didn't realize he was doing it?" "You should go ask Singer," he said.

So I did — he was signing books outside the lecture hall and as the line ended I asked him my question. His answer was even better than I imagined: "We would if we knew how to do so without making things worse and disturbing the ecosystems and so on." "Thanks!" I said, impressed. He spied the large white book I was hugging to my chest. "Are you reading Kolakowski?" he asked. "Yep," I said smiling. "Had to read that when I was studying Marx a long time ago. It's heavy," he said. "Quite literally!" I replied, hefting the 1200 page book. He smiled.

"I have to say, though," I said, feeling guilty, "that I don't agree with your *Darwinian Left* stuff." "That's OK," he replied. "You don't need to agree with everything I write." Then he wandered off, looking for the next thing to see.

I had to get that off my chest, because it was the one thing bugging me about Singer. Somehow later in life Singer had become a sociobiologist, one of that vulgar group of psuedoscientists who insist — despite all evidence — that humans are genetically programmed to do all everything a right-wing politician could imagine. (Sociobiology having gotten a bad name, they now call themselves evolutionary psychologists.)

In his book *A Darwinian Left*, however, Singer explains that this is no reason for the left to despair. If people are actually born stupid, that's only more justification for left-wing policies. We need to provide the stupid people with the extra resources to live on equal terms as the smart people. Steven Pinker cites this book (along with Singer's *The Expanding Circle*) several times in his execrable *Blank Slate* to prove that his noxious views aren't necessarily right-wing. (Neither Pinker nor Singer, of course, provide any real evidence to show this actually is the way humans are.)

That said, as usual Singer's conclusions do follow from his premises — if you do make that one small change to the way you think the world works, then his conclusions about what we should do to remedy it undoubtedly follow. I just wish he'd check his assumptions.

That aside, it seems unfair to dismiss Singer on the basis of a small blemish on an incredibly long and varied career — Wikipedia lists over forty books he's written or co-authored. His thoughtfulness and clarity in sharing it is an example to us all.

November 13, 2006

CAUSES OF CONFORMANCE

Institutions require people to do their bidding. A tobacco company must find people willing to get kids addicted to cigarettes, a school must find teachers willing to repeat the same things that they were taught, a government must find public servants willing to enforce the law.

Part of this is simply necessity. To survive, people need money; to get money, people need a job; to get a job, people need to find an existing institution. But the people in these positions don't usually see themselves as mercenaries, doing the smallest amount to avoid getting fired while retaining their own value system. Instead, they adopt the value system of the institution, pushing it even when it's not necessary for their own survival. What explains this pattern of conformance?

The most common explanation is an active process of beating people in: politicians get paid campaign contributions (legalized bribes) to meet the needs of the wealthy, employees get bonuses and penalties for meeting the needs of their employers, kids get threatened with time-outs and bad grades if they don't follow the demands of their teachers. In each case, the people are forced through a series of carrots and sticks to learn the values of the people in charge.

This is a fairly blatant form of conformance, but I suspect it's by far the least effective. Studies on punishment and rewards show that dealing them out lessens the victim's identification with the enforcer. Hitting me every time I don't do my job right may teach me how to do my job, but it's not going to make me particularly excited about it.

Indeed, punishments and rewards interfere with a much more significant effect: cognitive dissonance. Cognitive dissonance studies have found that simply by getting you to do something, you can be persuaded to agree with it. In a classic study, students asked to write an essay in favor of a certain position were found to agree more with the position than students who could write for either position. Similarly, people who pay more to eat a certain food claim to like it more than people who pay less.

The basic theory is that people work to lessen the disagreement between their beliefs and their actions and in most cases it's simply easier to change your beliefs. Quitting your job for the government is tough and painful; and who knows if you'll soon find another? So it's much easier to simply persuade yourself that you agree with the government, that you're doing the right and noble thing, that your work to earn a paycheck is really a service to mankind.

Of course, it also helps that everyone you're surrounded by feels the same way. Culture is another important influence on our beliefs. Another raft of social psychology studies find that people are willing to deny even obvious truths to fit in with a group. In the famous Asch studies on conformance, a group of confederates were seated around a table, with the subject of the experiment on the end. Everyone at the table was given a sheet with three lines, one obviously longer than the other, and then was asked to name the two lines of identical length. All of the confederates gave an obviously wrong answer and by the time the question got to the guy at the end, he ended up conforming and giving the wrong answer as well.

Similarly, spend your days in government offices where people simply take it for granted that they're doing the right thing, and you're likely to pick up that tacit assumption yourself. Such ideas are not only frequently stated, they're often the very foundation of the discussion. And foundational ideas are particularly hard to question, particularly because they're so taken for granted.

But perhaps the most important effect for conformance is simply selection. Imagine that nobody was corruptible, that all the carrots and sticks in the world couldn't get someone to do something they thought morally wrong, that they stood fast in the face of cognitive dissonance, and that their moral fiber was so strong that they were able to resist a less conscientious culture. Even then, it wouldn't make much difference. As long as there was enough variety in people and their moral values, all an organization would need to do is simply fire (or fail to promote) everyone who didn't play their game.

Everyone knows you climb the corporate ladder by being a "team player". Those who make a fuss or don't quite live up to expectations simply get passed over for a promotion. The result is simply that — without any explicit pressure at all — the people in positions of power happen to be the ones who identify with the organization's aims.

It's easy to look at the rather more flashy pieces of punishing people for failing to follow orders or living in a culture of conformity. But for those who want obedient employees, sometimes the most effective technique is simply failing to say yes.

December 28, 2006

BUSINESS 'ETHICS'

Moral Mazes (one of my very favorite books) tells the story of a company, chosen essentially at random, and through careful investigation from top to bottom explains precisely how it operates, with the end result of explaining how so many well-intentioned people can end up committing so much evil.

This week's scene takes place inside a textile processing plant at Weft Corporation, where the company's poor low-paid workers are suffering from byssinosis. Byssinosis, also called Brown Lung Disease, is when your lungs fill up with cotton dust. Eventually your throat closes up and you suffocate to death. The company insists the whole thing is a stunt made up by Ralph Nader and other liberal do-gooders. But one day they change their tune:

Weft, as well as all the other large and medium-sized American textile companies, was actually addressing the cotton dust problem, but in a characteristically indirect way. As part of a larger modernization effort, the firm invested $20 million in a few plants where executives knew such an investment would make money. ... The investment had the side benefit of reducing cotton dust levels ... One manager who was in charge of the project ... comments on whether dust control was a principal factor in the decision...:

No, definitely not. Would any sane, rational man spend $15 million for a 2 percent return? ... Now it does improve the dust levels, but it was that if we don't invest the money now, we would be in a desperate [competitive] position fifteen years from now. ... It was on these bases that the decision was made.

Publicly, of course, Weft Corporation, as do many other firms, claims that the money was spent entirely to eliminate dust, evidence of its corporate good citizenship. Privately, executives admit that without the productive return, they would not have — indeed, given the constraints under which they operate — could not have spent the money. And they have not done so in several other plants and only with great reluctance, if at all, in sections of otherwise renovated plants where it is more difficult to ... achieve simultaneous cost and dust reduction.

(Robert Jackall, *Moral Mazes*, 158f)

What does Jackall mean that the executives "could not have spent the money ... given the constraints under which they operate"? Another story in the book about the chemical corporation Alchemy illustrates his point:

Consider, for instance, the case of a large coking plant of the chemical company. [Coking is a chemical process for distilling coal.] Coke making requires a giant battery to cook the coke slowly and evenly for long periods; the battery is the most significant piece of capital equipment in a coking plant. In 1975, the plant's battery showed signs of weakening and certain managers at corporate headquarters had to decide whether to invest $6 million to restore the battery to top form. Clearly, because of the amount of money involved, this was a gut decision.

No decision was made. The CEO had sent the word out to defer all the unnecessary capital expenditures to give the corporation cash reserves for other investments. So the managers allocated small amounts of money to patch the battery up until 1979, when it collapsed entirely. This brought the company into breach of contract with a steel producer and into violation of various Environmental Protection Agency (EPA) pollution regulations. The total bill, including lawsuits and now federally mandated repairs to the battery, exceeded $100 million. I have heard figures as high as $150 million, but because of "creative accounting," no one is sure of the exact amount.

This simple but very typical example gets to the heart of how decision making was intertwined with a company's authority structure and advancement patterns.

... Had they acted decisively in 1975 — in hindsight, the only substantively rational choice — they would have salvaged the battery and saved their company millions of dollars in the long run.

In the short run, however, ... they would have been taking serious personal risks in restoring the battery. ... their political networks might have unraveled, leaving them vulnerable to attack. ... A manager at Weft Corporation reflects:

People are always calculating how others will see the decisions they make. ... They know that they have to gauge not just the external ... market consequences of a decision, but the internal political consequences. And sometimes you can make the right market decision, but it can be the wrong political decision.

(Mazes, 81-84)

Had the manager in charge of the plant with the ailing battery done the replacement, his department would be six million dollars less profitable. When it came time to compare managers for the next promotion, he would seem massively less efficient than the guy running the plant next door. He'd be passed by and his corporate ascendency would be over.

Corporate managers simply aren't allowed to be moral, or even reasonable. And those who try are simply weeded out. Not only does the manager who replaced the battery get passed over for the job; the manager who was obedient enough not to gets promoted to a more powerful position.

December 11, 2006

THE GENIUS IS IN THE DETAILS

As best as we can tell, the human brain works by mastering a specific thing and then "giving it a name", wrapping the whole thing up into a bundle and pushing it down a level, so that things can then be built with it as a component. You see this all over the place — it's how science works, it's how you program, it's even how people deal with their friends ("let's do the mall again").

So it would seem natural to think that smart people would work on a very high level, dealing not in details but in huge abstractions. They would have turned everything into a component, no longer worrying about its details, and built things out of the results.

Bizarrely, this seems entirely untrue. The smartest people I know disdain abstractions, preferring to speak in concrete specifics. Take Paul Buchheit, the genius behind Gmail. When he talks about building web applications, he doesn't think about high-level things like the underlying semantic structure of the data — instead he talks about the little "heads" that read data off of the hard disk and how fast they can move.

Another friend, also incredibly bright, doesn't refer to other people that way. He doesn't say "oh, he's an expert in X" or "he's really smart about X"; instead he says "he's thought a lot about X" — breaking down the abstractions of expertise and intelligence into something much more concrete: spending time thinking about something.

At first glance these seem like mistakes. Why should a brilliant web app programmer be thinking about hard disk heads? Isn't that something someone else should take care of? And why is my smart friend only concerned with how much time someone has spent on something? Aren't there other factors involved?

But if you look the other direction, you see the same pattern. Clueless business guys love speaking in big abstractions, talking about "information superhighways" that act as "more efficient content delivery systems" that will "monetize the genre" by "disintermediating the legacy players". These guys are speaking exactly as you would expect smart people to — thinking at a high level, working with the big ideas — yet the things they say are so incredibly stupid that they either don't mean anything or mean something that's actually impossible.

So what's going on here? As we noted at the beginning, the brain works by mastering the details and then giving them a name. But the business guys took the easy way out: they just mastered the names. If you asked them exactly how a content delivery system worked, they wouldn't be able to tell you. They know only the high-level thing, with none of the details.

And it's the details that make it so interesting — and so powerful. Anyone can master the names of big concepts and combine them like so many puzzle pieces; it's knowing how they work that takes time. And the smart people have made that investment. So perhaps it's just natural that they want to stay it a little closer to it than most.

December 4, 2006

TWO CONCEPTIONS OF TASTE

Taste is difficult to define and even harder to justify, so let us just take it for granted for a moment. (Alright, for those who don't get the picture, here's a quick attempt: taste is the ability to create elegance. The people who made the iPod clearly have taste; the people who made Windows do not.) Unfortunately for me, it seems like a lot of people in the US don't have much taste. (Try watching the infographics on the network evening news, for example.) But even among people who have taste, I've noticed there are two kinds: positive and negative.

Negative taste is the ability to tell when something is bad. Positive taste is the ability to make something that is good. Indeed, one might even say that there is only one kind of taste and positive taste is simply negative taste plus skills. But since taste is generally inferred from creations, it's probably simpler to treat them as two different things.

People with negative taste can make things that look really nice, but they also look very plain. I think the founders of Google have negative taste. John Gruber, as far as I can tell, mostly does. Same with Paul Graham. (As do I, for that matter.) People with negative taste make things by trying something very simple and then stripping away pieces until it looks good. They can detect goodness, but not create it, so they're limited to designs with very few variables, because then they can go thru all the options and pick out the ones that look OK.

People with positive taste, on the other hand, can make things that genuinely look good. This gives them a lot more freedom in their designs (they can use colors other than white!). Truly good designers have positive taste. Unfortunately for people like us, Apple seems to have hired most of them and put them to work building fairly bland web sites.

Of course, taste applies to far more fields than design. One could apply the same idea to writing. Positive taste writers can write beautiful flowing prose that looks you in. Negative taste writers can only write beautiful things by staying simple.

People with negative taste can recognize people with positive taste and hire them. People with no taste, on the other hand, fail to see the difference, resulting in disasters like the graphic design department of American Airlines.

People with negative taste can also be critics, which brings us to Joe Clark's famous comment[1] "Actually, no, it is not the responsibility of the critic to solve the problem. Pauline Kael was not expected to rewrite and redirect the films she disliked."

People with negative taste can pick out the bad movies. They just can't make great ones.

Followups: John Siracusa, Hypercritical[2] (2009)

December 1, 2006

1. http://lists.w3.org/Archives/Public/w3c-wai-ig/2004JulSep/0237.html
2. http://arstechnica.com/staff/fatbits/2009/05/hypercritical.ars

A MOMENT BEFORE DYING

There is a moment, immediately before life becomes no longer worth living, when the world appears to slow down and all its myriad details suddenly become brightly, achingly apparent.

For Alex, that moment came after exactly one week of pain, seven days of searing, tormenting agony that poured forth from his belly. Alex never liked his belly. Growing up he was always fat, surrounded by a family of bellowing, rotund

Americans, who had a room in their house with wall-to-wall, floor-to-ceiling cabinets, all entirely filled with bags and boxes of various pre-processed semi-organic assemblages, which they used to stuff their faces at all hours of the day.

Alex had body image issues. He'd avoid mirrors because he couldn't bear to look at himself, his large bulbous cheeks obscuring his fine features. He avoided photos, covering his face or ducking out of the way when the click of the camera came, for the same reason: he didn't want to be confronted with the physical evidence of his disgusting nature, thought he could not go on living if he had to face the truth.

It wasn't until he got away from his family that he discovered his weight was not an immutable characteristic, like the fingerprints he often mused about burning off, like the dental records which had caused him so much adolescent anguish, like the DNA he'd heard so much about in school. He would take off his shirt and stare at his stomach in the full-length mirror. It was there, of course, hideous as ever, but also appreciably smaller. Its size, he realized, could change.

So Alex starved himself. Cut down from three meals a day to simply two and then to only one. And even that became superfluous most days. Alex simply wasn't hungry.

He watched his stomach dwindle, monitored his progress on the electronic readout of his at-home scale, charted the numbers on his computer, admired the plunging trendlines.

He was doing so well. He told all his friends. The secret to losing weight, he would explain, is simply not eating. You just get used to it after a while. He looked at the beggars outside his window and refrained from giving them change so that they too could experience this miracle. He changed the channel when the radio began speaking about starvation in Africa. "Starvation isn't so bad," he scoffed. "You get used to it after a while." He wondered whether the USDA thrifty food budget could be further reduced.

He stopped going out. His friends always wanted to meet him for meals, or for drinks, events in which Alex simply wasn't interested anymore. Before long, Alex's friends were no longer interested in him.

Alex started eating in cafés, ordering a small pastry, sitting in a comfortable chair, listening to the music play over the loudspeakers. Soon he stopped doing even that.

Alex read on the Internet about death. There was a theory, increasingly well supported, that eating is what killed you. They found that rats on extremely restricted diets, rats who ate very few calories, lived impressively long. They saw the same results with other animals, up to and including chimpanzees. They suspected, but could not prove, the same was true of humans. Every little bite of food was another step towards death.

Alex started eating again. His appetite grew as slowly as it had declined but within months he was back to eating three meals a day. Food suddenly gave him pleasure again. He savored the tastes on his tongue.

One night he and his friends decided to try a new restaurant. But when the food came, Alex couldn't eat it. He thought it smelled funny. He let it sit there, his plate lying on the table, his food seething, untouched.

The next night Alex couldn't sleep. He'd wake up, feeling searing pains in his stomach, as if the food winding its way through his gut had spikes and was tearing apart the walls of his intestine.

He suffered like this for days, rolling on the floor in agony, unable to resist eating but every bite he ate causing him unimaginable pain. And still, he could not stop.

Five days in, it seemed like the worst had passed. The pains came less frequently, the pains were less intense. He actually slept that night.

The day Alex killed himself, he was awoken by pains, worse than ever. He rolled back-and-forth in bed as the sun came up, the light streaming through the windows eliminating the chance for any further sleep. At 9, he was startled by a phone call. The pains subsided, as if quieting down to better hear what the phone might say.

It was his boss. He had not been to work all week. He had been fired. Alex tried to explain himself, but couldn't find the words. He hung up the phone instead.

The day Alex killed himself, he wandered his apartment in a daze. The light streaming through the windows gave everything a golden glow, which had the odd effect of making the filth he'd become surrounded with seem cinematic.

Alex wanted to go outside for one last meal, but he had trouble making the appropriate connections. Jacket, shoes, pants, wallet. Each lay in a different spot upon the floor. Alex knew they went together, he drew lines connecting them in his mind's eye, but it didn't see to fix anything, his eyes just kept bouncing from one item to another.

Finally, he summoned the intelligence to put them on. The world seemed funny afterwards. He noticed the way the key turned in the lock, like a hand rotating in front of his face, an interplay of light and shadow, objects in space. He noticed the packages sitting at his doorstep, begging him to open them, but their labels insisting that they were addressed to someone else. He noticed the frail old ladies who refused to obey the walk — don't walk signs and instead walked slowly, backs hunched, across a major intersection.

He went to a new café across the street, the one place he hadn't been to yet. Light streamed in through the huge picture windows, making the whole place seem bright and airy. So much light, in fact, that the outside seemed a glow, as if the café was suspended in the middle of a powerful white light. People held lowered, indistinct conversations. People on his left, people on his right, people behind him. But one conversation seemed to be coming from the ceiling. It might have been a trick of the acoustics. He looked up and saw two speakers staring back at him and listened closely.

The café was not playing music. It was playing a recording of two people's lowered, indistinct conversation.

The day Alex killed himself, he had a sudden, powerful craving for a Key Lime Sugar Cookie. It was odd the power the Key Lime Sugar Cookie had over him. Alex did not particularly like limes of any sort. In fact, the idea of an actual actual, as with all fruits, thoroughly disgusted him. He hated how when he ordered sparkling water at fancy restaurants they would place a lime wedge on the top of his glass, how he had to confront the disgusting object every time he tried to take a sip, how touching the lime, even to remove it, was so disgusting as to be simply out of the question.

And yet, here it was, this cookie, with the lime flavor baked into the center and large transparent grains of sugar embedded in the top, begging for him, begging for one last taste. The cookie was sold exclusively by a publicly-traded chain of cafés that tried hard to seem international, giving itself a foreign-sounding title and printing the names of major world cities on every door, even though it had not expanded much beyond the eastern half of the United States. Alex purchased the cookie.

He noticed the way he couldn't quite form the words to request it, simply presented the cookie in front of the cashier and twitched his head, assuming (correctly) that in context the request would be understood. He noticed the way his hands moved haphazardly to remove the appropriate amount of money from his wallet. He noticed the way his change spilled out onto the counter as he tried to find the quarter with which to complete the transaction. He noticed the way he wobbled as he walked as he took the now-purchased cookie outside.

The day Alex killed himself, he savored his one remaining cookie, the sweetness of the embedded sugar grains, the bizarre flavor of what must have been lime. He used his tongue to wipe the remaining crumbs from his teeth, tossed the now-empty bag it had come in into the trash, and stepped out into the middle of the street.

January 18, 2007

THE SOCIOLOGIST'S CREED

"Men make their own history, but they do not make it as they please; they do not make it under self-selected circumstances, but under circumstances existing already, given and transmitted from the past. The tradition of all dead generations weighs like a nightmare on the brains of the living."

(Karl Marx, The Eighteenth Brumaire of Louis Napoleon)

January 2, 2007

THE ACTIVIST'S CREED

"True, those who have abandoned the life of a free man do nothing but boast incessantly of the peace and repose they enjoy in their chains. But when I see the other sacrifice pleasures, repose, wealth, power and life itself for the preservation of this sole good, which is so disdained by those who have lost it, when I see multitudes of entirely naked savages scorn European voluptuousness and endure hunger, fire, the sword and death to preserve only their independence, I feel it does not behoove slaves to reason about freedom."

(Jean-Jacques Rousseau, Second Treatise on Inequality)

February 11, 2007

THE INTELLECTUAL'S CREED

[T]he ideas of economists and political philosophers, both when they are right and when they are wrong, are more powerful than is commonly understood. Indeed the world is ruled by little else. Practical men, who believe themselves to be quite exempt from any intellectual influences, are usually the slaves of some defunct economist. Madmen in authority, who hear voices in the air, are distilling their frenzy from some academic scribbler of a few years back. I am sure that the power of vested interests is vastly exaggerated compared with the gradual encroachment of ideas. Not, indeed, immediately, but after a certain interval; for in the field of economic and political philosophy there are not many who are influenced by new theories after they are twenty-five or thirty years of age, so that the ideas which civil servants and politicians and even agitators apply to current events are not likely to be the newest. But, soon or late, it is ideas, not vested interests, which are dangerous for good or evil.

(John Maynard Keynes, General Theory, last page)

March 5, 2009

GETTING PAST

He called me into his office. It was an imposing room, wood paneling and a window opening on to a picturesque view of the water. An ornate light fixture hung from the ceiling, illuminating the mahogany desk, neatly organized with boxes OUT and IN, with a stack of paper, with a pad for writing on. There was no computer. He didn't need a computer. A computer would have ruined the look.

The walls were lined with bookshelves and the bookshelves were lined with management texts. Books on how to make people eat cheese, how to make them say yes, how to make them think positive thoughts, how to make them get rich. Books on locks and unlocking, thoughts and unthinking, beings and unbeing.

"Take a seat, Geoffrey," he said, looking at me from behind glasses, a tailored suit hanging on his frame. I obeyed, as I always did. It was an order.

"There's been concern around the office," he said. No agent. Not "people are concerned", not "I'm concerned", simply that "there's been concern", as if it was some poisonous gas that had been leaking out of my cubicle, green fumes floating in mid-air.

"There's been concern that you're not being a team player." A sports metaphor. Here we are, all rocketing towards the goal, filing our TPS reports in tandem, and me? I'm not being a team player. I'm sitting in the corner playing Minesweeper or one of those online flash games with the little jewels. The team's let down. I'm holding everyone up.

"I think that the best way forward is for us to get past this," he explains. Isn't that always the case? If we're on a path, and there's a rock, then obviously we have to go past it to go forward. We could go a different direction, but then we wouldn't be going forward anymore. But how did I become a rock?

"It's clear to all of us," he says. But who's "us"? There's only him here. "It's clear to all of us that your heart's not in it." I imagine myself, lying on the surgery table, the bright light shining from above, with an army of hims surrounding me; they're the us. One of him asks another for the scalpel, takes it, begins cutting out my still-beating heart. Aha, they think, his heart's not in it — it's still in him.

They toss the heart in the trash and file out. They need to interview another job candidate.

February 8, 2007

NEUROSIS #9

So here I am. We're somewhere over a dark patch in the middle of the country and I'm in the window seat in the last row in the plane. The guy in front of me's leaning all the way back, but I'm in the last row so my seat doesn't go back, and I have to lift my legs up to stretch out a muscle that was sitting funny while I was asleep. So here I sit, scrunched up in the the last row of the plane, my thighs hugged against my chest, my knees digging into the seat in front of me, my back curved funny from being unable to recline. But that's not the problem.

No, the problem is that I am terribly, almost unbearably, thirsty. My mouth has been dry for hours, we're long past that. Now I'm so thirsty that the color has drained from my face, because there simply is no fluid left to keep it there. I am so thirsty that it's beginning to feel like there's no water around to hydrate my brain so my neocortex is getting and shrivelling up. It's an odd feeling, your brain shriveling up. It makes it hard to think. But I guess that's not really the problem either.

The problem, the real problem I suppose, is that I can't ask for anything to drink. I am perfectly justified — I was asleep during the drink service, I am quite terribly thirsty, my flight is unusually uncomfortable to begin with — yet I cannot bring myself to do it. As the flight attendants walk briskly by, I fail to catch their eyes. And the a man sitting in the seat next to me on the aisle has headphones on, so I can't exactly interrupt him. I could ring my flight attendant call button, but I've never quite been able to bring myself to do that. I'm so close to the flight attendants anyway.

If I rang the call button, I tell myself, I wouldn't ask for a Sprite. I'd just ask for water. Asking for a Sprite, it'd seem like I was interrupting them just so I could get my soda fix. Like I was some sort of petulant child who had to have his soda and was going to throw a temper tantrum if they didn't get it. Like a troublemaker, the kind of person they look down on. But water? Water they'd understand: it was a genuine medical request, a normal, physical human need. Something totally worth taking the extraordinary step of pressing the flight attendant call button.

But I can't bring myself to do it. It seems like such an imposition.

This, I suppose, is the actual problem: I feel my existence is an imposition on the planet. Not a huge one, perhaps, not a huge one at all, but an imposition nonetheless. When I go to a library and I see the librarian at her desk reading, I'm afraid to interrupt her, even though she sits there specifically so that she may be interrupted, even though being interrupted by for reasons like this by people like me is her very job. At the fast food restaurant, I feel embarrassed taking time to pick through my pocket for appropriate change, so I always give them whole bills, then feel embarrassed when they have to take the time to count me out change. When someone asks me what high school I'm going to, I feel awkward explaining to them that I've gone to high school and to college and then started a company and sold it, so I just stutter a bit and then tell them that my high school is outside of Chicago.

I realize this is neurotic. Maybe not the high school thing, maybe that's just politeness, but certainly the thing right now, the brain shriveling with the knees digging and yet still the fear of asking for some water. "This is neurotic, Aaron," I say to myself. "You are being neurotic. It is not normal to be this shy. And geez, certainly you of all people have little justification for being so undemanding."

I am a good person, I mean. I work hard, I happily pay my taxes, I think of ways to make the world a better place, I always look the woman behind the counter in the eye and say "thank you, thank you," as if I really mean it, as if I really do appreciate the effort it took for her punch my order into her cash register and withdraw the right amount of change. And I do! So I deserve this, I deserve my glass of water, my can of soda. I am not like one of those people who goes around robbing banks and mugging old ladies and then stands in front of me in the supermarket line, throwing a tantrum about how dare the clerk not accept my credit card. No, I am perfectly justified in asking for a glass of water. I know all this, and yet, somehow, I still feel like an imposition.

Normally, it's not so bad feeling this way. Normally, I just sit in my quiet little room and do the small things that bring me pleasures. I read my books, I answer email, I write a little bit. I'm not such a nuisance to the world, and the kick I get out of living can, I suppose, justify the impositions I make on it. But when life isn't so fun, well, then I start to wonder. What's the point of going on if it's just trouble for us both?

My friends will miss me, I am told. And I guess it's somewhat better around friends. For some reason asking them for things doesn't seem quite so bad. Perhaps we've established some rapport, perhaps I feel I've given *them* enough to justify my small requests, perhaps I feel like my friends are special people who think along the same lines I do and thus understand my needs. (Inner critic: "Yeah, only a fellow genius would understand your special need for *water*. Jesus, what a dweeb.") But even so, I feel reticent. Even among my closest friends, I still feel like something of an imposition, and the slightest shock, the slightest hint that I'm correct, sends me scurrying back into my hole.

I know, I know, I'm wrong, I'm wrong to feel this way. My friends love me. They remark, spontaneously, about how nice it is to have me around. They invite me over to their houses to hang out. Indeed, at this very moment, two of my very favorite people to hang out with are actually fighting — fighting! — over the supposed privilege of having me live with them. "I just want to point out," one says, "that I have never tickled you." "I just want to point out," replies the other, "that I have never gotten you to attach clothespins to your face."

Clearly, rationally, I am in the wrong. These people like me. (Inner cynic: "If only to have someone around to tickle and pinch.") No, no, they genuinely like me. But the idea that people might actually want to be around me takes an amazing amount of getting used to. Last night, for the first time, I invited some people over to my apartment. I've never done this before. But, to my amazement, they all came. They even brought their friends. I ran out of chairs. The idea that a group of people would want to come over to see me was kind of stunning. Someone even brought wine.

OK, so perhaps there is a small group of people who, whether through quirks of genetics or some childhood trauma, appear, as best as I can tell, to actively enjoy my company. (Inner elitist: "Or just need excuses to drink wine?") But this does not excuse my impositions on the store clerk, the librarian, the man inquiring after my high school who I downright lied to — *lied* to! — just to avoid pointing out the error of his preconceptions, the bus driver who I had to distract with my inability to use the new stored-value payment machines, or the waiter at that restaurant I went to the other day who, I later realized to my endless mortification, I forgot to properly tip. (Waiter, if you're out there, please send me your address so I can mail you your tip! I'm so sorry!) These people did not request the dubious pleasure of my company. I have no justification for bothering them with my requests.

February 7, 2007

EVERYTHING GOOD IS BAD FOR YOU

While we were developing Reddit, we always used to run into people who'd recognize us and come up to say hi. "Oh, wow," they'd say to us. "I can't tell you how much your site has killed my productivity. I check it a hundred times every day." At first, we just laughed these comments off. But after a while, I begun to find them increasingly disturbing. We'd set out to make something people want — but what if they didn't want to want it?

For too long, simple popularity has been the only metric of a startup's success. Another startup, known as Twitter, has recently broken into the mainstream. And I constantly hear people saying things like "Yeah, well, I know it seems like a pointless waste of time. But it's so popular!" As if anything so *popular* had to be worthwhile.

Cory Doctorow recently made a similar argument[1]. When he publishes his books online, he notes, people are always telling him they don't like reading off a screen. And yet, these very same people spend every free hour of the day reading email and weblogs and news articles off a screen. "It's like watching someone shovel Mars Bars into his gob while telling you how much he hates chocolate," Doctorow complains. Doctorow's conclusion? Blogs are just better.

But I think Mars Bars are just the right analogy. Everyone in America knows that it's easy to accidentally find yourself stuffing your face with junk food when you're not paying attention. But no one would seriously maintain that junk food is better than fine cuisine. It's just easier.

Similarly, if you printed out all the blog posts and news articles and emails the average timewaster reads in a month and placed the resulting hulking volume down next to a copy of, say, *War and Peace* (which it would no doubt dwarf), it's hard to imagine the average person saying they'd actually prefer to sit down and read the first. (If *War and Peace* doesn't strike your fancy, substitute a similarly large tome.) But reading bite-sized blog posts is by far *easier*.

The same goes for reading stories on Reddit or your friends' pointless twits about their life. Looking at photos of sunsets or reading one-liners takes no cognitive effort. It's the mental equivalent of snack food. You start eating one and before you know it you've gone through two cans of Pringles and become a world expert on Evan Williams' travel habits.

We need to stop pretending that this is automatically a good thing. Perhaps Procter & Gamble doesn't care of their making us into a nation of fat slobs, but there's no reason why programmers and the rest of the startup world need to be so amoral. And no doubt, as pictures of cats with poor spelling on them become all the rage, people are beginning to wonder about where all this idiocy is leaving us. Which is where apologists like Doctorow and Steven Johnson step in, assuring us that Everything Bad is Good For You.

It isn't. YouTube isn't going to save us from an *Idiocracy*-style future in which everyone sits at home and watches shows like "Ow! My Balls!" (in which a man is repeatedly hit in the balls) — YouTube's damn-near creating that future. As I write this, YouTube's #1 featured video is titled "Farting in Public".

It doesn't have to be that way, of course. Nobody prefers farting to thought. It's just that, as David Foster Wallace noted about television, "people tend to be extremely similar in their vulgar and prurient and dumb interests and wildly different in their refined and aesthetic and noble interests." Similarly, no one (Doctorow included, I suspect), actually prefers blog posts to novels, it's just that people tend to have more short chunks of time to read blog posts than they do long chunks of time to read novels.

Technology was supposed to let us solve these problems. But technology never solves things by itself. At bottom, it requires people to sit down and build tools that solve them. Which, as long as programmers are all competing to create the world's most popular timewaster, it doesn't seem like anyone is going to do.

March 29, 2007

1. http://www.locusmag.com/Features/2007/03/cory-doctorow-you-do-like-reading-off.html

AARON'S PATENTED DEMOTIVATIONAL SEMINAR

Thousands of people out there are willing to give you a motivational seminar, but only Aaron's Patented Demotivational Seminars are going to actually admit they demotivate you. I've collected thousands of actual facts from real scientists and the verdict is in: people don't matter, except for a couple of rare exceptions, and you're not one of them. Sorry.

Let's start at the beginning, shall we? The universe is a bunch of random particles shooting through space following a handful of simple laws. Through completely random and unintentional properties, some of those particles bounced together to form you. But, I swear, it was a total accident. They didn't even realize they were doing it at the time and if they knew they'd probably feel kind of guilty about it.

For a long time, it was pretty clear that most people didn't matter. The average person didn't leave their town or village and so only interacted with a small handful of people who lived near them, most of whom found them annoying. The Internet has changed all that. Now the average person doesn't leave their computer and so only interacts with a small handful of spammers who read their LiveJournal, most of whom find them annoying. Luckily for posterity, their LiveJournal will probably disappear within their lifetime due to a hard drive crash or some other kind of poor server maintenance.

But let's say you want to make a difference in the world. You can learn a skill and go into a profession, where you get bossed around and told exactly what to do by people more powerful than you. (Obeying them is called "professionalism".) It's completely futile; had you not gone into the professional (or if you decide to disobey orders) they would have found someone else to do the exact same thing.

The same is true even if you're the one giving orders. Imagine about the most powerful job you can think of. Let's say you're a US Supreme Court Justice, able to change the laws of the world's only superpower with the stroke of your pen. Well, big deal. Had you not been appointed to the Supreme Court the President who appointed you would have found some other judge who would have made the same changes to the law. Yeah, you get to wear a robe and feel powerful, but when you look at the cold, hard, scientific facts, you're not making a lick of difference in the world.

Want to actually make a difference? You'll have to buck the system instead of joining it.

March 27, 2007

THE SECRET BEHIND *THE SECRET*

The #1 bestselling book in America is a 216-page volume called *The Secret*, based on a DVD of the same title. "Truly life-changing information," exclaims the publisher on Amazon.com. "A new era for humankind," exults the web site. "This is The Secret to everything — the secret to unlimited joy, health, money, relationships, love, youth: everything you have ever wanted. […] [It] utterly transformed the lives of every person who ever knew it… Plato, Newton, Carnegie, Beethoven, Shakespeare, Einstein."

What is this incredible secret? Namely, that the universe is governed by a heretofore unknown Law of Attraction, as yet undiscovered by conventional physicists, that the world rearranges itself to conform to your thoughts. Or, as one proponent put it, the universe "is akin to a big mail-order department," in which you "'order' what you get by sending energetic messages out to the universe."

This stuff is so blatantly absurd that it's not really worth debunking. And it's silly enough that Barbara Ehrenreich has already written the definitive mockery[1] ("Thoughts exert a gravitational-type force on the world, so that 'whenever you think something, the thought immediately attracts its physical equivalent.' If you think money — in a totally urgent, focused and positive way, of course — it will come flying into your pockets."). Twice[2] ("I don't have to write this blog, I can simply visualize it already written — or could, if I'd bothered to read the whole book and finish the DVD.")

But, drawing on some of Ehrenreich's other work, I'd like to discuss they *why* of this book. The book's success is easy enough to explain. As the Canadian publisher put it[3] in an interview with the *Toronto Star*, "Basically, human beings are lazy. If you tell them you can get rich just by thinking about it, obviously, they're going to buy it."

But these books also have a more insidious effect. As Ehrenreich notes, by making your lack of wealth and a good job into personal problems, you discourage people from looking at the social systems that created and sustained those problems. By telling them their thoughts control the universe, you can persuade them to do things like — as one Secret-endorsing book encouraged — "Place your hand on your heart and say … 'I admire rich people!' 'I bless rich people!' 'I love rich people!' 'And I'm going to be one of those rich people too!'"

And, in reverse, by telling people that bad things are caused by their negative thoughts, you get to persuade them to stop thinking about bad things. "I'm a really big believer in The Secret," a young black woman recently explained at a Secret-related book reading. "But I also believe that discrimination and racism are real. How can you harmonize those things?"

"You just said you believe in discrimination," explained the guru. "You be-*live* it. I'm going to ask you to stop believing it, because if you focus on the negative, you project it yourself."

That's right — if you stop believing in the existence of discrimination, it'll stop happening to you. No need to fight to end it! Those black people banned from lunch counters in the South? They weren't simply believing hard enough. Those studies showing that resumes with black-sounding names on them received far fewer callbacks as identical ones with white-sounding names? The researchers didn't take into account their thoughtwaves.

Following this idea goes to some pretty dark places and the authors take it all the way. "I really love what you're doing," said a young man at the same event. "But how, for example, was 9/11 attracted to the people in those buildings? That's something I can't understand."

"Sometimes, we experience the law of attraction collectively," explains the guru. "The US maybe had a fear of being attacked. Those 3,000 people — they might have put out some kind of fear that attracted this to happen, fear of dying young, fear that something might happen that day. But sometimes, it is collective."

When you manage to convince people that even getting murdered is their own fault, you've truly found the secret of success. For the already powerful, that is.

March 26, 2007

1.   http://query.nytimes.com/gst/fullpage.html?res=9B00E5DF113CF937A2575BC0A
     9639C8B63&sec=&spon=&pagewanted=all
2.   http://ehrenreich.blogs.com/barbaras_blog/2007/02/the_secret_of_m.html
3.   http://www.thestar.com/article/193263

SICK

I'm sorry I haven't been keeping up with *Bubble City*. I've spent a lot of the last few weeks lying in bed and drinking fluids. (With occasional breaks to play Rock Band, much to the annoyance of my neighbors.) Once again, I've been sick — this time, with four different illnesses.

I have a lot of illnesses. I don't talk about it much, for a variety of reasons. I feel ashamed to have an illness. (It sounds absurd, but there still is an enormous stigma around being sick.) I don't want to use being ill as an excuse. (Although I sometimes wonder how much more productive I'd be if I wasn't so sick.) And, to a large extent, I just don't find it an interesting subject. (My friends are amazed by this; why is such a curious person so uncurious about the things so directly affecting his life?)

One of my goals for this blog is to describe what it's like to be in various situations and it struck me that I've never said much about what it's like to be sick. So I figured I'd try to remedy that. (Unfortunately, being sick has made this slightly more difficult. I started this post on thanksgiving and now it's almost four days later.)

Cold: All the time I feel tired and woozy. My throat is sore and I'm constantly searching for kleenex to address my nose. Sometimes I feel too hot, like I'm burning up. I'm always thirsty. Concentrating on anything is difficult. I just feel kind of wasted.

Upset stomach: Huge pains grind through my stomach, like it's trying to leap out of my body. Food is always followed by pain, followed by running to the bathroom. I'm afraid to go out because I wouldn't want to get too far from a toilet. I'm always thirsty and the dehydration makes me angry and confused. At times the pain is excruciating and even after it goes I spend some time just reeling from it.

Migraine: Ever felt someone's nails dig into your scalp? Imagine that their nails are knives and they're scratching thru your brain and you can begin to imagine what a migraine feels like. Light, sound, touch — everything makes it worse, making the most painful pains even more painful. Even when you quell it with a pill, you still end up feeling woozy and disconnected, as if the pill is just barely keeping the pain at bay.

Depressed mood: Surely there have been times when you've been sad. Perhaps a loved one has abandoned you or a plan has gone horribly awry. Your face falls. Perhaps you cry. You feel worthless. You wonder whether it's worth going on. Everything you think about seems bleak — the things you've done, the things you hope to do, the people around you. You want to lie in bed and keep the lights off. Depressed mood is like that, only it doesn't come for any reason and it doesn't go for any either. Go outside and get some fresh air or cuddle with a loved one and you don't feel any better, only more upset at being unable to feel the joy that everyone else seems to feel. Everything gets colored by the sadness.

At best, you tell yourself that your thinking is irrational, that it is simply a mood disorder, that you should get on with your life. But sometimes that is worse. You feel as if streaks of pain are running through your head, you thrash your body, you search for some escape but find none. And this is one of the more moderate forms. As George Scialabba put it, "acute depression does not feel like falling ill, it feels like being tortured ... the pain is not localized; it runs along every nerve, an unconsuming fire. ... Even though one knows better, one cannot believe that it will ever end, or that anyone else has ever felt anything like it."

The economist Richard Layard, after advocating that the goal of public policy should be to maximize happiness, set out to learn what the greatest impediment to happiness was today. His conclusion: depression. Depression causes nearly half of all disability, it affects one in six, and explains more current unhappiness than poverty. And (important for public policy) Cognitive-Behavioral Therapy has a short-term success rate of 50%. Sadly, depression (like other mental illnesses, especially addiction) is not seen as "real" enough to deserve the investment and awareness of conditions like breast cancer (1 in 8) or AIDS (1 in 150). And there is, of course, the shame.

So I hope you'll forgive me for not doing more. And hey, it could be worse. At least I have decent health insurance.

November 27, 2007

STARTING OUT IN THE MORNING

For a long time, I have woken up in the morning with nothing. Recently, because I have been sick. Before that, because I was split up among many jobs. Before that, because I nominally had a real job. I miss the days when I woke up with purpose, when I lived to toil at some grand accomplishment. The feeling that all of life is in the service of some larger goal. It's fantastic.

I have been finally getting over my too-long illness, nursing myself back to strength by reading. When I was a kid, I used to take Saturdays to read, really read, devouring five or six books in one sitting. I haven't read like that in years, but now I'm doing it again — checking out stacks of books from the library and setting upon them one by one. It's fantastic.

And I don't just breeze thru the pages, I roll around in bed and pace the floor and sit in the bath fighting my brain around their words, knowing that there's some way it all makes sense, some way it can fit together, if only I can summon the strength to grab it. I wake up with thoughts of books in my heads, questions, anecdotes, stories. It's fantastic.

I feel like the books are bringing me back — back not only to health, but to the world of thought and action, the world of accomplishment, the world of doing something grand with oneself. It's fantastic.

December 28, 2007

THE THEORY OF THE GAME I

I have to admit, there's a part of me that gets no small enjoyment out of the fact that the first piece I wrote for a paying publication is nominally a review of a book on pick-up artists that actually ends up spending most of its time on glosses the history of American dating, discussions of foundational experiments in control of the emotions, the history of behaviorism in psychology, and the computer functionalist philosophy of mind. In other words, the typical article for *Other*.

I originally planned to post the review here to my blog, but instead I bumped into Annalee Newitz while I was writing it, she expressed interest in it so I sent her the draft I had and next thing I knew it was getting included in the next issue of the magazine. Reading back over it, I'm not sure I have a more to say in its favor other than it's definitely the weirdest review of *The Game* that will likely ever be published.

A couple paragraphs got removed in the print version I have and the editors added subheads to break up the flow, but here's the original piece as I sent it to them: (see next article — Ed.)

(Explanation in advance: I know fans of computer functionalism (what a weblog to have such readers!) are going to attack me for my oversimplification of their views. Well, if you want, I'm happy to attack your views at length and the conclusion comes out basically the same. So bring it on.)

December 24, 2007

THE THEORY OF THE GAME II

For a couple of weeks, it seemed like all my friends were reading a thick black book with a leather cover and gold-edged pages. "Is that The Bible?" I finally asked them. "It might as well be," said one. "It's a guide to picking up girls," another explained. I scrunched my face. "Oh, no no no," the smartest one there said. "Think of it as an ethnography of a community of pick-up artists."

The Game, if you want to put it that way, is a participant-observation study of a new Internet-fueled underground. It is an odd fact of life that, in our repressed and sexist society, a man's worth is in part measured by his ability to pick up women. (And vice versa, of course, but the book almost exclusively takes the man's point of view.)

We think of dating (like just about everything else in society) as the natural way for people to find partners, even though it was only invented in the past century. For most of even American history, kids were matched up by their parents. But as industrialization gave children disposable time (along with high schools to soak much of it up), dating was invented as a way for children to exercise their newfound mating freedom in a relatively controlled way.

Like everything else in high school, dating success was quickly picked up as an indicator of success in the neverending "popularity contest" and the same mentality followed the kids out of the schools and into the bars. The pick-up artists (or PUAs) take this sorry fact to its frightening conclusion. They approached the task of getting girls as almost a scientific question: what procedure will maximize digit-production in the human female?

The most striking result of this amateur research project was that being attractive is unnecessary. Sure, looks mattered to some extent, but the amazing thing was that even geek guys could get the girl. It was like they'd discovered some sort of magic spell: this dorky looking guy would walk up to the cutest girl in the bar and within fifteen minutes he'd have peeled her away from her boyfriend and had her giving him her number.

In this way, the book is a sort of intelligence porn: you don't need to be cute, cool, or sexy to get girls — you just need to be smart. With careful analysis and practice, you can learn to convincingly imitate any of those things. It's just a matter of discovering the right algorithms, like you do when you're writing a computer program. (Which probably explains the subculture's incredible popularity among computer programmers.)

What was going on? Part of it was genuinely devious. One practitioner did things like ask the girl to think of a time she'd been really embarrassed while making a particular hand signal. The hand signal became associated with blushing in her head, so that every time he made hand signal the girl begun blushing, a physical response she naturally misinterpreted as attraction. ("It's strange," she mused, "because you're not my usual type.")

But for the most part the tactics are much more straightforward: angle up to the girl so she can't easily turn her back to you, win over her friends first so they won't get in your way, give her subtle insults so she'll want to win you over, wear odd things so you'll stand out, use a standard script to be entertaining. For example, a standard line is to go up to a girl and ask her if she believes in magic spells. ("Yeah, well I don't either," you then say, "but my friend had this love spell supposedly cast on him and now he's all crazy for this girl.")

Why do these things work? Girls go to bars to meet guys, guys go to bars to meet girls. Unfortunately, there are lots of people there and they all act basically the same. Stilted, awkward conversations about the boring minutiae that everyone has in common. ("Oh, I like *Gilmore Girls* too!") Even if someone is attractive, it's a pain to stand around having to think of things to say to them for any reasonable amount of time.

The pick-up artist, by following a script of interesting-sounding things to say, by bringing props that the girl can easily comment on, by basically orchestrating the entire conversation in advance, comes into this room of copycats like a breath of fresh air. "Wow, this guy is so different," you think. "Being around him feels so fun and natural. It's like we really click." And just like the girl who misinterpreted blushing as attraction, you misinterpret planning as character. The guy isn't especially interesting; he's just bothered to pick up a script.

One problem with following our feelings is that our feelings are easy to misread. In a classic psychology study, Stanley Schachter and Jerome Singer shot up a couple hundred students with adrenaline, telling them it was a vitamin that improved vision. Half the kids were told the vitamin had side effects (their heart would beat fast, their hands would shake) and they acted pretty normally. But the rest searched for some external reason they were feeling that way — and started acting goofy or angry, throwing wads of paper at people or using things in the lab room as hula hoops.

It's the same reason clifftops seem romantic. Your body sees the long, steep drop and your heart starts pumping with fear. But your brain looks at the beautiful person next to you and starts thinking those heartbeats are love. The PUAs just took this time-tested method to the next level. They figured out which techniques were most effective at manipulating a woman's feelings. Then, like game theorists, they broke down the entire male-female interaction into steps and figured out which technique belonged where. (If the girl comes on too strong at first, use a neg to back her off for a bit. But if she's starting to leave, try to lure her back with a game.)

As you might guess, a system based upon treating women as objects and works by discovering ways to deceive them doesn't really work over the long-term. But when you're picking up new girls every night, it takes a while to notice that.

And once you're that deep in, you ask yourself, what does last? The book is full of stories of nice girls being snatched away from their sweet, devoted boyfriends by the counterfeit charm of a pick-up artist. When you have a stock set of phrases that make girls like you 90% of the time, you can't help but wonder if girls just aren't very bright. You treat them like objects, you find techniques that succeed on them as objects, and then you think of them as objects. And who wants a long-term relationship with an object?

The more ambitious PUAs begin seeing everyone this way. One of the book's more frightening characters, Tyler Durden, spends all his time analyzing others behavior, breaking it down into components, and then adopting it as part of his own affected personality, like some kind of sci-fi villain that does its evil deeds by adopting the forms of others. Durden begins seeing everyone as an object to either study or control, staging elaborate confrontations and emotional intrigues to achieve dominance in the pick-up community.

At the turn of the century, as machines became involved in large swathes of human life, psychology responded by insisting that humans were simply a special kind of machines. Unable to come up with an "objective" explanation for subjective experience (that is, consciousness), J. B. Watson and B. F. Skinner begun denying it existed, insisting that humans were nothing but patterns behavior, learned through schedules of positive and negative reinforcement administered by society. Change the patterns of reinforcement and you change the behavior; there was no need to get involved in messy issues like "feelings" or "opinions". Opinions aren't real, the behaviorists insisted. You can't hold one in your hand.

Skinner took these assumptions to their logical conclusions, writing a novel titled Walden Two, in which all human pain and suffering are alleviated by having society be controlled by a Master Reinforcer who makes sure people only get rewarded for socially optimal behaviors (and thus, according to Skinner, people only carry out socially optimal behaviors). Skinner intended Walden Two as a utopia, but the story reads like a dystopia more frightening than even *Brave New World*. At least in Huxley's world people had inner lives that had to be pacified. Skinner doesn't even give them that.

Behaviorism has since been widely discredited in the field of psychology, but it lives on in the world of computer programmers and their philosophical allies, where it is now called functionalism. People aren't machines anymore, now they're computer programs. You don't even have to perform the same behaviors to be considered human, you just have to calculate the same mathematical functions. (In the future, these technologists breathlessly explain, we will simply upload our brains to our computers, where we can continue to live forever in the computer's universe simulator.)

Whereas Skinner searched for the patterns of reinforcement that underlay people's behavior, the programmers now search for the algorithms. And while this research project (known as "artificial intelligence") has been a stunningly total failure, the fact that we can't find these algorithms doesn't seem to have shaken anyone's faith that they're out there to be found.

Instead, the AI proponents cheer loudly every time someone gets a computer to do something we think of as a human task. "Aha!" they proclaim. "Computers can beat humans at chess. How can we deny them humanity now?" But their computers don't play chess at all like humans do. They do not think about strategies or attempt to accomplish certain goals. Instead, they use their vast processing power to calculate millions of possible moves and countermoves, and then rank them based on how favorable they are.

The Game is like the AI version of dating. Instead of working to connect with people and entertain them, its practitioners search for statements that women seem to find entertaining and endlessly repeat them. Sure, they might succeed in picking up women, just as computers can succeed in beating humans in chess, but to think they're doing the same thing as normal people is to make a horrible mistake.

December 24, 2007

MONEY & CONTROL

"I never give money to those people," she said. "They're only going to spend it on drugs, anyway." And what's so wrong with that?, I wondered. I can see why one might want to discourage Harvard students from spending all their time getting stoned (although, I have to say, I don't see anyone doing that), but if your life is spent sitting outside, hungry, cold, and miserable, drugs seem like a pretty decent use of the money.

But, more importantly, since when is that your call to make? That you live in a nice house with a bulging wallet and he lives on the street is due to an enormous number of random factors that could just as easily have been reversed. And even if you're arrogant enough to believe you're a better person in some way — smarter, harder-working, more ambitious — since when does being better give you the right to tell other people how to live their lives? Is Tiger Woods allowed to just come along and take the chocolate out of your shopping cart at the supermarket?

It is a sad fact of reality that you have money and he has none and that, as a result, he needs the money to buy material goods. But no *moral* consequences can be derived from this. Just because history has given you the *power* to choose whether this person can acquire certain material goods doesn't give you the *right* to make that call.

Now it's true, you don't have to give him money at all. Most don't. But if you feel that other people deserve to live a life without privation, at least let them choose how to live that life.

Perhaps an example closer to home will help. Remember when your father offered to help you buy a house if only you went back to school? That was the same thing — trying to use the fact that he had money and you didn't in order to get you to do what he wanted. For years, he'd been trying to get you to go back to school; and you didn't, because it was your decision and you didn't want to. But then he realized he could use the money to control you. Remember how that chafed?

At the time you brushed it off as "his money, his call". But don't you see how that's not true? Whether you go to school or not was never his call. And while it's certainly within his rights to help you buy a house, using that to try to and control you was wrong. You deserve to make your own choices about your life — we all do.

Including that man there.

April 20, 2008

MONEY & WORTH

The streets of San Francisco are lined with poor people looking for a little spare change. Many different strategies are tried — some just shake a jar, others call for help, some make specific small requests, and a fellow I saw today just kept sunnily repeating "a nickel and a smile will last a long while" in an endearing tone. Others, however, try to earn their keep — playing music, doing tricks, selling special papers like *Spare Change*.

I have a strong urge to help out the first group, those who simply ask, but helping the second has always struck me as odd. People tell me that it's better if the poor receive their money by doing work, because it lets them retain some dignity, but I've never quite bought that. After all, how much dignity do you get when your income comes from people patronizingly pretending to buy a newspaper specially created for this ruse?

But there's a much more serious problem with only giving the poor money for doing things. It encourages them to think their worth as a person is defined by their success in the capitalist economy.

Now there is a grain of truth to this delusion. There are many useful jobs for which society can compensate you. (Although even that, frankly, requires a level of non-useful skill at fitting into the general capitalist system.) But that's about it. There are many useful jobs that society doesn't compensate well. There are many useful people who can't do any of those jobs because society never trained them or gave them the opportunities required. And even if, perchance, there existed someone who cannot and even with training and opportunity could not do anything useful, it seems clear to me that their simple existence as a human being endows them with some inalienable value. (If human beings didn't have value, then we would have no one to do useful things for.)

People on the street don't deserve our money because they can pretend to do certain menial jobs. Nor should their sense of dignity be bound up in doing them. Instead they, like everyone else, deserve our money because they are people and if we cannot care for other people, then we have precious little else.

April 20, 2008

MOVING ON

In November 2006, I moved to San Francisco because I had to: my company got acquired and us moving out was a condition of the agreement. It was the first time I'd ever actually lived in San Francisco, as opposed to just visiting, and I quickly realized that although it was a fun place to visit, I couldn't stand living here.

Even after all this time, I can't really put my finger on what it is I don't like — in fact,

I suspect it's probably harder for me now to explain it than it was when I first came here. The first thing that comes to mind is how *loud* the city is. I want a place where I can live quietly and focus on my work; but San Francisco is filled with distractions. There are always crews tearing up the street, trains that are delayed, buses that have broken down, homeless people begging, friends having parties, and so on. It's impossible to concentrate and without my concentration, I feel less like me.

The other big problem is that San Francisco is fairly shallow. When I go to coffee shops or restaurants I can't avoid people talking about load balancers or databases. The conversations are boring and obsessed with technical trivia, or worse, business antics. I don't see people reading books — even at the library, all the people are in line for the computer terminals or the DVD rack — and people at parties seem uninterested in intellectual conversation.

And so I'm moving back to Cambridge, Massachusetts — Harvard Square in particular, the one place I've ever been to that brings a special delight to my eyes, that warms my heart just to see. Surrounded by Harvard and MIT and Tufts and BC and BU and on and on it's a city of thinking and of books, of quiet contemplation and peaceful concentration. And it has actual weather, with real snow and seasons and everything, not this time-stands-still sun that San Francisco insists upon.

I miss Boston; I'm excited to go back.

But I'm also sad to leave my responsibilities in San Francisco. One of which I'd particularly like your help with. I've been honored and overjoyed to help Lawrence Lessig get his Change Congress[1] project off the ground. If you haven't heard, he's trying to build a national movement to get the corruption out of Congress; to pass public financing of public elections, earmark reform, and other pressing concerns.

But they need a full-time day-to-day tech organizer. Someone who knows how to blog and who the bloggers are and can keep them in touch with the community. Someone who knows enough about technology to know the tools that can be built and should be. And someone with enough drive and talent to make sure those things get built. It's a dreamy job and I hope there's someone out there who will take it from me. A more formal write-up[2] is on the Change Congress blog.

Thanks for everything.

June 16, 2008

1. http://change-congress.org/
2. http://change-congress.org/blog/2008/06/13/lawrence-lessig-and-joe-trippi-are-looking-best-ne

LAST GOODBYES

It's minutes to midnight and I'm hurriedly packing. Early tomorrow morning I catch a flight to Boston and start my new life. I haven't really gotten much of a chance to pack until now, because I've spent the past few days in a rush of meetings, getting in my last goodbyes for everyone I know in San Francisco.

It's been great seeing everyone, but like most locals, they're all puzzled as to why I'm leaving. I've been struggling to explain why. When I say the weather, everyone just laughs. When I say San Francisco is too loud, they start arguing. When I say it's the people, they tell me to find a better group of friends.

And the thing is, they're right. It's none of these. I've been spectacularly unable to articulate it, but the real answer is simpler and more prosaic. And now, after great thought and struggle, I realize the answer is simply this: *Cambridge is the only place that's ever felt like home.* It's that simple. And when you put it that way, it's clear why I have to go.

So goodbye Stanford, goodbye Palo Alto; goodbye south bay, goodbye peninsula; goodbye Change Congress, goodbye Creative Commons; goodbye Mission, goodbye SOMA; goodbye friends, goodbye loved ones; goodbye San Francisco, home to everyone I've ever loved. You'll always have my heart.

June 19, 2008

NYT PERSONALS

Michael Francis McElroy for The New York Times

Attention attractive people: Are you looking for someone respectable enough that they've been personally vetted by the *New York Times*, but has enough of a bad-boy streak that the vetting was because they 'liberated' millions of dollars of government documents? If so, look no further than page A14 of today's *New York Times*:

Aaron Swartz, a 22-year-old Stanford dropout and entrepreneur who read Mr. Malamuds appeal, managed to download an estimated 20 percent of the entire database: 19,856,160 pages of text.

Then on Sept. 29, all of the free servers stopped serving. The government, it turns out, was not pleased.

A notice went out from the Government Printing Office that the free Pacer pilot program was suspended, pending an evaluation. A couple of weeks later, a Government Printing Office official, Richard G. Davis, told librarians that the security of the Pacer service was compromised. The F.B.I. is conducting an investigation.

Continuing on the blog[1]:

In the technology world, Mr. Swartz is kind of a big deal, as the saying goes. At the age of 14, he had a hand in writing RSS, the now-ubiquitous software used to syndicate everything from blog posts to news headlines directly to subscribers.

[O]ver the course of six weeks, Mr. Swartz was able to download 780 gigabytes of data — 19,856,160 pages of text — from Pacer. The caper grabbed an estimated 20 percent of the entire PACER network, with a focus on the most recent cases from almost every circuit.

When the government abruptly shut down the free public program, Mr. Malamud saw it as a sign of possible trouble ahead. "Who shuts down a 17-site national program with no notice whatsoever?" he recalled thinking. "I immediately saw the potential for overreaction by the courts."

Mr. Malamud told Mr. Swartz: "You need to talk to a lawyer. I need to talk to a lawyer." Mr. Swartz recalled, "I had this vision of the Feds crashing down the door, taking everything away."

He said he locked the deadbolt on his door, lay down on the bed for a while, and then called [to warn] his mother.

But when lawyers told Mr. Malamud and Mr. Swartz that they appeared to have broken no laws, Mr. Malamud sent Mr. Swartz a message saying, "You should just lay low for a while."

Mr. Swartz said that he waited for a couple of months, but "nobody came knocking on my door. I started breathing a little more easily."

Want to meet the man behind the headlines? Want to have the F.B.I. open up a file on you as well? Interested in some kind of bizarre celebrity product endorsement? I'm available in Boston and New York all this month — contact me by email, Facebook, and web form.

More:

- John Schwartz, "An Effort to Upgrade a Court Archive System to Free and Easy2,"*New York Times*, February 12, 2009
- public.resource.org, "A Cleaner PACER[3]" ("32 districts, 735.9 GBytes, 19,856,160 pages")

UPDATE: Schwartz expands on his story in Steal These Federal Records — Okay, Not Literally[4].

February 13, 2009

1. http://thelede.blogs.nytimes.com/2009/02/13/steal-these-federal-records-okay-not-literally/
2. http://www.nytimes.com/2009/02/13/us/13records.html?pagewanted=all
3. http://public.resource.org/uscourts.gov/
4. http://thelede.blogs.nytimes.com/2009/02/13/steal-these-federal-records-okay-not-literally/

A NEW KIND OF WRITING?

There are two kinds of nonfiction: *science writing* and *journalism*. Science writing is when you're trying to explain an idea. You have a concept in your head and you try to get it across. There are lots of tools you can use to do this: you can give an example, you can tell the story of how you thought of it, you can draw a picture. But the concept is the important thing.

In journalism, you're telling a story. Someone did one thing, which led to something else, which led to this other thing. Occasionally you pause to take a step back and make some larger point: the story might have some moral or illustrate some larger principle or lead you to a conclusion. But the important thing is always the story.

Of course, this is how science advances. Something weird happened over here, so we measured it carefully and took detailed notes. (These are the experimentalists.) When you put all these weird things together, they kind of fit a larger pattern. (These are the theorists.) The theory then leads to more experiments and the new experiments lead to more theory. You inch forward, bouncing between experiment and theory, journalism and science writing, to a larger understanding of the world.

But, of course, just as science requires both, the best science writing requires both. This is what makes *This American Life*'s show "The Giant Pool of Money[1]" still so unsurpassedly brilliant. It took a question everyone wanted to know the answer to — why did the economy melt down? — and explained it not by just illustrating the concepts, as many science writers did, or just telling stories of the people involved, as journalists did, but by doing both, moving between the two modes so you could understand not just the theory but how it worked.

It seems like an obvious idea, especially when you lay it out this way, but I really can't think of any other good examples. Take three of my very favorite books: Robert Jackall's *Moral Mazes*, Robert Karen's *Becoming Attached*, and William Foote Whyte's *Street Corner Society*[2]. All are absolutely brilliant, among the best examples of the genre while conveying facts of incredible importance. Jackall is very cinematic: his book consists of well-chosen scenes and all the theory comes in the cuts between them. (As soon as I finished reading it, I wanted to turn it into a movie.) But the two — scenes and theory — exist in a weird sort of balance. Neither of them (with a few exceptions) really take over and drive the work the way both do in "The Giant Pool of Money" but instead they water each other down: the scenes are always illustrating a theory and the theory consists largely of scenes.

Karen embeds the theory within his story by telling the story of the theory's development. Because he does this without condescension, it's as good an introduction to the science as can be imagined. It's a very clever technique, and a very powerful one (I certainly wouldn't change it), but it's a different one and doesn't have the same power.

Whyte, by contrast, spends his book telling the story of one example. From it, he draws out all the important theoretical principles (basically inventing every major branch of sociology for the next century) but the theory is always illustrating his one story, just as Jackall's scenes are always illustrating his theory.

Malcolm Gladwell probably comes closest to a genuine mixture of the two, but his work is marred by the fact that he kind of makes up all his science. His stories are never illustrating some established scientific principle or even a new one he has that he wants to stand up to scrutiny, but instead his principles are always invented ad hoc to serve his stories, with the same fidelity a typical This American Life episode has to its theme. As Ira Glass comments[3] on "Six Degrees of Lois Weisberg[4]": "the article could be half the length and still hit all its big ideas, and it's only longer because Gladwell has found so many things that interest and amuse him, and that's the engine that drives the whole enterprise. … pretty much everything in the story after section five is, to my way of thinking, just there for fun."

As I've hinted at before, I'm hard at work on a book of my own, and of course I plan to write it this way. But surely I can't be the first. Anyone else have any good examples?

UPDATE: I'd forgotten how good a book *Fast Food Nation* is. It follows almost exactly this style. In general, it seems larger books written by magazine writers might, since magazine articles (story, story, moment of reflection) are the building blocks of the form, but I'm still having trouble thinking of other examples. *Outliers* is *much* better than the other Gladwell books on this front.

May 5, 2009

1. http://www.thislife.org/Radio_Episode.aspx?episode=355
2. I wanted to say Robert Caro's The Power Broker for the alliteration, but Whyte really is a better example because he doesn't study an extreme outlier.
3. http://us.penguingroup.com/nf/Book/BookDisplay/0,,9781594482670,00.html?sym=EXC
4. http://www.gladwell.com/1999/1999_01_11_a_weisberg.htm

A LIFE OFFLINE

I have literally had a computer since birth; the Internet came not long after that: I still remember email addresses supplemented by UUCP bang-paths. Hardly a day has gone by in which I haven't checked my email for what must be a decade.

The Internet has kept me connected to people — as a child, all my best friends were online; as an adult, all my coworkers are. My jobs do not take place in an office; they take place over email, where time and place do not matter. The upside, is that I can go anywhere and still do them. The downside, is I cannot get away from them.

I need to take a break. My life has become entangled with technology and pressure that I hardly know any other way of life. So I'm planning to spend the month of June (June 6 to July 4, to be exact) offline. I'm packing up the laptop and the cable modem and sending them someplace far away. I'm going back to the world of paper and books.

Of course, my phone is now a computer too, so that will also have to go. I don't have a landline, so if folks want to talk to me they'll have to write letters. I (amazingly) don't have any clocks or calendars, so I won't even know what time it is. All of which means no more meetings or coordinating to hang out with people. I suppose people could call on me, but honestly, I wish they wouldn't — at least at first.

I don't feel like the kind of person who could survive on Walden Pond — I'm a finicky eater and not a huge fan of animals in any capacity. So locking myself in my apartment seems about as close as I can get. There will of course be the clerks at stores and people on the street, but for the most part I'll be alone.

I've experimented with it a little — both my phone and my laptop have died recently — and it's liberating. Walking down the street or waiting in lines, I find myself checking my phone compulsively, using it to send my mind to some other world of email or news. Without it, I feel grounded. And my laptop is even worse — a beckoning world of IMs to friends, brain-gelatinizing television shows, and an endless pile of emails to answer. It's like a constant stream of depression. A day without it made me feel like I was human again.

I want to be human again. Even if that means isolating myself from the rest of you humans.

What if there's an emergency? Has there ever been an emergency? The biggest urgent things seem to be that my servers go down. Which sucks, but I need to be able to walk away from that. If you have things hosted on one of my machines, contact me now and I'll try to get you enough privileges that you can fix things if they break. If something's really an emergency, I'm sure you'll find me.

May 18, 2009

MY LIFE OFFLINE

Everyone wants to know how my month offline was. They ask it casually, like "How's work going?" or "What'd you do this weekend?" But it's not a casual question. It was a huge, incredible, transformative experience. Those 30 days felt like six months. My habits changed, my relationships changed, my identity changed, my personality changed — hell, the physical shape of my body changed dramatically. I went through four legal pads trying to describe what it was like. I'm still not sure I really know.

One thing is clear, though: my normal life style isn't healthy. This doesn't seem like the kind of thing that requires a break to learn. I imagine people with unhealthy lifestyles *know* they're unhealthy. They come home after work and say "I can't go on like this," they cry randomly in elevators. But I didn't know. Life online is practically the only life I know. Sure, I guess things were different when I was very young — I remember, after getting my first email account, wishing someone would email me so I'd have an email to answer (even then I knew I'd soon be missing those empty-inbox days) — but for most of my life, this has been it: a jumble of interruptions and requests and jobs and people, largely carried out alone. It never let up, so I never saw anything different. How was I to know there was anything wrong?

But the last few weeks have made it clear there was — is. These weeks haven't felt that different my other weeks online, really — same jumble of work and people and interruptions as always. The usual sense that I'm never really *here*, I'm always worried about the million things around the corner: a todo list that goes for pages, a thousand emails to respond to, hundreds of blog posts to read, twenty open tabs, a dozen IM windows, a text message to answer, a Twitter stream to catch up on. I never used to think about these things as a benefit or a distraction — I didn't think about them at all; they were just how life online was. This was the era of multitasking and I was its child. If I felt anything about it, it was pride — a kind of joy in (mostly) managing to handle a thousand different things thrown my way at once. But I never knew what life was like when things *weren't* constantly being thrown at you. Until it stopped, I never knew how awful it really was.

I am not happy. I used to think of myself as just an unhappy person: a misanthrope, prone to mood swings and eating binges, who spends his days moping around the house in his pajamas, too shy and sad to step outside. But that's not how I was offline. I loved people — everyone from the counter clerk to the old friends I bumped into on the street. And I loved to go for walks and exercise in the gym and — even though there was no one around to see me — groom. Yes, groom: shower and shave and put on nice clothes and comb my hair and clean up my nails and so on, all things a month ago I would have said went against my very nature, things I never did before *voluntarily*.

But most of all, I felt not just happy, but firmly happy — solid, is the best way I can put it. I felt like I was in control of my life instead of the other way around, like its challenges just bounced off me as I kept doing what I wanted. Normally I feel buffeted by events, a thousand tiny distractions nagging at the back of my head at all times. Offline, I felt in control of my own destiny. I felt, yes, serene.

When I was very young, my parents introduced me to a book called Flow. It argued that people good at their jobs went into a sort of flow state — they were "in the zone" — where the normal stress of the world faded away and all their concentration was focused on the task at hand. It wasn't "fun" the way ice cream or sex is fun — it didn't make you smile, just look grimly determined — but it was somehow more than that. It was *fulfilling*. And that was even better than a smile.

I go into such states when programming or writing and they are indeed fantastic, but also weirdly hollow. When you come out the real world — with its mundane stresses and distractions — comes crashing back in, and the moment of flow seems like just another temporary escape, an elusive dream. And it's a hard one to get back.

I still had flow states while offline — stronger than ever, in fact: I spent an ecstatic afternoon and evening writing longhand in a trance, pouring out the first forty pages of the book I've been researching; afterward, I was on a bigger high than I've ever had in my life — but they didn't feel like escapes. Normal days weren't painful anymore. I didn't spend them filled with worry, like before. Offline, I felt solid and composed. Online, I feel like my brain wants to run off in a million different directions, even when I try to point it forward.

A friend asked me if I knew I was privileged to be able to take such a break. It seemed a silly question: I feel privileged every day. As I write, my best friend is broke and homeless, much of the world struggles just to stay alive. I feel privileged to own a mattress, let alone take a break.

I realize everyone's lives are filled with work and people and distractions — the situation brewing at the office, the sump pump breaking down at the house, the family member who's fallen ill. I realize it must seem like the greatest arrogance to think one could escape life's mundane concerns, like asking to live on a cloud, floating above the mere mortals. But it was that arrogance that made me think I could contribute to adult mailing lists when I was still in elementary school, that arrogance that made me think someone might want to read my website when I was still just a teen, that arrogance that had me start a company as a college freshman. That sort of arrogance — not bragging, but simply inwardly thinking I could do more than was expected of me — is the only thing that's gotten me anywhere in life. I see no reason to stop now.

I don't know how I'm going to carve a life away from the world's constant demands and distractions. I don't know how I'm going to balance all the things I want to do with the pressures and responsibilities they bring. But after my month off, I do know one thing: I can't go on like this. So I'm damn well going to try.

July 24, 2009

WRITING A BOOK
PART ONE — AMBITION

So I'm writing a book. In some sense, this is nothing new. I've wanted to write a book since I was probably five and since then I must have started seriously writing drafts of half a dozen, before abandoning them. But this one feels different somehow. I really think I'm going to finish it.

I don't want to say what it's about publicly yet (hint: it has to do with politics), but it's ambitious — perhaps ridiculously so; when I tell people at parties about it they look at me as if trying to determine whether I've gone mad. My goals for it are ambitious too: I want it to be popular (how hard is it to be a 'national bestseller'?), I want it to be great writing (accurate, nuanced, and hard-to-put-down), and I want it to make a difference (get people organized, change government policy). Oh, come on. Now *you're* giving me that look.

I suppose most authors want these things, but it doesn't seem like they try particularly hard. And in a way that's understandable: writing 300 coherent pages is hard enough — why add all these additional requirements? But I have high standards for books. (I'm almost always disappointed.) I figure the least I can do is try my best to live up to them myself.

Just as I've always wanted to write a book, I've always wondered how you write one. The problem is that the kind of people who would write books on how they write books are usually pretty dreadful writers and I can't stand their poor writing, let alone their sense of superiority. (This is why I kept throwing *On Writing Well* against the wall.) But I've never written a book before, so I don't feel superior, and I'm at least trying to be a great writer. So for people in the same boat, I thought I'd write about what it's like.

It started with an email. I'd written a blog post on management that had gotten some attention, including a link from the famed Jason Kottke. Apparently the New York literati all read Jason's blog, because an editor at a publishing house followed the link and read my piece and thought it might make a decent book. He worked for the business book imprint of a major-name publisher and invited me to give him a call and discuss the idea further.

Normally when I come up with book ideas, I don't tell more than a couple people about them. I've certainly never talked to anyone at a major-name publisher before. So getting this email was thrilling. I'd always imagined I'd have to pitch my book to publishers someday, but now publishers were coming to *me*, and asking for a book! It gave the whole thing a seriousness those other book projects lacked.

I told him I was heading to New York soon and he invited me to lunch at the Knickerbocker. It was the kind of place you imagine New York businesspeople meet for lunch: guys in suits, wood-paneled walls, I think I might have even spotted a cigar.

The editor was very excited and encouraging, but as we talked I grew increasingly discouraged. I began to remember how much I hate business books with a passion, how ridiculously dumb and faddish they are. For his part, the editor complained about how the rest of the world didn't take business books seriously. They sold ten times better than normal books, he said, but the *New York Times* refuses to list any of them on their prestigious nonfiction bestseller list (there's a special section just for business bestsellers that's only published monthly and buried away).

Furthermore, the books are apparently sold in the most degrading ways — motivational talks at the Learning Annex were mentioned. I'd always imagined myself as more of a *Charlie Rose* guy. I wanted to write a bestseller, it was true, but mostly for the respect, not the money. For the people I hang out with, I suspect writing a bestselling business book would bring me only ridicule.

Afterward I met with a prominent book agent that my friend introduced me to — apparently one of the town's top ten. She was brilliant and enthusiastic and full of energy. Spending an hour batting around ideas with her was lots of fun. Her shelves were lined with the famous books her authors had published and I began to dream about a future among those names.

But that was just the intro, for the details she handed me off to an associate, who explained the next step was to turn my idea into a rough outline. So I went back to where I was staying and tried to do just that. But I just couldn't. I went for walks, I pounded my head against the desk, I tried moving words around on the screen, but I couldn't seem to find a way to make the business book idea make sense. The fundamental problem was simple: who would take business advice from a teenager?

As I was working on it, another idea (we'll call it the politics book) began nagging at the back of my head. I tried not to think of it, but it wouldn't go away. The more I told it to bug off, the louder it nagged. Finally, I decided I would get the business book out of the way quickly and then do the politics one. But as my idea for the business book fell apart in my hands, the plan for the politics book grew clearer and clearer. I began talking about it, getting excited about it, even doing a whole outline for it. It seemed so perfect, so *right*. Finally, my girlfriend asked why I didn't just do that book instead.

The associate agent was tepid (I guess politics books don't sell as well), but intrigued enough to suggest I pursue it. He said the next step was to work on expanding my description of the introduction. And somehow I got it in my head that the best way to do this would be to just try and write it.

Which meant I needed to figure out how to write.

July 27, 2009

WHY I AM NOT GAY

Until recently, men having sex with men was disapproved of in American culture. Actually, "disapproved of" isn't really the right word — it was immoral, illegal, disgusting. People who did it lived in secrecy, under the constant threat of blackmail for their actions.

In the tumult of the 1960s, various out-groups — blacks, Chicanos, Native Americans — begun organizing themselves and demanding to be respected and given their due. And men-who-had-sex-with-men decided that they were an out-group — they were gay — and they deserved rights too.

In doing so, they transformed an action (having relationships with someone of the same gender) into an identity ("being gay"). And, using the normal human mechanisms for distinguishing between people in your club and those not in it, they closed ranks. Gay men didn't have sex with women. Those who did weren't gay, they were "bi" (which became a whole new identity in itself) — or probably just lying to themselves. And straight men had to be on constant guard against being attracted to other men — if they were, it meant that deep down, they were actually gay.

This new gay identity was projected back through history — famous historical figures were "outed" as gay, because they'd once taken lovers of their own gender. They truly were gay underneath, it was said — it was just a homophobic society that forced them to appear to like the opposite sex.

Along with the identity went an attempt at justification. Being gay wasn't "a choice," they argued — it was innate. Some people were just born gay and others weren't. To a culture that tried to "correct" gay people into being straight, they insisted that correction was impossible — they just weren't wired this way. (They even provided a ridiculous genetic explanation for how a species with a small percentage gay people might evolve.)

This might have been a good thing to say — maybe even necessary in such a homophobic culture — but in the end it has to be seen as simply wrong. Having sex with other people of your gender isn't an identity, it's an act. And, like sex in general among consenting adults, people should be able to do it if they want to. Having sex with someone shouldn't require an identity crisis. (Nobody sees having-sex-with-white-people as part of their identity, even if that's primarily who they're attracted to.)

People shouldn't be forced to categorize themselves as "gay," "straight," or "bi." People are just people. Maybe you're mostly attracted to men. Maybe you're mostly attracted to women. Maybe you're attracted to everyone. These are historical claims — not future predictions. If we truly want to expand the scope of human freedom, we should encourage people to date who they want; not just provide more categorical boxes for them to slot themselves into. A man who has mostly dated men should be just as welcome to date women as a woman who's mostly dated men.

So that's why I'm not gay. I hook up with people. I enjoy it. Sometimes they're men, sometimes they're women. I don't see why it needs to be any more complicated than that.

September 8, 2009

A SHORT COURSE IN ETHICS

How are we to live? Most people seem to agree that there are "right" things and "wrong" things and we should try to do the right ones, but they're less clear on how to figure out what the right ones are.

Some say there are certain moral rules (don't murder, don't steal) that we must follow to be right. But how do you decide what those rules are? Many such rules have been proposed; how do we pick the good ones?

If you ask someone to justify a rule, they usually do it by listing its *consequences*: if we don't steal, God will reward us; everyone will be happier if we stop killing. In the end, it seems like everything boils down to consequences: good acts are those which accomplish good things.

So how do we decide what good things are? Doesn't everyone have their own idea of what's good? Instead of trying to promote one particular person's notion of what's good, it seems like we should balance everyone's good. In most cases, it's impossible for us to know what's actually good for a person, so this usually means taking their word for it and trying to give them what they *want*.

(Cases where people don't seem to want what's good for them are usually cases where people are confused about what they want. I may think I really want to eat this whole box of cookies but later I'll realize I really wish I hadn't.)

But everyone wants different things — how do we balance their desires? It seems like the only fair thing to do is to treat everyone equally. Of course, this doesn't mean treating every want equally: if one person wants a yacht and another person wants a dry place to sleep tonight, the second want seems much stronger than the first; filling it will accomplish more overall good.

Here's another way to look at this. Imagine that before we were born, we all sat up in the heavens and talked about how to design the world. None of us yet know which bodies we would be born into or which parents we'd have, so none of us can possibly be biased. Aren't we all going to want to promote the greatest good overall? We'll make sure the worst-off aren't particularly worse-off in case we're one of them, and we'll make sure the rest aren't especially handicapped in case we're one of them[1]. If we have to choose between a world with one more yacht for Larry Ellison and one with one more dry place to sleep for a woman in poverty, we'll probably pick the dry place.

So we have our simple moral principle: when faced with a question, pick the answer that will accomplish the most overall good. Two friends both want to borrow my TV tonight, but one already has a TV and just wants it so he can watch two channels at once, while the other can't afford even a single television. Our principle suggests the TV goes to the second.

But our principle doesn't just apply to the questions we're obviously faced with. Surely there are many other people who want a TV and have even less than my friend. By our logic, they would seem to deserve the TV even more, even though they didn't happen to be asking me for it and thus forcing me to confront the question.

It seems like we need to think more carefully about the implicit question of each moment: what do I do now — with my time, my money, my possessions? And it seems like we need to apply the same moral rule.

The conclusion is inescapable: we must live our lives to promote the most overall good. And that would seem to mean helping those most in want — the world's poorest people.

Our rule demands one do everything they can to help the poorest — not just spending one's wealth and selling one's possessions, but breaking the law if that will help. I have friends who, to save money, break into buildings on the MIT campus to steal food and drink and naps and showers. They use the money they save to promote the public good. It seems like these criminals, not the average workaday law-abiding citizen, should be our moral exemplars.

Such a thorough-going conception of ethics seems incredibly difficult. Surely it requires severe changes in our life. The traditional notion of ethics is much easier — there are some bad things (stealing, lying, cheating) and we need to try our best not to do them. But, as in any field, it's important to separate the truth from what's convenient. People are often criticized for not doing what they think is right (hypocrisy), but not believing in what's right because it's hard to do is far worse!

I am convinced that the account here is largely correct, but I certainly don't live up to its demanding standards. And that's OK. One of the conclusions of this argument is that it's impossible to be perfectly moral. By accepting that, and keeping it in the back of my mind, I do a little better each day.

For a long time, people told me eating meat was wrong and I refused to believe them, because I thought it would be impossible for me not to eat meat. Then one day, I accepted that they were right and I was doing the wrong thing and I decided I could live with that. I wasn't perfect. But shortly after I decided that, meat started seeming less and less attractive, and I started eating less and less, and now I don't eat it at all anymore.

Accepting you're immoral is the first step to being a more moral person.

September 14, 2009

1. This thought experiment comes from philosopher John Rawls, although its conclusion has been modified by Peter Singer

HONEST THEFT

Yesterday (see article "A Short Course in Ethics") I mentioned the case of my friends who save money by living at MIT. They sleep on couches in the common rooms, break into the showers in the gym, and steal food and drink from the cafeterias. They use the money they save on necessities to promote the public good. I suggested that they're actually behaving more morally than the average citizen. This seems shocking, so let's look at the objections in depth.

There's the obvious argument that by taking these things without paying, they're actually passing on their costs to the rest of the MIT community. But for most of these things, there are no costs: no MIT students use the couches or the showers at night. And while it's true that taking MIT food and drink probably does increase the university's costs slightly, this concern doesn't seem too consistently applied. Do you think it's wrong to take one of the free refreshments at an MIT event? The consequences seem about the same.

Even if they were costing MIT money, it seems this could be justified. MIT receives enormous sums from the wealthy and powerful, more than they know how to spend. Much of it gets spent on unneeded luxuries for their already-elite students. Redistributing it to the town's poorer residents seems potentially justified.

Others claim that this lifestyle results in increased security costs. I don't see how that's true unless the students get caught. Even if they did, MIT has a notoriously relaxed security policy, so they likely wouldn't get in too much trouble and MIT probably wouldn't do anything to up their security.

A more serious complaint is that this "erodes the social contact." Peter Singer (no contract theorist he!) puts this more clearly in his book *Democracy and Disobedience*: In any society people are going to have disputes. Everyone's better off if these disputes are resolved without resorting to force. Thus in most societies there are governments to help resolve disputes peacefully. Resorting to force when you don't like their resolution could tip things back to the bad state of people resolving things through force in general.

I don't think this is a particularly plausible concern. My friends (understandably) keep quiet about their lifestyle. If anyone, I am the one undermining the social contract by

AARON SWARTZ

publicizing it. But let's keep me out of this analysis for a second. It's hard to see how sleeping on MIT couches will lead to violent revolution.[1]

It's possible there are other objections to this style of life. Or perhaps some objectors are right — and not only shouldn't we steal from MIT, but we shouldn't take advantage of their largesse either. But thinking about these questions — as opposed to blindly following rules — is what it means to be a moral person and instead of eroding the social contract it seems much more likely to strengthen our moral sense.

Singer identifies one other concern, particular to democracies. (He thinks the previous concern is especially relevant in democracies, since there's not much improvement revolution can lead to, but in the end he decides this isn't too relevant since modern "democracies" aren't actually democratic.) He suggests that it's wrong to participate in politics and vote like everybody else, but then refuse to follow the rules when the decision ends up being something you don't like.

I think this is a fairly silly objection and basically impossible to justify on utilitarian grounds. (The book is Singer's doctoral thesis and is weirdly agnostic on utilitarianism. It's also not particularly well-written, so my apologies if I'm missing part of Singer's argument.)

Imagine it's a presidential election year and the major issue is that candidate A has promised to make kids in public schools wear uniforms while candidate B opposes it. (Imagine also that the president has the power to accomplish this rule change by simple executive order.) Whatever happens, you refuse to send your child to school wearing a uniform — you plan to keep dressing them as you do now. You have two choices: vote for candidate B or not cast a vote for president.

Singer suggests that if you vote for B and A wins, you ought to make your child wear the uniform. It's hard to see how this helps anyone. Nobody knows whether you voted for president or not (it's a secret ballot), no good (as far as I can see) comes from not voting. Indeed, if you vote for B, you make it more likely that everyone avoids this unjust law and you make it more likely you won't have to resort to civil disobedience and erode the social fabric.

It's hard to see how any intuitive notion of obligation can trump this.

September 15, 2009

1. Singer identifies one other concern, particular to democracies. (He thinks the previous concern is especially relevant in democracies, since there's not much improvement revolution can lead to, but in the end he decides this isn't too relevant since modern "democracies" aren't actually democratic.) He suggests that it's wrong to participate in politics and vote like everybody else, but then refuse to follow the rules when the decision ends up being something you don't like.

    I think this is a fairly silly objection and basically impossible to justify on utilitarian grounds. (The book is Singer's doctoral thesis and is weirdly agnostic on utilitarianism. It's also not particularly well-written, so my apologies if I'm missing part of Singer's argument.)

Imagine it's a presidential election year and the major issue is that candidate A has promised to make kids in public schools wear uniforms while candidate B opposes it. (Imagine also that the president has the power to accomplish this rule change by simple executive order.) Whatever happens, you refuse to send your child to school wearing a uniform — you plan to keep dressing them as you do now. You have two choices: vote for candidate B or not cast a vote for president.

Singer suggests that if you vote for B and A wins, you ought to make your child wear the uniform. It's hard to see how this helps anyone. Nobody knows whether you voted for president or not (it's a secret ballot), no good (as far as I can see) comes from not voting. Indeed, if you vote for B, you make it more likely that everyone avoids this unjust law and you make it more likely you won't have to resort to civil disobedience and erode the social fabric.

It's hard to see how any intuitive notion of obligation can trump this.

WANTED BY THE FBI

I got my FBI file today. (Request yours![1]) As I hoped, it's truly delightful. It has only minor redactions for reasons of personal privacy (basically, they deleted agents' names and so on). It all started when the — actually, I'll let the file tell the story:

February 6, from Washington Field to Chicago:

UNCLASSIFIED
FEDERAL BUREAU OF INVESTIGATION

Precedence: ROUTINE
Case ID #: 288A-WF-238343 (Pending)
Title: UNSUB(s); US COURTS — VICTIM; COMPUTER INTRUSION — OTHER
Synopsis: To set lead to locate Aaron Swartz.
Enclosure(s): Attached is an Accurint Report for Swartz.
Details: The U.S. Courts implemented a pilot project offering free access to federal court records through the PACER system at seventeen federal depository libraries. Library personnel maintain login and password security and provide access to users from computers within the library. PACER normally carries an eight cents per page fee, however, by accessing from one of the seventeen libraries, users may search and download data for free.

Between September 4, 2008 and September 22, 2008, PACER was accessed by computers from outside the library utilizing login information from two libraries participating in the pilot project. The Administrative Office of the U.S. Courts reported that the PACER system was being inundated with requests. One request was being made every three seconds.

[…] The two accounts were responsible for downloading more than eighteen million pages with an approximate value of $1.5 million.

[…] Data that was exfiltrated went to one of two Amazon IP addresses.

Investigation has determined that the Amazon IP address used to access the PACER system belongs to Aaron Swartz.

The following information was provided for the IP address:
Name: Aaron Swartz
Address: 349 Marshman Avenue, Highland Park, IL 60035
Telephone: 847-432-8857

A search in Accurint and Swartz's personal webpage confirmed this information. Swartz's social security account number is [...]. The telephone subscriber for telephone number [REDACTED] is [REDACTED].

NCIS report for Aaron Swartz was negative. A search for wages for Swartz at the Department of Labor was negative.
[…]
Washington Field Office requests that the North RA attempt to locate AARON SWARTZ, his vehicles, drivers license information and picture, and others, at 349 Marshman Avenue, Highland Park, IL 60035. Since SWARTZ is the potential subject of an ongoing investigation, it is requested that SWARTZ not be approached by agents.

February 15, Manassas, VA:

Set Lead 1: (Info)
[…]
AARON SWARTZ has a profile on the website LINKEDIN, at www. linkedin.com/in/aaronsw. SWARTZ is listed as a writer, hacker and activist based in the San Francisco Bay Area. SWARTZ's education includes Stanford University, Sociology, 2004. SWARTZ's experience includes the following:
[…]
SWARTZ has a profile on the website FACEBOOK. His networks include Stanford '08 and Boston, MA. The picture used in his profile was also used in an article about SWARTZ in THE NEW YORK TIMES.

SWARTZ's personal webpage, www.aaronsw.com, includes a section titled "Aaron Swartz: a life time of dubious accomplishments". In 2007, SWARTZ began working full-time as a member of the Long-Term Planning Committee for the Human Race (LTPCHR).

February 19, Manassas, VA:
  On February 17, 2008 [sic], SA [REDACTED] received an email
from [REACTED] Administrative Office of the US Courts, with
links to two published articles regarding the compromise of the
PACER system.

  On February 12, 2009, [REACTED] published an article in THE
NEW YORK TIMES titled "An Effort to Upgrade a Court Archive
to Free and Easy". For the article, [REDACTED] interviewed
[REDACTED] and AARON SWARTZ regarding the compromise of the
PACER system.

  The following information is found in the article: […]

February 24, Chicago:
  Synopsis: Lead covered by Chicago North RA
  Enclosure(s): Illinois DL/ID Image of Swartz and Accurint
  Vehicle/Residence Reports for Swartz address.

  Details: Attempted to locate AARON SWARTZ, his vehicles,
  drivers license information and picture, and others at 349
  Marshman Avenue, Highland Park, IL 60035.

  Successfully located drivers license photo for SWARTZ. Drove
  by address in an attempt to locate SWARTZ or vehicles related
  to the residence, but was unsuccessful. House is set on a
  deep lot, behind other houses on Marshman Avenue. This is a
  heavily wooded, dead-end street, with no other cars parked on
  the road making continued surveillance difficult to conduct
  without severely increasing the risk of discovery. However,
  divers license and Accurint information lists address above.
  Other family members are listed as current residents and four
  vehicles are currently registered to Susan Swartz who resides
  at above address. Illinois database checks for SWARTZ yielded
  negative results. SWARTZ has no arrests, no registered vehicles
  or property.

  Chicago considers this lead covered.

March 9, Manassas, VA:
  AARON SWARTZ posted a weblog titled "NYT Personals" [on
  February 13 — AS] at http://www.aaronsw.com/weblog. In the
  weblog, SWARTZ quotes the NEW YORK TIMES article in which he
  was interviewed. SWARTZ also posts "Want to meet the man behind
  the headlines? Want to have the F.B.I. open up a file on you
  as well? Interested in some kind of bizarre celebrity product
  endorsement? I'm available in Boston and New York all this
  month".

March 23, Manassas, VA:
  On March 10, 2009, [REDACTED] of THE ADMINISTRATIVE OFFICE OF

THE US COURTS (US COURTS) provided the following information:

[…] When asked to clarify how a user knows what constitutes unauthorized access and how a user would have known that they had to be in one of the seventeen libraries to access PACER, [REDACTED] had [REDACTED] prepare a response.

[REDACTED] provided the following information:

AARON SWARTZ would have known his access was unauthorized because it was with a password that did not belonged to him.

April 14, Manassas, VA

On 04/14/2009, SA [REDACTED] called (847) 432-8857 in an attempt to speak to AARON SWARTZ. A female answered the telephone and stated that SWARTZ was not available […] SA [REDACTED] left a message for SWARTZ to return her call and the female stated that she would email that message to SWARTZ.

SWARTZ called SA [REDACTED] and left a message on her voicemail stating he could be reached at […]. This number is a T-Mobile cellular number and returned negative results in Telephone Applications.

SA [REACTED] spoke to SWARTZ, at telephone number […], and explained that the FBI is looking for information on how SWARTZ was able to compromise the PACER system so that the US COURTS could implement repairs to the system and get PACER running again. SWARTZ stated that he would have to talk to his attorney first and would call SA [REDACTED] back at a later time.

April 16, Manassas, VA:

On 04/16/2009, SA [REDACTED] returned a telephone call to ANDREW GOOD, (617) […]. GOOD is AARON SWARTZ's attorney in Boston, MA. GOOD wanted assurance that if SWARTZ was interviewed, what he said would not be used to jeopardize him. SA [REDACTED] explained that assurance could not be given but that we were in an information gathering phase. GOOD refused the interview without the assurance.

April 20, Washington Field Office:

CASE ID #: 288A-WF-238943 (Closed)
[…]
CCIPS Attorney [REDACTED] closed the office's case. Based on the CCIPS closing, Washington Field is closing this case as of this communication.

I've just sent away for the CCIPS file.

October 5, 2009

1. http://foia.fbi.gov/privacy_instruc.htm

IS THE DMCA A SCAM?

I received my first DMCA takedown notice today. I published publicly-available IRS information about the nonprofit Kwaze-Kwasa [USA] Inc. Kwaze-Kwasa sent a letter to my ISP asking that it be taken down. I do not know why they want to keep this public information off the Internet, but I do know that the law lets them.

For those who aren't familiar, the Digital Millennium Copyright Act contained a section known as OCILLA (distinct from its also-famous anticircumvention provisions) that regulates publishing copyrighted material online.

There are three big parties with interests in this subject: copyright holders, who want strong tools to keep copyrighted material offline; ISPs, who don't want copyright law to apply to them' and Internet users, who want to be able to publish and read interesting content. OCILLA was largely written by ISPs and pretty much maximizes their interests at the expense of copyright holders and users.

I'm very glad that copyright holders get the short end of the stick — they want to modify the law to make sites like YouTube illegal, just because some people upload copyrighted material to it. If they had their way, websites based around user-generated content would pretty much be impossible.

But I am frustrated the law doesn't do enough for users. The takedown notice I was sent was obviously bogus — it didn't even allege a copyright violation, since the information I published wasn't even copyrightable (it was all basic facts and statistics published by the US government). Yet my ISP informed me that if I didn't take the page down, they'd take my entire website offline. And they have to do that because if they don't, they can be sued under the copyright law and could face very heavy penalties.

To get the page back up, I have to swear under penalty of perjury that I think the takedown was a mistake (yet the sender of a takedown does not have to swear that they think the takedown is valid!), consent to a lawsuit if the sender disagrees, and wait two weeks. Two weeks!

In short, the DMCA lets you get any page taken off the Internet for two weeks. This isn't just a law itching for abuse; it's a law being abused.

November 14, 2009

AGAINST REFLECTIVE EQUILIBRIUM
OR, WHAT IS ETHICS FOR?

Imagine you were an early settler of what is now the United States. It seems likely you would have killed native Americans. After all, your parents killed them, your siblings killed them, your friends killed them, the leaders of the community killed them, the President killed them. Chances are, you would have killed them too, and you probably wouldn't have seen anything wrong with this.

Indeed, it probably wouldn't even have occurred to you to think about the morality of this. If you did, it would probably seem just. They were trying to kill *you*! And your family! Going after them was just self-defense! (It wasn't, of course; you invaded *their* land.)

Or if you see nothing wrong with killing native Americans, take the example of slavery. Again, everyone had slaves and probably didn't think too much about the morality of it. That was just the way the world was. If you were asked about the big moral questions you faced, you'd probably think of things like the proper time to pay back a loan, or lying to your wife, or maybe a child's duty of obedience to their father.

Today, looking back on people who murder native American and keep slaves, those seem like comparatively small potatoes. Sure, we justify it by saying that they were just people of their time, but still… It's hard to get over the fact that George Washington ordered his general to "lay waste all the settlements around…that the country may not be merely overrun, but destroyed." (He also ordered that they not "listen to any overture of peace before the total ruin of their settlements is effected. Our future security will be in…the terror with which the severity of the chastisement they receive will inspire them.") It somehow colors everything he says. Whatever he may have thought about loan repayment or lying, slavery was the big moral question of his time, and (in practice, at least) he got it wrong.

We don't kill native Americans much these days and we don't keep slaves, but it's hard to believe that our era must be morally perfect. Surely if people back then could make such huge moral blunders, we could be making similar ones right now. And ethical philosophy is useless if it can't help us avoid such huge mistakes.

Some people suggest that the way to do ethical philosophy is to listen to our intuitions. "I do not think our intuitions about cases are less reliable than those about principles," Frances Kamm argues.

But of *course* our intuitions about cases are less reliable! If we could simply trust our intuitions, we wouldn't need ethical philosophy at all. If something was wrong, we would just know it was wrong. There would be nothing philosophy could tell us.

Obviously this is absurd. Lots of people do things that seem clearly unethical while thinking they're in the right. Perhaps Kamm thinks these mistakes are merely the result of temporary passions and that from her desk at Harvard she can consider such question with a more objective eye.

But, as I have shown, people's intuitions about cases are *systematically* distorted. Sitting at a desk wasn't enough to persuade George Washington to stop killing native Americans. His mistake wasn't the result of some momentary passion, but of an entire culture that had normalized mass murder and a society that depended on it. To think that he would just suddenly sit down and go "Hmm, murdering Indians feels wrong to me" is ridiculous. The only way he would possibly conclude that is by taking seriously his principles.

I grew up eating animals. I saw nothing wrong with this. My parents ate them, my siblings ate them, my friends ate them, people on TV ate them, the President ate them. I doubt I stopped to think about the morality of eating animals any more than I stopped to think about the morality of brushing my teeth. If you asked me for my intuition, I would have said eating animals was just fine. It was only when I stopped eating animals that my intuitions began to change.

December 30, 2009

THE ANTI-SUIT MOVEMENT

I don't like wearing suits. In part, this is simply a question of personal taste — I find them uncomfortable and overpriced, and I don't like the way they look. But it's also a question of principle. Suits — and the other trappings of "respect" that go with them, like titles and sir's and the rest — are the physical evidence of power distance[1], the entrenchment of a particular form of inequality.

As a result, when I go to events I try to avoid wearing a suit if I can. But sometimes not wearing a suit just feels really out of place. When you show up to a room of people in suits wearing a t-shirt and jeans, people don't think you're taking a brave stand on principle; they just think you're unkempt.

Yet these things do change. In the 1950s, college kids went to class in suits and addressed their professors as sir. The 1960s changed all that. Today, at most colleges, wearing a suit to class would be the weird thing to do.

This seems like a traditional collective action problem. If one person doesn't wear a suit, they seem weird, but if everyone doesn't wear a suit, they're all fine. But the idea of doing political organizing around not wearing a suit just seems bizarre. It's hard to know who to organize — each event has a different group of people — and even if you could find the people and they agreed with you, asking folks to join a no-suit pact just seems weird.

So suits are emblematic of this strange kind of politico-cultural issue — a political question that's not amenable to a political solution. And yet, from the 1960s, we know that these battles can be won. Does anyone know how?

March 16, 2010

1. http://en.wikipedia.org/wiki/Geert_Hofstede

HOWTO: READ MORE BOOKS

I've read a hundred books a year for the past couple years. Last time I mentioned this, a couple people asked how I could read so many books. Do I read unusually quickly? Do I spend an unusual amount of time reading? I did a simple calculation: The average person spends 1704 hours a year watching TV. If the average reading rate is 250 words per minute and the average book is 180,000 words, then that's 142 books a year. To my surprise, I wasn't reading nearly enough books. So I've taken some steps to read more:

1. Block your favorite blogs. I definitely have the mental habit noted in this xkcd cartoon: at the first sign of mental difficulty, I tab to a different window and begin typing the URL of a favorite blog. This habit is purely automatic, I do it without even thinking about it. As a result, I spend many, many hours a day reading blogs and following their links.

To overcome this habit, I added all my favorite blogs to an /etc/hosts file that redirects them to a bogus IP. Now when I type their URLs, I get an error message. I did the same with Hulu and other sites I use to watch TV shows; if you have a real television, be sure to get rid of it too. Now I usually try visiting a couple different blogs before my conscious self realizes what's happening, but this happens soon enough and, over the past couple weeks, I've managed to pretty much train myself out of this bad habit.

Now I either focus on the problem at hand or think enough about it to take a break and go for a walk, eat something, drink some water, read a book, or take a nap.

2. Order lots of books at the library. Most people think the way you read more books is by spending more time reading. But I've found that, like exercise, this is an effect and not a cause. I spend time reading when I have a great book to read. When I don't, I feel no urge to read and when I do start reading something, I put it down quickly. But if I'm reading a great book, I spontaneously come up with times and places to read it.

But figuring out which books are great in advance is hard. People's experiences about which books they find compelling depend somewhat on their interests and finding accurate critics is problematic. So the best way I've found to see whether a book is good is to just start reading it.

My local library system (Minuteman) allows you to request up to 20 books online and then delivers them to the branch library nearest you. So whenever someone makes a book recommendation or I hear about a book that seems interesting, I request it online. Then I go and pick up a stack of books at the library every week or so.

I begin reading them and finish the ones that are exciting enough to finish and return the ones that are unpromising enough to give up on. Then I return them all and get some more.

I also find that the due dates and the growing pile of books provides additional impetus to read them. And the habit doesn't cost me any money this way, so I don't feel guilty about it. (I'm sure you can come up with reasons I should feel guilty, but the fact remains that I don't.)

3. Alienate everyone close to you. The biggest consumer of time is undoubtedly other people, in large measure because talking to other people is so fun that you don't notice time going by. By keeping yourself away from other people (living alone is a good start), you free up an enormous amount of time for reading. I find this is particularly useful in reading books, since books can usually substitute for human company: you can take them with you on the train and to meals and curl up with them at night and so on.

Getting rid of other hobbies no doubt also helps. (And, unlike people, books don't encourage you to have other hobbies.) I didn't have any other hobbies, so this was less of a problem for me, but you may want to think about the things you do instead of reading books and stop doing them.

4. Keep the temperature low. A common problem is falling asleep while reading. But I find it's difficult to fall asleep when I'm cold (whereas it's very easy to sleep when I'm warm), so I keep the temperature quite low in my apartment during the day. Even when I'm snuggled up in bed, I'm usually cold enough that I can't fall asleep.

I suspect few people will take all of this advice, but hopefully some of it is useful to you.

March 2, 2010

HOWTO: LOSE WEIGHT

The standard advice for losing weight is to eat less and exercise.

Exercise is almost worthless as a weight-loss strategy: the number of calories you burn through exercise is miniscule and typically more than made up by your instinct to eat a little extra after exercising. Increased exercise is a *consequence* of losing weight, not a cause — when you lose weight you will have more energy and it will be easier to move, so you will then exercise. You have to lose weight first.

That leaves eating less. I have found three strategies to be effective here:

1.   **Get rid of all snacks**. It used to be when I was hungry, I'd just grab a snack from the kitchen. It got so I basically did this without thinking and, as a result, I ended up eating a lot of snacks. Now the only food I have is unprepared; if I want to eat, I have to consider it and take the time to actually cook something or travel to someplace that sells prepared food.

2.   **Drink more water**. There are lots of reasons to drink more water, but it's also a great way to lose weight. A lot of what feels like hunger is actually thirst, while having water in your stomach seems to counteract certain feelings of hunger. Furthermore, burning fat requires extra water.

Don't be afraid to be hungry. This is no doubt my most controversial tactic, but I do tend to think the body has a "set point" for the number of calories it's used to consuming. Lowering that set point may mean ignoring a bout of hunger or two and possibly even going a whole day without eating. But after that, your body gets full after eating much less. Again: I'm not saying more than a day — this isn't anorexia — but a one-day fast is far from unheard of. This may be easier for me since I almost always eat meals alone, making it no big deal if I skip them. People who eat meals with others may need to get used to only eating a side dish or just nibbling at their order.

Losing weight has been better than I ever imagined. Not only am I dramatically thinner, but I have more energy, I waste less time eating, and I now like the way I look. I'm much more flexible and mobile and, most incredibly, I've gotten taller — this at the age of 23. (A lot of people are skeptical that I've actually grown taller, but the changes are measurable and dramatic and come with all the symptoms of height growth I remember from my childhood (including the strange urge to stretch vertically on a regular basis). I suppose it's possible the height difference simply results from better posture, but that seems worth counting.)

I do not propose a new diet or some new theory. These are very simple commonsense tips: remove temptation, get enough water, remove obligation. But I've found they've been enough for me to lose dramatic amounts of weight. I used to be embarrassingly chubby, now people worry I have anorexia.

March 1, 2010

THAT SOUNDS SMART

How do you tell if what someone is saying is smart? Most people's first instinct is to think that things they can't understand must be smart. After all, to say such things they must have learned them and aren't people who have learned more about something generally smarter than people who haven't? Thus the common phenomena of people trusting jargon-laden statements.

One problem with this method is simply that jargon can be faked. It's not too hard to make up a bunch of longish words that sound complicated. And if you don't understand them, you'll have a hard time telling whether they're real or made up.

But the more serious problem is that this method is exactly backwards. Smart people actually say things that are very simple and easy to understand. And the smarter they are, the more clear what they say is. It's stupid people who say things that are hard to understand.

Part of this is because stupid people say things that aren't true, things that aren't true don't make sense, and things that don't make sense are hard to understand. But you can also look at it from the other end: if you genuinely understand something — really, truly understand it — then it doesn't seem complicated and you can explain it rather simply.

But the larger consequence is that if you're smart the world doesn't seem very complicated. This might seem obvious, but the obvious thought is rather different. The obvious thought is: The world doesn't seem complicated to smart people. But this isn't what smart people actually think. They think the world isn't complicated, period.

This is because when they try to explain part of the world they understand to someone, they explain it clearly, and, as a result, that person now understands it. This is proof that it's not just uncomplicated for them, it's uncomplicated for everyone.

But, I suspect, for most people the world is a strange and mysterious place, governed by principles they do not understand, which affect them severely but cannot be controlled, only coped with as best as possible. This is certainly how most people regard their computers.

By contrast, when I listen to smart people some part of the world I only dimly understood or never considered becomes immediately clear. Even if I don't agree, I never have any trouble understanding. Listening to them, is like breathing pure oxygen and I cannot get enough.

This means the tradeoff between being expert and being popular doesn't actually exist. People who truly understand their subject should have no trouble writing for a popular audience. And, in fact, their writing will probably better than that of the professional popularizers.

A good example of this was the early days of the blog Freakonomics. It had two writers, a successful economist and a popular journalist. The two had worked together on the bestselling book of the same name, with the general assumption that it was the journalist who had made the economist's work clear. But reading their individual posts on the blog, you could see it was the reverse: the economist was a much clearer writer than the journalist.

Another result is that you find the really smart things in unexpected and undervalued places. Smart writing won't be in formal and difficult-to-understand journal articles, but in the profanity-laced angry rants you'll find on someone's blog. That's where the smart people are, even if everybody else just thinks they're dumb.

June 18, 2010

ON INTELLECTUAL DISHONESTY

Dishonesty has two parts: 1) saying something that is untrue, and 2) saying it with the intent to mislead the other person. You can have each without the other: you can be genuinely mistaken and thereby say something false without intending to mislead, and you can intentionally mislead someone without ever saying anything that's untrue. (The second is generally considered deceit, but not dishonesty.)

However, you can be intellectually dishonest without doing either of these things. Imagine that you're conducting an experiment and most of the time it comes out exactly the way you expect but one time it goes wrong (you probably just screwed up the measurements). Telling someone about your work, you say: "Oh, it works just the way I expected — seven times it came out exactly right."

This isn't untrue and it isn't intentionally misleading — you really do believe it works the way you expected. But it is intellectually dishonest: intellectual honesty requires bending-over-backwards to provide any evidence that you might be wrong, *even if you're convinced that you are right.*

This is an impractical standard to apply to everyday life. A prospective employer asks you in a job interview if you can get to work on time. You say "Yes", not "I think so, but one time in 2003 the power went out and so my alarm didn't go off and I overslept". I don't think anyone considers this dishonesty; indeed, if you were intellectually honest all the time people would think you were pretty weird.

Science has a higher standard. It's not just between you and your employer, it's a claim to posterity. And you might be wrong, but what if you're not around for posterity to call you up and ask you to show your work? That's why intellectual honesty requires you show your work in advance, so that others can see if you're missing something.

December 14, 2011

RAW NERVE

RAW NERVE

This is a series of pieces on getting better at life.

1. Take a step back
2. Believe you can change
3. Look at yourself objectively
4. Lean into the pain
5. Confront reality
6. Cherish mistakes
7. Fix the machine, not the person

The best posts are probably 2 and 4.

Bonus pieces:

- What are the optimal biases to overcome?

Related reading:

- The Flinch[1] (for part 4)
- Everything is Obvious[2]
- Ray Dalio's Principles[3]

Aaron Swartz
August 18, 2012

1. http://www.amazon.com/gp/product/B0062Q7S3S
2. http://www.amazon.com/gp/product/0307951790
3. http://www.bwater.com/Uploads/FileManager/Principles/Bridgewater-
   Associates-Ray-Dalio-Principles.pdf

TAKE A STEP BACK

For most of my life, I saw my job as just making good choices. I was the decider, tasked with making the best selection from the options life presented. I could play with this friend or that one, go to this college or that one, take this job offer or the other one.

Even my problems I dealt with this way. If someone was annoying me, I'd choose to avoid them. If something was bugging me, I'd choose to stop thinking about it. I mostly kept my eyes on what was in front of me.

But recently I've started appreciating the virtues of stepping back and trying to see the bigger picture. Instead of just picking the best option, I try to invent new ones. Instead of just avoiding the stuff that bugs me, should I start making plans to fix them.

It's given me a weird feeling. I feel more in control of my life, more able to cope with my problems. I feel like I'm charting my own destiny, instead of following some track. It's hard to explain, but it's a feeling like I'm getting stronger — not physically, but psychologically. It's a good feeling. I feel like I'm growing as a person.

So I started wondering: *Is there more where that came from?* I realized I've never stopped to ask whether I could get better at life. After all, in my day job, I'm constantly looking for ways to learn and grow — reading the latest books and articles about the field, talking to other people with similar jobs and hearing what's worked for them. Why aren't I doing the same thing for life?

It turns out to be surprisingly hard. Life comes with no instruction manual and the advice parents give is all over the place. TV and the newspapers don't offer much more than narrow Quick Tips and I never saw a course in this stuff at school. There are self-help books and self-improvement courses, of course, but they seem overly practical: they're usually less about working through tough problems and more about energizing you to Get Up And Go! And there's philosophy about The Good Life, but it seems to go too far in the other direction: there's very little in there for someone to practically apply.

The blogs are a weird mix. There are the blogs on "life hacks," which are full of gadgets and gizmos that seem to cause more problems than they solve. There are the anti-procrastination blogs, where the author has a constant stream of epiphanies that all seem to amount to "just put away the distractions and get stuff done." And there are the charlatans, who tell you that all your wildest dreams can come true if you just follow their patented advice.

So instead of an obvious place to go, I've just been finding little bits and pieces in all sorts of strange places: psychology experiments, business books, philosophy, self-help, math, and my friends. But since there's no community around it, it's hard to discuss it with anyone (trying to persuade other people to be interested in what you're interested in is a fool's game).

So I figure I'll just start writing about it here and see if anyone cares. Maybe it'll grow into something, but even if it doesn't at least I'll clarify my thoughts and hopefully get a few good suggestions for further reading.

I don't have a name for what I'm talking about or even a good sense of what it is. I'm hopeful that will become clearer with practice. But in the meantime, what's helped you get better at life?—at thinking, deciding, working, thinking. Whether it's a gadget or technique or book or person, I'd love it if you posted what you've found most helpful in the comments.

August 18, 2012

BELIEVE YOU CAN CHANGE

Carol Dweck was obsessed with failure. You know how some people just seem to succeed at everything they do, while others seem helpless, doomed to a life of constant failure? Dweck noticed that too — and she was determined to figure out why. So she began watching kids, trying to see if she could spot the difference between the two groups.

In a 1978 study with Carol Diener, she gave kids various puzzles and recorded what they said as they tried to solve them. Very quickly, the helpless kids started blaming themselves: "I'm getting confused," one said; "I never did have a good rememory," another explained.

But the puzzles kept coming — and they kept getting harder. "This isn't fun anymore," the kids cried. But still, there were more puzzles.

The kids couldn't take it anymore. "I give up," they insisted. They started talking about other things, trying to take their mind off the onslaught of tricky puzzles. "There is a talent show this weekend, and I am going to be Shirley Temple," one girl said. Dweck just gave them even harder puzzles.

Now the kids started getting silly, almost as if they could hide their failure by making it clear they weren't trying in the first place. Despite repeatedly being told it was incorrect, one boy just kept choosing brown as his answer, saying "Chocolate cake, chocolate cake."[1]

Maybe these results aren't surprising. If you've ever tried to play a board game with kids, you've probably seen them say all these things and more (Dweck appears to be missing the part where they pick up the game board and throw all the pieces on the floor, then run away screaming).

But what shocked her — and changed the course of her career — was the behavior of the successful kids. "Everyone has a role model, someone who pointed the way at a critical moment in their lives," she later wrote. "These children were my role models. They obviously knew something I didn't and I was determined to figure it out."[2]

Dweck, like many adults, had learned to hide her frustration and anger, to politely say "I'm not sure I want to play this anymore" instead of knocking over the board. She figured the successful kids would be the same — they'd have tactics for coping with failure instead of getting beaten down by it.

But what she found was radically different. The successful kids didn't just live with failure, they loved it! When the going got tough, they didn't start blaming themselves; they licked their lips and said "I love a challenge." They'd say stuff like "The harder it gets the harder I need to try."

Instead of complaining it wasn't fun when the puzzles got harder, they'd psych themselves up, saying "I've almost got it now" or "I did it before, I can do it again." One kid, upon being a given a really hard puzzle, one that was supposed to be obviously impossible to solve, just looked up at the experimenter with a smile and said, "You know, I was *hoping* this would be informative."[3]

What was wrong with them?

The difference, Dweck discovered, was one of mindset. Dweck had always thought "human qualities were carved in stone. You were smart or you weren't, and failure meant you weren't." That was why the helpless kids couldn't take it when they started failing. It just reminded them they sucked (they easily got confused, they had "a bad rememory"). Of course it wasn't fun anymore — why would it be fun to get constantly reminded you're a failure? No wonder they tried to change the subject. Dweck called this the "fixed mindset" — the belief that your abilities are fixed and that the world is just a series of tests that show you how good you are.

The successful kids believed precisely the opposite: that everything came through effort and that the world was full of interesting challenges that could help you learn and grow. (Dweck called this the "growth mindset.") That's why they were so thrilled by the harder puzzles — the easier ones weren't any sort of challenge, there was nothing you could learn from them. But the really tough ones? Those were fascinating — a new skill to develop, a new problem to conquer. In later experiments, kids even asked to take puzzles home so they could work on them some more.[4]

It took a seventh-grader to explain it to her: "I think intelligence is something you have to work for...it isn't just given to you... Most kids, if they're not sure of an answer, will not raise their hand... But what I usually do is raise my hand, because if I'm wrong, then my mistake will be corrected. Or I will raise my hand and say... 'I don't get this. Can you help me?' Just by doing that I'm increasing my intelligence."[5]

In the fixed mindset, success comes from proving how great you are. Effort is a bad thing — if you have to try hard and ask questions, you obviously can't be very good. When you find something you *can* do well, you want to do it over and over, to show how good you are at it.

In the growth mindset, success comes from growing. Effort is what it's all about — it's what makes you grow. When you get good at something, you put it aside and look for something harder so that you can keep growing.

Fixed-mindset people feel smart when they don't make mistakes, growth-mindset people feel smart when they struggle with something for a long time and then finally figure it out. Fixies try to blame the world when things go bad, growthers look to see what they can change about themselves. Fixies are afraid to try hard — because if they fail, it means they're a failure. Growthers are afraid of not trying.

As Dweck continued her research, she kept finding this difference in all sorts of places. In relationships, growth-mindset people looked for partners who would push them to be better, fixies just wanted someone who would put them on a pedestal (and got into terrible fights when they hit problems). Growther CEOs keep looking for new products and ways to improve, fixies cut research and tried to squeeze profits from old successes. Even in sports, growther athletes got better and better through constant practice, while fixies blamed their atrophying skills on everyone around them.

But Dweck applied a growth mindset to the question of mindset — and discovered that your mindset could itself be changed. Even small interventions — like telling students they were doing well because they tried hard, rather than because they were smart — had huge effects. With more work, she could change totally fixed-mindset people into fervent growth-mindset ones.

She herself changed, converting from a fervent fixed-mindsetter, always looking for excuses to prove how smart she was, to a growther, looking for new challenges. It was hard: "since I was taking more risks, I might look back over the day and see all the mistakes and setbacks. And feel miserable. [You feel like a zero]… you want to rush right out and rack up some high numbers." But she resisted the urge — and became a leading psychologist instead.[6]

The first step to getting better is believing you *can* get better. In her book, *Mindset*, Dweck explains how to start talking back to your fixed mindset. The fixed mindset says, "What if you fail? You'll be a failure." The growth mindset replies, "Most successful people had failures along the way."[7]

Now when I first heard about this work, I just thought: that's nice, but I already do all this. I believe fervently that intelligence can change and that talents can be learned. Indeed, I'd say I'm almost pathologically growth mindset. But even I began to notice there are some things I have a fixed mindset about.

For example, I used to think I was introverted. Everyone had always told me that you were either an extroverted person or an introverted person. From a young age, I was quite shy and bookish, so it seemed obvious: I was an introvert.

But as I've grown, I've found that's hardly the end of the story. I've started to get good at leading a conversation or cracking people up with a joke. I *like* telling stories at a party a story or buzzing about a room saying 'hi' to people. I get a rush from it! Sure, I'm still not the most party-oriented person I know, but I no longer think we fit into any neat introversion/extroversion buckets.

Growth mindset has become a kind of safe word for my partner and I. Whenever we feel the other person getting defensive or refusing to try something because "I'm not any good at it", we say "Growth mindset!" and try to approach the problem as a chance to grow, rather than a test of our abilities. It's no longer scary, it's just another project to work on.

Just like life itself.

August 18, 2012

1. Carol I. Diener and Carol S. Dweck, "An Analysis of Learned Helplessness: Continuous Changes in Performance, Strategy, and Achievement Cognitions Following Failure," *Journal of Personality and Social Psychology*, 36:5 (May 1978), 451 – 462.
2. Carol Dweck, Mindset: *The New Psychology of Success* (2007), 3.
3. Carol S. Dweck and Ellen L. Leggett, "A Social-Cognitive Approach to Motivation and Personality," *Psychological Review*, 95:2 (1988), 256 – 273.
4. Claudia M. Mueller and Carol Dweck, "Praise for Intelligence Can Undermine Children's Motivation and Performance," *Journal of Personality and Social Psychology*, 75:1 (July 1998), 33–52.
5. *Mindset*, 17.
6. *Mindset*, 225.
7. Carol Dweck, "How can you change from a fixed mindset to a growth mindset?," *mindsetonline.com* (visited 2012-08-18).

LOOK AT YOURSELF OBJECTIVELY

In the 1840s, hospitals were dangerous places. Mothers who went in to give birth often didn't make it out. For example, at Vienna General Hospital's First Obstetrical Clinic, as many as 10% of mothers died of puerperal fever after giving birth. But there was some good news: at the Second Clinic, the number was just 4%. Expectant mothers noticed this — some would get down on their knees and beg to be admitted to the Second Clinic. Others, hearing new patients were being admitted to the First Clinic that day, decided they'd rather give birth in the streets.

Ignaz Semmelweis, an assistant at the First Clinic, couldn't bear it. He began desperately searching for some kind of explanation for the difference. He tested many things without success. Then, in 1847, Semmelweis's friend Jakob Kolletschka was performing an autopsy when a student accidentally poked him with a scalpel. It was a minor injury, but Kolletschka got terribly sick and ultimately passed away, with symptoms rather like the what the mothers had. Which got Semmelweis wondering: was some "deathly material" on the corpses responsible for the deaths?

To test this, he insisted the doctors begin washing their hands with chlorinated lime (which he found best removed the stink of death) before handling the pregnant women. The results were shocking. In April 1847, the mortality rate was 18.3%. Semmelweis instituted handwashing in mid-May and by June the mortality rate had crashed to 2.2%. The next month it was even less and later that year it reached zero — for the first time ever.

You'd think doctors would be thrilled by this incredible discovery. Instead, Semmelweis was ridiculed and attacked. He was fired from the hospital and forced out of Vienna. "In published medical works my teachings are either ignored or attacked," he complained. "The medical faculty at Würzburg awarded a prize to a monograph written in 1859 in which my teachings were rejected." Even in his native Vienna, hundreds of mothers continued to die every year.

Semmelweis turned to alcohol and his behavior became increasingly erratic. In 1865, he was committed to a mental institution. There he was beaten by the guards, placed in a straitjacket, and locked in a dark cell. He died shortly thereafter, at the age of 47, from an infected wound.[1]

Why did doctors so stubbornly reject Ignaz Semmelweis? Well, imagine being told *you* were responsible for the deaths of thousands of your patients. That you had been killing the people you were supposed to be protecting. That you were so bad at your job that you were actually worse than just giving birth in the street.

We all know people don't like to hear bad news about themselves. Indeed, we go out of our way to avoid it — and when we do confront it, we try to downplay it or explain it away. Cognitive dissonance psychologists have proven it in dozens of experiments: Force students through an embarrassing initiation to take a class, and they'll insist the class is much more interesting. Make them do a favor for someone they hate, and they start insisting they actually like them. Have them make a small ethical compromises and they'll feel comfortable making bigger and bigger ones. Instead of just accepting we made a mistake, and shouldn't have compromised or done the favor or join the class, we start telling ourselves that compromising isn't so bad — and when the next compromise comes along, we believe the lies we tell ourselves, and leap at making another mistake. We hate hearing bad news about ourselves so much that we'd rather change our behavior than just admit we screwed up.[2]

It doesn't help much when our friends point out what we did wrong. If we're so scared of hearing from ourselves that we made a mistake, just imagine how much we hate hearing it from someone else. And our friends know this: the answer to "Does this outfit make me look fat?" is not supposed to be "yes." We may joke about our friends' foibles behind their back, but we rarely do so to their face. Even at work, a lot of effort goes into making sure employees are insulated from their superior's most negative assessments. This is what we're taught: make five compliments for every criticism, sandwich negative feedback with positive feedback on each side, the most important thing is to keep up someone's self-esteem.

But, as Semmelweis showed, this is a dangerous habit. Sure, it's awful to hear you're killing people — but it's way worse to *keep on killing people*! It may not be fun to get told you're lazy, but it's better to hear it now than to find out when you're fired. If you want to work on getting better, you need to start by knowing where you are.

Semmelweis was defeated about as much as a man can be defeated. But nothing the other doctors could do to him would change the facts. Eventually scientists proved the germ theory of disease and Semmelweis was vindicated. Today, he's an international hero: universities and hospitals are named after him, his house has been turned into a museum, Austria even put his face on a €50 gold coin. Meanwhile, the doctors who opposed him are now seen as close-minded killers.

Try as you might, you can't beat reality. Semmelweis was right: those doctors *were* killing people. Firing him, driving him out of the country, writing long books disproving all his claims — none of it could change that frightening fact. The doctors may have thought they were winning the argument at the time, but they were big losers in the long run. And so were all the families that lost a loved one because they refused to admit their mistake.

But imagine if they had. When you're being attacked, conceding you screwed up seems like the worst thing you can do. If even you won't stand up for yourself, how can anyone else believe in you? Admitting your mistakes seems like giving up; it just proves that your opponents were right all along. But is it really so bad?

When Oprah started defending fabulist James Frey, she was savaged by the press. So she invited her critics on the show and apologized, saying "You were right, I was wrong." It didn't destroy her reputation; it rescued it. When the space shuttle *Columbia* exploded, launch manager Wayne Hale took full responsibility: "The bottom line is that I failed to understand what I was being told…I am guilty of allowing Columbia to crash." He was promoted. When JFK admitted the responsibility for the Bay of Pigs fiasco was "mine, and mine alone," his poll numbers soared.[3]

Imagine the same thing in your own life. If your boss started taking responsibility for your organization's problems instead of blaming others, wouldn't you like him more? If your doctor told you honestly that she had screwed up a procedure, instead of trying to cover up the mistake, wouldn't you prefer that? If a politician came clean that their policy proposals had failed, wouldn't you be more likely to trust him?

In moments of great emotional stress, we revert to our worst habits: we dig in and fight harder. The real trick is not to get better at fighting — it's to get better at stopping ourselves: at taking a deep breath, calming down, and letting our better natures take over from our worst instincts.

Even if seeing ourselves objectively is the best option, all our natural instincts all point the other direction. Not only do we try hard to avoid bad news about ourselves, we tend to exaggerate the good news. Imagine you and Jane are both up for a promotion. You want it bad, so you stay late, you work weekends. Sure, some things still slip through the cracks — but even those mistakes have really good reasons! Jane never does anything like that.

But if she did — would you even know? We see the world from our own perspective. When we have to cancel hanging out with friends to do extra work, we always see that — and feel the sacrifice. But when Jane does it, we see and feel nothing. You only get to see your own perspective. And even our mistakes make sense from our perspective — we see all of the context, everything that led up to it. It all makes sense because we saw it happen. When we screw up, it's for a reason. When other people screw up, it's because they're screwups.

Looking at ourselves objectively isn't easy. But it's essential if we ever want to get better. And if we don't do it, we leave ourselves open to con artists and ethical compromisers who prey on our desire to believe we're perfect. There's no one solution, but here are some tricks I use to get a more accurate sense of myself:

- **Embrace your failings**. Be willing to believe the worst about yourself. Remember: it's much better to accept that you're a selfish, racist moron and try to improve, than to continue sleepwalking through life that way as the only one who doesn't know it.

- **Studiously avoid euphemism**. People try and sugarcoat the tough facts about themselves by putting them in the best light possible. They say "Well, I was going to get to it, but then there was that big news story today" and not "Yeah, I was procrastinating on it and started reading the news instead." Stating things plainly makes it easier to confront the truth.

- **Reverse your projections**. Every time you see yourself complaining about other groups or other people, stop yourself and think: "is it possible, is there any way, that someone out there might be making the same complaints about me?"

- **Look up, not down**. It's always easy to make yourself look good by finding people even worse than you. Yes, we agree, you're not the worst person in the world. That's not the question. The question is whether you can get better — and to do that you need to look at the people who are even better than you.

- **Criticize yourself**. The main reason people don't tell you what they really think of you is they're afraid of your reaction. (If they're right to be afraid, then you need to start by working on that.) But people will feel more comfortable telling you the truth if you start by criticizing yourself, showing them that it's OK.

- **Find honest friends**. There are some people who are just congenitally honest. For others, it's possible to build a relationship of honesty over time. Either way, it's important to find friends who you can trust to tell to tell you the harsh truths about yourself. This is *really hard* — most people don't like telling harsh truths. Some people have had success providing an anonymous feedback form for people to submit their candid reactions.

- **Listen to the criticism**. Since it's so rare to find friends who will honestly criticize you, you need to listen extra-carefully when they do. It's tempting to check what they say against your other friends. For example, if one friend says the short story you wrote isn't very good, you might show it to some other friends and ask them what they think. Wow, they all think it's great! Guess that one friend was just an outlier. But the fact is that most of your friends are going to say it's great because they're your friend; by just taking their word for it, you end up ignoring the one person who's actually being honest with you.

- **Take the outside view.** As I said before, we're always locked in our own heads, where everything we do makes sense. So try seeing what you look like from the outside for a bit, assuming you don't know any of those details. Sure, your big money-making plan sounds like a great idea when you explain it, but if you throw that away, is there any external evidence that it will work?

August 18, 2012

1. "Ignaz Semmelweis", Wikipedia (visited 2012-08-13).
2. Carol Tavris and Elliot Aaronson, *Mistakes Were Made (but not by me): Why We Justify Foolish Beliefs, Bad Decisions, and Hurtful Acts*, (2007), ch. 1.
3. *Mistakes Were Made*, ch. 8. A larger study of public companies also found that companies which admitted screwing up tended to have higher stock prices. Fiona Lee, Christopher Peterson, and Larissa Z. Tiedens, "Mea Culpa: Predicting Stock Prices From Organizational Attributions," *Personality and Social Psychology Bulletin*, 30: 12 (December 2004), 1636–1649.

LEAN INTO THE PAIN

When you first begin to exercise, it's somewhat painful. Not wildly painful, like touching a hot stove, but enough that if your only goal was to avoid pain, you certainly would stop doing it. But if you keep exercising… well, it just keeps getting more painful. When you're done, if you've really pushed yourself, you often feel exhausted and sore. And the next morning it's even worse.

If that was all that happened, you'd probably never do it. It's not that much fun being sore. Yet we do it anyway — because we know that, in the long run, the pain will make us stronger. Next time we'll be able to run harder and lift more before the pain starts.

And knowing this makes all the difference. Indeed, we come to see the pain as a sort of pleasure — it feels good to really push yourself, to fight through the pain and make yourself stronger. Feel the burn! It's fun to wake up sore the next morning, because you know that's just a sign that you're getting stronger.

Few people realize it, but psychological pain works the same way. Most people treat psychological pain like the hot stove — if starting to think about something scares them or stresses them out, they quickly stop thinking about it and change the subject.

The problem is that the topics that are most painful also tend to be the topics that are most important for us: they're the projects we most want to do, the relationships we care most about, the decisions that have the biggest consequences for our future, the most dangerous risks that we run. We're scared of them because we know the stakes are so high. But if we never think about them, then we can never do anything about them.

Ray Dalio writes:

> It is a fundamental law of nature that to evolve one has to push one's limits, which is painful, in order to gain strength — whether it's in the form of lifting weights, facing problems head-on, or in any other way. Nature gave us pain as a messaging device to tell us that we are approaching, or that we have exceeded, our limits in some way. At the same time, nature made the process of getting stronger require us to push our limits. Gaining strength is the adaptation process of the body and the mind to encountering one's limits, which is painful. In other words, both pain and strength typically result from encountering one's barriers. When we encounter pain, we are at an important juncture in our decision-making process.[1]

Yes it's painful, but the trick is to make that mental shift. To realize that the pain isn't something awful to be postponed and avoided, but a signal that you're getting stronger — something to savor and enjoy. It's what makes you better.

Pretty soon, when you start noticing something that causes you psychic pain, you'll get excited about it, not afraid. *Ooh, another chance to get stronger.* You'll seek out things you're scared of and intentionally confront them, because it's an easy way to get the great rewards of self-improvement. Dalio suggests thinking of each one as a puzzle, inside of which is embedded a beautiful gem. If you fight through the pain to solve the puzzle, you unlock it and get to keep the gem.

The trick is: when you start feeling that psychological pain coming on, don't draw back from it and cower — lean into it. Lean into the pain.

In agile software development, there's a phrase: If it hurts, do it more often.[2]

For example, imagine Jane and Joan are working on a software project together. They both have a copy of the code; Jane is making the error messages friendlier while Joan is adding a new feature. They both work on their task for days and days until it's finally done. Now they face a problem: they need to *merge* their different changes back together.

Maybe you've had this problem, either with code or with text documents: you send a draft of a report to two friends, both suggest different changes, and you have to merge all their changes back into the original document. It's incredibly annoying — and doing it with software is way worse. So people put it off. Jane thinks "you know, let me just make the thank you messages a little nicer before we merge" and Joan thinks "you know, let me add just one more feature before we merge".

They keep putting the merge off, and every time they do the task gets bigger and more painful. But they have to do it eventually. By then, the merge is so big that it takes days of painstaking work just to piece together the already-written code. It's an arduous, painful process — which makes Joan and Jane just want to put it off even longer next time.

The agile approach, however, is to do the opposite: merging hurts, so we'll do it more often. Instead of merging every couple weeks, or every couple months, we'll merge every single day, or every couple hours. Even if Jane and Joan aren't even close to finished with their work, they'll check in what they have so far (maybe with some special code deactivating it until it's finished) so they don't end up in merge hell later on. These very small merges tend not to be painful at all, they're so easy that you hardly even notice.

The same principle shows up all across software development: from testing to releasing, your natural inclination is to put off painful things, when doing them more often actually is much easier.

And I don't think it's limited to software. I think the same principle would work even if, for some odd reason, you were required to touch a hot stove for an hour. Procrastinating and putting it off until you had no choice but to hold your hand to the stove for a full hour would end up being very painful. But if you did it in small frequent bits, just quick taps of the stove with your finger that eventually added up to an hour, it wouldn't be so bad at all. Again, the trick is not to run from the pain.

Of all the self-improvement tricks I've learned, this one was by far the most surprising — and by far the most impactful. I spent most of my life hemmed in by my talents. I knew I had strengths and weaknesses and it just seemed obvious I should find jobs that fit my strengths. It seemed crazy to take a job that probed my weaknesses.

Sure, there were somethings, over there, that I wished I was better at, but they seemed so far away. Meanwhile, there were lots of things over here that I was good at. Why not just keep doing them? Sure, I realized intellectually that I could get better (see "Believe you can change") at the other stuff, but it hardly seemed worth the pain of trying.

I'd learned not to shrink from hard truths, (see "Look at yourself objectively") so I'd literally have this conversation with myself: "Yes, I know: if I got better at selling things to people [or whatever it was], I'd be much better off. But look at how painful I find selling: just thinking about it makes me want to run and hide! Sure, it'd be great if I could do it, but is it really worth all that pain?"

Now I realize this is a bogus argument: it's not that the pain is so bad that it makes me flee, it's that the importance of the topic triggers a fight-or-flight reaction deep in my reptile brain. If instead of thinking of it as a scary subject to avoid, I think of it as an exciting opportunity to get better, then it's no longer a cost-benefit tradeoff at all: both sides are a benefit — I get the benefits of being good at selling and the fun of getting better at something.

Do this enough times and your whole outlook on life begins to change. It's no longer a scary world, hemming you in, but an exciting one full of exciting adventures to pursue.[3]

Tackling something big like this is terrifying; it's far too much to start with. It's always better to start small. What's something you've been avoiding thinking about? It can be anything — a relationship difficulty, a problem at work, something on your todo list you've been avoiding. Call it to mind — despite the pain it brings — and just sort of let it sit there. Acknowledge that thinking about it is painful and feel good about yourself for being able to do it anyway. Feel it becoming less painful as you force

AARON SWARTZ

yourself to keep thinking about it. See, you're getting stronger!

OK, take a break. But when you're ready, come back to it, and start thinking of concrete things you can do about it. See how it's not as scary as you thought? See how good it feels to actually do something about it?

Next time you start feeling that feeling, that sense of pain from deep in your head that tells you to avoid a subject — ignore it. Lean into the pain instead. You'll be glad you did.

September 1, 2012

1. Ray Dalio, Principles (2001), part 2 (visited 2012-09-01). This whole section was inspired by his argument.
2. I first heard this phrase at a ThoughtWorks training. See also Martin Fowler, "FrequencyReducesDifficulty," Bliki (28 July 2011).
3. See, for example, Derek Sivers, "Push, push, push. Expanding your comfort zone," sivers.org (13 August 2012).

CONFRONT REALITY

We are all capable of believing things which we know to be untrue, and then, when we are finally proved wrong, impudently twisting the facts so as to show that we were right. Intellectually, it is possible to carry on this process for an indefinite time: the only check on it is that sooner or later a false belief bumps up against solid reality, usually on a battlefield.

— George Orwell, "In Front of Your Nose"[1]

If you want to understand experts, you need to start by finding them. So the psychologists who wanted to understand "expert performance" began by testing alleged experts, to see how good they really were.

In some fields it was easy: in chess, for example, great players can reliably beat amateurs. But in other fields, it was much, much harder.

Take punditry. In his giant 20-year study of expert forecasting, Philip Tetlock found that someone who merely predicted "everything will stay the same" would be right more often than most professional pundits.[2] Or take therapy. Numerous studies have found an hour with a random stranger is just as good as an hour with a professional therapist.[3] In one study, for example, sessions with untrained university professors helped neurotic college students just as much as sessions with professional therapists.[4] (This isn't to say that therapy isn't helpful — the same studies suggest it is — it's just that what's helpful is talking over your problems for an hour, not anything about the therapist.)

As you might expect, pundits and therapists aren't fans of these studies. The pundits try to weasel out of them. As Tetlock writes; "The trick is to attach so many qualifiers to your vague predictions that you will be well positioned to explain pretty much whatever happens. China will fissure into regional fiefdoms, but only if the Chinese leadership fails to manage certain trade-offs deftly, and only if global economic growth stalls for a protracted period, and only if…"[5] The therapists like to point to all the troubled people they've helped with their sophisticated techniques (avoiding the question of whether someone unsophisticated could have helped even more). What neither group can do is point to clear evidence that what they do works.

Compare them to the chess grandmaster. If you try to tell the chess grandmaster that he's no better than a random college professor, he can easily play a professor and prove you wrong. Every time he plays, he's confronted with inarguable evidence of success or failure. But therapists can often feel like they're helping — they just led their client to a breakthrough about their childhood — when they're actually not making any difference.

Synthesizing hundreds of these studies, K. Anders Ericsson concluded that what distinguishes experts from non-experts is engaging in what he calls *deliberate practice*.[6] Mere practice isn't enough — you can sit and make predictions all day without getting any better at it — it needs to be a kind of practice where you receive "immediate informative feedback and knowledge of results."[7]

In chess, for example, you pretty quickly discover whether you made a smart move or a disastrous error, and it's even more obvious in other sports (when practicing free-throws, it's pretty obvious if the ball misses the net). As a result, chess players can try different tactics and learn which ones work and which don't. Our pundit is not so lucky. Predicting a wave of revolutions in the next twenty years can feel very exciting at the time, but it will be twenty years before you learn whether it was a good idea or not. It's hard to get much deliberate practice on that kind of time frame.

I've noticed very ambitious people often fall into this sort of trap. Any old slob can predict what will happen tomorrow, they think, but I want to be truly great, so I will pick a much harder challenge: I will predict what will happen *in a hundred years*. It comes in lots of forms: instead of building another silly site like Instagram, I will build an *artificial intelligence*; instead of just doing another boring experiment, I will write a grand work of social theory.

But being great isn't as easy as just picking a hard goal — in fact, picking a really hard goal avoids reality almost as much as picking a really easy one. If you pick an easy goal, you know you'll always succeed (because it's so easy); if you pick a really hard one, you know you'll never fail (because it will always be too early to tell). Artificial intelligence is a truly big problem — how can you possibly expect us to succeed in just a decade? But we're making great progress, we swear.

The trick is to set yourself lots of small challenges along the way. If your startup is eventually going to make a million dollars, can it start by making ten? If your book is going to eventually persuade the world, can you start by persuading your friends?

Instead of pushing all your tests for success way off to the indefinite future, see if you can pass a very small one right now.

And it's important that you test for the right thing. If you're writing a program that's supposed to make people's lives easier, what's important is not whether they like your mockups in focus groups; it's whether you can make a prototype that actually improves their lives.

One of the biggest problems in writing self-help books is getting people to actually take your advice. It's not easy to tell a compelling story that changes the way people view their problems, but it turns out to be a lot easier than writing something that will actually persuade someone to get up off the couch and change the way they live their life. There are some things writing is really good at, but forcing people to get up and do something isn't one of them.

The irony, of course, is that the books are totally useless unless you take their advice. If you just keep reading them, thinking "that's so insightful! that changes everything," but never actually doing anything different, then pretty quickly the feeling will wear off and you'll start searching for another book to fill the void. Chris Macleod calls this "epiphany addiction": "Each time they feel like they've stumbled on some life changing discovery, feel energized for a bit without going on to achieve any real world changes, and then return to their default of feeling lonely and unsatisfied with their life. They always end up back at the drawing board of trying to think their way out of their problem, and it's not long before they come up with the latest pseudo earth shattering insight."[8]

Don't let that happen to you. Go out and test yourself today: pick a task just hard enough that you *might fail*, and try to succeed at it. Reality is painful — it's so much easier to keep doing stuff you know you're good at or else to pick something so hard there's no point at which it's obvious you're failing — but it's impossible to get better without confronting it.

September 9, 2012

1. http://orwell.ru/library/articles/nose/english/e_nose
2. Philip Tetlock, Expert Political Judgment: How Good Is It? How Can We Know? (2006). I don't have my copy handy, so I checked this description against Philip Tetlock, "Reading Tarot on K Street," The National Interest (September/October 2009), 57–67.
3. Robyn M. Dawes, House of Cards: Psychology and Psychotherapy Built on Myth (1996).
4. Hans H. Strupp and Suzanne W. Hadley, "Specific vs Nonspecific Factors in Psychotherapy: A Controlled Study of Outcome," Archives of General Psychology 36:10 (1979), 1125–1136.
5. Tetlock, "Reading Tarot," 67.
6. K. Anders Ericsson, Ralf Th. Krampe, and Clemens Tesch-Römer, "The Role of Deliberate Practice in the Acquisition of Expert Performance," Psychological Review, 100:3 (July 1993), 363–406.
7. Ericsson, "Role," 367.
8. Chris Macleod, "'Epiphany Addiction'," Succeed Socially (visited 2012-09-09).

CHERISH MISTAKES

This is a tale of two nonprofits.

At one, they hate making mistakes. How else could it be? "We're not ever going to enjoy screwing up," they told me. But this attitude has a lot of consequences. Everything they do has to go through several layers of approval to make sure it's not a mistake. And when someone does screw up, they try to hide it.

It's only natural — you know you're going to get in trouble for screwing up, so you try to fix it before anyone notices. And if you can't do, then your boss or your boss's boss tries. And if no one in the organization can fix it, and it goes all the way to the executive director, then he tries to figure out a way to keep it from the press or spin it appropriately, so the world never finds out they made a mistake.

At the other nonprofit, they have a very different attitude. You notice it the first time you visit their website. Right in their navigation bar, at the top of every page, is a link labeled "Mistakes." Click it and you'll find a list of all the things they screwed up, starting with the most horribly embarrassing one (they once promoted their group under false names).

And it goes on to discuss mistakes big and small, core and peripheral. They previously used flaky phones that would cut out during a call, annoying people. They were insufficiently skeptical in some of the most important claims they made. At times, their admissions have the tone of a chastised teenager forced to write an apology, but together they provide a remarkable record of all the mistakes, both crucial and mundane, you might reasonably make when starting something new.

It's not that this group likes making mistakes — you can feel the annoyance and embarrassment seeping through the page — but they don't shirk from them either. They identify their mistake, admit them publicly, and devise steps to avoid them next time. They use it as an opportunity to get better.

I wrote before (see "Believe you can change") about Carol Dweck's studies of successful and unsuccessful kids, but there's one bit that really jumped out at me. Given a really tough puzzle to solve, one growth mindset kid just smiles and says "Mistakes are our friend."[1]

Mistakes are our friend. They can be an exasperating friend sometimes, the kind whose antics embarrass and annoy, but their heart is in the right place: they want to help. It's a bad idea to ignore our friends.

That's a hard attitude to take toward mistakes — they're so embarrassing, our natural instinct is to want to hide them and cover them up. But that's the wrong way to think about them. They're actually giving us a gift, because they're pointing the way toward getting better.

If we try to ignore them, they'll keep nagging at us. We'll run into them again and again in different guises. You'll say "Don't be silly, that wasn't a mistake — I meant to do that." And then you'll eagerly do the same thing next time (cognitive dissonance again — see "Look at yourself objectively"). Or else you'll say "Yes, yes, of course that was a mistake — it won't happen again." But as you hurry to move on, you don't change anything, and so it does happen again.

The trick is to confront the mistake, fess up to what went wrong, and think about what you can change to keep it from happening again. Usually just promising not to do it again is not enough: you need to dig into the root causes and address those.

Sakichi Toyoda, the founder of the Toyota car company, developed a technique called "Five Why's" for handling this. For example, sometimes a car would come off the Toyota production line and not start. Why? Well, imagine it was because the alternator belt had come loose. Most car companies would stop here and just fix the alternator belt. But Toyoda understood that was dodging the mistake — it would just lead it to come back again and again. So he insisted they keep asking "Why?".

Why was the alternator belt loose? Because it hadn't been put on correctly. Why? Because the person putting it on didn't double-check to see if it had fit in correctly. Why? Because he was in too much of a hurry. Why? Because he had to walk all the way to the other side of the line to get the belts and by the time he got back he didn't have enough time to double-check.

Aha! There, on the fifth why, we find the real cause of the mistake. And the solution is easy: move the box of alternator belts closer. But if we'd stopped at any earlier point (say, by just yelling at the alternator belt guy to always remember to double-check), we wouldn't have actually fixed the problem. The same mistake would have happened again and again. Only by digging all the way to the root cause did we realize we needed to move the box of belts. The mistake pointed the way to the solution.

The last time I wrote about two nonprofits, someone commented to say they were "outright nauseated" by my post. "[T]he website is not the place to signal humility and argue against your own conclusions. All that would demonstrate is naivety and incompetence," they insisted. And maybe they're right: maybe having a mistakes page at the top of your website goes much too far.

I've written before (see "Look at yourself objectively") why I disagree, but even if they're right that you shouldn't tell the world about your mistakes, you need to at least tell yourself. It's much too easy to conveniently forget about all the stuff you screwed up. And so even though it happens again and again, you never notice the pattern.

By forcing yourself to write it down, to keep a log of the problems you've run into, you begin to see patterns. You start seeing the things you get better at and the things you keep flubbing. And then you know what to work on for next time.

September 17, 2012

1.   Carol Dweck, *Self-Theories: Their Role in Motivation, Personality, and Development* (2000), 10.

FIX THE MACHINE, NOT THE PERSON

The General Motors plant in Fremont was a disaster. "Everything was a fight," the head of the union admits. "They spent more time on grievances and on things like that than they did on producing cars. They had strikes all the time. It was just chaos constantly. ... It was considered the worst workforce in the automobile industry in the United States."

"One of the expressions was, you can buy anything you want in the GM plant in Fremont," adds Jeffrey Liker, a professor who studied the plant. "If you want sex, if you want drugs, if you want alcohol, it's there. During breaks, during lunch time, if you want to gamble illegally — any illegal activity was available for the asking within that plant." Absenteeism was so bad that some mornings they didn't have enough employees to start the assembly line; they had to go across the street and drag people out of the bar.

When management tried to punish workers, workers tried to punish them right back: scratching cars, loosening parts in hard-to-reach places, filing union grievances, sometimes even building cars unsafely. It was war.

In 1982, GM finally closed the plant. But the very next year, when Toyota was planning to start its first plant in the US, it decided to partner with GM to reopen it, hiring back the same old disastrous workers into the very same jobs. And so began the most fascinating experiment in management history.

Toyota flew this rowdy crew to Japan, to see an entirely different way of working: The Toyota Way. At Toyota, labor and management considered themselves on the same team; when workers got stuck, managers didn't yell at them, but asked how they could help and solicited suggestions. It was a revelation. "You had union workers — grizzled old folks that had worked on the plant floor for 30 years, and they were hugging their Japanese counterparts, just absolutely in tears," recalls their Toyota trainer. "And it might sound flowery to say 25 years later, but they had had such a powerful emotional experience of learning a new way of working, a way that people could actually work together collaboratively — as a team."

Three months after they got back to the US and reopened the plant, everything had changed. Grievances and absenteeism fell away and workers started saying they actually enjoyed coming to work. The Fremont factory, once one of the worst in the US, had skyrocketed to become the best. The cars they made got near-perfect quality ratings. And the cost to make them had plummeted. It wasn't the workers who were the problem; it was the system.[1]

An organization is not just a pile of people, it's also a set of structures. It's almost like a machine made of men and women. Think of an assembly line. If you just took a bunch of people and threw them in a warehouse with a bunch of car parts and a manual, it'd probably be a disaster. Instead, a careful structure has been built: car parts roll down on a conveyor belt, each worker does one step of the process, everything is carefully designed and routinized. Order out of chaos.

And when the system isn't working, it doesn't make sense to just yell at the people in it — any more than you'd try to fix a machine by yelling at the gears. True, sometimes you have the wrong gears and need to replace them, but more often you're just using them in the wrong way. When there's a problem, you shouldn't get angry with the gears — you should fix the machine.

If you have goals in life, you're probably going to need some sort of organization. Even if it's an organization of just you, it's still helpful to think of it as a kind of machine. You don't need to do every part of the process yourself — you just need to set up the machine so that the right outcomes happen.

For example, let's say you want to build a treehouse in the backyard. You're great at sawing and hammering, but architecture is not your forte. You build and build, but the treehouses keep falling down. Sure, you can try to get better at architecture, develop a better design, but you can also step back, look at the machine as a whole, and decide to fire yourself as the architect. Instead, you find a friend who loves that sort of thing to design the treehouse for you and you stick to actually building it. After all, your goal was to build a treehouse whose design you like — does it really matter whether you're the one who actually designed it?[2]

Or let's say you really want to get in shape, but never remember to exercise. You can keep beating yourself up for your forgetfulness, or you can put a system in place. Maybe you have your roommate check to see that you exercise before you leave your house in the morning or you set a regular time to consistently go to the gym together. Life isn't a high school exam; you don't have to solve your problems on your own.

In 1967, Edward Jones and Victor Harris gathered a group of college students and asked them to judge another student's exam (the student was a fictional character, but let's call him Jim). The exam always had one question, asking Jim to write an essay on Fidel Castro "as if [he] were giving the opening statement in a debate." But what sort of essay Jim was supposed to write varied: some of them required Jim to write a *defense* of Castro, others required Jim to write a *critique* of Castro, the rest left the choice up to Jim. The kids in the experiment were asked to read Jim's essay and then were asked whether they thought Jim himself was pro- or anti-Castro.

Jones and Harris weren't expecting any shocking results here; their goal was just to show the obvious: that people would conclude Jim was pro-Castro when he voluntarily chose write to a pro-Castro essay, but not when he was forced to by the teacher. But what they found surprised them: even when the students could easily see the question *required* Jim to write a pro-Castro essay, they still rated Jim as significantly more pro-Castro. It seemed hard to believe. "Perhaps some of the subjects were inattentive and did not clearly understand the context," they suspected.

So they tried again. This time they explained the essay was written for a debate tournament, where the student had been randomly assigned to either the for or against side of the debate. They wrote it in big letters on the blackboard, just to make this perfectly clear. But again they got the same results — even more clearly this time. They still couldn't believe it. Maybe, they figured, students thought Jim's arguments were so compelling he must really believe them to be able to come up with them.

So they tried a third time — this time recording Jim on tape along with the experimenter *giving him the arguments* to use. Surely no one would think Jim came up with them on his own now. Again, the same striking results: students were persuaded Jim believed the arguments he said, even when they knew he had no choice in making them.[3]

This was an extreme case, but we make the same mistake all the time. We see a sloppily-parked car and we think "what a terrible driver," not "he must have been in a real hurry." Someone keeps bumping into you at a concert and you think "what a jerk," not "poor guy, people must keep bumping into him." A policeman beats up a protestor and we think "what an awful person," not "what terrible training." The mistake is so common that in 1977 Lee Ross decided to name it the "fundamental attribution error": we attribute people's behavior to their personality, not their situation.[4]

Our natural reaction when someone screws up is to get mad at them. This is what happened at the old GM plant: workers would make a mistake and management would yell and scream. If asked to explain the yelling, they'd probably say that since people don't like getting yelled at, it'd teach them be more careful next time.

But this explanation doesn't really add up. Do you think the workers liked screwing up? Do you think they enjoyed making crappy cars? Well, we don't have to speculate: we know the very same workers, when given the chance to do good work, took pride in it and started actually enjoying their jobs.

They're just like you, when you're trying to exercise but failing. Would it have helped to have your friend just yell and scream at you for being such a lazy loser? Probably not — it probably would have just made you feel worse. What worked wasn't yelling, but changing the system around you so that it was easier to do what you already wanted to do.

The same is true for other people. Chances are, they don't *want* to annoy you, they don't like screwing up. So what's going to work isn't yelling at them, but figuring out how to change the situation. Sometimes that means changing how you behave. Sometimes that means bringing another person into the mix. And sometimes it just means simple stuff, like changing the way things are laid out or putting up reminders.

At the old GM plant, in Fremont, workers were constantly screwing things up: "cars with engines put in backwards, cars without steering wheels or brakes. Some were so messed up they wouldn't start, and had to be towed off the line." Management would yell at the workers, but what could you do? Things were moving so fast. "A car a minute don't seem like it's moving that fast," noted one worker, "but when you don't get it, you're in the hole. There's nobody to pull you out at General Motors, so you're going to let something go."

At the Toyota plant, they didn't just let things go. There was a red cord running above the assembly line, known as an andon cord, and if you ever found yourself in the hole, all you had to do was pull it, and the whole line would stop. Management would come over and ask you how they could help, if there was a way they could fix the problem. And they'd actually listen — and do it!

You saw the results all over the factory: mats and cushions for the workers to kneel on; hanging shelves traveling along with the cars, carrying parts; special tools invented specifically to solve problems the workers had identified. Those little things added up to make a big difference.

When you're upset with someone, all you want to do is change the way they're acting. But you can't control what's inside a person's head. Yelling at them isn't going to make them come around, it's just going to make them more defiant, like the GM workers who keyed the cars they made.

No, you can't force other people to change. You can, however, change just about everything else. And usually, that's enough.

1. This story has been told several places, but the quotes here are from Frank Langfitt with Brian Reed, "NUMMI," *This American Life* 403 (26 March 2010; visited 2012-09-23). Quotes are taken from the show's transcript which sometimes differ slightly from the aired version.
2. Some of the concepts and terms here were inspired by Ray Dalio, *Principles* (2001), part 2 (visited 2012-09-01).
3. Edward E. Jones and Victor A. Harris, "The Attribution of Attitudes," *Journal of Experimental Social Psychology* 3:1 (January 1967), 1–24.
4. Lee Ross, "The Intuitive Psychologist and His Shortcomings: Distortions in the Attribution Process," *Advances in Experimental Social Psychology* 10 (1977), 173–220.

September 25, 2012

WHAT ARE THE OPTIMAL BIASES TO OVERCOME?

I've noticed that some people have complimented my series Raw Nerve by saying it's a great explanation of cognitive biases. Which always amuses me, since the series grew out of frustrations I had with the usual way that term gets used. There's a group of people (call them the cognitive bias community) who say the way to be more rational — to get better at making decisions that get you what you want — is to work at overcoming your biases. But if you're overcoming biases, surely there are some lessons that will help you more than others.

You might start with the most famous ones, which tend to be the ones popularized by Kahneman and Tversky. But K&T were academics. They weren't trying to help people be more rational, they were trying to prove to other academics that people were irrational. The result is that they focused not on the most important biases, but the ones that were easiest to prove.

Take their famous anchoring experiment, in which they showed the spin of a roulette wheel affected people's estimates about African countries. The idea wasn't that roulette wheels causing biased estimates was a huge social problem; it was that no academic could possibly argue that this behavior was somehow rational. They thereby scored a decisive blow for psychology against economists claiming we're just rational maximizers.

Most academic work on irrationality has followed in K&T's footsteps. And, in turn, much of the stuff done by the wider cognitive bias community has followed in the footsteps of this academic work. So it's not hard to believe that cognitive bias types are good at avoiding these biases and thus do well on the psychology tests for them. (Indeed, many of the questions on these tests for rationality come straight from K&T experiments!)

But if you look at the average person and ask why they aren't getting what they want, very rarely do you conclude their biggest problem is that they're suffering from anchoring, framing effects, the planning fallacy, commitment bias, or any of the other stuff in these tests. Usually their biggest problems are far more quotidian and commonsensical, like procrastination and fear.

One of the things that struck me was watching Eliezer Yudkowsky, one of the most impressive writers on the topic of cognitive biases, try to start a new nonprofit. For years, the organization he founded struggled until recently, when Luke Muehlhauser was named executive director. Eliezer readily agrees that Luke has done more to achieve Eliezer's own goals for the organization than Eliezer ever did.

But why? Why is Luke so much better at getting what Eliezer wants than Eliezer is? It's surely not because Luke is so much better at avoiding the standard cognitive biases! Luke often talks about how he's constantly learning new rationality techniques from Eliezer.

No, it's because Luke did what seems like common sense: he bought a copy of *Nonprofits for Dummies* and did what it recommends. As Luke himself says[1],it wasn't lack of intelligence or resources or willpower that kept Eliezer from doing these things, "it was a gap in general rationality."

So if you're interested in closing the gap, it seems like the skills to prioritize aren't things like commitment effect and the sunk cost fallacy, but stuff like "figure out what your goals really are", "look at your situation objectively and list the biggest problems", "when you're trying something new and risky, read the For Dummies book about it first", etc. That's the stuff I'm interested in writing about.

August 29, 2012

1.   http://lesswrong.com/lw/cbs/thoughts_on_the_singularity_institute_si/6klg?context=1#614h

FAREWELL

LOSING AARON

After his son was arrested for downloading files at MIT, Bob Swartz did everything in his power to save him. He couldn't. Now he wants the institute to own up to its part in Aaron's death.

— Janelle Nanos, Boston Magazine[1], January 2014

There was a point, during the two years of legal proceedings that would overtake, and then shatter, both of their lives, when Bob Swartz and his son Aaron found themselves with a bit of free time. They had arrived at the Federal Reserve building, in Boston, to meet Aaron's lawyer — one of dozens of meetings Bob would arrange in hopes of fending off the 13 felony counts against his son. But they were early, so they took a walk.

Aaron was Bob's first child, the oldest of three boys, and he was a fragile, thoughtful kid from the very beginning. Growing up, Aaron and his brothers, Noah and Ben, had unfettered access to the nascent Internet, creating and coding projects of their own design. Evenings were spent building robots with Legos, playing Myst or Magic: The Gathering. Dinner-table conversations might concern the merits of a particular font, or Edward Tufte's theories of information. "It was a house of ideas," Bob says.

Aaron taught himself to read at age three, and became bored with school shortly thereafter. By ninth grade he became an anti-school activist, arguing that rote drills and homework assignments couldn't teach kids how to think. Instead, he chose to be "unschooled," documenting his progress on a blog he called Schoolyard Subversion. "He lived more of his life online than he did with his friends," Bob says. "There was a degree of alienation that occurred, especially as he got older. He was working on the Internet and that was sort of terra incognita." But Aaron found a network of friends online — many far older than he — who shared his interest in the future of the Web. Bob understood his dark-eyed, curious son's enthusiasms. They spent time together in their Highland Park home, bonding over books as Aaron mowed through the family's canon. One summer, they cataloged several thousand of their books according to the Library of Congress classification system. One night a fight erupted over standards. Aaron won.

Another time, Bob took Aaron to the Crerar Library at the University of Chicago, just as his own father had once taken him. Bob led Aaron through the stacks, pulled a book off the shelf, and cradled it in his hands. It was from the 1800s, a marvel. He told his son libraries were portals into the knowledge of the world.

Whenever Aaron needed advice, his father would share an insight from life or literature. "You always answer things in stories," Aaron would say. That afternoon, as Bob and Aaron circled the block, they discussed the events of the past few months — Aaron's arrest, when he was forced to the pavement; his strip search and solitary confinement upon arraignment; the increasingly circuitous route the U.S. Attorney's Office was taking in negotiating the charges; their legal fees, which would soon clear $1 million; the looming felony conviction that Aaron feared. Aaron said he felt as though he'd been living in a version of *The Trial*, Kafka's classic novel, which follows the incoherent prosecution of a defendant named Josef K.

Aaron had read the story in 2011, shortly after his arrest, and called it "deep and magnificent" on his blog. "I'd not really read much Kafka before and had grown up led to believe that it was a paranoid and hyperbolic work," he wrote. Instead, he'd found it "precisely accurate — every single detail perfectly mirrored my own experience. This isn't fiction, but documentary."

Bob had admired Kafka, but didn't remember the plot of *The Trial*. He asked Aaron to remind him how the story ended.

Aaron just stared at him.

"They killed K., Dad," Aaron told him. "They killed him."

Just a few months later, on January 11, 2013, nearly two years from the date when he was first arrested by a Secret Service agent in Central Square, Aaron Swartz hanged himself in his Brooklyn apartment. He was 26 years old.

MIT may be the world's most prestigious engineering school, with touchscreen maps installed in its building lobbies, but it remains a remarkably difficult place to navigate. To find room 485 in the Media Lab building, you pass through a series of silver double doors, then skirt a workshop where a garden of mechanical flowers gleam purple and silver under iridescent lights. There are no bumper stickers or flyers taped to the hall window of room 485; the blinds are closed. The only sign it's occupied at all is the magnetic poetry on the door. Most of the tiles are a random scramble, but nine have been arranged to form the lines: *Construct the future to be better for your children.*

Bob Swartz is inside.

Bob has kind brown eyes and a brow crowned with gray fuzz. He wears a striped button-down shirt, khakis, a brown belt, a Tag Heuer watch with a simple brown leather strap, and sensible shoes. He swivels in his chair with one leg tucked underneath him. The room is small, only about 10 by 14 feet, but there are seven office chairs. "This is where the chairs hang out," he jokes. There is weariness in his voice. "I feel bad putting them out in the hall."

Bob lives in Highland Park, Illinois. For more than a decade, he has traveled to the MIT campus each month to consult on intellectual-property aspects of Media Lab creations. After Aaron's arrest, these trips took on a new urgency: He had to file motions, meet with attorneys, plead with MIT administrators. Now, in the wake of his son's death, coming here has become an exercise in grief.

"I see Aaron on every corner," he says. "I pass by the building. I see MIT police. I remember, I remember him…" he sighs. "We spent a lot of time here. There are all sorts of painful aspects of what happened. They come back."

In January 2011, just a few blocks from where Bob sits, Aaron was arrested for downloading 4 million copyrighted articles from JSTOR, an online archive of academic journals (JSTOR stands for Journal Storage). JSTOR charges libraries as much as $50,000 in yearly subscription fees to access its archive, but at the time, MIT's open-network policy meant any visitor to campus could take advantage of MIT's subscription privileges by using a guest login. Even so, Aaron was charged with excessive and unauthorized access to the university's network under the Computer Fraud and Abuse Act (CFAA).

United States Attorney Carmen Ortiz, in the midst of a prosecutorial tear that would lead the Globe to name her 2011's Bostonian of the Year, held up Aaron's indictment as a warning to hackers everywhere: "Stealing is stealing whether you use a computer command or a crowbar, and whether you take documents, data, or dollars," she said at the time. "It is equally harmful to the victim whether you sell what you have stolen or give it away."

In fact, Aaron faced stiffer maximum penalties than if he had used a crowbar: 35 years in prison and a fine of up to $1 million. "I said to him, 'I'll use every sinew in my body and every synapse in my brain to get you out of this mess,'" Bob says.

Bob pleaded with MIT's administrators and lawyers to intervene. Joi Ito, the Media Lab's director, also petitioned the university to consider it a "family matter" and speak up regarding the charges of Aaron having "unauthorized access" on a campus where anyone, anywhere, could log into the JSTOR system — or any library database — with a simple Ethernet connection. But instead, MIT took a position of "neutrality." It made no public statements for or against Aaron's prosecution or about whether he should be imprisoned. This is the other reason why Bob's visits to MIT are so painful: He can't walk through campus without feeling that MIT betrayed his son.

"I always felt that MIT would act in a reasonable and compassionate way and that MIT wasn't the issue," Bob says. "I didn't understand the depths of what MIT had done at that point."

Bob has developed a routine during his Cambridge visits. He rooms at the Kendall Hotel. In the evenings, he'll stroll to Emma's for a pizza, or visit the Coop bookshop in Harvard Square. Some days he eats at Legal Sea Foods, where he often overhears drug developers debating the risk of funding new research. This bothers him. He believes people should be willing to take risks, to try and to fail, and that through failure comes change and invention.

"It all came from my father," Bob says.

Bob's father, William Swartz, was a successful Chicago businessman who parlayed his wealth into social activism. He founded the Albert Einstein Peace Prize Foundation, and was active with Pugwash, the nuclear disarmament group that won the Nobel Prize when Aaron was eight. Through Pugwash, William befriended Jerome "Jerry" Wiesner, the 13th president of MIT and a cofounder of the Media Lab. When Bob was a teenager, his father would send him to pick up Wiesner at the airport when he came to town. "Jerry had an incredible heart about things and was just an extraordinary human being," Bob says. In his memories, Wiesner embodied all that MIT stood for: compassion and creativity, challenging authority, and pure scientific inquiry.

Bob was never accepted to MIT — his dyslexia led to mediocre grades in high school — but he convinced the university to let him complete some undergrad and graduate work there as a special student in the math department. He arrived just as MIT was beginning to embrace, and celebrate, its hacker ethos. At MIT, a hack can mean benignly breaking into a computer system, but it can also mean breaking into the university's underground network of tunnels, inflating MIT balloons during the Harvard-Yale game, or measuring bridges in Smoots.

"Hacking was investigating a subject for its own sake and not for academic advancement, exploring inaccessible places on campus, doing something clandestine or out of the ordinary, or performing pranks," wrote Brian Leibowitz, editor of The Journal of the Institute for Hacks, TomFoolery, and Pranks at MIT. What started as a series of stunts evolved into elegant acts of cunning that have come to define the institution's values. "Hackers believe that essential lessons can be learned about the systems — about the world — from taking things apart, seeing how they work, and using this knowledge to create new and even more interesting things," Steven Levy writes in Hackers: Heroes of the Computer Revolution. "They resent any person, physical barrier, or law that tries to keep them from doing this."

Bob's eyes brighten when he's asked about his own history of hacks. He says nothing, but just offers a sly grin; it's the same smile he passed along to his son.

In time, Bob took over his father's business and adapted it into a software company. He married and raised three boys of his own, who picked up his penchant for computing. "Before the World Wide Web existed, we were using the Internet," Bob says. "We all understood very early on that the Internet was going to change everything."

Aaron began to teach himself simple computer programs while still in elementary school. When he was 12, he accompanied Bob to MIT and sat in on Philip Greenspun's Web-development class. "I was so excited by the class that I immediately went home and tried to make something," Aaron wrote to a friend years later.

Even then, Aaron saw the Web as a platform for freely sharing. A year before Wikipedia launched, he built an open-source encyclopedia, which he submitted to Greenspun's ArsDigita contest for teen programmers. As a finalist, he met the inventor of the Web, MIT professor Tim Berners-Lee. He followed that up by coauthoring some of the first codes for RSS feeds, at age 14; working on the frameworks for Creative Commons with famed Harvard Law professor Lawrence Lessig, at 15; and helping to build the website Reddit, the sale of which made him a millionaire a week before his 20th birthday.

Like his father, Aaron was never an MIT student — he had done a brief stint at Stanford, but found it intellectually lacking. Instead, he worked with Lessig as a Safra fellow in Harvard's Berkman Center for Internet & Society, and began to focus on the political potential of his coding skills. He cofounded Demand Progress, an activist group that railed against Internet censorship. He juggled projects on open access, rethinking copyright restrictions, and ending corporate corruption, and had coauthored a Guerilla Open Access Manifesto, which argued that public access to scholarly journals was a moral imperative. Aaron approached every stage in his life with an unbridled idealism. Whenever he grew frustrated or disappointed, Bob always encouraged him to learn from failure. Aaron's goal, he says, was simply to "make the world better."

Aaron lived in Central Square, moving fluidly between Harvard and MIT's campus. At MIT, he visited friends and family, including his brothers, who interned at the Media Lab. Aaron's girlfriend at the time, Quinn Norton, described his familiarity with MIT: Aaron "had a history of hacking," she said in an interview with MIT after his death. Sometimes when she'd call him he'd tell her, "Can't talk now, in the middle of breaking into a building at MIT with a bunch of students."

"It was a fun place where he could do that," she said. "And I think he did it at MIT because it was in the spirit of the things that he did, and other people he knew did, at MIT."

Norton told MIT that Aaron was in the habit of gathering big data sets, and that she'd helped him scrape millions of books in the public domain from Google Books: "It was a game. He was a data pack rat…He really loved mashing them with scripts and going through and analyzing them and trying to pull stuff out of them.… I think that he somewhat reasonably thought that if MIT didn't like it they'd just tell him to stop."

Aaron was a child of the Internet, and as news of his suicide began to filter online, the Web heaved in mourning. Berners-Lee took to Twitter: "Aaron dead. World wanderers, we have lost a wise elder. Hackers for right, we are one down. Parents all, we have lost a child. Let us weep." Larry Lessig ended his online requiem with "I will always love you, sweet boy. Please find the peace you were seeking. And if you do, please find a way to share that too."

The Swartz family released a more pointed statement. "Aaron's death is not simply a personal tragedy," it read. "Decisions made by officials in the Massachusetts U.S. Attorney's office and at MIT contributed to his death.… MIT refused to stand up for Aaron and its own community's most cherished principles." At Aaron's funeral, Bob was even more raw. "Aaron did not commit suicide but was killed by the government," he said, making headlines worldwide, adding, "We tried and tried to get MIT to help and show compassion…[but] their institutional concerns were more important."

In March, Bob made his way back to campus for Aaron's memorial service. He wrote the words he would speak that day in his office in the Media Lab building. Dressed in a dark-gray suit, he stood at the podium and cited the work of other digital visionaries who flouted the law: Steve Wozniak and Steve Jobs, Bill Gates, Mark Zuckerberg, and the founder of Polaroid, Edwin Land. "These people did exactly what MIT told them to do, they colored outside the lines…but today's MIT destroys those kinds of people," he said.

Now it's summer, and the August sunlight filters in through his office window. Back in January, MIT asked professor Hal Abelson, a leader in the open-access movement, to lead an investigation into MIT's role in Aaron's death, and this is the first time Bob has been on campus since the report's release a few days earlier. Abelson interviewed dozens of people: Aaron's friends and family, law enforcement officials, Aaron's attorneys, MIT's attorneys, and two sets of administrative officials at MIT (Susan Hockfield's departure as president would lead to an administrative overhaul and a do-si-do of new appointments). The university's administrators had held off his requests for meetings until it was completed, but just yesterday, he'd been able to sit down with MIT's president, L. Rafael Reif, for nearly an hour. He was heartened to see a portrait of Jerry Wiesner over Reif's desk. He told the president that the questions associated with Aaron's death go to the soul of MIT. "There was a complete lack of compassion in the way that they handled the case," he says now. "And that is the tragedy. And to the extent that that doesn't change, MIT will have completely lost its way."

It was supposed to be the work of a ghost. In late 2010, after creating the fake user profile Gary Host — shortened to "ghost" on the email login — Aaron began downloading files from JSTOR. Sometime in November, he left a laptop hidden in a basement utility closet in MIT's Building 16, where it could conceivably continue to download for days without notice.

When JSTOR noticed the bulk downloads, it blocked the ghost email address, and notified MIT. But the downloading continued, and JSTOR locked MIT out of its archives. On January 4, 2011, campus police found the laptop in the closet and called Cambridge police. The detective who took the call was also a member of the New England Electronic Crimes Task Force, which includes representatives from the U.S. Secret Service. In short time, a host of officers descended on campus. They were unsure of what exactly was under way, but they suspected an international breach: When the Secret Service arrived, Bob says, the first thing they asked was whether any of the university's classified research was threatened.

Officers placed a video camera in the closet, while the Secret Service agent on the case, Michael Pickett, asked the school's Information Services & Technology staff for relevant electronic records. Without a subpoena, attorneys in MIT's Office of the General Counsel released the materials to Pickett.

The suspect returned to the closet later that afternoon, but when MIT police arrived he was gone. Only the camera saw him: a lean young man with dark, shoulder-length wavy hair, wearing a dark coat, a gray backpack, and jeans, and carrying a white bike helmet. Two days later, after those images had been distributed to MIT police, campus officers were alerted that someone had entered the closet yet again. They watched via video feed as their suspect removed the laptop, this time with a bike helmet obscuring his face. Later that day, MIT police captain Albert Pierce spotted a young man who resembled the suspect biking through campus on Vassar Street.

Pierce followed the suspect north on Mass. Ave. through Central Square, eventually overtaking him just past the intersection. He called for backup, and another MIT officer and Special Agent Pickett quickly responded. Pierce pulled up alongside the cyclist, showing him his badge and ID. The suspect said he didn't talk to strangers and that Pierce wasn't a "real cop," then ditched his bicycle, taking off toward Central Square. Pierce tried to chase him on foot, but returned to his car. By then, the other officers had arrived, and the two cars followed the suspect onto Lee Street.

Aaron Swartz was apprehended on a quiet block about a mile from MIT's campus, in front of a row of stately three-story townhomes. Special Agent Pickett put him in handcuffs. He was charged with breaking and entering in the daytime and with intent to commit a felony. He was just a few blocks from home.

Bob was walking off a plane in San Francisco when his wife, Susan, called him with the news: "Aaron has been arrested at MIT." Bob called Aaron immediately. He said he'd been roughed up, that officers took his bike, backpack, and laptop. "He sounded scared," Bob remembers.

Bob was alarmed, but this wasn't Aaron's first brush with the law. Four years earlier, the FBI had investigated Aaron for a bulk download of the Public Access to Court Electronic Records (PACER) website, a government-run court archive. The open-government activist Carl Malamud believed that public documents should be free to the public, and encouraged activists to liberate the files through a free trial PACER was offering libraries. Aaron told Malamud that he'd written a script that could make downloads outside the library network, but Malamud told him to stick to the appropriate channels. Aaron went ahead and used his script anyway, downloading some 2.7 million files.

That time, Aaron warned his parents the FBI might pay them a visit. Bob and Susan were upset, but tried not to show it. "I wanted him to understand that he had our support," Bob says. "It didn't seem to us that screaming and yelling at him was productive, so we didn't."

The FBI and the Department of Justice did send a surveillance team to the Swartz home, but never brought charges. Malamud and Aaron had not broken any laws, and besides, their mass downloads exposed glaring privacy gaps where the government had failed to redact Social Security numbers, names of informants, and other problematic information from the files. As Bob recalls, "It kind of came and went."

This time felt different. A few weeks after his arrest, law enforcement told Aaron he could come pick up the possessions they had confiscated. Aaron called Bob: "Dad, will you come with me to pick up my bike?" he asked.

"Of course," Bob said.

Bob and Aaron walked to the Vassar Street headquarters of the MIT police. As they sat in the station, looking through bullet-proof glass, "It was like, what are we doing here?" Bob remembers. Aaron was miserable and depressed. The MIT cops returned his helmet, backpack, and bicycle, but kept a USB drive that he had used for the downloads. "Now it's up to the Secret Service," Bob remembers the cop saying.

"The two of us looked at each other and said, 'This is a lot more serious than we thought.'"

In open-access corners of the Internet, Aaron's fellow hackers still search for an answer: What had he planned to do with the downloaded files? Most acts of civil disobedience are done publicly, without ghost logins or hidden laptops. Aaron could have done his downloading in the open: MIT's open-network policies at the time allowed anyone visiting campus to access services like JSTOR. That openness, coupled with the university's celebrated history of hacker culture, could have led Aaron to think he'd be more likely to be chastised than indicted. But it doesn't explain why he resorted to clandestine maneuvers.

Only Lessig, who for a short time served as Aaron's lawyer, has said he knows for certain what Aaron's plan was. But he's not sharing. Instead, he has dropped coy hints. In a lecture at Harvard shortly after Aaron's death, he floated possible scenarios. In one, Aaron was planning to release the files to third-world countries. Another theory: He planned to analyze the data to search for evidence of corrupt science, just as he had done with a legal database under Lessig's guidance at Stanford.

To Bob, the latter explanation seems more likely. "There was one conversation we had where he indicated that the goal of these documents was to do a meta analysis of them," Bob says. "He described, similarly, looking at funding associated with the documents."

But the reasons didn't matter in the end, he says. He knows they hardly mattered to the prosecution.

The real question is this: Did Aaron know, that fall, the danger he was putting himself in?

"There was no question in my mind he understood how this had gone terribly awry, and he was very upset about it," Bob says. "We didn't need to have those conversations as to why he did it, or what was going through his head, because that wasn't the question."

There's a story he told Aaron then, just after the arrest. "Look at my hand," he said to his son, pointing to a scar in the webbing between his index and middle fingers. "When I was a student, I was working in the darkroom at New College, and I was putting a rubber stopper into a glass tube. And every time I put in the rubber stopper the glass tube shattered, and I said to myself, You know, I'm going to put that glass tube through my hand, but I persisted, and I put that glass tube through my hand. And I went to Sarasota Memorial Hospital and the doctor there was not the best and he sewed back my finger and he left that web in my hand. Because I should have stopped — I knew."

Stephen Heymann, the lead attorney on Aaron's case, is known for his steadfast, inflexible approach to his prosecutions. He comes from a distinguished legal background: His father, Philip Heymann, is a Harvard Law professor who worked as a Watergate prosecutor. Philip Heymann also served as deputy attorney general in the Clinton White House, where he befriended Ortiz and Eric Holder, who would later become attorney general.

The younger Heymann has made a name for himself pioneering the prosecution of computer crimes within the U.S. Attorney's Office in Massachusetts. For nearly three decades, he has defended the laws outlined by the Computer Fraud and Abuse Act, and as the chief of the Cybercrime Unit within the U.S. Attorney's Office, he oversaw the first court-authorized electronic surveillance of a computer network. In 2000 he worked on the case against Jonathan James, a 16-year-old who had breached NASA's network. James became the first juvenile sent to a prison for hacking crimes.

The CFAA was Congress's hysterical reaction to WarGames, the 1983 film in which a teenage Matthew Broderick hacks into NORAD's nuclear arsenal. The aim was to protect U.S. bank and defense computers from international cyber threats, but as the Internet has evolved over the past three decades, so has the CFAA. The Justice Department has extended its scope and now uses it to bring charges for a wide range of online infractions, some as trivial as lying on one's MySpace page.

Heymann's work to enforce the CFAA has also helped to shape it. In 1994 he led the prosecution of MIT student David LaMacchia, who was charged with using the university's networks to copy $1 million worth of software, which he then posted online for others to use. Like Swartz, LaMacchia faced jail time and felony charges. Unlike Swartz, his case was thrown out by a judge, who deemed his actions "heedlessly irresponsible" but let LaMacchia off because he showed no intent to profit from his actions.

In legal circles, this Robin Hood approach to software distribution became known as the LaMacchia Loophole. In 1997 Congress passed a law that strengthened criminal punishment for copyright infringement, even if the owner did not intend to make a profit. The measure was an early predecessor to the Stop Online Piracy Act (SOPA) legislation that was floated in Congress in 2011 — legislation that Aaron campaigned against, and which was eventually quashed.

For Bob and Aaron, Heymann was the face of the state. Aaron's attorneys approached Heymann shortly after Aaron's arrest, asking him to drop the charges. The meetings did not go well; Heymann refused to accept a settlement that did not involve jail time. At an impasse with Heymann, Bob and Aaron approached JSTOR. The company was much more open to negotiation, and in June 2011, the sides reached a civil settlement. Aaron paid a $26,500 fine. A spokesman said JSTOR considered the case closed: "We [have] no interest in this becoming an ongoing legal matter."

Nonetheless, the criminal case slouched forward undeterred. As Aaron's indictment neared, Heymann offered him a plea deal: If he agreed to one felony count, he could get three months in jail, followed by a period of probation and time in a halfway house.

Negotiations continued, but in the end Aaron told Heymann no. He would fight the felony charges and go to trial.

Later, Heymann would tell MIT that he was "dumbfounded" by Aaron's decision, and claimed that Aaron was "systematically re-victimizing" the university by choosing to go through proceedings. Publicly criticizing MIT at a trial, Heymann said, was akin to "attacking a rape victim based on sleeping with other men."

In the ensuing months, Aaron was banned from the Harvard and MIT campuses. Secret Service agents tore apart his apartment. Heymann subpoenaed Aaron's girlfriend, Quinn Norton, to give grand jury testimony. That was bad enough, but even before the jury convened, Norton agreed to meet with Heymann — against Aaron's pleas. Norton would say later that she thought she could talk Heymann into dropping the prosecution. Instead, he grilled her until he had what he needed: Norton mentioned that Aaron had coauthored the Guerilla Open Access Manifesto (remarkably, the prosecution had failed to read through the blog posts of the Internet activist they had intended to charge). For Heymann, this was a key piece of evidence: It established a motive.

Aaron was devastated. If Norton hadn't met with Heymann, he believed, the prosecutor might never have found the manifesto for himself. He was furious. And more, Norton would tell an MIT investigator later, he was terrified "that anyone that talked to him would be treated like I was, so he didn't talk to anyone…. I considered myself radioactive, he considered both of us radioactive — anyone we talked to could suddenly be pulled into this nightmare."

Bob believes that Norton's cooperation with the prosecutors was a betrayal that left Aaron bereft. The couple's relationship dissolved shortly thereafter.

A few days before the indictment, Aaron's attorney called the U.S. Attorney's Office and agreed that Aaron would voluntarily surrender. But Bob says the prosecutors insisted on arresting him: "They strip-searched him. They took away his shoelaces. They put him in solitary confinement and left him there. They brought him out in handcuffs. And then, after his bond was posted, they left him in a cell for a couple of hours, with no explanation. It was just sadistic."

The U.S. Attorney's Office holds that it did not take the previous FBI investigation into account when it made the decision to prosecute Aaron, but Aaron's activist ties did seem to strike a chord. On the day of his indictment, Aaron sent 11 tweets, many of which linked to an article on the Demand Progress site that shared details of his case. This "wild Internet campaign" was a "foolish" move that shifted the case "from a human one-on-one level to an institutional level," Heymann would say later.

Aaron was charged with wire fraud, computer fraud, and "unlawfully obtaining information from" and "recklessly damaging" a "protected computer." There would be 13 felony counts in all. At the time of the indictment, the U.S. Attorney's Office said he could face 35 years in prison.

Aaron had ulcerative colitis, and his family feared that his health would deteriorate if he went to prison. He was growing increasingly depressed. "The endless plea negotiations, discussions of jail, what jail to go to, what the halfway house was going to be like…they were torture," Bob says. "They were torture for me but far more torture for Aaron. He couldn't deal. I dealt with the legal aspects of the case because it was very hard for him to do that. And, you know, it destroyed his feelings of security."

In an interview in December, Carmen Ortiz's first assistant attorney, Jack Pirozzolo, spoke with me about the case. "Steve [Heymann] is a cautious, careful prosecutor.... He has taken the tragedy of Mr. Swartz's suicide very hard. We as prosecutors have a job to do. We follow the evidence wherever it leads and recommend charges based on the evidence and the applicable law. In this case, the evidence of criminal conduct led to Mr. Swartz, and I don't think there can be much debate about that," he told me. He holds that the rule of law must be applied regardless of someone's talents, stature, or political beliefs. "As far as I am aware, Congress hasn't told us that there is a certain set of rules for MIT students and another set for everyone else.... A person's affiliation with MIT or Harvard does not bestow immunity from the consequences of breaking the law.... Mr. Swartz was obviously a talented guy, but our system can't work if we apply a set of rules to one group of people and not another because we approve of their talents. There is, in some sense, a breathtaking double standard that's being applied here."

To Bob, Heymann's actions went beyond the duties of a prosecutor.

"He clearly doesn't have a sense of what he's doing to people," Bob says of Heymann. "And this isn't the first time."

The pressure that Aaron was under was not unique. In 2008, Jonathan James, the juvenile hacker Heymann had convicted in 2000 at the age of 16, found himself again under suspicion. At the time, Heymann was leading an investigation into the largest identity-theft ring in U.S. history, and James was implicated. He was never charged, but Secret Service agents ransacked his home and put a tracking device on his car.

On May 18 of that year, he was found dead in his home from a self-inflicted gunshot wound. In his suicide note, he wrote that he'd become convinced that he would be scapegoated as a key member of the hacker ring because of his past conviction. "The feds play dirty," he wrote.

The relationship between Heymann and MIT was complicated, and only came to light much later.

Abelson's 182-page report, released in July, provides a remarkable glimpse of a university wrestling with its public persona. And while the report would ultimately find that MIT was justified in its neutral stance, the university often appears incurious and callous in its pages.

For example: Just days after JSTOR first noticed Aaron's bulk download and notified MIT, an MIT Information Systems & Technology staffer wrote an email explaining that the university did not require user authentication to access JSTOR. Yet the bulk of the allegations against Aaron dealt with him "exceeding authorized access" to the MIT network under the CFAA. "At no time, either before or after the arrest of Aaron Swartz, did anyone from the prosecution inquire as to whether Aaron Swartz had authorized access to the MIT network," Abelson wrote. When it came to the most fundamental question in the case — was Aaron authorized to access MIT's network or not? — MIT maintains that the feds simply never asked.

And MIT never spoke up.

MIT has maintained that its policy in Aaron's case was to remain neutral — which in practice meant, "do nothing." This was not without precedent. MIT had taken a similar stance when its students had tangled with law enforcement, and Aaron was not even a student.

Bob maintains that in Aaron's case, MIT's "neutrality" was in fact an abdication. By its silence, Bob says, the administration betrayed its mission. MIT has consistently sold itself as a leader on open access to scholarship — its professors create and share curricula over OpenCourseWare, and in 2009, they voted to make all of their scholarly articles available on the Web. Even as Heymann pursued Aaron for downloading millions of journal articles on MIT's campus, the university was touting the launch of MITx, a program that would provide free online courses to millions of students around the world.

While claiming neutrality, MIT's IS&T employees initially handed over many records to Heymann without a subpoena. Even later, Heymann and the Secret Service were permitted to call or email any staffer at will, an unusual privilege. In those exchanges, MIT staffers, either wittingly or unwittingly, helped Heymann build his case. What MIT describes as neutrality looks to Bob an awful lot like complicity with the prosecution. Abelson seemed to agree, writing that MIT's dispassionate approach, in fact, "was not neutral in outcomes."

Another key question in the prosecution's case was determining damages. MIT staff tallied up more than $5,000 worth of man-hours lost and "out-of-pocket costs," bumping the allegations into felony territory. But Abelson found that MIT padded the number: By his calculations, the university's only expenses were the cost of installing the video camera and making photocopies for the prosecution.

More examples of MIT's complicity turned up in files that Aaron's defense team obtained from the feds during discovery. When the Secret Service had trouble accessing Aaron's computer, it contacted MIT for help, emails show. The IS&T staff helpfully explained how to hack into it. Then there's the chummy note from an IS&T security analyst who had worked closely with the Secret Service. On the day Aaron was indicted, the analyst emailed Heymann: "Nicely done Steve and kudos! …it's just a true relief and very refreshing to see your accuracy and precision."

"They call this neutrality," Bob says.

Abelson's report also chronicles Bob's ordeal. From the time of the indictment through the end of 2011, Abelson found, Bob tried to persuade MIT to change its stance. He tried, and failed, to get Aaron an appointment at the Media Lab, in the hopes that it would garner him university support. Aaron's attorneys reached out to MIT to attempt to reach a settlement, but MIT rebuffed them. Bob pleaded: "Why are you destroying my son?"

In fall of 2011, Bob's wife, Susan Swartz, fell severely ill. Bob pulled back from the legal proceedings to focus on tending to her, and Aaron changed lawyers. In spring of 2012, Aaron's new attorneys tried in vain to schedule an appointment with MIT to discuss a plea initiative. Twelve calls went unanswered from May through September.

In September 2012, Bob again asked MIT to publicly state that it did not want jail time for Aaron. It refused. The university's general counsel told Abelson they believed publicly backing Aaron would actually hurt his case.

Tensions at MIT heightened in October after Aaron's lawyers filed a motion alleging the university was "acting in concert" with the prosecution, violating federal law and Aaron's Fourth Amendment rights protecting him from unreasonable search and seizure. The motion sought to suppress the indictment and all information gathered during the investigation. MIT was afraid its employees might have to defend themselves on the stand, which Abelson concluded served to further align the university's interests with the prosecution.

In the dwindling months of 2012, as both sides began to prep for hearings and it became increasingly apparent that Aaron's case would go to trial, squabbles over documents erupted. MIT continued to provide materials to Heymann's office under subpoena, but Heymann was not sharing them with the defense; when Aaron's lawyers asked MIT to send copies of the same documents, MIT's counsel referred them to the U.S. Attorney's Office. Bob soon came to believe that Heymann had never anticipated that the case would see a courtroom. The attorneys exchanged barbs over judicial misconduct.

These debates were still very much in play when the attorneys from all parties were notified that Aaron had taken his own life.

"I feel like I could put a brick through a window," Bob says in late October as he shuffles down Ames Street in Kendall Square. He left his overcoat back in the Media Lab building, and the wind is piercing his thin jacket. Bob is frustrated. The government is shut down, meaning his efforts to enact "Aaron's Law," federal legislation that would reform the CFAA, have been stymied. Bob wants to publish the discovery documents the prosecution gathered while making its case, but MIT has been dragging its feet, quibbling over redactions. And he's found that it's been harder to change the university than he had hoped.

When the Abelson report was released, President Reif promised a series of forums that would be held throughout the fall. The first one wasn't scheduled until December, nearly a year after Aaron's death. "MIT has dedicated thousands of hours to understanding what happened and to thinking about where we go from here," says university spokesperson Nathaniel Nickerson, explaining the delay. In the absence of school-sponsored meetings, students have been talking about Aaron's ordeal in small circles, if they feel comfortable talking about it at all.

Students and faculty in and around the Media Lab have said that what happened to Aaron has led to a chilling effect. If it could happen to him, it could happen to any of them. They've been reluctant to share their thoughts on official MIT online forums, which require a university sign-in. "I've had people ask me to post for them," says Nathan Matias, a graduate student at the Media Lab. "They've told me that they fear repercussions."

The Abelson report stated that MIT's decision makers had ignored the charges against Aaron until a year after the indictment, and never "form[ed] an opinion about their merits." The report also chastised students and faculty for not bringing concerns about the case to the administration before Aaron's suicide. The implication that too few students and faculty stepped forward to support Aaron infuriates some of his supporters. "Any time somebody is in jeopardy or puts the university in any sort of risk, they're thrown under the bus," says Willow Brugh, a Media Lab research affiliate. "Why would anyone possibly speak up against an issue like this?... It's absolute bullshit. In order to have academic integrity, you need to have to a safe space for people to dissent."

Ethan Zuckerman, the director of the Media Lab's Center for Civic Media, says the Abelson report also raises questions about the university's hacker culture. "MIT has long prided itself on creating a space for experimentation, including experimentation that involves bending or breaking rules," Zuckerman says. "This is a university that's internationally known for student pranks like putting a police car on the dome. One of the first questions, I think, is: Does this only apply when you're having fun? Or does this apply when you're engaged in politics or social change?"

"I think the worry is that the institute, which was always freewheeling, fun-loving, and impish-behavior-tolerating, is becoming captive to a set of lawyerly and administrative dictates," says computer science professor and former Harvard dean Harry Lewis, who taught both Mark Zuckerberg and Bill Gates. "Universities are much more beholden to officials in the federal government, state, and local government, to stay on their good side. But there's something lost when the lawyers and the people who have to make the business of the university run get to influence decisions that have real educational and philosophical and student-life-related consequences."

The Abelson report addresses this danger. It notes that "MIT is respected for world-class work in information technology, for promoting open access to online information, and for dealing wisely with the risks of computer abuse. The world looks to MIT to be at the forefront of these areas. Looking back on the Aaron Swartz case, the world didn't see leadership."

Bob has become convinced that MIT chose not to lead — and instead acted in its own self interest. The university has more than $940 million in government contracts for the classified research it conducts in its Lincoln Laboratory, and its IT networks are constantly under threat from China and other hostile hackers. MIT's report says as much: "A laptop attached to the network has the potential to perform a wide range of activities, and the MIT network has access to many services and databases that are critical for MIT research and education, some that involve sensitive information and government applications." Bob reasons that MIT chose not to cross Heymann so as not to alienate the New England Electronic Crimes Task Force — or endanger its federal grants.

The university's executive vice president and treasurer, Israel Ruiz, told me that MIT's dependence on federal grants did not factor into its decision to remain neutral, and that the university will evaluate future criminal instances on campus on a case-by-case basis. "We all know that we need to do a better job," he told me. "Unfortunately we cannot repeat history…we're trying to move forward."

Bob sighs as he trudges back to his office at the Media Lab building. The wind shifts and pushes a handful of brittle leaves in his path. He crushes them under his feet. "We couldn't change things," he says.

"Aaron had all these resources. He was bright, he had a very competent legal counsel, he had money, he had a family that supported him, and he was destroyed by the legal system." He shakes his head, and rubs his eyes with his hand. "I was better connected to people at MIT than almost anyone else, right? What happens in these instances where people don't have these connections and this sort of level of determination? They get completely crushed.

"What kind of justice is there in a world, in that instance? Because most people don't have anywhere near the resources that we've applied to this. I don't think I'm stupid, and I don't think I give up easily. But most people. Most people do."

The house of ideas is tucked back at the end of a very long drive, off a leafy road in Highland Park. The minivan parked outside is a sensible beige, with a sticker on the driver's side door, a small rectangle with a black-and-white photo of a dark-haired young man and the words: "Justice for Aaron Swartz." On the bumper is another: "Hacking is not a crime."

Inside, shelves buckle with books: a gold-embossed edition of the Talmud, manuals on coding in Python, a huge tome on Matisse, a guide to visiting family-friendly ranches. Stacks of magazines slump under the coffee table; portraits of brown-haired boys line the mantel. In one photo, the eldest stands to the left of his father, arms pulled behind him. He wears a slight smile. It's the same as his father's.

The house is not far from Lake Michigan, and every morning the father wakes and tries to walk, under the pretense of exercise, but really as a way to think. Lately, though, the shoreline has been under construction, so he's been walking the ravines he used to play in as a child. He can still tell you exactly the way the paths twist and wind. The thoughts, they follow him too.

Other times, he'll go to his office in a nearby industrial park. It's really more of a workshop, full of machines: 3-D printers and Russian microscopes, high-tech ovens and machining tools. He picks through the parts, distracts himself trying to make things work.

"What I like to say about this stuff you see on this table," he tells me there one day, "is that all I do all day is failed experiments."

He picks up a handful of 2-inch carbon-fiber square grids — each about the size of a poker chip — and shows them to me. It's obvious that these are the rejects. They've melted in places, or have tiny threads of carbon fiber or rough edges. They are imperfect.

"This is a failure, too," he says, holding one between his fingers. "It's just better than all the other failures."

He once wrote in a letter to MIT's president, L. Rafael Reif: "We, you and I, have failed my son, Aaron. I promised him that I would use every synapse in my brain and every sinew of my body to get him out of his predicament. I failed. However, I have seen MIT fail, too."

Does he still feel this way? I ask.

"Of course. There's a duality there, right? Clearly I failed. There's no question, my son is dead. On the other hand, do I feel that I didn't try hard enough? Yes. Do I feel guilt about not trying hard enough? No. If you understand the distinction I'm trying to make. Could I have done more? Of course I could have done more. Because you can always do more. Did I put everything in that I possibly could? Did I work as hard pretty much as I knew how? Yes. Do I wish I did more? Yes.

"But I don't go home at night and say, 'Well, you didn't care.' Because I did. I cared about it more than anything else." His voice catches. "And I don't go home at night and say, 'I didn't try.' Because I tried. Everything I could figure out. But I failed."

He points at the carbon pieces he'd just held in his hands. "With that stuff you get as many chances as you want," he says. "But with this I don't get another chance."

1. http://www.bostonmagazine.com/news/article/2014/01/02/bob-swartz-losing-aaron/

Made in the USA
Middletown, DE
12 August 2018